PRINCIPLES AND METHODS
OF SOCIAL RESEARCH

SECOND EDITION

WILLIAM D. CRANO
CLAREMONT GRADUATE UNIVERSITY

MARILYNN B. BREWER
OHIO STATE UNIVERSITY

2002

LAWRENCE ERLBAUM ASSOCIATES, PUBLISHERS
MAHWAH, NEW JERSEY   LONDON

Senior Editor:	Debra Riegert
Textbook Marketing Manager:	Marisol Kozlovski
Editorial Assistant:	Jason Planer
Cover Design:	Kathryn Houghtaling Lacey
Textbook Production Manager:	Paul Smolenski
Full-Service Compositor:	TechBooks
Text and Cover Printer:	Hamilton Printing Company

This book was typeset in 10.5/12 pt. Times, Italic, Bold, Bold Italic.
The heads were typeset in Engravers Gothic, Zapf Humanist and Revival.

Lawrence Erlbaum Associates, Inc., Publishers
10 Industrial Avenue
Mahwah, New Jersey 07430

Library of Congress Cataloging-in-Publication Data

Crano, William D., 1942–
    Principles and methods of social research / William D. Crano, Marilynn B. Brewer.—
2nd ed.
        p.   cm.
    Originally published: Boston : Allyn and Bacon, © 1986.
    Includes bibliographical references and index.
    ISBN 0-8058-3903-8 (alk. paper)—ISBN 0-8058-3904-6 (pbk. : alk. paper)
        1. Social sciences—Research.   2. Social sciences—Methodology.   I. Brewer, Marilynn
B., 1942– II. Title.

H62 .C692   2002
300′.7′2—dc21   2001040851

Books published by Lawrence Erlbaum Associates are printed on
acid-free paper, and their bindings are chosen for strength and
durability.

Printed in the United States of America
10 9 8 7 6 5 4 3 2 1

Dedicated to our mentor, Donald T. Campbell

CONTENTS

PREFACE

We wrote our first book on research methods fresh out of graduate school. Having both trained at Northwestern University under the watchful eye and, at times, thumb, of Donald Campbell, we were heavily invested in the experimental method, and the particular mindset that Campbell and Stanley (1966) had championed in their classic monograph, *Experimental and Quasi-Experimental Designs for Research*. It seemed to us then that the most certain avenue to advance in the social sciences was via the experimental road. In some ways, we still adhere to this proposition. Despite a host of worthy competitors, we believe the experiment remains the single most certain method to uncover causal relationships. Further, the experimental model provides a useful standard against which to evaluate the quality and utility of research findings based on non-experimental techniques. As a reference point, the experiment is useful even in settings that do not admit to the experimental method.

At the same time that we learned and absorbed the critical importance of experimental techniques, we were learning about the developing quasi-experimental approaches, which Cook and Campbell (1979) elaborated so elegantly, and which in no small measure helped establish the sub-field of evaluation research. In so doing, development of the quasi-experimental approaches also contributed to the developing recognition in the field that applications of our methods in socially relevant field settings was not an unworthy activity. In this book, we discuss the research emphases that have developed on the basis of hard thinking about experiments and their limits, their potential for social good, their application, and their misapplication.

That the experiment is not the *only* method available to social scientists is abundantly clear, perhaps more so today than yesterday. Similarly, the strict conditions that govern the appropriate use of the experiment are perhaps more obvious and accepted than in earlier times in the field. And yes, we recognize more clearly now than before that features inherent in the method itself can cause serious problems in inference, if not controlled. These issues have become increasingly central features of methodological disquiet over the years, and this ferment has been beneficial. The apprehension regarding the proper use of the experiment, its weaknesses as well as its strengths, reflects the developing sophistication of the research enterprise in the social sciences in general. We would like to think that our earlier volumes on research methods played a role in this process, though there is little evidence, experimental or otherwise, to support this contention.

With new developments over the years, the primacy of the experiment as the central tool of the social researcher has eroded. Now, we are better armed in our quest for scientifically sound understandings, with an ever-greater diversity of methods and techniques. The new methods we can bring to bear on an issue of social-scientific interest have expanded almost exponentially over the years, and this expansion has helped create the avalanche of new knowledge we are attempting to absorb and integrate. In large part, these new approaches and, at times, new ways of thinking about methods, motivated this revision of our methods text. The idea that research methodology is static is simply not supported by any evidence. To be sure, the fundamental principles of logic and proof have not changed much over the last millennia or so, but the methods that translate these principles into action, into trustworthy research data, continue to evolve at a rapid pace. Keeping abreast of the methodological possibilities now available to the social scientist is difficult, but not impossible. This book provides one avenue for such an updating.

Given the continuous development of the field, a feature of this book that may well keep it more current and useful than one might originally assume is our focus on understanding the principles that govern the use of a particular method, rather than on understanding how a given method can be used to answer a specific question. This book is more about *why* than about *how*—it is, as we stated in an earlier volume, a book *about* methods, not *of* methods (Crano & Brewer, 1986). Over the years, it has become obvious to us that researchers who understand the principles governing a particular approach produce better research than researchers who know "how to do it," but do not clearly understand why. It is for this reason that we do not provide detailed statistical computations to accompany each of the many methodological approaches we present. Such presentations focus on the *how*, rather than on understanding fundamental principles. In our experience, students learning a new method are better served by focusing on the method itself, understanding its logic, strengths, weaknesses, and the appropriate contexts for its application. This approach pays greater dividends than one that requires hours in a computer lab performing a series of calculations whose underlying mathematics is not well understood. We do not mean to undervalue proper statistical training. It is indispensable. But in the spirit of first-things-first, we are committed to the proposition that proper methods facilitate proper analyses, which in turn foster proper inference, which may produce better understanding. Using good statistics on methodologically suspect data usually does not accomplish much.[1]

There never has been a single, *right* way to support a position. Today, with the multitude of available methodological possibilities, this proposition is more true than ever. Researchers with a command of their techniques are more likely to be able to act in the methodologically opportunistic manner that is necessary to respond to ever changing research demands and contexts. Sometimes, natural, unplanned occurrences provide important venues for studying important issues. A state's imposing a 3-strikes law on habitual criminals, the rolling electrical blackouts in California, a hurricane, flood, or fire, provide the context to study issues of social importance, if the researcher is creative and opportunistic *and* has the variety of methodological skills necessary to move from one setting

---

[1] At points in the book we do provide formulae, calculation directions, etc.; however, we do this primarily to enhance the usefulness of a method, or to provide the reader a better picture of a technique, thus allowing for a deeper understanding of the technique itself.

to another without losing track of the question at hand. Understanding the principles that serve as the foundation for various research techniques, which, in effect, are the expression of the principles, allows the researcher to move seamlessly from one context to another without breaking stride. This is why we have stressed principles so strongly, even when discussing particular applications. We do not diminish the value of learning research by doing it. Indeed, we believe strongly that to become a good researcher, one must *do* research. However, in doing research, a continual focus on the principles that underlie the particular research technique in use should always be at the forefront.

Our focus on principles, and the diversity of techniques covered here, of necessity, opens this book to a broad range of social scientists. We created our original book on methodology to help train social psychologists. However, over time, along with the field, we have developed a much broader methodological orientation. Today, social psychologists are fundamentally *social scientists*, and must be conversant with the research techniques that formerly had been the purview of cognitive science, communication research, sociology, and political science. In addition, the widespread participation of social psychologists in more applied areas—evaluation research, marketing, organizational studies, and public health—has required that we expand our coverage appreciably. This expansion reflects the reality of the new demands that are now placed on the competent social scientist. We believe that the broad coverage makes this book appropriate for all of these specialties—that psychologists, communication scientists, evaluators, marketers, even public health trainees will find much of utility in our presentation.

We constructed this book, like our earlier ones, to foster our emphasis on principles. The beginning section of the book is concerned with the process of fitting methodological designs to research aims, and with the fundamental issues of reliability and validity—issues that lie at the heart of all scientific investigations. The material of the first three chapters is elemental; it must be considered in any research endeavor, no matter what method is to be employed.

The second section concentrates on fundamental research design strategies. We first consider the laboratory experiment. Then, using the laboratory experiment as a point of reference, we discuss field experiments, correlational designs, including structural equation models, quasi-experiments, and survey designs. The principles of each method are linked back to those that form the logical foundation of the experiment. In this way, we can illustrate the strengths and weaknesses of each design relative to a common (gold) standard.

We focus the third section of the book on data collection techniques, including systematic observational methods, content analysis, and scaling, along with methods for assessing dyads and groups, and measuring implicit thoughts and feelings—social cognitions. These various data collection techniques are all commonly used in one way or another across the social sciences, and a good understanding of their requirements allows readers both to judge the quality of studies using them, and to design studies of their own.

The final section of the book contains chapters on meta-analysis—the quantitative synthesis of research results across many studies—and on the social responsibility and ethical requirements of the social research methodologist. This last chapter probably should have been the first, because its counsel and requirements must inform all research, from beginning to end. This chapter is meant to sensitize readers to the enormous power the researcher wields, and counsels concerned moderation in its application. We believe that the ethical issues that we face in our day-to-day research lives are relatively consistent across methods. The ethical principles we adopt as researchers, that is, should govern our actions, whether they take place in field or laboratory settings. The details of time and context and research issue are in some ways immaterial to the underlying ethical principles, which should guide our actions in any venue. To make this point most forcefully, we have written a separate chapter, which should serve as a strong point of reference for the researcher, rather than providing a series of ethical caveats that are spread thinly throughout the various chapters of this book.

There is no doubt that the material we present is at times difficult, but the book's structure will help mitigate the difficulties that otherwise might arise. The first chapters in each section are fundamental to all that follows, and were developed to serve as general introductions to the sections. We have presented this material as clearly as we know how, avoiding unnecessary complications. We believe that conscientious students will not have trouble understanding the material. This is not to say that we have oversimplified the complexities of the information contained here. To have watered-down the presentation would have presented a misleading picture of the dedication needed to produce, even to understand, good research. To assist readers who might wish to delve more deeply into a specific topic, we have appended a list of suggested readings to the end of each chapter. These suggestions enrich the materials presented, and provide a more elaborated treatment of the issues discussed in the chapter.

As in all of our previous methodological writing, we have dedicated this book to our common mentor, Donald T. Campbell. Our dedication represents more than merely a pro forma nod to a good and famous man. Rather, it reflects a true appreciation for a person who made an enormous impact on the social sciences in general, and on our own lives in particular. Campbell conveyed the sense of mission, of the importance of our work as social scientists, while at the same time insisting by deed, more than by word, that the work should be fun. He encouraged us to pursue our individual substantive interests, and enabled those pursuits by providing us a powerful methodological foundation. This foundation has served us well over the years, and we are hopeful that this book might help supply the beginnings of a similar underpinning for at least some of its readers.

Campbell always encouraged us to approach a design or a result with a healthy skepticism. As scientists, it pays to be skeptical, but this sense should not drift into cynicism, a constant danger that must be avoided. As skeptical social scientists, we are aware of the many demands that must be met before a result or method is adopted; as cynics, the problems are always insurmountable, the demands never met, the results never of value. A skeptical methodological mindset fosters progress by motivating us to find better ways to investigate important issues; the cynical mindset prevents us from trying. Not trying is the polar opposite of the sermon Campbell preached.

In addition to Don Campbell, many others—too numerous to mention—have played an important role in the development of this book. We are happy to acknowledge at least some of their contributions. We are especially grateful to Dr. Radmila Prislin and Dr. Michele Alexander, both of whom read and commented on the entire volume and provided valuable suggestions for updating this revision of our text. Their encouragement and at times, challenging observations, helped us develop a better final product. In addition, we are grateful to Lawrence Erlbaum and our editor Debra Riegert for encouraging this project and making room for a new edition of Crano and Brewer in their methodology series.

Finally, and as always, we thank the members of our respective families—Suellen and Christine—whose encouragement and understanding throughout this entire process were a constant part of the psychological landscape.

Principles and Methods
of Social Research

PART

I

Introduction to Social Research Methods

I

1

BASIC CONCEPTS

When two American astronauts landed on the moon in the summer of 1971, their activities included an interesting and, for some, surprising demonstration. They showed that when the effects of friction are eliminated, a light object (a feather) and a heavy object (a hammer) will reach the ground at the same time when dropped simultaneously from the same height. This verification of a basic principle of high school physics delighted many viewers of the live televised broadcast, but probably few of them considered the fact that for hundreds of years before Galileo (who is thought to have predicted this outcome originally), Western scholars had accepted Aristotle's hypothesis that heavy objects would fall faster than lighter ones. For most of us, Aristotle's assumption seems intuitively correct, even though we know that it is contrary to scientific theory and empirical fact. Not all scientifically demonstrated phenomena contradict "common sense" intuitions in this way, but this case serves to illustrate the difference between science and intuition as bases of understanding the physical and social world.

The emphasis on subjecting all theoretical concepts, hypotheses, and expectations to empirical demonstration—that is, of testing our ideas—is basically what distinguishes the scientific method from other forms of inquiry. And the principles of scientific methodology, which lend structure to the manner in which such inquiries occur, is what this book is all about. More specifically, this book is intended to represent broadly the methods that have been derived from basic principles of scientific inquiry and to show how they apply to the study of human cognition, affect, and behavior in its social context.

Science and Daily Life

It is important to understand that the research principles and techniques presented throughout this text are not reserved solely for the investigation of scientific theories. At issue, in many instances, are questions of a more personal nature—the consensus surrounding one's personal beliefs, the relative quality of one's performance, the wisdom of one's decisions—and in these circumstances, too, the application of the scientific method can prove useful. At first glance, using scientific principles to guide one's own decision-making processes (or to judge the quality of their outcome) might appear somewhat extreme; however, in light of much current research on human judgment that demonstrates the frailty of our decision-making powers, such an approach makes good sense, especially when issues of personal importance are involved.

The susceptibility of people's judgmental processes to a host of biasing influences is well documented (e.g., Dawes, 1988; Kahneman, Slovic, & Tversky, 1982; Nisbett & Ross, 1980). Research suggests that it is risky to depend solely on one's own opinions or intuitions in evaluating the quality of a judgment or an attitudinal position. If Aristotle could be fooled, imagine how much more likely it is that *we* can be mistaken, especially in situations in which we are highly involved. To develop an intuitive grasp of the difficulties that can affect the quality of even simple decisions, consider the following scenario (adapted from Ross, Greene, & House, 1977):

> Suppose that while driving through a rural area near your home you are stopped by a county police officer who informs you that you have been clocked (with radar) at 38 miles per hour in a 25-mph zone. You believe this information to be accurate. After the policeman leaves, you inspect your citation and find that the details on the summons regarding weather, visibility, time, and location of violation are highly inaccurate. The citation informs you that you may either pay a $20 fine by mail without appearing in court or you must appear in municipal court within the next two weeks to contest the charge.
>
> How would you respond to the following questions?
> What % of your peers do you estimate would pay the $20 fine by mail?___%
> What % would go to court to contest the charge?___%
> What would you do? Would you pay the fine, or contest the charges?___Pay___Contest

Now consider your estimates of your peers' behavior in light of your decision to pay or to contest the fine. Were these estimates influenced by your decision? Although you might not think so, considerable research suggests that they probably were (e.g., Fabrigar & Krosnick, 1995; Marks & Miller, 1987). In actuality, approximately 46% of those posed with the speeding scenario said they would opt to pay the fine, whereas the remainder opted to contest it (Ross et al., 1977). However, if you thought that you would have paid the $20, there is a good chance that you assumed more of your peers would have acted similarly than if you decided to "beat the rap." On the other hand, those who would have gone to court are more likely to have assumed that more of their peers would have done so too.

The *false consensus effect*, as this phenomenon has been termed, is an apparently common, and relatively ubiquitous, judgmental bias. In the absence of direct information, individuals tend to use their own personal perspective on a situation to estimate what others would do or think. Such a bias, of course, can have a substantial influence on the quality of our assumptions and the propriety of our behaviors. What's more, this bias intensifies as a consequence of the decision's importance. Contrary to what you might expect, the more important the decision (or the belief, or the action), the more likely we are to assume that there are many other people who would decide, or believe, or act exactly as we do (Crano, 1983).

Clearly, our decision-making apparatus is far from foolproof. Like Aristotle, we are inclined to rely heavily, perhaps too heavily, on our own insights, feelings, and interpretations and to assume that other reasonable people would feel and act just as we do. There is no simple solution to problems of this type, but there is an available alternative, namely, to test our intuitions, decisions, and opinions, rather than merely to assume that they are valid or commonly accepted. The means by which we accomplish such tests are the same as those used in the investigation of formal theory, which, as noted, represent the central focus of this book.

The specific purpose of this chapter is to acquaint readers with the fundamentals of scientific research and to introduce several important themes that run throughout the text. There are a number of controversial issues in the philosophy of science—such as the status of induction or the logical framework for theory verification (cf. Bhaskar, 1978, 1982; Kuhn, 1970; Manicas & Secord, 1983; Popper, 1959, 1963; Secord, 1982)—but these concerns are avoided here in favor of a more descriptive presentation of the "ground rules" of scientific inquiry as agreed to by most social scientists.

The common feature of all approaches to the methods of science is the emphasis on observable phenomena. No matter how abstract the generalization or explanatory concept at the theoretical level, the concepts under investigation must be reduced to, or translated into, observable manifestations. So, for example, the very rich and complicated concept of aggression as a psychological state is translated in the research laboratory to a subject's pushing a button that delivers an electric shock to another. Once this "translation" occurs, the very powerful methods of scientific inquiry can be applied to the phenomena of interest. Often, these methods suggest that our understanding of the phenomenon was not correct, and that we should develop alternative hypotheses or generalizations. These alternatives, in turn, are translated into a new set of "observables," and the process is repeated. From this perspective, the conduct of scientific inquiry can be viewed as a cyclical process, which progresses from explanation to observation to explanation. From hypotheses regarding the nature of a phenomenon come deductions, which guide observations, which affect future generalizations, which, in turn, foster the development of new hypotheses, etc. This chapter explores the phases of this cyclical progression most relevant for social psychological inquiry.

FROM CONCEPT TO OPERATION

Figure 1.1 represents pictorially the translation of theoretical concepts into research operations. In the first phase of the translation process, the researcher's general idea is stated specifically in the form of a conceptual hypothesis. There are many ways that such hypotheses are formed, and we consider some of these in the next section.

Hypothesis Generation

The development of hypotheses is one of science's most complex creative processes. As McGuire (1973) observed, we have been reluctant to attempt to teach students this art, believing it to be so complex as to be beyond instruction. However, by following the lead of some of the field's most creative researchers, we can learn something about the means that they employ in developing their ideas.

One of the most important, and certainly the most widely used, methods of hypothesis generation involves the logical deduction of expectations from some established theory. The general form of hypothesis deduction is:

Theory X implies that B results from A.
We hypothesize that if X is true, producing A will result in the occurrence of B.

There are many factors that prompt us to emphasize the importance of theory in the social sciences, and one of the most crucial of these is the role of theory in the development of

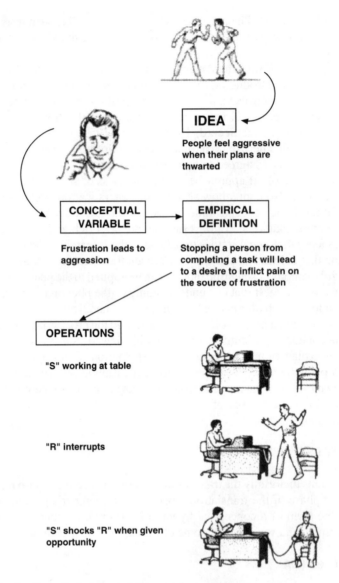

FIG. 1.1. Turning theoretical concepts into research operations.

hypotheses, a role that allows for the continued advance and refinement of our knowledge of social behavior.

Related to the deductive technique is a method that employs conflicting findings as a means of developing hypotheses. Typically, this approach searches for a condition or variable whose presence or absence helps to explain observed variations in research findings. This approach helps to refine theory by providing a more strict specification of the conditions under which a particular outcome can be expected to occur (or not to occur). An example of the use of the "conflicting findings" technique to clarify a theory is provided in research that sought to examine the relationship between ambient temperature and the tendency of people to act aggressively. Experimental research conducted in laboratory settings by Baron and his colleagues (Baron & Bell, 1975, 1976; Baron & Lawton, 1972;

Bell, 1992; Bell & Baron, 1990) consistently demonstrated that high temperatures *inhibited* the influence of aggressive models. Under normal circumstances, aggressive actors could induce considerable aggression on the part of naive subjects; however, when the ambient temperature of the laboratory was raised, subjects' aggressive tendencies diminished. These findings from the laboratory were in marked contrast to those observed by Anderson and his colleagues (e.g., Anderson & Anderson, 1984; Anderson & De Neve, 1992; Carlsmith & Anderson, 1979) outside the laboratory when they examined the average temperatures of the days on which major riots took place in the United States. They found a positive relationship between these two variables—Riots were *more* likely to occur when temperatures were high, suggesting that heat provokes rather than inhibits the spread of aggressive behavior.

One possible means of reconciling these apparently conflicting results involves an explanation based on the uniqueness, or prominence, of the temperature in the two research settings. In naturalistic settings (as reviewed in Anderson & De Neve, 1992), we adjust to the temperature. Whereas a heat wave is obviously uncomfortable, it is consistent, or constant. We experience the discomfort more as a dull ache than as a searing pain, but because this irritation is relatively constant, we do not consciously identify our discomfort as being caused by the heat. Under these conditions, an extraneous event in the environment—such as a confrontation between a policeman and a minor traffic offender—might be misinterpreted as the source of discomfort. Thus, the reactions of a crowd of people are likely to escalate when temperatures are high and have been for some time.

In the case of the laboratory research of Baron and his colleagues, however, the high ambient temperature of the laboratory typically came on very abruptly. Subjects walked into the laboratory from a relatively normal environment and found themselves in the middle of a heat wave. Under this circumstance, participants readily identify the source of their discomfort, and this discomfort is unlikely to "transfer" to (or be identified with) other stimuli. This explanation of an apparent contradiction of findings from two different programs of research gave rise to a new theory, known as "excitation transfer," which has been used to explain interesting behaviors ranging from violent anger to intense attraction (Zillman, 1979, 1996).

Another source of hypothesis generation comes from observation of seemingly paradoxical behavior. For example, in a classic study, Festinger, Riecken, and Schachter (1956) found that an extremely reclusive "doomsday" cult became much more publicity conscious, much more active in pushing their beliefs, *after* their prophecy concerning the end of the world had been shown to be obviously incorrect. This was in stark contrast to their typical behavior before the disconfirmation. The researchers' attempts to make sense of this apparently paradoxical behavior helped to lay the foundations of Festinger's (1957) classic theory of cognitive dissonance.

Yet another method of hypothesis development requires that we attend closely to the common, everyday behavioral tactics that people employ in dealing with others. For example, how can some used-car salespersons promise a car at an impossibly low price, later rescind their offer, and still succeed in selling an automobile that is considerably more expensive than that which was agreed on originally? Why is it that we are much more likely to agree to a rather major imposition if we have recently given in to a much smaller request? Social scientists attuned to issues of this sort have been able to develop some interesting and potentially valuable ideas on the basis of their observations and to apply these insights to topics ranging from inducing charitable donations to AIDS prevention to fostering organ donations (see Burger, 1999; Cialdini, 1988; Dillard, 1991; Eisenberg, 1991).

The case study is yet another source for hypotheses. By concentrating intensively on a specific person or interaction, we sometimes can discern systematic or regular relationships among variables or behaviors, and these, in turn, can provide the stimulus necessary for developing a testable proposition. Some of the most noteworthy examples of the use of the case study in the development of theory are provided by Freud and Piaget, both of whom used this approach extensively (some would say exclusively) in developing their theories.

Although the list is far from complete, we hope it provides some idea of the range of possibilities available to the social scientist in developing testable hypotheses (see McGuire, 1973, 1997; Campbell, Daft, & Hulin, 1983; for a more complete set of suggestions). After the hypotheses have been developed, we move to a perhaps less "artistic," but nonetheless creative phase, that of operationalization.

Operationalization

Historically, the social sciences are still quite close to the speculative stages of their initial development. It was not much more than 100 years ago that psychology as a field of study was tied to an approach known as introspectionism. In studies of the introspective variety, research participants were exposed to some stimulus presented by the investigator and then asked to describe their internal reactions to it. In this way, the early psychologists attempted to enter directly into the "black box" and thereby gain insight into the nature of the human organism. It was common that the investigator's own students would play the role of participant in these types of studies, and often, the same participant would be used in repeated experiments. Today's social researchers, possessing information unavailable to their predecessors, consider the introspective approach both risky and naive. For one thing, we have learned that people do not always have access to subjective experience in a way that can be verbalized (Nisbett & Wilson, 1977). We also have learned that participants involved in a scientific study may be overly willing to "please" the investigator by helping to confirm the research hypotheses (see chap. 6, this volume). In the early days of introspectionism, participants were often well aware of the particular theoretical position under investigation, and there was probably a great deal of informal pressure on these students to "confirm" the hypotheses of their teachers. Thus, introspectionism left a lot to be desired as a method of objective scientific inquiry. Nevertheless, the era of introspectionism was a valuable phase in the development of psychology in particular, and the social sciences in general, because it presented a bridge between the purely speculative, philosophical, explanations of human behavior and the more rigorous scientific approach.

The transition to objectivity in social research was marked by a strong emphasis on operationalization—the translation of abstract theoretical constructs into concrete procedures and indicators that can be observed, recorded, and replicated. The requirement for explicit description of research procedures did much to clarify theoretical issues and place the social sciences on firmer ground as scientific disciplines.

The translation of conceptual variables to scientifically researchable variables generally takes place in two steps. The first involves the redefinition of the abstraction in empirical terms; that is, the variable is specified in such a way as to be potentially observable or manipulable. Of course, what can be observed is inevitably a function of perceptual skills and available instrumentation; for example, what can be seen with the naked eye is different from what can be observed with the aid of a high-powered electron microscope. Thus, what is "objective" or observable must be defined in terms of the current limitations of our senses and technology. (See chap. 16, this volume, for recently developed methods that allow scientists to "read" the unverbalized content of the human mind—content that previously was not available for scientific investigation.) In general, an observation is considered sufficiently objective if independent researchers with similar training and available technical aids can agree on its evaluation or assessment.

The second step of concept translation involves a specification of the procedures and instruments required to make the actual observations, detailed sufficiently so that other scientists could duplicate the observation for purposes of replication or validation. This stage of research is referred to as the *operationalization of the conceptual variable* and requires close attention as the most rigorous aspect of scientific methodology. For purposes of empirical testing, it is essential that very specific and precise delineation of the phenomena of interest be provided. However, it should be made clear that this specification of research operations is not the end product of the scientific investigation, but merely a necessary step in the research process.

The Imperfection of Operationalizations.

Most social scientists do not regard the operationalization phase as the endpoint of their investigative efforts. Their operationalized constructs are put to use in testing and refining theory. As we emphasized earlier, the operational definition is the result of a specification of the research processes employed in the investigation of a given phenomenon in such a way as to make it directly observable. One's measurement instrument, for example, might be labeled an attitude test, but what is being observed, and hence, what constitutes the operationalization of "attitude," are the directly observable pencil marks that an individual has made on the questionnaire we have provided. Most theories in the social sciences, however, are concerned with processes somewhat removed from what is directly observed. (We are not especially interested in the pencil-marking behavior itself.) When discussing anxiety, or communication skill, or attitude change, for example, we are dealing with internal cognitive processes that are only indirectly and imperfectly inferred from an individual's observable actions. It thus becomes extremely important to note whether the operationalization has any psychological reality, that is, whether the processes that constitute the operation meaningfully reflect the underlying processes that give rise to the observable responses. Put another way, the researcher must be concerned with the degree of overlap between the operation and the internal processes it is purported to represent.

In the social sciences, theoretical concepts are generally of a high level of abstraction, but they must be defined through operations that can be carried out with available technological aids. We move, for example, from the conceptual definition of a construct like "attitude" (e.g., a consistent internal disposition to approach or avoid an attitude object) to the more empirical realm of endorsements of positively or negatively evaluative statements regarding the attitude object, and finally to the specification of a set of items and instructions that provide the actual measure of attitude in a particular research study (see chap. 15).

Specific operations are always imperfect definitions of any given theoretical construct because the product of any particular observation is a function of multiple sources—including observer errors, instrumentation errors, environmental and contextual conditions—many of which are totally unrelated to the conceptual variable of interest. In the physical sciences, many of the factors that affect instrument readings have been identified and can be minimized or corrected; even so, some slight variations in measurements, which do not correspond to variations in the attribute being measured, do occur. In social science research, these unidentified sources of variation are considerably more profound; even those factors that are identified are seldom successfully eliminated or controlled. Campbell (1969a) represented this state of affairs well when he observed:

Measurements involve processes which must be specified in terms of many theoretical parameters. For any specific measurement process, we know on theoretical grounds that it is a joint
function of many scientific laws. Thus, we know on scientific grounds that the measurements
resulting cannot purely reflect a single parameter of our scientific theory....Let us consider in
detail...a single meter, the galvanometer. The amount of needle displacement is certainly a
strong function of the electrical current in the attached wire. But, it is also a function of the
friction in the needle bearings, of inertia due to the weight of the needle, of fluctuations in the
earth's and other magnetic and electrical fields, of the strong and weak nuclear interactions in
adjacent matter, of photon bombardment, etc. We know on theoretical grounds that the needle
pointer movements cannot be independent of all of these, i.e., that the pointer movements
cannot be *definitional* of a single parameter....Analogously, for a tally mark on a census-
taker's protocol indicating family income, or rent paid, or number of children, we know on
theoretical grounds that it is only in part a function of the state of the referents of the question.
It is also a function of the social interaction of the interview, of the interviewer's appearance,
of the respondent's fear of similar strangers, such as bill collectors, welfare investigators,
and the law, etc., etc. A manifest anxiety questionnaire response may in part be a function of
anxiety, but it is also a function of vocabulary comprehension, or individual and social class
differences in the use of euphoric and dysphoric adjectives, or idiosyncratic definitions of
key terms frequently repeated, of respondent expectations as to the personal consequences
of describing himself sick or well, etc....(pp. 14–15)

Given these considerations, it is of critical importance for social scientists to recognize
that their theoretical concepts are never perfectly embodied in any single method of
observation.

Multiple Operationism.   Because of the imperfect correspondence between conceptual variables and their observable manifestations, we subscribe to the principle of multiple operationism. This principle involves the recognition that no single operation provides
enough information to adequately "define" a theoretical concept. Instead, the concept
must be multiply represented through a number of observation techniques. Ideally, these
techniques should be as different as possible on irrelevant dimensions. Any single operationalization of a concept is in error to the extent that it does not completely overlap
with the internal psychological state it is purported to represent. However, if many diverse
measures of a phenomenon are employed, it is probable that they will have nonoverlapping
sources of error. They will each miss the mark to some extent, that is, but will miss it in
different ways. Multiple, diverse measures with nonoverlapping sources of error allow
the researcher to "triangulate" on the concept. This methodological triangulation is the
logical outcome, and central advantage, of multiple operationism. The common variations
among heterogeneous observations, all of which focus on the same construct, provide the
information necessary to adequately identify, or define, the component of interest (Crano,
1981, 2000).
    To gain an intuitive feel for the concept of multiple operationism, consider an individual
just waking from a night's sleep and wondering exactly what time of day it is. Our usual
procedure for assessing time is to consult a clock, but clocks vary as instruments of time
keeping. Some are based on electrical power impulses, some are battery operated, some
run on mechanical spring loading, and so on. The interesting thing about these variations
in power source for our various timepieces is that the clocks are each subject to different
kinds of potential inaccuracy, or error. Electric clocks are affected by power failures or
temporary disconnection from a central power source; batteries die down; and springs
can be over- or under-wound, or fatigued by long use. Consequently, consulting any

single clock, whatever its type, leaves some room for doubt about the accuracy of its time assessment. When three different clocks all agree on the time, our confidence is increased, although just how confident we are depends on whether the three timepieces share any common source of inaccuracy or bias. If all three clocks are electrically powered, they could have been simultaneously affected by the same 20-minute power outage during the middle of the night, and hence all be reporting the same inaccurate reading. When three clocks with three different sources of power all agree, however, our confidence is considerably enhanced. When the three do not agree, the nature of their disagreement and our knowledge of the different types of inaccuracy to which each clock is susceptible can help us to track down the sources of error and zero in on the correct time.

From Operation to Measurement

The product of most scientific observations is expressed in terms of some measurement. *Measurement* simply refers to the assignment of numbers to specific observations in such a way as to reflect variations among those observations. The level of measurement, or the degree of correspondence between number assignment and extent of variation in the attribute being observed, depends on the rule of number assignment being applied. The simplest level of correspondence is represented by the *nominal rule* of measurement, which requires only that different numbers be assigned to observations or events that can be differentiated on some specified dimension(s). The basic requirement of nominal measurement is one common to all empirical research, that is, the ability to obtain agreement among observers on the assignment of labels. Application of nominal scaling is illustrated in social psychological research by the use of categorical rating systems of interpersonal communication, in which numbers are arbitrarily assigned to represent categories of verbal behavior, such as the respondent 'asks a question' or 'supports another's position' (see chap. 11).

Somewhat more complex than the requirements for the application of the nominal rule are those measurements that apply the *ordinal rule*, which specifies that the ordering of number labels correspond to the rank ordering of observations on the attribute of interest. Ordinal scales are commonly employed to make ratings of social situations along such dimensions as "degree of anxiety arousal (high, medium, low)," "socioeconomic status (upper, upper middle, middle, etc.)," and the like. More measurement sophistication is achieved with the application of the *interval rule*, under which the variations in numbers assigned reflect equal gradations in the degree of the different observations. Measures of social attitudes derived from Thurstone scaling techniques (see chap. 15) provide examples of interval scales in social psychological research. A fourth level of measurement requires the application of the *ratio rule* of number assignment under which the values of the numbers reflect, in equal intervals, the difference between the observations and some standard derived from an absolute zero point. For interval scaling, it is sufficient that the numbers reflect *comparative* values of different observations rather than measurements against some absolute standard, but the latter is required for ratio scales. The use of ratio scales is relatively rare in social psychological research, but some measurement techniques, such as measures of the amount of time taken to make a response or the amount of pressure exerted on a hand-press device, do meet the requirements of a ratio scale. A decision tree that illustrates the level of measurement we are using (or contemplating) is presented in Fig. 1.2.

For practical purposes, the essential difference among these four levels of measurement is the extent of correspondence between the number and the subtle variations in the attribute or construct being measured, that is, in the "fit" between number and observation. The higher the level of measurement, the greater is the degree to which the data are represented in the number assignments. We do not always shoot for the highest level of measurement,

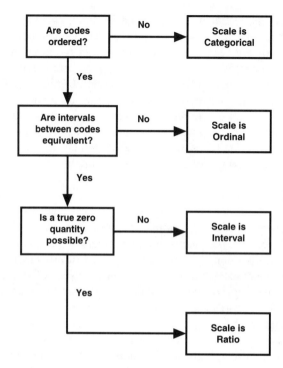

FIG. 1.2.   Decision-tree to determine level of measurement.

however, because they make increasingly greater demands on data quality. Higher levels of measurement also make available more sensitive statistical techniques. Thus, the ability to interpret observations in terms of higher order measurements adds considerable precision to the research process, but the assignment of numbers does not automatically create precision if there is some possibility that the rules of number assignment have been violated.

THE ROLE OF THEORY IN SOCIAL PSYCHOLOGICAL INQUIRY

It is traditional to think of scientific theories as convenient data-summarizing generalizations that are helpful in guiding decisions about the content and interpretation of future observations, but that are discarded when the obtained observations do not fit the conceptual framework. We feel, however, that the actual role of theory in most scientific endeavors differs somewhat from this ideal. In our view, a formal theory is a template, or a pattern, against which various data sets are compared. The extent of the "match" between theory pattern and data pattern provides an indication of the usefulness of the theory. Of course, the match is rarely, if ever, perfect, but with the continual modification of the template, an increasingly better fit can be obtained. However, even when the fit between data and theory is unsatisfactory, the theory is rarely discarded until an alternative that provides a better match with the data is available.

Theory Testing as a Process

As suggested in the preceding paragraph, the interplay between theory and data is not entirely an objective process. Kuhn's (1970) still stimulating and controversial analysis of scientific "revolutions" has produced increased awareness of the influence of social factors on the process of scientific advance (Horwich, 1993). The acceptance of particular theoretical positions is determined at least partly by the prevailing social climate, and frequently in large part by the personalities of the advocates of competing theoretical perspectives. Nor is all vigorous and valuable research necessarily inspired by formal theoretical considerations. Some active areas of research in social science have been derived from essentially exploratory investigations, inspired more by hunches and guesswork than by formal theory.

For example, following much speculation on the inevitable conservatism of group decision making, Stoner (1961) compared responses made by individuals on a test concerned with their willingness to advocate risky decisions with those of six-person groups. He found (to the surprise of many) that the average group decision was significantly more risky than the average individual decision. This finding, which was labeled the group "shift-to-risk" phenomenon (or the "risky shift") generated much further research. However, the extensive program of research evident in this area was not stimulated simply by an interest in risk taking, per se, but by the controversy that developed over theory-based explanations that were advanced to account for the group effect on the riskiness of decisions. The outcome of this collective research effort demonstrates that under some circumstances, groups do indeed make riskier decisions than the individuals who constitute the group, whereas in other circumstances, the opposite is the case (Blumberg, 1994; Isenberg, 1986). As is often the case in social psychology and communication science, the most active, visible, and extended areas of research are those that are inspired by the theory-testing process and the competition of alternative theoretical explanations.

Ideally, the theory-testing process begins with the derivation (from the theoretical structure) of implications that can be stated in the form of hypotheses regarding the existence of relationships among observable variables. Most of these derived hypotheses are of the general form: "If theory U is true, then, with irrelevant factors eliminated, the occurrence of variable A should be related to the occurrence (or condition) of Variable B." Comparisons between these predicted relationships and the actual outcomes of controlled observations comprise the testing process, through which the original theory is subjected to continuous potential disconfirmation (although the failure to obtain the predicted results in any particular case can always be attributed to the inadequacy of the empirical statement or the research operations to reflect the theoretical position). Successive failures of empirical investigations to disconfirm the derived hypotheses create incremental acceptance of the theoretical position. This process continues until some outcome is encountered that cannot be explained by the current theory at a time when some alternative is available which accounts for all the previous findings and the otherwise inexplicable result.

This continuous process of theory purification can be illustrated with the following example: *A gunslinger of the Old West rides into a town, and the terrified inhabitants form the impression (i.e., hypothesis) that "Joe is the fastest gun in the territory."* The clear implication of this position is that in a contest against any other gunman, Joe's gun will be fired first. The expectation can be "proved" only one way—that is, by showing that alternative hypotheses (i.e., that other gunmen are faster) are incorrect. Each time Joe's skill is pitted against that of someone else and the predicted outcome is attained, the theoretical allegation gains credibility. The more challenging the rival, the more encouraging Joe's victory. If Joe were to shoot the local schoolmarm, for example, he would generate little enthusiasm for his claim. Conversely, if he were to meet and outshoot an internationally famous desperado, confidence in the hypothesis would increase appreciably.

However, if on just one occasion Joe's gun fires second (or not at all) in such a contest, a logical alternative—which can account for all the outcomes—suggests itself, namely, that "Joe was fast, but Irving is faster." To the extent that the critical result actually reflected relative ability (rather than some extraneous factor such as Joe's gun jamming, or his having been shot from behind), the new theoretical position is likely to replace the old. However, even if the critical case did not occur, and Joe were to knock off the top 200 on the "hit parade," the original hypothesis would still not be completely secure because there would always be the nagging realization that sometime, somewhere, the disconfirming case might come along.

This analogy might at first seem silly, but parallels can be drawn between the Old West and the new social science. Today, a scientist rides into town and proposes the hypothesis that X causes Y. Others dispute this, claiming that A causes Y, or B causes Y, or C causes Y. Some of these alternatives will be clearly implausible, and the scientist will have little trouble discrediting them. If our researcher's explanation holds up against a number of highly plausible alternative explanations, he or she will have strengthened the theoretical case considerably. Like the gunman, unfortunately, the scientist can never be completely sure that the competitive (theory-testing) process has eliminated all rivals.

There are, of course, degrees of uncertainty. A scientist whose hypothesis has been tested only once or twice should be more concerned about its validity than one whose theory has been shown to be consistently successful in the face of strong, plausible challenges. Thus, the general approach to be emphasized throughout this text consists of various strategies whose major function is the falsification of as many competing hypotheses as possible. Through this continuous process, the gradual purification of theory can be accomplished, though certainty is never assured. Again, however, it must be stressed that even long-term success and widespread acceptance is no guarantee that a theory is true or valid or even optimally useful.

In the case of successive gun battles, one disconfirming outcome can eliminate the possibility of further testing of the original theory. In the case of scientific theory, no position ever stands or falls on the result of a single observation. Every individual observation is subject to a number of potential explanations. Only the total pattern of multiple test outcomes determines the goodness of fit between theory and data. Thus, the process of theory testing, as well as the concept of measurement, is best viewed in terms of multiple operationism. A theory frequently stands in the absence of perfect fit between its implications and every data outcome until some alternative theory becomes available which accounts for more of the actual observations. The more convergence there is between the outcomes of successive heterogeneous investigations and the implications of a particular theoretical position, the less likely it becomes that some alternative explanation will become available to replace it, although the possibility of such an alternative can never be ruled out entirely.

The process of theory testing described here is represented in the series of Euler diagrams of Fig. 1.3.

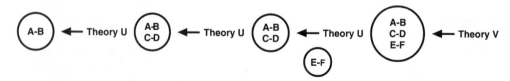

FIG. 1.3. Euler diagrams illustrating the process of theory development.

1. A relationship (A–B) is observed between two empirical variables, which is consistent with Theory U, although several other theoretical explanations of the same relationship (not shown here) are available.

2. Another relationship (C–D) is also observed and is consistent with Theory U, but not the other theories that related A and B. This new relationship rules out alternative explanations of A–B that are not also consistent with the C–D findings. Theory U is bolstered.

3. A third relationship (E–F) is observed which is inconsistent with the implications of Theory U. The status of Theory U is tentative.

4. The explanations of Theory U are replaced by those of Theory V (which may be a modification of U or an entirely different theoretical proposition) because the latter is consistent with all of the formerly observed outcomes and also with the new findings (E–F).

Within this framework of theory testing, the purpose of good research design is to conduct each empirical investigation in such a way as to minimize rival alternative explanations for the relationships under investigation and to plan programs of research in such a way as to represent the theory being tested under a maximum of heterogeneous conditions to successively rule out potential alternative theoretical positions.

THE CONDUCT OF RESEARCH: AN OVERVIEW OF THIS BOOK

The preceding section on the role of theory in social research presents a view of research as an iterative, cumulative process extended across time and persons. Any single research study can and should be regarded as a part of this larger enterprise—something like an individual piece in a giant jigsaw puzzle. No one study is sufficient in and of itself to prove or disprove a theory or hypothesis, but each study contributes in some unique way to the total picture. For the individual researcher, however, the major focus of attention is the design and conduct of one research project at a time. It is the purpose of this book to introduce students of social research to the basic tools needed for that purpose.

The stages of any individual research study are diagrammed in Fig. 1.4. We have already discussed, briefly, the principles involved in translating conceptual variables into empirical operations. We divide the operationalization of our research ideas further into two basic

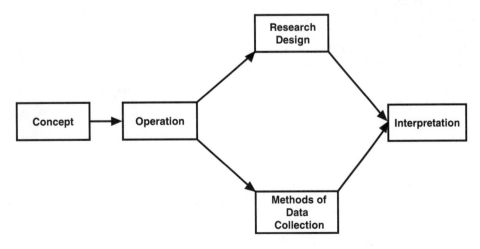

FIG. 1.4. Stages of research.

steps. The first is the selection of an overall research design—the master plan that defines the type of study we are conducting. Research design includes decisions as to the setting in which the research is to be undertaken, the relevant variables to be included, and whether or not the researcher controls or manipulates critical features of the situation. The second step is that of choosing the specific methods of data collection that are to be used in the study. How are the selected variables of interest to be assessed and what are the respective roles of the researcher and the subjects in the data collection process?

The combination of research design and data collection methods defines the nature of the research study. When the design and methods have been carried out, the final stages of the study involve analysis and interpretation of the resulting data. Statistical analyses are highly specialized and their treatment falls beyond the scope of this book. Correct interpretation of the results of such analyses, however, must take into account the design and methods by which the data were obtained, and these are the features of the research process that we focus on throughout this text.

The organization of this volume generally follows the stages depicted in Fig. 1.4. The remaining chapters of this first part are devoted to general issues in the operationalization of theoretical concepts and the selection of research design and methods of measurement. Part II presents more detailed discussion of specific research designs that may be employed, elaborating on a basic distinction between experimental and nonexperimental research approaches. Part III details procedures associated with specific data collection methods, with attention to the relative strengths and weaknesses of each. Specific issues of analysis and interpretation are raised as they are relevant to materials covered in these two sections. Finally, part IV of the book addresses more general issues that cross-cut all methods of research in the social sciences. These general issues include the social and ethical responsibilities associated with the conduct of social research and advancing the cumulative progress of behavioral and social science through combining and synthesizing findings from multiple individual investigations. In these final chapters, we hope to make clear that science is a collective enterprise undertaken in the context of societal values.

SUGGESTED READINGS

Kuhn, T. S. (1970). *The structure of scientific revolutions*. (2nd Ed.). Chicago: University of Chicago Press.

McGuire, W. J. (1997). Creative hypothesis generating in psychology: Some useful heuristics. *Annual Review of Psychology, 48*, 1–30.

Nisbett, R., & Ross, L. (1980). *Human inference: Strategies and shortcomings of social judgment*. Englewood Cliffs, NJ: Prentice-Hall.

2

FITTING RESEARCH DESIGN TO RESEARCH PURPOSE: INTERNAL AND EXTERNAL VALIDITY

Although a wide range of potential research methods is covered in the following chapters, research strategies in the social and behavioral sciences can be divided roughly into two general types—*surveys* and *experiments*. The former include all observations that occur in "natural" (i.e., nonlaboratory) settings and which involve a minimum of interference over people's normal behavior or choices. Experiments (which can be conducted either in laboratory or field settings) include those observational studies in which data are collected under conditions where behavioral choices are limited or in some way constrained by the controlled manipulation of variables and measures selected by the researcher. The advantages and limitations of these two types of research strategies tend to be complementary, so an effective program makes use of both in different states of the research process.[1] Experimental methods are particularly advantageous for determining causal relationships. They also are ideally suited for specifying systematic relationships among sets of isolated and rigidly controlled variables. However, for research in human behavior, the very control that marks the advantage of experimental techniques places limitations on the representativeness of the phenomena they are used to study.

Surveys, on the other hand, have the value of "real world" context and the availability of mass data in developing information about human actions. However, these advantages are bought at the cost of a lack of control over nonsystematic variation in the variables of interest. The inability to exert control over critical variables can result in interesting, but scientifically inconclusive, findings. The relative value of experimental versus survey research methods depends to a large extent on the importance of making inferences about the causal relationships among the variables being studied (Brewer, 2000).

---

[1]The word *program* is used loosely here to refer to accumulated evidence relevant to a particular theoretical position, whether planned and executed by a single researcher or research team, or derived from the uncoordinated efforts of independent researchers working in the same area.

CAUSATION

The overall purpose of most research studies is to investigate a predicted relationship between the occurrence of some variation of one variable, *A*, and the occurrence of variations of another variable, *B*, in the same setting. Variables may be states of the physical or social environment (e.g., weather conditions, the number of people present in the situation), properties of a stimulus (e.g., the facial expression in a photograph, the content of a message), or characteristics of a person or a person's behavior (e.g., mood state, degree of aggression). Relationships can be between two environmental variables (e.g., the relationship between variations in the coldness of the weather on the number of people who are in an outdoor setting), between an environmental or stimulus variable and an individual characteristic or trait (e.g., the relationship between the state of the weather and the average mood of people exposed to it), or between two characteristics of an individual (e.g., the relationship between mood and aggressiveness). To say that there is a relationship between two such variables means that if the state of one variable differs or changes, we can expect that the state of the other will also change or differ. So, for example, if we measure people's mood on a sunny day and then again on a cloudy day and there is a difference in mood such that mood is more negative on the second occasion, then we can say we have shown a relationship between the state of the weather and individuals' moods.

The more precise the theoretical specification of a predicted relationship, the more closely the obtained data can be matched against the prediction. The nature of the relationship may be specified in terms of the form it will take, that is, what kind of changes in *B* will accompany particular changes in *A* (see chap. 8 for a description of some of the functional relationships that may be specified), and what the *causal direction* of the relationship will be. Directionality may be differentiated into three types.[2]

1. *Unidirectional causation*, in which changes in *A* are predicted to produce subsequent changes in *B*, but changes in *B* are not expected to influence *A* (e.g., increases in the temperature-humidity index are accompanied by an increase in aggressive responses of rats, but the degree of aggressiveness of rats does not affect weather conditions).

2. *Bidirectional causation*, in which changes in *A* lead to changes in *B* and, in addition, changing *B* produces changes in *A* (e.g., perceiving threat produces feelings of anxiety, and increasing anxiety enhances the perception of threat).

3. *Noncausal covariation* (or third-variable causation), in which changes in *A* are indirectly accompanied by changes in *B* because both *A* and *B* are determined by changes in a third variable, *C* (e.g., birth rate and consumption of beef steak rise or fall with increases or decreases in the cost of living index).

---

[2]This discussion of causal–noncausal relationships is not affected by the possibility of multiple "levels" of causation. The relationship between any stimulus–response pairing may be examined in terms of organism–environment interactions, sense receptor–effector sequences, or changes in biochemical structure. It is our view that accounts of phenomena at each of these levels of explanation are equally legitimate, provided that the implications of explanations at one level are not contradictory to the implications of those at other levels. For behavioral scientists, causal links are usually described in terms of changes in the overt behavior of an organism relative to changes in the external environment or stimulus features. To be acceptable, however, explanations of these links must be compatible with known limitations of the neurophysiological capacities of the organism and with conditions determined by the requirements of physical survival and social organization.

Causation versus Covariation

The simple observation that B varies when A varies is not sufficient to demonstrate which of the previously mentioned cases holds. To determine that any particular directionality exists, alternative explanations for the observed relationship must be ruled out. Both cases 1 and 2 must be distinguished from case 3 by demonstrating that when A changes *in isolation from* changes in any other factors, subsequent changes are observed in B.[3] Case 1 can be distinguished from case 2 by observing whether modifications in B following changes in A can produce further changes in A. Finally, the validity of the predicted causal variable in a case of type 3 can be determined by noting whether the relationship between A and B can be eliminated if C (and only C) is held constant (i.e., not permitted to vary). All of these differentiations are possible only under conditions in which variations in the relevant variables can be observed uncontaminated by related variations that are not relevant to the theoretical issue. Thus, the greater the precision of the theoretical specifications, the greater the rigor required in hypothesis-testing research to rule out irrelevant details.

Moderators and Mediators of Causal Relationships

In addition to specifying the nature and direction of a causal relationship under study, it also is important to distinguish between two different types of "third variables" that can influence causal relationships—moderators and mediators (Baron & Kenny, 1986). Sometimes causal relationships can be either augmented or blocked by the presence or absence of factors that serve as moderator variables. To take another weather-related illustration, consider the causal relationship between exposure to sun and sunburn. Although there is a well-established cause–effect link here, it can be moderated by a number of factors. For instance, the relationship is much stronger for fair-skinned individuals than for dark-skinned persons. Thus, fair skin is a moderator variable that enhances the causal relationship between sun exposure and burning. However, this does not mean that the sun–sunburn relationship is spurious. The moderator variable (skin pigmentation) does not cause the effect in the absence of the independent variable (sun exposure). Other moderator variables can reduce or block a causal sequence. For instance, the use of effective suntan lotions literally "blocks" (or at least retards) the causal link between the sun's ultraviolet rays and burning. Thus, a researcher who assesses the correlation between sun exposure and sunburn among a sample of fair-skinned people who never venture outdoors without a thick coat of 30 SPF sunblock would be ill-advised to conclude that the absence of correlation implied the absence of causation. Moderator relationships can be represented notationally as follows:

---

[3] When an observed relationship is found to have been mistakenly interpreted as a causal relationship of type 1 or 2, when it is actually a case of type 3, the relationship is said to be *spurious*.

Like Baron and Kenny (1986), we think it is important here to distinguish between third variables that serve as *moderators* and those that serve as *mediators* of a cause–effect relationship. With moderator effects, the causal link is actually between X and Y, but the observed relationship between these two variables is qualified by levels of variable C, which either enhances or blocks the causal process. A mediational relation, on the other hand, is represented as follows:

$$X \longrightarrow C \longrightarrow Y$$

In this case, the presence of C is necessary to complete the causal process that links X and Y. In effect, varying X causes variations in C, which, in turn, causes changes in Y. To return to our weather examples, the effect of rain on depression may be mediated by social factors. Rain causes people to stay indoors or to hide behind big umbrellas, hence reducing social contact. Social isolation may, in turn, produce depression. However, rain may not be the only cause of social isolation. In this case, rain as an independent variable is a sufficient, but not necessary, cause in its link to depression. To demonstrate that X causes Y only if C occurs does not invalidate the claim that X and Y have a causal relationship; it only explicates the causal chain involved.

Moderator variables are reflected in interactions between two or more independent variables, as is discussed more fully in chapter 4. Mediational hypotheses are usually tested way of correlational analyses and are covered in chapter 8.

PHASING OF RESEARCH

The bulk of the preceding discussion has been devoted to research as a venture in causal hypothesis testing. Such a preoccupation with the *verification* (theory testing) phase of scientific investigation is typical of social research in general. The total research process, however, does not begin with the testing of hypotheses and the verification of theory, but rather with the naturalistic observation of human behavior. Observation is quite often an informal activity of people who are interested in the people and things around them. There is probably no way to describe adequately the skill that enables one to decipher the interrelationships that exist in the environment, but without this skill, the chances of generating useful social theory are slim.

Given sufficient observation of natural phenomena, the social scientist is in the position to enter into the second phase of the research process, namely, that of classification. By noting the various circumstances under which the critical phenomenon is modified or affected, the scientist has begun the generation of a very rudimentary theory. At this stage of the cycle, there is greater stress on the accuracy of observation. At the same time, the validity of the classificatory rules employed in the ordering of observations is continually reassessed, particularly if the observational data prove not to be amenable to easy classification.

With the completion of the classificatory phase, the researcher is in a position to initiate the verification process. At this point different sciences diverge, depending on the nature and source of their data. Although all sciences are empirical, not all are experimental. Some areas of investigation—for example, astronomy—involve phenomena that cannot be brought under the manipulative control of the researcher and can only be observed naturally. However, where experimentation is possible, it is the most powerful research strategy available for determining the source and direction of relational events. Essentially, the purpose of the hypothesis-testing experiment is to clarify the relationship between two (or more) variables by bringing the variation of at least one of the elements in the relationship under the control of the researcher; that is, the experimenter determines when and how changes in this variable occur. The element that is subjected to this controlled variation is referred to as the *independent variable* because its manifestation is manipulated independently of its "natural" sources of variation. Its variations are referred to as experimental *treatments* or *manipulations*. The other element of the relationship under investigation, which is observed but not controlled by the experimenter (although its allowable manifestations may be somewhat limited by the particular research setting) is referred to as the *dependent variable* because it is expected to be influenced by the manipulations of the independent variable. If the experimental research is adequately controlled (see chaps. 4 & 5), the observed variations in the dependent variable will be attributable to the effects of the independent variable. Thus, the experiment provides a critical setting for demonstrating the nature of the relationship between theoretically relevant variables, but as such it is only one phase in the theory-building process.[4]

In many ways, the efforts of the observation and classification periods determine to a great extent the potential value of the outcome of the verification process. If, during these earlier phases, the interrelationships between the dependent and independent variables were accurately assessed, then the probability that the experimental investigation will confirm earlier intuitions and add to the store of trustworthy social knowledge is high. A trial-and-error approach to experimentation sometimes opens up new and meaningful lines of investigation, but premature emphasis on the verification phase of research also can lead to a misdirection of attention to the interrelationships of variables having no real or important connection. If important progress is to be made in this field, investigators must realize that research is not completely summarized by a discrete, one-shot investigation of a hypothesis, but rather is a process whose earlier phases are as critical as the more prestigious validation procedures.

The successful verification of a suspected relationship within the limited conditions of the experimental laboratory does not complete the research process. The artificially controlled nature of the laboratory experiment introduces the possibility that an observed relationship exists only under the restricted conditions of a particular research setting. To rule out this threat to the validity of a theoretical proposition, the relationship must be empirically demonstrated under a variety of controlled and natural conditions. If it turns out that the predicted relationship consistently exists under some conditions, but not under others (e.g., increasing monetary incentives increases work output in large manufacturing companies, but not in small ones), the theory must be able to account for these limiting circumstances or risk being supplanted by one that does. To insure that our theoretical concepts and hypotheses have been adequately tested, our research repertoire must contain a number of heterogeneous methods and techniques.

FORMS OF VALIDITY

The stage of research at which a particular investigation falls should dictate the research strategy the investigator adopts. This choice, in turn, should be guided by considerations of two types of validity—internal and external validity (Campbell & Stanley, 1963). These

---

[4]Lachenmeyer (1970) made a strong argument for the role of experimental methodology in all phases of theory construction, including the development of observational techniques and measurements, fact-finding exploratory research, and the verification of the existence of hypothesized relationships. In our view, however, the unique features of the experiment make it most useful as a hypothesis-testing device.

forms of validity reflect on the quality of different, but critically important, aspects of the research process. *Internal validity* has to do with the certainty with which one can attribute a research outcome to the application of a treatment or manipulation that is under the rigid control of the researcher. Internal validity is about the extent to which causal inferences can legitimately be made about the nature of the relationship between the treatment and the outcome. *External validity* is concerned with the issue of generalizability. Assuming that a research finding is internally valid, external validity has to do with the extent that it can be generalized to other respondent groups, to other settings, and to different ways of operationalizing the conceptual variables.

Typically, the exposition of these forms of validity is reserved for discussions involving experimental methods, and in the case of internal validity, this is proper because the issue of internal validity is concerned with the appropriate interpretation of the relationship between an independent and a dependent variable, the central feature of all experimentation. However, considerations of generalizability are equally important in evaluating the worth of experimental and nonexperimental research, and as such, should be considered in both experiments and survey research contexts. Before beginning this discussion, however, three closely related issues—the role of statistics, the field/laboratory distinction, and the contrast between basic and applied research—are considered.

The Role of Statistics, or Statistical Validity

Just as the choice of research method must be conditioned on considerations of the nature of the phenomenon of interest, so too must the role of statistical techniques be evaluated with respect to the general goal of eliminating or reducing the plausibility of rival alternative hypotheses for the events under investigation. One potential rival explanation that plagues social research at all stages of investigation is the operation of "chance." The phenomena of interest to the social sciences are generally subject to considerable nonsystematic variation, that is, variations from individual to individual and, within individuals, from time to time. Given such uncontrolled (and unexplained) variability, the occurrence of any observed pattern of data is always potentially attributable to the operation of chance, or random happenstance. The purpose of most inferential statistical tests is to assess the validity of this rival explanation of results in terms of the probability, or likelihood, that the obtained data pattern could have occurred by chance. That is, statistical inference allows us to assign a probability to one type of threat to internal validity—the operation of chance as a possible cause of any relationship between independent and dependent variables. The results of a statistical inference test tell us the probability of a *Type I* error of inference—the likelihood that a result would be obtained when the *null hypothesis* (no true relationship between the independent and dependent variable) is actually valid. Statistical significance is achieved when this probability is so low as to render the chance explanation implausible. Usually, a value of .05 or less (i.e., an outcome that could have occurred by chance no more than 5 times in 100) is chosen as the cut-off value.[5]

When the probability of a Type I error is not low enough to make the null hypothesis implausible, we have to worry about making a *Type II* error of inference—failing to reject the null hypothesis even when it is false (i.e., there really is a relationship between the independent and dependent variables but we have failed to detect it strongly enough).

---

[5] In the social research literature, the use of statistical significance testing has come under challenge (Hunter, 1997), but for many reasons, it still represents current practice (Abelson, 1997; Estes, 1997).

Reducing the probability of Type II errors depends on designing experiments with sufficient power (see Cohen, 1992) to detect effects above and beyond random variation. The power of an experiment (or of a survey study) depends in part on the number of participants that are measured (in general, power is increased as the number of participants included in the study increases) and also on the precision and reliability of the measures that are used (see chap. 3). Ideally, our studies will have sufficient statistical power so that we can adequately assess the probability of a Type I error without risking high probability of making a Type II error.

For the purposes of testing the role of chance, statistical analyses are very powerful and necessary research tools indeed. However, the time and effort required to master the theory and calculations essential for the use of statistical significance testing techniques have led many students of social science to confuse statistical sophistication with expertise in research design. Statistical considerations are not the beginning and end of our research design concerns. Indeed, in our view, proper research design almost invariably simplifies the statistical analyses that we require (see Smith, 2000). The statistical analyses that are chosen should depend first on their relevance to the theoretical issues being addressed, and second, on the nature of the design. Complicated statistics cannot compensate for poor design. Teaching the student to avoid the pitfall of equating current tools of analysis with the purpose of research methodology is a major aim of this text. Our sentiments lie with those of Agnew and Pike (1969) who observed:

> It is our view that the researcher who works outside the laboratory should, if anything, be more sophisticated about the principles of measurement, research design, statistics, and rules of evidence than the laboratory researcher. Note that we are talking about principles of research design, not about rituals. Though more difficult to teach, it would be preferable to provide the student with an appreciation of the main rules of evidence used in science. Hopefully, the student would then be able to select research tools that fit his research interests, rather than looking for a research problem that will fit his research tools. (p. 142)

Field versus Laboratory Research

For a long time in social psychology, a controversy existed between the proponents of field research and those who favored laboratory experimentation. The field researchers claimed that only in real-life settings could we discover anything of value—that the responses of participants who were studied within the cold, antiseptic environment of the social psychological laboratory could not be viewed as valid representations of the behavior they would have emitted in more normal, everyday circumstances. The laboratory experimentalists, on the other hand, argued that so many theoretically extraneous events occurred in the natural environment (the field) that one could never be certain about the true relationship that existed among any given set of variables.

As is the case with most arguments of this type, both sides were partially correct, and both were partially wrong. To be sure, there are numerous examples of laboratory research that is so devoid of reality that its practical or scientific utility must be seriously questioned. It is just as obvious, however, that not all laboratory research is social psychology is psychologically "unreal" (see Aronson, Wilson, & Brewer, 1998). In many areas of investigation (e.g., in communication, persuasion, group interaction), we have gained much valuable information about the complicated nature of human social interaction. To argue that nothing of value can come out of the social laboratory is to deny the obvious.

On the other side of the argument are the laboratory researchers who contend that so many uncontrolled events occur in the relatively free-form field environment that no clear specification of relationships between or among theoretically implicated measures is possible. As before, there are plenty of examples that would serve to "prove" the contentions of the critics of field research. The inability of these researchers to randomly assign respondents to various conditions of a study—indeed, the inability of the investigator even to control the presence or absence of very powerful factors that would obviously have major influences on critical behaviors—are two of the more telling problems frequently mentioned by the critics. These problems are real and are part of the standard set of difficulties the field researcher faces whenever studies of this general nature are attempted. With the increasing sophistication evident in much contemporary field research, however, it is becoming ever more apparent that these difficulties can be surmounted, or, if not completely offset, their effects at least identified. Many recent research methodology texts focus specifically on the complete or partial solution of the many problems encountered in field research settings.

In brief, in our view there is a place in the social sciences for both field and laboratory research; each reinforces the value of the other. The findings obtained in the laboratory are retested in the field, where their robustness is put to a severe test. If the findings hold, then a potentially important addition to our knowledge base is gained. Likewise, the less-than-completely controlled observations of the field researcher can be brought to the laboratory for more rigorous examination. If these observations prove valid within the more strict confines of the laboratory, their value is already established, given their initial development in the "real world." Thus, field and laboratory research not only do not compete, they complement each other in real and important ways. Today's social science appears in agreement with this assessment. Many of our most precise research endeavors are, in fact, field experiments (see chap. 7), and some of our most powerful generalizations were born in the "sterile" confines of the laboratory (Mook, 1983). The integration of field and laboratory research methodologies, that is, of combining surveys and experiments, is examined in the forthcoming chapters. But before we begin this examination, we consider one final differentiation between general types of investigation, this one involving the distinction between basic and applied research.

Basic and Applied Research

Viewing the research process as the accumulative reduction of plausible alternatives to a particular theoretical account provides a context for some consideration of the traditional distinction between basic and applied research. Essentially, the difference between the two lies in whether relatively long-term or short-term gains are expected from the outcomes of the research. The *applied* label refers to those research efforts that are directed toward affecting a particular phenomenon in some preconceived way (e.g., which of several advertising campaigns will produce the greater number of product sales; which serum formula will terminate the symptoms of skin cancer most effectively; which remedial program will reduce illiteracy in the urban ghetto). Because the goals of applied research are relatively concrete, feedback on the effectiveness of any experimental manipulation is immediate. For *basic* research, on the other hand, the goal of each research project is to contribute to that ephemeral universe of knowledge, or, in somewhat more specific terms, to add to the accumulative pattern of data that will ultimately determine the survival value of alternative theoretical interpretations of the phenomena under investigation (e.g., *which* theory of consumer motivation; *which* etiology of skin cancer; *which* explanation of the nature of mass illiteracy). In this enterprise, the value of any particular research contribution can only be judged from a historical perspective.

The differential value of applied and basic research does not lie in any major differences in rigor of research methodology or clarity of results (Bickman & Rog, 1998). Rather, from the perspective provided in this chapter, the essential difference lies in the relative probability that results of research programs will contribute to the development of a broadly based explanatory theory or to a limited exploration of some causal relationship. To the extent that applied research is restricted to the examination of variations in a particular *A–B* relationship, it is unlikely to uncover some explanatory principle that accounts for *C–D*, *E–F, and A–B*. The applied social researcher is likely to limit the research explorations, for example, to sources of tension between blacks and whites in contemporary American society. A basic research program, on the other hand, would be more likely to be concerned with the general phenomenon of ethnocentrism in intergroup relations, thus involving the investigation of black–white relations, *as well as* interethnic relations, international relations, and all other manifestations of the phenomenon (probably including interactions among lower animals within an evolutionary framework).

It is the contention of many who are committed to basic social research that its long-run benefits, in terms of the alleviation of social problems, will be greater than those of applied research. However, just as the distinction between long-term and short-term is a relative one, the difference between applied and basic research is a matter of degree. To the extent that applied researchers are open to creative variations in their research problems, it becomes probable that they will serendipitously arrive at findings that will have broad theoretical impact. On the other hand, the more the basic researcher becomes involved in the permutations or combinations of a particular *A–B* relationship, or the more committed he or she becomes to a minor theoretical point (i.e., the closer one comes to the stereotypic version of the "ivory tower" scholar), the less likely it is that the research will contribute to a meaningful expansion of the explanatory power of the discipline, no matter how *in*applicable the results of the research may be!

BASIC ISSUES OF INTERNAL VALIDITY

As we have just indicated, the purpose of the design of experiments is oriented toward eliminating possible alternative explanations of research results (i.e., variations in scores on the dependent variable) that are unrelated to the effects of the treatment (independent variable) of interest. When an experiment is adequately designed, changes in the dependent variable can be attributed to variations in the treatment, which is manipulated by the investigator; that is, response differences on the dependent variable can be accounted for by differences in exposure (or lack of exposure) to the experimental treatment. These differences may occur between measures on the same persons taken before and after exposure (the *pretest–posttest design*) or between measures on different groups which have been exposed to different conditions (*the comparison-group design*). In either case, if any obtained differences can be attributed directly to the experimental treatment, the study is said to have internal validity. If factors other than the experimental treatment could plausibly account for the obtained differences, then the internal validity of the study is threatened. The existence of such rival factors is usually referred to as a *confounding* of the experimental treatment because the potential effects of the variable under investigation cannot be separated from the effects of these other variables. A research study is said to be confounded, or internally invalid, when there is reason to believe that obtained differences in the dependent variable would have occurred *even if exposure to the independent variable had not been manipulated.* Potential sources of such invalidity that could affect almost any research program have been identified and discussed by Campbell and Stanley (1963). The eight major threats to internal validity that they discussed may be summarized as follows:

1. *History.* Differences in scores on the dependent variable measured at two different times may result from events that have occurred during the passage of time between measures, and these events events are unrelated to the experimental treatment.

2. *Maturation.* One general class of effects that may occur over the passage of time between measures on the dependent variable involves changes in the internal conditions of the participants in the study, such as growing older, becoming more tired, less interested, and so on. These are termed maturation effects even though some representatives of this class (e.g., growing tired) are not typically thought of as being related to physical maturation.

3. *Testing.* Participants' scores on the second administration of the dependent variable may be affected by the fact of their having been previously exposed to the measure.

4. *Instrumentation.* Changes across time in dependent variable scores may be caused by changes in the nature of the measurement instrument (e.g., changes in attitudes of observers, increased sloppiness on the part of test scorers, etc.) rather than by changes in the participants being measured.

5. *Statistical regression.* Unreliability, or error of measurement, will produce changes in scores on different measurement occasions, and these scores are subject to misinterpretation if participants are selected on the basis of extreme scores at their initial measurement session. (This threat to internal validity is discussed more fully in chap. 9.)

6. *Selection.* When dependent variable scores for two or more different groups of participants are being compared, differences between groups could be due to special selection procedures employed in constructing the comparison groups.

7. *Experimental mortality.* If groups are being compared, any selection procedures or treatment differences that result in different proportions of participants dropping out of the experiment may account for any differences obtained between the groups in the final measurement.

8. *Selection-history interactions.* If participants have been differentially selected for inclusion in comparison groups, these specially selected groups may experience differences in history, maturation, testing, and so on, which may produce differences in the final measurement on the dependent variable.

An example of a simple research study may help to clarify how these factors may operate to make it impossible to determine whether the independent variable of interest is actually responsible for producing changes in the dependent measure. In this hypothetical study, the attitudes of a group of college students toward their school's administrators are measured. One week after the initial measurement, the same group of students is exposed to an administrator's speech (the experimental treatment), which advocates stricter discipline for students. The student group is then measured again on the attitude test. In this simple pretest–posttest design involving only one group, the researcher is interested in whether the speech communication changes attitudes expressed on the test. However, with this design, any attitude changes (or lack of change) in the group occurring between pretest and posttest could not be directly attributed to the effects of the communication because of the many uncontrolled factors that could provide rival alternative explanations. For instance, during the passage of time between pretest and posttest, some event might have occurred on campus (*history*), which altered attitudes instead of the communication. The school authorities, for example, might have voted a major tuition increase.

It should be noted here that although individual histories may cause individual changes in test scores, only commonly experienced events, which affect most of the group in the same way, will produce systematic changes between the pretest and posttest scores; that is, individuals may have varied (historical) experiences, some of which tend to increase attitude scores and some of which tend to decrease scores. Across individuals these will cancel out, unless most of the individuals have the same experience, which exerts a consistent effect, in one direction, on all of their scores.

Similarly, the class of variables categorized as *maturation* effects could account for changes in attitude scores. It is possible, for instance, that as students become older and more experienced, they generally become more tolerant or accepting of authority figures. The longer the time period between pretest and posttest, the more likely it is that maturation or intervening historical events will provide plausible rival explanations for any obtained attitude change.

A third rival explanation could arise from the possibility that pretesting produces sensitivity to the issue, which causes changes in responses to the second test. For some kinds of dependent variables, particularly achievement tests, test-taking practice effects usually lead to improved performance on a second measure, even if different questions are used. Unlike history or maturation, these *pretest sensitivity* or *practice effects* are more likely to provide plausible alternative explanations of results with shorter intervals between pretest and posttest.

Another type of measurement effect could occur if there were possible differences in scoring procedures employed between the pretest and the posttest (*instrumentation effects*). This would be especially likely if the attitude test was in the form of an essay exam (where scorers could shift standards between tests) rather than an objectively scored (e.g., multiple-choice) test. Whenever measurements are in any way dependent on subjective judgments of scorers or observers, as is often the case with social psychological variables, biases of the measurer may produce instrumentation effects. For instance, in the previously mentioned study, the researcher himself may have presented the pro-authority speech. If he were strongly personally committed to influencing the participants, and if he were scoring an essay-type attitude test under these circumstances, he might be much more likely to detect pro-authority statements in the essays after the speech than during the pretest, thereby introducing scoring differences in favor of his own bias. Even with well-trained objective scorers, subtle differences in attitudes or conscientiousness over time may produce systematic instrumentation effects.

Instrumentation effects can be controlled by requiring several unbiased scorers to agree in their judgments or by scoring pretests and posttests at the same time without letting the scorers know which is which. Unfortunately, other rival factors cannot be so readily eliminated within the simple pretest–posttest design. Ideally, the factors of history, maturation, and testing could be controlled if we could measure each participant at the same point in time both with and without the experimental treatment. Then any differences between the two measures could be interpreted as due to the effect of the treatment and nothing else. As long as we are bound by the restrictions of Aristotelian logic, however, the best we can do is to measure two different groups of participants that are equivalent in terms of the effects of the rival factors. If one of these groups is then exposed to the experimental treatment and the other is not, then any changes in the experimental (or treatment) group above and beyond those that occur in the control group (the one receiving no treatment) can be attributed to the experimental variable. In other words, even though history, maturation, et cetera, may produces changes *within* the two groups, any difference *between* the groups can be accounted for by the experimental treatment that was administered to one but not to the other.

Random Assignment and Experimental Control

As was previously noted, the design of experiments is intended to eliminate threats to internal validity. The prototype of a good experimental design is one in which groups of people who are initially equivalent (at the pretest phase) are randomly assigned to receive the experimental treatment or a control condition and then assessed again after this differential experience (posttest phase). A graphic depiction of this *pretest–posttest– control group design* is presented in Fig. 2.1. As noted, random assignment of participants to the experimental and control groups must be assumed if the design is to be considered a true experiment.

The success of the two-group experimental design depends primarily on the assumption that experimental and control groups are equivalent on all factors except exposure to the independent variable. The ideal of comparability between two groups with respect to all variables other than the ones under experimental investigation may be met in either of two ways. Some variables may literally be "held constant," that is, maintained at the same level for all participants in all groups (e.g., testing everyone at the same time of day, using the same experimenter for all participants, etc.). Other variables may be allowed to vary randomly with the assumption that there will be no systematic differences between the sets of participants in the two comparison groups on these extraneous sources of variation. This is accomplished through the technique of *randomized assignment* to groups.

Randomization requires that all individuals available for a particular research study be potentially able to participate in either the experimental or the control group, and that only chance determines the group to which any individual is assigned. When enough participants are available, this chance assignment assures that there are no systematic differences between the groups initially and also that there is no reason to believe that they will experience any systematically different histories during the research period, other than the experimental treatment.

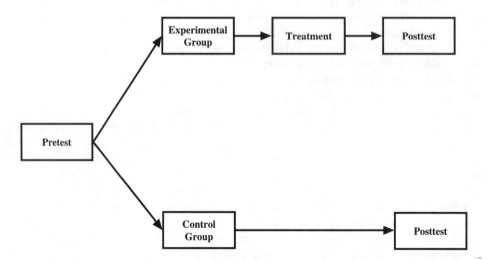

FIG. 2.1. Diagram of a pretest–posttest–control–group design.

If any basis other than chance is used to assign participants to groups, then participant selection may account for differences on the dependent variable. Particularly hazardous is any selection procedure that permits participants themselves to determine to which treatment they will be exposed. Such self-selection on the part of the research participants makes it impossible to tell whether the treatment affected dependent variable scores or whether differences in scores were determined by the personal characteristics of the individuals who chose to expose themselves to the experimental treatment. For example, in educational research dealing with remedial teaching programs, it is unwise to expose volunteers to the program and then to compare their progress with that of a "control" group of students who refused to take part in the program. If any differences in achievement show up, it is impossible to determine whether they were brought about by the remedial program or whether characteristics of the volunteer participants, such as greater motivation to improve, were responsible for the performance differences. Only volunteer participants who were randomly assigned to a no-remedial-treatment condition could provide an equivalent control group for comparison with the experimental group.

The self-selection of participants to experimental or control conditions can cloud the interpretability of a study, but other forms of selection artifacts can also arise when randomization is not employed, and these sometimes can prove even more difficult to recognize than simple self-selection. Unfortunately, in some research circumstances, nonrandom selection is nearly impossible to avoid. Under such circumstances, extreme caution must be exercised in the interpretation of research findings. To illustrate this point, we expand our example of an experimental testing program.

Suppose that the government developed a program designed to offset the academic deficiencies of children whose parents fell below federal poverty guidelines. Only poor children, in other words, were eligible for this program. How would the researcher determine whether the educational program was succeeding? A pretest–posttest–control group experimental design would seem ideal for the investigator's purposes, but who would constitute the control group? From our previous discussion, it is clear that one would not compare the academic achievement of treatment group participants with that of children who were eligible for the program, but who had failed to volunteer for it. Too many differences already exist between volunteers and nonvolunteers to trust such a comparison (see Rosenthal & Rosnow, 1975).

Alternatively, one could sample from a group of children who were not eligible for the program. However, these "control" children would be from a higher economic stratum than that of the experimental group, and we already know from years of educational research that there is a positive relationship between socioeconomic status and academic achievement. Thus, a comparison of this type would almost surely show large initial (pretest) differences between the groups, in favor of the (richer) control-group participants. Such a difference would reflect the selection artifact that is operating here.

Another possibility would be to systematically search for children in the control group whose pretest scores matched exactly that of children in the experimental condition. If a suitable match could be found for every participant in the experimental group, then by definition the average pretest scores of the two groups would be identical. Whereas this might seem an appealing solution to some, it is fraught with difficulties because it implicitly assumes that the histories, the maturation rates, and so on, of the two samples will be identical over the course of the study. This is a risky assumption at best, and in light of considerable research (e.g., Cronbach & Snow, 1977), palpably unlikely in the present circumstances. We know that children of higher socioeconomic status are academically advantaged relative to their poorer peers and that this "achievement gap" widens as time goes by. This "selection x maturation interaction" artifact is often difficult to recognize and even more difficult to offset. Likewise, if the histories of the two groups differed systematically over the course of the experiment (a likely possibility if the treatment extended for any period), we will encounter an interaction of "selection x history," whose effects can bias the results just as surely as that of the simple selection bias discussed earlier.

Solutions to the problems introduced by selection artifacts are not simple. Generally, complex statistical techniques are employed in the attempt to assess, if not offset, the biases that can occur when the assignment of participants to conditions is not random (see chap. 9 for a more extended discussion of this issue). It should be kept in mind that these statistical "fixes" are not ideal, but rather akin to a salvage operation. Clearly, if randomization can be accomplished, it should be.

Participant Loss

The advantages of random assignment for internal validity are assured as long as the initial equivalence of the experimental and control groups can be maintained throughout the study. Unfortunately, research involving volunteer participants is never free of the possibility that at some time between random assignment to groups and the posttest, some of the participants may drop out of the experiment and become unavailable for final testing. If the groups are initially equivalent, and if this drop-out rate (referred to by the more morbid as *participant mortality*) is determined by random factors, then the loss of participants should not be any different for the experimental and control groups and does not pose a threat to internal validity. If we have pretested all participants at the beginning of the experiment, we can check the pretest scores for those participants who have dropped out. If those scores are essentially the same for drop-outs from both the experimental and the control groups, we have some assurance that the two groups are still equivalent except for effects of the experimental treatment.

If there is something about the experimental treatment that enhances or otherwise affects the chances of participants dropping out of the study, a serious problem is introduced because the initially equivalent groups may become differentially selected groups by the time of final testing. For instance, if after random assignment to research groups, participants in the experimental treatment group learn that they are going to be subjected to a severe electric shock as part of their participation, many of them may find excuses for discontinuing their involvement in the experiment. Thus, at the time of post-treatment testing, the experimental group would be composed almost entirely of unusually brave or unusually compliant participants, unlike the control group, which had not been exposed to the same selective pressures.

The good researcher must be aware that participant selection is a potential problem not only at the initial stage of assigning participants to groups but throughout the study, and will attempt to design the experiment such that differences between the treatments received by experimental and control groups will not themselves introduce differential tendencies to drop out of the experiment. In the example given earlier, for instance, the experimenter could see to it that both experimental and control groups were led to expect that they might receive an electric shock (even though only the experimental group would actually receive it). This procedure would not prevent participants from dropping out of the study, but it would assure that such drop-outs were equally distributed between experimental and control conditions.

Sometimes participants are dropped from an experiment by the researcher, either during the course of the experiment or at the time of data analysis. For instance, on identifying one or two participants who show unusual performance after the experimental treatment, the researcher might examine the background information for these participants, conclude that they were highly atypical, and thereby justify the removal of their data from the final analysis. If the participants in the control group are not also examined for similar atypical cases, the researcher has applied a differential selection rule which may result in an apparent "treatment effect" that would not have appeared if all the data had been included. In general, it is not permissible for a researcher to eliminate participants at any point after assignment to groups has occurred, although weeding out the participant pool prior to random assignment is sometimes acceptable.

Other Sources of Invalidity

Complete control over experimental treatments is necessitated by the fact that inferences drawn from control group studies are acceptable only when the treatments to which the experimental and control groups are exposed differ only on the variable under consideration (i.e., all other conditions are held constant). For example, in physiological research dealing with the effects of surgical removal of the brain, some animals are subjected to the full surgery (the experimental group), whereas others go through a "sham operation," in which they undergo all of the phases of the surgery except the actual removal of the brain section. The sham operation control is used to assure that differences between experimental and control animals are attributable to effects of the surgical ablation and not to experiences associated with general operative procedures, such as anesthesia or post-operative shock. Similarly, a researcher interested in the effects of anxiety-producing situations must be sure that the conditions to which the experimental and control groups are exposed differ only in anxiousness and not in such extraneous variables as the relationship between participant and experimenter.

The Fallible Observer.   One source of internal invalidity that can threaten an experiment, even when random assignment has been used, is that derived from the researcher's expectations about how the experiment will (or should) turn out. Chapter 6 discusses research indicating how such expectations can influence, in relatively complex and subtle ways, the nature of the experimenter–participant interaction. However, more direct experimenter effects may influence the outcome of a study independent of any effects on participant responses. Such effects are generated by unintentional differences in criteria applied by observers to participants in different groups, unintentional misinterpretation of participants' responses, unintentional errors of data recording and analysis, and the like.[6] (Such factors would be considered "instrumentation" effects in our earlier discussion of threats to internal validity.)

   A valuable example of the effects of observer bias on the (mis)recording of participants' responses was provided by Kennedy and Uphoff (1939). These experimenters asked individuals who were classified on the basis of their belief or lack of belief in extrasensory perception (ESP) to take part in a test of ESP ability. Using a standard card-guessing task, the participant-observers were to "transmit" the symbol portrayed on each of a set of cards to another individual and to record the guesses made by this "receiver." The persons whose ESP was being tested were, in fact, experimental accomplices, and the "guesses" they made were pre-recorded. The principal dependent measure of this investigation was

---

[6]The word *unintentional* is stressed here because such effects can occur even when the experimenter makes an honest effort to avoid them.

the number of times the participant-observers erred in recording the accomplice's responses. Of 11,125 guesses, only 126 (1.1%) were misrecorded. Given the magnitude of
the recording task, an *error rate* of 1.1% would not seem overly bothersome. However,
closer examination of the direction of these errors as a function of the individual student-
observer's beliefs in ESP proved revealing. Of the 57 errors tending to increase telepathy
scores, 36 (63%) were committed by "believers" in ESP. Conversely, 18 of the 27 errors
(67%) lowering telepathy scores were made by the "unbelievers." These errors, then, were
definitely influenced by the observers' prior beliefs, and were clearly not random, though
they admittedly were small, as is typical of findings in this area of research.

Control Variables.   As the previous examples illustrate, the ideal of *ceteris paribus*—
that there be no differences in conditions to which comparison groups are exposed except
the experimental variable under consideration—is seldom perfectly met in practice. The
experimental and control groups can never be treated precisely alike in every detail; some
minor variation can be ignored as irrelevant. However, it pays to be aware of details—
today's irrelevancy may become tomorrow's major breakthrough.[7] The need for careful
control over experimental variables has driven some social researchers to limit themselves
to laboratory research and ritualized research techniques. However, it is our hope that
greater awareness of the principles that underlie research methods will encourage investigators to apply their ingenuity to achieving controlled variations in a variety of potential
research settings.

BASIC ISSUES OF EXTERNAL VALIDITY

The design issues we have been discussing thus far in the chapter are concerned almost
exclusively with the internal validity of a research study. In many ways, internal validity
is the *sine qua non* of good experimental research. The essence of experimental design
is to control the assignment of participants to treatment groups and the conditions of
treatment delivery in such a way as to rule out or minimize threats to the internal validity
of the study, so that any differences observed in the dependent measures can be traced
directly to the variations in independent variables introduced by the experimenter. Even
when internal validity is high, however, there may arise questions about the validity of
interpretations of causal effects obtained in any given study, particularly their applicability
or generalizability outside of the experimental setting. These concerns constitute questions
of external validity, which can be further divided into questions of (1) generalizability
of operationalizations and (2) generalizability of results to other places and participant
populations (see Cook & Campbell, 1979).

Validity of Operationalizations

Concerns over the validity of operations refer to the correct identification of the nature of the
independent and dependent variables and the underlying relationship between them, that
is, to what extent do the operations and measures embodied in the experimental procedures
of a particular study reflect the theoretical concepts that gave rise to the study in the first
place? Threats to this form of validity arise from errors of measurement, misspecification

---

[7]At one time, for example, rat researchers paid no attention to whether their animals were handled or
petted between experimental sessions; now, handling is recognized as an important determinant of learning
performance.

of research operations, and, in general, the complexity of stimulus features that constitute our experimental treatments.

The complex experimental manipulations characteristic of social research are marked by what Aronson et al. (1998) call "multiple meaning"; that is, their impact on participants may be due to any of several factors inherent in the treatment situation, many of which may be completely extraneous to the conceptual variables of interest. In such cases, researchers cannot be sure that any effects obtained actually reflect the influence of the one construct they were attempting to represent in their experimental operations. Confidence in interpretation is enhanced if a series of experiments is conducted in which the conceptual variable is represented by a number of different experimental manipulations that vary as much as possible, having in common only the one basic factor of (theoretical) interest. When different techniques produce the same result, attributing the effect to the common conceptual variable is substantiated.

As an illustration of the construct validation of an experimental manipulation, we consider an experiment undertaken by Aronson and Mills (1959) to test the hypothesis that undergoing a severe initiation to join a social group enhances the attractiveness of that group to the initiate. In their original experiment, Aronson and Mills convinced female college students that they needed to pass an "embarrassment test" to qualify to participate in a series of group discussions on various sensitive topics. In one version of the experimental procedures, the initiation test was relatively mild, but the severe initiation condition required that the participant read aloud (in front of a male experimenter) a considerable amount of sexually explicit material and a list of obscene words. As predicted, those participants who underwent the severe initiation were more favorable in their later evaluations of the group discussion (which was actually quite dull) than were the participants in the mild initiation condition.

Aronson and Mills (1959) designed their experimental approach as an operational representation of some concepts derived from dissonance theory. The basic idea being tested was that the participant needed to justify effort expended in qualifying for the group discussion, and they could do so by evaluating the goal of their effort—the group discussion—as worth that effort. The greater the effort involved, the greater the need for justification and hence, the greater the need to positively value the group experience. When the experiment was published, however, a number of alternative explanations for the effect of initiation severity on attraction ratings were proposed. Most of these alternatives revolved around the fact that the Aronson and Mills procedures for manipulating "effort" involved a potentially sexually arousing experience. If that were the case, then the carry-over of sexual excitement to evaluations of the group discussion, rather than effort justification, may have accounted for the positive effects of the severe initiation condition.

To rule out this alternative interpretation, Gerard and Mathewson (1966) designed a replication experiment with a different operationalization of effort expenditure. In this second experiment, electric shock, rather than the reading of obscene materials, was used as the severe initiation experience, and the shocks were represented as a test of "emotionality," rather than as an "embarrassment test." Having thus removed sexual arousal as a component of the experimental manipulations, Gerard and Mathewson obtained results that confirmed the original findings—participants who underwent painful shocks to join a dull group evaluated that group more positively than did participants who underwent very mild shocks. This replication of the basic effect with different experimental operations confirms, at least indirectly, the effort-justification interpretation of the original study and provides support for the external validity of the initial experimental manipulations. The Gerard and Mathewson experiment represents a *conceptual replication* of the earlier Aronson and

Mills study. The role of such replication studies in the validation of social science theory is discussed in more detail in chapters 7 and 18.

Generalizability

Once a research study has been completed, the investigator is usually interested in reaching conclusions that are generalizable across people and across settings. Results that are applicable only to particular persons at a particular time or place are of little value to a scientific endeavor that aims at achieving general principles of human behavior. *Generalizability* refers to the robustness of a phenomenon—the extent to which a relationship, once identified, can be expected to recur at other times and places under different environmental conditions. Threats to this form of external validity arise from possible *interaction* effects between the treatment variable of interest and the context in which it is delivered, or the type of participant population involved. An experimental finding lacks external validity if the nature of the effect of the independent variable would be reduced or altered if the setting or the participant population were changed. Because so many of the laboratory experiments in social psychology are conducted with college students as participants, it has been suggested that the truth of the causal relationships we observe may be limited to that particular population. If it happens that college students—with their youth, above-average intelligence, health, and socioeconomic background—respond differently to our experimental treatment conditions than would other types of people, then the external (but not internal) validity of our findings would be suspect. However, this population-based hypothesis is subject to the same rules of evidence as any other.

Just as the validity of measurement depends on an adequate representation of variation in the theoretical concept, participant generalizability depends on the extent to which the participants included in a study represent the potential variability of the human organism. We have already discussed the principle of random assignment of participants to treatment conditions, but further randomization is required to assure generalizability of results, namely, random *selection* of the sample from the entire population of relevant persons. (In chap. 10 we consider a number of different forms of respondent sampling.) As with random assignment, the ground rule of random participant selection is that all persons in the population of interest are equally likely to be included in the research sample. Such random sampling is a rarely realized ideal in social research. Limited resources and participant availability make it impossible and, in many cases, the necessity for keeping experimental and control groups equivalent further limits the participant pool. Under the typical volunteer participant conditions, the usual procedure is to randomly sample from some readily available population and then to generalize to those persons who cannot be assumed to be systematically different from those who took part in the research study. This still places severe limitations on generalizability of findings—research results obtained from college sophomores can hardly be automatically assumed to apply to a population that includes grade school dropouts and people over 60—but the cost and impracticality of true random sampling usually make this limitation a necessity.

One way to overcome the lack of generalizability of most research studies is to repeat essentially the same design with different populations of persons as they become available. To the extent that research results are reproduced with different types of persons, generalization across all persons becomes more convincing. Even a failure to replicate findings with different population adds to our understanding of the phenomenon being investigated by identifying the limitations of the effects of the variables under study.

Apart from *generalizability across participants*, the reproducibility of any research findings may be limited to the conditions under which the phenomenon was studied. *Condition replicability* involves two aspects: the internal conditions of the research participants across time, and the external physical and social environment in which the research is carried out. Too often, replication of research studies is conducted with the aim of reproducing, in precise detail, the exact conditions of the original research. Apart from the inevitable futility of such an approach to replication, it is not consistent with the aim of identifying principles and relationships that have some survival value across heterogeneous circumstances. Conclusions are of limited value if they cannot satisfy this criterion of robustness in the face of altered research conditions.

Possibly the most serious limitation to generalizability of research results arises from the limitations imposed by the necessities of experimental design and the restricted environment of the scientific laboratory. The social psychological laboratory setting represents a unique and isolated social experience, in which the researcher exercises unusual control over the environmental conditions to which the participant is exposed and which limit the participant's available choices of behavior. In many respects, this is the strength of the scientific approach to understanding social phenomena, for until simple principles are isolated and identified, the complex gamut of social relations will remain unfathomable. However, the unusual relationship that occurs between researcher and participant, and the participant's awareness of being an object of scientific investigation, may produce phenomena that are unique to the laboratory setting. Until the implications of such research are examined under broader social conditions, any conclusions drawn are at best tentative.

SUGGESTED READINGS

Baron, R. M., & Kenny, D. A. (1986). The moderator-mediator variable distinction in social psychological research: Conceptual, strategic, and statistical considerations. *Journal of Personality and Social Psychology, 51*, 1173–1182.

Campbell, D. T., & Stanley, J. C. (1966). *Experimental and quasi-experimental designs for research*. Chicago: Rand-McNally.

Mook, D. G. (1983). In defense of external invalidity. *American Psychologist, 38*, 379–387.

3

MEASURING CONCEPTS: RELIABILITY AND VALIDITY

Chapter 1 discussed the inevitable imperfection of any single measure as an operationalization of a theoretical concept and the consequent need for multiple operationism. The translation between an abstract theoretical conception and its operational realization is always incomplete. Even so, although all translations (i.e., measures) are imperfect, individual measures vary in the adequacy with which they characterize the underlying conceptual variable of interest. Some measures come closer than others to representing the true value of the concept, in part because they are less susceptible to sources of systematic error or random fluctuation. The quality of a given measure is expressed in terms of its *reliability* and *validity*. Briefly, reliability is the consistency with which a measure assesses a given concept; validity refers to the degree of relationship, or the overlap, between an instrument and the construct it is intended to measure.

RELIABILITY

The concept of reliability derives from classical measurement theory, which assumes that the score obtained on any single measurement occasion represents a combination of the *true score* of the object being measured and random *errors* that lead to fluctuations in the measure obtained on the same object at different occasions (Gullicksen, 1950). The standard classical test theory formula, modified slightly to fit with our particular position on reliability, is expressed as follows:

$$O = T + \sum e_{r+s},$$

where O = observed score, for example, a score on a math test, a behavioral check-list, or an attitude scale, T = true score, and $\sum e_{r+s}$ = the sum of random and systematic errors that combine with true score to produce the observed score. The standard formula usually lists only random error; it does not take account of systematic error, or combines it with random error. In our view, both random and systematic error can affect the observed score, but in different ways, and hence we have modified the more standard formula.

True score represents the replicable feature of the concept being measured. It is not "true" in the sense that it is a necessarily perfect or valid representation of the underlying construct. "True" in the present context signifies replicability, the component part of the observed score that would recur across different measurement occasions in the absence of error. In this sense, the true score actually represents reliability, which at its heart, has to do with measurement consistency or generalizability across participants and contexts. As the classical test theory formula indicates, an observation devoid of error would perfectly represent the true score or, to put it another way, would be perfectly reliable.[1]

A common example may help clarify the meaning of true score. Often, when using a standard bathroom scale, we notice our weight fluctuating. In fact, weighing ourselves twice, almost simultaneously, often results in different readings. Has our weight changed? Probably not, but factors extraneous to "true" weight have varied from the first to the second weighing (the tension of the scale's spring, the placement of our feet on the scale, etc.). These extraneous factors are error. They really do not have anything to do with how much we weigh. They degrade the relationship between true and observed scores. The greater the proportion of error, the less the observed score reflects the underlying true score, and the more unreliable the measure is said to be.

To understand the relationship of reliability and measurement error, it is important to distinguish between *random* and *systematic* sources of error. Random error is due to chance events—an inadvertent misrecording, an incorrect summation of scores, an overstretched spring on a bathroom scale, a foul mood induced by an argument with one's parent, and so on—which tend to increase the variability of scores in nonsystematic ways. Such errors not only reduce the accuracy of measurement, they also affect the measure's sensitivity to detecting differences between different groups of research participants. Truly random error tends to cancel out across the groups that are being compared, assuming that the number of observations (or participants) is sufficiently large. Theoretically then, if the group is large enough, random errors will sum to zero. This is not to suggest that random error is harmless, however, because it tends to increase variability of scores, and increased variability tends to affect tests of statistical significance such that greater differences between groups are needed before the true differences between groups can be judged real or trustworthy (or statistically significant).

If we consider the standard inferential statistical test, the truth of this observation becomes obvious. Most common inferential statistical tests (e.g., t tests, analyses of variance, etc.) compare the average scores obtained between different groups and divide this difference by the variance within the groups. Error affects the denominator in this equation, making it larger. Thus, an unreliable measure requires a greater difference between groups (the numerator) to conclude that their difference is reliable. With greater error, we have less power to detect real differences. With less error, however, the denominator shrinks. We thus have greater power to detect a difference and deem it statistically reliable, that is, to conclude that our finding is not the result of random or chance fluctuations in the data.

In contrast to random error, systematic error can best be conceptualized as *systematic measurement bias*, consistently and artificially inflating or deflating the scores within a given group of participants. Because bias is systematic and not random, it does not cancel

---

[1]Even though perfectly reliable, a score would not necessarily be a *valid* indicator of the underlying theoretical construct. Perfect reliability suggests merely that the observation is perfectly replicable. What the observation means, that is, the question of validity, is not addressed here.

between groups; rather, it exacerbates differences over and above those that actually exist. In addition, the systematic nature of bias tends to decrease variability of scores within a group, thereby lowering the denominator in the statistical test. Thus, smaller differences between groups are judged incorrectly as being reliable, or statistically significant. Given the systematic, cumulative nature of biased measurements, an increase in group size simply enhances the apparent (but not real) differences between groups.

An example of a hypothetical experiment will help to clarify this conceptual differentiation. Suppose that an experimental treatment (e.g., harsh criticism) tends to decrease the likelihood that people will succumb to a persuasive communication. In our hypothetical experiment, two groups of undergraduate participants perform a filler task. In one group, the participants are told privately that they performed horribly, that they probably should not be in college, and that their future employability in other than menial labor is highly doubtful. The controls are given no feedback on their performance. Both groups then are exposed to a persuasive message that argues for a moratorium on all future enrollment increases at their university. The critical dependent measure is an attitude scale that assesses the extent of their agreement with the message they have received. Scores can range from 0 to 20, with higher scores indicating greater agreement with the speaker's position.

The true scores of the treatment (criticized) and control (not criticized) groups are presented in the first two columns of Table 3.1. A statistical test of the difference between mean scores of these two groups would disclose a significant difference, with the control participants demonstrating greater agreement with the message.

Suppose, however, that our attitude-measuring device contained random error, which either raised or lowered actual test scores. Overall, however, being random (or unbiased), the error averaged out to 0. Then the scores that we obtained would be those derived through an addition of columns 1 and 3 (true score + error component) for the treatment group, and columns 2 and 4 for the control group. Notice that the same absolute amount of "error" was added to each group's scores. Thus, the respective column sums remain the same. Yet, on re-analysis, the same statistical test that had disclosed a significant difference when comparing columns 1 and 2 would now disclose no significant difference between the groups when comparing columns 5 and 6. This reversal of fortune is attributable to the increased variability of scores when the random error components are added to each column. With these results, we would be forced to conclude, incorrectly, that our manipulation had no effect on attitude change. This form of erroneous conclusion is termed a *Type II error*.

To complete the example, suppose now that our observer expected results exactly opposite to those suggested by the "true" scores of columns 1 and 2. This expectation so colored the experimenter's perceptions that the error scores of the treatment group were all positive, that is, they increased the scores of this group, whereas the ratings of the control participants were decreased by their respective error scores. This systematic inflation of the treatment group (column 7) scores, and systematic deflation of the control group's ratings (column 8) reduces variability of scores and results in a statistically significant mean difference between the groups. However, the results would lead the observer to conclude that the critical treatment indeed had a real effect, but that it tended to increase the susceptibility to attitude change of those receiving it. The effects as inferred from an examination of the true scores of columns 1 and 2 would support exactly the opposite conclusion. The biased observations of the experimenter results in a finding completely at odds with the reality of the relationship between criticism and attitude change. Erroneously finding a statistically significant result that is not truly attributable to the treatment is termed a *Type I error*.

TABLE 3.1

Results of a Hypothetical Experiment, with "True" Scores, "Error" Components, and Their Combinations

Participant #	(1) True Score Treatment Group	(2) True Score Control Group	(3) Treatment Group Unbiased Error	(4) Control Group Unbiased Error	(5) Treatment Group True Score + Unbiased Error	(6) Control Group True Score + Unbiased Error	(7) Treatment Group True Score + Error (Bias)	(8) Control Group True Score – Error (Bias)
1	8	12	+2	+6	10	18	10	6
2	6	10	−1	−6	5	4	7	4
3	7	9	+4	−1	11	8	11	8
4	9	10	−4	+4	5	14	13	6
5	9	11	+1	+2	10	13	10	9
6	12	14	−6	−7	6	7	18	7
7	6	12	+4	+1	10	13	10	11
8	10	13	−8	+5	8	18	18	8
9	4	12	−2	+1	8	13	6	11
10	3	10	+10	−5	13	5	13	5
Sum =	74	113	0	0	74	113	116	75

Assessing Reliability

Systematic errors in measurement become part of an individual's "true score" on that measure and hence affect its validity as a measure of the conceptual variable of interest. Type I errors are mistakes of valid inference. They represent a misidentification of the causal factor that actually is responsible for an observed finding. Thus, *bias* helps create Type I errors. It fosters conclusions of a difference between groups when, in fact, none exists. Random errors, on the other hand, affect the measure's reliability. Random error lessens the chances of finding a true difference between groups when, in fact, a true difference exists. As such, random error fosters Type II errors. When measures are taken on a large group of individuals with a given instrument, the variability in obtained scores is due partly to differences among those individuals in their true scores on the measure, and partly to random fluctuations. Technically, the reliability of a measure is defined as the proportion of total variance in observed scores that is due to true score variability. A perfectly reliable instrument would be one in which this proportion was equal to 1.00, or in which true score equaled observed score. A perfectly unreliable score, on the other hand, would be one in which the observed score equaled the sum of the error components, and true score contributed nothing to the observed score. It is hard to imagine a measure this bad, but theoretically it could exist.

Although the technical definition of reliability presented in the prior paragraph is standard, the actual meaning of the term *reliability* varies, depending on how it is assessed and when the definition was made. In the past, reliability usually referred to the degree to which participants' scores on a given administration of a measure resembled their scores on the same instrument administered at some later point in time—or the extent to which two judges, observing the same behavior, produced the same ratings of the behavior. If the test–retest scores tended to be very similar (i.e., highly interrelated), the measure (or the judges) was said to be reliable. Or, if parallel forms of a test—two forms of the test that are thought to measure the same construct—were highly correlated, the test was said to be reliable. However, reliability also has come to mean the degree to which components *within* a particular measure are related to one another. Both of these features of reliability are important and should be considered when evaluating the quality of an instrument.

Internal Consistency.   The question of internal consistency is concerned with the extent to which the components of a measuring instrument are interrelated, that is, predict or produce the same or similar results. The idea of internal consistency is usually applied to a measure, such as an ability test or attitude scale, that is composed of a set of individual items. It is assumed that all the items of the scale measure essentially the same underlying construct. The same logic is applied when the "measuring instruments" are human observers, or judges. In this case, the question is, "Have the judges seen the same thing (as inferred from their assigning more or less identical scores to the observations)?" The answer to the question is assessed by the extent to which the observers' observations overlap.

If the items that purportedly constitute a measure of a specific belief or behavior in fact measure a variety of different constructs, then there is little to justify their being combined as a representation of a single construct. Similarly, if observers are judging the same phenomenon (say, a group interaction) using different criteria, then combining their individual observations into a global summary score makes no sense. As Nunnally (1967) observed, "a test should 'hang together' in the sense that the items all correlate with one another. Otherwise, it makes little sense to add scores over items and speak of total scores as measuring any attribute" (p. 251). To justify the combination of items in deriving an individual's overall score on such a test, the internal consistency of the item set must be established.

One of the earliest means used to assess the internal consistency of a scale is a method known as the *split-half* technique. In this method, a measure consisting of set of items is administered to a sample of respondents. For the purpose of analysis, the items that constitute the scale are divided into two groups of approximately equal number, and the sums of the two sets of items are calculated.[2] If there is a high degree of interrelatedness among items (this is necessary if the central assumption is to be granted), then the relation between total scores from the two halves of the scale should be strong, thus indicating that the items are focused on the same underlying attitude or aptitude. If the two halves of the measure do not "hang together," this suggests that the scale items might not all be measuring the same underlying construct.

An alternative to the once common split-half technique is now more commonly employed to determine a scale's internal consistency. This approach, called Cronbach's (1951) *coefficient alpha*, represents an indispensable aspect of the scale construction process. Coefficient alpha is a measure of the hypothetical value that would be obtained if all of the items that could constitute a given scale were available, and randomly put together into a very large number of tests of equal size. The average correlation between all possible pairs of these "split-half" tests is approximated by coefficient alpha.

Determining the alpha coefficient of a scale is relatively simple, if one has a computer available (or if a relatively short test is being used). Computationally, we determine coefficient alpha as follows:

$$r_{tt} = \frac{k}{k-1}\left(1 - \frac{\sum \sigma_i^2}{\sigma_T^2}\right)$$

where r_{tt} = coefficient alpha (α), the estimate of whole-scale reliability,
k = the number of items in the scale,
$\sum \sigma_i^2$ = the sum of the variances of each of the individual items, and
σ_T^2 = the variance of the total scale.
The degree of internal consistency is usually considered acceptable if this coefficient is .75 or better, though the actual value depends on the extent of error the investigator is willing to tolerate.

From the internal consistency computational formula presented, we can infer that the number of items in a scale plays an important role in the scale's (internal consistency) reliability, as do the interrelationships that obtain among the items. If the items are highly interrelated, alpha will be high. In addition, the formula suggests that, all other things being equal, the more items, the greater will be the scale's coefficient alpha. Thus, one simple means of enhancing alpha is to "lengthen" the scale, that is, to add items to it. If participants' responses to the new items are similar to their responses on the original set (i.e., if the correlations between new and old items are high), the addition will enhance the coefficient of internal consistency. The qualification presented at the beginning of the previous sentence suggests that considerable care be exercised when developing new items to add to an established set. Of course, this method of enhancing reliability is subject to the law of diminishing returns. Adding a good item to a 5-item scale will have a much

---

[2]Various means are used to split the total item set in half: Even numbered items are contrasted with odd numbered items, the first half compared with the second half (probably a poor choice because of possible fatigue effects on the part of participants), the total item set is randomly split into two groups, and so forth.

greater effect on internal consistency than adding a good item to a 15-item scale. If the average correlation between items is reasonable (say, greater than .25), adding an item to a scale already containing 9 or 10 items will have relatively little effect on coefficient alpha. Further, the higher the existing inter-item correlations, the less the effect of added items.

It sometimes happens that the coefficient of internal consistency is unsatisfactory even with relatively lengthy tests. One possible solution in situations such as these is to inspect relations among pairs of items and eliminate those items that do not relate well with the majority of other items. Another simpler method is to assess all item-total relations, that is, the correlation between participants' scores on each item and their total score over all items.[3] If a specific item is measuring something very different from that of the others in the item set, its relation with the total score will be weak. This information will alert the scale developer that this particular item can be deleted and substituted with one that (hopefully) better represents the concept under investigation.

Our emphasis on internal consistency should not be taken to mean that all of the items on a scale should be mere clones of one another. Ideally, the items of a scale should share a common focus, but they should be entirely different in all other aspects that are irrelevant to this focus (see Andrews & Withey, 1976; Eagly & Chaiken, 1993; John, Hampson, & Goldberg, 1991). For example, consider these two items, developed for a scale of attitudes toward ecological issues:

- The Federal Government should rule that automobiles must be constructed so that hydro-carbon emissions are completely reduced.
- All communities must employ both primary and secondary sewage treatment facilities before pumping wastes into public waters.

An individual's response to either of these items will be determined by a number of factors. The first item will be affected not only by the respondent's concern for the protection of the environment, but also by attitudes toward governmental intervention in private business, beliefs regarding the feasibility of complete elimination of hydrocarbon emissions, and so forth. Similarly, agreement with the second items will be affected by beliefs about the effectiveness of primary and secondary sewage treatment, the ecological integrity of the water supply, and so on, in addition to attitudes regarding the environment, the central issue of the scale.

Thus, both items potentially tap factors that are irrelevant to the to the issue of concern to the researcher, but these irrelevancies are different across items. Such heterogeneity of item content will produce some inconsistency of response (and hence, lower alpha), but as long as many such items are used, all sharing one common response determinant (though, perhaps, numerous noncommon determinants as well), the total set of responses will provide a better measure of the central attitude than any single item. In this context, the item-total relationship proves useful in determining whether an item is a good representative of the construct under study.

It is possible for items on a test to be too closely related (Cattell, 1972; Dawson, Crano, & Burgoon, 1996). Consider the following example:

---

[3]It is good practice to adjust these "item-total correlations" statistically, so as to remove the influence of the particular item under consideration on the total score. This adjustment becomes especially important when the scale is composed of relatively few items, because in such cases, the contribution of any given item to the total score is great.

- Today's Volkswagen is a wonderful automobile.
- The new Volkswagen Beetle is a terrific car.

Clearly, we would expect the degree of relationship between responses to these two items to be very high. However, because they provide little, if any, nonredundant information, their consistency does not contribute much to the overall quality of the measure.

When attitude scales are constructed with an emphasis on item variability, it can happen that participants' responses are so inconsistent over the entire item-set that few items meet the test of acceptable item-total interrelationship. In this circumstance, it is important to determine whether the items, in fact, do focus on one central, underlying construct, or if the measure is *multidimensional*, that is, if it taps a number of different constructs. To inspect this possibility, the entire matrix of item intercorrelations can be factor analyzed. This type of analysis provides the researcher with information regarding the actual number of constructs or "scales" that may exist in the instrument under construction, as perceived by the respondent sample. On the basis of this information, the investigator may decide to retain only a subset of the original items (e.g., those that form the most internally consistent subset, as indicated by a reliability analysis on the various subcomponents of the overall instrument) and to develop additional items to add to this subset in constructing an improved scale. The other items would be discarded or used as a separate scale with its own internal consistency coefficient.

For example, suppose we administered a number of items that we believed tapped people's feelings about the preservation of the environment, but our results suggest that the items do not form an internally consistent whole. If we were to factor analyze the item set, we might find that one group of items that "hang together" very well all have to do with participants' feelings of obligation to future generations. Another set of items that hang together might all have to do with the financial implications of environmental depredations. These items do not relate much with the "future generations" items. In this case, we have two possible scales, probably both of which are in need of further work, and both of which measure aspects of environmentalism worthy of study. We could add more items to each to create two more reliable measures, and readminister one or both to a new sample. This procedure will enable us to determine the extent to which the new items hang together with the original set(s) of items. Eventually, an iterative process of this nature will enable the investigator to generate a scale, or scales, of acceptable internal consistency. The skill and insight of the scale constructor, the complexity of the issue under consideration, and the investigator's understanding of the issue and the respondent sample used will all play a role in the ultimate success of the scaling process.

Temporal Stability. The development of measurement scales possessing a high degree of interrelatedness among the items is one of the primary tasks of the test constructor. However, there is a second feature of reliability, called *temporal stability*, whose significance also merits consideration in our discussion of test construction. Questions pertaining to this aspect of scale quality are concerned with the degree to which the data obtained in a given test administration resemble those obtained in a second testing, which employs the same scale and the same respondent sample.

In considerations of temporal stability, researchers generally make use of one of two techniques, the most common of which is called the *test–retest* method. In this technique, a set of items is administered to a group of participants and then, at some later time, the test is readministered to the same group. Participants' scores on the first administration are compared to the scores they obtain on the second; a large, positive relation is taken as evidence of (temporal stability) reliability.

The major problem with the test–retest method is that the information it provides can prove ambiguous. Consider a few extreme examples: suppose an investigator was to employ a test–retest procedure with a delay of 3 min between test administrations. Chances are good that the relation between participants' scores on the tests would be nearly perfect. This would not, however, necessarily indicate that the scale was reliable. There is a delicate balance that must be struck when deciding on the appropriate interval between test administrations. Apparent reliability will be enhanced artificially if participants can remember their previous responses and wish to appear consistent. Conversely, a very long delay between administrations can diminish temporal stability because people do change over time. Thus, even a very good test can appear unreliable if the temporal separation between administrations is extreme.

It is difficult to specify the "ideal" temporal lag between scales when using the test–retest method. Sometimes, even a modest time lag will artificially reduce the test–retest relationship. For example, suppose that we constructed a scale to measure attitudes toward a well-known politician and administered this scale to a sample of 500 respondents. Two days later, we readministered the same scale to the same respondents. A 2-day lag would not seem overly long. However, what if, during that interval, the politician had been implicated in a juicy, well-publicized, public scandal. These things have been known to happen in U.S. politics. In this case, we could have little hope that the scale would prove temporally stable. The attitudes of those who originally were favorably disposed toward the now-discredited public servant would be expected to change drastically, whereas those of people who had always hated the fallen politico would remain substantially the same. Such a change pattern would adversely affect the obtained test–retest relation. In this case, changes in the observed score would suggest unreliability, even if the error components of the measure were minimal. "History," rather than "instrumentation," would be the cause of the apparent lack of temporal stability of the scale.

A procedure known as the *equivalent* (or *alternate*, or *parallel*) *forms* method was developed to circumvent some of the problems introduced by a temporal separation between test administrations. In this technique, the scale developer constructs two different tests, both of which are thought to assess the same underlying construct. Both tests are administered to the same participants at the same time. If a high relationship is obtained between scores on the two tests, it is interpreted as an indication of the reliability of the instrument(s). The rationale here is the same as that of the split-half approach, except that the two ("equivalent") forms are considered whole tests.

The major difficulty encountered in this situation is that a weak relationship between equivalent forms is not completely informative. It is conceivable that this result indicates that the scales are indeed unreliable. However, it might also be the case that the equivalent forms simply are not equivalent. In attempting to determine the reasons underlying a lack of interrelatedness between two theoretically identical measures, the investigator sometimes must devote more time than would be demanded in the development of an entirely new set of scales.

As can be seen, questions of temporal stability can cause some difficulty for the test constructor. What's more, the information that a test is temporally stable usually is not considered sufficient evidence of a scale's reliability because it is possible that a scale could elicit stable responses across time and still not be internally consistent. To satisfy the full set of criteria of scale reliability, it is desirable that the scale demonstrate both temporal stability and internal consistency. Nonetheless, though temporal stability does not provide a complete estimate of a scale's reliability, it is important because it furnishes a comparison against which the effects of agents of change can be assessed. Thus, if a test is known to be temporally stable, then the explanation of changes between test administrations can be directed at external agents—for example, a social intervention, a historical event, maturation, and so on.

Cronbach and his colleagues proposed a more ambitious approach to reliability estimation, termed *generalizability theory* (Cronbach, Gleser, Nanda, & Rajaratnam, 1972). This approach recognizes that irrelevancies (error) can be introduced into a test by many different factors, or *facets*, to use their terminology. These irrelevancies can reside in observers, items, contexts, occasions for measurement, participants, and so forth. The more generalizable the instrument (i.e., the more consistent it is across occasions, respondents, contexts, etc.) the better or more trustworthy the instrument is. Cronbach et al. (1972) provide a framework for conceptualizing these different error sources and for determining their individual impact on the measure under consideration. The generalizability approach has won adherents among psychologists (e.g., see American Psychological Association, 1985), but as yet has not been widely adopted in practice. At a minimum, it provides a more comprehensive outline of the multitude of factors that may affect a score, and alerts the researcher to the wide variety of factors that may affect the utility of an instrument.

VALIDITY

Constructing measuring instruments that meet the criteria of reliability (in terms of internal consistency and temporal stability, or inter-observer agreement) satisfies a basic requirement for the *operationalization* phase of a scientific investigation. In chapter 1 of this text, however, we made a distinction between the adequacy of an operation in terms of objectivity and replicability, and its adequacy as a manifestation of a theoretical construct. This distinction marks the difference between the reliability of a measuring device and its validity. Whereas the former is the *sine qua non* of scientific research, the validation of operations relative to the hypothetical concepts under investigation is crucial from the standpoint of theory development. It is easily conceivable that the procedures usually followed to generate a reliable scale of individual differences could lead to an internally consistent, temporally stable instrument that had no relationship whatever to the theoretical attribute that had motivated the research in the first place. Consistency of responses, from item to item or from time to time or from observer to observer, although necessary, is not sufficient to guarantee a scale's validity. Although some degree of response consistency is essential in the diagnosis of any underlying attribute, the validity of a measuring instrument must be studied through the use of operations beyond those applied to assess reliability.

Basically, the validity of a scale refers to the extent of correspondence between variations in the scores on the instrument and variation among respondents on the underlying construct being studied. Theoretically, the true score represents a measure of the replicable "shared variation" or of the "common factor" that underlies participants' responses to all items. Whether this response factor adequately reflects the particular conceptualization that the investigator wants to measure, however, is still a matter for investigation. It is important to keep this point in mind when validating any measure. Validation always requires empirical research beyond that used in the scale construction (reliability) phase of instrument development. This validation process will invariably focus on the relationship of the scale with some other indicators of the construct under investigation. The mere fact that a scale's items appear to tap the construct under study (i.e., has "face validity," to use a well-worn but practically meaningless term) is simply not sufficient.

Nunnally (1967) noted that validity is a relative, descriptive term, not an all-or-none property, and his view accords with Messick's (1989), which defined validity as a "judgment of the degree to which evidence and theoretical rationales support the *adequacy* and *appropriateness*" of a construct (p. 13). This definition suggests that validity is not a thing, a feature of a measure, but rather an aspect of the interpretation of a measure. As such, validity is always open to question, review, and revision. It is never a closed issue, but rather a continuous process. It is "the best available approximation to the truth or falsity of propositions" (Cook & Campbell, 1979, p. 37); but the judgment must always be tempered by recognition that the best available evidence may change, and thus the evaluation of validity of a construct also may change.

This view suggests that the researcher always attempt to determine the extent to which the scale is valid in the particular application in which it is employed. The fact that previous research demonstrated the usefulness of a scale does not necessarily imply that it will be valid in another setting, with different respondents, or at different times. Too often, validity is conceptualized as a static, enduring property, such that once a scale is validated, it is viewed as valid for all time. This interpretation is inconsistent with the more realistic view of validity as a transient, relativistic, descriptive quality. Because validity changes from time to time and from sample to sample, it should be periodically reevaluated to ensure that what once was a valid indicator of some theoretical construct (e.g., attitude) remain so (see Campbell, 1960, for an extensive discussion of the concept of validity).

As an example of the instability of scale validity, consider the changing "validities" of an attitude scale developed to tap opinions regarding the justification of war. Would this scale, developed in the 1950s cold war climate to measure relatively broad, general feelings about war, be likely to provide valid information when used in the context of an investigation of participants' feelings about the government's intervention in political strife in Latin America today? Probably not. A person who might feel that war was indeed justified under certain circumstances might answer this scale very differently if it were used to assess governmental actions in Latin America, and he or she felt that the United States had no business meddling in the affairs of neighbors to the south. In other words, our hypothetical scale, which might provide a valid indicator of people's general attitudes toward the justification of a defensive war, in which the survival of the country was at stake, could prove to be completely invalid as an indicator of participants' specific attitudes toward a particular war or war-related governmental policy at a particular point in time.

With this general introduction to what the concept of validity is, and what it is not, we now consider some specific subcategories of validity that are of central concern to social scientists. An appreciation of these more specific features of validity provides a more complete understanding of the concept of validity as it is applied in the scaling of stimuli or of individuals, which are considered in chapters 14 and 15, respectively. In discussing these various forms of validity, it is important to keep in mind that they all are component parts of what is generally termed *construct validity*. Ultimately, we are concerned with the validity of the measure for the construct of interest. The various subforms, or components, of construct validity are important insofar as they reflect on the underlying construct, whether that construct is an attitude, attribute, process, or consistent behavioral predisposition.

Predictive Validity

The procedures designed to assess the validity of a scale should vary according to the purposes for which the instrument is devised. The form of validity that probably can be grasped most simply, that is the most intuitively obvious, is *predictive validity*. Predictive validity is of major concern when the purpose of a measure is to predict either the likelihood, or the extremity, of some behavior of interest. The behavior itself becomes the criterion, and the accuracy with which the scale predicts the specific level or extremity of the criterion is taken as an indication of the scale's (predictive) validity. A test of reading readiness, for example, should enable an investigator to discriminate the "ready" from the "unready," that is, to predict which children are most likely to succeed (or fail) in grasping the fundamentals of this essential skill. To test the degree of such discrimination, a researcher could administer the test to a group of preschoolers and relate these results to the scores the children receive on a standardized test of reading achievement after their first year of formal schooling. The resulting relationship would suggest the predictive validity of the readiness test.

In judging the utility of prediction to establish the validity of a scale, three important limitations should be kept in mind. First, because many factors can influence the magnitude of a relationship, predictive validity in and of itself is not sufficient to establish the validity of a measure. A failure to obtain a strong relationship in the foregoing example might have been due to a massive failure of the instructional system to teach reading effectively to any of the children in the sample, or it might have indicated that the standardized test was not appropriate to the sample.

A second difficulty with this validation approach is that it can be relatively uninformative even if scale scores are strongly related to criterion scores. Whereas a strong predictive relationship is certainly encouraging, it does not explain why such a relationship occurred. In the absence of theory relating the measure to children's performance, the validation process is much less informative, and much less useful, than it needs be.

A third, more practical limitation on the usefulness of prediction in establishing the validity of a scale has to do with the relative absence of useful criteria in social science. Few of the variables of our field are as easily quantified as standardized first-grade reading achievement. Typically, our scales are constructed to assess complex, abstract qualities. In these instances, predictive validation approaches are not useful because appropriate criteria against which predictions might be compared do not exist. For this reason, predictive validation approaches are most widely used when dealing with scales of fact, that is, for issues on which there are consensually agreed-upon answers. In these instances, typically, criteria do exist (or can be constructed), and the full power of the predictive validation approach can be realized. Predictive validation approaches are less useful when constructing measures of opinion, on which the answers reflect matters of choice or palate, which vary from person to person, and on which there is no necessary consensually correct answer.

Content Validity

Content validity is concerned with the extent to which the content of a measure represents (or samples) the complete range of the construct under consideration. In establishing the content validity of a test of eighth-grade mathematics, for example, we would be concerned with whether or not the scale adequately sampled the range of mathematical skills that an eighth grader should know. If the test focused exclusively on addition and subtraction, it is obvious that it would not have sampled enough of the hypothetical domain of interest, and some modifications and additions would clearly be indicated.

With factual materials (i.e., when developing tests of knowledge or ability), constructing scales with adequate content validity is not overly difficult. The domain of interest is relatively well specified, and a representative sample of items can be drawn from this pool of potential questions. When the researcher is dealing with other psychological or social variables, however, the situation typically is not so clear-cut. For example, suppose a researcher wanted to study cognitive complexity. The number and type of items needed to adequately represent this attitudinal domain is not immediately apparent.

Assessment of content validity is a subjective operation. Unlike estimates of predictive validity, there is no simple statistical measure of the degree to which this validation requirement is met. To help ensure content validity, many researchers begin the scale construction process by generating large numbers of diverse items, all judged as focused on the attribute or domain of interest. Assumptions of this type, however, are based almost solely on the subjective estimates of the researcher who constructed the scale, and as such, are subject to bias. A more secure means of assuring content validity is through the use of expert panels, whose opinions regarding the adequacy of coverage of a particular scale, although far from infallible, provide more trustworthy information than that of an investigator working independently.

Construct Validity

An orientation more amenable to the validation of scales concerned with abstract, theoretical factors is evident in techniques used to establish the *construct validity* of measures. A *construct* is a hypothetical variable—a name a researcher gives to a set of beliefs, attributes, processes, or predispositions thought to be interrelated and forming a meaningful whole. Construct validation is an approach whose aim is to establish the reality of a psychological concept; it is a test of whether or not the hypothesized construction plausibly exists. If it does, then it should enter into predictable relationships with other constructs. Construct validation is the process of searching for these expected relationships. The importance of constructs in social science cannot be overestimated. After all, "Science is primarily concerned with developing measures of constructs, and finding functional relations between measures of different constructs" (Nunnally, 1967, p. 85).

Of the many ways in which construct validity is assessed, perhaps the most common is called the *known groups* method. In this validation approach, a measure of a hypothesized construct is given to different groups of people who are known to differ on an attribute that is the focus of the instrument. If the scale actually measures what it purports to, then these groups should have different scores, and these differences should be predictable in advance of the test's administration. For example, if an investigator has devised a scale to measure prejudice against African Americans, then the average scale score of a mob of Ku Klux Klanners should be different from that of that of a group of members of the American Civil Liberties Union. If no differences are found, or if the differences are in a direction opposite to that expected, then it is clear that the validation process has failed—either the theory on which the expected relations are based is in error or the test itself is not a good indicator of racial attitudes.

The known groups method has been used in a number of different situations to test the goodness of a range of scale types (e.g., Crano & Crano, 1984; McGahuey et al., 2000; Rokeach, 1960; Webster & Kruglanski, 1994; Wheeler & Austin, 2000) and generally proves a convincing technique in establishing the case for validity. For example, Wheeler and Austin (2000) were interested in validating a scale to measure adolescent women's grief responses. They assembled a sample of young adolescent women, 13–19 years of age, some of whom had recently suffered a perinatal loss. As indicated by the authors' "Loss Response List," those women who had lost their babies exhibited significantly more grief and depression than the women who had not endured such a loss. The differences were as might be expected on the basis of theory and common sense, and lent support to the validity of the measure.

Although the known groups method is quite useful, there are some contexts that preclude its use for all practical purposes. Sometimes, for example, the appropriate groups will not cooperate. At other times, the quality under consideration does not suggest identifiable groups who would be expected to differ greatly on the construct. An investigator studying self-esteem, for example, might have a hard time finding established, identifiable groups known to differ on this quality. As such, the application of the known groups technique is limited by the focus of the construct. Thus, in many areas of social research, alternative procedures must be employed to establish validity. In such situations, an approach originally proposed by Campbell and Fiske (1959) may sometimes prove useful.

Convergent and Discriminant Validity

When attempting to validate a construct, an investigator must develop a set of hypotheses regarding other constructs with which his or her particular conceptualization should be (or should not be) related. If a measure is to be judged a valid indicator of the construct, then the hypothesized relationships should exist, and measures purportedly assessing these various conceptualizations should be related. This process is termed *convergent validation*, which is meant to establish the extent to which the new measure adheres to other, related indicators of the construct it is designed to epitomize. These other indicators may be scales or similar types of measurement instruments, but they could also be peer reports, coded observational records, or some other nonscalar data form.

Convergent validation subsumes other, more specific validity forms such as predictive validity, concurrent validity, and so on. Crano (2000) wrote:

> In the ideal case, indicators that are as dissimilar as possible are used to estimate the convergent validity of a measure. This view distinguishes the search for convergent validity from the assessment of reliability, in which maximally similar measures are sought. In the quest for convergent validity, measures as dissimilar as possible are developed and used so as to increase the likelihood that they share different sources of error. . . . The more similar the measures, the greater the probability that they are prone to the same irrelevancies, thereby compounding error. (p. 40)

For example, suppose a researcher wanted to develop a measure of religiousness. One might expect this measure to relate to other measures with which religiousness is thought to covary. For example, we might expect this measure, if it is valid, to relate to such indicators as charitable contributions, being compassionate to sick people, and attending religious services. If these expected relationships do not materialize, two possibilities arise: The most obvious is that the scale in question is not an adequate measure of the construct (it is assumed that the instruments measuring the variables with which the critical scale is theorized to relate—giving to the poor, being compassionate, etc.—are all relatively valid). The second possibility is that the scale is valid, but that the theory on which the hypothesized relationships are based is incorrect, and thus no relation between the constructs should be expected.[4] However, if other measures of religiosity do exhibit the hypothesized pattern of interrelationships with the validating scales (compassion, attendance at services, etc.), the investigator is left with the first alternative, that is, the measure probably is invalid and in need of reconceptualization.

---

[4]One might argue, for example, that attending religious services does not necessarily indicate high levels of religiousness.

When the predicted pattern does occur, these findings are taken as supportive evidence for the scale's validity. Consistent with our general orientation to deductive science and the scientific method, it should be obvious that even perfect confirmation of the hypothesized relationships does not *prove* the measure's validity, but rather suggests its utility. So in the present example, if the new religiosity measure were strongly related to compassion for the sick, giving to the poor, and so on, we might be confident that we were on the right track, but it would be wrong to assume that we had arrived at our destination.

THE MULTITRAIT–MULTIMETHOD MATRIX

Operations that assess the relationships between a new measure and other established measures with which the new test is thought to relate are termed *convergent validation techniques* (Campbell & Fiske, 1959) because, in essence, the measures converge on, or define, a hypothesized network of interconnected traits, processes, dispositions, behaviors, or all of these. This convergence of expected relationships is the essence of convergent validity. A successful convergent validation operation not only suggests that the critical scale is an adequate measure of the construct in question, but also bolsters the theoretical position that was used to develop the hypothesized interrelationships that formed the basis of the validation process.

A parallel series of operations, termed *discriminant validation techniques* (Campbell & Fiske, 1959), also can be used to assess scale quality. These techniques are generally used in conjunction with studies of convergent validity. In the convergent validation process, we generate a series of hypotheses regarding probable interrelationships that are expected between the measure of the construct under development and other, perhaps more established, construct measures, independent of extraneous factors (e.g., similar methods of measurement). In discriminant validation, we devise a series of variables with which the construct is not expected to relate. If the critical scale is to be judged valid, and the investigator's hypotheses are correct, then no (or a very weak) relationship between measures of the critical variables should occur. If such results are obtained, they would be taken as evidence for the scale's discriminant validity. Both convergent and discriminant validity, subclasses of the more general concept of construct validity, are investigated in the multitrait–multimethod matrix approach. Each of these two validity forms provides different and useful information about the quality of an instrument.

The multitrait–multimethod matrix (MTMMM) is a logical extension of the complementary principles of multiple operationism and triangulation introduced in chapter 1 of this text. In this (MTMMM) approach, multiple measures are used to assess the degree to which measures of theoretically related constructs adhere, over and above the relationship that might come about simply as a result of their sharing common methods of measurement. The technique involves computing a correlation matrix that reveals the relationships among a set of carefully selected measures. The measures are selected to represent a combination of several different (theoretically relevant) constructs assessed by several different methods of measurement. Each construct is measured by each and every measurement technique. Analysis focuses on the interrelationships among measures theorized to assess the same construct. These relationships are compared with those involving measures of different constructs that happen to be measured by the same measurement technique. Obviously, in most instances, the particular form of measurement technique is not relevant theoretically. The pattern of interrelationships between traits sharing the same and similar and different methods of measurement help determine the construct validity of the measures under study.

TABLE 3.2

Illustration of a 3 (Traits 1, 2, 3) × 3 (Methods A, B, C) Multitrait–Multimethod Matrix, Where Trait 1 = Self-Esteem, Trait 2 = Sociability, and Trait 3 = Intelligence, and Method A = Standardized Self-Report, Method B = Peer Check List, and Method C = Behavioral Observation

	Traits	Method A			Method B			Method C		
		1	2	3	1	2	3	1	2	3
Method A	1	(.90)								
	2	.50	(.88)							
	3	.40	.30	(.75)						
Method B	1	**.58**	.20	.18	(.92)					
	2	.25	**.56**	.11	.70	(.91)				
	3	.17	.09	**.48**	.60	.51	(.83)			
Method C	1	**.57**	.20	.19	**.69**	.41	.30	(.93)		
	2	.23	**.59**	.16	.44	**.68**	.29	.71	(.89)	
	3	.18	.12	**.48**	.34	.28	**.61**	.82	.66	(.82)

Note. Reliabilities are the parenthesized values on the main diagonals. Validity coefficients are in bold type. Heterotrait–monomethod values are enclosed in solid lines. Broken lines enclose heterotrait–heteromethod values.

A concrete example may help explicate this approach. Suppose a social developmentalist were interested in creating a self-esteem measure for young children using behavioral observation. On the basis of theory, the researcher believes that self-esteem should be strongly related to sociability and also, but much less strongly, to intelligence. To use the MTMMM approach, the researcher finds two established scales of self-esteem. The first of these scales uses self-ratings to measure self-esteem, the second, peer ratings. The new measure, remember, uses behavioral observations. Then, the researcher finds *established* scales of sociability and intelligence, which are measured by the three different techniques used to measure esteem (self-ratings, peer ratings, and behavioral observation). These nine tests are administered to a sample of 200 kindergartners. The resulting matrix of (hypothetically) obtained relationships is presented in Table 3.2.

Four Critical Entries in the Matrix

In examining this set of results, Campbell and Fiske (1959) recommend that we consider four important components of the matrix before attempting to form an assessment of convergent and discriminant validity. These critical components are:

- The (parenthesized) reliabilities of the three methods of measurement. These values, contained in the main diagonal of the matrix, are considered first. The reliabilities of the measures must be strong enough to encourage further consideration of the data. If they are not, there is not much point to inquire about validity. However, as shown, the reliabilities of our hypothetical measures are strong.

- Adjacent to the reliability diagonals, enclosed in solid lines, are the heterotrait–monomethod triangles. These entries reflect the correlation between the *different* traits that are assessed by an *identical* measurement method. Thus, in the topmost data triangle of Table 3.2, we find the relation between self-esteem and sociability, self-esteem and intelligence, and sociability and intelligence when all of these traits are measured by self-report ($r = .50$, .40, and .30, respectively).

- Next, we consider the heterotrait–heteromethod triangles, which are enclosed in broken lines. These values reflect the relationship between *different* traits assessed by *different* methods of measurement. In Table 3.2, the correlation between sociability as measured by peer checklist and self-esteem as measured by self-report is of moderate magnitude (i.e., $r_{B2A1} = .25$).

- The final entries to be considered are the monotrait–heteromethod values, which lie on the diagonal the separates the heterotrait–heteromethod triangles. These *validity diagonals*, as they are termed, reflect the association of presumably *identical* traits assessed by *different* methods of measurement. They are presented in bold type in Table 3.2.

Evaluative Mechanics of the MTMM Matrix

We use these various entries to assess construct validity. In their classic paper, Campbell and Fiske (1959) suggested that four important requirements be met before we conclude that our measures are valid indicators of a construct. The first is that the entries in the validity diagonals (the monotrait–heteromethod values) be statistically and practically significant. This requirement is the only one that is concerned with convergent validity. It is reasonable to require these values be strong because they are meant to express the association between different measures of the (presumably) identical trait. For most theoretical purposes, measurement method is considered incidental, or theoretically vacuous. As such, it should not interfere with values on traits or constructs of interest. We have convergent validity when there is a strong overlap among the various assessments of traits that are considered identical (and which differ, presumably, only in the manner in which they are measured). Thus, in our example, all three of our measures of self-esteem should correlate strongly. This is a reasonable requirement if we are to infer that they measure the same underlying construct. If they do not, it is possible that the method we used to measure self-esteem, which plays no role in our theory, is impinging on our results.

The second requirement, which is concerned with discriminant validity, is that each validity value exceeds the correlations of the entries of the rows and columns in which it is located. In the language of the MTMMM, the monotrait–heteromethod values should exceed associated heterotrait–heteromethod associations. This too, is a reasonable requirement. It means that the relationship between different measures of the (presumably) same trait should be stronger than different measures associating different traits. Discriminant validity is called into question if the association of different traits determined by disparate measures exceeds that involving identical traits (also measured by means of dissimilar methods). In such a case, theoretically irrelevant measurement variance rather than trait overlap may be the main cause of the association.

A third requirement of the MTMMM approach is that the validity values exceed the entries in relevant heterotrait–monomethod triangles. This "common sense desideratum" (Campbell & Fiske, 1959, p. 83) requires that the relationship between different measures of the same trait should exceed the relation between different traits that merely happen to share the same method of measurement. Again, to the extent that this is not true, we are left to conclude that systematic (if theoretically irrelevant) measurement variance may be controlling outcomes to an unacceptable degree. As seen in Table 3.2, the results of our hypothetical study are not generally consistent with this third requirement.

The final requisite of the MTMMM technique is that the same patterns of trait inter-relations be observed in the heterotrait triangles irrespective of measurement overlap; that is, the pattern of trait interrelations should be the same in the monomethod and the heteromethod blocks. Such a requirement would be met if method were truly incidental, as required. The patterning of traits should be maintained whether the traits are measured by the same method (as in the monomethod triangles) or by different methods (the heteromethod triangles).

Over the years, researchers have used these "rules of thumb" to interpret the outcome of MTMMM research. Since its introduction, the technique has stimulated more than 2,000 published studies. Even so, considerable controversy still surrounds the question of the proper statistical method to decompose the matrix, but these issues do not concern us here (for discussion of some of the issues involved in the analysis of the MTMMM, see Crano, 2000; Marsh & Bailey, 1991; Mellon & Crano, 1977; Schmitt, Coyle, & Saari, 1977; Schmitt & Stults, 1986). In a reprise of their technique more than 30 years after its publication, Fiske and Campbell (1992) avoided the statistical slugfest surrounding the technique and instead observed that the "criteria proposed in the original article seems like a sound first step, especially when one has an extended research program and sees the particular matrix as only a step toward constructing an improved set of measuring procedures" (p. 394). This is wise advice indeed. It reemphasizes the procedural nature of validity, the need for continual assessment and refinement of instruments, and the fact that validity ultimately is a data-informed judgment, not a state of being.

Threats to Measurement Validity

The different validation operations we have presented should not be viewed as mutually exclusive. Each of these approaches provide valuable, necessary information, and should be employed whenever possible. The aim of each is to supply information that facilitates construction of a more and more refined measure of some cognitive or behavioral attribute. It is through such operations that valid measures of theoretically relevant conceptualizations ultimately emerge.

If, as we hold, validity is not an all-or-none property, but rather a relativistic, descriptive quality that indicates the extent to which theoretically expected variations on the attribute of interest are reflected on the critical scale, then the more valid the scale, the greater should be this correspondence. We must acknowledge that the score a person receives on a scale is never a pure, totally accurate picture, completely determined by the attribute or construct in question, but rather is the product of a complex interaction of many factors, only one of which is the attribute or construct of theoretical interest. Methodologists have identified a number of irrelevant factors that (more or less) systematically influence attitude scales. It is important that these factors (known variously as *response sets* or *response biases*) be understood and controlled because they can systematically influence participants' responses and thus lower validity.

Response bias exists to the extent that the measurement operations influence the obtained results. The degree to which data are affected by these operations, or by other factors that are independent of the construct under consideration, partially determines the extent of the scale's invalidity. At the most extreme level, we could envision a situation of complete invalidity, in which the way that questions are worded totally determines participants' responses, independent of the content or meaning of the items. Under ideal conditions, the opposite is sought: Item format and question wording are designed so as to be irrelevant, and only the content of the questions determines responses. This ideal is never met, but an understanding of some of the potential threats to attaining this ideal can enhance the degree to which it will be approximated.

Mood.   Perhaps not surprisingly, a respondent's mood may have a strong impact on the responses he or she gives to a social query. An interesting example of mood effects is provided by Schwarz and Clore (1983), who asked people to tell them about the quality of their lives. The telephone survey was conducted over a wide geographic area, and some of the respondents were enjoying a bright sunny day when they answered. Others were in a part of the country in which it was raining when the survey was done. Quality of life responses were quite different depending on the weather. Obviously, the quality of one's life is controlled somewhat by weather, but it is enlightening to see how strongly such transitory effects can affect answers to questions that are meant to tap a more stable state. In an interesting extension of their research, Schwarz and Clore (1983) asked some of their respondents what the weather was like before beginning their questionnaire. Among these respondents, weather had no effect on quality of life responses. Why? Presumably because when the source of their transitory mood state was brought to mind, they were able to discount it when answering the survey. This same result has been replicated in many different studies. When German respondents were asked to report on the quality of their lives, for example, they reported much higher quality of life scores if the German national soccer team had won their games in the World Cup Playoffs than if they had lost (Schwarz, Strack, Kommer, & Wagner, 1987; see Schwarz & Strack, 1991, 1999, for extended discussions of mood on subjective well-being).

Social Desirability.   In many measures of social variables, the respondent essentially is asked to present a self-report concerning some more-or-less important belief, value, attitude, or behavior. There are some situations in which an individual's beliefs, values, attitudes, and/or behaviors are at variance with those approved by common social norms. Under such conditions, the respondent might be tempted to respond in a "socially desirable" way by misrepresenting true feelings and responding in a manner that is consistent with social mores. Variations in respondents' sensitivity to the demands of social desirability, or differences in people's perceptions of what is and is not socially desirable, can invalidate a scale. The findings of many early surveys of adolescent sexual behavior offer a good illustration of this point. In many of these reports, we discovered that a high proportion of adolescent men had engaged in sexual intercourse, whereas relatively few women of this age had done so. Such findings suggest a number of interesting possibilities: It could be that a small number of dedicated women were indeed picking up the slack for their less active sisters. It is more likely, however, that the cultural values approving sexually experienced males and virginal females were well learned by the time a person reached adolescence, and respondents' reports of their activities were at least in part a function of these learned values, rather than of actual behavior.

In attempting to solve the problems that a bias of this type can generate, it is useful to speculate on the factors that cause it. The social desirability response bias occurs because of a lack of self-knowledge on the part of the respondent, his or her refusal to be completely frank or honest, or both. There is little that can be done when an individual simply does not know himself or herself well enough to give answers based on fact and reality, rather than some idealization formed in part by the demands of the society. On the other hand, administering scales anonymously can combat problems attributable to a lack of candor. If respondents can be assured anonymity, it would seem more likely that they would be willing to supply honest answers, even if these answers were contrary to established social beliefs or practices.

Language Difficulty. A more tractable problem arises when a verbal measure uses language that is different from that characteristically employed by the respondent sample. In Wilson and Patterson's (1968) scale of conservative attitudes, for example, the word *apartheid* appears. The definition of this word probably was quite apparent for almost all of Wilson's sample of British respondents. Personal experience in attempting to employ this scale in the United States has shown that a widespread understanding of this term cannot be assumed. Because most scales of opinion are intended to be fairly general instruments, capable of being administered to a variety of respondents, it is advisable to determine in advance whether the meaning of the items that constitute the scale is the same as that originally intended. A preliminary interview of respondents drawn from the test population can supply a relatively inexpensive, rapid, and usually accurate determination of the "understandability" of the items on a scale. If the language used is too difficult or is misinterpreted, an alternate wording should be adopted. In brief, the language of the scale should be adapted so as to fit the language of the sample.

Extreme-response Sets. There is some evidence in the attitude scaling literature suggesting that reliable differences exist among people in terms of the tendency to employ (or to avoid) the extreme response alternatives of rating scales. Some people, it seems, characteristically use the middle parts of scales, whereas others characteristically employ the extremes. Researchers have correlated this tendency with intelligence, conservatism, dogmatism, and other personality attributes, but the results of such investigations are not clear-cut. There seems to be no way to design a scale that is impervious to this potential bias; however, we do have available statistical methods to determine the degree to which "extreme-response sets" occur on any given administration (see Nunnally, 1967, pp. 612–613). Research generally suggests that the extreme-response tendency does not greatly affect validity, but it is conceivable that on some issues, this bias could have a powerful impact on results. Remember, a bias that skews the responses of only 5%–10% of the sample could have a powerful effect on the outcome of a statistical analysis (Crano, 1997).

Acquiescence. People's tendency to acquiesce to, or agree with, positively worded statements is the final stylistic response trait to be considered. A positively worded statement is one on which agreement indicates a position favorable to the attitude object under investigation. Research indicates that some people characteristically acquiesce or agree with positively worded statements. Known variously as the tendency to "guess true," "acquiesce," "agree," or "yeasay," this variable has generated more research on stylistic biases than any other. This interest was probably stimulated by the development of Adorno, Frenkel-Brunswick, Levinson, and Sanford's (1950) theory of the "authoritarian personality." The California F (for fascism) Scale was one of the principal measurement devices employed in the assessment of authoritarianism, and over time, became a very popular scale, being used in hundreds of investigations. Indeed, more than 50 years after the publication of the classic work of Adorno et al. (1950), research interest on authoritarianism and its measurement is still intense (Altemeyer, 1988, 1996; Ray, 1985).

All the items on the original F scale were worded positively, and thus, higher levels of agreement with the items resulted in high authoritarianism scores. Some researchers hypothesized that the characteristic to agree with positively worded statements, rather than the content of the statements per se, might be responsible for some respondents' authoritarianism scores. Thus, the scale was not measuring authoritarianism so much as it was the tendency to agree with positively worded statements. To test such suspicions, specially constructed F scales consisting of positively worded items that were designed to be opposite in meaning to the original items were constructed. If item content were the major determinant of respondents' scores, a strong negative correlation between the original and the derivative F scale items would be expected. Instead, substantial *positive* correlations were obtained, thus supporting those who hypothesized the existence of an acquiescence response set.

Results of this type stimulated considerable research, which was focused not only on the F scale but also on response sets in general (see, e.g., Altemeyer, 1988; Block, 1965; Chapman & Campbell, 1957a, 1957b, 1959a, 1959b; Jackson & Messick, 1962; Wrightsman, 1965). Much of this research employed item-reversal techniques of the type discussed earlier. A major conceptual difficulty with this approach is that it is sometimes impossible to know when an item has truly been reversed. Consider the following item:

Capitalism represents the most equitable economic system.

One might reverse this item by substituting the word *socialism* or *communism* for *capitalism*; another possibility would change the word *equitable* to *inequitable*. Still other reversals of the original item are possible and, unfortunately, an individual might logically agree or disagree with both the original and its reversal. In this example, for instance, a respondent might feel that neither capitalism nor socialism nor communism was an equitable economic system. The predicted negative correlation between apparently reversed scales might well not occur given a sufficient number of reversals of this type. In light of the difficulties discussed, such a finding would not necessarily indicate the presence of an acquiescence response bias, but rather the failure to develop good reversals.

Interpretational problems of this type led Rorer (1965) to question the very existence of response sets. In an influential paper, Rorer argued that the response style question was a pseudo-issue and need not be considered a real danger to the validity of scales. This reaction to the complexities and interpretational difficulties of this research area is understandable, but probably too extreme. Campbell, Siegman, and Rees (1967), following Rorer, were able to demonstrate convincingly the presence of response biases in both the *F* scale and selected subscales of the Minnesota Multiphasic Personality Inventory (MMPI). The effects of these stylistic biases were not great, but this is very different from saying that they did not exist.

Like all the other set or stylistic biases, that of acquiescence has been shown to be a real phenomenon, whose potential effect on the validity of an instrument is not great; however, their impact on the outcome of an analysis could be sufficient to substantially alter the conclusions we might draw from it. If one is committed to the development of increasingly sensitive, reliable, and valid measurement instruments, even minor distortions should be eliminated. The typical strategy used to control for the acquiescence bias is straightforward: Use approximately equal numbers of positively and negatively worded items, so that the scale is balanced in terms of item wording. This solution is so simple that it should be standard practice; it is more common today than in earlier research. As a result, today's scales generally are less susceptible to the weak but consistent stylistic biases that can affect responses.

CONCLUDING REMARKS

To construct a measure that can be used to assess people's attitudes, attributes, thought processes, or behavioral predispositions reliably and validly requires substantive knowledge, technical competence, and a certain intuitive feel for the ways that people think and feel and act. Knowledge of correlational statistics is also helpful, and with increasingly sophisticated computer programs available at most research installations today, the computational work involved in these analyses becomes a non-issue. Even more than in most areas of research, however, "learning by doing" is crucial here. One learns how to write good items by writing items. One learns how to construct good measures by practice. Coupled with strong theoretical knowledge of the phenomenon of interest, and related phenomena, these experiences in scale construction help ensure the validity of the new measure. The lessons that we teach ourselves in endeavors of this type are at least as important as those that others teach us.

SUGGESTED READINGS

Crano, W. D. (2000). The multitrait-multimethod matrix as synopsis and recapitulation of Campbell's views on the proper conduct of social inquiry. In L. Bickman (Ed.), *Research design: Donald Campbell's legacy* (Chap. 3, pp. 37–61). Beverly Hills, CA: Sage.

Cronbach, L. J., Gleser, G. C., Nanda, H., & Rajaratnam, N. (1972). *The dependability of behavioral measurements: Theory of generalizability for scores and profiles.* New York: Wiley.

Nunnally, J. C. (1967). *Psychometric theory.* New York: McGraw-Hill.

II

RESEARCH DESIGN STRATEGIES

4

DESIGNING EXPERIMENTS: VARIATIONS ON THE BASICS

Chapter 2 introduced the concepts of internal and external validity, two important forms of experimental validity, and provided some information on the basic structure of the experiment in light of internal validity requirements. This chapter expands on this basic structure to consider variations in the ways in which experiments can be designed, set up, and executed.

VARIATIONS IN EXPERIMENTAL DESIGN

To summarize our earlier discussion, the classic "true" experimental design (Campbell & Stanley, 1963) involves the following steps:

1. Obtaining a pool of participants.
2. Pretesting them on the dependent variable of interest.
3. Randomly assigning each participant to experimental or control groups.[1]
4. Carefully controlling for differences in the application of the experimental treatment between the two groups.
5. Remeasuring both groups on the dependent variable at some time following the experimental treatment.

These steps are diagrammed in Fig. 4.1. Variations on this basic structure include elimination of the pretest, the addition of multiple experimental treatments, and the repeated

---

[1]In much of our discussion, we assume that experiments are conducted with individual persons as the unit of analysis. However, in some cases, experimental treatments are delivered not to individuals (independently assigned) but to groups of persons (e.g., small work groups or even whole classrooms). In this case, the group, rather then the component individuals, becomes the unit of analysis. More discussion of the issue of randomizing individuals or groups is provided in chapters 5 and 17.

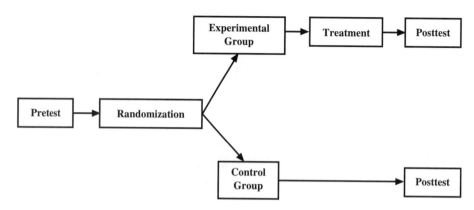

FIG. 4.1.   Pretest-posttest control group design.

use of the same participants in all conditions of the experiment. This chapter addresses each of these modifications in turn.

Pretest Sensitization

The pretest in this basic design allows us to demonstrate that those assigned to the two different treatment conditions did not differ in their response to the dependent variable at the outset of the experiment. Ideally, after random assignment the two groups are essentially the same, on average, in their pretest scores within the limits of chance variation. Pretests also serve other purposes in controlling for individual differences, as is discussed later in this chapter and in chapter 8.

Although pretesting has a number of benefits, the basic pretest–posttest–control group design is often altered to offset a potential problem that can be introduced by the pretest itself. This problem is termed *pretest sensitization* and refers to the possibility that the pretest can make participants in the experimental group unduly sensitive to the treatment to which they are exposed. Under these circumstances, the effect of the treatment may be artificially enhanced—the treatment appears stronger, or more effective, than it would be when applied to people who were not previously exposed to the pretest. It is also possible that the presence of a pretest can dampen the effectiveness of an experimental treatment if, for example, it alerts participants to the fact that the experimenter is trying to change their position and arouses their resistance to such change. Either of these pretesting effects are especially likely if the pretest is administered in the same session as the experiment itself, just prior to the introduction of the experimental manipulation.

An example may help to clarify the sensitizing bias. Suppose that we wanted to learn about the racial attitudes of a large group of research participants. The experimental treatment to be employed is a communication that we hope will influence participants to be less biased in their attitudes toward interactions with other racial groups. We administer the treatment and find it to be successful: The experimental participants are much less biased on the posttest measure than are those in the control group (who did not receive the communication), though both groups were identical on pretest attitudes.

From these results we cannot be sure that the experimental communication alone would be an effective means of changing people's racial attitudes. It is possible that the pretest might have sensitized the experimental participants to the treatment and thereby altered its effectiveness. Perhaps as a result of the pretesting, participants were led to think about the validity of their racial beliefs. Those in the experimental group—already sensitized to the subject—were especially susceptible to the communication when they received it. The participants in the control group might also have been induced to think about their racial attitudes because of the pretest, but because they were not exposed to the communication, they did not show as much attitude change.

One way to reduce this problem would be to administer the pretest measure some time in advance of the experimental treatment, at least a few days or weeks prior to participation in the experiment itself. Assuming that the participants do not make a strong connection between the earlier testing and the experiment, the passage of time should reduce any sensitization associated with the pretest measure. However, this does not always work. If the pretest involves an important or emotionally loaded issue (e.g., the previously mentioned racial attitudes illustration or some measures of self-esteem or self-concept), respondents may ruminate about their responses after they have taken the test. Under these circumstances, it is possible that the pretest leads to a change in attitudes over time. Thus, when participants enter the experiment, the pretest no longer reflects their current attitude or position. Even when this kind of sensitization is not likely, it is not always possible to administer a pretest at a different time. Participants may only be available for one session.

To solve this problem, researchers often eliminate the pretest as part of the experimental design. This is especially likely in experimental contexts in which a pretest would have to be administered in the same session as the experimental treatments and may bias results by unduly sensitizing participants, and thereby making them more (or less) susceptible to the treatment. The result is the posttest-only control group design, diagrammed in Fig. 4.2. In this case, we have no direct test of the assumption that those assigned to the two conditions were initially "equivalent" on the dependent variable. But random assignment allows us to presume initial equivalence of experimental and control groups (within the limits of chance), so there is no need for pretesting to establish that the groups are the same prior to the introduction of the experimental treatment. Of course, this assumption rests on the use of a relatively large number of participants. Random assignment of a pool of fewer than 20 people is not likely to produce equivalent groups if individuals vary a lot on the dependent variable of interest. A general rule of thumb is that the pool of participants must be

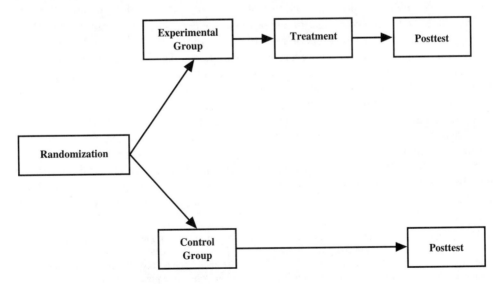

FIG. 4.2. Posttest-only control group design.

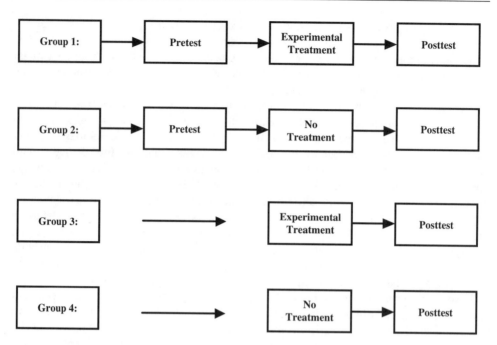

FIG. 4.3. Solomon four-group design.

large enough to randomly assign at least 25–30 individuals per condition to take advantage of randomization as a method for achieving initial equivalence of treatment conditions.

The posttest-only control group design has several advantages in reduced cost and effort, along with the avoidance of the pretest sensitization bias. However, it has one disadvantage in that it prevents the researcher from assessing the potential effects of pretesting on the experimental treatment under study. This disadvantage can be overcome by combining the pretest–posttest and posttest-only control group designs, in what is called a *Solomon four-group design*. In this variation, participants are randomly assigned to one of four groups, two of which are pretested and two of which are not. One of the pretested groups and one of the untested groups are then exposed to the experimental treatment; the others are not, and this produces the division of participants represented in Fig. 4.3.

The use of this design permits several effects to be evaluated in the same experiment. Equivalence of groups 1 and 2 on the pretest suggests that the randomization procedure has been effective, and posttest results across all four groups can then be used to assess the effects of both the treatment variable and of pretesting. Any effect of the experimental treatment, above and beyond testing and other rival factors, can be determined by comparing the posttest results of the two experimental groups (1 and 3) with those of the control groups (2 and 4). Effects of pretesting alone can be obtained by comparing the posttest scores of groups 2 and 4, whereas any effects of pretesting on sensitivity to the experimental treatment can be detected in differences between groups 1 and 3, who have received the same treatment but differ in their prior exposure to a pretest measure.[2]

[2]A review of research (Lana, 1959) making use of this four-group design indicated that loss of generalizability of findings because of pretesting effects was minimal. However, Rosnow and Suls (1970) found that the pretesting effect operates differentially in groups of volunteer and nonvolunteer subjects. Because this issue remains unresolved, investigators are urged to exercise cautions when interpreting studies that make use of pretests, especially in contexts in which pretest sensitization is a reasonable possibility.

EXPANSION OF EXPERIMENTAL TREATMENTS

So far we have been considering experimental designs in which the independent variable consists of the presence or absence of a single experimental treatment (the treatment–control group design). However, there is no reason that more than one variation of an experimental treatment cannot be made within the same experiment so long as certain rules for enlarging the number of treatments are followed. First, instead of presence versus absence of the experimental treatment as the basic comparison, we may compare groups that have been exposed to different *amounts* or *kinds* of the independent variable. Then, in addition to determining whether the existence (presence or absence) of the treatment makes any difference in the dependent variable, the researcher can determine whether variations in the treatment also make a difference. These variations may be quantitative—different amounts of the variable (e.g., 0 vs. .3 cc. vs. .6 cc. of a drug, or high vs. medium vs. low anxiety inducement)—or qualitative—different ways of producing the independent variable (e.g., anxiety induced by social conditions vs. anxiety induced by physical danger). The number of variations of a given experimental treatment (including its absence) is referred to as the number of *levels* of that variable. Thus, the basic treatment–control group design is a two-level experiment; introducing additional variations of the same experimental treatment (independent variable) expands the design to three or four levels or more.

Factorial Designs

Levels of one experimental treatment may be combined with levels of another treatment to further expand the experimental design. For complete interpretability of results, these variables should be *factorially* combined; that is, conditions should be constructed such that all levels of each variable are combined with all levels of the others(s). There are several reasons why we might want to expand an experiment beyond a single variable. One of the most important of these is to allow for the identification of interaction effects, which are discussed later in this chapter. Conceptually, the concept of interaction is relatively easy to illustrate. For example, suppose we are interested in the persuasive effects of group consensus on individual beliefs. We believe that high consensus in a group will shape group members' opinions rather strongly, but only when the issue at hand is not highly relevant to the individual. When the issue is highly self-relevant, group members will resist the apparent consensus and may even go so far as to adopt a more radical antigroup position than they held before the consensus became known. They might respond in this way because they resent the apparent restriction on their individual freedom that the consensus estimate implies (Burgoon, Alvaro, Grandpre, & Voloudakis, in press). Low group consensus, on the other hand, is not expected to have much impact, no matter the self-relevance of the issue. We could not test this hypothesis by manipulating only one variable, so we combine them in a factorial design. The patterns of change that occur in the high self-relevance condition as a consequence of high or low consensus would be contrasted with those that occur when self-relevance is low.

A second important reason to combine factors is to enhance the power of our designs to detect theoretically meaningful differences. The variance associated with a factor is controlled, or accounted for, when that factor is a part of the experimental design. If the factor is not a part of the design, its variation is unexplained, and must be classed as error, or "unaccounted for" variance. This added variance lowers the power of our design to detect differences, and hence may lead to Type II error, mistakenly failing to reject the null hypothesis (see chap. 2). To return to our example, suppose that we did not consider self-relevance, but rather hypothesized that high group consensus would have a strong persuasive effect on group members' beliefs. Our prediction would be confirmed if we happened to use issues the participants did not find highly self-relevant. However, if we had stumbled on highly self-relevant issues for our participants, our hypothesis would be disconfirmed. By adding self-relevance to the experimental design, we have controlled, and explained, the variation associated with this factor, and created a more comprehensive and fine-grained theoretical view of the effects of consensus on group members' expressed beliefs. Moreover, the overall error rate of our experiment has been lowered, and our consequent power to detect real differences enhanced.

Creating the Design. With a factorial design, we can assess the effects of variation in one independent variable while systematically varying one or more other independent variables as well. Each independent variable that is manipulated in a factorial design is a *factor*, and the number of conditions (or *cells*) in the design is equal to the product of the number of levels of all its factors. For a two-factor design, for example, the combined treatments might be as shown in Table 4.1. In this illustration, Variable 1 has five levels, and Variable 2 has four levels. This design would be designated a 5 × 4 factorial. It consists of (5 × 4) 20 separate conditions, formed by the factorial combination of the two independent variables.

For a three-variable design, the two-variable case is repeated for each level of the third variable, as in Table 4.2. Note that the number of treatment groups, and therefore the number of participants that are required, increases geometrically as variables are added to the design. This fact automatically places some practical limits on the number of variables that can be included in any single study; theoretically, however, the number of variables that can be combined is practically limitless. Table 4.2, for example, presents a 3 × 2 × 3

TABLE 4.1
Two Variable (5 × 4) Factorial Design

		Variable 2		
Variable 1	*Level 1*	*Level 2*	*Level 3*	*Level 4*
Level 1	Condition 1-1	Condition 1-2	Condition 1-3	Condition 1-4
Level 2	Condition 2-1	Condition 2-2	Condition 2-3	Condition 2-4
Level 3	Condition 3-1	Condition 3-2	Condition 3-3	Condition 3-4
Level 4	Condition 4-1	Condition 4-2	Condition 4-3	Condition 4-4
Level 5	Condition 5-1	Condition 5-2	Condition 5-3	Condition 5-4

TABLE 4.2
Three Variable (3 × 2 × 3) Factorial Design

			Variable 3	
Variable 1	*Variable 2*	*Level 1*	*Level 2*	*Level 3*
Level 1	Level 1	Condition 1-1-1	Condition 1-1-2	Condition 1-1-3
	Level 2	Condition 1-2-1	Condition 1-2-2	Condition 1-2-3
Level 2	Level 1	Condition 2-1-1	Condition 2-1-2	Condition 2-1-3
	Level 2	Condition 2-2-1	Condition 2-2-2	Condition 2-2-3
Level 3	Level 1	Condition 3-1-1	Condition 3-1-2	Condition 3-1-3
	Level 2	Condition 3-2-1	Condition 3-2-2	Condition 3-2-3

TABLE 4.3

Solomon Four-Group Design as a 2 × 2 Factorial
Combination of Source and Pretest Variation

	Pretest	No Pretest	
Treatment	Group 1	Group 3	Treatment
No treatment	Group 2	Group 4	Main effect
	Pretest main effect		

factorial design. If we wish to randomly assign 25 participants to each cell of the design, we would require 25 × 3 × 2 × 3 participants, a total of 450. If we wished to add another three-level factor to the design and still maintain the same number (25) of participants per cell we would need exactly three times as many participants as in the three-way (3 × 2 × 3) design of the table. Obviously, then, there are practical constraints on the number of conditions that can be run in a factorial design, and both the number of factors and the number of levels of each factor must be limited.

It is preferable, but not mandatory, that the same number of participants be exposed to each of the cells of the design, which represent the various combinations of treatments. Then, the effect of any single treatment variable can be obtained by comparing dependent variable scores of all participants who were exposed to the first level of that variable with those exposed to the second level, the third level, and so on. Differences on the dependent measure attributable to variations of the levels of a single variable are called *main effects*. In obtaining the main effect of a given variable, the effects of the other variables are ignored because they are held constant across all levels of the variable under consideration by the factorial design. In other words, equivalence of groups is maintained because an equal number of participants in all levels of the variable have been exposed to each of the variations of the other independent variables.[3]

The Solomon Four-Group Design: An Illustration. We have already considered one factorial design in our discussion of the use of pretesting in true experiments. In this design, two factors are systematically varied—presence or absence of a pretest, and presence or absence of the experimental treatment—each with two levels. Thus, the four-group design depicted in Fig. 4.3 can be rewritten in factorial form as in Table 4.3. Using this design, the overall effect of having received the experimental treatment versus not receiving it (ignoring pretesting conditions) is obtained by comparing scores of participants in Row 1 (Groups 1 and 3) of the table with those in Row 2 (Groups 2 and 4). The overall effect of pretesting on posttest scores is obtained by comparing participants in Column 1 (Groups 1 and 2) with those in Column 2 (Groups 3 and 4). In obtaining the treatment effect, we can ignore the effect of the pretesting variable because both treatment and control groups have equal numbers of randomly assigned participants who have been pretested or not pretested. Thus, any pretesting effects have been "held constant" across the two treatment conditions. The same logic holds when we wish to consider the effect of pretesting, independent of treatments. As can be seen, among the pretested group, an equal number of participants have served in the treatment and control conditions, and this equality is found in the

---

[3]Strictly speaking, we can employ different numbers of subjects in the various treatment combinations of a factorial design, and at times this may be desirable. If certain assumptions of proportionality are met, common statistical techniques (cf. Winer, 1971) allow us to estimate treatment effects. However, both analysis and interpretation are simplified when equal ns are employed.

nonpretested group as well. Thus, treatment variations "cancel out" when assessing the effects of pretesting.

Interaction Effects

As we have seen, a factorial design allows us to look at the effects of each independent variable with the other variable controlled for. The overall effect of each variable is called the *main effect* of that factor (i.e., the effect of variations in the levels of that factor, when variations in the other factor have been systematically controlled). As noted previously, the main effect of each variable can be detected with greater power and efficiency when other influential variables have been systematically controlled in a factorial design rather than being allowed to vary randomly. However, the primary advantage of the use of factorial designs in which two or more experimental treatments are combined lies in the opportunity to detect whether the effects of one variable are in any way influenced or altered by variations in the level of the other variable(s). Such influences are termed *interaction effects*. The pretest sensitization effect discussed earlier in this chapter is an example of a type of interaction effect. In the four-group design depicted in Table 4.3, sensitization would produce differences in the effect of the treatment depending on whether the pretest had been present or not. In this case, the difference between Group 1 and Group 2 (pretest present) might be greater than the difference between Group 3 and Group 4 (no pretest). That would mean that the pretest sensitized participants in such a way as to enhance the effect of the treatment manipulation. Thus, the effect of the treatment is altered by the presence or absence of pretesting.

Most interactions of theoretical interest are those that involve two or more manipulated treatment variables. For example, suppose that we were interested in the effects of various types of leadership on the productivity of small work groups and, further, whether the stress of outside competition influences these leadership effects. To address this issue, we might design an experiment in which groups of participants (say, four people per group) were brought together in a work setting, given tools, materials, and instructions, and asked to produce *widgets* (small pieces of equipment).

The groups could be set up so that the leadership role was either very democratic or very authoritarian—a factor with two levels of experimental treatment. Further, participants could be informed that they were competing with another group, whose production figures would be constantly available to them. (To enliven the proceedings, we could promise a $50 prize to the most productive group. Notice that all groups are promised this reward, so it is a constant, not an experimental treatment.) We could experimentally vary the information the groups received such that the "other" group always seemed much more productive, about the same, or much less productive than the participants' own group. This second factor, which we will operationally define as *competitive stress*, would be a three-level variable.

By combining these two variables factorially, the experiment takes the form of a 2 (democratic vs. authoritarian leadership) × 3 (high, medium, or low competitive stress) factorial design. Our dependent measure, the number of widgets produced by each partic-ipant group, constitutes our index of group productivity, the dependent measure.

Suppose that we randomly assigned 15 groups to each of the six conditions formed by the factorial combination of our two experimental treatments.[4] The average productivity of the groups in each condition is depicted in Table 4.4. A very quick scan of the results

---

[4]Note, this is an illustration of an experiment in which groups, rather than individuals, would be the unit of analysis (see note 1, this chapter).

TABLE 4.4

Mean Number of Widgets Produced as a Function of Leadership
and Competitive Stress

		Competitive Stress		
		Low	Medium	High
Leadership	Authoritarian	25	35	45
Style	Democratic	45	35	25

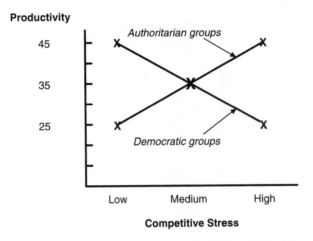

FIG. 4.4. Effects of competitive stress and group on productivity [see Table 4.4].

in the table indicates that neither the leadership nor the stress variables alone produced a substantial main effect. Why? Because summing across the conditions of leadership style, we see that the groups exposed to high competitive stress produced 70 pieces of equipment on average, just as did the groups exposed to medium and low stress. Similarly, the democratically run groups produced 105 widgets on average, neither more nor less than the authoritarian groups.

Although there is no evidence of a main effect for either treatment variable in these data, by simply looking at the data pattern (always a good idea) it becomes clear that the manipulations did have an influence on the groups' productivity. Leadership style per se had no differential impact on productivity, but *in combination* with level of competitive stress, its influence was substantial. The interaction of these two variables suggests that under conditions of low stress, a democratically structured group will out-produce groups that are directed in a more authoritarian fashion. However, as the stress of competition increases, authoritarian groups increase in productivity, whereas democratic groups become less productive. Because of this interaction effect, we cannot specify the nature of the effect of leadership style on production without knowing the stress conditions under which the group is operating.

Common Forms of Interaction Effects. Interactions can take many different forms. The most common interaction forms are *divergent* interactions and *crossover* interactions. The productivity data of Table 4.4 from our previous example provide an illustration of a crossover form of interaction. The basis for this terminology is evident from the graphic portrayal of these results in Fig. 4.4. As shown in this figure, the productivity levels of

TABLE 4.5

Widget Production as a Function of Leadership and Competitive
Stress: Example of a Divergent Interaction

| | | Competitive Stress | | |
		Low	Medium	High
Leadership	Authoritarian	25	35	45
Style	Democratic	25	15	5

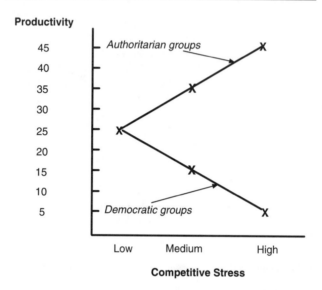

FIG. 4.5.   Effects of competitive stress and group on productivity [see Table 4.5].

the authoritarian and democratic groups cross over, in this case at the medium level of competitive stress.

A divergent interaction effect is illustrated in the data of Table 4.5, which is depicted graphically in Fig. 4.5. (Note that the divergent effect could just as well take on the appearance of a *convergent* interaction if the levels of competitive stress were reversed, i.e., if the high level were presented first and the low level last on the horizontal axis. Convergent and divergent interactions are simply alternative forms of the same interaction effect.)

As shown in this last illustration, democratic and authoritarian groups are equally productive under low levels of stress, but as stress increases, the production rates of the groups diverge: The democratic groups become less productive, the authoritarian groups more so. A main effect of leadership style also becomes evident in this example: Across stress conditions, the authoritarian groups produced more widgets overall than did the democratic groups. However, interpretation of this main effect has to be tempered in light of the interaction effect obtained. Authoritarian groups do not out-produce democratic groups under all conditions, but only when competitive stress is medium or high.

The Issue of Independence.   It should be noted that, just as random assignment to experimental conditions presumes control over exposure to the independent variable, factorial designs presume that two or more experimental treatments can be *independently* manipulated. Sometimes, however, the nature of two variables is such that the levels of one cannot be produced independently of the other. Suppose, for example, that one wanted to study the effects of high or low anxiety-producing conditions in combination with the effects of the attractiveness of the experimenter on the complexity of children's speech. Suppose further that our experiment required that anxiety be induced by the behavior of the experimenter. In such a design, it is unlikely that the two "independent" variables would really be independent because it is not likely that participants would find a person who was scaring them to death to be attractive. This example indicates the importance of going beyond the mere mechanics of factorializing. Some thought is required in the combination of independent variables to ensure that meaningful experimental conditions have been created. Although almost any set of independent variables can be combined on paper, the way they are perceived by participants is critical.

Blocked Designs

As we mentioned earlier, the effectiveness of random assignment in creating initial equivalence among our various experimental conditions depends on the "law of large numbers." Only when a large pool of participants is initially available can random sorting guarantee a "cancelling out" of individual variation across cells of the experimental design. If the initial pool of participants is relatively small and diverse, the researcher may be concerned that randomization may not distribute participants evenly between different experimental groups. When only a small initial pool is available, and particularly when this pool includes a few extreme cases, random assignment may not produce the desired equivalence between conditions. When this is the case, or when it is desirable to gain greater control over sources of variation, participants may be sorted into categories before assignment to experimental groups. This variation in random assignment is called a *blocked* design.

The participant pool is first blocked, or ordered according to levels, on some relevant variable (e.g., dividing participants into groups that are high, medium, or low on some measure of intelligence, or sorting participants by sex). Then, from within these groupings, participants are randomly divided between experimental and control groups so that each of the resulting groups has an equal number of members from each block. As long as this assignment of preclassified participants is determined by chance, the assumption of random assignment is not violated, and the initial equivalence of experimental groups is assured. One form of a blocked design makes use of a pretest on the dependent variable (usually a pretest that has been administered sometime prior to the experimental session). All participants in the pool are first categorized into groups based on similarity of pretest scores. Then participants within each of the groups, or blocks, are randomly assigned to experimental and control conditions, as diagrammed in Fig. 4.6.

A blocked design is a form of factorial design. The blocking variable is one factor, which is then crossed with the experimental treatment factor (or factors, if there is more than one independent variable). In terms of experimental manipulation, however, this is known as a *mixed* design. Experimental variables are those which can be manipulated by the researcher and randomly assigned to participants. Blocking variables are not manipulated or randomly assigned—they are characteristics that the participant comes to the experiment with, already predetermined. (As researchers we are not in a position to experimentally manipulate an individual's sex or intelligence or pre-existing attitudes and values; we can only measure these factors as part of our experimental procedures.) Blocking increases experimental control by assuring that differences among participants are equalized across experimental conditions.

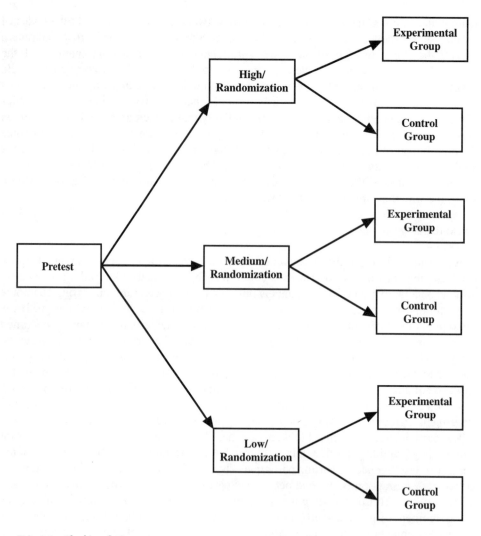

FIG. 4.6.   Blocking design.

Blocking also permits testing interactions between the experimental variable and participant characteristics. For instance, it may be that the effectiveness of a particular persuasive communication depends on the level of intelligence of those who hear it. A complex argument may be processed, understood, and accepted by recipients who are high in intelligence but misunderstood or rejected by those with lower levels of intellectual capacity or cognitive skills (see McGuire, 1997; Rhodes & Wood, 1992; Wood & Stagner, 1994). A simplistic argument, on the other hand, may appeal to people of average intelligence but be dismissed by high IQ individuals. If intelligence of the audience is ignored, it may appear that there is no difference in the overall effectiveness of complex or simple arguments. However, if participant intelligence is measured before the experimental communication is delivered, and participants are then divided into high, medium, and low IQ blocks prior to random assignment, differences in effectiveness of the two types of communication could be observed between the different IQ groups. This way, we learn more about the conditions under which different types of communication might be effective. Although intelligence cannot be manipulated by a researcher, it can be recognized as a *moderator variable*, that is, a factor that alters (inhibits or enhances) the effects of a particular experimental treatment.

REPEATED MEASURES AND COUNTERBALANCING

In most experimental designs, any one participant is exposed to one and only one experimental condition. Although this condition may represent the factorial combination of a number of experimental treatments, it is still true that the participant is assigned to only one cell of the extended experimental design. In some experiments, however, the same participants may be used in more than one cell of the experimental design. Such designs are called *repeated measures* studies because participants are repeatedly measured on the dependent variable, once after each treatment exposure. Variables that are manipulated in this way are called *within-subject* factors in an experimental design.

The pretest–posttest–control group design is an example of a repeated measures design. In this design, all participants are measured once prior to any treatment and then again after the experimental group has been exposed to the treatment variable. Thus, the first testing can be used as a no-treatment base of comparison for assessing treatment effects. In other repeated measures experiments, individual participants are exposed to a series of different treatment conditions and measured after each. Every participant may be exposed to all possible treatments, or participants may be randomly assigned to different sets of treatments.

Just as pretest sensitization effects can influence the results of a pretest–posttest experiment, the effects of one experimental treatment may carry over in some way to influence the effects of succeeding treatments. Thus, the order in which treatments in a repeated measures study are administered may have a major effect on its results. There is no way that order effects can be eliminated from the pretest–posttest design because, by definition, the pretest measure has to be taken first, before any other experimental treatment is administered. With successive treatments, however, varying the order in which different participants receive the treatments can control for the impact of treatment order effects. For maximum interpretability of results, treatments should be presented to different participants in *counterbalanced* order. For instance, if each participant is to be exposed to four messages— one from a pleasant communicator (treatment A), one from a neutral source (B), one from an unpleasant communicator (C), and one for whom no source is identified (D)— a counterbalanced ordering would be achieved by varying order of presentation as in Table 4.6.

Notice that counterbalancing does not necessarily involve using every possible order of all conditions (for designs with five or more experimental treatments, this would run int'

TABLE 4.6
A Counterbalanced Design

	Order of Communication Presentation			
	1	*2*	*3*	*4*
Group 1	A	B	C	D
Group 2	B	D	A	C
Group 3	C	A	D	ʳ
Group 4	D	C	B	

unwieldy possibilities). The conditions of counterbalancing are met if (a) each treatment occurs once and only once in each position, and (b) each treatment is immediately preceded by every other treatment once and only once across the presentation orderings. In our example, for instance, A is preceded once by B (Group 4), once by C (Group 3), and once by D (Group 2). The only other requirement for counterbalancing is that the number of participants in each group be equal, so that each ordering is used an equal number of times. Using this procedure, each group of participants receives one of the different orderings, and order becomes a blocking variable in the overall experimental design.

Repeated measures designs, with counterbalancing, have the advantage of assuring the equivalence of groups exposed to different treatments because each participant, in effect, serves as his or her own "control group." However, repeated use of the same participants is just not possible for all types of experimental variables. In many cases, one level or combination of variables would severely interfere with, or preclude, administering any other treatment combinations. The effects of some variables are cumulative. In studies involving intake of different amounts of drugs or alcohol, for instance, the experimenter could not administer a second dosage level to the same participant until all traces of the first dose were eliminated from that participant's system; otherwise, the repeated doses would accumulate and obliterate any differences in the effects of dose level. Other experimental treatments are such that once participants have been exposed to one of them, their fatigue, level of awareness of experimental purposes or procedures, or lack of naiveté, may make them unsuited for use in further experimental conditions. However, there are some types of experimental manipulations that lend themselves to repeated measures designs more readily. For instance, in real life, people are often exposed to information about several different persons or to multiple news stories in succession on a particular topic. So, in experiments where the independent variable involves different content of information about persons or events, exposing the same participant to different levels of the manipulation may be reasonable. Even in these cases, however, the order in which a particular condition is received may make a difference. But the counterbalanced design makes it possible to assess such order effects and take them into account in interpreting the effects of the experimental treatment.

RECAP

This chapter started with the basic two-group pretest–posttest experimental design and demonstrated how elements can be added to or subtracted from that basic design in order to create useful variations in the structure of an experiment. The levels of an independent variable can be expanded from two conditions to multiple variations. More than one independent variable can be manipulated in a single experiment using factorial designs. Pretesting can be excluded or included and used either as a blocking variable or in a repeated measures design. Deciding among these different design features must be done on the basis of the purposes of the experiment (including theories about potential interaction effects among different variables) and one's knowledge or intuitions about factors such as sensitization, carryover, and order effects.

Whatever form the experimental design takes, the design stage is still just the blueprint of the experiment itself. The design tells us what variables are being manipulated, at how many different levels, and in what combinations. Once this blueprint has been put into place, the real task is constructing the conditions and procedures through which the intended design will be implemented, that is, the *operations* of the experiment. As with any construction, building each experiment always involves some unique features, decisions to be made, and problems to solve. However, there are some general principles and guidelines for constructing experimental procedures that can help maximize the internal validity of the results of the experiment, and contribute to external validity as well. The following chapter covers some of these general principles in a step-by-step approach to conducting a laboratory experiment.

SUGGESTED READINGS

Campbell, D. T., & Stanley, J. C. (1966). *Experimental and quasi-experimental designs for research*. Chicago: Rand-McNally.

Smith, E. R. (2000). Research design. In H. Reis & C. Judd (Eds.), *Handbook of research methods in social and personality psychology* (pp. 17–39). New York: Cambridge University Press.

Winer, B. J., Brown, D. R., & Michels, K. M. (1991). *Statistical principles in experimental design*. New York: McGraw-Hill.

5

CONSTRUCTING LABORATORY EXPERIMENTS

The preceding chapter discussed the design of experimental studies at a relatively abstract level to introduce basic principles of planning and constructing a laboratory experiment. This chapter considers how to *implement* an experimental design, in terms of the basic construction of a laboratory experiment, and describes the different forms of experimental treatments that are used in contemporary social research. The chapter also covers aspects of the experiment that, while not formal features of the design, can nevertheless have a great impact on a study's outcome. Although this text is not meant to be a nuts and bolts "how to do it" book, this chapter contains details and information that should provide a useful guide to the conduct of experimental research.

Figure 5.1 presents a skeletal framework for constructing a laboratory experiment, outlining the elements that comprise any experimental study. In developing an experiment, the researcher in effect creates an "alternate universe," a small but self-contained environment in which the main "action" of the study takes place. Each step in the construction has to be defined and controlled by the experimenter, and this control constitutes an important feature, both the strength and the weakness, of the experimental method.

Select Participant Pool

The first step in developing any study is arranging for the availability of a pool of eligible participants. This is the essential first step because it will control many of the later decisions the experimenter must make, including the particular form of treatment, the measures to be used, the extent to which the researcher is a part of the experimental context, and so on. This step also may be one of the most difficult for the experimenter to control. (We discuss some of the ways in which participants may be recruited for participation in experiments later in this chapter). At this point, we assume that a pool of participants is potentially available for the study. It is the researcher's role to define which participants are eligible to take part in the investigation. For some purposes, for practical or theoretical reasons, the researcher may wish to limit the investigation to individuals with particular characteristics, such as only male participants or only those of a specific age range, race, or religion. In

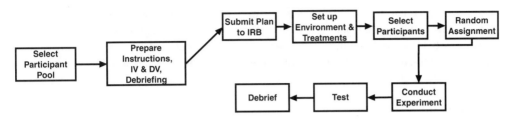

FIG. 5.1. Framework for constructing the experiment.

such cases, experimenter control may be purchased at some cost to external validity (see chap. 7).

Deciding on Sample Size

Having secured a pool of eligible participants, the next decision to be made concerns the *number* that will be actually included in the experiment itself. The issue here is one of statistical power. It is important to ensure that a sufficient number of participants has been included to detect meaningful differences between experimental conditions above and beyond random variation. If the number of participants is too low, statistical inference will have low power; that is, we will fail to identify a difference where one might actually be present (a Type II error; see chap. 2).

How do we know how many participants will be sufficient? The most widely accepted method is to perform a power analysis prior to conducting the experiment. Cohen (1992) provided a useful table for estimating necessary sample sizes for the most common statistical tests used in social research. The formula depends on choosing the size of the effect that one would like to be able to detect.[1] For practical purposes, in social research we generally aim for medium effect sizes. In a two-group experiment, this would require 64 participants to have sufficient power to detect a real difference at the $p < .05$ level of statistical significance. To detect a much smaller effect, the sample would increase exponentially. The same two-sample experiment would require 393 participants to have sufficient power. Practical constraints usually limit the potential power of our research endeavors. (See chap. 2 for methods of increasing power in addition to simply increasing the number of participants).

Prepare Materials

Once the participant pool has been identified, and specific groups defined as eligible for participation, the experimenter can organize the various features that will define the experiment. Instructions must be prepared, independent variables and dependent measures planned and constructed, and debriefings written. The debriefing is the experimenter's honest explanation of what the study is about, and it is an indispensable part of the study, especially if voluntary participants are used in the research.[2] Most experimental treatments can be developed in such a way that it is unnecessary to deceive participants (this issue is considered in detail in chap. 19). However, if deception is planned, the experimenter

---

[1]Following Cohen (1988), differences between two groups of .8, .5, and .2 standard deviation units are defined as large, moderate, and small effect sizes, respectively.

[2]In some research, participants are not aware of their being under investigation, and in some instances, as will be seen later in this chapter, it is impractical or impossible to debrief.

must develop a plan to offset its effects in a careful post-experimental debriefing. A good general rule is that participants should leave the study feeling as good about themselves as they did when they entered it. If the experimental treatments put participants' self-esteem at risk, or if they were misinformed in any way, this potential damage must be offset at the study's completion.

Submit to IRB

The central features of the experimental design, that is, the instructions, dependent and independent variables, and debriefing, must be submitted for approval to a committee specifically constituted to protect the welfare of research participants. In most universities, this body is called the Institutional Review Board (IRB) or, less formally, the "human participants committee." It is imperative that no research involving human participation ever be conducted without prior approval of the IRB. Failure to meet this requirement can have serious consequences for an investigator and sanctions on the entire institution. Recently, researchers in the medical school of a colleague's institution were accused of conducting research that had not been sanctioned by the university's IRB. The offender's research project, which was funded by the federal government, was terminated, and moreover, the entire research enterprise at the university was brought to a halt. No research involving participants, human or otherwise, was permitted until the problems were remedied. All ongoing projects had to be re-reviewed. This took months, and during that time, students and faculty were not allowed to conduct research that made use of human beings. Imagine being a Ph.D candidate whose dissertation research was about to begin or, worse yet, about to reach completion. Imagine attempting to do an empirical study for one's senior thesis or fourth-year project or research methods course assignment. These opportunities were lost because of an investigative team whose actions brought the entire research enterprise under a cloud of suspicion.

Set Up Environment

Assuming that the IRB has reviewed the proposed study and finds that it does not entail undue risk to the human participants who will be involved, the researcher must now set up the experimental context. In considering all of the elements of an experimental setting, we must distinguish between those features of the context that are to be held constant, and those that are to be systematically manipulated. Experimental contexts are characterized by both a physical environment and a social environment. Because social experiments involve the use of mindful and cognizant persons, the participants must be given some kind of information or instructions regarding what the experiment is about and what they are supposed to do. Apart from the specific features that are to be manipulated as the independent variable (or variables), it is critical to good experimental design that these other features be defined and controlled by the experimenter in such a way that they do not interfere with the intended independent variable.

Most environmental features, other than the independent variable of interest, will be controlled by assuring that they are kept the same for all participants in all experimental conditions. The same laboratory space is used for all conditions; the same set of instructions are recorded and played for all participants; the same experimenter runs every session, and so on. Some features cannot be held constant in this way. It is difficult, for instance, to run all sessions of an experiment at the same time of day, and the same experimenter may not be available for every session. In these cases, the researcher must control the situation in such a way that variations in the aspects of the situation are evenly distributed across the experimental conditions. Some experimental sessions may be run at 10:00 a.m. and others at 5:00 p.m., but every treatment condition must be equally likely to occur at the early sessions and the later ones. For example, suppose create a simple experiment with one treatment and one control condition. It would be a mistake to conduct all the treatment runs in the mornings, and to test the control participants only in the evening sessions, because differences might ensue as a result of factors associated with the times of day at which the participants were studied (e.g., fatigue, hunger, etc.), rather than the treatment variable itself. In our example, the manipulation is perfectly confounded with time of day, rendering an unambiguous interpretation of results impossible. Similarly, it would be a mistake to have one experimenter conduct all the experimental runs, and another all the control sessions. To do so would create an uninterpretable outcome because we will have perfectly confounded treatment/control conditions with experimenter and thus, could not be certain if differences occurred because of the experimenters, or the experimental condition to which our participants were assigned.

EXPERIMENTAL TREATMENTS

We classify experimental manipulations into three broad types, depending on whether they involve variations in the physical, social, or instructional features of the experimental context. *Social manipulations* are usually dependent on some action of another human being within the experimental situation, often a research accomplice working for the experimenter. *Environmental treatments* entail the systematic manipulation of some aspect of the physical setting. *Instructional manipulations* usually are presented to the participant by the experimenter as part of the description of the purposes and procedures of the study (the "cover story"). Usually, different treatment varieties are combined in same study, but for illustrative purposes we discuss them as "pure" types.

Environmental Manipulations

Most experiments require some intervention into the physical environment so that the experimental treatment can be effected. Sometimes the environmental intervention is quite dramatic. Consider, for example, an experiment by Latané and Darley (1968) conducted as part of their investigation of diffusion of responsibility in groups. They hypothesized that an individual's reaction to an emergency would be determined by the presence or absence of other people in the setting. A lone individual was expected to react promptly to signs of an emergency, but when others were present, the responsibility for action was expected to diffuse throughout the group and reduce the probability that anyone would respond at all. To test this hypothesis, Latané and Darley arranged a situation in which a participant arrived at the laboratory and was directed to a waiting room, either alone or in the company of other participants. In the room was a sign instructing the participant(s) to begin work on a questionnaire. Soon after participants began the questionnaire, thick, dark smoke began to pour into the room through a ventilator. The amount of time participants stayed in the room after the smoke appeared constituted the dependent variable of the study. As predicted, the more people in the room, the longer it took anyone to respond.

In this example, the environmental intervention (smoke pumped through the ventilator) constituted a part of the setup or staging of the experiment. It was held constant for all experimental conditions; in other words, although it affected the experimental context, it was not an experimental manipulation as all participants experienced it. The independent (manipulated) variable was the number of people present, not the physical situation. In other experiments, some aspect of the physical environment is the manipulated independent variable.

Good examples of environmental manipulations may be found in the study of objective self-awareness (Duval & Wicklund, 1972; Vallacher, 1978). In this area of research, variations in the extent to which participants focus on themselves, versus the external environment, are thought to have important implications for psychological processes and consequent behaviors. Accordingly, researchers have concocted different environmental treatments that affect participants to become self- or other-focused. One of the early studies in the field made use of a video camera (Insko, Worchel, Songer, & Arnold, 1973). In some conditions of the study, a video camera was trained on participants as they performed. In the other conditions, the camera was carefully stowed away. This manipulation of the experimental context was used to help test Duval and Wicklund's (1972) theory.

Stimulus Manipulations

The given examples of environmental manipulations all involved manipulations of the context in which the participant would make some kind of behavioral response or reaction. Another form of environmental manipulation is used in experiments in which participants are given some visual or verbal materials and asked to make a judgment or decision about the content of those materials. In such *judgment experiments* (Aronson et al., 1998), the experimental treatment consists of variations in aspects of the stimulus materials that are presented. For instance, in much of the experimental research on impression formation, or person perception, participants are given a verbal description of some individual person (sometimes with a photograph accompanying the description) and are asked to judge how much they would like this person, or what traits or personality the individual might have. In these studies, specific pieces of information about the individual stimulus person are varied (e.g., age, ethnicity, physical or psychological traits, specific behaviors) to determine how those particular features influence judgments of the person as a whole. In social psychology, this research paradigm for studying person perception was introduced in classic experiments conducted by Solomon Asch (1946) and has been used regularly since then to study how impressions are formed and how social stereotypes influence judgments of individuals (Jones, 1990).

Social Manipulations

Social features of the experimental environment include the presence versus absence of other people and the behavior of others toward the experimental participant. The classic use of a social manipulation is exemplified in classic studies of conformity, also conducted by Solomon Asch (1948, 1951). In these experiments, Asch paired a naive participant with varying numbers of experimental confederates. The study was introduced as an investigation of perceptual processes. On each trial of the experimental session, a stimulus line was presented, along with three comparison lines, and the participant's task was to judge which of the comparison lines most closely matched the stimulus line in length. The stimuli were designed so that the correct choice was quite obvious, and did not demand a fine discrimination (see the illustration in Fig. 5.2). The experimental session was set up so that on each trial the naive participant responded after most of the confederates; the judgments given by the confederates were preprogrammed so that on selected trials they all chose the clearly incorrect alternative.

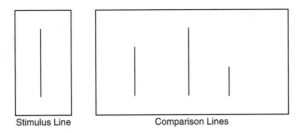

FIG. 5.2. Example of stimulus and comparison lines used by Asch (1948).

Asch's experiments were conducted to determine how this behavior on the part of other people in the setting would influence the overt choices made by the naive participant. Results indicated that participants could resist the group's influence best when only one or two confederates were present; the addition of a third confederate dramatically increased the degree of conformity, but further increases in group size had no substantial additional effect.

An independent variable involving manipulation of the number of persons present in a group is conceptually simple, but when experimental confederates are involved, the cost can be high. In some of Asch's experimental conditions, as many as 15 confederates were employed for every one participant! Assuming even a minimal rate of pay for accomplices, this can prove very expensive.

To circumvent the excessive cost entailed in an Asch-type conformity experiment, Crutchfield (1955) designed an electrical apparatus that he used to simulate the responses of confederates. The general trend of social research has been in the direction of such mechanization in the manipulation of the social environment (though today, computer terminals and video displays often replace devices such as that used by Crutchfield). Such mechanization has advantages in creating a more homogeneous, carefully controlled treatment, avoiding potential biasing effects introduced by overzealous confederates. However, some research (e.g., Levy, 1960) has indicated that "electrical confederates" generally do not have as powerful an impact as human accomplices on participants' responses.

An intermediate solution to the issue of human versus artificial social manipulations involves the use of people who are presented via audio- or videotape. This approach has the advantage of presenting the participant with an apparently human interactant, while, at the same time, maintaining strict comparability in what is offered to different participants in the same experimental condition. With modern technology, these simulated interactions can be made to appear quite realistic. For instance, in experiments conducted by Lord and Saenz (1985), the researchers wanted to place participants into a social situation in which they believed they were "solos" (e.g., the only woman in a group of 5 men). In reality, all of the other members of the participant's "group" were videotaped actors whose responses were prerecorded. The real participant was placed in a small room with a video camera, believing she was interacting with other participants via "live" video broadcasting. To make the experience as real as possible, the participant herself was actually videoed and saw herself on her video monitor whenever it was her turn to speak. This feedback made the manipulated interaction quite compelling, and no participants reported being suspicious about the actual presence of other participants at the time they were debriefed about the actual purposes of the study. Similar elements of realism have been used in simulated interactions on computer "chat rooms," where some of the participants are actually simulated group members prescripted by the experimenter (Gardner, Pickett, & Brewer, 2000).

Instructional Manipulations

By far the most common form of experimental manipulation is that dependent on differences in instructions provided by the experimenter to the participants in the study. In the most common form of this general treatment type, the instructions provided to the different treatment groups are identical except for the substitution of a few words or sentences. Thus, it is extremely important that participants are paying attention so they "receive" the experimental treatment.

If participants are alert and motivated, even small differences in wording can prove to have powerful effects. Consider, for example, an ingenious study by Zanna and Cooper (1974) who were studying the effects of misattribution of arousal on people's judgments. Zanna and Cooper gave participants a pill, which actually consisted solely of milk powder, but participants were instructed in ways that produced different expectations about the pill's supposed effects. Participants in the "arousal" treatment condition were told, "This M.C. 5771 capsule contains chemical elements that are more soluble than other parts of the compound. In this form of the drug these elements may produce a reaction of tenseness prior to the total absorption of the drug, 5 minutes after the ingestion. This side effect will disappear within 30 minutes" (p. 705).

Participants who were randomly assigned to the "relaxation" condition were given the same pill and the identical instructions, except that the word *tenseness* was replaced by *relaxation*. This simple variation in wording established different participant expectations and interpretations of their own bodily reactions which, in turn, altered their response to the rest of the experiment.

Instructional manipulations are not always presented in the initial instruction phase of an experimental session. For example, in one investigation of the effects of monetary payment on people's intrinsic interest in a task, Crano and Sivacek (1984) developed the following scenario: Participants were brought individually to the laboratory and asked to write an essay in favor of the legalization of marijuana, a position that pretesting indicated most participants already favored. Some were merely asked to do this to "help out" the experimenter, whereas others were offered $5 to do so. A third condition provided an alternative means of paying participants. In this manipulation, as the experimenter was asking the participant to help him out, there was a knock on the door, and a colleague asked the experimenter to step into the hallway for a moment. There, he explained (loudly enough so that the participant could be sure to overhear) that he had completed a survey research project and still had $15 left in his participant payment fund. He then asked the experimenter if he would award $5 to three of his participants as this would "save him considerable bookwork" with the agency that had funded his study. The experimenter agreed, returned to the participant, and now offered $5 to write the pro-marijuana essay. This manipulation allowed the researchers to investigate the differential effects of different forms of payment.

Apparently "accidental" instructional treatments of this type are common in social psychological research, and probably constitute one of the social scientist's most powerful tools. Indeed, it is not without justification that Aronson and Carlsmith (1968) observed, "it might be said that part of being a good experimental social psychologist involves learning to say 'whoops' convincingly" (p. 45).

The Manipulation Check

We have stressed the importance of participants' engagement in the study if instructional manipulations are to be used. The reason for this is obvious. We need to know that our treatments have been perceived or interpreted as we intended them to be. To help ensure this, we ask our participants whether they in fact noticed the variations built in to the study via our experimental manipulations. Such questions constitute our manipulation check.

To illustrate the use of a manipulation check, we return to an example we used in chapter 4, in which an experimenter wanted to study the effects of anxiety arousal and experimenter attractiveness on the complexity of children's speech. To do this, the experimenter was dressed to appear either very attractive or very unattractive, and then attempted either to arouse or dampen anxiety during the study. We warned earlier that these two variables probably could not be combined independently in a single experiment, arguing that a person who is scaring us probably will not be viewed as attractive. However, this observation is based on a hunch, not empirical data. We can test our hunch regarding the (non)independence of these factors by asking participants to indicate the extent to which they found the experimenter attractive and also their level of anxiety. These measures should be administered in addition to the main dependent measure, the variable that is the central focus of the study. If the treatments operated as planned, then the measure of anxiety would suggest that the participants exposed to the anxiety-producing experimenter were more anxious than those exposed to the low anxiety-producing one. However, ideally, experimental variations in anxiety would not be associated with participants' ratings of the experimenter's attractiveness. Similarly, we would hope that participants in the highly attractive experimenter condition would view the experimenter as more attractive than those exposed to the unattractive experimenter, irrespective of the anxiety condition to which they had been randomly assigned. We would not want this variable to affect participants' ratings of anxiety, however. If such effects did occur, it would be hard to argue that our independent variables were truly independent. In such cases, we either must refine our treatments, so that their effects do not "bleed into" one another or, less desirably, apply analytic procedures in an attempt to account for the carry-over effects of one variable on the other. This latter approach is risky because most of our common statistical approaches assume the independence of observations. In this case, the data clearly are not independent, and hence not amenable to common statistical treatment.

The manipulation check is informative even in settings in which variables are not likely to impinge on each other. For example, suppose we are interested in determining the effects of fear arousing anti-HIV advertisements on the at-risk sexual behavior of adolescents. After exposing a group of these participants to a series of such ads, we monitor their reported behavior over the next 6 months. If we were to find no differences in reported behavior between those exposed to the ad campaign and those who were not, we might be tempted to conclude that fear arousal does not affect behavior, at least, not the at-risk sexual behavior of adolescents. We might be correct in this interpretation, but it might rather be the case that the ads failed to generate fear. Our theory about fear arousal and behavior might be perfectly predictive, but our fear arousal treatment might have failed miserably. If we had been smart enough to administer a manipulation check at the conclusion of our treatment ("How frightening are these ads?" "Were you more worried about HIV after the presentation than before?" etc.), the proper interpretation of our results would be more certain.

Manipulation check information also helps us to determine if our treatments are operating as we think they did. Suppose, continuing our example, we find that our ad campaign had a powerful effect. That is, adolescents who received a very frightening series of advertisements about HIV and AIDS were much less risky than those who did not. We could stop here, write up our results, and send them off to the nearest newspaper or scientific journal. However, it would be much more informative if we had manipulation check data that indicated that the participants who were most afraid after our presentation were also the most likely to avoid risky sexual encounters. This information would bolster our theoretical interpretation and lend weight to our explanation.

It should be obvious that manipulation check information can be of enormous advantage to the experimenter. Such data can be helpful even when the experimental treatment has apparently failed. The information such checks can provide, no matter the apparent success of our experiment, is so important that they should be used whenever possible. Neglecting to collect manipulation check data for other than the most compelling reason is, in most cases, shortsighted. Nonetheless, we need to caution that such checks, while potentially informative, are not necessarily perfect indicators of whether our experimental manipulations have been received as intended. Particularly when some self-report measure is used for the manipulation check, participants may not always be able to state explicitly what they have experienced or understood (Nisbett & Wilson, 1977). Thus, manipulation checks can be used in conjunction with the results on the dependent variables in an experiment to help understand the findings, but they should be used only as one aid in the process of interpretation.

Assign Participants

Having emphasized the importance of random assignment in developing true experimental designs that allow for causal inference, we do not go into detail about randomization other than to reinforce the fact that true randomization requires that any person in our sample be equally likely to participate in any of the experimental conditions. This is the central requirement of random assignment. Without it, we cannot claim that our assignment was random. There are many different ways to implement random assignment once experimental conditions have been designed and constructed, and we cannot go into extensive detail about all of those methods here. However, there are a few basic principles about the mechanics of random assignment that we can present at this point.

There are basically two different ways in which randomly assigning individual participants to particular experimental treatment conditions can be accomplished. One is to use some process of randomization (e.g., a coin toss, roll of a die, or use of a table of random numbers) one-by-one for each participant as he or she arrives at the experimental session. For instance, if we have a 2 × 2 experimental design, resulting in four different treatment conditions, we would label the various conditions 1, 2, 3, and 4. Then as each participant showed up, we would consult a table of random numbers, place a finger on an arbitrary starting point, and then run down (or up) the column on the page until either a 1, 2, 3, or 4 were encountered. Whichever number comes up first, that is the condition the participant would be assigned to.

Randomly assigning participants on a one-by-one basis is one ideal form of random assignment procedure. However, it has a disadvantage: We have to run a large number of participants in a short period of time to be sure that the resulting randomization spreads participants evenly across all our conditions. (With randomization, we can by chance run into a string of 1s all in a row, so that participants get "bunched up" into one treatment until chance evens things out.) This is not particularly problematic if we are running large numbers of participants in a single session. In that case, random distribution will work quite well. However, if our experimental procedures require running individuals one or two or three at a time, this random assignment procedure may not work so well. The alternative is a form of "block randomization" (see chap. 10) in which conditions are randomly ordered in advance, before participants arrive at sessions. All possible conditions are numbered and then randomly ordered, and then this random ordering is repeated in blocks until the total number of intended participants is reached. For example, using our previous 2 × 2 design, the four conditions would be ordered (via a table of random numbers) with whichever number came up first being first, the one coming up next being second, and so forth. Once all four had been included, the process would be repeated for the next block, and so on. If we were planning to run 25 participants per condition, this process of randomly ordering the four conditions would be done for 25 blocks. Once the ordering was predetermined, the first participant who shows up would be assigned to the first condition in the preordered set and so forth until all conditions had been conducted.

Technically, random assignment should be implemented in such a way that each individual participant in the experiment has an equal chance (at the outset) of being assigned to any of the conditions, independently of any other individual's assignment. Both one-at-a-time and blocked randomization procedures meet this criterion, as long as individual participants are allocated separately to their randomly determined treatment condition. In practice, however, it is sometimes the case that a particular experimental treatment is delivered to all of the participants who show up at a particular session at the same time. For instance, perhaps we have an instructional manipulation that is to be delivered verbally, aloud, by the researcher. At the same time, we have a stimulus manipulation that is contained in written materials distributed individually to each participant. Now say that we are conducting experimental sessions in which five participants are participating at the same time in the same room. We can still randomly assign each participant to some different variation of the written stimulus materials because each participant does not see what the others have received. However, everyone hears the verbal instructions read aloud by the experimenter, so only one version can be delivered. In this case, the instructional treatment is randomly assigned to the whole session, and all five participants get the same version. Random assignment is implemented across sessions, but not within sessions. Technically, this is a violation of the principles of random assignment at the individual level because there may be nonindependence among participants in the same session (see chap. 17 for discussion of how this affects statistical analyses).

Most of the time, this violation of random assigned is not particularly problematic, but it can lead to loss of data at times. For example, suppose we want to study the effects of discomfort on people's judgments of various governmental policies (e.g., welfare, job training, universal health insurance). We have a laboratory that holds 20 participants at a time. We want to make some of them uncomfortable to determine whether discomfort will make them less likely to support government-funded welfare, job training, and health insurance. To do this, we play loud white noise during the "discomfort" condition. The controls are studied under normal circumstances. If we wanted to have 60 participants in each of our two conditions, we would need to conduct six sessions—three involving randomly assigned experimental participants and three involving control participants. We want the sessions to be identical in all respects except the presence or absence of the treatment. However, suppose that during one of the sessions, one of our participants became very ill and suffered a seizure. This disruption might render the data of this session noncomparable with that of the other sessions, and we would probably have to drop the data from that session, losing all 20 participants. For this reason, it is a good general rule that, if experimental treatments are assigned to sessions, one should conduct a large number of sessions, with only a few participants (e.g., no more than five) in any one session.

CONDUCTING THE EXPERIMENT

The experiment is the sum total of all that we have discussed to this point. It is the combination of our experimental manipulations and measures, enmeshed within a well-considered physical context (usually this context is a laboratory, but it need not be). Once participants have experienced the conditions that constitute the experimental treatment to which they have been assigned, the final step of conducting the experimental session is the measurement of the dependent variable(s). Just as the experimenter has controlled the stimulus situation in the experiment, he or she also determines the types of participant behaviors that will be observed and measured. Dependent variables can include a wide range of response types, including overt behaviors, questionnaire responses, and cognitive and physiological measures. (The methodological issues involved in developing and using these different types of response measures are covered in detail in chapters 11–17 of this book.)

Enhancing Experimental Realism

The frequent use of subtle, instructional manipulations as the independent variable in experiments highlights the importance of participant involvement and attention as a critical factor in good experimental research. In this connection, Aronson et al. (1998) draw an important distinction between experimental and mundane realism, concepts that are closely tied to the manner in which experiments are set up and the types of manipulations used. If the setting of an experiment has real impact on participants, that is, if the experimental arrangements literally force participants to attend to the task requirements of the research (and focus less on themselves), the study is said to have a high degree of *experimental realism*. In other words, experimental realism is achieved if participants are unable to intellectualize their reactions and are responding to the experimental situation in a way that approximates their natural, spontaneous behavior.

Mundane realism refers to the degree to which various features of the experiment (e.g., instructions, treatments, measurement operations) mirror real world, nonlaboratory events that participants might encounter in their day-to-day experiences. For instance, some experiments involve asking college students to write essays or take tests, events that are quite usual in the daily life experiences of the average student. Note, however, that this same experimental procedure would have considerably less mundane realism for participants who were middle-aged truck drivers for whom such tasks might be considerably more exotic.

Mundane and experimental realism are not mutually exclusive. Whenever possible, a good research design will establish both. However, of the two, experimental realism is the more important for validity of results. The mere fact that an event occurs in real life does not endow it with importance, and an experimental situation that mirrors a dull real world experience will probably prove to be dull and uninvolving. Individuals in this type of setting will tend to become apathetic and may fail to respond to the experimental manipulation simply because they failed to attend to it. Some of the treatments employed by social researchers are so subtle that the participant must be closely attuned to the experimental situation if the manipulation is to have any impact. If respondents are bored or apathetic, this needed degree of attention cannot be assumed. It is clearly worth the time and effort that it takes for social researchers to keep their participants interested and involved.

SOCIAL SIMULATIONS AND ANALOGUE EXPERIMENTS

The techniques for conducting laboratory experiments discussed in the preceding sections of this chapter place emphasis on achieving experimental realism within the laboratory setting. The major concern is that the experimental procedures create an environment that is involving and impactful for the research participants, even if the situation is peculiar to the laboratory setting and bears no direct resemblance to events the participant is likely to encounter in life outside the laboratory. Where but in the laboratory, for instance, would individuals engage in a dull and boring task and then be asked to describe that task to another person as fun and interesting, as were participants in Festinger and Carlsmith's (1959) classic dissonance research experiment? In that study, the investigators deliberately used the research context as an excuse to induce participants to engage in a behavior contrary to their ordinary experience. The fact that the requested behavior had no structural similarity to events outside the laboratory was irrelevant to the purposes of this particular investigation.

Now we shift attention to laboratory studies in which there is an explicit intention to emulate events that occur in the "real world." In such studies, the degree of correspondence between the situation created in the laboratory and the real-life situation it is intended to represent becomes a major concern. There two different types of laboratory experiments that share this concern for real-world correspondence. The first is the *role-playing simulation*, in which participants are asked to actively imagine that they are actors in a given real-world situation and to respond as they believe they would in that context.[3] The other is a type of research that we refer to as the *analogue experiment*. An analogue differs from a simulation in that participants are not playing an explicitly defined role but are responding directly to a specially constructed situation that has been designed to reproduce or mimic selected features of a real-world situation.

Social Simulations

When used for research purposes, simulations are intended to preserve many of the advantages of controlled laboratory experiments while approaching conditions that are more generalizable to the real world. A well-designed simulation has the potential to isolate the social phenomenon of interest without destroying its natural contextual meaning because participants can "actively imagine that all the normal constitutive relations of a social situation are satisfied" (Greenwood, 1983, p. 243). Because of these added "imaginative" elements, the treatment conditions of a simulation study are inevitably more complex and multidimensional than those of the basic laboratory experiment. Hence, the potential increase in generalizability is attained with some sacrifice of precision in the specification of the independent and dependent variables.

Passive Role-Playing Simulations. Various types of simulation research differ in the extent of active role playing that is involved. At one end of the spectrum are studies employing what Greenwood (1983) called "passive-interpretive role-playing," which might also be described as *mental simulations*. In such studies participants are provided with a written or verbal description of a situation or scenario, and their role in it, and are asked to estimate or predict how they (or others) would behave in that situation.

Such role-playing studies have been used for theory-testing purposes on occasion. Rosenberg and Abelson (1960), for example, placed participants in a role-playing situation in order to test some hypotheses derived from balance theories of attitudes and attitude change. In this study participants were asked to imagine themselves in the role of a

---

[3]In some types of simulation research, the human participant is replaced by a computer model of the processes under investigation. Such computer simulations are very valuable tools for theory development (Abelson, 1968; Hastie & Stasser, 2000). Their status as empirical research, however, is ambiguous and such forms of simulation are not covered here.

department store manager. As part of the context of their role playing, participants were given a set of attitudes toward a particular employee (Mr. Fenwick) and his plans to mount a modern art display in the rug department of the store. The affective relationships assigned to different participants were varied to produce different states of psychological inconsistency or imbalance. Participants were then given three different communications to read, each of which was designed to change their attitude toward some aspect of the situation. A measure of final attitudes was used to determine which communications had been accepted by the role-playing participants and the extent to which this corresponded with predictions derived from formal balance models. Although the results confirmed balance theory predictions to some extent, they also indicated that acceptance of communications was affected by motives other than restoration of cognitive balance (e.g., avoiding negative interpersonal affect). Thus, even though it did not involve a real interpersonal situation, this role-playing study did prove capable of testing the theory in the sense of subjecting it to potential disconfirmation.

Some forms of passive role playing have been suggested as possible alternatives to the use of deception in experimental social psychology (e.g., Carlson, 1971; Kelman, 1967; Mixon, 1972; Schultz, 1969). The argument here is that if role-playing participants can be given a complete subjective understanding of the experimental conditions that would be used in a real study, their estimates of how they would behave in that situation can substitute for actual participation in such situations. During the 1960s and 1970s, a number of role-playing studies were conducted to determine whether the results obtained would match or reproduce the findings from previously conducted deception experiments. Horowitz and Rothschild (1970), for example, compared reports from two forms of simulation against the data from an earlier Asch-type conformity study conducted by Gerard, Wilhelmy, and Conolley (1968). Darryl Bem (1965, 1967) conducted a series of "interpersonal simulations" of classic dissonance experiments (Brehm & Cohen, 1959, 1962; Festinger & Carlsmith, 1959), and the outcomes of Milgram's (1965) studies of obedience have also been subjected to role-playing simulation (Freedman, 1969). In terms of their ability to reproduce experimental findings, the results of such role-playing studies have been mixed (see Miller, 1972). Even when the findings are parallel, it remains ambiguous whether the results of a passive role-playing simulation can be interpreted in the same way as those obtained under the real experimental conditions (see Cronkite, 1980).

Active Role Playing.   While passive role playing has some potential value for theory testing, the more widely used forms of simulation involve more active role-playing efforts in which participants actually act out their responses in the simulated social situation. The primary version of this research method is the so-called role-playing game. In this form, participants are given roles to play within a specified social system. The parameters of the system are under the control of the experimenter and within this context, the participants make choices and decisions befitting their perception of the roles they have been given. The behavior choices of each participant and their consequences for the behaviors of other participants in the system constitute the major dependent variables in this research design. Participation in such games is usually extended over a considerable period of time and experience indicates that motivation and involvement among role players run quite high. Elaborate simulation exercises have been developed, ranging from simulations of small decision-making groups, such as jury deliberations (Bornstein, 1999) or management teams (Cohen, Dill, Kuehn, & Winters, 1964), business organizations and market economies (Klein & Fleck, 1990), to whole societies (SIMSOC, Gamson, 1969) and intercultural relations (Hofstede & Pedersen, 1999).

Within the fields of social and organizational psychology, some of the research on small group interaction has been extended through the use of role-playing techniques. For example, McGrath and his associates examined the process of interpersonal negotiation within the context of a collective bargaining structure (McGrath, 1966; McGrath & Julian, 1963; Vidmar & McGrath, 1967). Among the variables they studied within this framework are the representational role obligations of participants, the effectiveness of mediators, the extent of conflict of interests, leadership capacity, and other personality characteristics of participants. Many of the results of this simulation research have been compared with and supported by field studies of labor negotiations. Other organizational simulations have been used in the laboratory to study the uses of social power (e.g., Goodstadt & Kipnis, 1970), sex differences in social influence strategies (Instone, Major, & Burker, 1983), and organizational memory (e.g., Moreland, Argote, & Krishnan, 1996).

Probably the most dramatic simulation of a social subsystem is represented by the prison simulation designed and conducted by Philip Zimbardo and his colleagues at Stanford University (Zimbardo, Haney, Banks, & Jaffe, 1973). Zimbardo created a mock prison in the basement of a college building and recruited college student participants who were randomly assigned to play the roles of "guards" and "prisoners" in the simulated setting. Zimbardo was attempting to demonstrate the powerful effects of institutionalization and deindividuation on interpersonal behavior. As with Milgram's (1963) earlier studies of obedience, however, the results of the simulation were more extreme than expected as the participants became fully involved in their respective roles. Although the simulation had been intended to extend across a 2-week period, Zimbardo felt forced to cancel the study at the end of 6 days because of the escalating cruelty on the part of the guards toward the prisoners, who were showing signs of progressive apathy and depression.

Bargaining and Negotiation Games. There is a great deal of social research on the decisions and behavior of individuals in two-person bargaining games. Although the format of most of this research resembles the usual laboratory experiment rather than simulation designs, some background information on the paradigm of experimental games research is useful to a discussion of the extension of these games into simulation settings.

Most of such experimental games research to date revolves around the use of the "prisoner's dilemma" situation, which receives its name from the following analogy:

> Two suspects are taken into custody and separated. The district attorney is certain that they are guilty of a specific crime, but does not have adequate evidence to convict them at a trial. He points out to each prisoner that each has two alternatives: to confess to the crime the police are sure they have committed, or not confess. If they both do not confess, then the district attorney states he will book them on some very minor trumped-up charge, such as petty larceny and illegal possession of a weapon, and they will both receive minor punishment; if they both confess they will be prosecuted but he will recommend less than the most severe sentence. If one confesses and the other does not, then the confessor will receive lenient treatment for turning state's evidence whereas the latter will get the book slapped at him. (Luce & Raiffa, 1958, p. 95)

The maximal joint outcome for both prisoners is attained if neither confesses. However, each of the individuals has to face the risk that if he refuses to confess while the other does confess, his own outcome will be very bad. Thus, each is motivated to attempt to maximize his own personal gain by confessing. If both act on this motivation, as the district attorney wants and expects them to do, their joint outcome will be less than optimal.

		Player B's Choice	
		1	2
Player A's	1	3,3	0,5
Choice	2	5,0	1,1

FIG. 5.3. Prisoner's dilemma game joint payoff matrix.

The prisoner's dilemma is represented in the social psychological laboratory in the form of a "non-zero sum" or "mixed-motive" two-person game. On each trial of such a game, each of the two players makes a choice between two alternatives and the outcome or payoff from his choice is determined by the nature of the choice made (simultaneously) by the other player. The potential choices and outcomes are represented by the joint payoff matrix, shown in Fig. 5.3.

The first value in each cell represents player A's payoff (in coins or chips) and the second, player B's, if that cell represents the joint choices of the two participants. In this type of matrix, choice 2 is the low-risk, "rational" choice for each player, but if both players make this choice on each trial, their joint payoff will be only one coin each. The maximum joint payoff of three coins each can be achieved only when both players choose choice 1. However, if one player chooses choice 1 while the other sticks to choice 2, the resulting payoffs will be highly uneven. Thus, the optimization of income for both players can be achieved only through joint cooperation in which each player can choose choice 1 with some measure of confidence that the other player will do so too. In the typical experimental games study, the dependent measure is the total number of competitive (choice 2) and cooperative (choice 1) choices made by each player, along with the related measure of total joint payoffs.

In some studies, the behavior of one player in the two-person game is determined by the experimenter, either by using a confederate who makes predetermined choices or, more recently, by having choices provided by a preprogrammed computer. In one such study, Komorita (1965) reported no significant reciprocation of cooperative responses from the simulated partner, but Scodel (1962) and Bixenstine and Wilson (1963) found that cooperation could be significantly increased when the partner provided a sequence of choices switching from highly competitive to highly cooperative. In a large computerized study, Axelrod (1984) invited experts in game theory and bargaining research were invited to submit strategies for playing multiple rounds of the prisoner's dilemma game (PDG) in a computerized "tournament." When all submitted strategies were played against each other in a pairwise manner, the strategy that produced the best outcomes in the long run was that of "tit-for-tat." In this strategy, the player makes the cooperative choice on the first round of play and from then on reciprocates the choice made by the other player on the previous round. Results from these kinds of gaming simulations have contributed to theories about the evolution of cooperation in human society.

As a paradigm for studying interpersonal decision making, the PDG can be considered a "minimalist" situation. To preserve the dilemma aspects of the situation, players are not allowed to communicate with each other or directly negotiate the choices that they make. The basic structure of the dilemma situation is built in to more realistic, dynamic, role-playing simulations in the bargaining and negotiation literature (see McDonald, 1998).

International Relations Simulation.   Some of the richest outcomes of role-playing research are from the area of simulated international relations. It is not surprising, perhaps, that this area of research should have been the first to lend itself to simulation research as the real-world political arena provides so few opportunities for testing relevant social science theories.

One example of simulation in this area is the Inter-Nation Simulation (INS), developed at Northwestern University (Guetzkow, Alger, Brody, Noel, & Sidney, 1963). In the INS, individual participants (decision makers) play roles of government representatives of imaginary nations participating in an international government organization. Variations in inputs and outcomes are possible at three levels of operation: (a) characteristics of the decision makers and their role definitions, (b) characteristics of the participant nations, and (c) the nature of the supranational alliance structure. Some examples of the use of INS include a study by Brody (1963) of the impact of changing nuclear power relationships on communication and alliance patterns; Raser and Crow's (1968) study of relationships among power levels and threat intensity and group cohesion, goal seeking, and resorting to violence; Druckman's (1968) investigation of the development of ethnocentrism; and a study by Zinnes (1966) of the relationship between hostile perceptions and hostile communications among nations.

Because of the real-world analogies built into INS studies, it is a temptation to generalize the findings to predict outcomes in the real international arena. Some findings encourage this extrapolation, such as indications that the use of role experienced participants (State Department employees and diplomatic representatives at the United Nations) does not seem to alter results obtained from college student participants. However, other findings suggest caution. The study by Zinnes (1966) compared outcomes of an INS with results from an analysis of World War I documents and found that the predicted relationship between hostile perceptions and hostile messages was borne out in the simulation but not in the historical data. Any time such comparisons can be made, an opportunity is created for exploring the limitations of relevant theories.

Outcomes of explorations with the INS structure have led to the development of further simulation models. Increased complexity, for example, has been introduced in an expansion called International Processes Simulation (IPS; Smoker, 1968) and the Balance of Power game (Chapin, 1998).

Simulations as Research. All active role-playing simulations involve a combination of programmed relationships among variables specified by the researcher and unprogrammed activity on the part of the human decision makers. The increased complexity of many simulations has necessitated the use of computers for providing programmed input as well as for storing running records of all output variables. Many simulations have been developed as educational or training tools rather than specifically for research purposes. As a consequence, each simulation has many different components and lots of room for planned or unplanned variations. Using simulations as experiments involves systematically varying one or more aspects of the simulation design across different "runs" of the simulation. Each run (no matter how many participants are involved) amounts to a single replication, so it would take 10 or 20 simulation sessions to conduct even a simple two-condition experiment. As simulations are time- and effort-intensive (some Internation Simulations, e.g., run over a period of days or even weeks), this amounts to a very costly way of doing experimental research. More often, experimental variations will be introduced within sessions of a simulation, as a type of pre–post or repeated measures design. For example, a study by Raser and Crow (1964) investigated the effects of the development of an invulnerable retaliatory force by one nation in the international system. In the real world, the development of such a force would inevitably occur with many other changes, any of which could account for subsequent events, but within the INS, this development could be systematically introduced or removed by experimental intervention in a way that eliminated other plausible explanations of its effects. Thus, simulations can be adapted to test specific research hypotheses when time and resources are available.

Analogue Experiments

In simulation research, the "real world" is represented in the laboratory through the researchers' instructions to role-playing participants and the latter's ability to imagine themselves in the situation portrayed. The logic of an analogue experiment is quite different. In this type of research, participants are not asked to act out a role in an "as-if" context, but are presented with a real situation to respond to directly. The difference between an analogue experiment and other basic laboratory experiments is in the design of the stimulus situation and its relationship to some specified event or problem existing outside the laboratory. An analogue is designed to preserve an explicit relationship between the laboratory setting and some real-world situation of interest; for every feature of the external situation that is considered theoretically relevant, there is a corresponding feature contained in the laboratory situation. In this sense, an analogue is like a roadmap of a particular geographical region, where there is a one-to-one correspondence between features on the map and specific features of the actual terrain (e.g., highways, rivers, mountains, etc.) but where other features that exist in the real setting (e.g., trees, houses) are not represented on the map. If the features represented in the analogue situation have been appropriately selected, participants' responses to that situation should provide an accurate "mapping" of their responses to the corresponding situation in real life.

Analogue experiments have been used for some time in various aspects of clinical research. Animal models, for instance, are regarded as analogues to human physiology in much medical research, and experimenter-participant roles are treated as analogues to the therapist-patient relationship in both medical and clinical psychological research. The use of analogue experimentation in social science research, however, has been relatively rare, despite its potential role in closing the gap between research in the laboratory and in the real world. Partly this may be because such experiments are not easy to design, as they require concern for both experimental realism and accurate simulation of mundane events. Analogues have been successfully employed in a number of areas, however. By calling attention to specific examples of such applications, we hope to increase awareness of the analogue experiment as a potentially valuable research tool.

Analogue experiments vary in the level of social organization that is being represented in the laboratory setting. Some experiments focus on events or problems faced by single individuals, with emphasis on the intra-individual processes that mediate responses to such experiences. Others attempt to structure whole social groups, in the laboratory situation, with an emphasis on the interpersonal processes operative within that social structure.

One example of the use of analogue experiments to assess intrapersonal decision processes was prompted by a specific real-world event—the killing of Kitty Genovese outside a New York apartment complex in 1963. Ms. Genovese was pursued and murdered by her assailant over a period of 30 min, despite the fact that her cries for help could be heard by as many as 38 people in nearby apartments. This event, and the extensive newspaper coverage it generated, led social psychologists Bibb Latané and John Darley (1968, 1970) to speculate about the psychological processes involved in an individual's decision whether or not to intervene in such emergency situations, and how those processes might be affected by the actual or inferred presence of other people who are also potential helpers. Their theorizing led to a series of experiments on bystander intervention, in which individuals in the laboratory were faced with various decision crises parallel to those in real-world emergency situations.

Among the studies of bystander intervention, the experiment most closely analogous to the original news event was that conducted by Darley and Latané (1968). In this experiment, participants were involved in a communication study in which each participant sat in a separate small room and communicated via intercom with the other participants. After a brief warm-up introduction, the participants were asked to speak, one at a time, about their college experiences. Midway through his presentation, in which he had mentioned his history of epileptic seizures, one participant (actually a tape recording prepared by the experimenters) said he felt lightheaded. Following this, his speech became blurred and disoriented, eventually sounding like gasping for help. After a moment, a thud was heard over the intercom and then silence.

The independent variable in this experiment was the size of the group participating in the study at the time of the emergency. In one condition, participants believed that they and the "victim" were the only two participants in the session, whereas in other conditions, each participant believed there were one to four other participants present at the same time. As in the real-world event, participants were visually isolated from the potential victim and from other participants, and, as in the real emergency, each had to decide whether a response to the emergency was called for and whether he or she was personally responsible for making such a response. The results confirmed Latané and Darley's (1968) predictions about the effects of other bystanders. When participants believed they were the sole potential helpers in the situation, 85% responded within less than a minute by seeking help from the nearby experimenter. When participants believed there were others present, however, the probability of responding within a short interval dropped dramatically as the number of others present increased, with only 31% responding when they believed there were four other participants available.

Analogues of Collective Decisions. Like the Kitty Genovese case, many contemporary real-world problems reflect situations in which individuals have to make decisions under conflict between their own interests and that of others. Dwindling fuel supplies, electrical brownouts, depletion of fresh water supplies, and air pollution are all cases in which individuals acting in their own self-interest can lead to collective disaster. One solution to the negative consequences of social dilemmas requires that individuals restrain their own self-interested behavior (take shorter showers, car pool to work, reduce heat in their homes) in the interest of the collective good. Unilateral restraint on the part of any single individual is useless, however, unless a large proportion of other individuals exercise the same restraint. Yet, if many others exercise such constraint, a single individual doesn't need to. Hence the dilemma.

Because it is difficult to experiment with large-scale social problems such as the conservation of energy and other scarce resources, various stripped-down versions of social dilemmas have been designed for the laboratory in order to study individual and group decision-making processes in the face of such choices (see Messick & Brewer, 1983). In a sense, the PDG described earlier is a two-person version of such collective choice analogues. However, research using the PDG came under heavy criticism for losing sight of any parallels between decision making in the PDG setting and real-world decision-making contexts. To avoid falling into the same trap, analogues of collective decision problems have been designed with careful attention to their real-world counterparts.

Of the collective dilemmas that have been designed for laboratory investigations, the most clearly analogous to conservation situations is the replenishable resource task, versions of which have been used in a number of group studies (Brechner, 1977; Kramer & Brewer, 1984; Messick et al., 1983). The basic structure of this task is the existence of a common pool of points (worth something of value, e.g., money or experimental credits) to which each of the participants in an experimental session has access. On each trial or round of the experimental task, every participant is permitted to draw from the common resource pool a selected number of points (which becomes theirs to keep) up to some maximum limit, after which the pool is replenished by some proportion of the pool size remaining after participants have drawn off their portions. The replenishment rate is set in such a way that if the participants as a group restrain their total take on each trial to a level below the maximum possible, the resource pool size can be maintained at its original level 'indefinitely. However, if the total take on each trial exceeds the replenishment function, the pool will gradually be depleted until there is no longer any common resource on which to draw.

The participants in this resource dilemma situation are not being asked to act as if they were making decisions about conservation of energy or some other simulated experience. Instead, they are making actual decisions about real scarce resources in the scaled-down laboratory setting. What is hoped is that the task has been structured so that the basic elements of the decision to be made are the same as those operative in the dilemma situations that exist outside the lab. As in real, large-scale collective problems, individual participants must make their decisions about resource use in the absence of knowledge about what other participants are doing and without coordination of choices. If these structural elements accurately parallel those in the real-world situation, then researchers can use the laboratory analogue to determine how variations in contextual features (e.g., availability of feedback about the state of the resource pool, forms of communication among participants, identity of the group, etc.) can alter the decisions that are made on the collective level. Such research can be used simultaneously to test hypotheses about basic psychological or group processes and about the effectiveness of potential interventions that might be implemented in the real world to influence the conservation of scarce resources (Messick & Brewer, 1983; Torres & Macedo, 2000).

Analogues of Intergroup Relations.   Another recurring social situation that has been subjected to considerable experimental research is that associated with the desegregation of previously isolated social groups. Most societies are characterized by division into recognized subgroups based on demographic, economic, religious, or all three of these categories. Historically, it is often the case that such subgroupings are also associated with physical or geographic separation so that the various groups have opportunity to develop distinctive identity and cultural traditions in at least partial isolation from each other. When political and economic factors force increased contact between members of such groups, these prior group identities (and associated intergroup hostilities, distrust, or stereotypes) often interfere with the establishment of new forms of interdependence and interpersonal associations between representatives of different categories.

Although most of the research on the process and outcomes of desegregation has been conducted in field settings, the effects of category identity on interpersonal behavior have also been investigated in laboratory experiments. Many of these studies have employed a "minimal intergroup situation" (Tajfel, Billig, Bundy, & Flament, 1971; Brewer, 1979), in which an arbitrary categorization of an otherwise homogeneous group of participants is introduced, and participants have no direct contact or interdependence with members of either their own or the other category. The use of this research paradigm is clearly intended to study processes of social categorization at their most basic level, and it is not intended that the minimal situation be representative of any real-world intergroup settings. Recently, however, Brewer and Miller (1984) suggested how this minimal paradigm can be expanded to be more explicitly analogous to desegregation situations outside the laboratory.

The skeletal version of the Brewer and Miller analogue includes three components: (a) creation of two distinct categories subdividing a group of participants, (b) provision of opportunity for members of the two categories to interact for some specified time in isolation from each other, and (c) creation of a new task environment in which representatives from the two categories come into contact under conditions of cooperative interdependence. These elements of the experimental paradigm are intended to capture the basic features of any intergroup desegregation situation, the presence of distinct category identifiers (made visually salient by colored name tags or uniforms), a period of isolation between groups, and a contact situation in which intergroup hostilities interfere with the requirements of cooperative interdependence. To these basic elements can be added other features that also mimic specific real-world situations, such as introducing differences between the categories in initial status or power, differences in numerical representation, or in access to resources or skills, and other asymmetries. Given these initial conditions, the characteristics of the contact situation can then be varied to determine their effect on intergroup acceptance within the contact setting and on its generalization to other category members beyond that setting.

It should be noted that even with a number of structural embellishments, the laboratory analogue will always be a "stripped down" representation of intergroup contact situations in the real world. In particular, it would be virtually impossible to capture in the lab the sense of historical and cultural tradition that marks intergroup distinctions in society at large. Nonetheless, experience with the analogue paradigm indicates that it can engage, at least temporarily, much of the emotional significance attached to other social category identification. During the initial period of category segregation, members of the two subgroups do appear to establish a sense of "ingroup–outgroup" differentiation, express evaluative biases in favor of their own category, and exhibit apprehension about future interaction with members of the other category. Given this level of involvement, the analogue can provide a relatively low-cost method for testing the potential effectiveness of various intervention strategies designed to increase the positive effects of intergroup contact. By utilizing analogue experiments in this way, promising avenues of policy research can be identified and potentially costly mistakes avoided in the social arena.

SUGGESTED READINGS

Aronson, E., Wilson, T., & Brewer, M. B. (1998). Experimentation in social psychology. In D. Gilbert, S. Fiske, & G. Lindsey (Eds.), *The handbook of social psychology* (4th ed., Vol. 1, pp. 99–142). Boston: McGraw-Hill.

Milgram, S. (1963). Behavioral study of obedience. *Journal of Abnormal and Social Psychology, 67,* 371–378.

Tajfel, H. (1970). Experiments in intergroup discrimination. *Scientific American, 223,* 96–102.

6

EXTERNAL VALIDITY OF LABORATORY EXPERIMENTS

It is often thought that the use of laboratory experiments in social research involves achieving internal validity at the cost of external validity, or generalization of results to the world outside of the laboratory. Because of this, critics both within and outside the social sciences have argued that the experimental approach that structures so many of our research endeavors is inadequate or inappropriate for the study of social beings. A common criticism of the social experiment concerns its artificiality, or reactivity, and the consequent impossibility of determining the adequacy of generalizations based on experimental data. After reviewing nearly 20 years of research in his field, for example, Cronbach (1975) appeared to have despaired even of the possibility of developing lasting and useful generalizations from social research. A similar theme was sounded by Gergen (1973, 1976), who found social psychology to be more a historical than a scientific enterprise. Our theories, he argued, are little more than post hoc descriptions of the particular set of historical circumstances in which they are developed. As circumstances change, so too must these time bound descriptions.

Gergen coined the term *enlightenment effects* to identify one central factor that makes it difficult for experimental social research to arrive at stable and lasting generalizations. Owing to the rapid diffusion of information in our society, Gergen argued, social research findings soon become common knowledge. Thus, when people are put in the role of participants, they are likely already to understand the nature of the phenomenon under investigation, and to act in a way that confounds the issue in question. For example, if participants act "as they ought," the findings that ensue are not necessarily indicative of people's real, unbiased, out-of-laboratory responses. On the other hand, if they act in ways that are purposely contrary to theoretical expectations, we encounter the same difficulty. There appears no easy, logical solution to the "enlightenment" problem if we grant the unlikely assumption of a highly motivated and well-read public that attends closely to all the latest developments in social science.

While evaluations of the Gergen/Cronbach variety are far from widely accepted (they were strongly opposed by rebuttals from Greenwald, 1976; Godow, 1976; Harris, 1976;

Hunter, Schmidt, & Jackson, 1982; Manis, 1976; and Schlenker, 1974, 1976), the intensity of the reaction to these redefinitions of the appropriate role of the social researcher, especially that of the experimental social researcher, suggests that they struck a nerve. Though these critiques were discomforting, they were valuable because they motivated social researchers to become much more conscious of the factors that could compromise the ultimate contribution of their work. As a result, the field now is much more concerned with issues of generalizability and applicability than it was a short time ago.

In responding to the points raised by the critics of "scientific" social research, it is important to realize that most of their discussion revolves about the role of the controlled laboratory experiment. The attraction of the experiment as a model form of research is based on its power to elucidate causal relationships. However, as we repeat throughout this text, the laboratory experiment is one of many research models available to the behavioral scientist, and of these, it is perhaps the most stringent in its requirements. The proper utilization of experimental methods requires the satisfaction of a number of prior conditions. One of these is that sufficient knowledge concerning the phenomenon of interest exists, so that the manipulations and measures employed will be appropriate. Another condition requires the experimenter to have a sufficient grasp of the research setting so as to preclude the effects of extraneous variables from influencing the results of the investigation. This condition implies that the research task be sufficiently involving to offset the occurrence of Gergen's enlightenment effects.

The question of the generalizability of our research findings is never definitively settled. However, although certainty can never be attained, it can be approximated, or approached, and the approximation can become more and more exact if we are increasingly sensitive to the forces that influence behavior within and outside the experimental laboratory. So, for the remainder of this chapter we consider aspects of the laboratory experiment that affect the trustworthiness of experimentally based generalizations. Although our observations cannot and do not hope to answer all of the objections that have been raised by the critics of experimentation in social psychology, it becomes clear that our recommendations provide a much firmer ground for generalization if followed than if ignored. It also becomes clear that the issues of generalization that have been raised in the context of the controlled experiment apply as well to alternate research tactics.

GENERALIZABILITY ACROSS PARTICIPANTS

The principal components of all social psychological experiments are participants, experimenters, measures, and the manipulations employed by the experimenter to influence participants' behavior. The first part of this chapter concentrates on aspects of the participant sample and the manipulations to which participants are exposed. In the last part, questions and findings concerning the actions of the experimenter in experimental investigations—and the potential impact of these behaviors on the internal as well as external validity of an experiment—are discussed.

Restriction of Participant Populations

Many of the critics of social psychological experimentation have argued that, from the viewpoint of generalization of findings, the individual typically used in psychological research (i.e., the college sophomore) is perhaps the poorest choice possible. In fact, it has been stated in the past that there is possibly nothing more dissimilar to the average "man in the street" than the college sophomore. Barclay, Crano, Thornton, and Werner (1971) presented a detailed account of the stresses and strains seemingly inherent in university life, and it would be surprising if those exposed to these forces were not quite different from those who were not. To mention a few examples, the average college sophomore is more intelligent than the typical person on the street; usually healthier; more concerned with the social forces operating on the physical and social environment; sensitive to the various communication media and thus better informed; and plays a greater and more active role in exerting control over the factors influencing daily life.

The impact of these differences in some social psychological investigations is probably great (Sears, 1986). In many others, however, the use of college sophomores as participants could be expected to have only a minor, if any, influence. In a great proportion of investigations, the processes under study axe so basic that the special peculiarities of the college sophomore could not reasonably be expected to impinge on results.

In a situation in which basic human processes are under study (and it is in precisely this type of situation that the experiment is most advantageously employed), it seems reasonable to assume that the particular idiosyncrasies of the individuals sampled should have relatively little effect on the results obtained. Even if this were not the case, the use of unusual populations still might be encouraged, if the experimenter cannot find other, more nearly "average" groups. Consistent with the general orientation of Campbell and Stanley (1963), we argue that the development of a psychology of the college sophomore (or of any other esoteric group) is better than no psychology at all. Once determined from a restricted population, principles of behavior can then be applied systematically to other groups in order to test whether participant characteristics limit the generalizability of the original findings.

Participant Awareness

Unfortunately, these arguments confront only one aspect of the "participant" issue. Many critics of laboratory experimentation object not simply because a sample from an unusual population is employed in experimental social research, but because the responses of any individual conscious of the fact that he or she is under observation could be expected to be very different from those of persons who do not possess this information. This argument is an important one, but it fails to consider the degree to which this "self-consciousness effect" might operate within any given experiment. In some cases, the participant's awareness of being observed is probably the most salient feature of the total experimental situation. If this is so, then the obtained results of such a study should be viewed with caution, but certainly not dismissed from consideration. In other instances, however, because of the situation created by the experimenter or the impact of the various manipulations used, it seems quite likely that the participant's awareness of being studied would be greatly diminished, and would thus have little effect on the results of the investigation.

In most cases, the experimenter should attempt to construct situations that reduce the self-consciousness of participants as much as possible. A number of options are available, some of the most effective of which depend on the choice of experimental treatments and the manner in which they are implemented. For the moment, we consider variations in participants' perceptions of their role and the ways in which these perceptions can influence the outcome of an investigation.

Participants' self-definitions of the part they will play in a study are probably formed long before they enter the laboratory and undoubtedly are influenced by the degree of freedom they felt to commit themselves to the research. On the basis of freedom of choice considerations, participants can be generally classified into one of three categories: voluntary participants, involuntary participants, and nonvoluntary participants.

Voluntary Participants. Individuals in this category are aware that they are under investigation, but have made a conscious decision that the gains involved in their participation outweigh the possible losses (measured in terms of time spent, privacy invaded, etc.). The outcome of their involvement in the experiment, in other words, is viewed as positive. This decision can be prompted by a number of factors: monetary incentives, altruism, attainment of greater personal insight, possibly contributing to human science, and so on. If this positive mental set is maintained during the experiment (i.e., if the manipulations do not force participants to revise their estimates of gains and losses), then it is doubtful that such participants would willfully attempt to subvert the experiment. This is not to say that the individuals become unaware of the fact that they are being studied, but rather that they consider this potential invasion of privacy to be part of the bargain and are willing, as long as the gain-to-loss ratio remains positive, to respond in an honest manner.

It sometimes happens that the voluntary participant proves to be too willing to cooperate, too willing to help the experimenter confirm his or her hypotheses. Rosenthal and Rosnow (1975), in an extensive review of the volunteer participant literature, found volunteers to be better educated than nonvolunteers and to have higher occupational status, higher need for approval, higher intelligence, and better adjustment than nonvolunteers. If these factors combine in an overly cooperative volunteer, that is, a participant intent on helping confirm the research hypotheses, they can reduce the generalizability of the study.

Involuntary Participants. These individuals have proved to be the bane of many good experiments. Participants who feel that they have been coerced to spend their time in an experimental investigation and consider it unjustifiable often vent their displeasure by actively attempting to ruin the study. The feeling of coercion on the part of experimental participants can be stimulated in a number of different ways. In many universities in the United States, for example, introductory psychology students are expected to serve in some minimum number of experiments as part of course requirements. In the armed forces, draftees are commonly tested, and sometimes experimented on, often without their consent. Individuals of minority groups, because of their relative rarity, often find themselves the targets of sometimes unwanted scientific scrutiny. Persons forced to comply with the demands of some higher authority can generate a good deal of resentment, which can seriously affect the outcome of the study. Dissatisfaction with "guinea pig" status in many situations is both understandable and justified. Unless the experimenter can demonstrate that participation in the study is not a one-sided proposition, but rather a cooperative venture in which both parties can gain something of value, there is no reason to expect willing acquiescence to the participant role. Sometimes payment can be used to help the participant justify participation in the study. More satisfactory is the experimenter's explanation of the reasons for, and the importance of, the investigation. It is surprising how willing individuals are to serve in studies they perceive to be of great potential scientific importance.

Whether participants are more accurately described as voluntary or involuntary, some rationale for their participation should always be provided at the beginning of the experiment. No one likes to waste time, even if paid to do so. By informing participants of the importance of the research project in which they are serving and of the importance of their role in the research process, the experimenter can develop a sense of positive commitment on the part of the participants. In many circumstances, informing participants of their role is a condition for their participation. Most IRBs today, for example, require that participants be appraised of their rights at the beginning of the study, which includes information regarding the time involved, the potential risks their work might entail, and the potential contribution of their efforts.

Nonvoluntary Participants. These individuals unknowingly enter into an experimental situation, are exposed to an experimental treatment, and their responses are observed and recorded. They are not aware that they are part of a study until after the completion of the research, at which point the investigator may (or may not) explain the nature of the study to the "participants." The popularity of the nonvoluntary participant is increasing within social research, with good reason. Because they are not aware of their participation in a study, it is obvious that the reactions of nonvoluntary participants cannot be described as artificial or laboratory dependent. Results based on the reactions of such individuals should enjoy a high degree of external validity, or generalizability. A discussion of the ethical considerations involved in the use of nonvoluntary participants is deferred until the final chapter, but because our argument is that this practice is sometimes defensible, some description of the ways in which these participants can be employed are presented here.

Many issues can be investigated experimentally in naturalistic surroundings with nonvoluntary participants if one is attentive to the investigative possibilities offered by contemporary events. Consider an example from the literature on attitude–behavior consistency. Since the classic and controversial research of LaPiere (1934), social psychologists have wondered whether people's attitudes were accurate indications of their future behavior. Considerable research has been devoted to this issue, and the results are not entirely clearcut. Many theories have been advanced to explain the conditions under which attitude–behavior consistency might, or might not, be expected to occur. One such theory has to do with the participant's "vested interest" in the attitude in question. Sivacek and Crano (1982) hypothesized that attitude–behavior consistency would be enhanced when the attitude was "hedonically relevant" to the participant, that is, if the behavior it suggested actually made a difference in the participant's life.

Social circumstances in Michigan at the time this idea was being developed provided an opportunity to test the hypothesis. In the fall of 1978, state citizens were asked to decide by ballot whether the legal drinking age should be raised from 18 to 21. The researchers recognized that this issue offered an ideal way to test the "vested interest hypothesis" and used students at Michigan State University as the participants of their research. Sentiment on the campus was almost uniformly opposed to this referendum. However, on consideration, it is clear that the law would affect only the youngest participants (i.e, only those who would not turn 21 by the time of the law's change, should the referendum pass). According to Sivacek and Crano's idea, therefore, these people would be most willing to "back up" their attitude with concrete behavior (i.e., demonstrate a high degree of attitude–behavior consistency). Those for whom the law's change had little hedonic relevance (i.e., those who would be 21 by the time the new law was implemented) were not expected to act in accordance with their attitudes, at least not to the same extent as their younger peers.

To test this hypothesis, large numbers of students were polled on a number of issues of concern—of course, one of these issues was the upcoming referendum. Participants were then divided into three groups according to age: those in the low vested interest group would be 21 years of age before the change in law was effected; those in the high vested interest category would be 19 years old, or less, at the time of the change (and hence, could not legally drink for 2 years); participants falling between these extremes were defined as being of moderate vested interest.

Interestingly, the attitudes of students in all three categories were identical. Everyone, it seemed—at least most students—thought the referendum was a bad idea. But was everyone equally likely to act in accord with this belief? The results of the study suggest that they were not. When participants were called 2 weeks prior to the election and asked if they wished to work for a (fictitious) organization to help defeat the referendum, significantly more participants in the high vested interest group (47%) volunteered their time than those in the moderate (26%) or low vested interest (12%) categories. In addition, these younger participants were more willing to pledge more of their time. (In the interests of fairness, after participants were informed about the experiment, they were given the option of volunteering their time with an organization that was actually working against the law change. Given the landslide that accompanied the law's passage, however, their actions probably made little difference to the outcome of the election.)

This example demonstrates that an issue of long-term interest and importance in social research can be investigated through the use of nonvoluntary participants. None of the individuals contacted in this research thought they were participants of a psychological investigation. Thus, it is unlikely that they biased their responses in order to please the investigators or help support their hypothesis.

An interesting methodological addition characterized this study. A critic of the research might wonder whether or not younger students were more willing than older ones to volunteer for social causes. This tendency, if it exists, would suggest an alternative interpretation of the findings: It was not vested interest, but a general tendency of younger students to volunteer, that caused the differences found in Sivacek and Crano's (1982) research. To render this alternative implausible, the researchers conducted another survey that asked students who favored marijuana reform to volunteer to work on behalf of this agenda item. No differences associated with age were found, suggesting that young students were not more prone than older students to work on social issues.

Even given this added study, however, it is not possible to argue that the findings regarding vested interest are necessarily generalizable to the world at large. Consider the sample. As noted, it consisted of students at Michigan State University during the fall quarter of 1978. Was this group representative of the general population? Of the population of American university students? Of the population of midwestern university students? In addition, although it was left unstated, it is true that only those who had a phone and answered it during the time of the experiment were included in the study. It is conceivable that these people differed in systematic ways from those who could not be contacted or who did not have a telephone.

Were people of the same age range as those of the sample, in general, as likely to be as intensely interested in the outcome of the drinking referendum as the students? Would attitudinal intensity make a difference? None of these questions were addressed in the research, and thus, as would be hypothesized by Cronbach, there might well exist any number of interacting variables that would qualify the general observation that vested interest influences attitude–behavior consistency.[1]

Nonvoluntary participants are typically used in field research situations, outside the laboratory, where participants do not know they are taking part in an experiment. Recently, some studies have been designed so that the naive participants entering (or leaving) an experimental laboratory are treated and tested before they realize the experiment has begun (or after they think it has ended). For example, Brehm and Cole (1966) administered their experimental manipulation to unsuspecting participants while they were sitting in

---

[1]Later research (Crano, 1997; Lehman & Crano, in press) used representative national samples to test the vested interest hypothesis, and the results support the model.

a room waiting for the experiment to begin. The investigators attempted to induce a feeling of obligation on the part of the participant toward an experimental accomplice, to determine whether this feeling would influence the participant's later reaction toward the confederate once the "real" experiment began. The manipulation took the following form: After arriving at the laboratory, participant and confederate were informed that there would be a 10-min delay before the experiment was begun. The confederate asked permission to leave for a few moments and returned to the laboratory a short time later. In one of the experimental conditions, he brought a coke for the naive participant; in the other condition, he simply returned and the experiment was begun. This apparently innocent, charitable action on the part of the confederate constituted the principal independent variable manipulation of the study, and it seems quite probable that no participant even guessed that it was part of the experiment.

In an imaginative study of the influence of various personality factors on people's tendency to help a person in distress, Wilson and Petruska (1984) brought people into their laboratory and had them complete a number of personality measures. Participants left the laboratory alone or in the company of an experimental accomplice who presumably had just completed the same set of questionnaires. As the participant walked away from the laboratory setting, having "finished" the study, he or she was confronted by a person who was in need of minor assistance. Wilson and Petruska wanted to know whether the personality factors they had identified on the measures that participants completed in the laboratory were related to the likelihood that the participant would help a person in need and, further, whether the presence or absence of a nonintervening accomplice would influence the participant's behavior. As in the Brehm and Cole (1966) study, Wilson's participants probably had no suspicion that they were being studied; the experiment was over, as far as they knew. As such, their responses were free from the self-consciousness that might have occurred as a consequence of their being aware that they were subjects of study in a psychological laboratory. When studying responses that might reflect negatively (or positively) on the morality of the participant, it seems reasonable, perhaps even desirable, to follow the Wilson and Petruska example and try to conduct research on participants who are not unduly influenced by the laboratory setting.

Participant Roles

In an interesting discussion of the effects of participant characteristics on research out-comes, Webber and Cook (1972) attempted to summarize the roles that participants most frequently adopt in experimental settings. In their system, they identified four general participant types: (a) good participants, who attempt to determine the experimenter's hypotheses and to confirm them; (b) negative participants, who also are interested in learning the experimenter's hypotheses, but only in order to sabotage the study (Masling, 1966, referred to this type of reaction as the "screw you" effect); (c) faithful participants, who are willing to cooperate fully with almost any demand by the experimenter, who follow instructions scrupulously and ignore any suspicions they might have regarding the true purpose of the study; and (d), apprehensive participants, who worry that the experi-menter will use their performance to evaluate their abilities, pesonality, social adjustment, and so forth, and react accordingly in the study.

This categorization is compatible with, and amplifies, the voluntary–involuntary–nonvoluntary participant distinction that we have drawn. We assume that almost all par-ticipants are at least partly apprehensive about taking part in an experiment, although this apprehension probably diminishes with experience. Involuntary participants are most likely to be negativistic, as are voluntary participants who find that the cost/benefit ratio of their participation is not as favorable as they thought when they originally signed up for the study. The good and the faithful participant roles are most likely to be assumed by voluntary participants. Nonvoluntary participants, of course, being unaware that they are being studied, are unlikely to assume any of the roles that Webber and Cook defined. Although some experimenters find little support for these role distinctions (e.g., Carlston & Cohen, 1980), some very careful and thoughtful research (Carlopio, Adair, Lindsay, & Spinner, 1983) has produced evidence that is in essential agreement with the participant categories that we have discussed.

In many studies of participants' motivation in psychological experiments, it has been found that individuals would go to great lengths to "please" the experimenter, that is, to help confirm the research hypotheses. Although Orne (1962) was not the first to investigate this issue (e.g., see Pierce, 1908), he was able to demonstrate quite clearly the almost incredible degree to which participants were willing to help the experimenter. Presenting participants with approximately 2,000 pages of random numbers, instructing them to sum each two adjacent numbers and to continue to work at this task until his return, Orne found almost no one willing to quit this ridiculous task even after 5 hours had elapsed. Adding a final step to this process (i.e., asking participants to tear the completed pages into "a minimum of 32 pieces," throw these into the waste basket, and begin again) had almost no effect on the participants' persistence. Other similarly self-defeating tasks were continued beyond reasonable limits. When questioned about their unusual perseverance, participants in these experiments often responded with a guess that the experiment was concerned with endurance, and thus their actions were quite appropriate. Repeated performances of this type have alerted psychologists to the tremendous degree of behavior control the experimenter can exert in the laboratory.

Nowhere was this fact more evident than in the studies of Stanley Milgram (1963, 1965). While investigating the effects of a wide range of variables on "obedience" behavior, Milgram's basic experimental procedure took the guise of a two person (teacher–student) verbal learning study. In these studies, the naive participant acted as "teacher," whose task it was to shock the "student" each time the student committed an error of memory. In fact, an experimental accomplice played the role of student and actually received no shocks. The shock generator was a rather formidable-looking apparatus, having 30 switches, and corresponding voltage levels ranging from 45 to 450 volts, with written descriptions of these voltages ranging from "Slight Shock" to "Danger: Severe Shock." The accomplice was placed in another room and purposely gave many wrong answers. In response, the teacher was to increase the level of punishment. The dependent measure of this study was the level at which the naive participant refused to administer further punishment to the "student." When the 150-volt level was reached, the accomplice demanded to be set free, to terminate the experiment. Though he was unseen, his protestations, amplified from the other experimental room, were truly heartrending. At this point in the investigation, almost all naive participants indicated their willingness to end the study. The experimenter, however, always responded, "You have no other choice, you must go on!" An incredibly large percentage of the participants did just this. In one of these studies (Milgram, 1965), for example, 61% of the individuals tested continued to the very end of the shock series!

When questioned about their actions, Milgram's participants responded in a manner similar to that of Orne's. Their rationale was that they were an integral part of a scientific investigation, and they were determined to fulfill their commitment to this study, even though this might entail some discomfort. It should be stressed that these participants did not enjoy themselves in this study. Milgram's filmed records indicate that many individuals vehemently protested the demands to continue the experiment and demonstrated clear signs of extreme nervousness and tension. Even so, many continued. It would appear that under the auspices of a scientific investigation, people are willing to commit themselves to boring, tedious, meaningless, and even blatantly immoral actions, actions which they very well might refuse to perform outside the laboratory setting.

Apart from the moral and ethical implications of this investigation, we must also consider findings of this type from the standpoint of generalizability. Were the participants willing to perform their questionable behaviors only when asked to do so for the sake of science? If so, we must question whether the relationships discovered will continue to hold outside of the laboratory setting. But suppose the participants were willing to perform as told whenever an important value (duty, allegiance to a higher law, etc.) was involved. In that case, Milgram's research might be applicable in a wide variety of circumstances.

EXPERIMENTER EXPECTANCY AND BIAS

To this point, we have shown how the researcher's decisions regarding the basic features of the experiment can influence the internal and external validity of the investigation. Should we use voluntary, involuntary, or unvoluntary participants? Should experimental realism be enhanced at the expense of mundane realism? These decisions, under the conscious control of the experimenter, have great bearing on the quality, and ultimate contribution, of the research enterprise. However, in addition to these deliberate choices, there are other aspects of the setting that generally are not consciously controlled, but which also can have considerable influence on the quality and generalizability of the results of an investigation. These influences originate in the experimenter or in the experimental setting. We have learned that the mere presence of the experimenter in the research setting can operate as a subtle but nevertheless potentially powerful "treatment," differentially affecting participants' responses as a result not of the experimental manipulation, but of the experimenter's own expectations.

Rosenthal (1966) and his associates demonstrated in several studies that the expectations of an experimenter can seemingly be transmitted to his or her participants, be they elementary school children (Rosenthal & Jacobson, 1968), college sophomores (Rosenthal & Fode, 1963), or Spraugue-Dawley albino rats (Rosenthal & Lawson, 1964). Although controversy surrounds the medium of communication that is involved in such effects, the process has been demonstrated over a wide range of experimental contexts (Harris & Rosenthal, 1985, 1986).

Research on expectancy effects is not novel. At the turn of the century, Moll (1898) and Jastro (1900) devoted attention to this issue. The "double blind" method in pharmacological research (in which neither patient nor physician know whether a drug or placebo has been administered) was developed specifically to combat expectancy effects on the part of physicians. In examining research on this problem, Beecher's (1966) study of placebo effects is especially interesting. In this investigation, the effects of morphine, a powerful narcotic, were compared with those of a placebo in the control of moderate pain. Using a double blind procedure, no differences in pain alleviation were detected between the experimental and control (placebo) groups. Similarly, Reed and Witt (1965) apparently were able to induce hallucinations on the part of a participant who thought he had been given the hallucinogenic drug LSD when, in fact, a placebo had been administered. If effects of this profound nature can be produced through simple manipulations of participants' expectations, imagine how much more intrusive such expectations can be when the behaviors under study are not of major importance to the respondents.

In a series of replicated studies, Rosenthal and Fode (1961, 1963) convincingly demonstrated the presence of expectancy effects. Using a group of students in his experimental psychology course, Rosenthal ostensibly conducted a laboratory exercise in which the students were to serve as experimenters. Their task was to present a set of 10 full-face photographs to volunteers from the introductory psychology course. The volunteers' job was to make a judgment concerning the "successfulness" of the people depicted in the photographs. Up to this point, the study is completely straightforward. However, before they began, Rosenthal told half of his experimenters that previous research had demonstrated that the photos depicted successful people, and thus, they could expect relatively high ratings from the participant volunteers. The other experimenters were told the opposite. (In fact, the photos were chosen from a larger pool of pictures that had been administered to a large group of students; they were chosen because they had been rated essentially neutral with respect to "successfulness.") All student-experimenters then were told that, because the exercise was designed to give them practice in "duplicating experimental results," they would be paid twice the usual amount ($2/hour, rather than $1) if their results agreed with previous findings.

The ratings that the two groups of experimenters obtained were substantially different, in ways consistent with the expectancy hypothesis. Those led to expect positive ratings from the participants reported significantly more positive estimates than those who expected negative scores. In a replication of this study, in which the biased experimenter was removed to the extent that he did not even handle the photographs and was not in direct facial contact with the participants, Fode (1960) obtained results similar to those of the first investigation. Adair and Epstein (1967) removed the biased experimenter even farther from the experimental situation by tape-recording the instructions of the experimenters who had been led to expect either a high or low rating, and played these instructions to a new sample of participants. In both the face-to-face and the tape-recorded instruction conditions of this study, expectancy effects were obtained.

Rosenthal has argued that although intentional recording errors on the part of the student-experimenters were possible in these studies, they were not very likely to occur. Because the experimental setting allowed the participant to observe the recording of his ratings, Rosenthal reasoned that any recording errors of the experimenter would have been detected and corrected by the participant. Later studies in which the same general approach was employed have resulted in generally confirmatory findings (see Fode, 1965; Laszlo & Rosenthal, 1967; Marwit & Marcia, 1965; Masling, 1965, 1966; Shames & Adair, 1967; Silverman, 1966; Troffer & Tart, 1964).

Although experimenter-bias effects due to recording, observation, and computation errors are troublesome, their effects are not overly difficult to offset. More subtle and troublesome is the possibility in which the experimental participant, through some subtle and unintentional cues from the experimenter, decides to perform "correctly," that is, in a manner that he or she thinks will please the researcher (Webber and Cook's "good" participant role).[2] The interactive nature of the experimenter/participant relationship renders control extremely difficult in such situations. How could such cuing occur? Suppose that each time a "correct" response was made, the experimenter reinforced the participant (either verbally or nonverbally). The reinforcement could be extremely subtle and unintentional. A slight nod of the head, a hardly perceptible smile, or a leaning of the body toward the participant might be all that is needed to trigger a cooperative response. Returning to Rosenthal and

---

[2]It is also possible that the participant could assume any of the other roles described by Webber and Cook (1972), but we focus specifically on the problem encountered when the good participant role is adopted.

Fode's (1963) photo rating task, consider a participant's relief when, actively attempting to "psych-out" the study, he or she realizes that the experimenter gives a nod of the head, or smiles, or says "good" each time a high photo rating (or a low one, depending on the experimental condition assigned) is given. The problem has been solved, the information transmitted, and the participant has learned how to perform in the experiment to please the investigator.

If this reconstruction is correct, then the majority of expectancy findings can be explained in terms of the behaviors of an experimenter too anxious to confirm theoretical expectations. In the course of this pseudo-confirmation, this person

- systematically errs in observation, recording, or analysis of data (whether intentionally or not), or
- cues the participant to the correct response through some form of verbal or nonverbal reinforcement.

If this latter possibility obtains, the forms of the cue might well be more subtle than those previously discussed, but certainly need not be. Verbal reinforcement, for example, has been shown to be very effective in altering or maintaining sought-for responses.

Solutions to the Problems of Expectancy Bias

The design problem that must be overcome in controlling the first two forms of demand effects is twofold: It consists of controlling both observer bias and the intentional or unintentional cuing of the experimental participant. By properly controlling one of these factors, experimenters often take care of the other.

Monitoring.   From the previous discussion of observer bias, it would seem that a possible control consideration would entail more careful observation of the experimenter, to insure that his or her data transcription and analysis were accurate. This could be accomplished by recording the experimenter–participant interaction, and comparing the results, as presented by the experimenter, with those obtained through the unbiased observers. Unfortunately, this process does not preclude the possibility of a subtle, nonverbal cuing of the participant by the experimenter. As such, this addition can be, at best, only partially effective. Whereas a more rigorous observation of the experimental interaction is certainly worthwhile, it dose not solve completely the potential expectancy problem.

Blind Procedures.   A more effective solution, controlling the effects of both observer bias and participant cuing, borrows from the "blind" procedures developed in pharmacological research. The most obvious way in which this control can be effected is through the simple expedient of failing to inform those individuals interacting with participants about the nature of the experimental hypotheses. The reasoning underlying this control is that if experimenters do not know what is expected, they will be unlikely to pass on any biasing cues to the participant.[3] Similarly, any recording or calculation errors that might be made would be expected to be unbiased, not tending to affect systematically the experimental or control group scores.

---

[3]This would involve hiring experimenters or data analysts; the individual responsible for mounting the study could hardly be expected to do so without knowing his or her own hypothesis.

Unfortunately, experimenters, even hired experimenters specifically shielded from information about the theory under development, have been shown to be hypothesis-forming organisms who, over the course of an investigation, might evolve their own implicit theory of the meaning and nature of the work they are performing. This possibility can be assessed through an investigation of the variability of the experimental data over the course of the entire study. If scores tend to become more and more homogenous as the investigation progresses, the possibility that an implicit hypothesis has been formed (with the attendant expectancy problems) cannot easily be dismissed. Although such an analysis enables experimenters to evaluate the probability of the occurrence of implicit hypothesis formation, it does not suggest any realistic way of correcting for this effect.[4] Thus, the particular application of the experimental blind procedure would not seem to offer a real solution to the experimenter expectancy problem, unless the entire experiment could be completed before a series of implicit hypotheses could realistically develop. It seems likely that this hypothesis-generation behavior could be impeded if the experimenter was prohibited from discovering the nature of the results until the completion of the investigation, but often because of the very nature of the experimental situation, this is impossible.

A slight variant of this procedure does not presume to eliminate knowledge of the experimental hypotheses from the investigators, but rather limits their information about the experimental condition to which any participant or group of participants has been assigned. Often, it is possible to test both treatment and control participants in the same setting, at the same time, without the experimenter's knowledge of the specific condition into which any individual falls. This is especially likely when (written) instructional manipulations are used. For example, suppose that a market researcher wanted to decide between four spokespersons for a newspaper advertising campaign designed to help sell a new automobile model. Accordingly, the researcher develops four sets of news copy which are identical except that they are attributed to different sources: a noted consumer advocate, a Nobel-prize-winning physicist, a trusted TV personality, and a popular sports hero. To avoid problems of experimenter expectancy, the market researcher randomly mixes the four newspaper ads and distributes them to participants in groups of participants whose reactions to the new model car are then assessed. All four conditions of the experiment are run at the same time, in the identical experimental setting. Because the researcher does not know which participant received which communication source, it is obvious that experimenter expectancies could not influence the results. Thus, even though the researcher might hold a strong expectation that the consumer advocate's endorsement would prove most persuasive, experimenter bias could not operate on participants' responses if the researcher could not distinguish between those who received the ad copy attributed to this source and those whose copy was attributed to other sources.

Mechanized Procedures. Whereas this variant of the blind procedure can be employed in many different experimental settings, it cannot be used in all situations. In some settings, the experimental and control conditions cannot be studied simultaneously in the same location. In such cases, mechanization of the experimental procedures can provide the solution to the problem of experimenter expectancy. Instructions can be recorded, manipulations videotaped and presented to participants, respondents' answers written, recorded,

---

[4]This observation illustrates the important conceptual distinction between methodological versus statistical control. A methodological control of expectancy would, through appropriate experimental design procedures, render the contamination of results by "experimenter expectancy" extremely improbable. Conversely, statistical control would not rule out the possibility of the occurrence of experimenter effects, but, rather, would enable us to gauge their strength.

or videotaped, and data analyzed by impartial computers (or computors). The aura of data of this type, "untouched by human hands," helps render implausible the alternative hypothesis of experimenter expectancy if these devices are employed intelligently and not subverted by inappropriate actions on the part of the investigator. Studies of this type, however, sometimes can prove uninvolving, uninteresting, or unreal to the experimental participant. These reactions can, in turn, give rise to a host of contaminating features. This need not always be the case. In some instances, the mechanization procedure can prove so intrinsically interesting, or demanding, that the participant attends to very little else. The improper use of computer terminals to provide experimental stimuli or collect participants' responses is a case in point. The mechanics of responding can sometimes be so demanding or cumbersome that the experimental treatment is not even noticed. Reactions of this type have proved discouraging to some of our more mechanically minded investigators. Such problems, however, are far from unsolvable. With adequate preparation, a realistic, interesting, and sometimes even educational, experimental situation can be devised, and, as recent experience has demonstrated, the intelligent use of computers to present experimental treatments or monitor participants' reactions can represent a positive and important step in the solution of the problem of experimenter bias (for examples of computer use in experimentation, see Davis, 1999; Fletcher, 2000; Walther, 1993; Ware & Johnson, 2000; Welsh & Null, 1991).

Clearly, any list of control suggestions will, of necessity, prove incomplete. Many other approaches to the solution of the expectancy problem are possible, but are idiosyncratic to the experimental setting in which they are employed. The important consideration that should be kept in mind is that expectancy effects must be mediated through the experimenter. Possible explanations of the effect have focused on two possibilities, involving the experimenter's systematically biasing the results of an investigation by (a) misobservation, misrecording, and/or miscalculating the experimental data; or (b) through emission of significant cues to the appropriate or expected behavior, which the receptive participant can interpret and use as a guide to the correct response in the experiment. In the absence of certainty concerning which of the two sources of bias is responsible for the previously reported expectancy findings, both must be controlled. Often, experimental procedures designed to treat one of those potential sources of bias can efficiently counteract the biasing effects of the other. Given the choice of methodological or statistical control, the investigator should choose the former, as it is more efficient and less expensive. Blind procedures should be used where possible; mechanization, being more expensive and often creating a somewhat artificial social experience, should be retained for those situations in which the experimental blind is not possible.

THE MANY FACES OF EXTERNAL VALIDITY

External validity refers to the question of whether an effect (and its underlying processes) that has been demonstrated in one research setting would be obtained in other settings, with different research participants and different research procedures. Actually, external validity is not a single construct but represents a whole set of questions about generalizability, each with somewhat different implications for the interpretation and extension of research findings (Brewer, 2000). The following sections discuss three of the most important forms of external validity: robustness, ecological validity, and relevance. Each of these raises somewhat different questions about where, when, and to whom the results of a particular research study can be generalized.

Robustness: Can It Be Replicated?

The robustness issue refers to whether a particular finding is replicable across a variety of settings, persons, and historical contexts. In its most narrow sense, the question is whether an effect obtained in one laboratory can be exactly replicated in another laboratory with different researchers. More broadly, the question is whether the general effect holds up in the face of wide variations in participant populations and settings. Some findings appear to be very fragile, obtainable only under highly controlled conditions in a specific context; other findings prove to hold up despite significant variations in conditions under which they are tested.

Technically, robustness would be demonstrated if a particular research study were conducted with a random sample of participants from a broadly defined population, in a random sampling of settings. This approach to external validity implies that the researcher must have theoretically defined the populations and settings to which the effect of interest is to be generalized and then must develop a complete listing of the populations and settings from which a sample is drawn. Such designs, however, are usually impractical and not cost effective. More often, this form of generalizability is established by repeated replications in systematically sampled settings and types of research partipants. For instance, a finding initially demonstrated in a social psychology laboratory with college students from an eastern college in the United States may later be replicated with high school students in the midwest and among members of a community organization in New England. Such replication strategies are not only more practical, they also have potential advantages for theory-testing purposes. If findings do not replicate in systematically selected cases, we sometimes gain clues as to what factors may be important moderators of the effect in question (Petty & Cacoppo, 1996).

Generalizability across multiple populations and settings should be distinguished from generalizability to a particular population. A phenomenon that is robust in the sense that it holds up for the population at large may not be obtained for a specific subpopulation or in a particular context. If the question of generalizability is specific to a particular target population (say, from college students to the elderly) then replication must be undertaken within that population and not through random sampling.

External validity is related to settings as well as to participant populations. The external validity of a finding is challenged if the relationship between independent and dependent variables is altered when essentially the same research procedures are conducted in a different laboratory or field setting or under the influence of different experimenter characteristics. For example, Milgram's (1963) initial studies of obedience were conducted in a research laboratory at Yale University, but used participants recruited from the community of New Haven. Even though these experiments were conducted with a nonstudent sample, a legitimate question is the extent to which his findings would generalize to other settings. Because participants were drawn from outside the university and because many had no previous experience with college, the prestige and respect associated with a research laboratory at Yale may have made the participants more susceptible to the demands for compliance that the experiment entailed than they would have been in other settings.

To address this issue, Milgram (1974) undertook a replication of his experiment in a very different physical setting. Moving the research operation to a "seedy" office in the industrial town of Bridgeport, Connecticut, adopting a fictitious identity as a psychological research firm, Milgram hoped to minimize the reputational factors inherent in the Yale setting. In comparison with data obtained in the original study, the Bridgeport replication resulted in slightly lower but still dramatic rates of compliance to the experimenter. Thus, setting could be identified as a contributing, but not crucial, factor to the basic findings of the research.

Ecological Validity: Is It Representative?

The question of whether an effect holds up across a wide variety of people or settings is somewhat different than asking whether the effect is representative of what happens in everyday life. This is the essence of ecological validity—whether an effect has been demonstrated to occur under conditions that are typical for the population at large. The concept of ecological validity derives from Brunswik's (1956) advocacy of "representative design" in which research is conducted with probabilistic samplings of people and situations.

Representativeness is not the same as robustness. Generalizability in the robustness sense asks whether an effect can occur across different settings and people; ecological validity asks whether it does occur in the world as is. In the Brunswikian sense, findings obtained with atypical populations (e.g., college students) in atypical settings (e.g., the laboratory) never have ecological validity until they are demonstrated to occur naturally in more representative circumstances.

Many researchers (e.g., Berkowitz & Donnerstein, 1982; Mook, 1983; Petty & Cacioppo, 1996) take issue with the idea that the purpose of most research is to demonstrate that events actually do occur in a particular population. Testing a causal hypothesis requires demonstrating only that manipulating the cause can alter the effect. Even most applied researchers are more interested in questions of what interventions could change outcomes rather than what does happen under existing conditions. Thus, for most social psychologists, ecological validity is too restrictive a conceptualization of generalizability for research that is designed to test causal hypotheses. Ecological validity is, however, crucial for research that is undertaken for descriptive or demonstration purposes.

Further, the setting in which a causal principle is demonstrated does not necessarily have to physically resemble the settings in which that principle operates in real life for the demonstration to be valid. As Aronson et al. (1998) put it, most social psychology researchers are aiming for "psychological realism" rather than "mundane realism" in their experiments. Mundane realism refers to the extent to which the research setting and operations resemble events in normal, everyday life. Psychological realism is the extent to which the psychological processes that occur in an experiment are the same as psychological processes that occur in everyday life. An experimental setting may have little mundane realism but still capture processes that are highly representative of those that underlie events in the real world.

Relevance: Does It Matter?

In a sense, the question of ecological validity is also a question of relevance—Is the finding related to events or phenomena that actually occur in the real world? However, relevance also has a broader meaning of whether findings are potentially useful or applicable to solving problems or improving quality of life. Again, relevance in this latter sense does not necessarily depend on the physical resemblance between the research setting in which an effect is demonstrated and the setting in which it is ultimately applied. Perceptual research on eye-hand coordination conducted in tightly controlled, artificial laboratory settings has proved valuable to the design of instrument panels in airplanes even though the laboratory didn't look anything like a cockpit.

Relevance is the ultimate form of generalization and differences among research studies in attention to relevance is primarily a matter of degree rather than of kind. All social psychological research is motivated ultimately by a desire to understand real and meaningful social behavior. But the connections between basic research findings and application are often indirect and cumulative rather than immediate. Relevance is a matter of social process—the process of how research results are transmitted and used, rather than what the research results are (Brewer, 1997).

Is External Validity Important?

External validity, like other validity issues, must be evaluated with respect to the purposes for which research is being conducted. When the research agenda is essentially descriptive, ecological validity may be essential. When the purpose is utilitarian, robustness of an effect is particularly critical. The fragility and nongeneralizability of a finding may be a fatal flaw if the goal is to design an intervention to solve some applied problem. On the other hand, it may not be so critical if the purpose of the research is testing explanatory theory, in which case construct validity is more important than other forms of external validity.

In physics, for example, many phenomena can be demonstrated empirically only in a vacuum or with the aid of supercolliders. Nonetheless, the findings from these methods are often considered extremely important for understanding basic principles and ultimate application of the science. Mook (1983) argued compellingly that the importance of external validity has been exaggerated in the psychological sciences. Most experimental research, he contended, is not intended to generalize directly from the artificial setting of the laboratory to "real life," but to test predictions based on theory. He drew an important distinction between "generality of findings" and "generality of conclusions," and held that the latter purpose does not require that the conditions of testing resemble those of real life. It is the understanding of the processes themselves, not the specific findings, which has external validity.

In effect, Mook argued that construct validity is more important than other forms of external validity when theory-testing research is conducted. Nonetheless, the need for conceptual replication to establish construct validity requires a degree of robustness across research operations and settings that is very similar to the requirements for establishing external validity. The kind of systematic, programmatic research that accompanies the search for external validity inevitably contributes to the refinement and elaboration of theory as well as generalizability.

SUGGESTED READINGS

Orne, M. (1962). On the social psychology of the psychological experiment. *American Psychologist, 17*, 776–783.

Rosenthal, R. (1966). *Experimenter effects in behavioral research*. New York: Appleton-Century-Crofts.

Sears, D. O. (1986). College sophomores in the laboratory: Influences of a narrow data base on social psychology's view of human nature. *Journal of Personality and Social Psychology, 51*, 515–530.

7

CONDUCTING EXPERIMENTS OUTSIDE THE LABORATORY

The preceding chapters discussed various ways in which experiments conducted in laboratory environments can be made as realistic, involving, and impactful as possible. Even when such methods are used, however, it is still desirable to move outside of the laboratory, into field contexts, to extend and validate the results of any research program in the social sciences. As we state throughout this book, research should be conceived as a process in which observation gives rise to theory, which is followed by research. Variations between expectations and research results lead social scientists back to observation, to theory revision, and back to research, as shown in Fig. 7.1. It is important to note that neither laboratory nor field research is accorded primacy in this diagram. Each has its place, and each should be engaged in only after appropriate observation and theory development. This chapter reinforces this view by considering how experimental methods can be applied outside the laboratory, and how laboratory and field experiments can be used in conjunction with each other. Later chapters address nonexperimental research methods in field contexts.

The distinction between laboratory and field is basically one of setting, that is, the context in which the research is conducted. A laboratory is a designated location to which potential participants must go to take part in the research. A field study is one in which the investigator brings the research operations to the potential participants in their own environment or naturalistic setting. With the advent of the World Wide Web (WWW) as a venue for research, social scientists move even farther away from the sterile confines of the laboratory, more into the participants' own world, often into their homes or offices.

With the WWW, the distinction between field and lab becomes even more blurred than before. The school classroom, for instance, is sometimes converted into a "laboratory" for research purposes, and many laboratory studies have been conducted under the guise of some other activity, such as job interviews or group discussions. In general, however, laboratory and field experiments differ on the important dimension of how aware (or unaware) participants are of the fact that they are involved in a research study. In field settings—even when informed in advance that a research study is underway—participants

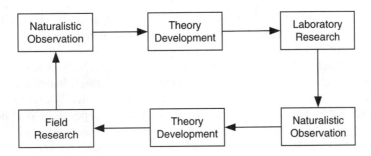

FIG. 7.1. The research cycle.

are less likely to be as highly conscious of the research goals as they are in a laboratory (or Internet) environment.

As a general research strategy, the movement between laboratory and field settings should be a two-way street. Many phenomena of interest to social scientists are first observed in naturalistic settings. In the complex environment of the real world, however, it often is difficult to pinpoint the specific effect one variable has on another. To test a particular cause–effect relationship, the potential causal variable of interest must be disembedded from its natural context or causal network, and the laboratory is an ideal setting for eliminating the salience or intrusiveness of extraneous contextual variables. Once the relationship has been established in the experimental laboratory or Internet experiment, however, the reasons for moving back into the field as a research site are the reverse of that just mentioned. It is important to re-embed the causal variable into its natural context, to be certain that its effect is not suppressed or reversed under conditions in which the phenomenon normally occurs.

RESEARCH SETTINGS AND ISSUES OF VALIDITY

The interchange between laboratory and field experiments is critical if we are to establish the external and construct validity of a research finding. Internal validity is, for the most part, inherent in a single study. With sufficient information about how an experiment was conducted, how participants were assigned to treatments, and how contextual conditions were controlled, we should be able to assess whether the results of that particular study are internally valid. However, issues involving construct validity or external validity can rarely be resolved within the context of a single experiment. These questions require multiple replications of the effect under consideration, ideally across many different research contexts, before meaningful assessments are possible.

Here it is important to distinguish between two types of replication research, where replication refers to the design and conduct of a new study that attempts to repeat the findings of an earlier one. In *exact replications*, an attempt is made to reproduce the procedures of the initial study, particularly the operationalizations of the independent and dependent variables, as closely as possible. Only the participants, the time, and the place (and, usually, the experimenter) are changed. The purpose here is to determine whether or not a given finding can be reliably repeated under slightly different circumstances. In *conceptual replications*, on the other hand, an attempt is made to determine whether a particular empirical relationship can be repeated when different experimental operations are used to represent the same theoretical concepts. To establish external validity of a research result, it is sufficient to demonstrate that the same treatment produces a similar result in different contexts with different types of participants. To establish construct validity, however, conceptual replications are required in which the operationalizations of both treatment and effect variables are as dissimilar as possible.

In principle, exact replications vary context while holding research procedures constant, whereas conceptual replications vary both context and procedures. In reality, variations in context and research operations are neither independent nor mutually exclusive, and both are closely related to alterations in the setting in which an experiment is conducted. In many cases, it is difficult to change the context in which a study takes place without altering the entire experimental setup, and this is particularly true when a replication involves the shift from laboratory to field or to Internet settings. The advantages of field experiments are best realized when the independent and dependent variables are significantly modified to be appropriate to the new context. Such modifications often involve a fundamental rethinking of the theoretical variables and a concern with conceptual, rather than exact, replication of the original study.

Although specific procedures may differ, the basic rationale for the conduct of either field or laboratory experiments is the same. For purposes of this chapter, however, we pay particular attention to the ways in which the conduct of a field experiment is most likely to differ from that of the typical laboratory or Internet experiment.

Selection of Participants

Field experiments generally differ from laboratory experiments in the extent to which participants are consciously aware that they are involved in a research project. The two settings (field and laboratory) also differ in the types of people who are likely to be recruited as participants. A major criticism of laboratory research in social psychology has been the extent to which it relies on college students as participants (see Krantz & Dalal, 2000; Sears, 1986). Field experiments often provide for a broader, or at least different, representation of participant populations, and these participant variations are even more evident in Internet research. Researchers sometimes select particular field sites specifically to reach participant groups of a particular age or occupation. For instance, they go to old people's homes to study the elderly, to schools to study young children, and to courtrooms to study lawyers. Other settings (e.g., the city streets) do not permit such control over participant selection, but do provide for a wide range of potential participants. It should be emphasized, however, that moving into field settings does not automatically guarantee greater representativeness of participants. Dipboye and Flanagan (1979) conducted an extensive comparative review of laboratory and field research in industrial-organizational psychology and concluded that field studies typically involved just as narrow a participant population (specifically, "male, professional, technical, and managerial employees in productive-economic organizations") as did the average laboratory study.

Control Over the Independent Variable

Although the essence of experimentation is systematic manipulation by the researcher of variations in treatment or conditions that constitute the independent variables of the study, the extent of experimenter-controlled manipulation in different research settings is a matter of degree. In some cases, the researcher creates experimental situations from scratch, controlling background context as well as experimental variations. In other cases, the experimenter controls less of the setting but introduces some systematic variation into existing conditions, as in the field experiment by Piliavin, Rodin, and Piliavin (1969) where the behavior of an experimental accomplice in a subway train was varied to study bystander helping in that setting.

In yet other cases, the experimenter does not manipulate any of the stimulus conditions directly, but selectively directs participants' attention to particular aspects of the stimulus field as the experimental treatment. This type of manipulation is illustrated by laboratory experiments in which variations in seating arrangements are used to alter participants' visual perspective on a social situation (e.g., Duval & Wicklund, 1973). Similar techniques have been used in field settings. In field studies of altruism, for example, researchers have attempted to manipulate the salience of the need for help through the use of cues such as the presence of a cane (Piliavin et al., 1969), the environmental context in which the research occurs (Vrij & Winkel, 1991), or the apparent distress of a victim (Darley & Batson, 1973).

In other field research contexts, the experimenter neither manipulates the stimulus conditions directly nor controls participant attention, but instead *selects* from among naturally occurring stimulus situations those that represent the independent variable of interest. Here the line between experimental and nonexperimental research becomes thin indeed, and the distinction depends largely on how well standardized the selected field conditions can be across participants. One good illustration of the use of selected field sites in conjunction with laboratory research comes from the literature on mood and altruism. Mood induction manipulations have been developed in laboratory settings. Typically, the inductions consist of either having participants read affectively positive or negative passages or having them reminisce about happy or sad experiences in their own past (see Forgas, 2000). Following the mood state induction, participants are given an opportunity to exhibit generosity by donating money or helping an experimental accomplice. Results generally show that positive mood induction elevates helping behavior. Despite multiple replications of this effect in different laboratories with different investigators, however, the validity of these findings has been challenged both because of the artificiality of the setting in which altruism is assessed and because of the potential demand characteristics associated with the rather unusual mood induction experience.

To counter these criticisms, researchers in the area took advantage of a natural mood induction situation based on the emotional impact of selected motion pictures (e.g., Underwood et al., 1977). Following pilot research in which ratings were obtained from moviegoers, a double feature consisting of "Lady Sings the Blues" and "The Sterile Cuckoo" was selected for its negative affect-inducing qualities. Two other double features were selected as neutral control conditions. A commonly occurring event—solicitation of donations to a nationally known charity with collection boxes set up outside the movie theater lobby—was selected as the measure of the dependent variable of generosity.

Having located such naturally occurring variants of the laboratory mood induction operation and altruism measure, the major research design problem encountered by the researchers was that of participant self-selection to the alternative movie conditions. Whereas random assignment of volunteer moviegoers was a logical possibility, the procedures involved in using that strategy would have recreated many of the elements of artificiality and reactivity that the field setting was selected to avoid. Therefore, the investigators decided to live with self-selection and to alter the research design to take its effect into consideration. For this purpose, timing the collection of charitable donations at the various movie theaters was randomly alternated across different nights, to occur either while most people were entering the theater (prior to seeing the movies) or while leaving it (after seeing both features). The rate of donation of arriving moviegoers could be used as a check on preexisting differences between the two populations apart from the mood induction.

Fortunately, there proved to be no differences in initial donation rates as a function of type of movie, whereas post-movie donations differed significantly in the direction of lowered contribution rates following the sad movies. This pattern of results, then, preserved the logic of random assignment (initial equivalence between experimental conditions) despite the considerable deviation from ideal procedures for participant assignment.

Two points should be emphasized with respect to this illustration of field research. First of all, the field version of the basic research paradigm was not and could not be simply a "transplanted" replication of the laboratory operations. Significant alterations were necessary to take full advantage of the naturalistic setting. The researchers had considerably less control in the field setting. They could not control the implementation of the stimulus conditions or extraneous sources of variation. On any one night, a host of irrelevant events (e.g., a break-down of projectors, a disturbance in the audience) may have occurred during the course of the movies, which could have interfered with the mood manipulation. The researchers were not only helpless to prevent such events, but would not have been aware of them if they did take place. In addition, in the field setting, the experimenters were unable to assign participants randomly to conditions and had to rely on luck to establish initial equivalence between groups.

The second point to be emphasized is that the results of the field experiment as a single isolated study would have been difficult to interpret without the context of conceptually related laboratory experiments. This difficulty is partly due to the ambiguities introduced by the alterations in design and partly to the constraints on measurement inherent in the field situation where manipulation checks, for example, usually are not possible. The convergence of results in the two settings greatly enhances our confidence in the findings from both sets of operationalizations. Had the field experiment failed to replicate the laboratory results, however, numerous possible alternative explanations would have rendered interpretation very difficult.

Random Assignment in Field Settings

Participant self-selection problems plague field experimentation in many different ways. In the field experiment on mood and helping behavior cited previously, random assignment to experimental conditions was not even attempted. Instead, the effects of potential selection factors were handled in other ways that involved an element of risk-taking. The pre-movie data collection served as a check on the assumption that people who attend sad movies are not inherently different from people attending other movies in their propensity to give to charities. But what if that assumption had proved false and there had been an initial difference in the rate of donations from attendants at the different types of movies? Such prior differences in behavior would have made interpretation of any differences in donations after exposure to the movies hazardous at best. In this case, the researchers were taking a gamble in counting on the absence of initial population differences. Presumably, they would not have gone ahead with the study if the differences in pre-movie donation behavior had been found. Personal experience, or better yet, pilot research, could have led them to expect that the factors determining which type of movie most people saw on a particular night were irrelevant to their propensity to give to charity.

In other settings, too, the research may rely on the essentially haphazard distribution of naturally occurring events as equivalent to controlled experimental design. Parker, Brewer, and Spencer (1980), for instance, undertook a study on the outcomes of a natural disaster—a devastating brush fire in a southern California community—on the premise that the pattern of destruction of private homes in the fire constituted a "natural randomization" process. Among homes in close proximity at the height of the fire, only chance factors, such as shifts in wind direction and velocity, location of fire fighting equipment, and traffic congestion, determined which structures were burned to the ground and which remained standing when the fire was brought under control. Thus, homeowners who were victims of the fire and those who were not could be regarded as essentially equivalent prior to the effects of the fire, and any differences in their attitudes and perceptions following the fire could be attributed to that particular differential experience. When comparisons are made between such naturally selected groups, the burden of proof rests on the investigator to make a convincing case that the groups were not likely to differ systematically in any relevant dimensions other than the causal event of interest.

One should not conclude from these examples that experimenter-controlled random assignment is always impossible in field experiments. In many cases, the nature of the experimental manipulation is such that the researcher can deliver different versions or conditions to potential participants in accord with a random schedule. Consider, for example, another study of helping behavior in which the effect of positive, rather than negative, mood was being investigated. As one manipulation of positive mood, Isen and Levin (1972) arranged that some users of a public phone booth would find a dime in the coin return slot of the telephone as they started to make their call. Although the researchers had no control over which persons would make use of the targeted phone booths during the course of the experiment, they could control the timing and frequency with which dimes were or were not placed in the booths. They alternated these conditions on a random basis and then observed the behavior of the next caller who happened to use the selected phone booth. With this kind of randomization, the researchers could be relatively confident that no prior-existing participant differences influenced their results.

In some field research efforts, the investigator may be able to assign participants randomly to experimental conditions but, once assigned, some participants may fail to participate or to experience the experimental manipulation. If such self-determined "de-selection" occurs differentially across treatment conditions, the experimental design is seriously compromised. One way of preserving the advantages of randomization in such cases is to include participants in their assigned experimental conditions for purposes of analysis regardless of whether they were exposed to the treatment or not (assuming, of course, that one is in a position to obtain measures on the dependent variable for these participants). This was the solution applied to the two field experiments conducted by Freedman and Fraser (1966) to test the effectiveness of the "foot-in-the-door" technique for enhancing compliance to a rather large, intrusive request from the researcher (e.g., to permit a five-person market survey team to come into one's home for 2 hours to classify household products). Of primary interest was the rate of compliance to this large request by participants who had been contacted previously with a small request (e.g., to respond to a very brief market survey over the telephone), in comparison to control participants who were not contacted until the time of the larger request.

The purpose of the manipulation in Freedman and Fraser's study was to test the effect of actual compliance to the initial small request on responses to the later one. However, the operational experimental treatment to which potential participants could be randomly assigned was exposure to the request itself. Approximately one third of those who were given the initial small request refused to comply and hence failed to complete the experimental manipulation. If these participants had been excluded from the study, the comparability between the remaining experimental participants and those randomly assigned to the non-initial-contact condition would have been seriously suspect. To avoid this selection problem, the researchers decided to include measures from all participants in the originally assigned treatment groups, regardless of their response to the initial request. With respect to testing treatment effects, this was a conservative decision because the full treatment was significantly diluted among those classified as being in the experimental group. As it turned out, the initial compliance effect was powerful enough to generate a significant difference between treatment groups (of the order of 50% vs. 20% compliance rates) despite the dilution of the experimental condition. If the results had been more equivocal, however, the researchers would have been uncertain whether to attribute the absence of significant differences to lack of treatment effects or to failure to achieve the experimental manipulation.

Assessing Dependent Variables in Field Settings

In many field contexts, the design and evaluation of dependent measures is parallel to that of laboratory experiments. In the guise of a person-on-the-street interview or a market research survey, for example, field researchers may elicit self-reports of relevant attitudes, perceptions, judgments, or preferences. Or, measures may be designed that assess participants' willingness to engage in relevant acts, such as signing a petition or committing themselves to some future effort. Finally, situations may be constructed to elicit the type of behavior of interest to the experimenter, such as providing participants with opportunities to donate to charity (Underwood et al., 1977), to help a stranger who has collapsed (Piliavin et al., 1969), or to trade in a lottery ticket (Langer, 1975). One advantage of experimentation in field settings is the potential for assessing behaviors that are, in and of themselves, of some significance to the participant. Instead of asking participants to report on perceptions or intentions, we observe them engaging in behaviors with real consequences. In such cases, our dependent measures are much less likely to be influenced by experimental "demand characteristics" or social desirability response biases. In laboratory settings, participants might check a particular point on a scale to please the experimenter or to look good; but we think very few people would choose someone as a roommate for the entire year unless there were more powerful reasons to do so.

Indirect Measures

In some field settings, the kinds of dependent measures typically employed in laboratory studies might be viewed as so intrusive that they would destroy the natural flow of events characteristic of the setting. For this reason, field experiments are often characterized by the use of indirect or concealed measures of the dependent variable under study.

In a sense, all measures of psychological variables are indirect, in that we have no direct access to the thoughts or perceptions of another person. However, conceptually, some measures are more indirect than others. Indirect measures are those for which the link to the variable of interest involves a hypothetical intervening process. For example, in an interesting study of the "illusion of control" over chance events, Langer (1975) sold 50-cent lottery tickets to participants under one of two conditions: In one condition, buyers were arbitrarily handed a particular ticket by the salesperson; in the other, buyers were allowed to select their own tickets from the available set. What Langer was interested in was the effect of the illusory "control" implied in this latter condition on participants' confidence that theirs might be a winning ticket. Rather than simply asking the participants how confident they felt, however, Langer used a less direct measure of this variable. Each participant was approached after obtaining a ticket and was told that someone else wanted to purchase a ticket and the seller had run out. The participants were then asked for how much they would be willing to sell their own tickets. The reasoning behind this procedure was that the asking price for the ticket would reflect the subjective utility of the ticket. This in turn reflects the probability that the participant attached to the ticket's winning a great deal of money. As predicted, those participants who had chosen their own tickets wanted significantly more money to sell their ticket than participants who had been given their tickets with no choice.

What is interesting about this use of an indirect measure is the likelihood that participants would have been embarrassed to report on their differential confidence had they been asked directly whether they thought they had a winning ticket; after all, they would know that the "objective" view would be that the probability was quite low and subject to purely chance factors. Assuming that the indirect measure used was closely related to true subjective confidence, it may have detected an effect that would not have appeared in the results of direct self-report (see also Langer, 1997, 2000).

Indirect measures are among a variety of techniques used by field researchers to make *unobtrusive measurements* of the dependent variable of interest (see Webb, Campbell, Schwartz, & Sechrest, 1996; Webb, Campbell, Schwartz, Sechrest, & Grove, 1981). Some unobtrusive measures are based on observations of ongoing behavior, utilizing methods of observation that interfere minimally or not at all with the occurrence of the behavior. For instance, voluntary seating aggregation patterns have been used as an index of racial attitudes under varied conditions of classroom desegregation; observational studies of conformity have recorded public behaviors such as pedestrians crossing against traffic lights or turn-signalling by automobile drivers; and studies of natural language often resort to eavesdropping on conversations in public places. Cialdini et al. (1976) used naturalistic observation of clothing and accessories to study what they call the "Basking in Reflected Glory" phenomenon. They recorded the wearing of t-shirts and other apparel bearing the school name or insignia by students in introductory psychology classes at seven universities each Monday during football season. The proportion of students wearing such apparel at each school proved to be significantly greater on Mondays following a victory by that school's team than on days following defeat. A simple monitoring of public displays provided quantitative confirmation of the hypothesized tendency to identify with success or to bask in reflected glory. Sigelman (1986) found a similar tendency after election day. He noticed that those who supported the winning ticket tended to keep their political signs and posters up longer that those whose candidates lost.

Other observational techniques may rely on the use of hidden hardware for audio or video recording of events that are later coded and analyzed. Finally, some techniques make use of the natural recording of events outside the experimenter's control, such as physical traces left after an event. One interesting illustration of the use of unobtrusive physical trace measures is provided in Langer and Rodin's (1976) field experiment testing the effects of responsibility on the well-being of residents of a nursing home. The major outcome of interest in that study was the general alertness and activity level of the residents following introduction of the experimental treatment. This was assessed not only by the traditional methods of participant self-report and nurses' ratings, but also by various specially designed behavioral measures. One of these measurement processes involved placing two inches of white adhesive tape on the right wheels of patients' wheelchairs. The tape was removed after 24 hours and analyzed for amount of discoloration, which served as an index of patient activity level. Unfortunately, the amount of dirt picked up by the tape turned out to be negligible for patients in all conditions, so the measure proved insensitive to treatment effects. Had the nursing home been less well cared for, the measure might have worked.

The results of Langer and Rodin's (1976) nursing home study serve to illustrate some of the problems and pitfalls of reliance on unobtrusive measures in field settings. The adhesive tape index did not produce any detectable treatment effect; however, other more direct self-report and behavioral measures demonstrated significant impact of the experimental treatment. Had the researchers been forced to limit their assessment of effects to the least obtrusive measure, they would have missed a great deal.

These results highlight the importance of pilot testing one's measures before relying on their use in a full study. In addition, they illustrate two potential problems with unobtrusive measures that must be considered. The first of these has to do with reliability. In general, the reliability of unobtrusive measures will not be as great as the more direct measures they are designed to mimic (Webb et al., 1981). As might be expected, therefore, the validity of dependent variable measures—the extent to which they measure what they are supposed to measure—is also likely to be of greater concern with unobtrusive measures. This concern comes about because the farther removed the actual measure is from the variable of interest, the less likely it is to prove valid. The rationale for this observation can be demonstrated simply. For instance, consider the number of steps involved in going from the dependent variable of patient activity level to the measurement of discoloration of white adhesive tape in Langer and Rodin's (1976) nursing home study. First, patient activity had to be translated into distance traveled in the wheelchair, which in turn had to be related to the amount of dirt picked up by different sections of the tape, which had to produce measurable differences in discoloration. In such a chain, many intervening processes can reduce the correspondence between the initial variable (activity) and the measured outcome, for example, the speed with which the wheelchair traveled, how often the floors were cleaned, whether the patient's movement was self-propelled or passive, occurred typically before or after floor cleaning, etc. Reliance on a single measure that could be affected by so many irrelevant factors is hazardous at best. The researchers, in this instance, did not rely on any single measure and so had some interesting findings to report at the end of the day. Imagine if their study rested on the analysis of the wheelchair tapes. In that case, they would have had nothing to say. Justification for our continued emphasis on multiple operationism is nowhere more evident than in studies of this type, which make use of creative unobtrusive measurement approaches.

Field Experimentation and Application

Conceptual replication highlights the advantages of combining laboratory and field experimentation for purposes of theory building, but the interplay between laboratory and field research is critical to the development of effective applications in social science as well. Basic experimental research may isolate important causal processes but convincing demonstrations that those processes operate in applied settings are essential before theory can be converted into practice. The research literature on psychological control provides a particularly good example of how a synthesis between field and laboratory experiments can work at its best. This research began with animal research in the laboratory (Brady, 1958), extended to field studies of stress in humans (e.g., Janis, 1958), then moved to laboratory analogues (e.g., Glass & Singer, 1972), and back to the field (e.g., Aspinwall & Taylor, 1992; Johnson & Leventhal, 1974; Mills & Krantz, 1979). Results from both types of settings repeatedly demonstrated the potent effect of the perception of control or responsibility on an organism's ability to cope with stressful events (Moghaddam & Studer, 1998; Taylor & Aspinwall, 1996). Even the illusion that one has control over the onset or the consequences of potential stressors is apparently sufficient to increase tolerance for stress and reduce adverse effects. As a result of these findings, procedures that are applicable in medical practice and the administration of health care institutions have been developed for inducing actual or perceived personal control (e.g., Thompson & Collins, 1995). At the same time, the fact that field applications permit testing research hypotheses in the presence of severe, noxious, or potentially life-threatening situations has contributed substantially to our basic theoretical understanding of the role of psychological factors in physiological processes.

A NEW RESEARCH VENUE: THE INTERNET

The Internet, or World Wide Web, has become a new and exciting venue for social research. Although the first studies conducted via the Internet are of recent vintage (some consider the survey study of Kiesler & Sproul, 1986, to be the first internet study, and research by Krantz, Ballard, & Scher, 1997, to be among the first published Web-based experiments), the potential of the net as a research venue may be enormous. The entire world, it seems, is wired, and the Web offers an opportunity to tap into it as a source of research participants.[1] The potential advantages of the web for research are numerous and include the capability to reach a huge audience of potential participants at low cost, reduced experimenter artifacts, greater generalizability of results owing to more diverse participant samples, and so on. Its disadvantages are less obvious, but nonetheless real (multiple submissions by the same participants, lack of attention to materials, hackers, high drop-out rates, etc.). Owing to the relative scarcity of research that has used the internet as a medium of scientific investigation thus far, much remains to be done. However, the utilization growth curve appears to be exponential, so it is important to consider this developing approach carefully. The Internet as a research site also is gaining popularity for the conduct of survey research (see chap. 10).

Methodological Concerns (Reliability and Validity)

Before considering some of the practical issues involved in using the Internet as a research venue, it makes sense to consider whether or not it should be used. The net has a number of strong proponents (e.g., see Birnbaum, 2000a; Reips, 2000), but even these researchers advise caution when mounting or interpreting Internet-based research. The issues that must be considered when using this new methodological venue are the same as those we face with the more traditional methods, and can be packaged neatly under the terms *reliability* and *validity*. When using the Web, issues of reliability are the same as those we confront when using conventional methods. The measures we use in WWW research must be reliable. This is not different from the requirement of the more standard approaches. In some ways, the Web offers greater potential to develop measures of high reliability. Buchanan (2000) suggested that with its abundance of available research participants, and their diversity relative to the standard college sophomore sample, developing measures of high reliability might be facilitated by using the Web. This observation makes sense. Developing scales of fact or opinion typically requires large numbers of respondents and in many research settings, these necessary large numbers are not available. They may be found on the Web, however, and if these participants are not substantially different from the norm, their use is clearly indicated.

---

[1] A recent estimate suggested that by 2003, more than half the households in the United States would be connected to the Net (Internet.com LCC, 1999).

The similarity of Web versus more traditional participants raises questions of both generalizability and validity. Research tentatively suggests that people who take part in Web-based research are different from the typical college sophomore. Web participants are more likely to be somewhat older and certainly from more diverse backgrounds and cultures; after all, the Web can attract participants from all over the world. However, whether these differences matter is difficult to determine, given the relative youth of the Web as a research engine and the lack of a large database on which to base our methodological appraisals.

Assessing the validity of Web-based research findings is difficult, just as it is in more traditional forms. Validity of Internet findings has been studied in two ways. One common approach is to conduct the investigation in the traditional laboratory and also on the Web. Investigators point to similarities of research findings between the Internet and the laboratory to suggest the validity of the Web-based research results. After all, the reasoning goes, if the findings of the lab and the Web are the same, then the Web results are not biased. Unfortunately, although this approach has some initial face appeal, it rests on a conformation of the null hypothesis to establish (convergent) validity. This is an unsatisfactory method of proof, despite its intuitive allure. The similarity of results from laboratory and the WWW may be attributable to a host of factors, none of which necessarily reflect on the quality of the Web as a research venue or its lack of reactivity vis-à-vis the more traditional research venue. Although it is unlikely that Web-based research will be underpowered, given the relative abundance of potential Web participants, it is possible that a comparative study would not have sufficient participants (and hence a lack of power) to detect a true difference between comparison groups. It also is possible that different sets of factors in the two research venues artificially cancel differences that otherwise might have occurred. For example, a lack of attention to an Internet-based personality inventory may well result in a lower than desired internal consistency coefficient; this same low coefficient may be found in a laboratory sample, but the result may come about because of a failure of the scale items themselves to adhere strongly to one another. Developing methods to enhance attention to the Web-based materials (more flashy presentation format, promise of payment for participation, etc.) would not solve the more fundamental problem of an item set that does not do a good job in measuring a particular psychological state or entity. Confirming the null hypothesis is not a satisfactory approach to establishing validity under any circumstance, and circumstances involving the WWW are not immune to this problem.

Unquestionably, a more powerful method to help establish the validity of Web-based findings is through the use of construct validation techniques, in which relationships based on theory and prior research are hypothesized, and found, on Web-based samples of research participants. If prior theory and research has led to certain expectations, and these expectations are met in the data derived from the Web, the validity of the results, and the research operations on which they are based, are bolstered.

Research by Williams, Cheung, and Choi (2000) supplies an interesting example of this form of validation. Williams et al. were interested in studying the relational tactic of ostracism, which involves ignoring and excluding another person from an ongoing activity. Considerable research has been focused on ostracism, and as might be expected, it suggests that social ostracism is quite aversive for its targets; even so, ostracized individuals often try to re-ingratiate themselves with the ostracizing group and are relieved when they succeed. Williams (1997; Williams & Zadro, in press) theorized that ostracism threatens four fundamental needs: belongingness, self-esteem, control, and meaningful existence. From this central axiom, he developed a model that predicts the psychological reactions that ensue in response to ostracism.

To study this need theory of ostracism, Williams et al. (2000) mounted a Web-experiment. Participants accessed their Web site and were asked to take part in a game with two other participants (actually, these others' responses were programmed). They were told that they should envision "throwing and catching a flying disc according to the messages that were shown on their screen." The messages systematically included the participants in the game or systematically excluded them: Some participants were randomly assigned to the condition in which the disk was thrown to them 67% of the time; others received the disk 33%, 20%, or never after the first throw. Measures taken immediately afterward showed that greater degrees of ostracism had greater aversive impact, as predicted on the basis of the model, with perceptions of belonging and self-esteem most severely threatened by ostracism.

This research strongly supported Williams' (1997) model and provides an interesting and useful model of a Web-based experiment. The study made use of more than 1,400 participants, from 62 different countries, and they ranged from 13 to 55 years of age. This magnitude of the participant sample, and its diversity, suggest that results that were discovered are probably generalizable beyond the boundaries of the standard "college sophomore" sample.

As shown in this study, the validity standards required of Web-based research are not different, or any more difficult, than those applied to the more traditional research fare. In both cases, validity is established through convergence of results expected on the basis of theory. In the standard laboratory, confirmatory results are not usually used to claim the utility of the laboratory as a research site; this is a given. With the Internet, however, confirmatory research may serve the dual function of validating both theories and research approaches.

Practical Considerations

A roadmap on how to make use of the WWW to facilitate research is beyond the scope of this book. However, there are a number of such books available, and the interested researcher should consult these or the Web sites that have been made available to help facilitate social research (e.g., Birnbaum, 2000b; Jones, 1999).[2] Some of these sites are happy to cooperate with researchers in mounting Web-based experiments. For example, a WWW site at the University of Mississippi (www.olemiss.edu/PsychExps/) actively encourages experimenters to use the site to conduct research. Further, it encourages researchers to make their data available to the social science community and provides an archive of data that has made use of the experimental facilities made available on the Web site. Researchers at the site have used these data to study the validity of Web-based research (e.g., McGraw, Tew, & Williams, 2000). More efforts of this type are bound to evolve with the further development of the Web as a research facilitator, efforts that could help develop large archives of social science data amenable to secondary analysis.

One of the central attractions of the Web for research purposes is the almost unlimited participant pool it promises. Getting participants is facilitated by a number of mailing lists that are available on line. Various user groups interested in the particular issue under

---

[2]Some useful Web sites to view ongoing research are (a) a list of online social psychology studies by Scott Plous (www.wesleyan.edu/spn/expts.htm); (b) Reips' experimental psychology laboratory (www.psych.unizh.ch/genpsy/Ulf/Lab/WebExpPsyLab.html); and (c) Yahoo's site (www.yahoo.com/social_science/psychology/disciplines/personality/online_tests). In addition, the American Psychological Society maintains a useful site (http://psych.hanover.edu/APS/exponnet.html) which lists ongoing research in which the Web surfer may participate. All of these lists, and the experiments they host, provide the researcher with some useful ideas about how to proceed.

study can be contacted and its members invited to participate. In addition, e-mails can be sent to various listserves that might contain subscribers interested in the topic under study. Many of the sites that have been noted to this point have lists of studies that are being run. People who like to participate in psychological research go to these sites to find research of interest. Perhaps as important as soliciting participation is keeping participants in the study once they have signed on. There is some evidence to suggest that the dropout rate of Web experiments is much greater than that of the standard laboratory study. This result is readily anticipated. The social pressure to stay in a study once begun is much less on the Web than it is in a laboratory, in the presence of the experimenter and perhaps other participants. If a study proves boring to Web participants, they are likely to vote with their feet—or mice—and leave the study. Researchers making use of the Web have tried to attenuate drop-out by running studies that involve payment (or lotteries) for those who complete the research, by developing interesting and appealing Web sites, and by keeping the time demands low (typically, 15 min or less). These fixes have introduced problems of their own. For example, if there is a monetary award promised, researchers must be aware of the possibility of multiple submissions, that is, of participants taking part in the experiment more than once, to gain more money or to enhance their chances of winning a large lottery. A number of different solutions to the multiple submission problem have been used (see Musch & Reips, 2000), but none is foolproof or particularly convenient. The dropout problem must be solved if the full research potential of the Web is to be realized. At this point, the Web offers almost unprecedented opportunities for research. Using the Web, in the best of all possible scenarios, social scientists can:

- conduct experiments of much greater complexity than would be possible in a laboratory;
- draw on a much greater range of participants, helping to ensure participant generalizability;
- avoid experimenter demand; and
- lessen possible experimenter bias.

It remains to be seen if these promises are met in practice. With sufficient ingenuity, we believe the Web can be an extraordinarily useful adjunct to social research. To ignore the possible benefits of Web-based research would be foolhardy. However, to fail to see the Web's many potential pitfalls would be equally shortsighted. We are optimistic that the potential difficulties involved with Web research will be met. It seems a safe bet to assume that the ingenuity the social sciences have brought to bear on other promising, but problematic, methodological factors will be brought to bear on the Web and that the Internet will become a potentially important part of the researcher's tool kit.

SUGGESTED READINGS

Birnbaum, M. H. (Ed.). (2000). *Psychological experiments on the internet*. San Diego: Academic Press.

Langer, E. J., & Rodin, J. (1976). The effects of choice and enhanced personal responsibility for the aged: A field experiment in an institutional setting. *Journal of Personality and Social Psychology, 34*, 191–198.

Webb, E. J., Campbell, D. T., Schwartz, R. D., Sechrest, L., & Grove, J. (1981). *Nonreactive measures in the social sciences*. Boston: Houghton-Mifflin.

CHAPTER

8

CORRELATIONAL DESIGN
AND CAUSAL ANALYSIS

The initial chapters of this book focused on considerations relevant to the development and use of experimental designs. In these designs, participants' exposure to a treatment or manipulation is totally controlled by the researcher; the major purpose of such control is to reduce or eliminate the plausibility of alternative explanations of change in the dependent variable. In research of this type, there is a clear distinction between the independent (or causal) variable, which is controlled or manipulated by the experimenter, and the dependent variable, which is allowed to vary freely. In many areas of research in social science, however, experimental control over important variables is either impossible, unethical, or, at the very least, completely impractical.

The experimenter studying the effects of organismic characteristics such as sex, age, or height, or such relatively enduring personal attributes as religious affiliation, for example, is in no position to manipulate these variables. People arrive at the laboratory with predetermined levels of these characteristics, and these features of the individual are beyond the immediate influence of the experimenter. Similarly, if participants' levels of a relevant variable are determined by their responses on a measuring instrument, such as a scale of authoritarianism, extraversion, or need for cognition, the experimenter again is not in a position to manipulate the initial level of this variable. It is a feature of the participants themselves. In most situations of this type, the experimenter can no longer determine whether variations in the independent variable cause changes in the dependent variable; rather, the research question becomes whether the variables under investigation are in some way related to one another. The type of analysis thus becomes correlational, rather than causal.[1]

In most common correlational approaches, the variables are allowed to vary freely, and the researcher records the extent of their *covariation*, that is, the extent to which

---

[1]Relatively recent statistical developments in social science in "structural equation modeling" or "path analysis" do facilitate the causal interpretation of correlational results, if certain stringent requirements are met. We discuss some of these techniques, and their requirements, later in this chapter.

changes in one are related to (but not necessarily caused by) changes in the other. The most common correlational study is one in which response–response types of relationships are being investigated, as, for example, when an individual's responses on one measuring instrument are being compared with his or her responses on another measure, or set of measures. A person's score on a scale of religiosity, for instance, might be correlated with his or her score on an instrument designed to measure authoritarianism. Participants' responses on both measures are unconstrained by the researcher; the question is the extent to which scores on one measure are related to scores on the other. More specifically, does a particular individual's score on one measure give a clue to, or help predict, that individual's response to the second measure?

In some experiments, researchers first sort individuals into different "experimental" conditions on the basis of either organismic characteristics (sex, age, etc.) or responses made on some measuring instrument, and then study the effects of an experimental manipulation on the responses of individuals so assigned. Designs of this type are called "mixed," because they combine both experimentally controlled assignment to various treatment conditions and (correlational) participant self-selection to conditions, based on the particular variable or variables on which participants are classified. This type of experimental design is equivalent to the "blocked design" discussed in chapter 4.

To provide a simple example, suppose that based on participants' scores on an intelligence test, an investigator constitutes two experimental groups, one composed of intelligent people, the other of unintelligent people. The researcher then administers a 10-page persuasive communication to each person, attributed to a source of either a high or low credibility. The design of this study is depicted in Table 8.1. In such designs, the variable that is "controlled" through selection (i.e., intelligence) is treated as an independent variable for the purposes of statistical analysis. However, the temptation to interpret results as if control-through-selection were equivalent to experimental manipulation must be avoided.

For example, suppose that the results of the study showed a "main effect" for intelligence such that the highly intelligent participants were more persuadable than the dull participants. This result would not necessarily indicate that high intelligence caused increased persuadability. It could be that the tendency to remain open to persuasive communications resulted in (i.e., caused) an increase in measured intelligence. Because the independent variable was not experimentally assigned (no independent manipulation by the experimenter influenced the status of the participants' intelligence), we are unable to decide between these possibilities. Instead, we must be content to note that a positive relationship between intelligence and persuadability exists (at least in this example) and resist the temptation to offer causal explanations of this relationship. When participants' level on an independent variable is determined by self-assignment, random manipulation of exposure to this variable is necessarily impossible; such variables, therefore, can enter

TABLE 8.1
Example of a Mixed Design, With One
Manipulated and One Blocked Factor

		Source Credibility	
		Low	High
Intelligence	Low		
	High		

an experimental design only as "control" factors and never as experimental (causal) treatments. If the control factor is categorical (e.g., "male/female," "Protestant, Catholic, Jewish, etc.") it is called a "blocking" variable, and it is treated as a factor in the analysis (see chap. 4). If the control factor is a continuous measure (e.g., IQ), it is called a *covariate*. In such cases, associations between variations in the covariate and the dependent variable are assessed and accounted for in the analysis. Typically, in such analyses (e.g., analysis of covariance), we attempt to determine the effect of the covariate on the outcome and then analyze the relationship between independent variables and outcomes after accounting for the covariate's effect. For example, we might be interested in the effects of a program designed to improve public speaking skills. We randomly assign participants to training or control conditions and at the completion of training, administer a test of public speaking. However, we may be concerned that participants' prior public speaking experience might have an effect on our results. We cannot control this factor—the participants bring it to the experiment as part of their past histories—but we can measure it in advance of the experimental session and account for its effects. Suppose we find, as we might expect, that the covariate is related positively to speaking skill. This is reasonable, insofar as people who are experienced public speakers should be better at it than those who never have had to speak in public. However, we are still interested in the effects of our treatment after accounting for this difference. The analysis of covariance approach allows us to estimate the effect of our treatment over and above that attributable to the covariate, in this case, prior public speaking experience.

TYPES OF CORRELATION

The major advantage of correlational research is that it permits the free variation of both variables of interest so that the degree of relationship between them can be determined without the loss of information inherent in the experimental design. Recall that in experimental research, variation in the independent variable is limited by controlled manipulation; likewise, manifestations of the dependent variable often are limited by virtue of the research setting and of the "allowable" response options offered by the experimenter on the dependent measure.

Consider, for example, a research design in which participants of different degrees of anti-Semitism are compared on their responses to an experimental situation that involves their working with a Jewish partner. Like most cognitive variables, anti-Semitic prejudice can be measured on a continuous scale, and this allows the possibility of identifying considerable variation between individuals. However, the demands of blocking experimental designs require that responses on the dependent variable be compared across groups of participants. Therefore, incorporating a variable such as anti-Semitism into an experimental research setting necessitates redefining variation among individuals according to some categorical scheme, such as "high," "medium," or "low" manifestations of the variable of interest. Thus, for purposes of the research design, individuals with some variation in degree of anti-Semitic feeling will be considered members of the same "experimental" grouping, and they will be treated as if they were equivalent on this variable.

At times, this categorization can result in an unsatisfactory and unnecessarily gross use of information. For example, consider the data of Table 8.2. This illustration presents the scores of 10 participants on a scale of anti-Semitism, arranged in order from lowest to highest. Now suppose the researcher wished to "assign" these participants to two "experimental" groups of equal size. To do so, he or she could use a common decision rule,

TABLE 8.2
Illustration of a Median Split Categorization of Participants
into High and Low Anti-Semitic Groups

Participant #	Anti-Semitism Score	Experimental Group
6	3	
9	28	
1	30	Low
10	49	
4	50	
	MEDIAN	
2	51	
5	53	
8	67	High
3	75	
7	88	

called a median split; that is, the group would be divided at the median, the "middlemost" score, with those above the median termed the "high anti-Semitic group," and those below the median the low group.

As Table 8.2 shows, dividing participants into discrete classifications on the basis of a continuous measure can have some clearly undesirable features. The four participants nearest the median have very similar scores, yet two of them (Participants 10 and 4) have been defined (by the median split) as being in the low anti-Semitic group, whereas the other two (Participants 2 and 5) have been placed in the high group. This classification holds despite the fact that the scores of Participants 10 and 4 on the critical scale are more similar to those of Participants 2 and 5 (who have been classified in a different group) than they are to the other participants in their own experimental group, and this same observation could be made for Participants 2 and 5. As Table 8.2 illustrates, participants with scores of 3 and 50 are classified as being identical in terms of their anti-Semitic sentiments (they are both in the "low" group), whereas those with scores of 50 and 51 are defined as different! Problems of this nature are avoided in correlational studies, where the total variation on both "independent" and dependent measures is used, rather than truncated. This approach enhances the potential for accurately recording and employing the true extent of covariation between measures.

Linear Correlation and Regression

Some correlational statistics (e.g., the correlation ratio [eta]) provide information only on the extent of relationship between the two variables being measured. Others provide information on both the degree and type of relationship. Specifically, the most commonly computed correlation—the Pearson product-moment correlation coefficient—is used to determine the extent of linear relationship, that is, the extent to which variation in one measurement is accompanied consistently by direct or inverse variation in the other measure. The scatter plots appearing in Fig. 8.1 are provided to illustrate the difference between linear and nonlinear relationships for measures of two variables, designated X and

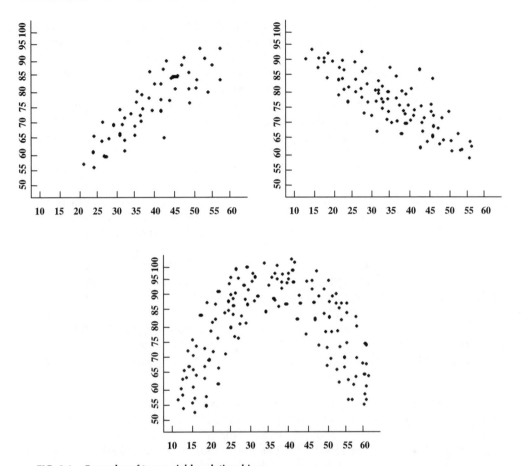

FIG. 8.1. Examples of two-variable relationships.

Y.[2] The points on each graph represent the coordinates of test scores on X and Y for particular individuals.

Graph (a) in Fig. 8.1 illustrates a positive linear relationship. In this circumstance, individuals who have relatively low scores on the X measure also tend to have relatively low scores on the Y measure, and those with high X scores also have high Y scores. An example of two variables that would be expected to exhibit such a relationship would be intelligence and academic performance. Conversely, Graph (b) represents a negative, or inverse, linear relationship in which relatively high X scores are accompanied by relatively low Y scores, and vice versa, such as the relationship that would be expected between measures of education level and criminal activity.

Graph (c) in Fig. 8.1 illustrates a nonlinear, or curvilinear, relationship in which increases in scores on X sometimes are accompanied by an increase in Y and sometimes by a decrease in Y. Such a relationship might be found, for example, between measures of anxiety, or tension, and performance on a complex intellectual task. At very low levels of anxiety (the X score), due to lack of motivation, fatigue, or boredom, performance

---

[2] Scatterplots are common graphic devices for indicating the nature of the relationship between two variables by representing simultaneously the relative standing of all individuals on both measures.

(Y score) is poor. As anxiety levels (X scores) rise above this minimal level, performance improves until a point is reached at which anxiety begins to interfere with efficiency of performance. As anxiety increases beyond this level, performance decreases.

The nonlinear relationship of Fig. 8.1(c) points out the importance of representing a wide range of variation on both variables before drawing any conclusions about the nature of the relationship between them. It also should be noted in the case represented by Graph (c) that despite the orderly relationship between X and Y scores, the product moment correlation between them would be approximately .00 because the relationship is not well represented by the linear measure. This highlights the importance of representing the relationship between two variables graphically, before trying to interpret the meaning of an obtained correlation value.

Only when the relationship between two measures is essentially linear does the product-moment correlation accurately assess the degree of relationship. In such cases, the value of the correlation coefficient (r) will indicate the magnitude and direction of linear relationship. The value of r may vary from -1.00 to $+1.00$, with the sign being an indication of the direction of relationship (positive vs. inverse) and the deviation from .00 an indication of the extent of relationship. An r of $+1.00$ would represent a perfect positive linear relationship. In such a case, the scatterplot of X and Y scores would form a straight line, indicating that the relative standing of any individual on the X measure would correspond exactly to that individual's relative position on the Y measure. Such perfect relationships are very rare, but the closeness of the existing relationship to this ideal is indicated by the size of the r value, which may be interpreted in either of two ways: proportion of common variance or accuracy of linear prediction.

Proportion of Common Variance. The squared value of the product–moment correlation (r^2) is known as the *coefficient of determination* because it provides an estimate of the proportion of "shared variation" between the two measures being correlated. The higher this value is, the greater is the amount of variation in one measure that is accounted for by variation in the other. When $r^2 = 1.00$, the degree of common variation is 100%. This means that if the X variable were "held constant" (i.e., only individuals with the same score on the X measure were considered), variation in Y would be eliminated (i.e., all would have the same Y).[3] With correlations that are less than perfect, the value of r^2 indicates the proportion by which variation in Y would be reduced if X were held constant, or vice versa. It should be emphasized, however, that the existence of shared variance between two variables does not indicate whether one variable causes the other.

Accuracy of Linear Prediction. The nature of the linear relationship can be depicted through the use of a scatterplot, which is a graphic representation of the set of X and Y scores that are obtained when two measures are taken on a sample of respondents. The straight line drawn through this set of points is called a *regression line* (see Fig. 8.2). The regression line in the scatterplot represents a formula for predicting one measure (Y) on the basis of a score on another measure (X). The linear prediction formula is $Y' = bx + a$. In other words, the expected score (Y') is equal to some constant, "a," which is added to the individual's score on X, which has been multiplied by another constant ("b"), which represents the rate of change on Y scores per unit change in X.[4] For example, suppose we

---

[3]Note that r^2 would be equal to 1.00 whether the correlation value equals $+1.00$ or -1.00. The coefficient of determination indicates degree of linear relationship irrespective of direction.

[4]The value of b is directly related (but not necessarily equal) to the value of r, being positive when the linear relationship is direct, and negative when it is inverse.

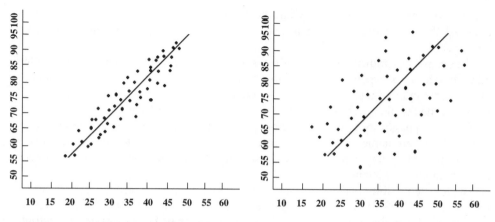

FIG. 8.2.   Scatterplots and regression.

know that grades in organic chemistry (scored on a 100-point scale) are related to scores on the science section of the MCAT (medical school) examination. Based on considerable empirical research, we have developed a formula that predicts a person's MCAT science score. Our hypothetical prediction formula takes the following values: $Y' = .13X + 1.6$, where Y' is the predicted MCAT score, and X is the chemistry grade. Thus, a person who earned 80 points (of 100) in organic chemistry would be expected to score 12.0 on the MCAT science section.

The scores generated on the basis of the regression formula are predicted values; they do not always correspond exactly to the actual scores for all individuals with a specific X value, which are depicted in the scatterplot. The degree of variation, or the distance of scatterplot points from the linear regression line, is directly related to the value of $1 - r^2$. Thus, the higher the correlation coefficient (r), the less variation around the regression line, that is, the tighter the fit between the actual Y values and the points on the line, and thus, the greater the accuracy of the linear prediction. Figure 8.2 illustrates this relationship with a comparison between two pairs of measures that are represented by the same regression line, but different correlation values. In the case of Graph (a), with a relatively high correlation, the variation of actual scatterplot points from the regression line is small. Thus, for any individual, the deviation between his or her actual score on the measure and that predicted from the X score is potentially quite small. In Graph (b), on the other hand, the deviation is much greater because the relationship (r) is much weaker. The size of the linear correlation directly reflects the accuracy of prediction.

We should point out that prediction or regression analysis, like correlation, does not imply causation. When prediction equations are based on existing covariation between two measures, the source of covariation is not specified. We have been dealing with the generalized equation for predicting Y from X, but the procedures could just as well have been used to predict X from scores on Y. The choice of "predictor" and "criterion" is often arbitrary, except when the predictor variable is one that temporally precedes the criterion variable.

Interpreting Null Results

Whenever the results of a product–moment correlational analysis indicate an approximately .00 linear relationship between two measures, there are four potential explanations for this lack of correlation. First, and most simply, there may be no systematic relationship between the two variables. This would be the expected outcome, for example, if one assessed the correlation between measures of broad-jumping ability and intelligence among adult males.

The second possibility, which already has been illustrated, is that there is some systematic relationship between the two variables, but the relationship is essentially nonlinear. Observing a graphic representation of the obtained data in the form of a scatterplot, as recommended earlier, best assesses the plausibility of this explanation.

The third possibility is that one or both of the measures involved in the correlation is flawed, or unreliable. Imperfection in measurement always diminishes the apparent relationship between variables; the greater the imperfection, the more serious its effect on the correlation coefficient.

The fourth possibility is that the lack of correlation may be an artifact of limitations of measurement. The size of the correlation between any two variables will be automatically attenuated (diminished) if the range of scores on either or both measures is restricted or truncated. This attenuation may be the result of a limitation of the opportunity for systematic relations to appear, or it may reflect a change in the nature of the relationship across different levels of one of the variables.

A case of attenuation due to limited observations is illustrated in Fig. 8.3 in which Graph (a) represents the relationship between measures on X and Y across a wide range of scores on both variables. The trend of the relationship is clearly linear and positive, although for every value of X there is some variation in scores on Y (i.e., the relationship is not perfect; the observations do not all fall on a straight line). Graph (b) provides a blow-up of the limited range of values represented in the area sectioned off in Graph (a). Within this restricted range of X scores, the effect of nonsystematic variation obliterates the linear trend in the relationship between X and Y. If the correlation were computed between these two measures for individuals with very little variation in their scores on X, the resulting value would be much closer to .00 than would be representative of the whole relationship. Mathematically, there has to be some variation in both measures to compute any meaningful coefficient of correlation. If all individuals have the same score on either or both measures, the computed correlation will automatically be .00.

Figure 8.4 illustrates a case in which the relationship between two variables could be misrepresented if the range of values measured on one of the variables were unrepresentative of the total range possible. This graph presents, roughly, the relationship

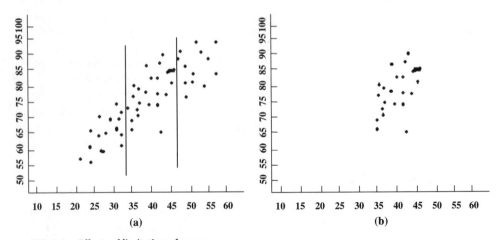

FIG. 8.3.   Effects of limitation of range.

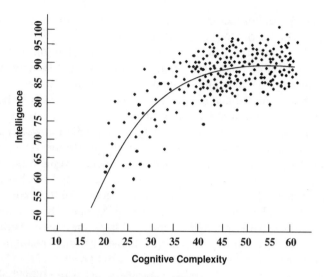

FIG. 8.4. Relation of cognitive complexity and intelligence.

that obtains between measures of cognitive complexity (see Streufert, 1997; Suedfeld, Tetlock, & Streufert, 1992) and intelligence. In the lower ranges of IQ scores, there is a systematic increase in scores on the complexity variable as intelligence increases. However, as the range of IQ reaches a ceiling, as it would in a sample of university students, the variation in complexity scores is no longer systematically related to IQ. This attenuation of relationship among participants at the upper levels of intelligence led early investigators (whose participants were primarily college students from very selective schools) to conclude that cognitive complexity and intelligence were independent. Only after a wider range of intelligence was represented in this research did the true nature of the relationship become apparent.

Multiple Correlation and Regression

Just as the experimental designs discussed in chapter 4 were not limited to the manipulation of a single independent variable, correlational analyses are not limited to the investigation of the relationship between two variables at a time. A researcher may wish to know in what way the combination of several different variables relates to some particular measure. For example, we may be interested in how well a group of factors such as level of education, economic status, and parental background combine to correlate with individual measures of racial prejudice. For such interests, the most commonly used analytic technique is the "multiple regression correlation," in which a weighted combination of scores on the "predictor" measures is used to create a predicted value on the variable of interest (the "criterion" measure) and then the linear correlation between individual predicted scores and actual criterion scores is computed.[5] The larger this overall correlation value (R), the

---

[5]The combination of predictor variables is usually linear, producing a prediction equation of the general form: $Y' = a + b_1X_1 + b_2X_2 + \cdots + b_iX_i$, where the constant, a, and b-weights, are assigned to maximize the fit with actual Y scores. The prediction equation can also include interactions between predictor variables by entering a new predictor variable, which is the multiplicative product of the relevant variables (see Aiken & West, 1991).

better the combined predictor factors "account for" the variation in the criterion measure. The degree of variation accounted for is indicated by R^2.

Because the weights assigned to each predictor in the multiple regression formula are calculated to maximize prediction for the specific sample data on which they are computed, generalizing the resulting equation to new data sets inevitably reduces the relationship between predicted and obtained criterion values. This is so because the analysis proceeds on the assumption that the sample data are free from error. As such, any measurement error specific to the sample on which the prediction weights are calculated affects these values. Because error is random, a new analysis (either repeating the study on the same sample or employing another group of respondents) would be subject to different sources of error, and the predictor weights could be expected to change accordingly. Therefore, R values should be reported with some correction for this expected "shrinkage" (see McNemar, 1969). The extent of shrinkage is affected by the size and composition of the original respondent sample and by the quality of the measures employed in the multiple correlation. Higher quality (i.e., more reliable) measures result in less shrinkage. Theoretically, with perfect measures, no shrinkage would occur.

Another useful solution to the "shrinkage" problem makes use of a "hold-out sample." In this approach, some portion of the respondent sample is purposely held out of the main analysis, in which the specific weight of each predictor variable is determined. These weights then are employed on the data of the *hold-out sample* in calculating a new multiple R. If the weights that were determined in the main analysis successfully replicate the R^2 in the group of hold-out respondents, confidence in the utility of the prediction formula is bolstered.

USES AND MISUSES OF CORRELATIONAL ANALYSIS

From a research orientation, the main problem with the evaluation of freely occurring variables is that they usually have natural covariates; that is, the occurrence of the variable of interest is confounded by the co-occurrence of other factors that naturally accompany it. To take a simple example of a naturally occurring variable, suppose that a researcher is interested in demonstrating a predicted relationship between weather and psychological mood. Specifically, the investigator has hypothesized a positive relationship between rain and depression: the more rain, the greater one's score on a depression inventory. However, even if the research effort confirms the existence of a positive correlation between the occurrence of rain and degree of depression, the investigator is a long way from identifying rain as the critical causal factor. Frequently co-occurring with rain are other weather conditions such as low barometric pressure, gray skies, and heavy cloud cover, any of which provide plausible alternative explanations for the occurrence of psychological depression. Only if these other factors could be held constant (i.e., if comparisons could be made between rainy days and nonrainy days in which air pressure and cloud conditions were the same) could rain be isolated as the determining factor. Unfortunately, nature does not ordinarily provide us with an adequate sampling of such comparable conditions, so until researchers can bring the occurrence of rain under experimental control, they must be aware of the limitations on the interpretation of their correlational data.

The natural covariates that confound interpretation of the results of correlational research may occur in any of three forms:

The Hidden Third Factor. An observed relationship between any two variables may be affected by a third source of variation that is accidentally or causally linked with one of the

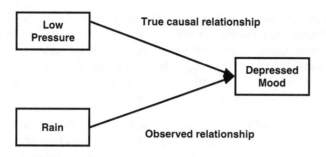

FIG. 8.5a.   Illustration of the effect of a hidden third factor.

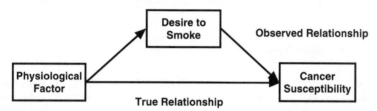

FIG. 8.5b.   The "third cause" explanation of the smoking-cancer relationship.

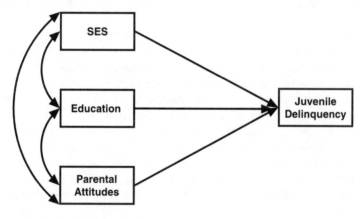

FIG. 8.5c.   Example of multidimensional causation.

observed variables. The rain–depression illustration previously discussed is an example of this potential confound in which the natural link between rain and low barometric pressure may confuse our interpretation of the true nature of the causal relationship. For instance, the actual relationships may be as depicted in Fig. 8.5a.

In other cases, the third factor may be a causal variable that accounts for the common variation in both observed variables. Such a "third cause," in the form of some unknown physiological factor, has been proposed as an alternative explanation for the obtained relationship between cigarette smoking and lung cancer, as depicted in Fig. 8.5b. As long as studies of the relationship between smoking and disease are limited to the observation of people who are already (through self-selection) smokers or nonsmokers, such third-factor explanations can never be completely eliminated (although the convergence of results from multiple sources of data, including experiments on lower animals, have made these alternative hypotheses highly implausible).

Multidimensional Causation.   Determining the nature and strength of the relationship between two variables is particularly difficult if the observed independent variable is only one of several interrelated factors that contribute to variation in the dependent variable, as in the situation depicted in Fig. 8.5c. In such cases, the existence of a directional relationship is not likely to be inappropriately perceived, but the relative contributions of a particular source of variation may be misjudged.

Confounding of the Independent and Dependent Variables.   Determining the nature of the relationship between two variables also is difficult if the effect of one of the variables cannot be extricated from that of the other. Such, for example, is the problem that confronts the researcher interested in whether high prestige schools produce exceptionally good scholars, as opposed to the alternative possibility that good scholars seek out high prestige schools.

Prediction versus Hypothesis-testing

Because many of the covariates that confound naturally occurring phenomena cannot be extricated, there has been a temptation among behavioral scientists to substitute correlational analyses for experimental control in attempts to sort out the factors that contribute to variation in variables of interest. Many of these attempts reflect an inadequate understanding of the context of testing and measurement within which most of our commonly used correlational techniques were developed.

Measurement theorists are very clear that there is a distinction between a measuring instrument and the underlying conceptual variable it is designed to represent, and we have emphasized this position in our earlier discussion of validity (chap. 3). Any single measurement is only a partial and inadequate reflection of individual variation on the dimension or construct of interest. As discussed earlier, the score obtained on any given measurement is made up of both "true score" and "error" components, the true score representing reliable, relatively stable characteristics of the individual or event being measured, and error representing random, temporary factors that affect a response only at a particular point in time. An assessment of the degree of error contributions to scores is essential to any understanding of what is being measured, but the reliable true score component of any measure may also contribute to misinterpretation of test results.

Sometimes a measure may tap some dimension completely different from the one intended, but more subtle errors arise from multiple determinants of true scores that include the relevant variable of interest. Other contributing factors could be such things as reliable tendencies to avoid extreme responses, or other such methods factors, as discussed in chapter 3.

Knowledge of the various sources of true score and error components of any measuring instrument is relatively unimportant if one is interested only in the development of prediction equations. If scores on one measure are consistently related to scores on another measure, then the former can be used to predict the latter, no matter what the underlying source of covariation may be. Thus, for instance, scores on a high school achievement test may adequately predict academic performance in a college setting without indicating whether the source of common variation is basic intelligence, motivation, study habits, parental income, or ability to cheat on tests! Prediction, however, is not equivalent to explanation. Yet many correlational techniques that are appropriate to the evaluation of measures as predictors have also been used to test the validity of theoretical concepts.

If, as we hold, valid explanation requires a comprehensive theoretical understanding of the relationships among variables, then the failing to distinguish between prediction and explanation is a dangerous practice.

One common example of the misuse of prediction correlations is the use of partial correlations to statistically eliminate the effects of natural covariates of a variable of interest. The basic partial correlational methodology involves calculating the intercorrelations among two predictor variables (which are themselves interrelated) and a criterion variable. The purpose of the partial correlational method is to determine whether there is any common variance between the criterion and one of the predictor variables after the source of variation common to the second predictor has been removed from both measures.

To return to our weather research illustration, partialling would involve obtaining measures of the correlation between rain and barometric pressure, between rain and depression, and between barometric pressure and depression. Then the rain–depression relationship would be subjected to partial correlation analysis in order to determine whether there was any degree of relationship "left over" after the common variation with air pressure had been accounted for.

Within the context of prediction analysis, in which the partial correlation was developed, there is no problem in interpreting the value of a partial r. The partial correlation between predictor and criterion measure indicates the contribution of that predictor to an improvement in the accuracy of prediction over what it would be if only the other (partialled out) predictor were to be used. If the partial $r = 1.00$, there is no point in using both predictors because the second adds nothing to validity of prediction. Thus, to return to our example, if the correlation between rain and depression, with barometric pressure "partialled out," were .00, this result would indicate that noting the presence or absence of rain would not improve the simple correlation between depression and barometric pressure. However, a partial r value significantly greater than .00 indicates that the combination of both predictors results in a better prediction of the criterion than if either predictor were used alone.

For purposes of hypothesis testing, the mere existence of a significant partial correlation can be easily misinterpreted because such a result does not indicate how, or why, the improvement in prediction occurs. The partial value may indicate that the two variables under consideration share some theoretical determinant that is not shared by the other, partialled-out variable. On the other hand, it may indicate that the two predictors are both measures of the same common underlying construct, but they do not share the same sources of error variation. Accepting the former interpretation is equivalent to assuming that the partialled-out variable has been measured without error or any other unique sources of variation—an assumption that may hold with respect to the measurement of rainfall and air pressure, but certainly not for the kinds of conceptual variables common in social science research! Periodic warnings have appeared in the literature against the use of partial correlations to test underlying conceptual variables without regard to the contribution of error variation to the size of the partial correlation (e.g., Brewer, Campbell, & Crano, 1970; Sechrest, 1963; Stouffer, 1936), but the practice continues nonetheless.

CAUSAL MODELS

Fortunately, in recent years more sophisticated multivariate-analytic approaches have become available to assist investigators evaluate the total pattern of intercorrelations among multiple measures in a theory-testing framework. Bentler's (1995) EQS and Jöreskog and Sörbom's (1993) LISREL are two popular programs used in the statistical analysis of structural models. Variously termed *path analysis, structural equation modeling, structural modeling, covariance structure modeling*, and so on, the common goal of all such techniques is to allow evaluation of the plausibility of a set of hypothesized relationships that exist among a set of constructs and measured variables (scales, measures, operationalizations). We make a distinction between models on the basis of the kinds of variables used. If all measures are treated as the construct, the model is called a path analysis. This is appropriate for variables that can be measured directly (e.g., student attendance, gender, etc.). Often, however, the variables of interest cannot be measured directly. In that case, we use multiple indicators to capture the construct of interest, which is called a *latent variable*. So, for example, if "parental support" is included as part of a model, we might use several indicators to capture this variable (e.g., parents' attendance at school meetings, their ratings of their child, the child's homework completion rate, school grades, etc.). Models making use of latent variables are called structural equation models, or covariance structure models. Such models are relatively commonplace in those social sciences in which experimental manipulation is difficult (e.g., political science, economics, sociology) and they are becoming more widely used in psychology as well (see Hoyle, 1995; Schumacker & Lomax, 1996). Our earlier remarks on multiple and partial correlation will prove useful in our discussion of causal models, as these basic correlational techniques are fundamental in the development of such models.

Although there are different varieties of path or structural equation models, all require the researcher to postulate a set of relations that exist among a set of variables, in other words, to propose a theory of relationships among variables. The usual goal of most such models is to specify a *causal* relationship, or a set of causal relationships, that link theory-relevant variables. These models typically are closed systems. That is, they explicitly acknowledge that the causal factors may be only a small sample of the possible causal factors that affect a particular variable; they are not meant to describe the total universe of causes. However, it is important that relations among all variables be specified in advance if the model is to be used as a test of a theory.

A general example will help introduce structural models. Suppose a researcher believes that Constructs A and B operate as causes (though perhaps only two of many possible causes) of Construct C. A and B are not theorized as being causally related, though they may be associated (or correlated). Such a model could be represented as in Fig. 8.6a.

To test this set of hypotheses, the researcher must develop a *measurement* model, which is a specification of the various measures that operationalize the underlying latent variables (or constructs), and that indicates the relationships (causal and otherwise) between and among the components of the model. As shown in Fig. 8.6b, the graphic specification of the measurement model is considerably more complex than that of the structural model, because the researcher has used more than one measure to specify each latent variable (a very good practice), and each measure is associated with its own unique error component. These error components for latent variables are called *disturbances*.

Mediation.   As shown in Fig. 8.6b, each construct (Variable A, B, C) is estimated by three independent measures (a1, a2, a3, b1, etc.). Each of these measures is prone to error, as indicated by the error components (e1a, e2a, e3a, etc.). The theory as presented is quite simple. Two variables $(A \& B)$, which are associated but not causally linked, are postulated to operate as direct causes of some other variable (C). This direct causal model does not exhaust the possibilities, however. In most discussions of path analysis or structural equation modeling, a distinction is made between direct and indirect

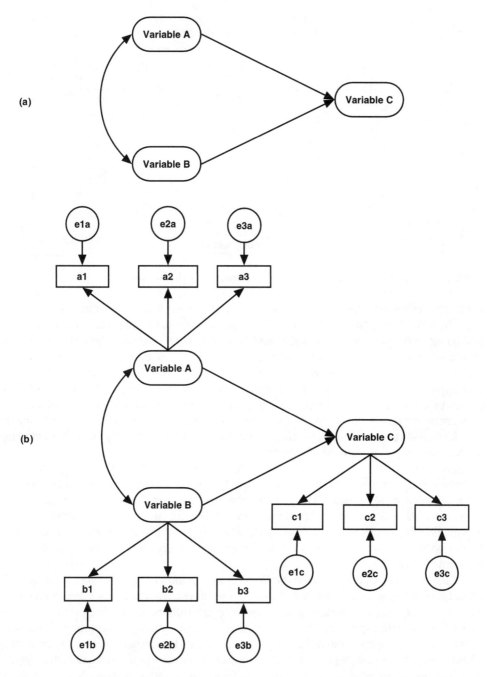

FIG. 8.6. Examples of structural equation model (a) and its associated measurement model (b).

effects. With direct effects, a change in one variable is directly reflected by a subsequent change in another, as in the example of Fig. 8.6. Conversely, some variables are thought to influence others only indirectly; that is, their influence on a variable is mediated by another variable (or set of variables). An example from the literature will help illustrate this distinction. In his book *The Attraction Paradigm*, Donn Byrne argued that attitude

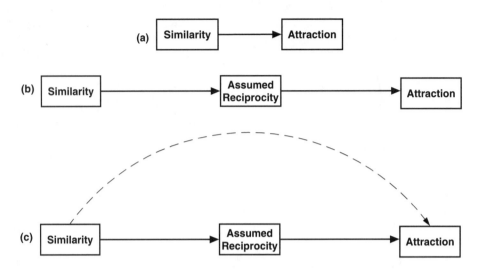

FIG. 8.7. Hypothesized relationships between attitude similarity and attraction.

similarity causes attraction; that is, we tend to like those who have attitudes similar to
ours. To demonstrate this, Byrne (1971) measured participants' attitudes on a number of
issues and then systematically manipulated the extent to which these attitudes were shown
to be consistent with those of a hypothetical other. When asked whether they thought that
they would like to be friends with, and work with, this other person, participants in the
high apparent similarity condition were much more likely to report positive responses than
those in the low similarity groups. This finding supported Byrne's hypothesis of a direct
effect between similarity and attraction (diagrammatically, this prediction is illustrated in
Fig. 8.7a). Although somewhat simpler than the structural model of Fig. 8.6a, both models
propose direct effects with no mediation.

Later research (Condon & Crano, 1988; Napolitan & Goethals, 1979) suggested that
the relationship demonstrated by Byrne was, in fact, mediated by a third variable, namely,
the assumption of reciprocity. This explanation was based on the idea that we like others
who are similar to us because we assume they will like us. In other words, although there
is a relationship between similarity and attraction, it is not direct, but rather is mediated
by the assumption of reciprocated liking. Diagrammatically, this alternative explanation
is summarized in Fig. 8.7b.

To test these competing hypotheses, Condon and Crano (1988) measured participants'
attitudes on several issues and then showed these same participants the completed questionnaire of another (purported) participant. The information on this second instrument
was designed so that apparent similarity could be systematically varied among the participants. Some participants found the "other" person agreed with them on every issue, some
found almost no common ground, and some were between these extremes. Participants
then were asked to judge (a) how similar they were to the other person, (b) the extent to
which the other person liked them (assumed reciprocity), and (c) how much they thought
they would like the other person (attraction).

The results of correlational analyses supported both the direct and the mediational
hypotheses. Although the simple correlation between similarity and attraction was statistically significant ($r = .64$), this result appeared to be mediated by the assumed reciprocity–
attraction relationship ($r = .81$). Indeed, when the influence of assumed reciprocity was
removed from the similarity–attraction relationship, the resulting partial correlation

($r = .18$) was substantially less than the original correlation (as indicated by the dashed line in Fig. 8.7c). Given this pattern of data, it is reasonable to observe that the mediational model is more plausible than the direct effect hypothesis. The mediational interpretation is not contradictory to the direct effect idea; rather, it enhances and elaborates it and thereby helps to refine our ideas about the nature of the relationship between similarity and attraction.

The logic of this comparison between causal models is the logic of path analysis, or structural equation modeling. Contrary to some claims, these approaches do not "prove" the existence of a causal relationship any more than a successful experiment "proves" a theory (Crano & Mendoza, 1987). Rather, as Reis (1982) observed, the confirmation of a hypothesized structural relations model lends confidence in its validity and, in some cases, helps to render implausible some alternative explanations. This is especially the case when two competing orientations are pitted against one another.

Although this example is a relatively simple application of causal modeling, with a slight enhancement, it can be used to introduce some concepts and principles that are used frequently in the path analysis literature and thereby help readers follow research using these techniques. First, however, we expand our theoretical model somewhat. Suppose that on the basis of considerable theory and research, we think that there are two very important causes of people's attraction to others, namely, attitudinal similarity (as in the example presented earlier) and physical beauty.

Considerable research, for example, demonstrates that we are more attracted to good-looking people than to those who are not (Dion, 1980; Dion, Berscheid, & Walster, 1972; Dion & Dion, 1995). The effects of both variables, however, are mediated by other factors. Similarity is thought to be mediated though reciprocated liking, and beauty is hypothesized to be mediated through social competence, which in turn is mediated through reciprocated liking. The rationale for these latter expectations is relatively simple: Good-looking children are more pleasant to interact with than unattractive children (Berry & McArthur, 1985, 1986) and, as a consequence, receive more attention from parents and other adults. As a result of such socialization experiences, these children learn more social graces and become more socially competent than unattractive children, who usually do not receive such attention. We are also more likely to assume that a socially competent person likes us because he or she is less likely to embarrass us, to criticize us too harshly in front of others, and so on. As a result of this chain of events, we can predict that physical attractiveness (beauty) causes attraction, but this effect is mediated through intermediate effects involving social competence and assumed reciprocity of liking.

Although the verbal description of this theory of attraction is somewhat complicated, a model depicting all of the relationships that we have discussed can be presented very economically, as is demonstrated in the path diagram of Fig. 8.8, to which we refer in the following discussion.

Types of Variables. In interpreting this model, it is important to distinguish between *exogenous* and *endogenous* variables. An exogenous variable is one for which no cause is postulated within the model. Attitude similarity in Fig. 8.8 is one such variable (as is beauty). This is not meant to imply that nothing causes attitude similarity between people, but rather that these causes, whatever they may be, are outside of the boundaries of our theoretical system. An endogenous variable is one that, at least in part, is affected by a variable or variables that are part of the theoretical model we have developed. In our illustration, social competence, assumed reciprocity, and attraction are examples of endogenous variables: Each is the effect of some causal variable in the model.

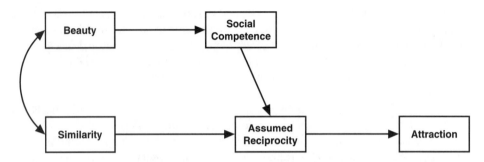

FIG. 8.8.   Examples of a path diagram linking physical beauty, attitude similarity, and attraction through the mediators of social competence and assumed reciprocity.

Types of Relationships.   Note that two different types of arrows connect the variables of Fig. 8.8. Most common in this diagram are the single-headed arrows, as, for example, those linking social competence with assumed reciprocity, and assumed reciprocity with attraction. Connections of this type imply causal hypotheses; thus, social competence is hypothesized to be a cause of assumed reciprocity (though perhaps only one of many), which in turn is thought to be a cause of attraction. But notice the connection in Fig. 8.8 between beauty and similarity. Here, a double-headed arrow connects the variables. Relationships indicated by connections of this type indicate that a causal relationship has not been hypothesized between the variables; the variables might be correlated, but the relationship is not theorized as causal. As noted, both beauty and similarity are exogenous, and hence, their causes are beyond the predictive boundaries of our theory. A third type of relationship also is possible, namely, no relationship. In these instances, no arrow connects the variables. In Fig. 8.8, no direct relationship is predicted between beauty and assumed reciprocity, and thus, no arrow connects these two variables.

Types of Models.   In addition to the types of arrows that connect the variables in a structural equation model, the direction of the arrows also is important in determining the complexity of the analyses that must be employed in solving the equations represented by the causal paths. Notice that the directional flow of the arrows in Fig. 8.8 is consistently from left to right and, furthermore, that no paths ever return to a variable that has already been involved in a relationship. Models of this type are called recursive, and are amenable to relatively straightforward statistical analysis.

Nonrecursive models, on the other hand, allow for causal paths to "backtrack." In models of this type, a variable can be both a cause and an effect of another. If the model of Fig. 8.9 allowed for the possibility that social competence was both a cause and an effect of assumed reciprocity, the diagram of Fig. 8.9 would indicate this. Now the model becomes nonrecursive, given the possibility of reciprocal causation. Models of this type are more difficult to analyze, and necessitate postulating numerous assumptions before they can be assessed statistically (see Kenny, 1979). At least for the beginning path analyst, nonrecursive models probably should be avoided.

Identification.   One of the central difficulties of nonrecursive models concerns the problem of underidentification. Identification is a term that refers to the relative number of unknowns in a set of equations. As you might recall from introductory algebra, it is impossible to solve an equation if it contains more unknown quantities than known quantities. This same problem afflicts structural equation models. If we have more unknowns

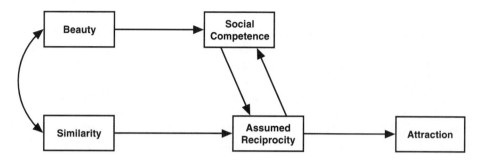

FIG. 8.9.   Example of a nonrecursive path diagram.

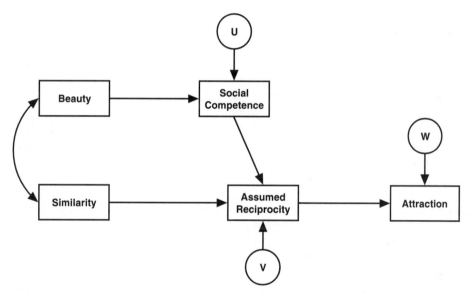

FIG. 8.10.   Path diagram with uncorrelated disturbance terms.

(i.e., paths) than knowns (correlations between measures), the solution of the set of structural equations that constitute the model becomes impossible.[6] In situations in which we have more correlations (knowns) than paths (unknowns), the model is overidentified. This generally is a desirable circumstance because it allows for greater certainty in the estimation of causal paths and also permits us to test models by determining whether two different estimates are approximately equal. A final possibility is a model that is "just identified"; that is, the model has exactly the same number of known as unknown quantities. In most such circumstances, the set of equations that make up the model generally can be solved to provide estimates of the hypothesized causal paths.

Disturbances.   A final technical point that deserves mention in this discussion of path models concerns the concept of disturbances. To appreciate this idea, it is useful to refer to Fig. 8.10, which bears a strong resemblance to an earlier illustration, with a

---

[6]To determine the number of "knowns," use the following formula: $K = n(n - 1)/2$, where K = number of knowns, and n = number of measured variables. If the number of paths in our model exceeds this number, the model is not solvable.

few additional variables (U, V, and W) included. These additions are called *disturbance terms*. Generally, when designing a causal model, we recognize the fact that we have not defined or measured all of the possible causes of our endogenous variables. In Fig. 8.9, for example, we hypothesized that beauty is a cause of social competence, but we also realize that it probably is not the only cause. The disturbance term "U" indicates our recognition of this fact. This term is analogous to an "error term" in an analysis of variance. It reflects all of the unmeasured, unspecified causal determinants of an endogenous latent variable, in this case, all of the causal determinants of social competence in addition to beauty. The terms V and W represent the disturbance terms of assumed reciprocity and attraction, respectively.

Disturbance terms are conceptualized as exogenous variables; that is, their causes are beyond our theoretical model. They are assumed to be independent of each other and of any prior causal variables in the model. This assumption of independence between disturbance terms is necessary to maintain a just-identified or overidentified model. Of course, this assumption, which greatly simplifies (indeed, in some cases, makes possible) the calculations of causal paths, should not be made if it is logically or theoretically untenable.

Although many new terms were introduced in this discussion of structural equation models, much of this material bears a strong relationship to terms and concepts that already have been considered at length in this book. In fact, the ideas that underlie structural equation (causal) modeling are the same as those that lie at the heart of the experimental method. In both approaches, we begin with a theory or a set of hypotheses regarding the relationships among a set of variables. These relationships are clearly stated. For many, a major strength of the structural modeling approach is that it forces us to explicitly detail the relationships that we think exist among our variables. Having specified our model, we collect data that bear on the hypothesized relationships. In structural analysis, we must attend to a number of technical issues regarding the identifiability of the model, the relationships between disturbance terms and endogenous variables (and the relationships among disturbance terms), the recursivity of the model, and so on, but all of these issues are secondary to the theoretical specification of the model itself. If our theory is reasonable, the set of structural equations that we obtain will make sense, and if our theory is pitted against another, the structural equation approach will enable us to choose between the more plausible of the two.

As was stated earlier, however, in no case will the structural modeling approach allow us to state with certainty that the model we have constructed provides the complete and true specification of the causal parameters of the variables of interest. One reason for this is that there are a great many possible path models that can be constructed from any given set of variables; as the number of variables in the model becomes large, the number of possible structural models becomes astronomical, and one (or many) of these alternatives might explain the set of relationships much more compelling than the model that was originally developed. However, it would be difficult to make an assessment of this sort even if all possible models were specified, given the current lack of statistical tools with which to compare the "fit" of data to alternative models. Yet another reason for caution in interpreting causal models is implicit in our reference to disturbance terms. Generally, the paths between these terms and the endogenous variables are stronger than are those involving our predicted causal (exogenous–endogenous) relationships. In this case, our predicted model might be explaining only a miniscule portion of the possible variance associated with a given set of relationships. Such a result would be comparable to a multiple regression study in which our set of predictor variables was only weakly related to the criterion (i.e., with a relatively unsubstantial R^2). In this case, even if the result is statistically significant, it is obvious that the predictors we have chosen do not provide a very complete picture of the factors associated with the criterion.

As in the experimental method, a path model can never be proven correct, or valid, no matter how plausible the obtained results. Rather, the approach helps us to render alternative explanations of causal relationships implausible. Just as in the experimental methods, a structural model gains credence by a process in which alternative explanations of the critical relationships are shown to be less plausible than the theory under examination. It is important to understand, however, that these techniques have to be reserved for research circumstances in which considerable information about the phenomenon of interest already exists. Unless used for hypothesis development, a possibility suggested by Crano and Mendoza (1987), the structural equation approach demands an explicit statement of predicted relations among variables (causal and otherwise) derived from some empirical or conceptual framework. This is a very different process from the analysis of correlations in exploratory research, in which the patterns of association among variables often are not predicted in advance, but rather observed after the data are collected. The misuse of inferential statistical analyses and tests on such post hoc observations is rampant in social science research where the principles underlying these analyses are apparently misunderstood.

SUGGESTED READINGS

Crano, W. D., & Mendoza, J. L. (1987). Maternal factors that influence children's positive behavior: Demonstration of a structural equation analysis of selected data from the Berkeley Growth Study. *Child Development, 58*, 38–48.

John, O. P., & Benet-Martínez, V. (2000). Measurement: Reliability, construct validation, and scale construction. In H. Reis & C. M. Judd (Eds.), *Handbook of research methods in social and personality psychology* (pp. 339–369). Cambridge, England: Cambridge University Press.

Schumacker, R. E., & Lomax, R. G. (1996). *A beginner's guide to structural equation modeling*. Hillsdale, NJ: Lawrence Erlbaum Associates.

9

QUASI-EXPERIMENTS AND EVALUATION RESEARCH

The preceding chapters drew a clear distinction between research classified as *experimental* and research that is *correlational*. In correlational research, the investigator's role is that of an observer. All variables of interest are permitted to vary freely in their natural context. In a real sense, all the variables in correlational studies are dependent variables. The researcher's job in these research contexts is to assess this variation and to tease out the patterns and interrelationships that exist among the critical measures. On the other hand, in experiments, the researcher actively intervenes in the normal pattern of covariation, systematically controlling variation in the independent variable (or variables) to assess its causal impact. For purposes of internally valid cause–effect analysis, controlled manipulation of the causal variable and random assignment of subjects to the manipulated conditions are the necessary hallmarks of true experiments.

In many research contexts, the distinction between experimental and correlational studies may not be all that clear-cut. For example, in our discussion of field experiments, we mentioned studies in which the researcher *selects* rather than creates the levels of the independent variable, or cases in which "random" assignment occurs naturally rather than by experimental intervention.[1] Such studies preserve the logic of experimental design but lack the degree of experimenter control that characterizes "pure" experiments. By the same token, some correlational studies are conducted in the context of interventions into a given social situation (e.g., studies that investigate the reactions of an established group to the introduction of a new member), thus mixing aspects of experimental and correlational design. The distinction, then, between experimental and correlational research should be seen as a continuum rather than a strict dichotomy.

Somewhere between true experiments and pure correlational research studies are those research situations in which some systematic intervention in a social setting has been made for the purpose of assessing its causal effects, but the exposure of participants to this

---

[1]We use the term *random* advisedly here because unless the researcher has complete control over the selection or assignment of research units, the process is not truly random.

treatment variable is not randomly determined. This could occur because the intervention involves some pervasive treatment affecting all participants in the social setting at once; or it could be that some participants are exposed to the treatment while others are not, but who is or is not exposed is determined by self-selection, administrative decision making, or some other nonrandom assignment process. These situations bear some resemblance to the basic treatment-control experimental design, in that a treatment is introduced at a specifiable point in time or space. Thus, outcomes in the presence of the treatment variable can be compared with outcomes occurring in its absence (across times or persons). But as a research design, the structure of the situation lacks a critical element necessary for internal validity. In the absence of random assignment, it is much more difficult to separate effects caused by the introduction of the treatment from effects caused by prior group differences, historical events, and the like.

EVALUATION RESEARCH

One situation in which interventions into a social system can be studied is on the occasion of the introduction of a new social program or government policy designed to alleviate a particular social problem or condition. Such interventions may range from the introduction of new forms of distribution of tax revenues at the national level (e.g., the New Jersey guaranteed income experiment), to new procedures in the criminal justice system at the state or local level (e.g., the effects of the introduction of "three-strikes" laws), to the introduction of new teaching methods at the classroom level (e.g., using Logo to teach geometry). Most of the time, determining the effectiveness of such programs or policy changes is largely a political process, derived from the claims of program managers, beneficiaries, and interested community members. In some cases, however, attempts are made to assess the effects of such interventions more systematically and scientifically with structured empirical observations and quantitative measures of outcomes to program participants. This extension of social science methodology to the assessment of effects of social programs is generally known as *evaluation research*. In recent years, evaluation research has developed into a major field of applied social science (cf. Campbell, 1969c; Scriven, 1993; Struening & Brewer, 1983). Actually, assessment of program effects is only one of several ways in which empirical research can and has entered into the formation and evaluation of social policy. Among the various functions that quantitative research may serve in the policymaking process, the following are probably most important and widely recognized.

Needs Assessment

At early stages of policy formation there is a need for accurate information about the extent and distribution of a given social problem. At this point personal testimony and experience can be supplemented with quantitative data derived from survey or observational studies. Since 1975, for example, the federal government has supported the *Monitoring the Future* project, a longitudinal study of the attitudes and actions of U.S. high school and college students and young adults, focusing particularly on their opinions toward, and use of, legal and illegal drugs. The survey supplies a useful picture of trends in drug usage among young persons. *Monitoring the Future* was not designed to assess needs in the classic sense, but the information it supplies can be used to infer general trends that may signal the need for intervention. Indeed, data from the project helped motivate the federal government to mount a massive media program to counteract rising adolescent drug abuse.[2] Needs assessment research is essentially descriptive, and its quality depends primarily on the adequacy of measures and sampling techniques employed. In the case of the Monitoring the Future and the National Household Surveys, the research is performed by a highly competent surveying organization; the results produced are trustworthy.

Program Development

Pilot studies of programs at their initial conceptualization stage provide a research opportunity for testing program concepts in controlled experiments on a small scale. The purpose of evaluation research at this stage is not to assess the final impact of the program, but to provide feedback to program designers that can lead to changes or alterations in program development. Research conducted in the service of program design is often referred to as *formative evaluation* (Scriven, 1967).

Feasibility Studies and Efficacy Research

Once a social program or intervention has been designed, the next question is whether or how the program can be implemented on a large scale through existing agencies or institutions. Feasibility studies are conducted on a small scale to determine whether the program as planned can be delivered within various organizational contexts. The purpose of such small-scale field testing is to decide whether or not the program components can be implemented as intended on a more wide-scale basis, and if so, whether the services reach the targeted population. The type of data collected for this kind of study include administrative records and books, direct observation of service delivery, and interviews with service recipients to ensure that the treatment was delivered as planned.

Program efficacy studies are also conducted on a small scale to determine whether the expected effects from the planned intervention occur as planned (see Donaldson, in press). In efficacy research, the treatment is very carefully implemented and monitored on a highly constricted respondent population. The idea is to ensure that the treatment works as planned. To ensure the best possible outcome, the treatment is delivered under the most ideal conditions possible. Obviously, if the treatment does not operate as planned, there is no sense in attempting to deliver it to a larger population of recipients, in conditions that might work to diminish its effect. The efficacy study presents the "best of all possible worlds," in that it is much more under the tight control of program developers than the actual intervention will (or can) be. As such, it provides the best chance for treatment effectiveness. Failures at the program efficacy stage can spell disaster for the larger intervention.

Program Effectiveness Evaluation

Variously called *summative evaluation, impact evaluation*, or *outcome evaluation*, research to assess whether a social program has had an effect on the social problem it was designed to alleviate is perhaps the primary form of evaluation research. Not all evaluation tasks call for effectiveness research, however, and it is important to distinguish this function from the others. The effectiveness question is inevitably one of causal hypothesis-testing

---

[2]The *National Household Survey on Drug Abuse*, which is also supported by the federal government, has a similar substantive focus, but is concerned with older as well as younger respondents.

and therefore requires that a number of prior conditions be met that make the program potentially subject to such rigorous evaluation. Among the requisite conditions for effectiveness evaluation are (a) that the goals or objectives of the program be sufficiently specified to allow for definable outcomes, (b) that the program be well enough defined to determine whether it is present or absent in a given situation or time, and (c) that some basis for observing or estimating the state of outcomes in the absence of the program be available for comparison to program outcomes. All of these conditions are not easily met, and many of the problems associated with program evaluation can be traced to instances in which evaluators or policymakers have attempted to do effectiveness assessments in settings where feasibility, efficacy, or developmental evaluation efforts would have been more appropriate.

Cost–Benefit Analysis

Beyond determining whether a program has any effect at all, analysis of program benefits relative to program costs requires assessment of the *degree* of program effect along some interval scale. In other words, the research must determine how much change in the outcomes of interest can be attributed to the program. Relatively few full-fledged cost–benefit evaluations have been done of social programs, partly because of the difficulties of obtaining valid estimates of program effect sizes, and partly because of the absence of a common yardstick for measuring both costs and benefits in the social domain. For example, although we can calculate the costs involved in developing and airing an anti-tobacco ad, we cannot compute the costs of the potential annoyance or anxiety associated with its implementation or the benefit of lessened morbidity and mortality associated with people's acceptance of its central message. Nonetheless, some research models are available for comparing the size of effects associated with alternative programs that share common goals but different dollar costs (see Bickman & Rog, 1998; Levin, 1983; Nas, 1996; Thompson, 1980).

SPECIAL CHARACTERISTICS OF EVALUATION RESEARCH

As a part of the research enterprise, program effectiveness evaluation shares much of the logic and purpose associated with any other hypothesis-testing experimental research. However, the conduct of evaluation research does have some special contextual and functional characteristics that make it a somewhat different form of social research.

Political Context

The primary distinguishing characteristic of evaluation research is its explicitly political character. All social research may have direct or indirect political implications to some extent, but the essence of evaluation research is political decision making. The decision whether to do a systematic evaluation, how it is to be conducted, and how the results are to be used, are all made in the political arena. Because almost all social programs are controversial to some extent, with advocates and detractors, evaluation studies inevitably become part of the controversy. These contextual factors frequently have an impact on the nature and quality of research design that is possible in the setting. Randomization, for instance, which is a relatively simple matter in the laboratory context, can be a political hot potato when special interests are at stake. For example, imagine attempting to implement random assignment to either a highly sought-after preschool program or a control condition.

Parents who want their children to take part in the program are not likely to accept the argument that a causal analysis of the treatment requires that their child be passed over.

Separation of Roles

In most experimental research, the investigator who plans the study and designs the outcome measures also determines how the independent variable is to be operationalized. However, in most evaluation research studies, the individuals responsible for research design and measurement are not the same as those responsible for design, delivery, and implementation of the treatment (program). Hence most evaluation projects are characterized by a split between "program people" and "research people," with occasional conflicts of interest and purpose. At worst, program personnel may feel threatened and defensive about the presence of an evaluation research component (after all, "evaluation" is an emotionally loaded term) and may deliberately undermine research efforts wherever possible. At best, the program implementers and research team feel they are part of a common effort but will inevitably face differences in priorities associated with their different functions. One common source of conflict between program and research staff revolves around the desirability of making changes in the program or program delivery during the course of the research. Ideally, for experimental purposes, the treatment variable should remain constant throughout the study, but program personnel are subject to continual pressure to alter or improve aspects of the treatment or policy in response to new information (perhaps from the research results themselves). Usually some compromise between program rigidity and program flexibility is required in these cases.

Scriven (1997) made a further distinction between evaluator and evaluation consultant. The evaluator's role is to judge the value of a program, whereas the evaluation consultant's role is to evaluate but not generally to make judgments of merit or to advocate for one position over another. Scriven held that the evaluator should maintain some degree of independence from the project, if possible, so that a less biased judgment can be made and so that this judgment can be used to support one position over another.

Confusion Between Process and Outcome

Another source of difference between program personnel and research staff is their relative concern with process versus outcome. Program implementers tend to want to know how their program is doing (e.g., is it reaching the intended population, are clients happy with the services received, etc.), whereas researchers want to know what effect the program is having (i.e., are the clients different or better off when they have received the services). Of course, it is very unlikely that a program will have an impact on outcomes of ultimate interest unless the process of program implementation has been successful, and a good evaluation study will include assessments of many of these intervening factors. However, it is important, but not always easy, to maintain a distinction between these two levels of program effects.

QUASI-EXPERIMENTAL RESEARCH DESIGN

Ideally an evaluation research study would employ a true experimental design including random assignment of participants to treatment versus nontreatment conditions, or to different levels of the treatment program. Randomization is possible in many field settings, and good examples of the use of randomized experiments for program evaluation are available in all areas of social policy (see Boruch, McSweeney, & Sonderstrom, 1978), including a large-scale experiment on the implementation of a "negative income tax" program (Kershaw & Fair, 1976), a 16-city study of the effects of innovative electric rate structures on energy conservation (Crano & Messé, 1985), and a study of an anti-HIV intervention program in Maryland, Georgia, and New Jersey (O'Leary et al., 1998). In some situations, good arguments can be made for the use of random assignment through lottery as a method of allocating a scarce resource or service in the interests of fairness (see Brickman, Folger, Goode, & Schul, 1981; Wortman & Rabinowitz, 1979).

In many cases, such random assignment is not feasible for practical or political reasons. Sometimes it is impossible to control who will make use of available services or programs (who will or will not choose to watch a public television program or to attend an open clinic, etc.). At other times, programs can be delivered selectively, but the selection decision is outside the researcher's control and based on nonrandom factors such as perceived need, merit, or opportunity. Under these circumstances, the evaluation researcher will look to various quasi-experimental design alternatives in an effort to sort out treatment effects from other sources of change. Quasi-experimental designs maintain many of the features of true experiments but do not have the advantages conferred by random assignment. The absence of random assignment is a defining feature of *quasi-experiments*, and requires the researcher to seek factors that help offset the problems that arise because of it (see Campbell & Stanley, 1963; Cook & Campbell, 1979). The remainder of this chapter is concerned with various quasi-experimental designs and the issues that are associated with their use in social research.

Regression Artifacts and Assessment of Change

Because new social programs are introduced into ongoing social systems for the purpose of altering or improving some aspect of that system, the ultimate question for evaluation research is whether or not the system or the persons in it have changed as a result of the program. To understand how the nature of research design affects our ability to assess change meaningfully, we must first consider *statistical regression* as a potential artifact in the measurement of change. The concept of regression artifacts was briefly introduced in chapter 2 as a potential threat to the internal validity of a research study. We elaborate more fully here just how regression effects can operate to undermine the validity of cause–effect interpretations.

A brief history of the origin of the term *regression* provides some insight into the nature of this effect. The term was first used by Francis Galton (1885) in a paper entitled "Regression towards mediocrity in hereditary stature," in which he reported the results of his study of the relationship between the average height of parents and their adult offspring. One reported finding of this study was that the children of very tall parents were, on the average, not quite as tall as their parents, whereas the children of very short parents were, on the average, not quite as short. In general, the heights of offspring of extreme individuals were closer to the overall population average than their parents were.

The trend observed by Galton is often referred to as the "regression fallacy" because it is frequently misinterpreted as indicating a long-term tendency toward mediocrity. The implication is that across generations, variation in height becomes smaller and smaller as the concentration of cases around the mean height becomes greater. In actuality, the variation does not necessarily change from generation to generation because even though the offspring of extreme parents tend to be closer to the mean than their parents were, the offspring of more average parents are equally likely to vary away from the mean, closer to the two extremes. The impression of a movement toward the mean is an artifact of the initial selection of extreme cases.

The appearance of regression toward the mean is an inevitable consequence of comparing pairs of scores on imperfectly related measures. Whenever the correlation between two measures (like parental height and offspring height) is less than 1.00, there will be some deviation between scores on the first variable and corresponding scores on the second. If the first measures are selected for their extremity (i.e., to represent the highest or lowest values in the distribution), there is bound to be a bias in the direction that these variations in the second measure must take. In other words, for the tallest parents in a population, differences between their heights and those of their children will usually be such that the children are somewhat shorter, simply because there isn't much room for variation in the other direction. Similarly, deviations from the heights of extremely short parents most often will be in the direction of increasing height because of the same selection bias.

It is important to distinguish between research findings that result from artifacts and those that reflect real effects. An artifact is an artificial finding, or "pseudo-effect," that results inevitably from the nature of the relationship between measuring instruments or from the method of data collection employed in an investigation. In Galton's example, regression does not reflect some genetic defect on the part of extreme parents which results in mediocre offspring. Extremely tall parents generally produce tall children and extremely intelligent parents usually have highly intelligent children. However, the relationship between characteristics of parents and offspring is not perfect. Because of this, the selection of extreme cases among parents biases the direction of differences between parents and children in a way that has nothing to do with the laws of genetics. The artificiality of the regression effect can be seen more clearly when it is noted that it also works in reverse: Extremely tall children have parents who are, on the average, closer to the mean. Obviously, children's height could not have caused parents' height; this relationship is spurious.

Regression and Reliability. The regression artifact afflicts social research most frequently as a result of measurement unreliability, which is responsible for imperfect correlations between two testings on the same measure. Test reliability was referred to in previous chapters, but a detailed consideration is useful here to clarify the role of unreliability in the occurrence of regression effects.

The basic elements of the measurement theory model of test–retest reliability are presented in Table 9.1. The data in this table illustrate that each test score is assumed to be made up of two components: true score and error (see chap. 3). The true-score component represents stable characteristics of the individual that are tapped by the measuring instrument. We assume that the true score for any individual being measured does not change between one testing and another unless some basic change has occurred in the individual's underlying response pattern. Thus, in Table 9.1 (which illustrates test–retest relationships under no-change conditions), each of the 20 hypothetical individuals is represented by one true score that contributes to the obtained score on both testing occasions.

In contrast to the stability of true score variation, the error component of test scores represents all the temporary, chance factors that happen to influence test responses at a particular point in time. The most important assumption of testing theory is that these chance factors operate randomly. That is, some individuals' scores are artificially raised by these variables whereas others are lowered, so that across individuals the error effects cancel out.[3] This characteristic of error scores is illustrated in column 2 of Table 9.1, where the algebraic

---

[3]Table 3.1 in chapter 3 illustrates the effect on test scores of error factors that are biased rather than random.

TABLE 9.1
Illustration of Random Error and Test–Retest Reliability

True Score	Error at Test 1	Total Score at Test 1	Error at Test 2	Total Score at Test 2
95	−5	90	+1	96
93	+2	95	−3	90
92	−6	86	0	92
90	+8	98	−7	83
87	+1	88	+1	88
85	−5	80	+6	91
85	+5	90	+3	88
80	−3	77	+1	81
78	+6	84	−7	71
75	+9	84	+6	81
75	−7	68	+4	79
74	−5	69	+1	75
73	+6	79	−8	65
70	−2	68	−4	66
68	−3	65	−2	66
65	−4	61	+3	68
63	+3	66	+5	68
60	−2	58	+4	64
58	+5	63	−3	55
55	−3	52	−1	54
Sum = 1521	0	1521	0	1521
Mean = 76.50		76.05		76.05

sum of the 20 error scores (which represent the extent and direction of random influences on each test score) is equal to 0. The test score obtained by combining the true-score component of column 1 and the error score from column 2 for each individual is given in column 3. It represents the observed score, that is, the score an individual would receive on the measure. Because the various error scores cancel each other out, the sum and mean of the obtained test scores are the same as the corresponding values for the true scores. However, the pattern of obtained scores is different from that of the corresponding true scores because of the effects of random error, and the variance of the two score distributions also is different.

If error scores are truly random, then the factors that determine the direction and extent of error on one testing should *not* be the same in a second testing of the same individual. That is, for any individual, the error component of the score on a first testing should be completely unrelated to the error score on a second testing. Thus, in column 4 of Table 9.1, a completely new set of error scores is given. These scores represent the random influences on responses for each individual at the time of retesting. Although the algebraic sum of these error scores is equal to 0, as on the first testing, the pattern of errors across individuals is entirely different from that of the first testing. The sum of true score and error for the second testing results in the obtained score values for Test 2. These are recorded in the final column of Table 9.1.

The combined effect of unrelated error components introduces discrepancies in test results for the same individuals across different testings. For any individual, a test score obtained from a second measurement is expected to deviate somewhat from that person's score on the same instrument at the first testing. The extent of deviation in scores between testings is a function of the degree of test unreliability. The more unreliable the test, the greater the error, and as such, the greater will be the deviations in scores from one administration to another. The degree of *similarity* in patterns of scores across different testings is known as *test–retest reliability*. Because reliability involves the relationship between two sets of test scores, it is measured in terms of the linear correlation between testings (see chap. 8). That is, the reliability coefficient is the value of the Pearson product–moment correlation between the test results of a set of individuals at time 1 with the results for the *same individuals* on the *same test* at time 2. For the data in Table 9.1, the value of the reliability coefficient is equal to .82.

As mentioned in chapter 8, the squared value of the correlation coefficient measures the extent of common variation between two measurements. In the case of reliability coefficients, the correlation value itself represents the proportion of true-score variation in the measuring instrument, or the extent to which differences in obtained scores reflect differences in true-score values rather than chance error. The lower the reliability correlation, the greater the proportional effect of error (which is defined as $1-r$), and the more random extraneous factors influence the value of obtained test scores. For our hypothetical data, the value of r indicates that 82% of the obtained variation in test scores can be attributed to true score differences, whereas 18% is due to random fluctuation. Unreliability in tests is responsible for the regression phenomenon in test–retest research studies.

The regression artifact is most easily understood in the context of a simple pretest–posttest research design where no control group is used and where research participants are *selected for their extremity* on the basis of pretest results. For instance, suppose that the data in Table 9.1 represent the results of two testings on a standardized English reading exam. The data have been collected to determine the effect of a specialized Latin course on reading ability. The instructor is interested in whether any improvement in reading scores occurs after the course has been provided for the top 25% of the students. The pairs of scores in Table 9.2 (taken from Table 9.1) illustrate what would happen if the top students were selected on the basis of pretest scores.

The decrease in mean score depicted in Table 9.2 would occur even if the Latin course had absolutely no effect—even if the *true* scores did not change for any of the individuals measured. Because of the effects of test unreliability, the top five scores have "regressed toward the mean," giving the appearance of a decrease in performance. Any actual increase in true-score performance would be suppressed in such a design because of the counter-effect of regression.

Regression toward the mean can create an apparent, or pseudo-improvement, effect if scores are selected from the lower extremes of pretest values. For example, if a remedial

TABLE 9.2
Selection of Top 25% from Table 9.1

Top 5 Pretest Scores	Corresponding Posttest Scores
98	83
95	90
90	96
90	88
88	88
Mean = 92.2	Mean = 89.0

TABLE 9.3

Selection of Bottom 25% from Table 9.1

Top 5 Pretest Scores	Corresponding Posttest Scores
65	66
63	55
61	68
58	64
52	54
Mean = 59.8	Mean = 61.4

reading program is provided for the students who scored in the bottom 25% of the test distribution presented in Table 9.1, the effect of regression in the absence of any true effect would lead to the appearance of change, as depicted in Table 9.3. In this case, any actual improvement in true scores would be artificially enhanced by the direction of the regression effect.

In either case, the selection procedure has the consequence of biasing the direction of deviations between pretest and posttest results. This occurs because the selection of the top pretest scorers inevitably involves overrepresenting cases of positive error scores (e.g., in the case of the top five participants from Table 9.1, the obtained scores are based in part on positive errors, which sum to $+16$, whereas the one negative error score is only -5). On the second testing, when random error scores are unrelated to those of the first, both positive and negative error scores are *equally* likely to occur, thus producing a sum of obtained scores that is necessarily lower than the pretest sum, which was based on an overabundance of positive error components. Similarly, the selection of the lowest obtained scores on one test overrepresents *negative* error components. Thus, the obtained score sum will inevitably be increased on a second testing in which more positive errors occur just by the rules of chance. (Again, the effect may be clarified by observing that it would also occur in reverse. That is, the top five posttest scores are based on errors that overrepresent positive values and correspond to pretest scores with more balanced errors and an average closer to the mean.)

The size of the regression phenomenon in pretest–posttest comparisons is directly related to the degree of unreliability in the measuring instrument used. A perfectly reliable instrument ($r = 1.00$) would reflect only true-score variation, and thus produce no regression effects because there would be no discrepancies between scores on first and second testings (apart from true-score change). For all practical purposes, however, perfectly reliable measures of social or personological variables are impossible to attain. Although the refinement of most tests is aimed at achieving reliability values of .80 or better, the remaining error component could produce considerable regression between testings for scores selected because of their extremity.

Statistical Control of Regression Artifacts. One method of controlling for the effects of regression in pretest–posttest research designs involves statistically removing the expected regression effect in computing difference scores. This is accomplished by comparing each individual's actual posttest score with a "regressed" score, a predicted posttest score based on the expected deviation from his or her pretest score.[4] Across all respondents,

---

[4]Regressed scores are obtained by multiplying the pretest score, in standardized score form, by the value of the reliability coefficient (i.e., the test–retest correlation).

the average obtained posttest score should not differ from the average of the regressed scores if no true-score change has occurred. If a significant difference between predicted and obtained scores does appear, it indicates that some change has occurred above and beyond that expected on the basis of mere regression.

The major difficulty with the statistical adjustment of regression effects is that it requires an accurate assessment of test–retest reliability in the absence of any real change. Computed values of the correlation between pretest and posttest scores suffer from the same sampling fluctuation as any other statistic, and in addition, the appropriate time period necessary for true test–retest reliability assessment is difficult to determine. Testing must be distant enough in time to assure that the sources of error on the second testing (e.g., mood, fatigue, misinterpretation of questions, guessing behavior) are completely different, for each respondent, from those of the first testing. The test–retest time period also should be appropriate to provide a base estimate of normal test-score fluctuation against which to compare treatment effects. It is rare that such an estimate of reliability would be available to assure accurate projections of regression effects.

Regression and Matching: Comparison Group Designs

It is fairly obvious how regression effects would influence change scores obtained from a single population with initially extreme test values. Because this effect is so well known, simple pretest–posttest designs comparing groups chosen on the basis of extreme scores are rarely used in program evaluation or other research contexts. The effects of regression artifacts can enter more subtly, however, whenever we have two or more respondent groups that are not randomly assigned to treatment and comparison conditions. This possibility arises because when the individuals participating in a social program have been selected nonrandomly, it is likely that they differ from nonparticipants (i.e., the comparison group) in some systematic way on the outcome measures of interest, even prior to the program experience. This initial non-equivalence makes it difficult to interpret any posttreatment differences between the two groups. Attempts to compensate for pretest inequality between experimental and control groups are frequently made through post hoc "matching" of participants, a procedure that is widely applied despite frequent warnings against its use (e.g., Campbell & Stanley, 1963; Hovland, Lumsdaine, & Sheffield, 1949; McNemar, 1940; Thorndike, 1942). Essentially, matching involves identifying the overlapping scores between the two groups and then making posttreatment comparisons only between the members of the two groups who attained similar scores on the pretest measure (or some related measures). In effect, this procedure amounts to an attempt to apply the blocking design of experimental research (discussed in chap. 2), but the blocking is accomplished after assignment to treatments has already been determined. A slight variation of this matching technique occurs when an experimental treatment group is composed by some special criteria and then a "control" group is created on an ex post facto basis by selecting from the general population (i.e., from among those who did not meet the special criteria for inclusion in the experimental group) a group of participants who "match" the predetermined experimental respondents on some specified pretest variables. In either case, interpretation of the results of such matched group designs is confounded by the potential effects of *differential regression*.

An extension of the sample data presented in Table 9.1 can illustrate the matched group differential regression problem. Table 9.4 provides a new set of data on pretest scores for 10 hypothetical cases comprising an experimental group representing a sample that is randomly drawn from a special *low-scoring population*. These cases do not represent the

TABLE 9.4

Pretest Scores for Experimental Group and Matched
Comparison Group

Predetermined Experimental Group			"Matched" Cases from Table 9.1
True Score	Error	Total	Test 1 Score Distribution
73	+3	76	77
74	−4	70	69
70	−2	68	68
65	+3	68	68
63	+4	67	66
68	−4	64	65
69	−5	64	63
62	−1	61	61
53	+5	58	58
50	+1	51	52
Mean = 64.7	0	64.7	64.7

TABLE 9.5

Posttest Scores With No Change in True Scores

Experimental Group Posttest Results			"Matched" Group Posttest Scores from Table 9.1
True Score	Error	Total	
73	+1	74	81
74	−2	72	76
70	+5	75	66
65	−3	62	79
63	+6	69	68
68	+2	70	66
69	−3	66	55
62	−5	57	68
53	−3	50	64
50	+2	52	54
Mean = 64.7	0	64.7	67.6

extreme scores of their population; rather, they are drawn randomly from it. They are to be compared with 10 cases selected from the pretest (Test 1) distribution in Table 9.1 that "match" the experimental pretest scores as closely as possible. By virtue of this selective matching, the initial means of the experimental and control groups appear to be equal. However, Table 9.5 illustrates what would happen on posttest scores in the absence of any treatment effect (i.e., with no change in true scores). The true scores of the experimental group participants are unchanged. Random-error differences introduce some change in the pattern of posttest scores compared with pretest values, but because these errors are random, the overall mean for these cases is unchanged and no regression occurs.

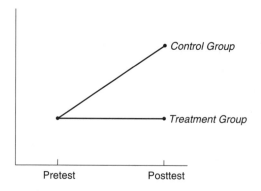

FIG. 9.1.   An illustration of asymmetric regression.

The 10 posttest scores from the control group, on the other hand, exhibit a tendency toward increases, with an overall mean almost three points higher than the pretest value. Referring to Table 9.1 provides an explanation for this increase. To match the experimental group scores, the 10 control cases were selected from the bottom extreme of the Test 1 score distribution. This selection of extreme cases introduced a bias into the study. Negative error scores were overrepresented among the "matched" (control) cases. On Test 2, therefore, the random occurrence of some positive error scores would inevitably produce an increase in total score values, that is, a regression toward the original group mean. Figure 9.1 illustrates how the mean scores derived from Tables 9.3 and 9.4 would appear in the absence of any real change.

Figure 9.1 depicts a case in which differential regression (one group exhibiting regression toward a grand mean while the other does not) causes the experimental treatment to appear to be detrimental: in the absence of any real effect, the final test scores are below those of the control group. Campbell and Erlebacher (1970) provide a detailed discussion of this type of regression artifact as it affects the interpretation of research on compensatory education programs. It is typical of the implementation of these programs that they are provided for particularly disadvantaged populations without random assignment. Thus, any attempts to evaluate their effectiveness through ex post facto comparison with a matched control group selected from the available general population introduces a regression bias that operates against the apparent value of the treatment. This is the situation represented in Fig. 9.1. On the other hand, whenever matching with a predetermined experimental group is such that the selection of matched cases draws from the upper extremes of the available control group, the bias of differential regression would be in the opposite direction, that is, in favor of the experimental group over the control on posttest results.

Differential regression produces even more extreme effects if the matched groups both are drawn as selected cases from initially different populations. In such cases, both groups are likely to exhibit regression effects, but toward different means. This is often the case when comparisons must be made between experimental and control groups composed of previously intact social units, as illustrated in Table 9.6. It is clear from these data that the initial differences between these two groups make the differences obtained on the Test 2 measure meaningless as an evaluation of the effectiveness of the experimental treatment. In the absence of any true-score change between pretest and posttest, there is still a significant difference between the two groups on the final testing. If there had been some change, it would have been impossible to interpret because it could have been a function of the initial group differences rather than the experimental treatment.

TABLE 9.6

Illustration of Initial Group Differences

	Group I (experimental treatment)					Group II (controls)			
True Score	Test 1 Error	Test 1 Total	Test 2 Error	Test 2 Total	True Score	Test 1 Error	Test 1 Total	Test 2 Error	Test 2 Total
75	−5	70	+1	76	53	+3	56	−1	52
73	+2	75	−3	70	49	−5	44	+3	52
72	−6	66	0	72	48	−3	45	−5	43
70	+8	78	−7	63	45	+5	50	−1	44
67	+1	68	+1	68	45	+2	47	+4	49
65	−5	60	+6	71	42	+7	49	−4	38
65	+5	70	+3	68	42	+3	45	+2	44
60	−3	57	+1	61	38	+4	42	−3	35
58	+6	64	−7	51	36	−8	28	+7	43
55	+9	64	+6	61	35	+2	37	−4	31
55	−7	48	+4	59	32	−2	30	+3	35
54	−5	49	+1	55	30	−5	25	−3	27
53	+6	59	−8	45	29	+3	32	+1	30
50	−2	48	−4	46	28	−1	27	−1	27
48	−3	45	−2	46	26	−6	20	+7	33
45	−4	41	+3	48	25	+5	30	−1	24
43	+3	46	+5	48	24	−9	15	−6	18
40	−2	38	+4	44	23	+6	29	0	23
38	+5	43	−3	35	21	+5	26	−6	15
35	−3	32	−1	34	16	−6	10	+8	24
Mean = 56.05	0	56.05	0	56.05	Mean = 34.35	0	34.35	0	34.35

TABLE 9.7
Illustration of Post Hoc Matching

Pretest Matched Scores		Corresponding Posttest Scores	
Group I	Group II	Group I	Group II
57	56	61	52
49	50	55	44
48	49	59	38
48	47	46	49
46	45	48	43
45	45	46	44
43	44	35	52
41	42	48	35
38	37	44	31
32	32	34	30
Mean = 44.7	44.7	47.6	41.8

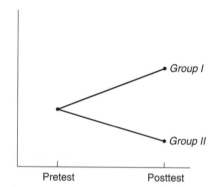

FIG. 9.2.   An illustration of divergent regression.

Under such circumstances, where the researcher is unable to determine the composition of comparison groups through random assignment, it is not uncommon to attempt to correct for initial differences by selecting cases from the original groups in a way that creates two new groups that appear to be equivalent on the initial measure. Table 9.7 illustrates such a selective matching from the groups in Table 9.6. The first two columns represent cases drawn from Groups 1 and 2, which are closely matched on the basis of Test 1 score results. The resulting means are *exactly* equal, and so it appears that the selection procedure has been successful in creating initially equivalent subgroups. However, the data in the next two columns, which present the Test 2 scores for the selected cases in the absence of any true-score change, reveal the fallacy of the apparent equivalence.

The matching procedure involved selecting cases from the opposite extremes of the two original distributions: the lower scores from Group 1 and the upper scores from Group 2. As a result, the directional bias in the selected pretest cases had opposite effects for the two sets of scores, causing one group to regress upward and the other downward. In this case, the differential regression pattern has the effect of artificially enhancing the appearance of effectiveness of the experimental treatment on the posttest measure. This effect is pictured in Fig. 9.2. Had the initial group means been reversed, regression would have led to a conclusion that the treatment had a detrimental effect.

Post hoc matching on the basis of any other pretreatment variable or combination of variables (e.g., age, socioeconomic status, intelligence, personality scores) is subject to the same regression phenomenon as long as the matching variables are imperfectly related to the posttreatment dependent variable measure. Such is the case, for example, with research that attempts to assess racial differences by comparing groups differing in race but "matched" on socioeconomic variables. In a society where race is still inextricably confounded with multiple cultural factors, such post hoc matching can only produce groups that are subject to differential regression effects and, thus, essentially uninterpretable results. In general, if one's research must depend on nonrandomly selected comparison groups, the evaluator is better off accepting and taking into account nonequivalence between the groups than resorting to matching techniques.

Time Series Designs as Quasi-Experiments

Problems associated with differential regression and other sources of nonequivalence make many nonrandom comparison group designs inadequate with respect to internal validity. Evaluation researchers have therefore looked for other kinds of baseline information that can replace or supplement comparison groups as a basis for assessing change.

The need for alternatives to the comparison groups design is especially obvious when a social program is introduced that affects an entire population (nation or state) at one time. In this case, the only method for assessing change is to compare conditions before and after the treatment is introduced (or determine the amount of treatment absorbed by each participant) and assess any differential outcomes as a result of these differences. If the only information available on pretreatment conditions is a single measure taken near the onset of the new program, serious problems of interpreting change are created. Consider, for example, a measure of the incidence of violent crimes in one state for the year before and the year after the introduction of a moratorium on capital punishment. Such a single pretest–posttest assessment of change is impossible to interpret without some knowledge of the degree of fluctuation expected between two measures in the absence of any true change.

The hypothetical crime statistics represented in Fig. 9.3 illustrate the problem. The change in rate between the two annual figures may be interpreted in several different ways. It may represent an actual increase in crime rate under conditions where capital punishment is removed as a deterrent. On the other hand, it may simply reflect the normal year-to-year fluctuation in crime rates, which, by chance, have taken the direction of an increase over this particular time period. To make matters worse, social experiments such as this one often are introduced under exceptional social conditions; ameliorative efforts are

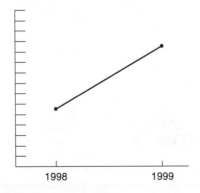

1998   1999

FIG. 9.3. Data from a two-point change measure.

more likely to be undertaken when undesirable conditions have reached some kind of peak or, in the case of our present example, public opinion may have been particularly amenable to an experiment in eliminating capital punishment following a period of exceptionally low crime. If this is the case, differences in measures taken before and after the experimental intervention may simply reflect regression back to normal rates.

Some indication of the relative degree of change that occurs after an experimental treatment may be obtained by comparing the change during the critical period with fluctuations between comparable time periods prior to the experimental period, that is, by observing the change within the context of a *time-series* analysis. Consider how the interpretation of the data from Fig. 9.3 is affected by the different contexts recorded in Fig. 9.4. Figure 9.4a suggests that the 1998–1999 change score represents normal year-to-year fluctuation in the crime index with no particular rise above previous years. Figure 9.4b indicates a rise, but one that is consistent with a general trend toward year-by-year increases established long before the introduction of the experimental treatment. Figure 9.4c presents 1998 (pretreatment) as a particularly low year, with 1999 representing a slight regression back toward previous rates. In all of these cases, there is no reason to

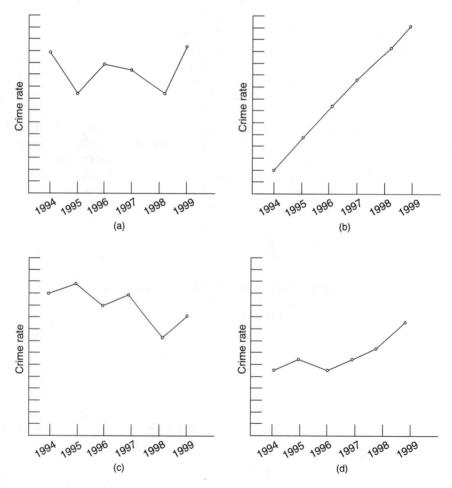

FIG. 9.4. Time trends by year.

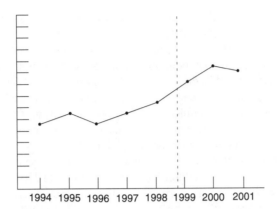

1994 1995 1996 1997 1998 1999 2000 2001

FIG. 9.5. Interrupted time-series data.

believe that the 1998–1999 increase would not have taken place even if the experimental moratorium on capital punishment had not been introduced.

Figure 9.4d provides an example in which the critical change period has a difference score significantly greater than previous levels of fluctuation, thereby indicating that some real change has occurred. We could be more certain of the meaningfulness of the change if the time series were extended for more years after treatment to determine whether the change in pattern of crime statistics was stable. Such an extended series is represented in Fig. 9.5, which illustrates the quasi-experimental design known as the *interrupted time series* (Cook & Campbell, 1979; McCain & McCleary, 1979; McDowell, McCleary, Meidinger, & Hay, 1980; Orwin, 1997).

Of course, knowing that a meaningful and stable change has occurred in a time-series analysis does not rule out sources other than the experimental intervention as possible causes of the change. Alternative explanations might be available, such as an abrupt increase in population density, changes in record-keeping procedures, or other factors related to crime rate that could have occurred simultaneously with the treatment. Statistical analyses of changes in time-series data are compounded by two problems in particular. One is that "errors" (i.e., extraneous factors that influence the data obtained at any one time point) tend to be correlated between adjacent measurements. That is, a particular chance event that affects the statistics obtained at one time is more likely to carry over to measures taken at the next succeeding time point than to other points in the series. Such carry-over errors (called *autocorrelated errors*) make it more difficult to pinpoint a change in the time series at the one specific time of interest to the evaluation researcher.

The second problem that plagues time-series analyses is the presence of *systematic trends* or *cycles* that affect the pattern of data over a specific time period. Changes due to the treatment of interest must be separated from normal changes that occur regularly across time. When data are obtained on a monthly basis, for instance, regular seasonal fluctuations that may operate across the year must be taken into account. (Crime statistics, for example, tend to be influenced by weather conditions, which produce seasonal changes that vary from region to region.) Such patterns introduce complications in the analyses of time-series designs, but they are not impossible to manage. Statistical procedures known as *prewhitening* can be applied to remove regularities in the time series before analyses of experimental effect are begun (e.g., Box & Jenkins, 1970).

An applied example of research that made use of an interrupted time series, and whose data were affected by both autocorrelated error and systematic trends, is provided in

Ramirez and Crano's study of California's "three strikes" law. This law, which took effect in California in 1994, made a 25-year-to-life sentence mandatory for anyone convicted of a third felony. Ramirez and Crano (in press) were interested in the effect of the law. Do criminals really calculate the cost–benefit ratio before committing a crime? To test this possibility, they studied monthly crime rates 12 years before and 5 years after the law's implementation. Crimes are cyclical in nature; for example, in each year of the study, crime spiked in December. We could speculate on the reasons for this, but this result certainly gives little comfort to those seeking peace on earth, good will toward men. In addition, the data were obviously autocorrelated. Numbers of crimes committed in June were more closely correlated to those of May and July than those of February and April. The statistical procedures made available by Box and Jenkins (1970) and Berry and Lewis-Beck (1986) provide the necessary corrections. The research provided an answer to the question, "Does the law work?" but the answer was equivocal. When studying crimes of passion (i.e., violent crimes), the three-strikes law affected the rate of crime in the long run, but it had no immediate impact. This result suggests that the law operated not as a deterrent, but rather because it took violent career criminals off the streets.[5] For nonviolent, "white collar" crimes, however, the three-strikes law appeared to have both a deterrent and an incapacitating effect. That is, it appeared to cause some criminals to avoid crimes, while at the same time incarcerating a proportion of those who made a living off such activities. Both effects cumulated to cause a dramatic decline in white collar crime. The law appeared to have no affect whatsoever on drug-related crimes.

Time Series and Use of Archival Data. It is rarely, if ever, the case that program evaluators have sufficient lead time prior to the introduction of a new treatment to obtain premeasures over an extended period specifically for the purposes of evaluation research. Hence, the use of time-series (quasi-experimental) designs generally relies on the availability of statistical records or other archival documents that have been kept for purposes other than research. Sometimes the only relevant historical materials available are written records (newspaper summaries, case records, personal letters, etc.) that must be subject to *content analysis* to be useful as research data. (The methods and purposes of content analyses are covered in chap. 13.) For now, we deal only with research based on the availability of quantitative records or statistical indices compiled by institutions or government agencies for various accounting purposes.

Fortunately for North American researchers, the United States has been something of a "statistics-happy" society for much of its recent history. In addition to the constitutionally mandated census of the entire population every 10 years (which provides valuable demographic information on a regular basis), numerous federal agencies are charged with maintaining statistical databases of records of births and deaths, hospital admissions and other health records, various indices of economic activity, records of arrests, convictions and other indices of criminal activity, unemployment statistics, and the like. Parallel record keeping goes on at state and local levels, which is important for evaluations of locally implemented social programs.

Use of statistical archives has a number of advantages, but also creates some disadvantages for research purposes. First, it limits the dependent measures or outcome variables that can be assessed to the type of information on which records happen to have been kept.

---

[5]Criminologists suggest that 90% of all crimes are committed by 10% of the population. As such, incarcerating a "career criminal" (termed *incapacitation*) would have a disproportionate effect on future crime rates.

Records kept for administrative purposes may or may not reflect the primary goals of the particular social program being evaluated. For instance, in evaluations of the criminal justice system, it is easier to obtain archival records on recidivism (re-arrests or imprisonment) than on more positive outcomes to program participants. In educational settings, information on achievement test results is much more likely to be available than are indicators of other types of student outcomes, such as social adjustment or moral development.

Another limitation imposed by reliance on archival records is the time interval covered by a given statistic, which may or may not be the unit of time ideal for research purposes. If statistics are accumulated on a daily basis, the researcher has considerable flexibility to aggregate data over any time period he or she chooses, but also has an imposing arrray of data to compile. On the other hand, if summary statistics have been maintained only on a yearly basis, the research will have to cover a very long period for a sufficient number of data points to be available for purposes of statistical analyses.

Finally, a major worry with many archival studies is the possibility that the nature or method of record keeping has been changed at various points in time. Record-keeping systems can be altered, usually for administrative convenience, in a number of ways. For one thing, the *criterion* for inclusion in the data file may be changed. Criminal statistics, for instance, can be dramatically affected by changes in the activities or actions on which police are required to file a report. Records may be altered in form or content, such as changes in categories of information or in times at which information is recorded. Sometimes, and this is especially relevant in medical research, new techniques of diagnosis will allow certain identification of diseases that could not always be clearly diagnosed before the new test. This change will produce data that suggest a rapid rise in the incidence of the disease. Sometimes the researcher will know enough about the diagnosis or record-keeping system to make conversions between different versions of the same information, but more often such changes render data noncomparable from one time to another. If changes in administrative record-keeping methods occur in close proximity to the introduction of a social program, such records become useless as measures of program-induced changes.

Comparison Time-series Designs.   Assuming that comparable statistical records are available across times and places, one way that the interrupted time series can be strengthened as a quasi-experimental design is to combine it with the comparison-group design. If a social program is introduced in one location or institution but not in some other, any pre-existing differences between the treatment and comparison site make it difficult to interpret any posttreatment differences. However, if time-series data based on the same record-keeping system are available for both sites, and if both are subject to similar sources of cyclical and noncyclical fluctuations, then the time-series data from the comparison group can serve as an additional base for evaluating changes in the experimental series. When the two time series are roughly parallel prior to the introduction of the experimental program, but diverge significantly afterwards (as illustrated in Fig. 9.6), many potential alternative explanations for the change in the latter series can be ruled out. As with any time-series design, statistical analyses of comparison series can be complex (Berk, Hoffman, Maki, Rauma, & Wong, 1979; Berry & Lewis-Beck, 1986), but the logic of the design is quite compelling and straightforward and it has been used to good avail in a number of evaluation settings.

A second method of forming a comparison for the interrupted time series is to include variables in the analysis that are parallel to the critical variables but which should not be affected by the interruption. For example, in Ramirez and Crano's three-strikes study, data on minor crimes were available. These crimes should have been affected by the same

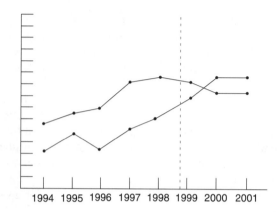

FIG. 9.6. Comparison time-series data.

extraneous variables as felonies (e.g., general economic conditions, social unrest, etc.), but were not affected by the enactment of the law. Thus, ideally, the law's passage would affect the rate of serious crime, but not misdemeanors.

Regression-Discontinuity Design

The final quasi-experimental design to be described here is applicable to cases in which exposure to a treatment program is based on some clear selection principle. The *regression-discontinuity* design relies on the existence of some systematic, functional relationship between the selection variable and the outcome measure of interest. If individuals are selected for inclusion in a special educational enrichment program on the basis of achievement test scores, for instance, we would expect those test scores (apart from any program effects) to be positively linearly related to later measures of educational attainment. Alternatively, if a need factor, such as poverty, was used as the basis of selection, we would expect in the absence of any program to find a negative relationship between poverty scores and later achievement.

The regression-discontinuity quasi-experimental design is meant to mimic a true experiment in which a group of participants at a cut-off point are randomly assigned to a treatment or a control condition. For example, suppose the State Department of Education has developed a program for children whose families fall below the poverty line established by the federal government. To test the effect of the program, we might take those falling slightly above and slightly below the poverty line and randomly assign them to the program or control condition. The effect of the program then could be tested in a true pretest–posttest control group experimental design. Such a design would be very difficult politically, however, and so the regression-discontinuity design was developed as an analogue to the true experiment. In the regression-discontinuity approach, if selection into the special program is associated with a specific cut-off point on the selection variable, we can use the outcomes of those who fall at or below the cut-off point as a comparison to those falling above the cut off. Although overall we would expect those below to perform differently (either much better or much worse) than those above, in the absence of a special treatment, we would not expect any abrupt change in outcomes for those falling near the cut-off point on either side. If such a change does occur, we can take this as evidence of a treatment effect above and beyond the expected selection effect (Thistlethwaite & Campbell, 1960). Such a regression-discontinuity effect is illustrated in Fig. 9.7 for the

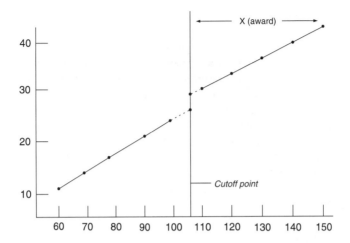

FIG. 9.7. **Regression-discontinuity results.**

case of a positive (merit-based) selection factor. A full treatment of the assumptions and statistical analyses for this design is available in Trochim (1984), Reichardt and Mark (1998), and Cook and Shadish (1994).

The regression-discontinuity design is less common than comparison time-series designs in program evaluation settings, partly because cases of selection based on a criterion cut-off score are relatively rare, and partly because it requires extensive data collection for individuals across the full range of scores on the selection variable. However, when regression-discontinuity analyses are used, they often are focused on important, socially relevant issues. For example, using this approach, researchers have investigated the effects of mandatory divorce counseling laws (Deluse, 1999), programs for mathematically gifted Black children (Robinson, Bradley, & Stanley, 1990), and the effects of being placed on the Dean's list on college students' later academic performance (Seaver & Quarton, 1976).

Regression-discontinuity is an interesting quasi-experimental design to consider, particularly in contrast to true experimental design. Whereas true experiments are based on pure randomization as the basis for treatment assignment, the regression-discontinuity design is based on equally pure *non*random selection. In either case, strict application of the selection rule permits cause–effect conclusions to be drawn with high internal validity, but any deviation from the selection principle compromises the validity of interpretation. Apart from being difficult to implement, the regression-discontinuity design is more susceptible than true experiments to problems associated with measurement error. In addition, it is essential that the data obtained in the analysis is linear, or the interpretability of the ensuing results is severely compromised. Given these problems, the regression-discontinuity design is not preferable to a randomized experiment, *if the latter is possible.* However, as a special case, the regression-discontinuity design does help to illustrate how research purposes can be adapted to policy conditions without total loss of interpretability. In the appropriate circumstances, the design provides information that may prove extremely useful for policymaking purposes, and this same evaluation could be made of many of the other designs outlined by Campbell and Stanley (1963), Cook and Campbell (1979), Bickman and Rog (1998), and many other researchers who have discussed and developed quasi-experimental designs. These designs are ideally suited to circumstances of social or practical importance that do not admit to pure experiments.

The quasi-experimental approach allows social science researchers to study these important issues and to make estimates of the strength of manipulated or naturally occurring "treatments." The confidence we can place in these estimates is usually not as great as that which we can derive from true experimental designs (which involve random assignment), but sometimes the issue is important enough that we are willing to pay this price to generate even a rough estimate of the strength of a relationship or the effectiveness of a treatment. With sufficient thought and effort, quasi-experimental designs can produce important insights, insights which, because of contextual constraints, might not have been researchable through the more standard experimental techniques. This chapter only scratched the surface of the wide variety of possible designs, but that is as it should be. The chapter was meant to lay the groundwork. The elaboration of the multitude of variations that can be developed is a function of the ingenuity, creativity, and motivation of the individual researcher.

SUGGESTED READINGS

Bickman, L., & Rog, D. J. (Eds.). (1997). *Handbook of applied social research methods*. Thousand Oaks, CA: Sage.

Cook, T. D., & Campbell, D. T. (1979). *Quasi-experimentation: Design and analysis issues for field settings*. Chicago: Rand-McNally.

Scriven, M. (1997). Truth and objectivity in evaluation. In E. Chelimsky & W. R. Shadish (Eds.), *Evaluation for the 21st century: A handbook* (pp. 477–500). Thousand Oaks, CA: Sage.

10

SURVEY DESIGN AND SAMPLING

In some very fundamental ways, survey research is different from the experimentally oriented methods that were described in the initial chapters of this book. Although, as in
experimentation, questions of bias are raised in the evaluation of all surveys, the major
critical focus is with external, rather than internal, validity. The usual question in survey
contexts is, "How well do the responses of a subset of a population (the total group to
which we wish our findings to generalize) actually represent the underlying perceptions or
feelings of the population?" Generally, we are not concerned with issues of internal validity (i.e., is the manipulation responsible for the obtained findings?) because surveys rarely
include manipulations—although survey researchers are increasingly using the technique
as a vehicle for experimentation. Typically, the issues of concern for the survey researcher
are different from those of the laboratory experimenter. This chapter provides an introduction to this alternate form of research. It is important to bear in mind throughout this
chapter that an important goal of much survey research is to provide estimates of population values that are as accurate as possible. Most of the technical aspects of survey
sampling have been developed in the service of this goal.

Assignment versus Selection

To draw the distinction between the experimental techniques and survey research, it is
useful to emphasize the distinction between sampling and assignment. Recall that in the
sections of the book devoted to experimental design (chaps. 1–5), we stressed the importance of random assignment of participants to conditions. In experiments, we are concerned
primarily with ensuring that participants are randomly assigned to the various conditions
of the study; often, however, we are less concerned with the characteristics of the pool
from which participants were drawn. The core requirement for random *assignment* is that
each person (or unit) in the pool has the same chance of being assigned to a specific experimental or control condition as any other person (or unit) in the pool. Random assignment
is essential if the full power of experimental techniques to foster causal statements is to be
realized. Most experimentalists realize that the generalizability of results is dependent on

the features of the pool from which the participants were drawn, but this is consideration is secondary. For example, if our participant pool consisted of all students enrolled in Psych 101 in the fall semester, then logically, the results are generalizable only to that group. Without additional data, it would be dangerous to generalize research findings beyond that group. Of course, we often are not content to generalize to such a restricted population, but to go farther involves some risk of overextending our results. This should not be interpreted as a criticism of experimentation, or of random assignment of individuals from restricted participant pools. Rather, it is intended to caution researchers not to overextend the boundaries of their findings. This observation also helps to draw a distinction between assignment, where consideration of features of the participant pool usually takes a back seat, and selection, where the features of the pool are of central importance.

The issue of *selection* (or *sampling*, the two terms being used synonymously here) is different from, and perhaps more fundamental than, that of assignment. Selection is not concerned with the rules that govern the placement of individuals from a large pool into the more constrained treatment or control conditions of a research design (i.e., with assignment), but rather with the issue of how those particular people got into the pool in the first place. Several forms of selection (simple random sampling, stratified, multistage sampling, etc.) are treated in this chapter, but first some important preliminary issues must be considered.

Census or Survey.   In the technical sampling literature, a distinction is made between a *census* and a *survey*. A census is generally taken to mean a complete enumeration of all of the units that possibly could be included in the investigation (sometimes called a *population* or *universe*), whereas a sample refers to a partial enumeration of the eligible units. In most work in the social sciences, the sampling approach is preferred to the use of the complete set of possible responding units because, *within some reasonable degree of error*, the survey sample will approximate the results that would have been obtained had a complete census been taken—and this can be done at a fraction of the cost associated with a complete enumeration of all unit.[1]

Precision.   The expression "within some reasonable degree of error" is emphasized because it leads to an issue of importance in any discussion of survey sampling, namely, *precision of estimates*. This term refers to how close a sample estimate is likely to be to the value that would be obtained if the whole population (census) had been included in the survey. Suppose we have available a list of all of the 45,000 students who attend a large midwestern university (technically, such a list is called a *sampling frame*). We know that 20,000 of these students live off campus, and we wish to determine the average rent these students pay, so we can compare this figure with that obtained in surveys of students from other universities. In addition, we want to know something about the distribution of rent costs over this population. How could we perform this study? We could contact all 20,000 off-campus students and (assuming that everyone participates and tells the truth) ask them to tell us the amount of rent they pay each month. We could calculate the average over the entire group of students, or we could group the data, as in the "Population 1" column of Table 10.1. The ensuing average, and the percentages of students within each

---

[1] In the United States, a census of the population is taken every 10 years. This is an incredibly costly endeavor, and in recent years, sophisticated social scientists have argued that a sample would be a cheaper and reliable alternative to the census. The less technically sophisticated have argued against the sampling alternative. This chapter illustrates the advantages and disadvantages of both positions.

TABLE 10.1

Monthly Rent Costs Distribution of Off-Campus Students

Rent Category	Population 1	Sample 1	Population 2	Sample 2
$0–$25	600	36	0	0
$26–$50	900	47	0	0
$51–$75	980	56	0	0
$76–100	2,840	149	4,000	220
$101–$125	3,700	183	6,000	290
$126–$150	3,800	177	7,000	315
$151–175	2,800	129	3,000	175
$176–$200	1,520	72	0	0
$201–$225	1,220	58	0	0
$226–$250	1,000	55	0	0
>$250	640	38	0	0
Total	20,000	1000	20,000	1,000
Mean	$135.22	$134.00	$124.25	$124.12
s.d.	57.25	59.60	24.34	25.40

rent category, would provide us with an exact measure of population values because, in fact, the entire population had been questioned.

Contacting all 20,000 off-campus students of our hypothetical university might tax our research resources beyond the breaking point, however, and so instead we decide to sample only 1,000 of the total population. To do this, we use a table of random numbers (details of using such a table are discussed later in this chapter) to select 1,000 people from the off-campus housing list, and we contact these individuals for our survey. Under these circumstances, we do not know the true population value (called the *population parameter*); however, we are able to estimate the parameter from the sample survey results, and the probable accuracy of an estimate is termed the *precision* of that estimate.

We can estimate the probable precision of a sample mean by determining the standard error (S.E.) of the mean, which is estimated for a simple random sample by the following formula:

$$\text{S.E.} = \sqrt{s^2/n},$$

where S.E. = the standard error of the mean (precision),
s = the standard deviation of the sample observations, and
n = the number of observations in the sample.
Variants of this formula are used for other sampling designs.

Under some circumstances, it is useful to modify the estimate of precision by a factor known as the *finite population correction*, or fpc, as follows:

$$\text{S.E.} = \sqrt{(1 - f)s^2/n}$$

where f = the sampling fraction, that is, the proportion of the total population included in the sample.

The fpc is included in the calculation of the precision estimate to reflect the facts that in simple random sampling, units are chosen without replacement, and that the population from which the sample is drawn is not infinite (as assumed in standard statistical theory).

The fpc suggests that sampling without replacement results in greater precision than sampling with replacement. When the sampling fraction is small (say, less than 1 in 20), the effect of the fpc on the standard error is minor. This follows logically because in situations involving a small sampling fraction, the likelihood of selecting the same unit more than once (when sampling with replacement) is minimal; hence, the effect of the fpc on the standard error in such circumstances is minimal. Thus, in practice, with small sampling fractions, the fpc often is not used in the precision formula.

In addition to the fpc, the formulas just presented contain two other clues about factors that can influence the precision of a sample mean. Notice that the size of the sample has much to do with the standard error (or precision). Indeed, in situations involving large populations, it is the sample size, rather than the sampling fraction, that plays the predominant role in determining precision. As sample size increases, the standard error decreases. However, the relationship is not one-to-one, because it is the square root of the sample size that appears in the formulas for the standard error. This means that if a researcher wishes to double the precision of a sample (if s and the fpc were to remain constant), he or she has to quadruple the sample size.

The other important term in the formula is the *standard deviation*, denoted by the term s, which represents the variability of the individual values in the sample. It is an estimate of the variability of the values in the population from which the sample was drawn. Obviously, the larger this term, the greater the standard error of the mean. In other words, the more variable the population on the characteristic of interest (in our example, monthly rent payments), the greater the standard error of the sample mean, and, consequently, the lower the precision of the sample mean. Consider Table 10.1 again. As shown here, the range of monthly rental payments in "Population 1" is relatively broad. A random sample of 1,000 respondents drawn on this population would produce results similar to those of the "Sample 1" column, where the standard deviation is $59.60. Now consider the distribution of "Population 2." Such a set of restricted values might be obtained in a town that exerted strict control over the rents that landlords could charge students. As can be seen in this example, the standard deviation of a random sample of the respondents drawn from this population is much smaller than that of the sample of Population 1. This is so because the variability of the true population values of Population 2 are themselves smaller than those of the first. To take an extreme example, suppose that all 20,000 off-campus students paid exactly $200/month rent. In this instance, a sample of a single off-campus student would provide an absolutely precise estimate of the population mean. A moment's reflection on the precision formulas reveals why this is so. When the population values are the same for all units, there is, by definition, no variation in these values. The standard deviation term in the formula, therefore, would equal exactly zero. The results of any division of this term (no matter what the sample size, n) also would equal zero. Thus, the more restricted the population values, the more precise the sample values, all other things being equal. Or, to put it another way, the fewer respondents will be needed to obtain a given precision level for the sample mean.

SAMPLING MODELS

Survey sampling is undertaken in the service of two fundamental goals: efficiency and economy. *Efficiency* refers to the attempt to balance considerations of cost with those of precision. One of the central preoccupations of many sampling approaches is to devise means by which the precision of estimates can be enhanced without either resorting to samples of unmanageable size or depending on the kindness of nature to provide population values of low variability. Other sampling approaches have been developed in the service of *economy*. These approaches (as in the case, say, of multistage sampling, discussed later) are undertaken not to enhance the precision–cost ratio, but rather to reduce the expenses involved in sampling and data collection. We now consider examples of both of these general sampling orientations.

The Simple Random Sample

A *simple random sample* is one in which every member of the population in question has an equal (and nonzero) probability of being selected every time a unit is drawn for inclusion in the sample.[2] The probability of selection is equal to the sampling fraction, and is simply calculated by dividing the number of units to be included in the sample by the total number of units in the population. Thus, in the examples of Table 10.1, the sampling fraction was 5% because 1,000 of a possible 20,000 students were to be sampled. Sampling approaches of this type are called *epsem designs*. In sampling theory, this term refers to "equal probability of selection methods." Simple random sampling, systematic sampling, and proportionate stratified sampling approaches are examples of epsem designs.

In selecting a simple random sample, the researcher has a relatively restricted set of procedural options. In situations involving a small population, one can enter each of the population units on individual elements (slips of paper, discs, etc.), mix the elements well, and choose the number planned for the sample. Picking names out of a hat is an example of this process: If all the names are entered, individually, on elements (e.g., slips of paper) of the same size, if the elements are mixed well, if the person doing the choosing does so without looking into the hat (or otherwise exerting an influence on the particular names that are chosen), and if the elements are not returned to the hat after being selected, we have a simple random sample. If any of these conditions are violated, the result cannot be considered a true simple random sample.

In research situations in which the underlying population is large, such a process becomes unwieldy. Reconsider the example of Table 10.1. Obviously, the "name in the hat" approach would be unwise in this situation. The sampling process would be so tedious that the research probably would never be completed. (Imagine writing the names of 20,000 people on index cards, putting these into a (very large) hat, mixing them, and choosing 1,000 cards at random.) In such cases, the use of a table of random numbers is highly recommended.[3]

The process begins with a determination of the required sample size. Guidelines for estimating sample size are presented later in this chapter. For now, assume as in the example that we have decided on a sample of 1,000 students from the total eligible population of 20,000. To choose the specific students that are to constitute our sample, we would number each of the names on our list, from 00001 to 20000. This list constitutes our sampling frame. Then, using a table of random numbers, we could select the first 1,000 different

---

[2]An issue in the definition of *simple* random sampling is whether sampling is conducted with or without replacement. Following Kalton (1983, p. 10), we take this term to refer to sampling without replacement; that is, once a unit is included in the sample, he, she, or it is not returned to the population, and thus, cannot be chosen again. Sometimes, the term *simple random sampling without replacement* is used to describe this form of sampling, and the term *simple random sampling with replacement* is used to described the equivalent technique in which the units sampled at one draw is returned to the population before the next draw is made. In practice, almost all sampling is done without replacement.

[3]Random number tables can be found in the appendix sections of most statistics textbooks and today can be generated on most personal computers with almost any basic statistical software.

5-place random numbers that corresponded with the numbers on the list of students. So, if we came upon the number 18921 when searching our random number table, we would include the 18,921st student on the list in our sample; however, the random number 22430 would not be used to select a unit into the sample because there are only 20,000 eligible students on our frame (i.e., there is no student whose "ID number" corresponds to that from the random number table). When employing a random number table, it is good practice to pick a starting point at random each time the table is used. This helps to assure that the same investigator does not always make use of the same set of random numbers when selecting samples.

Other potentially useful approaches for drawing random samples have been suggested for reasons of convenience in various sampling contexts. For instance, if the sampling fraction were 50%, a flip of a coin could determine whether or not a given unit would enter into the sample. During the war in Vietnam, young men's draft status was determined by their birth date. A lottery was conducted with dates of birth entered. Dates were drawn from a barrel, and those whose birth date was chosen early in the process were drafted before those whose number came up later in the drawing. This approach seems to have solved the problem of magnitude—imagine if every young man eligible for the draft had to be listed before the government could determine his place in the draft.[4] It is often the case even in these circumstances, however, that the use of a random number table proves the more convenient, and always the more sure choice, as the critique of Notz, Staw, and Cook (1971) suggested. It is good practice, therefore, to become proficient in the use of this aid. Indeed, if our recommendation were sought about the appropriate means of drawing a sample, it would be very simple: "Use a random number table."

Systematic Sampling

An alternate means of choosing the students from our off-campus renters list involves a technique known as *systematic sampling*. In this approach, as before, a specific sample size is determined. Then, the size of the sample is divided by the total eligible population to determine the sampling fraction. In our example, the sampling fraction is 1000/20000, or 1 in 20. A number between 1 and 20 is randomly chosen, and then every 20th person after that number is selected for the sample. Thus, if we randomly chose the number 15 as our starting point, we would include in our sample the 15th, 35th, 55th, 75th, and so on, student from the renters list. We would continue in this fashion until we had sampled exactly 1,000 students.

In some ways, systematic sampling resembles simple random sampling because all of the units in the sampling frame initially have an equal chance of being selected (systematic sampling is an epsem method). It differs from simple random sampling because the probability of different *sets* or groups of units being included in the sample is not equal. Thus, if 15 were chosen as our starting point, the probability of the 16th student being included in the sample is zero because our sampling interval is 20. However, the probability of students 15 and 35 both being included in the sample is 1/20 because if 15 is chosen (a 1 in 20 chance), then 35 is sure to be chosen as well. Estimating the precision of a

---

[4]Even so, the draft lottery was not without its critics. Notz, Staw, and Cook (1971) suggested that the numbers were not mixed well, and hence the drawing was not random. Men with birthdays in the first half of the year were more likely to be drawn early than those from the latter half. Apparently, the drum containing the birthdates was not agitated sufficiently. In a drawing with life-and-death implications, these niceties of sampling become more than academic.

systematic sample is difficult unless we are willing to make some simplifying assumptions. In practice, it is generally assumed that if the sampling frame is arranged haphazardly, the resulting (systematic) sample approximates a simple random sample (and hence, the precision formulas presented earlier may be used). This generally is a safe assumption unless the frame is ordered in a cyclical manner and the sampling interval coincides with the length of the cycle. For example, suppose a frame contained the names of all applicants for a marriage license. Suppose the names of the couples to be married are listed in order, with the woman's always coming before the man's. If we used an odd number as our sampling interval, our sample would be more or less evenly represented by men and women. However, an even numbered interval would produce a sample consisting entirely of men, or of women depending on our starting point. This kind of regularity is not what we seek in developing a survey. However, sampling frames with cyclical arrangements "are rarely met in practice, and situations in which they may occur are usually easily recognized" (Kalton, 1983b, p. 19).

Stratification and Stratified Samples

Moser and Kalton (1972) made the important point that the definition of randomness refers to the means by which a sample is drawn, not to the outcome of this process, which is the sample itself. Thus, it is conceivable that one could draw a random sample that, in fact, appeared to be anything but random. To return again to our rent example, suppose that one of our research issues concerned the question of whether the rent students paid was associated with class standing. Do off-campus seniors, for example, typically pay more rent than off-campus sophomores? To answer this question, we would require that both seniors and sophomores be included in the sample. However, it is possible that even if there were a fair number of sophomores on our "off-campus renters" list, our sample might contain none. Such a chance event would be extremely unlikely, but if we were extraordinarily unlucky, it could occur, even if our sampling technique were flawless.

To control the size of the samples selected from different subgroups of the population, survey researchers generally make use of a technique known as *stratification*, in which the population is divided into theoretically meaningful or empirically important *strata* before the sample is drawn. (This procedure is analogous to the use of blocking in experimental research, as discussed in chap. 4.) Sampling units (or respondents) then are chosen randomly from within each stratum, and this permits prespecified sample sizes to be selected for each stratum. Two forms of stratified sampling are possible, depending on the manner in which the sampling fraction is employed. Frequently, the same sampling fraction is used for all strata; in such a case, the result is called a *proportionate stratified (random) sample*. Sometimes, a different sampling fraction is employed within each strata; in this instance, the resulting sample is termed a *disproportionate stratified (random) sample*. Generally, the research issues themselves dictate whether a proportionate or disproportionate stratified sample is drawn.

To provide an example of situations that would call for the use of proportionate or disproportionate stratified sampling, consider the following scenario. Suppose that the democratic governor wanted to raise the state income tax, but was concerned about the effect that such an action might have on her political future. To obtain some prior information regarding the effect of such a move on her popularity and the differential impact that such a proposal might have on a number of different "constituencies" that were important to her continued effectiveness, she commissioned a survey to study the issue. Depending on the number and complexity of the populations (constituencies) of interest, this survey could take many forms, but we begin with a simple case.

Suppose we wanted to determine the reaction to the tax hike of people from two obvious constituencies, namely, registered Democratic and registered Republican voters. (For the sake of convenience, we assume that all voters in the state must register as belonging either to the Democratic or the Republican Party.) To survey these groups, (a) the list of registered voters in the state (the sampling frame) could be divided into Democratic and Republican strata, (b) some sampling fraction (say, 2%) decided on, (c) the appropriate number of people (in this case, 2% of the total number of registered Democratic and Republican voters) randomly chosen from each list, and (d) the resulting sample interviewed.[5] Because the same sampling fraction is employed in both strata, the sample is a proportionate stratified random sample (i.e., an epsem design). Note that in this approach, the sample size in a stratum is exactly proportional to the population size in that stratum. Thus, if Democratic voters constituted 65% of the population, 65% of the resulting sample would consist of Democratic voters.

In some instances, a proportionate sampling strategy does not provide a sample (within a stratum) sufficient for research purposes. For instance, if the governor wanted to analyze the data of the Republican voters on their own, a 2% sampling of the 35% of the total population who registered as Republicans might not prove sufficient. In this instance, a sampling fraction greater than that used to choose the Democratic Party stratum might be employed. This approach would render the sample a disproportionate stratified sample.

Suppose that the simple Democratic–Republican breakdown provided data that were too gross for the governor's purposes—a more fine-grained stratification process was called for. Accordingly, the lists of Democratic and Republican voters could be further subdivided by sex and county. (Although voter registration lists do not list voters' sex, we will assume that a semi-reliable estimate could be derived from given names—usually a bad idea.) The resulting lists (strata), formed by the combination of political party, sex, and county could then be sampled using a constant or uniform sampling fraction (again, say, 2%), and the results could result in a more precise (overall) estimate of voters' opinions. The sampling operations employed in this example are diagrammed in Fig. 10.1. In addition, assuming adequate sample size (within strata), such an approach also facilitates the analysis of individual strata. As in the previous example, given the use of a uniform sampling fraction, the sample takes the form of a proportionate stratified (random) sample.

As noted earlier, in some instances it is wise to employ different sampling fractions among strata. Returning to our beleaguered governor, suppose that she feels that people of high socioeconomic status (SES) might have a disproportionate influence on the outcome of the election. Accordingly, it is important that she know what the more affluent voters of the state think of her tax hike idea. To determine this, we could add another stratification factor, SES, to our original design. (As with sex, voter registration lists do not provide such information; however, we might use a proxy for SES based on each voter's address.) The stratified population from which the sample is to be drawn for County A might then look like that of Table 10.2. The same table would be repeated for each county, which operates as a factor in our design, much as a factor in a factorial design (chap. 4).

As shown in Table 10.2, there are relatively few voters in County A at the upper end of the SES categorization. Yet, we suspect that their opinions matter greatly because

---

[5]Later in the chapter, we discuss factors that help the survey researcher decide on the number of units to employ in the sample. In subsequent chapters, important considerations regarding the construction of the different types of measuring devices that can be employed in surveys are presented.

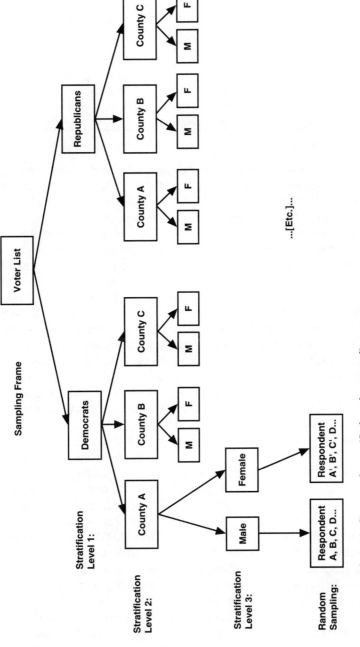

FIG. 10.1.   Schematic diagram of a stratified random sampling process.

TABLE 10.2

State Voter Population in Country A, Stratified by Party
Preference and Socioeconomic Status (SES)

	Democratic		Republican	
SES	Males	Females	Males	Females
Upper	800	1200	3000	1600
Upper-middle	3000	3600	9000	8000
Middle	20000	28800	31900	19100
Lower-middle	39000	41800	20000	22000
Lower	25000	24000	3000	4900

these are the people who control the communications media, who contribute the lion share to political campaign funds, and so forth. As such, the governor is interested in their reactions. Accordingly, we decide on a disproportionate sampling strategy. We will randomly sample 5% of the potential respondents in the upper SES categories (i.e., 100 Democrats—40 men and 60 women, and 230 Republicans—150 men and 80 women), 2.5% of those in the upper-middle strata (165 Democrats and 445 Republicans), and 0.5% of the respondents in the remaining strata. (As in proportionate stratified sampling, the actual sampling units—respondents, in this case—are chosen randomly, within the constraints imposed by the sampling fraction and the stratification rules.) This approach is called disproportionate stratified (random) sampling because all strata are not equally represented. The two highest SES strata are oversampled, relative to the other strata, to provide sufficient numbers of respondents to allow for separate within-stratum analyses. It is important to note, however, that when the overall precision estimate is calculated, the sample is weighted so as to compensate for the disproportionate oversampling of the two highest SES strata. In calculating the overall precision estimate, that is, responses are weighted to redress the imbalance of the sample in such a way as to statistically "remake" the sample into a proportionate stratified sample.

Why should the survey researcher go to the bother to stratify? Earlier, we suggested that one compelling reason was to offset the possible selection of an unusual distribution of respondents. Although possible, such an occurrence is unlikely. More importantly, proportionate stratification ensures that the distribution of respondent units in the sample is the same as that in the population, and this enhances the precision of our estimate. In other words, by controlling for the effects of a particular stratification variable, we reduce error in our estimates because differences that would have occurred as a result of the categorization difference are now controlled, or accounted for. For example, suppose that Republicans and Democrats characteristically respond differently to a Democratic governor's request for a tax increase. If we did not stratify on political party preference, the different responses would add to the standard error of our estimate, thereby lowering precision. Without stratifying, the differences that occurred as a result of party preference would not be accounted for. By using political party as a stratification factor, with proportionate stratification, we control for these party-related response differences, thereby buying greater precision.

Just as controlling for political party differences enhances the precision of our estimate, so too does stratification on the other factors employed in the examples presented. In general, it is true that the more stratification factors, the greater the precision of the estimate.[6] It must be understood, however, that to stratify, we must possess (a) population data on the stratification factors and (b) separate lists for the strata. In our example, this means that we would need to be able to identify male Democrats, male Republicans, female Democrats, female Republicans, and the counties in which they reside. In general, stratification adds to precision to the extent that the different strata characteristically respond differently on the issue under investigation. Thus, returning to our example, if men and women responded more or less identically to a tax increase proposal, then stratifying on sex would have little effect on precision; that is, the stratification factor would not account for any variation. If they responded very differently, however, then stratification would be a powerful addition to precision of estimates. The trade off here is clear: Stratification can be expensive and difficult, so to determine whether it is worth the costs involved, we should first decide whether or not the stratification factor is in some way related systematically to the variables under study.

Other Sampling Formats

Cluster and Multistage Sampling. In many research situations, the available sampling frame does not provide a list of all potential respondents; however, a good estimate of the *places* in which respondents might be found is available. For example, suppose we wished to sample the parents of public high school students in a large midwestern city. We are interested in their feelings about the adequacy of advanced placement courses. The school board is reluctant to give us the names of all parents or guardians. As such, we have no sampling frame, at least initially. We could proceed, nonetheless, by obtaining a detailed map of the city, which listed each block, and then randomly sample these natural clusters. In *cluster sampling*, we make use of the natural segment (or cluster) as the sampling unit. In this method, the sampling frame is identified (say, all blocks of houses in the city), and from this population, specific clusters (blocks, in this case) are chosen, either through simple or stratified random sampling. Once a cluster is chosen for inclusion in the sample, *all* members of the cluster are surveyed (in our example, all eligible parents of highschoolers within the chosen cluster, or block, would be surveyed).

In *multistage sampling*, a cluster is sampled from a sampling frame (as in cluster sampling), and then (unlike cluster sampling) the cluster is sampled as well. To return to our high school example, for a two-stage sample, we divide the total city into blocks and then choose some of these blocks for our sample. However, instead of surveying all members of the chosen blocks, we sample within them. Thus, only selected members of each of the chosen clusters are used. This procedure can be extended to more stages. For example, in a national election survey, we might break the nation into counties, then census tracks, then blocks within the chosen census tracks, and finally, households within the tracks, and specific voters within the household. Figure 10.2 illustrates the differences between cluster and multistage sampling.

One potential distorting influence that must be attended to when using cluster or multistage sampling concerns the fact that clusters generally are not of uniform size. For instance, in our high school example, not all of the selected blocks would contain the same number of parents. This problem is exacerbated when the cluster sizes are of great

---

[6]If forced to choose, the survey researcher generally should aim for more strata, even if relatively ill-defined, rather than fewer, more tightly constituted, highly differentiated strata. Greater precision per sampling unit is obtained in this way.

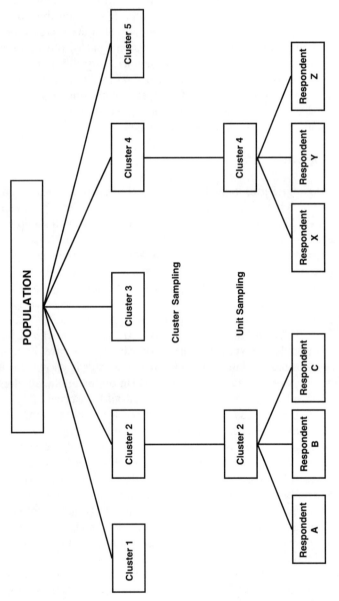

FIG. 10.2. Schematic diagram of cluster and multistage sampling approaches.

variability, as would be the case when counties are used as the primary sampling units in a state-wide or national sample, and individual households the elements to be sampled. In such cases, the potential respondents do not have an equal probability of selection, and the precision of the resulting estimates is thereby jeopardized.

An approach known as *probability proportional to size* sampling (PPS) has been developed to solve this potential problem. Kalton (1983b) discussed the details of this technique; for our purposes, it is sufficient to understand that the PPS sampling approach ensures that the likelihood of selection in a cluster or multistage sample is the same for all potential sampling units (or elements) no matter the size of the cluster from which they are drawn. Under such constraints, the sample is an epsem one, and the standard approaches for estimating precision may be used. PPS sampling should be used in cluster or multistage sampling designs.

Multistage sampling is particularly useful when the population to be studied is spread over a large geographic area. For example, suppose we wished to use face-to-face interviews to determine the proportion of a state's inhabitants who used some form of state-financed social service. Using a multistage sampling approach, we could make use of the state's natural segmentation into counties, and randomly select a given number of counties for the sample. At this point, we could randomly select towns within each of the chosen counties, neighborhoods within the towns, and blocks within the neighborhoods. Then, we could list the dwellings within the blocks, and (in the case of multistage sampling) sample individual respondents within the dwellings. Notice that by using this approach, there is no necessity for constructing a sampling frame for individuals, which in many instances would be prohibitively expensive, if not impossible. Instead, our interviewers need only learn the number of potential respondents within a household that has been selected for sampling, and then select among respondents by some pre-specified selection scheme (Kish, 1965, developed a widely used selection method to be used in these contexts. It is known as the Kish selection grid.) In research situations of the type described here, multistage sampling offers a practical alternative to simple (or stratified) random sampling, which requires complete sampling frames before the initiation of the research. However, the multistage sampling approach usually does not provide estimates that are as precise, and this is especially true if the clusters are homogeneous on the issues tapped in the survey.

To illustrate this point, suppose that the citizens of certain counties were impoverished relative to those of others (and hence, were more likely to make use of the social services offered by the state). If, by chance, either these or the other counties were overrepresented in the sample, the survey would provide inaccurate estimates. A relative overabundance of poorer counties would suggest that more people statewide made use of the state's services than was actually the case, whereas the opposite (though equally erroneous) conclusion would be drawn if the richer counties were inadvertently oversampled.

With the cluster and multistage sampling approaches, the precision of the survey estimates thus depends on the distributional characteristics of the traits of interest. If the population clusters are relatively homogeneous on the issues that are central to the survey, with heterogeneity between clusters, the results obtained through this method will be less precise than those obtained from a random sample of the same size. However, if the population clusters are relatively heterogeneous (i.e., if the individual clusters provide a representative picture of the overall population), multistage sampling will generate estimates as precise as simple random sampling. Notice that the heterogeneity of a sample has different implications for cluster and stratified sampling. With stratified sampling, increased heterogeneity within strata results in a *loss* of precision—the respondents (or sampling units) within strata ideally should be as similar as possible. With cluster or multistage sampling, however, increased heterogeneity within clusters results in an *increase* in precision.

A method that is almost always employed to offset the homogeneity problem involves the stratification of clusters in advance of their selection. Thus, counties can be stratified by population size, level of employment, and so on, using census or Department of Labor statistics; in the high school example, homerooms could be stratified by grade, male–female ratio, and so forth. By this prestratification process, we help ensure that clusters from different strata are represented approximately equally in the sample.

Two-phase Sampling. In two-phase (or double) sampling, all respondents (who might have been chosen by any sampling method, e.g., simple random, cluster, or multistage sampling) complete the basic survey. Then, either concurrently or some time thereafter, selected units in the sample are asked to provide additional information. In two-phase sampling, two (or more) surveys are conducted: the *basic* survey, in which all participate, and the *auxiliary* survey (or surveys), which employs a specified subsample of the main sample. Two-phase sampling is an extremely useful, and widely used, technique. The United States Bureau of the Census, for example, has used two-phase sampling in its population counts for more than 40 years. In the census, certain standard data are collected from all households; in addition, some households are asked to provide considerably more information.

Perhaps the most important use of two-phase sampling is in developing stratification factors. When the auxiliary data are collected subsequent to (rather than concurrent with) the basic survey information, the initial survey can be used to create stratification factors. Oftentimes, in two-phase sampling, relatively esoteric groups, which cannot be identified on the basis of readily available information, are sought for study. On the basis of the information obtained in the first-phase sample, the sought-after group is identified, and (usually) disproportionately oversampled, with a lesser sampling fraction being used for the remaining population. In this way, "rare" respondent groups can be identified in sufficient numbers to allow for their study.[7]

Panel Surveys. The "multisurvey" form of the multiphase sampling method must be distinguished from the panel survey, in which a prespecified sample of respondents (a panel) is surveyed repeatedly, over time. In panel surveys, the respondent sample is not successively "whittled down" over the course of the sampling phases, as is characteristic of multiphase sampling. The purpose of the panel survey is to assess the individual changes that might occur in the knowledge, opinions, actions or perceptions of the respondent sample over the course of time. Panel surveys have proved especially useful in public opinion contexts, in which the performance of a political figure is monitored over time, in surveys of people's perceptions of their economic well-being, in voter-preference studies, and so on (see Blalock, 1985; Duncan, 1984; Rahn, Krosnick, & Breuning, 1994; and Tanur, 1983; for a discussion of some of the applications and methodological difficulties that panel designs can involve). Given careful sampling, panel surveys can provide a sensitive index of the mood of an entire nation. Indeed, panel surveys have proved to be very powerful tools in predicting the shifting allegiances of the electorate and the consequences of such shifts on the outcomes of state and national elections.

---

[7]Although we limit our discussion to a simple two-phase sampling process, the number of ancillary surveys that can be undertaken is limited only by cost considerations and the patience of the respondents in the sample. When more than two sampling phases are used, the approach is termed *multiphase sampling*.

ADDITIONAL CONSIDERATIONS

Sampling Frame

To this point, our discussion of survey design and sampling has focused primarily on the various forms of sample designs that surveys employ and their advantages and disadvantages, especially in light of the concept of precision. There are additional factors that should be considered when using any sampling technique, however, and these are noted briefly in the pages that follow. The first of these is concerned with the sampling frame.

At one point or another in the development of any survey sample, some listing of the population must be obtained. This listing is called the *sampling frame*. As noted, in simple random sampling, the frame must be a listing of all the individual population units, whereas in cluster or multistage sampling, the initial listing is of the clusters that contain all the population units, and the subsequent listings are required only for the clusters selected at the first stage.

Two types of sampling frames are most commonly employed. The first of these consists of a listing of all of the names of a specified population, for example, the students of a university, the list of registered voters of a county or precinct, all subscribers of a magazine, or members of a professional organization. Such lists are convenient and can prove extremely useful for sample selection. However, possible limitations of the list must be clearly acknowledged. For example, suppose that we obtained a list of all of the subscribers to *Fortune Magazine*. Would it be legitimate to use this list as the sampling frame for a survey? Of course it would, if we were concerned with estimating characteristics or attitudes of this particular *population of subscribers*. It would be an inappropriate frame for sampling the U.S. population because the subscribers to this periodical are, on average, considerably wealthier and better educated than the typical person. The sampling frame needs to provide a complete coverage of the population to which inferences are to be made. Kish (1965) provided an extended discussion of factors that influence the quality of sampling frames.

Less obvious are the biases associated with using telephone directories as our sampling frame, a convenient, though not entirely satisfactory, sampling tactic. First of all, although approximately 95% of American households have telephones (Congressional Information Service, 1990), at least 25% of all residential subscribers do not have their names listed in the directory (Schuman & Kalton, 1985). Thus, it is dangerous to assume that a sample based on names drawn from a telephone directory is representative of the general population. Too many potential systematic differences (poverty, mobility, differential needs for privacy, latent paranoia, etc.) between those with and without telephones, and between listed and unlisted subscribers, make such a practice risky. The technique of random digit dialing, discussed later in this chapter, presents one way of offsetting the problem of unlisted telephone subscribers, but it does not address the fact that people who have telephones are quite different from those who do not (Thornberry & Massey, 1988).

A second form of commonly used sampling frame consists of a detailed map of a specific physical environment, such as a city or town, a precinct, ward, or neighborhood. Cluster or multistage sampling is used with sampling frames of this type. The use of maps in defining the sampling frame is common in surveys that seek to cover reasonably wide geographic areas. In general, however, their use is more difficult and demanding than survey designs that employ population lists as the sampling frame. In many situations, however, no adequate population lists are available; under these circumstances, maps become a useful sampling alternative.

Random Digit Dialing

In recent years, the use of the telephone as a data collection method for surveys has increased markedly. The technique of random digit dialing has been developed for telephone survey sampling. Although telephone surveys have been used for many years (e.g., see Cooper, 1964; Troldahl & Carter, 1964), they have recently received intense critical attention; this attention, in turn, has resulted in the refinement and further development of the telephone method of data collection. *Random digit dialing* was developed to overcome the frame deficiency of unlisted numbers in the telephone directory. As noted earlier, about 25% of U.S. residential telephone subscribers are unlisted, and it has been estimated that in some large metropolitan areas, as many as 40% of all residential phones are unlisted (Sudman, 1976). In such an instance, using the city's telephone directory as the sampling frame can result in considerable bias, especially if those who choose not to list their phone numbers are in some ways systematically different from those who do (see Brunner & Brunner, 1971, and Glasser & Metzger, 1975, for a discussion of this issue).

To overcome this limitation, survey researchers developed a number of ingenious solutions involving random digit dialing, some of which, unfortunately, have some rather major practical deficiencies. The simplest random digit dialing approach calls for the use of a random number generator to develop lists of telephone numbers. Those answering the number constitute the sample. The problem with this approach is that most of the numbers generated in this manner either are not in use, or are not assigned to residential dwellings (but rather to commercial enterprises, government agencies, etc.). Glasser and Metzger (1972) estimated that fewer than 20% of randomly generated numbers result in usable responses. When 80% of a survey researcher's calls are futile, the costs of the study are exacerbated intolerably.

An alternative scheme makes use of the list of all published numbers in combination with a randomization process. This option begins with the random selection of telephone numbers from the phone directory. Then, the last two digits of each of the chosen numbers are deleted and replaced by random numbers. This approach has the advantage of assuring the survey researcher that the numbers employed in the study are potentially in use, and this, in turn, dramatically increases the proportion of usable numbers, from approximately 20% when purely random numbers are used to approximately 50%. However, this approach has disadvantages because directory-listed prefixes may be biased in some way, and 50% is still an unacceptably high proportion of useless calls.

To improve on this procedure, Waksberg (1978) suggested an elaboration of the random number approach. In Waksberg's model (and most others making use of telephone data collection methods), the survey analyst obtains from the phone company a list of all area codes and (3-digit) prefix numbers (exchanges) currently in use in the area to be sampled. Then, every possible two-digit number is added to these numbers. This list of 8-place numbers constitutes the initial sampling frame. Numbers are sampled randomly from this frame, and then two additional random numbers are added to those selected, thus resulting in 10 numbers, consisting of a 3-number area code, a 3-number exchange (both of which are known to be currently in use), and the 4 additional numbers needed to complete the phone call. Each of these numbers is called. If the number is not a residential listing, it is discarded from further consideration. If, however, the number is that of a residential phone, it is sampled and used as the basis for further number generation, by randomly replacing the last two numbers of each successful "seed number."

The advantage to Waksberg's (1978) approach derives from the fact that the telephone company uses banks of 100 numbers; as such, the final two digits of a phone number are very informative with respect to the utility of the other 99 possible numbers that can be generated by random sampling of these numbers. If the phone number can be used, this implies that the remaining numbers will also fit the criteria employed in selection of sampling units; if it cannot be used, there is a strong likelihood that the remaining 99 possibilities also cannot be used. Following Waksberg's method can result in significant savings.

Telephone versus Face-to-Face Interviews

Use of telephones to conduct surveys is a recent innovation relative to the "standard" model, which involves a face-to-face interview. The most obvious reason why we would turn to the telephone is obvious: Telephone surveys can result in substantial savings of interviewer time and research funds. In fact, most large-scale national surveys today are done by telephone; the costs of doing otherwise would be prohibitive for most organizations. From the minute of its first use, researchers have debated the validity of telephone survey relative to the more standard model. In early attempts to validate a telephone interview approach, researchers compared their phone results with those obtained under the standard face-to-face conditions. If the results were similar, a vote was cast in favor of the telephone approach by virtue of its efficiency and cost savings. Differences between the two survey modes often were taken as evidence of the failure of the telephone survey to produce valid results. This interpretation is based on assumptions that rely more on tradition ("we've always done it this way") than logic. Consider a survey in which sensitive issues are the focus of inquiry—respondents' use of illegal drugs, or other illegal acts, risky sexual practices, and so on. In which context is the more honest answer to the following question to be obtained?

How many times in the last year have you driven while intoxicated?

Arguably, a person speaking anonymously over the phone might be more willing to give an honest answer to this question (assuming the answer was more than never) than a respondent facing his or her questioner across the kitchen table. The quasi-anonymity of the phone conversation would seem to promote more honest answers to sensitive questions. Hoppe and her colleagues (2000) suggest that this intuition is correct, as does research by McAuliffe, Geller, LaBrie, Paletz, and Fournier (1998). Both of these studies reveal rather small differences in respondents' answers to questions in telephone versus face-to-face interviews, and when differences occur, they suggest that the more valid answers are obtained over the phone because higher rates of socially undesirable behaviors are reported over the telephone. Boekeloo, Schamus, Simmens, and Cheng (1998) found higher rates of reporting of both drug abuse and sexual encounters in their sample of early teenagers using a telephone versus face-to-face interview, and concluded that the telephone survey is a reliable method of obtaining valid data. On the basis of findings of this kind, Noble, Moon, and McVey (1998) touted the use of random digit dialing for large-scale policy research and suggested that the technique produces results that do not appear to be less valid than those derived from more standard forms of face-to-face interviews. Greenfield, Midanik, and Rogers (2000) agreed with this observation and suggested that the telephone survey approaches in general appear to produce results similar to the more usual interview format. However, as Lavrakas (1993, 1998) suggested in his review of telephone survey methodology, caution should be exercised when using this approach. Because telephone service costs money, surveys making use of the telephone—even random digit dialing surveys—systematically undersample the poor, the undereducated, the disenfranchised, and people of low income and modest educational accomplishment. On some issues, this underrepresentation may produce biased results, whereas on others, these sociodemographic variations may be inconsequential. For an example of a context in which these differences may matter greatly, consider a survey research study concerned with people's attitudes toward government housing assistance for the poor. We know that the poor are less likely to have phones. As a consequence, their presumably positive responses to the government's program would be underestimated. The survey results would suggest that the general population was less favorably disposed to housing assistance than is actually the case. This problem is not specific to survey methods using random digit dialing, but to telephone surveys in general. In using the telephone survey—or any other research technique for that matter—it is imperative to assess in advance the potential interaction of content with research method, and to adjust the method accordingly.

CAPI, CATI, and CASAI: Augmenting the Technique

Many surveys make use of skip patterns. A *skip pattern* is a roadmap through the interview, which directs the researcher to omit certain questions depending on the respondent's earlier answers. For example, in one section of our survey, we might be interested in the respondent's educational history. If the person had finished only high school, it would be foolish to ask the year he or she graduated from college. The college and graduate school questions would be skipped on the basis of the respondent's earlier response, and we would jump to the next section of the survey. Following the skip patterns in a complex survey can be arduous for the researcher. The computer helps solve this problem. With readily available programming, computers can be used to skip to the appropriate survey items with 100% accuracy. When using face-to-face interviewing methods augmented by the computer, the general term for this technique is *computer assisted personal interviewing* (CAPI). CAPI is widely used today. Now, the researcher need only read the preprogrammed questions and enter the participant's responses on line. CAPI is a useful tool: It allows the researcher to use visual aids, if necessary, to clarify questions or alternative response choices, assures that the proper skip pattern is followed, and cuts costs by obliging the interview to enter respondents' data as soon as they are supplied. In the days of paper and pencil scoring, the researcher entered respondents' answers on paper, and these were later entered into the computer. Each step between response and analysis opens the door to error, so eliminating even one step in the data transfer process is a step in the right direction.

In addition to making research easier, more efficient, and more reliable, CAPI opens the door to a development in survey research that is becoming increasingly popular. CAPI facilitates experimental manipulations in survey research. For example, we might be interested in the effect of question order: Are items answered differently as a consequence of their coming before, or following, other questions? With CAPI, it is easy to manipulate question order to investigate this issue. Minor variations in question wording can be incorporated into the computerized script, and their effects assessed. CAPI has opened the door to a host of experimental interventions; coupled with the strict concern for sampling that is characteristic of the survey research approach, this invasion of experimental techniques promises to provide powerful data of impressive generality.

CATI—*computer assisted telephone interviewing*—is the CAPI equivalent for telephone surveys. CATI has long been a fixture in telephone interviewing and is a well-developed methodology, with a number of commercial software programs available to help develop the survey interview, skip patterns, experimental interventions, and so on.

Because it enjoys all the benefits of CAPI, CATI is used extensively in telephone surveys. The approach is economically appealing: It requires fewer qualified interviewers because the computer takes over many of the survey researcher's decisions.

A computerized analogue of the paper and pencil survey is called CASAI, *computer-assisted self-administered interviewing*. This method replaces the paper form with a laptop (typically), which presents the survey instrument to the respondent. This approach has all the advantages of the previously mentioned computer-assisted approaches; that is, skip patterns can be programmed, experimental manipulations built into the survey instrument, and so on. Another very important advantage of CASAI over the standard paper and pencil survey is that the computer can be programmed to refuse illegitimate responses. Sometimes, respondents inadvertently fail to answer all questions, or give answers that are impossible. A sophisticated CASAI program can alert the respondent that he or she has provided an answer that is illogical or impossible, or that an item has been skipped. In this way, incomplete data are drastically reduced; given the costs involved in selecting and recruiting survey respondents, this reduction of incomplete data results in important savings, in addition to maintaining the integrity of the sample.

A variant of CASAI is *audio-CASAI*, in which respondents are fitted with earphones and the survey questions are presented (via computer) aurally, and answers are received on the computer. This would not seem an immense advance, and perhaps it is not; however, for treating sensitive subjects, it offers many advantages. The respondent may answer questions without having to interact with the survey researcher. As such, it is hypothesized that audio-CASAI will lead to more honest responses. A second obvious advantage to the technique is evident when working with respondents who are not skilled readers. In this case, a verbal interview is conducted, although one of the interactants is a machine. All of these mechanized approaches have two central goals. The first is obvious: to cut costs of research. The second is less obvious, but perhaps even more important, and that is to enhance the reliability and validity of the research. Used wisely, computer-assisted techniques can satisfy both goals.

Answering Machines

As phone answering machines became an increasingly common feature of most homes, researchers have become worried that their telephone surveys would fall prey to large proportions of nonresponse. People would screen their calls, they reasoned, and as soon as a survey researcher made contact, they would assume that he or she was attempting to sell them something. They would not pick up the call, and if enough people did this, sampling would be compromised and the study ruined.

Survey researchers have good reason to worry about call screening. For years, un-scrupulous salespeople have used fake surveys to gain entry into people's homes. Many of us are sensitive to these invasions and are likely to avoid them whenever possible. Call screening via telephone answering machines offers a good opportunity to avoid unwanted calls of this type. Does the answering machine represent a threat to survey research? Oldendick and Link (1994) investigated this question across nine random digit dial surveys, and found that only 2%–3% of households used answering machines to screen calls. On the surface, this proportion does not represent a severe threat to the integrity of the survey. However, careful consideration of the characteristics of those who screen calls raises concerns. Oldendick and Link found that wealthy, white, educated, young, city dwellers were most likely to screen. This consistency in demographic characteristics re-quires that researchers remain vigilant on this issue. If the practice of call screening expands and remains consistently associated with demographic characteristics, survey researchers will face a difficult problem.

Internet Surveys

The development of computer-assisted self-administered questionnaires (CASAI) has made possible a new forum for survey research, namely, web-based and e-mail surveys. Instead of mailing self-administered questionnaires to potential respondents, individuals can now be contacted by e-mail or through the World Wide Web and directed to a website where they can complete a survey instrument online. This method of reaching a sample of respondents has many advantages with respect to cost and time and effort. The major problem with electronic surveying is sampling representativeness.

In most cases, the sampling frame for a web-based survey is the population of people who have access to computers and feel comfortable using them regularly (Kiesler & Sproull, 1986). In this sense, electronic surveying methods are in a similar position to that of telephone surveying in the 1950s when many households still did not have telephone lines. Even though the number of households with computer access is increasing at a rapid rate, it is still true that people who have Internet access are likely to be more affluent, have higher education, be younger, and less likely to be Black or Hispanic than the general population of the United States (to say nothing of the world population). Further, many web-based surveys are conducted on a volunteer basis. A general announcement of the availability of an opportunity to participate in a social survey is posted on popular websites and interested respondents are instructed how to participate. Not surprisingly, the samples generated by such methods are highly self-selected and not typical of the population at large.

Kiesler and Sproull (1986) were among the first to use the Internet for research purposes. Via the Internet, they sent a survey to a set of individuals randomly selected from a list of all e-mail addresses at a university. Concurrently, they sent the survey to other students from the list via traditional mail system. The researchers found no differences in response rates between the two groups. This substantive result was replicated by some researchers (e.g., Mehta & Sivadas, 1995), and challenged by the results of others (e.g., Schuldt & Totten, 1994).

In an effort to implement probability-based random sampling for internet surveys, some survey organizations recruit panels of respondents by contacting individuals through standard random digit dialing telephone survey sampling techniques. When potential respondents have been reached by telephone, they are then invited to become part of a survey research panel and provided with the necessary equipment to complete surveys online in exchange for their participation. For example, Knowledge Networks is one organization that has recruited a panel of nearly 100,000 potential respondents in this way and provides panel participants with Internet access via web TVs. Once individuals are in the panel, this constitutes a sampling frame for specific surveys. Random samples of the panel are drawn and sent electronic messages instructing them to complete a survey on a specified site. This sampling method is initially costly in terms of recruitment and provision of hardware, but it does produce samples that are close to comparable in representativeness to those obtained by standard random digit dialing telephone survey methods.

Sample Size

The question of sample size must always be addressed in developing any survey. How many respondents must we sample to arrive at a reasonable estimate of population values?

Before we can answer this question, however, we must answer a series of other questions, and once these issues are decided on, the sample size more or less defines itself. As in all other areas of survey sampling, the decision regarding the size of the sample involves trade-offs, most of which concern the complementary issues of cost and precision.

It seems intuitively plausible that the size of the sampling fraction would be an important determinant of the adequacy of the sample. Such is not the case, however. When the underlying population is large, precise sample results can be obtained even when the sampling fraction is very small. What matters most is the *absolute size* of the sample, rather than the size of the sample *relative to* the size of the population. A moment's reflection on the formula for the standard error of a simple random sample, given earlier in this chapter, shows why this is so. This formula demonstrates that the size of the sample, not the sampling fraction, determines precision.

The first decision that must be made in determining the size of the survey sample concerns the amount of tolerable error. The less precision required of the results, the smaller the sample needed. Thus, if we wish to obtain extremely precise findings (i.e., results that will estimate underlying population values with a high degree of accuracy) it must be understood that we will need to sample more respondents. Cost and precision go hand in hand.

Suppose we wish to estimate the proportion of the population that possesses a specific trait or characteristic, or holds a given belief or value. Having made the decision regarding the degree of precision necessary for our purposes, we must make a rough estimate of the proportion of the population that possess the trait or belief. For example, we might want to estimate the proportion of a city's electorate that would vote for the Democratic gubernatorial candidate. To estimate the necessary sample size with a certain degree of precision, we first have to estimate this percentage. Suppose that some prior, informal surveys indicated that the Democrat could be expected to garner approximately 58% of the vote in the city. Then, having decided on the necessary precision, we could determine the necessary sample size for a simple random sample by the formula,

$$n = p(1 - p)/(\text{S.E.})^2,$$

where n = the necessary sample size,
p = the estimated proportion of the city's population who plan to vote Democratic, and
S.E. = the standard error of the sample proportion (i.e., the amount of error we can tolerate).

Applying this formula, assuming a standard error of 5%, would yield the following:

$$n = .58(.42)/.05^2, \text{ or, } n = 97 + \text{respondents.}$$

It is unlikely in most contexts that a standard error of this magnitude would be acceptable. It results in a 95% confidence interval of $+/-10\%$.[8] However, this value provides a useful point of contrast for later calculations. It is informative to manipulate the two crucial parameters in the equation to determine the effects of differing precision needs, and the influence of the accuracy of the population proportion estimate, on sample size. Suppose that instead of a standard error of 5%, the governor decided that no more than a 2% standard error was acceptable. This is a more reasonable choice, as it results in a 95% confidence interval of $+/-4\%$. In this case, assuming the same 58% favorableness

---

[8]That is, the estimate is within 10% of the population percentage, with a 95% probability.

estimate, the size of the simple random sample necessary would change from 97+ people to more than 600! In fact, 609 respondents would be needed to arrive at a 2% standard error, assuming that 58% of the population favored the Democrat. And if a 1% standard error were sought, more than 2,400 respondents would have to be surveyed. Again, the interplay of cost and precision is obvious.

For the sake of simplicity, we ignore the finite population correction (fpc). However, when the sample consists of more than 10% of the population, the fpc should be used. The appropriate correction formula is:

$$n = Nn'/(N + n')$$

where n = the corrected sample size,
N = the population size, and
n' = the uncorrected sample size (derived from the earlier formula).

Thus, in a city of 50,000 voters, the sample size necessary to insure a 1% standard error would be $50,000 \times 2,400/(50,000 + 2,400)$, or $n = 2,290$ respondents. This figure assumes that all eligible voters actually vote. If this is not the case, then an additional correction is needed. Suppose that from past experience we know that not all of the city's eligible voters actually exercise their right to vote. In this case, we would revise our earlier revised estimate, by dividing this earlier figure by our estimate of the proportion of eligibles that actually will vote. Thus, if we expect that 80% of all eligible voters will exercise their franchise, we would require approximately 2,863 (i.e., 2290/.8) respondents for our survey.

In general, the accuracy of the population proportion estimate is not nearly as telling as the desired precision level in determining sample size; this is fortunate because the accuracy of this parameter estimate rarely is certain. To illustrate this point, suppose that in fact 58% of the electorate actually favored the Republican candidate, rather than the Democrat. In this circumstance, the needed sample size for any of the desired precision levels that we calculated earlier would not change. The positions of the population proportion estimates in the numerator of the formula would change, but this would not influence the outcome of the calculation. It is the deviation of the proportion estimates from an equal (50–50) split that influences sample size, and a moment's reflection shows why this is as it should be. If there is substantial inequality between respondents' preferences for one or another option (in this instance, in their choice of governor), then fewer respondents should be needed to assess this underlying population preference accurately. This is, indeed, the case. Thus, if we estimated that 90% of the population preferred the Democratic candidate, we would need only 250 people in our simple random sample to estimate the underlying population percentage who actually did plan to vote for her—if we were willing to settle for a 2% standard error, did not make use of the fpc, and assumed that all eligible voters would actually vote. Note that formulas presented here are applicable in the case of simple random samples. When other sampling designs of the type discussed earlier in the chapter are employed, the formulas must be modified somewhat.

A word of caution must be introduced at this point. The calculations of the size of a sample necessary to estimate a population parameter at a given level of precision will hold only if the sampling procedure itself is properly executed. If our basic sampling technique is flawed, then the number of respondents sampled will not matter much— the results of the sample will not accurately reflect population values. A classic example of this observation is provided in a real life case history that many think set back the cause of survey research for many years. This case, an often-told example in elementary sampling courses, took place in 1936. At that time, a popular magazine, the *Literary*

Digest, attempted a national poll to estimate who the electorate would choose as its next president: Franklin D. Roosevelt, the Democratic candidate running for his second term, or Alf Landon, the Republican nominee.

The results of the poll, printed in bold headlines at the beginning of the October 31, 1936, edition of the *Digest*, read:

Landon, 1,293,669; Roosevelt, 972,897
Final Returns in The Digest's Poll of Ten Million Voters

Obviously, the sample size chosen by the *Digest* was more than respectable, as it consisted of more than 10 million people! Yet, the *Digest*'s estimate was not only wrong, it was laughably off-base. Despite the *Digest*'s prediction, Roosevelt ended up with 523 electoral votes to Landon's 3! As a result, the headlines of the November 14 *Digest* read,

WHAT WENT WRONG WITH THE POLLS?
None of the Straw Votes Got Exactly the Right Answer—Why?

What did go wrong? Obviously, we cannot fault the *Digest* for having too small a sample. But just as obviously, the poll's results were disastrously off-base. How did a respected magazine, which had conducted similar polls in the past, with a high degree of success, make such a blunder? A brief review of the sampling procedures employed by the *Digest* will give some insight into these problems and hopefully illustrate the fact that sample size alone is not sufficient to guarantee accuracy of population estimates.

To perform their survey, the *Literary Digest* used telephone books and its membership list as the sampling frame. From their list, the *Digest* randomly sampled a large number of potential respondents, and sent them a "ballot," which was to be returned by mail. In retrospect, there are two glaringly obvious problems with this procedure: First, in 1936, the proportion of the population that owned telephones was not nearly as great as it is today. Those who did own phones were among the wealthy, a group that traditionally votes Republican. What's more, only 20% of the mailed ballots were returned. Again, there is evidence that suggests that more wealthy, better educated, people would do this. (The *Digest*'s own past polling experience had demonstrated this.) As such, the *Digest*'s sample was fatally flawed; it grossly oversampled those who, on the basis of important demographic indicators, would be likely to vote for a Republican presidential candidate, and grossly undersampled those who would likely vote Democratic. It is little wonder, under these circumstances, that the *Digest* predicted that the Republican would receive a landslide 57% of the vote when, in fact, he received only a fraction of this amount. The kinds of errors made by the *Literary Digest* are the stuff of which sampling legends are made.

Nonresponse

Attributable at least in part to the *Literary Digest* fiasco is the problem of dropouts or nonrespondents. Because sampling theory is based on probability theory, the mathematics that underlies sampling inference assumes *perfect* response rates. As Moser and Kalton (1972) observed:

> The theory is based essentially on the textbook situation of "urns and black and white balls,"
> and, while in agricultural and industrial sampling the practical situation corresponds closely

to its theoretical model, the social scientist is less fortunate. He has to sample from an urn in which some of the balls properly belonging to it happen not to be present at the time of selection, while others obstinately refuse to be taken from it. (p. 166)

Survey researchers have devised a number of ingenious methods to reduce nonresponse in data collection. In mail surveys, for example, cash incentives to participate and follow-ups sent to those who do not return the survey within a specified period of time have been shown to have a positive effect on the response rate (e.g., Armstrong, 1975; Heberlein & Baumgartner, 1978; Kanuk & Berenson, 1975; Linsky, 1975). In addition, considerable care is exercised in developing questionnaires of reasonable length, in personalizing the survey for the respondent, in guaranteeing anonymity, and so forth. Whether these tactics are effective in other forms of surveys (e.g., telephone, face-to-face interviews) is not established (see O'Neil, 1979).

In telephone and face-to-face interviews, a set of problems somewhat different from those of the mail interview is encountered. In phone and face-to-face research, we must distinguish "not-at-homes" (NAHs) from refusals. In the case of NAHs, survey researchers employ repeated attempts to contact the potential respondent. With refusals, different tactics are used. Some of the more established survey research organizations employ people with the descriptive job title of "refusal converters" to attempt to persuade recalcitrant respondents. In general, in the typical phone survey or face-to-face interview, most attempts to reduce the refusal rate focus on the means to gain "entry" or to develop rapport (see chap. 12, on interviewing, for an extended discussion of these issues). Many phone surveys, for example, attempt to induce respondents' compliance by presenting a set of nonthreatening, impersonal, and innocuous questions at the beginning of the survey. Having obtained the respondent's initial cooperation and commitment to the survey, the interviewer then moves on to more personal self-disclosures, which people ordinarily are reluctant to provide at the outset of the interview.

When the chosen methods to secure cooperation fail, as they sometimes do, survey analysts move to a different strategy, which involves the attempt to reduce the biasing impact of those who have been selected for the sample, but who are not present at the time the interviewer tries to contact them, or who refuse to cooperate with specific requests for information when they are interviewed. It is important to realize that these attempts are not solutions to the nonresponse problem, but rather means of attempting to reduce its biasing effect on the survey estimates. Detailing the technical aspects of these approaches is beyond the mission of this chapter (see Kalton, 1983; Kish, 1965; O'Neil, 1979; Politz & Simmonds, 1949); however, some of the more common techniques conceptualize the response–nonresponse distinction as a category on which members of the population can be stratified. If the researcher can obtain some information about the nonrespondents and compare it with that of the "respondent" stratum, then some means of estimating the probable response of the nonrespondents can be developed.

Other approaches (e.g., Cochran, 1977) make no inferences about the probable responses of the nonrespondents, but rather determine what the outcome of the survey would be if all of the nonrespondents had answered one way or the other (e.g., the technique may ask, "What if, had they participated, *all* the nonrespondents said that they planned to vote for—or against—the incumbent?"). This approach allows the researcher to draw boundaries on the percentage of the total sample voting for the incumbent. However, if the number of nonrespondents is sizeable, this range can be so great that the survey has no practical utility. There are many examples of correction approaches of this type available in the sampling literature—probably because the problem is so ubiquitous. The researcher interested in gaining the insights necessary to apply these solutions to his or her sampling problem, or to invent a solution that will work for a particular problem that might be encountered, is encouraged to consult this literature (e.g., see Daniel, 1975; Dillman, 1972; Dillman, Carpenter, Christenson, & Brooks, 1974; Dillman, Gallegos, & Frey, 1976; Kanuk & Berenson, 1975; O'Neil, 1979).

This chapter discussed the methods of drawing a sample, of estimating precision and sample size for simple random samples, and the like. However, considerations regarding the actual set of questions to be posed in the survey, the manner in which they are delivered, and their general form and content, have been set aside. In the next part of this book, five chapters are devoted to issues of this nature. We hope that the information presented here provides a useful background for this new information.

SUGGESTED READINGS

Hoppe, M. J., Gillmore, M. R., Valadez, D. L., Civic, D., Hartway, J., & Morrison, D. M. (2000). The relative costs and benefits of telephone interviews versus self-administered diaries for daily data collection. *Evaluation Review, 24,* 102–116.

Kalton, G. (1983). *Introduction to survey sampling.* Beverly Hills, CA: Sage.

Visser, P. S., Krosnick, J. A., & Lavrakas, P. J. (2000). Survey research. In H. Reis & C. M. Judd (Eds.), *Handbook of research methods in social and personality psychology* (pp. 223–252). Cambridge, England: Cambridge University Press.

DATA COLLECTION METHODS

CHAPTER

11

SYSTEMATIC OBSERVATIONAL METHODS AND NATURALISTIC RESEARCH

In the previous part of this book, we were concerned with general strategies used in the design and implementation of different types of research. In the next six chapters, we turn attention to methods of assessment and measurement used to collect the data that constitute the output of research studies. We begin this section with a general consideration of systematic observational methods. This is an obvious and appropriate starting point because all of the assessment or measurement techniques to be presented are dependent on some form of systematic observation. This chapter is fundamental to those that follow because it provides a general outline of the structural aspects that shape the overall character of all research that makes use of observational assessment techniques.

Although all science is fundamentally bound to observation, the term *systematic observational methods*, in our view, has come to refer to a diverse set of techniques that are employed to study behavior that:

- (Usually) occurs outside the formal boundaries of the laboratory,
- (Usually) is naturally instigated, that is, does not make use of a controlled experimental treatment,
- (Usually) places few restrictions on the allowable responses of the persons under observation,
- (Usually) emphasizes behavioral processes rather than outcomes, and
- *Always* entails a replicable system of assigning values to observed events.

This last condition separates *systematic* observational techniques from other observational methods that, while perhaps valuable, do not really fall into the realm of social science. Obviously, poets, novelists, and social critics may have important, profound insights into social phenomena. However, their work and visions, no matter how profound, no matter how useful, no matter how perceptive, cannot be counted as scientific because they do not depend on systematically collected and replicable data, continually refined via data-checking feedback, and so on—the process of scientific advance we advocated in the first pages of this book.

The tentative nature of the first four parts of our description of observational methods suggests both the range of research tactics that can be legitimately described as (systematically) observational and the variations that characterize researchers' uses of this general approach to accumulate scientifically informative data. Systematic observation can and often has been used in the laboratory, where behaviors are highly constrained, but in this chapter we focus our discussion principally on the use of observation in *natural* settings.

THREE ASPECTS OF NATURALISM

The naturalistic character of data obtained through observational methods is the most valued feature of research of this type—it is the major reason why research is conducted outside the friendly and facilitating confines of the laboratory. In his discussion of the dimensions of field research, Tunnell (1977) observed that there is some confusion about exactly how the naturalness of a research enterprise should be conceptualized. The criterion of naturalness, he observed, could be applied to the *behaviors* being studied, the *treatments* that are (or are not) applied, and the *setting* in which the research is conducted. Furthermore, these three factors could be combined in any number of ways, and these combinations would reflect the extent to which the total study could be judged as more or less naturalistic. At the extreme end of "unnaturalness," we have studies that constrain actions or require unnatural behaviors (i.e., actions that are not a usual part of the participant's behavioral repertoire), make use of strong manipulations, in unusual contexts. This set of descriptors provides a good summary depiction of many of our most revered laboratory experiments. At the other end of the naturalness dimension we have research that places no constraints on participants' behaviors, that does not impinge on the environment, and that occurs in natural settings. Tunnell's classification bears consideration, as naturalness is such a highly valued commodity among field researchers and others who champion the use of systematic observational techniques over the more constrained experimental laboratory approach. As seen from the above examples, however, all scientific research, even experimental research, can be viewed as a variant of systematic observation. The behaviors, settings, impingements, and settings on which the research is focused can vary widely, however, and Tunnell's system, as shown here, helps us situate the research along the three dimensions of naturalness.

Natural Behavior

A prime goal of almost all observational research is to study natural behavior. As discussed previously (e.g., chap. 7) impressive gains in generalizability can be realized if the behavior under study is naturally instigated and not made in response to the demands of the research situation or an experimenter. Behavior is thought to be natural to the extent that it is an existing part of the individual's response repertoire (i.e., it is not established to meet the specific demands of the study) and is unselfconscious (i.e., it is enacted without the actor's self-conscious awareness that he or she is the object of scientific scrutiny).

Although considerable research is conducted within the artificial confines of the laboratory, a growing number of investigations today, even those conducted in the laboratory, make use of natural behavior as the primary dependent measure. Latané and Darley's (1968) laboratory studies of factors that influence the likelihood that a person will come to the aid of another in an emergency provide research examples that combine experimental control with a relative lack of restriction on participants' behavior (see, also, Latané, 1997). Though focused on naturalistic behaviors, studies of this type strive for the precision and control that once were thought achievable only in the laboratory, and only under conditions of powerful constraint on the range of participants' allowable responses. There are many examples of attempts to transfer the control of the laboratory to naturalistic field settings and to study behavior that is generated by the participant, rather than specified in advance by the experimenter. In a clever field experiment, for example, Moriarty (1975) induced individuals sunning themselves at a crowded beach to feel more or less responsible for the welfare of another by having his experimental accomplice ask a fellow sunbather to watch his radio while he went "to the boardwalk for a few minutes." Soon after his departure, another of Moriarty's accomplices approached the empty blanket, picked up the aforementioned radio, and if not stopped by the "watchperson," ran off with it.

Participants' responses to the apparent theft of the property constituted the dependent measure. In this instance, the behavior that was emitted was naturalistic—participants' behaviors were completely unconstrained and unselfconscious (in the sense that most probably did not think they were part of a psychological experiment)—the possible responses ranged from physically restraining the thief, following him, calling for help, leaving the scene, or ignoring the entire episode. The naturalistic behavioral responses obtained in this research were used to study the impact of the specification of responsibility on prosocial behavior, or bystander intervention, and the findings of this research were deemed by many to be more trustworthy than those of many of the earlier investigations that were conducted in more artificial laboratory settings.[1] The stress on people's behavior, rather than their beliefs about behavior, is another feature that distinguishes the general observational approach. Willems (1976) summarized this position forcefully when he observed:

> To the ecologist, overt behavior simply is more important than many other psychological phenomena. For the ecologist, it is more important to know how parents treat their children than how they feel about being parents; more important to observe whether or not passersby help someone in need than what their beliefs are about altruism and kindness; more important to note that a person harms someone else when given an opportunity than to know whether his self-concept is that of a considerate person.... It is not readily apparent to me how all of the data on how-it-looks, how-it-feels, and what-people-think-they-want will become translated into understanding ... problems of long-term environmental adaptation and adjustment. (pp. 225–226)

Willems' point is well taken, but it would be a mistake to overextend this view to a position that people's internal states are unknowable or uninteresting. As is shown throughout this section, research methodologists have made giant strides in developing techniques to tap into cognitions, emotions, stereotypes, and other behavioral dispositions that guide overt actions and are sometimes not even recognized by their holders (see, especially, chap. 16).

Natural Treatment

In Tunnell's (1977, p. 428) view, a natural treatment is a "naturally occurring, discrete event ... that the subject would have experienced ... with or without the presence of a

---

[1]Incidentally, in Moriarty's (1975) study, 95% of those asked to watch the "victim's" belongings did intervene in the theft, whereas in a similar study that did not include a specific request, no one even tried to stop the staged theft of an expensive calculator in a college library (Austin, 1979).

researcher." By this definition, Moriarty's (1975) treatment (a staged theft of a radio) was not natural, because it probably would not have occurred without the researcher's active involvement. Although we are in general agreement with Tunnell's classification system, we find his natural treatment definition overly restrictive, and inconsistent with the general intention of fostering more, and better, field research. In our view, a treatment can be considered natural even if produced by the actions of an experimenter if (a) it plausibly could have occurred without experimenter intervention and (b) the participant is unaware of the fact that it did not. Thus, we would consider Moriarty's context and treatment "natural," even though it was completely fabricated by the researcher. In our view, the experimental manipulation of the situation did not destroy its naturalness (the theft of people's belongings on public beaches *does* occur) and the participants' responses suggest strongly that they did not suspect that they were, indeed, participants in a scientific investigation.[2]

The crucial consideration in judging the naturalness of a treatment is not whether the event in question has been staged, but whether the participants suspect that it has. By our reasoning, a naturally occurring event that really does fit Tunnell's definition could be viewed as "unnatural" if participants believe that it is part of an experimental manipulation. As an example of this, one of us had the unfortunate and embarrassing experience not long ago of stumbling while rushing down the aisle of a large lecture hall just before the beginning of class. Although many students could have assisted or at a minimum, helped gather the 20 pages of notes and reprints that had been dropped, no one did anything. When they were questioned (some would say grilled) later in class about their (lack of) response, many students volunteered that they thought the professor was only acting, and that his less than graceful landing was part of an experiment. In this instance, the naturalistic event was perceived as contrived by the students, who (we hope) reacted in an unnaturalistic manner by failing to assist another in need. Whereas most psychologists probably are not as clumsy, many have had experiences that are, at least conceptually, similar to this one.

An example of a natural treatment that satisfies both our and Tunnell's definition is provided in the research of Parker, Brewer, and Spencer (1980), which we discussed earlier in chapter 7. Recall that in this study, the researchers questioned the victims and near-victims of a major brushfire that struck near Santa Barbara, California. Some of the respondents' homes had been completely destroyed, whereas others' homes, even though they were in the immediate vicinity of the fire, were spared by the vagaries of a wind shift or some other chance events. In this research, two groups were constituted on the basis of the naturalistic treatment, the burnt out victims and those whose homes were spared. The treatment (a destructive brushfire) occurred without experimenter intervention, and the respondents knew this. As such, the treatment was natural. However, the behaviors that Parker et al. assessed (i.e., people's responses to an interviewer regarding the outcomes of their actions on the outcome of the event) does not satisfy our earlier definition of "natural." Natural behavior, in this instance, would have involved observing people in the act of attempting to save their homes at the time of the fire.

In our view, retrospection on past actions does not constitute natural behavior. The participant in research of this type generally is aware that he or she is being monitored, and even if this is not the case, the unknown relationship between the retrospection and the actual behavior (at the time it was emitted) renders the naturalness of such data suspect

---

[2]Whether a study of this kind would be viewed today as ethically defensible is an open question. We discuss questions of this type in chapter 19.

(Pezdek & Banks, 1996). As such, reporting behavior of this variety should not be viewed as naturalistic. It is important to understand that this does not mean that such reports, or the results they foster, are not valuable. To be sure, naturalness helps to bolster the assumption of generalizability, and the more naturalistic the study (in terms of setting, behavior, and treatment), the more likely the results are to generalize. However, what is natural is not necessarily important, and what is contrived is not necessarily without value.

Natural Setting

Generally in the social sciences, a *naturalistic observational investigation* refers to a study that has been conducted outside the laboratory. In Cook and Diamond's (1972) terms, a naturalistic setting is "a context that is not *perceived* to have been established for the sole or primary purpose of conducting research" (p. 2, emphasis added). As in our discussion of natural treatments, the respondents' perceptions of the setting, not the actions of the researcher, define the naturalness of the setting. By Cook and Diamond's definition, any setting can be considered natural if the respondent does not think it has been constructed for the purpose of research. Thus, a college classroom is a natural setting (at least for college students). Moriarty's beach scene is an obvious (good) example of a natural setting. It is reasonable to assume that people were unaware that the setting had been modified to allow for a systematic study of the effects of the specification of responsibility on helping behavior. The setting contributed to the credibility of the treatment. This last point bears emphasis: Even though we might take great care in the development of our hypotheses, manipulations, measures, and so on, it often is the case that we are lax in our choice of the setting in which our observation occurs. This is a mistake because an ill-chosen setting can defeat even the most well-designed study by rendering reliable data collection difficult or impossible. Weick (1968, 1985) has often reminded researchers of the importance of the choice of setting in determining the likely success or failure of observational research: "Greater deliberateness in the choice and arrangement of an observational setting can lead to sizable improvements in the precision and validity of observational studies. Any setting has properties that detract from clear observation, but these distractions are more prominent in some situations than in others" (Weick, 1985, p. 25).

It is important to understand that all three of the dimensions of naturalness that Tunnell has brought to our attention interact, and thus, could produce a situation in which the observed responses are very different from those we expect. In a study similar to Moriarty's (1975), Howard and Crano (1974) staged a theft of another's books. In our terms, the treatment, setting, and behaviors were completely naturalistic. The (natural) settings for this research were the Michigan State University library, the student union, and a popular on-campus grille. The treatments (the behaviors of the victim and the thief) were well-rehearsed and generated no suspicion. And, of course, the behaviors of the respondents in reacting to the theft were unconstrained. Even so, there was surprising (and unexpected) variation in the degree to which bystanders were willing to intervene (by stopping or identifying the book thief) in the three settings. Rather little help was provided the victim in the library, more in the lounge, and most in the grille. The authors reasoned that different norms dictated appropriate behavior in the settings, and were responsible for the variations in helping that were observed. Such norms can have a powerful influence on behavior even when events call for a radical departure from the usual, or prescribed, forms of action. Though unexpected, these findings were more credible because of the naturalistic circumstances in which they were observed.

Whereas Tunnell's (1977) three-dimensional analysis is useful, it is important to realize that a number of factors having to do with the design of the observational study will play a major role in determining the extent to which naturalness will be achieved on any one of them. Two of the most important of these primary design considerations are (a) the extent to which the observer is involved in the activities that are under investigation and (b) the type and form of coding system that is chosen to summarize the behaviors that are the focus of the study. These two factors lead to a series of more specific tactical considerations that guide the conduct of any given observational study, as will be seen on the pages that follow.

OBSERVER INVOLVEMENT IN THE SETTING:
THE PARTICIPANT-NONPARTICIPANT DISTINCTION

The degree to which an observer interacts with the individuals under study is one of the most important determinants of the form that the study will take, of the quality of the data that will be collected, and of the uses that can legitimately be made of the obtained results. Observer participation or interaction can vary tremendously, from complete participation in the situation under observation to removal in both time and space from those being studied. The technique that calls for the greatest intimacy between observer and observed—*participant observation*—is an "intense social interaction between researchers and participants in the milieu of the latter, during which time data, in the form of field notes, are unobtrusively and systematically collected" (Bogden, 1972, p. 3). According to McCall and Simmons (1969) participant observation has "given rise to more criticism and controversy in the past twenty years" than any other method of social research (p. 1). This is so because participant observation allows the researcher so much freedom in defining his or her appropriate realm of action, and demands so little systematization of observations. Indeed, Williamson and Karp (1977) observed that one of the most remarkable features of this approach was the lack of agreed-on rules or standard operating procedures used to guide its use. The venues and topics in which participant observation approaches have been employed are vast, ranging from studies of go-go dancers in the Philippines (Ratliff, 1999) to midwifery in Ontario (Bourgeault, 2000), to communication patterns between police and the poor in Vancouver (Schneider, 1998–1999) and, most recently, to participant-observation of communication in groups on the World Wide Web (e.g., Polifroni, von Hippel, & Brewer, 2001). Given this diversity of potential application, a good definition of this technique that encapsulates even a majority of participant observation research is difficult to develop. Schwartz and Schwartz (1955, p. 344) came closest, perhaps, in defining participant observation as "a process in which the observer's presence in a social situation is maintained for the purpose of scientific investigation. The observer is in a face-to-face relationship with the observed, and, by participating with them in their natural life setting, he gathers data. Thus, the observer is part of the context being observed, *and he both modifies and is influenced by this context*" (emphasis added). It is Schwartz and Schwartz's final clause that delineates the area of "criticism and controversy" mentioned by McCall and Simmons, and to which we return in discussing the relative advantages and disadvantages of participant and nonparticipant techniques.

The term *participant observation*, then, broadly describes the general research process in which an observer observes from within the context he or she wishes to study. The observer is accepted as a member of a group and uses this privileged status to gather information about the group. Typically, participant observation entails the simultaneous collection and analysis of data (Lofland, 1971) because in this technique, the processes of hypothesis generation and hypothesis testing often occur almost simultaneously.

Gaining Entry

To make best use of the technique of participant observation, the observer first must gain entrance into the group under study. A good example of some of the possible dangers and distortions involved in this entry process was provided by Festinger, Riecken, and Schachter's (1956) now classic study of the *Seekers*. Briefly, the Seekers were a group of persons who claimed to have had contact with extraterrestrial beings, the *Guardians*. These benevolent spacemen had informed the leader of the earthbound group that a major flood was soon to inundate the northern hemisphere. The Seekers themselves were to be transported by flying saucer, at the last minute, out of harm's way. Though the group was not large, belief in the prophecy was strong among its members.

Festinger and his associates, not sharing the faith, decided that this group provided a good opportunity to study the effects of disconfirmation of a strong expectation on people's future behavior. The best way to accomplish this investigation, they reasoned, would be to join the group, and thus obtain an "inside view" of the proceedings. Unfortunately, the Seekers were not a proselytizing group; membership was by invitation only. As the authors admitted, "our basic problems were . . . obtaining entree for a sufficient number of observers to provide the needed coverage of members' activities, and keeping at an absolute minimum any influence which these observers might have on the beliefs and actions of members of the group. We tried to be nondirective, sympathetic listeners, passive participants who were inquisitive and eager to learn whatever others might want to tell us" (p. 237). To gain entry into the group, members of Festinger's team hid their social science credentials, approached the Seekers and claimed "psychic experiences" of the type calculated to interest the members of the group. The experiences were constructed so that they could be interpreted in light of the Seekers' system of beliefs. The danger that these stories, necessitated by the selectivity of the Seekers, interfered with the natural equilibrium of the group was recognized: "Unhappily, [the ruse] had been too successful, for, in our effort to tailor a story to fit the beliefs of the members of the group, and thus gain their approval for our observers, we had done too well. We had unintentionally reinforced their beliefs that the Guardians were watching over humanity and were 'sending' chosen people for special instruction about the cataclysm and the belief system" (p. 241). Given the nature of the entrance requirements, however, the observers had little choice but to fabricate psychic experiences to gain admittance to the group. Unfortunately, the Seekers interpreted these myths as proof of the correctness of their beliefs. The actions of the researchers had the inadvertent effect of bolstering the Seekers' beliefs.

The necessary entry-gaining actions of Festinger's observers illustrate a point that should be recognized in all studies making use of participant observer techniques; that is, in almost all closed groups, the problem of entry (of the investigator) assumes great importance. The actions the nonmember performs in gaining admittance to the group under investigation can, to a major extent, affect the ongoing group process, and the quality of the data that are subsequently collected. Thus, in attempting to join a group for the purposes of participant observation, the most unobtrusive means possible should be used, so that the natural group situation remains so. Failing that, a detailed account of any possible interference resulting from the entry process should, as in Festinger's study, be included in any description of the research. This description does not solve the interference problem, but at least alerts the reader to possible distortions that might reside in the results.

A different approach to entry (and a different set of problems) is evident in Thorne's (1988) study of the draft resistance movement during the Vietnam War. Thorne first joined the anti-draft movement and later decided to use her experiences as a source of data for her thesis. To avoid deceiving her peers, Thorne discussed her plans, which were met with responses that ranged from "hostility to mild tolerance" (p. 134). Whereas Thorne avoided deceiving those who shared her political convictions, her openness may have altered the fundamental nature of the interactions that ensued *after* she disclosed her research plans. By disclosing her intentions, she was able to maintain truthfulness to a much greater degree than the observers of Festinger et al. (1956). It could be argued, however, that her disclosure affected the naturalness of the context just as strongly as Festinger's observers did.

These two extreme examples do not offer a clear solution to the problem of entry. Complete openness as to motive and approach is certainly more ethically defensible, but in no way does it solve the problem of the observer affecting the observed. Complete nondisclosure of techniques and motivation, as exemplified by Festinger et al. (1956), would appear to solve the problem of group members reacting unnaturally to one of their group; unfortunately, the manner in which observers gained entry, and the effects of their actions while in the group, can take a toll on the quality and credibility of the behavioral observations that are made.

Going Native

The entry problem is only one of the difficulties encountered when using participant observation. Just as there is a large literature in anthropology, psychology, and sociology devoted to the solution of entry problems, so too have social scientists been concerned with the problem of "going native." Overidentification with the observed group tends to blind the observer to many relevant aspects of the total situation, and draws attention to those events perceived to be of interest to the group, which may or may not be scientifically worthwhile. Given Thorne's (1988) identification with the draft resistance movement, one might question the quality of the data her research produced. Could she be an unbiased and nonjudgmental observer, given her political commitments?

Perhaps a hypothetical example will help to illustrate this point. Suppose an agnostic social scientist was interested in the patterns of interaction that occurred during prayer services of a Pentecostal sect; further, that during the course of observation of a church group, he became so deeply impressed by the fervor of the members that he entered into the activities and eventually attained complete membership in the organization. Would his account of the group's activities and practices prove of interest? Possibly. A more difficult question concerns the scientific value of his work. Remember, the fact of his conversion does not necessarily diminish our observer's scientific expertise. It is the manner in which this expertise is employed that gives cause for concern. Observer-bias problems aside, we must critically examine the relationships on which our observer chose to focus. It is conceivable that these might have been so idiosyncratic to his group, or so theoretically barren, that his account from a scientific perspective is worthless. This is not to suggest that the researcher cannot become close to those he or she observes (see Mehan & Wood, 1975; Thorne, 1988), but rather that the ultimate purpose of the interaction—the systematic collection of reliable information—be kept in mind at all times. It is the overly complete identification with the group under study, and the resulting failure to interrelate new with known information (a kind of scientific tunnel-vision), that proves so troublesome when the observer "goes native." Of course, not all observational research is equally susceptible to this problem. Festinger's observers, for example, were probably not remotely tempted to identify with the Seekers, nor was Alfred (1976), a participant observer of a Satanic sect.

Restricted Participation Techniques

By restricting the degree of observer participation in the situation under study, investigators can simultaneously control the problems both of entry and of going native. This solution has generated studies in which observers were, for the most part, unseen by the observed, their existence oftentimes not even suspected. The most extreme form of nonparticipant observation is of the type directed toward *archival records*, in which events previously recorded are adopted by the scientist for study. Webb et al. (1981) demonstrated how such unlikely sources as tombstones, pottery shards, obituaries, a city's water pressure, newspaper headlines, library withdrawals, even the U.S. Congressional Record, have all been employed as useful sources in the search for social information. We discuss one form of this kind of analysis in chapter 13.

Less remote from the actual events under consideration, and perhaps more common, are investigations of ongoing group or individual activity, in which the observer is partially or totally concealed. Total concealment requires an observational setting of a high degree of structure. Because the observer must remain undetected, it is essential that the group under study remain within the setting in which he or she is concealed. Attempts at completely concealed, nonparticipant observation have resulted in a variety of research operations that are sometimes interesting, often amusing, and almost always ethically questionable. Henle and Hubble's (1938) observers, for example, hid under beds in college dormitories to collect their data. This strategy is not recommended today. Less dangerous, but clearly questionable, was Carlson, Cook, and Stromberg's (1936) research in which observers eavesdropped on people's conversations in theater lobbies. The list could be extended indefinitely, but it is clear that concealed observation is usually an ethically questionable operation. Such research techniques should be considered only after all other options have proved fruitless (see chap. 19, and Mariampolski & Reichel, 1978).

Ethical considerations aside, in many situations concealment is impossible. Accordingly, social scientists have altered their research operations in such a way as to allow for *partial* participation of the observer with the observed. The tactic of limited participation, however, generates many difficult problems in its own right, as is illustrated by the number of different techniques developed for their solution. Soskin and John (1963), for example, somehow convinced a married couple who were about to embark on a two-week vacation to wear small radio transmitters during the entire vacation period. In this way, the observers had a complete sound recording of the couple's interactions. Clearly, the volunteers in this study knew they were being observed. The degree of observer participation in their lives, however, was not nearly so great as it would have been if Soskin or John had accompanied the couple during their vacation, following them wherever they went, and so on. As such, the degree of observer participation in this study was slightly less than complete, and somewhat more than that occurring when total concealment is employed.[3]

---

[3]It is interesting to note that after the first day of observation, the couple's references to the study in which they were involved, the recording apparatus, and so on, became extremely infrequent. This does not necessarily mean that the couple's behavior was unaffected by their participation in the study, however, but does suggest that awareness of observation decreases over time.

A variant on this theme makes use of structured diaries and time sampling (Leigh, 1993; Robinson & Goodbey, 1997; Wheeler & Nezlek, 1977), in which respondents complete a set of questionnaires regarding their mood, interaction partners, thoughts, actions, and the like, at time intervals specified by the researcher (say, daily, or at randomly determined sequences). Robinson and Goodbey (1997), for example, asked participants monitor their time allocations (leisure vs. obligatory) over the course of the day, and Leigh (1993) had participants note their alcohol consumption and sexual activity at the end of each day. The "observations" made under these circumstances are of the self-report, retrospective variety, but the naturalism of the setting in which the data collection takes place, the natural behavior under study, the short duration between action and recording, and the natural treatments that occur place this approach among the naturalistic methods employing partial observer participation.

In the *Experience Sampling Method* (ESM), respondents carry a pager; when the pager sounds, the respondent completes a set of questionnaires. Alternately, participants may be asked to complete a measure at a specified time (or times) each day. If a beeper is used, it usually is programmed to sound randomly once in every given block of time (say, once every 2 hours; Kubey, Larson, & Csikszentmihalyi, 1996; Larson & Csikszentmihalyi, 1983). The value of the diary approach is that it "catches" respondents in their natural milieu, and thus allows the researcher to associate the outcomes of various natural events with respondents' subsequent moods, intentions, behaviors, and the like. The added advantage of the ESM is that because data often are drawn on a random schedule, they are less susceptible to the cyclical biases that might occur if the diaries were always completed at the same time of day.

With sufficient creativity, the diary method (with time sampling) can be used to study a variety of important issues. Johnson and Larson (1982), for example, investigated the moods, and mood shifts, of bulimic women and contrasted these data with those of a group of nonbulimic women. (*Bulimia* is a disorder characterized by episodes of rapid consumption of massive amounts of food, followed by forced vomiting, the use of laxatives, or other purgatives.) Larson, Csikszentmihalyi, and their colleagues studied the (generally negative) effects of solitude on people's feelings, and the (generally positive) aftereffects of being alone (Larson & Csikszentmihalyi, 1978, 1980; Larson, Csikszentmihalyi, & Graef, 1980). It is difficult to envision the means by which solitude could be studied credibly in a laboratory context. Nezlek, Wheeler, and Reis (1983) employed a structured diary approach to study such issues as the initiation and control of interactions, the influence of physical attractiveness on beginning interactions, etc. These studies provide valuable insights into the effects that everyday events have on people's natural behaviors. As such, these kinds of diary-based approaches have become increasingly popular (see Reis & Gable, 2000).

In an interesting application, Peters and her colleagues used the ESM to study chronic pain (Peters et al., 2000). They reported no evidence of reactivity to the monitoring and found differences in reported pain taken by the ESM and reports taken retrospectively. Klumb and Baltes (1999) used the ESM to study the validity of retrospective reports in the aged, and the approach proved useful in this context as well. Findings derived from the ESM methodology, especially if integrated with other data obtained under different techniques, have the potential to greatly expand our understanding of social behavior. In general, approaches that combine more than one method of measurement bolster confidence in the validity of our results. This general orientation is certainly true in the case of the ESM.

Another example of partial (observer) participation is provided in studies of the patient–therapist relationship. In studies of this type, an observer (often, a student in training) attends the therapeutic hour, but strictly as an observer; that is, he or she does not interact in any way with either patient or therapist. A more common variant on this theme involves the filming of the therapeutic interaction for later study. Often, both therapist and patient know of the ongoing observation, but it is felt that this form of "participation" is less intrusive than that in which the observer is physically present. However, as might be expected, research indicates that people who know they are being watched tend to emit more socially valued behaviors. Roberts and Renzaglia (1965), for example, showed that the mere presence of a microphone had a measurable effect on the behaviors of both patient and therapist. Zegiob, Arnold, and Forehand (1975) found that people were more likely to play positively with children when being observed, and Samph (1969) observed more acts of altruism when people knew they were being watched than when they did not. These studies suggest that the mere fact of observation can bias the observational record. Despite this, today the use of audio or videotape recordings in social research is becoming increasingly common. These approaches have the advantage of allowing the researcher to examine and re-examine the behaviors of interest, at a time of his or her choosing. The capability of "taking a second look" usually enhances the reliability of any behavioral coding. The point at which techniques of this sort fall on the participant-nonparticipant continuum depends on the obtrusiveness of the recording device. If participants are unaware of the observation, the research can be judged nonparticipant (if, perhaps, unethical); if respondents are aware of the taping, and the recording machinery is an obvious part of the setting, then, as Roberts & Renzaglia (1965) demonstrated, the degree of observer interference can be as severe as it would have been had the observer been physically present.

A somewhat different form of participant observation was suggested by Mahl (1964), who found voice frequencies below 500 cps to be a good indicator of people's emotional state, yet apparently not under conscious control. As such, respondents can know they are being observed, yet be unable to alter the particular behaviors under investigation. Along these same lines, in an earlier series of investigations, Ponder and Kennedy (1927) found the reduction of the period between eye blinks to be a good indicator of emotional excitement, if the respondent was in a situation in which gross physical movements were impossible or impractical (e.g., while sitting in the witness chair in a courtroom, while waiting for a golf opponent to sink or miss a putt, etc.). The eye blink response has been used as a general indicator of psychological stress; recent research suggests that victims of wartime induced post traumatic stress disorder show exaggerated eye blink to startling stimuli (typically, bursts of white noise; e.g., Morgan, Grillon, Southwick, Davis, & Charney, 1996). Pupil dilation, too, has been found to provide some useful information about the internal state of the individual. Research by a number of investigators (e.g., Atwood & Howell, 1971; Hess, 1965; Hess, Seltzer, & Shlien, 1965) has suggested that pupil dilation, a response that people ordinarily do not monitor or attempt to control, provides a reasonable if indirect indication of interest (see Janisse, 1973, for a review of some of the pitfalls to be avoided when using this measure). Dabbs and Milun (1999) used pupil dilation as an indirect assessment device for measuring racial prejudice (as inferred from pupillary responses indicating greater attention to people of a different race). Thus, this measure, like those making use of lower vocal frequencies or eye blink latencies would appear to provide the social scientist with a useful, if limited, assessment of the psychological state of a respondent. For present purposes, the important aspect of these measures is that they provide examples of indicators of people's internal states, over which they sometimes can, but usually do not, exert conscious control. As such, measures of this type sometimes are valued over the more direct approaches because they are less likely to be used by the respondent to misdirect the investigator.

Participant Observation: When and Why

Given the problems of entry, of going native, and of observer interference in the natural actions of the group under investigation, to which studies employing observer participation are so susceptible, we might wonder why participant observation would ever be used. Cicourel (1964) provided perhaps the best defense of this approach when he observed, "More intensive participation has the advantage of affording the observer a greater exposure to both the routine and the unusual activities of the group studied. The assumption is that the more intensive the participation, the 'richer' the data" (p. 44). The personal relationships that can form in participant observation research can materially influence the quality of the data that are collected. For this reason, participant observers are urged to be friendly, nonthreatening, concerned with the group's welfare, and so forth. Indeed, there is a growing literature in the social sciences demonstrating Guba's (1980, p. 21) point that "Good guys get better data" (e.g., Douglas, 1976; Van Maanen, in press). The observer can best demonstrate friendliness, humanness, and so on, with the respondents when he or she is in relatively frequent contact with them, that is, in participant observation research.

Reacting to the question of when this technique should be used, Becker (1958) responded:

> Sociologists usually use this method [participant observation] when they are especially interested in understanding a particular organization or substantive problem rather than demonstrating relations between abstractly defined variables. They attempt to make their research theoretically meaningful, but they assume that they do not know enough about the organization *a priori* to identify relevant problems and hypotheses and that they must discover these in the course of the research. (p. 652–653)

If we accept Cicourel's and Becker's attempts at delineating the boundaries of this technique, then participant observation methods would seem to be most useful in situations of the exploratory, hypothesis-generating variety, in which great amounts of "rich," if not necessarily reliable, information are needed. The primary concern here is the accumulation of large amounts of data, not on the data's reliability or validity.[4] Once having identified a set of behaviors of interest, however, it follows that techniques involving far less observer participation should be favored. In this way, the potential interference that can be generated by the observer's presence in the group under investigation is circumvented. In Cicourel's (1964) view, the cost of this removal of the observer is calculated in terms of a loss of richness in the data; however, because behaviors for investigation in a hypothesis-testing study already have been chosen, and the observer is focusing on a very prescribed set of responses, the loss would seem inconsequential.

For the most part, the nonparticipant methods are most deficient in those areas in which the techniques that call for greater observer participation are strongest. Generally, nonparticipant techniques require the observer to conduct research in settings that restrict the mobility of the observed group, thus enabling the observer to maintain isolation from the group and, at the same time, insuring that the respondents remain within the observational

---

[4]In fairness, it should be noted that Becker found the participant observational approach suitable for hypothesis- or theory-testing, but he indicated that this operation could legitimately occur only after a number of prior requirements were satisfied (also see Kidder, 1981).

setting. Restrictions of this type can be employed while simultaneously maintaining the naturalness of the observational setting, behaviors, and treatment. When such mobility restriction is not possible, the use of nonparticipant techniques is ill-advised.

At every point on the participant–nonparticipant dimension, there are advantages to be gained, and dangers to be avoided. The careful investigator must assess the relative costs of one method in light of the advantages it offers. This assessment is dependent on many factors, most notably the amount of information one possesses about the issue under investigation, the availability of both settings and participants for observation, and the ethical propriety of the techniques that will be employed to capitalize on the advantages of the chosen approach.

CODING OBSERVATIONS

The observational researcher must not only decide on the degree to which he or she will participate in the behaviors under observation, but also the manner in which the actions and behaviors that are observed are to be recorded and codified. Figure 11.1 presents a flowchart of the steps to be taken in developing a coding system to be used in observational research. Each of these steps is considered in detail.

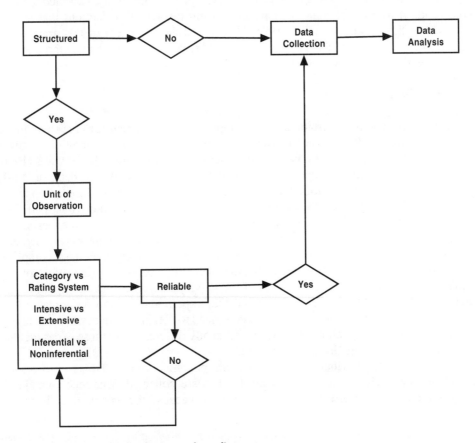

FIG. 11.1. Steps in the development of a coding system.

The Structured-Nonstructured Dimension

The differing theoretical orientations and research training backgrounds of social scientists have resulted in wide variations in the degree of structure of the coding systems they use in observational research. At one extreme on this dimension are the proponents of complete systematization of the observational data. These researchers argue that some structure must be imposed on the mass of input accruing to any observational study to investigate effectively any hypothesized relationship. Common in research of this type are coding systems that focus on a very limited and explicit portion of the possible range of behaviors that occur. In this way, reliable ratings of specific behaviors thought to have some theoretical importance can be established.

Those favoring less structured observational techniques have argued against attempts to focus on a limited range of behaviors. The "constriction" of the observational field, they suggest, results in a loss of valuable data that happen not to fall within the range of the chosen coding system. One of the most forceful and influential presentations on behalf of the nonstructured orientation is found in Glaser and Strauss's (1967) text, *The discovery of grounded theory*. In this book, observers are urged to enter into the research setting with no prior theoretical preconceptions.[5] Theory is to be constantly generated on the basis of the observations, and continually revised as new data are obtained. The resulting "grounded" hypotheses, based on the actual data they are developed to address, are expected to prove more valid, or true to life than those resulting from theoretical deductions that are not grounded in this manner (Strauss, 1991). The initial attractiveness of this approach is great; however, Glaser and Strauss's (1967) method raises some important methodological issues, to which we now turn our attention.

Early Data Returns

A major difficulty with the grounded theory approach is that conclusions based on initial observations inevitably influence the interpretation of subsequent observations—this is the essence of the approach. As mentioned earlier in this book, and in Rosenthal's (1966) volume on experimenter expectancy effects, the sequential analysis of data, or "early data returns," represents a subtle but nonetheless real source of bias. In examining the effects of early data returns, for example, Rosenthal, Persinger, Vikan-Kline, and Fode (1963) arranged for each of eight naive student-experimenters to test two experimental accomplices and then a group of naive participants. Half the experimenters obtained data from the accomplices that were consistent with their expectations, whereas the accomplices disconfirmed the other experimenters' hypotheses. When examining the effect of this manipulation on the recorded responses of the naive participants that all experimenters later studied, Rosenthal et al. (1963) found that experimenters who had obtained the confirmatory data *early* in the investigation continued to obtain such data when examining the naive participants. Their results were significantly different from those experimenters whose expectations were disconfirmed initially.

Clearly, the most obvious way to avoid this potential source of bias is to reserve all detailed inspection of results until all the data are collected. This recommendation is contradictory to the grounded theory approach, because the technique calls for the

---

[5]The use of any coding scheme presupposes the existence of some hypothesis or hypotheses. If there were none, then the observer focusing on a certain restricted set of behaviors (which all coding schemes assume) would have no reasonable basis for doing so.

continuous revision of both hypotheses and research direction as a function of the data as they are collected. The potential for observer bias is particularly high in the grounded theory approach.

Sampling Problems

In addition to the observer bias difficulties resulting from the sequential analysis of data, the manner in which nonstructured observations are collected also poses problems for the validity of the obtained results. The question of whether or not the "discovered" relationships are artifacts of the specific observational sample, or represent meaningful, generalizable discoveries, is difficult to address in research of this type. When an observer has no predetermined categories of behavior to attend to, those events that stand out in the specific research setting will be noticed (Borgida & Nisbett, 1977). These hypervisible events, however, will not necessarily occur in different settings. Concentrating on the conspicuous occurrences of a given situation can compromise the comparability of the obtained findings with those gathered in different settings. As Weick (1985) observed, "Routine activity is the rule, but it seldom gets recorded" (p. 44). Bertrand Russell (1930) made essentially the same point when he observed that great people were great only infrequently—most of the time, their lives were relatively humdrum.

Consider the dilemma of observers who employ no pre-specified observational system in their research. Literally hundreds of different behaviors occur in situations involving even very simple two-person interactions. Can the observer make any clear assertions regarding the generality of the behaviors that are observed? Unfortunately, the answer to this question must be no, because the noticeable behavior patterns that were observed might be specific to the sample chosen for observation. The problem of the situation-specific determination of what is observed or noticed is avoided when the investigator enters the research field with predetermined categories of behavior to guide and structure the observational activities.

It would be unwise to interpret this critique of nonstructured methods as a general condemnation of this approach. Insofar as the focus of these methods is generating testable hypotheses, we have no objection to their use. Barton and Lazarsfeld (1969, p. 182) advanced this position even more strongly, when they observed, "Research which has neither statistical weight nor experimental design, research based only on qualitative descriptions of a small number of cases, can nonetheless play the important role of suggesting possible relationships, causes, effects, and even dynamic processes. Indeed, it can be argued that only research which provides a wealth of miscellaneous, unplanned impressions and observations can play this role." It is when the theories or hypotheses suggested by such methods are accepted, without first having undergone the necessary verification process in more controlled settings that the potential dangers of nonstructured observation become real. Nonstructured techniques are valuable in generating hypotheses, but their use in hypothesis testing situations is always debatable.

STRUCTURED METHODS: CATEGORY SYSTEMS AND RATING SCALES

Whereas it might appear at first glance that nonstructured techniques provide a relatively simple means of conducting research, this is decidedly not the case. The ability to extract significant aspects of group or individual behavior, to filter from the mass of input those relationships of potential theoretical importance, to reconstruct from necessarily incomplete notes the pattern and flow of the observational record, is acquired only after intensive commitment to research of this type. It was partly for this reason, and partly in response to the call for more quantitatively based research techniques, that social scientists reoriented their observational methods in the direction of greater structure. The most extreme point of this development is represented by research in which rating scales are used to quantify and summarize the actions of the person or group under study. Rather than begin at this extreme in our discussion of structured observational techniques, we will direct our attention instead toward methods that make use of category systems. These techniques fall somewhere near the midpoint of the structuredness dimension, between the completely open, nonstructured varieties of research at one extreme, and the severely constricted rating-scale approaches on the other.

Every category system represents an attempt to quantitatively summarize the qualitative behaviors that occur in the observational setting. In its most simplistic form, this approach involves a simple count of the number of times specific categories of events occur. A category is a description of a behavior, or other observable aspect, of a group or individual. A set of these descriptions, quite literally, a checklist, constitutes a category system (or system of categories). Given a system of two or more categories, the observer's task is the notation of the number of times respondents' actions fall into the various categories that constitute the system. Categories should be mutually exclusive; an event coded as satisfying the demands for inclusion in a given category should not satisfy the demands of any other category. The question of the degree of intensity of occurrence is usually not a concern when category systems are used, unless different categories are defined by different intensities. Like a light switch (rather than a rheostat), the category is either "on" or "off."

The Unit Issue

A recurring issue in research making use of category systems concerns the unit of behavior to be considered when categorizing a social act—that is, when does one behavior stop, and another begin? The problem of unit definition has plagued social scientists for some time, probably first inviting the attention of the early anthropologists. The question then, as now, concerns the problem of the definition of the appropriate unit of study. For example, how was one to define a given culture? By geographical area? By common language? By common leaders, beliefs, kinship terms, or inheritance rules? The unit problem in observational research, though at a level of somewhat less grand proportion than that encountered by quantitative anthropologists (e.g., see Murdock, 1967; Murdock & White, 1969), nevertheless is very troublesome. In many cases solutions for specific category systems have been made by defining units with respect to the categories being employed. For example, in his analysis of small group interaction, Bales (1950) chose as the unit of behavior "... the smallest discriminable segment of verbal or nonverbal behavior to which the observer... can assign a classification" (p. 37). In other words, any act that *could* be classified was counted as a unit of behavior. In Leventhal and Sharp's (1965) coding system of facial expressions, *time* determines the unit; for a given, pre-specified period, observers code the expressions of the forehead and brow, then the eyes, then the mouth, etc. Given the physical restrictions of Leventhal and Sharp's observed group (women in labor) on whom this technique was employed, the time-determined unit offered a useful and unambiguous solution to the problem of the selection of the behavioral act for categorization. In observational studies of young children, however, the definition of an action by temporal criteria could invite catastrophe, because the mobility of such targets might be such that they were not available for observation when the time for observation occurred. Accordingly, many observers of children's behavior have used the child's attention span in defining the unit of observation. So, as long as a child attends to a given object (be it another child, a teacher, a toy, etc.), a single act for categorization is defined. When attention shifts to another object, this is entered as yet another "unit" for categorization. These examples represent the polar extremes of the determination of unit, from the objectively defined unit, time, to the respondent-defined unit, attention shift.

Somewhere between these extremes are systems in which the respondents themselves define the unit. For example, DePaulo, Kashy, Kirkendol, Wyer, and Epstein (1996) were interested in studying lying. When are lies told, why, to whom, and so on. They asked their volunteers to keep a diary, and to note all of their daily social interactions that lasted more than 10 minutes, and also all the lies they told during an interaction, no matter what its duration. The participants themselves defined the unit—that is, they were to count as a lie any action they took intentionally that successfully misled another person. It is risky to allow participants to define the unit of analysis; some respondents, for example, might have minimized their lying so as to appear more ethical or truthful. However, to adopt other unit-defining methods would be awkward, if not impossible, using the diary approach. Allowing the participant to define the unit was a conscious choice of the researchers that was dictated by the method. As can be seen, there are many gradations of unit definition. There is no general rule to guide the researcher in choice of unit of observation, other than the rule of common sense. As in DePaulo et al. (1996), it often is the case that the observational context itself will suggest, if not completely dictate, the unit and the manner in which it is defined.

Time: When and How Long

An important general consideration in developing category systems concerns time. When considering the temporal aspect of systematic observations, two general issues arise. The first of these has to do with the timing of observations. Some systems divide the behavioral stream in terms of temporal units. That is, over every time interval (say every 5, 10, or 20 s), a behavioral code is assigned to the individual or group under observation. In this approach, time defines the unit. Research of this form often is used to study recurring interdependencies between behaviors. In a study of young children's play behavior, for example, we might find that children's aggressive outbursts are often preceded by other children frustrating their desires.

A second way in which time is used in observational research is not as a segmenting system, but as a dependent measure, signifying the duration of a particular coded event. Returning to our children's example, we might code both the child's aggressive outburst and its duration. This form of measurement is becoming increasingly popular with modern video techniques, which can impart a running time signature on the interaction record (Bakeman, 2000).

Category System Construction

Given the number of available category systems, how can the investigator choose one over the others? Or, having considered the possible choices and rejected them all, what are the criteria the researcher should bear in mind in constructing his or her own category system? In the following paragraphs, we consider some important aspects of category system construction.

Intensity–Extensity of Systems. Perhaps one of the most important questions the prospective category-system constructor must answer concerns the degree of fine detail the observational data must have. Should one vie for a broad, general description of all major events that occur in the observational setting, or, rather, concentrate intensively on a particular set of precisely defined actions or behaviors, to the exclusion of all others? Clearly, this answer will depend on the nature of the phenomena under investigation. In the investigation by DePaulo et al. (1996), for example, the researchers were focused almost exclusively on lying. Other features of the participants' interactions might have been important or noteworthy, but their intense focus on participants' diary entries that had to do with lying would have rendered these other factors inconsequential for the immediate purposes of their research. Of course, there is nothing to prevent the researchers' later return to the diaries to investigate other features of social interaction.

Making use of an extensive system, which aims for broad coverage (at the expense of fine detail), an investigator can enhance the likelihood that all important events occurring within the observational period will at least have been noted, i.e., categorized. It usually is the case, however, that the more extensive the category system, the less complete are the recorded (or coded) details of any given event. Thus, whereas the researcher making use of an extensive coding scheme might well be able to describe the general outlines of the total interaction pattern, it is unlikely that these data will convey much precise information of any specific event.

Increased precision of description demands a constriction of observational focus. To describe an event intensively, the observer must ignore other, perhaps equally important incidents that happen to occur simultaneously. If one is concerned about the effects of a specific variable on a specific behavior or set of behaviors, this loss of general, summary information might not be bothersome. However, observational specificity assumes considerable knowledge of the events of possible significance in the interaction under investigation. For example, suppose that we wished to study nonverbal communication among members of a specific adolescent gang. To accomplish this, we construct an elaborate coding scheme through which the changing facial expressions of the observed individuals can be intensively studied. The coding scheme is so detailed that categories are provided for even the subtlest facial nuances. However, if after months of pretesting the system, training coders, gaining entry into the gang, and so on, we discover that a major value of the gang members is the maintenance of a poker-face at all costs, then our efforts will have been largely wasted. A more extensive, less detail-specific system might not have been defeated by idiosyncratic norms of this type. Conversely, if we had previously determined the major aspects of nonverbal communication within the gang, the use of a general, all-encompassing, and extensive coding system could have proved extremely inefficient. An extensive category system would provide not only much unnecessary, irrelevant data, but also would prohibit the investigator from intensively concentrating on the behaviors known to be of importance.

There is an obvious trade-off involved, then, in the choice of intensive versus extensive category systems. The decision regarding the type of system to use should be based primarily on the relative amount of information the investigator possesses about the phenomenon of interest. In an exploratory study, intensive concentration on a very specific set of behaviors (e.g., nonverbal displays) is risky because the arbitrarily chosen indicators often will convey little worthwhile information. While concentrating on specific actions, other more important details can be neglected. When the boundaries of the phenomenon in question have been clearly delineated, however, then the use of an intensive system that focuses specifically on the events known to be important is strongly suggested.

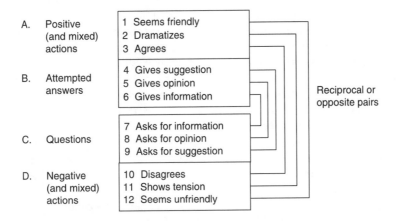

FIG. 11.2.   Categories of the Bales interaction process analysis.

Most of the widely used category systems lie somewhat between the extremes of complete coverage of all possible events and intense concentration on minute behavioral details. A good example of a fairly extensive (and widely used) category system, which is limited to the classification of interpersonal behavior, is provided by Bales' (1950, 1970) interaction process analysis (IPA), presented in Fig. 11.2. (See Bales & Cohen, 1979, and Bales & Isenberg, 1980, for extended discussions of this general approach.) In this system, the 12 coding classifications exhaust the total range of possible interactive behaviors that can occur between members of a small group.[6]

An example of a contrast to Bales' extensive system is the model of Caldwell (1968), who dubbed her system APPROACH, a procedure for patterning responses of adults and children. While calling for the use of many more categories than Bales' IPA (65 vs. 12), Caldwell's scheme is more restrictive in the events observed and recorded. In this case (as in most other systems of this type), nonextensivity reflects the researcher's desire to provide a system that is flexible enough and sensitive enough to allow for very fine distinctions to be made between highly similar behaviors.

The Number of Categories in the System.   Whereas they differ in terms of intensity/extensity of categories, the most striking contrast between the Bales and Caldwell systems is the difference in the absolute number of categories employed in each scheme. The choice of category number is an important consideration in constructing or choosing a coding system. Generally, the more complex the behavior to be observed, the more simple should be the category system. The logic of this assertion becomes clear upon examination. Keep in mind that with all category systems, decisions on the part of coders regarding the evaluation (i.e., categorization) of any given action are a vital part of the research process. Further, in the study of any complex set of behaviors, even the most intricate of systems will not be so complete as to handle every action that occurs. Thus, the combination of highly complex observational data and a large number of possible coding options (some of which require the observer to make extremely fine grained judgments among coding alternatives) can result in an overload in the capacity of even the most experienced, well-trained coder. Using fewer, more broad categories will tend to transform

---

[6]Note, however, that Bales' categories deal with the nature of the interaction, not its content.

the coders' function from one of split-second, often unreliable, decision making to that of more leisurely observation and broad, general categorization of events.

With the widespread use of videotaping, some of these issues are less important than has previously been the case. Despite videotape, it is still true that coders "burn out," so lessening the demands on them is a good long-term strategy. In much observational research, especially that conducted in settings that restrict respondents' movements (e.g., the research laboratory), videotapes of the critical interactions can be made, and these can be viewed as often as necessary to insure a reliable coding of behaviors. In this way, complicated coding schemes can be used to study even complex behavior. Such a combination will call for considerable re-reviews of the videotape, but with a sufficiently motivated cadre of coders, such a process can result in a highly informative analysis.

Studying behavior of the more simple variety demands a more elaborate classification system to ensure that the subtle behavioral differences that do occur in the situation will be noticed. An example of the types of behaviors that can be examined through the use of a complex coding scheme is provided by Caldwell (1968), whose observers were to note the actions and reactions of a single child (in a nursery school setting) to his or her surroundings. In this setting, coders had ample time to determine which of the sixty-five APPROACH categories described the responses of the observed child. Using the same system to classify the responses of adults in a group discussion situation would have proved considerably more difficult, because the adult's actions would have been more subtle, exhibited greater purpose, and occurred with greater rapidity and frequency. In this instance, Bales' IPA would be a more realistic and appropriate option, unless the group interaction were videotaped. With this technical aid, it is conceivable that a more intensive system (such as Caldwell's) might have proved feasible, but as noted, even with tapes, coders can be pushed beyond reasonable limits.

Dimensions versus Classifications.   A way of lessening the load on observational coders is to form dimensions of categories—in essence, to categorize our categories. DePaulo et al. (1996) provide a good example of such an approach. In their research on lying, they were interested in four different features of this behavior: the content of the lie (was it concerned with feelings, actions, plans, etc.), its reason, the type of lie, and the lie's referent. A schematic of this system is presented in Fig. 11.3. Researchers assigning codes to the lies respondents listed in their diaries could first code for content, then reason, type, and referent. Breaking the coding decisions along these dimensions lessens the difficulty of the coding task; this important as it enhances the likelihood of reliability, an important issue that we consider later in this chapter.

Frequency of Category Use.   As has been emphasized here, the construction of a useful coding system is dependent in large measure on the relationship between the system, the observational context, and the types of behaviors to be observed. To construct a coding scheme independent of some consideration of the settings in which it will be employed, and of the types of behaviors it will be used to classify, is foolhardy at best. Thus, we recommend that the effectiveness of any given coding system under construction be regularly and systematically investigated. The fact that a set of categories has been arbitrarily selected to constitute a coding system does not necessarily imply that none of these categories is superfluous, nor that some classifications should not be broken down into smaller, more precise units of analysis. This is not meant as an argument to reinvent the wheel with each new study, but rather that the coding scheme should be compatible with the research

Category	Dimension
1. Feelings	
2. Accomplishments or Knowledge	Content
3. Actions or Plans	
4. Facts or Property	
1. Protect Liar	Reason
2. Protect Other	
1. Total Falsehood	
2. Exaggeration	Type
3. Subtle (evasion or omission)	
1. Liar Him/herself	
2. Target of Lie	Referent
3. Another Person	
4. Event or Object	

FIG. 11.3.   Schematic diagram of the coding scheme of DePaulo et al. (1996).

terrain (see Bakeman & Casey, 1995, or Bakeman & Gottman, 1997, for a more extended discussion of this issue).

In the initial phase of category construction, it is best to employ the prospective system in a preliminary investigation, noting the frequency with which the various categories that constitute the system are employed. If a given category is consistently under-employed, it either should be broadened, to account for more of the behaviors that occur, or dropped from the system. Conversely, a category whose frequency of usage is considerably greater than all of the others should be divided into more discriminating classifications. Category refinement of this nature should proceed until the distribution of descriptive classifications as determined through preliminary investigation is not obviously disproportionate. Only when this phase of the construction process is completed should the investigator consider using the system in a real research setting.

Inference.   In addition to the potential problems mentioned above, the category system constructor is faced with a difficult decision when deciding upon the degree of inference the prospective system will require of coders. Should the classification system deal strictly with *observable events*, or, rather, call for the coder to make some estimate regarding possible motivations for, or intentions of, the actor under investigation? In deciding on inference level, the social scientist is faced with two desirable yet conflicting goals. If a category system is based solely on clearly visible behaviors, then the investigator need not be overly concerned about possible differences in interpretation of the same behavior by different observers. Such concrete, behavior-based category systems, however, often do not allow for the clear transmission of the "feeling" of the interaction. The subtle nuances of the observational situation are lost, often at great cost to the interpretation and integration of the obtained results. Heyns and Zander (1953) outlined the possible choices confronting the scientist quite well:

> At the simpler (noninferential) extreme, [the observer] might develop categories such as 'Shoves other children,' 'Calls other children names,' 'Asks for help,'.... On the other hand, he may use such categories as 'Shows hostility,' 'Demands submission,' [etc.]. In the latter case the observers are looking at the same behavior but are making inferences concerning it. (p. 390)

When determining the inference level of categories, much depends on the degree to which the coding operations of the investigation are removed from the actual observational setting. If the research operations call for the concurrent observation and codification of behavior, then inferences regarding the motivation underlying the observed events can cause problems. Interpreting a person's motives "on line" is difficult and time consuming. Coding on line does not allow the coder to sit back and think about an actor's internal state. Inference-making is facilitated if the coding and categorization operations are being made on videotaped actions, however. Often, it is useful to include both inferential and more direct, concrete categories in the same observational system. For example, in a study of attraction, we might assess eye contact between two people, the physical distance between them, etc., as well as asking the coder to estimate the extent to which they like one another. This recommended leniency in terms of inference is somewhat unorthodox in systematic observational research. The predominant school of thought recommends these methods be applied only to observable events and behaviors. Many value the methodology of systematic observation precisely because it is inference-free. We appreciate this view. Indeed, keeping coder judgments of underlying, unobserved cognitions to a minimum is bound to facilitate the reliability of a coding scheme. On the other hand, inferences about the motives, beliefs, or emotions underlying a given behavior can sometimes be quite obvious. These inferential judgments add richness to the coding scheme, if they can be made reliably.

Reliability

A primary consideration in the construction of any system concerns the issue of the reliability of categories. As Geller (1955) observed, "The fewer the categories, the more precise their definition, and the less inference required in making classifications, the greater will be the reliability of the data" (p. 194). Weick (1985) has outlined four types of comparisons that can be used in observational research to study reliability:

> First, the ratings of two persons observing the same event would be correlated, a measure that would rule out the errors of change in the person and the environment. Next, the ratings of the same observer watching a similar event at two different times would be compared (this would rule out errors of content sampling.) Then the agreement of two observers observing an event at two different times would be correlated. This measure ... would be expected to yield the lowest reliability of the four comparisons. Finally, the observations of a single observer watching a single event would be compared in a manner similar to odd-even item correlations in a test. This is a check on internal consistency or the extent to which the observer agrees with himself. If the category system is explicit and well defined, this measure of reliability would be expected to yield the highest correlation. (p. 38)

TABLE 11.1
Agreement Matrix Used in Calculating Cohen's Kappa

	Content Catagory	Observer B				
		1	*2*	*3*	*4*	*Total*
	1. Feelings	44	5	0	6	55
	2. Accomplishments	4	61	5	22	92
Observer A	3. Actions	2	5	38	0	45
	4. Facts	0	18	7	19	44
	Total	50	89	50	47	236

The most fundamental question of category reliability is, "Do the ratings of two or more observers who have witnessed the same event(s) coincide to an acceptable degree?" By acceptable degree, we mean beyond that which would occur by chance. For example, if we have a system of only two categories, and our observers agree 60% of the time, should we be satisfied? Recognizing that agreement in such a system would occur by chance 50% of the time, it is evident that a 60% intercoder agreement rate is not much to write home about. Cohen's (1960, 1968) kappa is a widely used index to assess the extent of agreement between coders while controlling for chance. Kappa's value can range from zero (no agreement whatsoever) to one (perfect agreement). Conceptually, the statistic is relatively straightforward. We begin with a matrix whose rows and columns reflect the various categories of the coding scheme. The rows represent the codings of Observer A, the columns those of Observer B. So for example, suppose we are using the category system that DePaulo et al. (1996) used to code lying, and are focusing on the first dimension of their system, namely the content of the lie. We could develop an agreement matrix by listing observers' codings, as in Table 11.1. The diagonal entries in the table represent the number of times the coders have overlapped (i.e., agree) on a given category. The nondiagonal elements represent disagreements. The greater the number of entries off the diagonal, the lower the kappa, and the lower the reliability of the coding system.

To calculate Kappa (κ), we first need to know the proportion of intercoder agreement. This is calculated by summing the diagonal entries and dividing by the total number of observations. In our example,

$$P_{\text{agree}} = (44 + 61 + 38 + 19)/236, \text{ or } 162/236, \text{ or } .686.$$

To find the proportion of agreements expected by chance, we multiply each column total with its respective row total, and sum these products. This sum would then be divided by the square of the total number of observations. In our example, this process would require the following calculations:

$$P_{\text{chance}} = [(50^{\star}55) + (89^{\star}92) + (50^{\star}45) + (47^{\star}44)]/236^2$$

$$= [(2750) + (8188) + (2250) + (2068)]/55696.$$

The end result of this series of calculations is 15256/55696, or .274.

To determine Kappa, we use the following formula:

$$\kappa = \frac{P_{\text{agree}} - P_{\text{chance}}}{1 - P_{\text{chance}}},$$

which in our example results in $\kappa = .567$; this is considerably less than the proportion of intercoder agreement that was found ($P_{agree} = .69$), and reflects the adjustment made for chance agreements.[7] This is not a particularly strong result. Generally, observational researchers suggest that a kappa of .75 or greater is an acceptable result; kappas between .6 and .75 suggest caution, and those less than .6 indicate a dangerous level of unreliability or intercoder disagreement (Fleiss, 1981). The agreement matrix of Table 11.1 gives some indication of the source of the problem, and by extension, its solution. To improve the coding scheme, or the coder training, we consider the off-diagonal entries. Are there cells off the diagonal that suggest an inordinate or unacceptable number of disagreements? In the hypothetical table presented here, it is clear that our two observers had most disagreement on the categorization of lies as involving either facts (Category 2) or accomplishments (Category 4). Such a result suggests that the researcher either clarify the definition of these two categories or spend more time training coders about the distinction, or both.

Weick (1985) held that the reliability of a coding system is a reflection of both the discriminability of the classifications that constitute the scheme and the efficacy of coder training. In the construction of category systems, intercoder agreement is of major importance because without it, very little use can be made of the collected observations. For example, suppose in our research we have obtained the intercoder agreement matrix of Table 11.1. The level of agreement is not satisfactory, but which coder's observation is the more accurate? We have no way to answer this question. It is equally difficult to determine the cause of disagreement, that is, whether it is attributable to insufficient coder training or to the nondiscriminability of some of the categories that constitute the coding system. Enhancing coder agreement often calls for nothing more than practice. Given sufficient practice with a coding scheme, most individuals can learn to employ reliably even the most complex of systems. Nondiscriminability of categories, however, represents a more difficult problem. If a single unit of behavior can be logically classified through the use of two or more different categories within the same coding system, this gives rise to intercoder disagreements that augmented training will not resolve.[8] The appropriate response to problems of this type is a restructuring of categories to delineate more clearly the boundaries of each. This, in turn, calls for additional coder re-instruction and reliability testing, to determine whether the sought-for increase in category differentiation has occurred.

All the previously mentioned aspects of system construction affect the reliability of the coding scheme. The reliability of a system will be enhanced if:

- The system is extensive, rather than intensive.
- The unit of analysis is observer-defined, rather than dependent on some action of the observed.
- The coding system consists of a small number of categories.
- Observation and classification are not concurrent processes (i.e., audio- or videotapes are used to allow for review of the observational data).
- Little or no inference is called for.

---

[7]Robinson and Bakeman (1998) kindly provide a computer program to reduce the drudgery of calculating Kappa.

[8]A good indication of nondiscriminability of categories occurs when the same observer, reviewing the same behaviors (typically through the use of videotape), assigns different scores from the first to the second observation. Results of this type suggest that the coding classifications cannot be employed with any degree of reliability.

This is not meant to suggest that the above considerations should always determine the type of category constructed, but rather to call attention to the fact that some types of categorization will be more subject to problems of unreliability than others.

Rating scales

Having chosen a category system and unit of analysis appropriate for the group under observation, the basic procedure of an investigation of this type is fairly straightforward. The unit of analysis is chosen, individuals or groups are observed, and if a given action of interaction described by system occurs within the unit of analysis, it is so noted. At the completion of the investigation, the researcher determines the frequency of occurrence of each category (and sometimes, the sequence of actions or the time at which the actions occurred). With this information, the investigator is able to determine the manner in which different manipulations (if used) affected the actions of the individual or group, and the sequence of dependencies among the behaviors under study. Sometimes, however, the frequency counts on which these determinations are based are viewed as insufficiently informative. In these instances, researchers often find that a more sensitive analysis of the processes under observation can be obtained using rating scales.

In its most simple form, a rating scale is an extension of a category system, in which a coder must decide not only on the classification of an event, but also evaluate its magnitude or intensity. This apparently minor addition adds considerably to the difficulty of the coding task. Consider the plight of an observer making use of Bales' IPA in coding the behavior of an individual in a small group interaction. The observed participant's response to another person in the group must be classified through the use of one of the 12 IPA categories. In itself, this can be a difficult job. Now suppose that the observer must determine not only the proper classification of an action, but also estimate the intensity of the response. Having decided that Person A has "shown solidarity" (Category 1) toward Person B, that is, the coder must then decide whether this extension of solidarity was mild, average, above average, or intense. The result of this approach is that the complexity of the coders' tasks is greatly increased, because they must not only categorize, but also rate (in terms of intensity, magnitude, duration, etc.) the critical behaviors. Inference levels are inevitably increased in this process, and the reliability of the total system thereby suffers.

In opposition to these disadvantages stands the possibility of increasing the information value of the obtained results. We return to Bales' IPA to show how this is so. Suppose that in the early days of the founding of the United States, we found ourselves observing the members of the Continental Congress in their deliberations on the Declaration of Independence. One member of the Congress, feeling great ambivalence over Jefferson's document, hesitantly states, "Yes, I suppose I can go along with this." You code this as an instance of Category 1, showing solidarity. Another member, perhaps better understanding the historical significance of his actions, jumps up and screams, "I will stake my fortune and my life on this document!" This action is also coded as an instance of Category 1. Clearly, these two acts are different, yet both receive the same score—the categorical (but quantity-free) IPA cannot denote even this obvious distinction in intensity. Through the addition of an intensity qualification, differences of this type are not glossed over, and a more descriptive picture of the interaction is conveyed. This addition assumes that the necessary categorization and intensity rating processes can be accomplished with some reasonable degree of reliability. If this is the case, and there are many technical aids to help secure reliability (e.g., taping of interactions, computer-assisted coding devices, etc.), then the use of rating scales is indicated, because such measures provide considerably more information than that obtained through the use of more simply employed category systems.

CONCLUDING REMARKS

In observational research, the progressive degree of control that is placed on the allowable actions of the observer is wide-ranging. At the least controlled pole, we have the open, unconstrained methods of the early ethnographers; this approach to the accumulation of information is very different from that of the highly structured, often ritualistic practices of today's experimentalists. We believe that the development of increasingly sophisticated methods to reduce the impact of the observer on the observed reflects the growth, evolution, and overall progress of the science of human behavior. As we suggested at the very beginning of this chapter, it is often the case that the more elementary, basic, "foundation-building" observational techniques have been neglected in favor of the more "advanced" experimental ones. This is usually a mistake. Schwartz and Jacobs (1979) highlighted the importance of observational methods when they stated, "Ordinarily (in the experimental methods), one has a hypothesis, knows pretty well what it means, and wants to know if it is true. Here (in the observational methods), one has a hypothesis, is pretty sure that is true, and wants to know what it means (wants to know *what* is true)" (p. 327).

It is our hope that this review has demonstrated that naturalistic observational methods, appropriately used, are as scientifically "respectable" as the more prestigious experimental techniques and even more useful in areas in which knowledge concerning the phenomenon under consideration is limited. The fact that a given experimental technique possesses a high degree of internal validity does not necessarily indicate its appropriateness for use in all situations (Mook, 1983). The behavior or relationship in question must guide the choice of which investigative method is to be employed. To approach a research problem from the opposite direction, with a prearranged methodology dictating the phenomenon to be studied, represents a mechanistic mentality that is incompatible with the aims of any science.

SUGGESTED READINGS

DePaulo, B. M., Kashy, D. A., Kirkendol, S. E., Wyer, M. M., & Epstein, J. A. (1996). Lying in everyday life. *Journal of Personality and Social Psychology, 70*, 979–995.

Reis, H. T., & Gable, S. L. (2000). Event-sampling and other methods for studying everyday experience. In H. T. Reis & C. M. Judd (Eds.), *Handbook of research methods in social and personality psychology* (pp. 190–222). New York: Cambridge University Press.

Weick, K. E. (1985). Systematic observational methods. In G. Lindzey & E. Aronson (Eds.), *The handbook of social psychology* (3rd ed., pp. 567–634). Reading, MA: Addison-Wesley.

12

INTERVIEWING

The research interview is a data collection method in which participants provide information about their behavior, thoughts, or feelings in response to questions posed by an interviewer. Unlike most of the observational methods discussed in chapter 11, interviews always involve some form of interaction between the investigator and the respondent, and this factor distinguishes the technique from self-administered questionnaire methods (see chap. 15) in which respondents sometimes never see, much less interact with, a researcher. The interactive nature of the interview, and its dependence on verbal or linguistic responses, constitutes at one and the same time its major strength and its major drawback as a method of social research.

It almost always is easier and cheaper to use written questionnaires completed by respondents than it is to expend the time and effort necessary for an interview (Bartholomew, Henderson, & Marcia, 2000).[1] Thus, it is important to consider the circumstances under which an interview approach is most appropriate. Probably the most important basis for choosing the interview occurs when the nature of the research issue demands a personal, interactive, method of data collection. This might be the case, for instance, when highly sensitive information is sought, or when certain responses call for more probing for details than one could cover in a standard questionnaire format. Interviews also might be required with special respondent populations who might not be able to handle the requirements of a questionnaire (e.g., young children, the elderly, or people for whom the language of the interview is not their first language). Further, if the problem of nonresponse is a serious threat to research validity, it may be more likely that personal contact will achieve higher response rates than the more impersonal questionnaire approach.[2]

---

[1] Questionnaire scale construction is discussed in detail in chapter 15.

[2] Interviews, of course, are used in many contexts other than basic research data collection. The clinical interview is a valuable tool of diagnosis and treatment in mental health settings, and extensive participant interviews often accompany the debriefing phase of a laboratory experiment. However, these specialized uses of the in-depth interview technique are beyond the purview of this text. This chapter focuses on the use of the interview in the general context of survey research.

Modes of Administration

Before beginning our discussion of designing and conducting interviews, it is important to note that interviews do not always entail face-to-face encounters between interviewer and respondent. *Telephone interviews* are extremely common and popular today, with good reason. Not many years ago, however, researchers were warned to avoid telephone interviews because it was generally assumed that people would be less willing (than in face-to-face encounters) to consent to be interviewed, and those who did agree to participate would be unwilling to give the interviewer more than 5 to 10 min of their time. Research focused specifically on this concern indicates that it is much less problematic than originally thought. Groves and Kahn (1979), for example, found that participation rates in telephone interviews were only 5% less than those involving face-to-face encounters, and Bradburn and Sudman's (1979) data demonstrated somewhat higher response rates to telephone, as opposed to personal, interviews—at least in urban areas. In addition, Dillman's (1978) research revealed that the response rate in telephone interviews was approximately 15% greater than that of mail surveys. In terms of respondents' willingness to participate in extensive telephone interviews, implications much the same as those drawn from the response rate research can be drawn.[3] The findings of Quinn, Gutek, and Walsh (1980), Dillman (1978), and Smith and Kluegel (1984) all suggest strongly that once committed to the telephone interview, respondents are *not* likely to disengage prematurely. Telephone interview studies lasting as long as an hour have been conducted with no appreciable drop-out problem (Kluegel & Smith, 1982). Herman (1977) coupled face-to-face with telephone interviewing. An interviewer went to the homes of those who refused a telephone interview or could not be reached via phone. She found that the quality of the phone interviewees was comparable to that of the face-to-face interviewer, although the phone interviewees were less likely to disclose personal information (e.g., for whom they voted).

In brief, there is much to recommend the use of the telephone as a major form of interview research. Telephone interviews are almost invariably less expensive to conduct than personal interviews, they can be accomplished with greater speed, and with greater researcher control over the behaviors of the interviewers, if the research is conducted from a central location containing a number of phones. Previously held beliefs regarding the potential drawbacks of this approach have been shown largely to be unfounded. Telephone interviews are no more susceptible to response rate or premature disengagement problems than face-to-face interviews. Consequently, telephone interviewing has become increasingly common, and it is a reasonable bet that this mode will continue to be the major method by which interviews are conducted.

Despite the many advantages of the telephone approach, it is important to keep in mind some potential disadvantages. In a face-to-face interview, the researcher is more likely to detect and correct confusion on the part of the respondent (Bartholemew et al., 2000). He or she is more likely to be able to clarify issues and to realize that a question does not carry the intended implication. This is an especially important advantage in the initial research phases in which the interview schedule (the list of questions to be employed) is being

---

[3]Of course, these findings presume that the respondent can be reached by phone in the first place. Given that approximately 95% of American households have telephones, this form of contact has not been problematic, at least in industrialized nations. However, in recent years the increasing use of answering machines, voice mail, and caller-id to screen out incoming phone calls has made access to potential participants for phone interviews somewhat more difficult (see discussion of sampling issues in chap. 10).

developed. The telephone interview also does not allow for the use of visual aids; this can prove to be important if complex questions or lengthy response options are to be provided the interviewee. Finally, the telephone interview does not provide the researcher with visual contact with the respondent. This can prove troublesome in situations in which visual cues are used to replace a number of otherwise lengthy or overly personal questions. In health surveys, for instance, a visual inspection of the respondent often proves useful. Similarly, the telephone approach would seem less than optimal in situations in which respondents' socioeconomic status is to be estimated by visual inspection of their neighborhood or dwelling. In these cases, the telephone interview is not necessarily less costly than the more personal face-to-face approach.

No matter what form the mode of interviewing assumes (telephone or face-to-face), the principles that govern good interview technique are the same. In the pages that follow, we present some "rules" that should govern the manner in which this approach is employed.

CHOICE POINTS IN THE DEVELOPMENT OF THE INTERVIEW

The interview is one of our most common data-gathering devices. It can be employed to study a wide range of issues, across widely varying samples of respondents. The methodological variations available in the choice of specific interview method, question format, and so on, are perhaps equally diverse. Nevertheless, there are a number of common characteristics that all research of this type shares, which reflect the decisions that the investigator must face at one time or another in the design of any interview study (see Fig. 12.1). We focus on these "choice points" in the following discussion to provide a general framework within which all of the many and varied forms of interview research might be conceptualized. This approach should provide a good basis for understanding the proper use of the interview as a tactic of scientific research.

Broadly, the strategic research operations characteristic of all interview studies involve the choice of (a) the type and form of questions to be employed, (b) the interview format, (c) the means by which the interview will be conducted, (d) the sample or population of respondents to whom questions will be addressed, and (e) the methods to be used in coding, aggregating, and analyzing respondents' answers. Earlier, in chapter 10, we dealt with considerations of sampling, and in chapter 13, we discuss the coding, aggregation, and analysis of verbal data. Accordingly, the task of this chapter reduces to a consideration of the first three choices. As is seen, however, consideration of these issues is far from

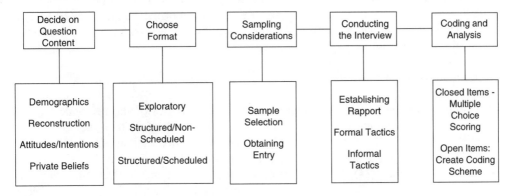

FIG. 12.1. Steps in designing an interview investigation.

trivial because the decisions made at the formative stages of the interview study have ramifications for all that follows.

Although social scientists have become increasingly conscious of the necessity for a systematic study of the best means of developing interview questions, there is surprisingly little in the way of research directed specifically toward this issue. Some texts (Dijkstra & van der Zouwen, 1982; Krosnick & Fabrigar, in press; Rossi, Wright, & Anderson, 1983; Sudman & Bradburn, 1982) do discuss some of the intricacies involved in this task, but most of the advice seems to boil down to "use common sense" and "draw upon practical experience." This is undoubtedly sound advice, but it provides little direction for the researcher in terms of specific item wording or format. Later in the chapter we discuss some of the factors that appear to have an impact on the likelihood that people will interpret the meaning of a question properly, but for the moment it is sufficient to keep in mind a few simple but effective rules of thumb in question construction:

- Keep the items as brief as possible—the longer the item, the more likely it is to succumb to one or another of the problems listed below.

- Avoid subtle shadings—if you want to know about something, ask about it as directly as possible.

- Avoid double-barreled questions, that is, questions that logically allow for two (possibly opposed) answers, for example, "Do you like this year's Fords or Chryslers?"

- Use language the respondents can understand (most people are not social scientists, so to use the jargon of the field is probably ill-advised).

- If at all possible, pretest items on a small sample of respondents drawn from the same population that will constitute the ultimate data source.

QUESTION/INTERVIEW CONTENT

The variety of issues that can be addressed in the interview represents one of the most appealing features of this methodology. This diversity, however, makes it difficult to categorize the types of questions that have been, and can be, used. Some researchers use a simple dichotomy to classify survey items: "Does the question focus on a public or a private action?" or "Is the item concerned with *fact* or *opinion*?" Experience suggests that these classifications are unnecessarily broad, and that the seeming simplicity of the categorization is more apparent than real. Schuman and Kalton (1985) suggested a more differentiated classification, which more sensitively describes the situations in which the interview might be used most profitably, and the forms of information that might be sought through the use of this technique. In the pages that follow, we will adopt their scheme with some minor modifications.

Sociodemographic Information

Questions concerned with descriptive personal characteristics of the respondent (age, religion, sex, race, income, etc.) are perhaps the most common of all items included in the interview. In general, there is reason to believe that answers to questions of this type can be trusted, especially if the item is clear and precisely worded (e.g., Parry & Crossley, 1950; Weaver & Swanson, 1974). So, for example, it would be better to ask "Date of birth" than "age" to learn the age of a respondent. The former is readily available in most people's memories and less likely to be distorted.

Two sociodemographic issues that sometimes defy this observation (for rather different reasons) are race, or ethnicity, and income. Given the relatively subjective nature of race (even social demographers are hard-put to provide an acceptable definition), and the even more subjective nature of ethnic origin in the United States, where the "melting pot" analogy is far more than symbolic, it is difficult to validate participants' responses to survey items of this type. Many view income as a private matter, and thus, questions on this issue typically generate a relatively large (something on the order of 5%–10%) refusal rate. Nonresponse (or item refusal) is preferable to a respondent's deliberate misreporting, but it does cause problems in later (analytic) stages of the research. In addition, there is cause for concern in interpreting even the responses of those willing to disclose personal income. For many, income varies as a function of the availability of overtime, seasonal fluctuations in worker demand, and so forth, and estimates of income are likely to be inaccurate. In other instances, especially when total household income is at issue, systematic underreporting is likely because of income sources that are typically overlooked (e.g., interest, dividends, irregular or seasonal employment), a less than complete knowledge of other household members' wages, and the like.

With problems of this nature, it is little wonder that many survey researchers now ask for the much less threatening information regarding the respondent's job, and then attempt to relate these answers to other items, or to extrapolate income or "social class" from them (see Cain & Treiman, 1981; Hodge, Siegel, & Rossi, 1964; Hollingshead, 1949). Given the near ubiquity of sociodemographic items included in almost all surveys, it is understandable why some researchers have recommended that a standardized set of such items be used in all interview research. We resist such a recommendation because it represents a move in a direction away from the tailoring of items to research issues, a central tenet of good research design. However, those who would like a survey of commonly employed measures (to be used in the development of their own specific item set) would be well-advised to consult VanDusen and Zill (1975).

A question that should occur to researchers in light of the potential problems involved with data of this sort is its relevance for the research issue. In many instances, specific types of demographic information are not at all relevant to the theoretical issue under investigation. An appropriate question then becomes, why ask the question if it has no relevance to the research issue, especially if it might compromise the interview? We realize that such information may serendipitously prove quite useful in later, secondary, analyses, but its potential cost should not be underestimated.

Reconstruction

The research interview is perhaps the most practical, and certainly the most common, means of investigating people's reconstructions of past events. Very often, events having important social implications occur so rapidly or unexpectedly that researchers are unable to observe behavior at the time the events occur. Floods, blizzards, prison riots, are but a few such occurrences whose analysis might provide valuable information for the social scientist. Less encompassing, but perhaps equally important, past events at a personal level (e.g., marriage, births, promotions, etc.) also can be a rich source of information, but such events typically leave few accessible traces. By a judicious use of the interview, such information becomes more available to the researcher.

This is not to say that the data about past events obtained through interview techniques are perfectly trustworthy. Some events are simply not important enough to the respondent to remember. Consistent with this observation, Sudman (1980) speculated that there are three important factors that influence the fidelity of recall of an event. They are:

- Uniqueness of the event (e.g., most middle-aged Americans can remember exactly where they were, and what they were doing, when they learned that President John Kennedy had been shot).

- The magnitude of the event's economic or social costs or benefits (e.g., we're more likely to recall the day we won the $1 million lottery than the time we lost $2 at the racetrack, and

- The long-term, continuing nature of the event (e.g., recall of an injury having long-term effects will be more memorable than one that, though as serious, has consequences of short or limited duration).[4]

Although, as Sudman (1980) indicated, the specific event under study will have a major influence on the likelihood of accurate recall, there is general agreement that the nature and form of the questions employed in reconstructive interviews also can have a significant effect on the accuracy of respondents' memory. Cannel, Miller, and Oksenberg (1981) suggested that instructions that stress the importance of complete answers have a positive effect on the completeness of people's responses. Indeed, they sometimes go so far as to ask the respondent to sign an agreement by which he or she acknowledges the importance of accuracy and completeness of answers.

Also shown to be effective in such situations is the use of longer, rather than shorter, questions. For reasons that are not entirely clear, people tend to give longer and more complete answers to longer questions, even if the longer question is merely a multiple restatement of the shorter version (see Ray & Webb, 1966). Thus, though briefer questions are generally to be preferred, longer questions may be employed when accuracy of recall is at stake. Finally, by reinforcing more complete answers, the interviewer can encourage respondents to provide more extensive, and presumably more accurate, responses. Although there is some danger that such reinforcement could bias participants' responses, if used judiciously this tactic appears capable of stimulating more complete answers without unduly influencing their content.

Attitudes and Behavioral Intentions

Another common use of the interview is in assessing people's attitudes and intentions. We distinguish between these terms because an attitude, an evaluative belief about a person or thing, may or may not carry with it any clear behavioral implications, whereas a behavioral intention is clearly an indication of an individual's decision to act in a certain manner (Ajzen, 1982). In chapter 15, we present a detailed discussion of the elements that must be considered in the development of attitude scales, and this information will not be repeated here.[5] However, Schuman and Kalton (1985) identified two aspects of survey questions—constraint and specificity—that are particularly relevant to interviews in which people's attitudes (or behavioral intentions) are the principal features of study.

---

[4]These factors probably interact with the specific event outcome in determining accuracy of recall. We know that pleasant outcomes are more likely to be remembered, especially those that have occurred recently; thus, winning $5000 in the lottery is probably more readily recalled than losing $500 in a poker game, not only because it is a more pleasant outcome, but also because it has a more enduring impact.

[5]It is important to note that the principles that govern the reliable (and valid) measurement of attitudes apply equally to the measurement of behavioral intentions.

Because these aspects of survey items may, in and of themselves, influence the way in which a participant responds, we will briefly turn our attention to them.

Question constraint refers to the fact that in most survey research, the respondent is asked a question and provided a prespecified and limited set of allowable responses. The form of the respondent's answers, that is, is constrained by the available choices. One of the most common constraints is the absence of a "Don't Know" or "No Opinion" response. Of course, if a respondent spontaneously gives one or the other of these responses, it typically is recorded as such (it would be foolish to force an answer when the respondent indicates no knowledge of the topic). However, research by Schuman and Presser (1981) demonstrated that the mere presence of an explicit "Don't Know" option has a significant effect on the proportion of respondents who are likely to answer in this manner. Questioning respondents under standard conditions about an obscure piece of legislation (the Agricultural Trade Act of 1978), Schuman and Presser found that two thirds of their sample had "no opinion." When an explicit "No opinion" option was made available to other respondents, however, the proportion of the sample that chose this alternative rose to 90%.

Given this apparent effect of the presence or absence of the "don't know" option, the investigator should evaluate whether the use of this response will increase or decrease the accuracy of information obtained from respondents. If the researcher judges that the respondent population includes a large number of people have no real knowledge of the issue at hand, then it is advisable to include this option (see, also, Bishop, Oldendick, Tuchfarber, & Bennett, 1980).[6] On the other hand, if the researcher judges that most people do have opinions on the issue, but that they are not altogether firm about them, the "don't know" option can result in considerable under-representation of opinions held.

The issue of *question specificity* calls attention to the fact that minor changes of wording can have marked effects on people's responses. Rugg (1941), for example, found that only 25% of respondents in a national sample were willing to "allow speeches against democracy." However, when the question was put to a comparable sample in slightly modified form, Rugg found that 46% were against "forbidding" such speeches. Evidently, the different connotations of the words "forbid" and "(not) allow" produced these differences, even though the implications of the two questions were identical.

Private Beliefs and Actions

Sometimes, the focus of an investigation is on behavior that is of a highly personal, secretive, or illegal nature. People engaging in such actions usually are not willing to be observed; however, surprisingly, they often are quite willing to discuss their experiences, especially if they can be assured of anonymity or confidentiality. Kinsey, Pomeroy, and Martin's (1948) study of sexual practices in the United States, Schaps and Sanders' (1970) investigation of marijuana usage, and Bradburn and Sudman's (1979) survey of drunken driving are examples of interviews focused on private actions. In their attempts to prevent HIV/AIDS infection, Aronson, Stone, and their colleagues have demonstrated that participants are willing both to disclose their rates of sexual contact and the likelihood that these encounters involved the use of condoms (Aronson, Fried, & Stone, 1991; Stone, Aronson, Crain, & Winslow, 1994).

Considerable research has been undertaken to determine the degree to which respondents under-report the extent of their involvement in private, or socially undesirable actions.

---

[6]If accuracy of response is absolutely essential, it is important that the respondent know that choosing the "don't know" option is not tantamount to an admission of ignorance.

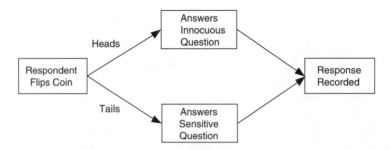

FIG. 12.2.   Schematic of the randomized response technique.

Although the research literature on this issue is mixed, it generally indicates that there is a tendency for people to distort, or to fail to admit to, actions that are illegal or viewed with disapproval by the society at large (see Abernathy, Greenberg, & Horvitz, 1970; Goodstadt & Gruson, 1975; Tracy & Fox, 1981). Attempts at solution of the underreporting problem typically take one of two forms. The most simple entails a concerted effort on the part of the investigator to secure respondents' commitment to the interview, to assure them that their answers will not be traceable, and to provide reinforcement and feedback over the course of the interaction (Cannell et al., 1981).

Other approaches involve somewhat more complicated arrangement in which each sensitive question ("Have you ever had an abortion?") is paired with an innocuous one ("Do you like chocolate ice cream?"). The particular item of each pair to be answered is randomly assigned to the respondent at the time of the administration (see Fig. 12.2). Because the interviewer does not know which of the two items the respondent is answering, anonymity is assured. The analysis of data of this type proceeds on the assumption that the researcher knows the proportion of the sample who were assigned the innocuous or the sensitive question, knows (or can estimate) the proportion of the population that would answer the innocuous question positively or negatively, and finally, knows the number of positive (or negative) responses obtained on a specific question pair over the entire sample. With this information, one can estimate the number of respondents who answered the sensitive question affirmatively (see Warner, 1965; Schuman & Kalton, 1985).

Miller (1984) suggested a simpler technique, which involves providing respondents with lists of behaviors, and simply asking them to tell the number of such activities in which they have engaged. One group receives the innocuous list, the other respondents a list containing all of the innocuous actions *plus* the critical sensitive behavior of interest. Differences in the absolute number of all reported behaviors between the two respondent samples provide an estimate of the percentage of the total population that has engaged in the sensitive behavior. Because the respondents need only report an overall number, the technique is much less intrusive than one in which every behavior need be admitted or denied. However, the "random response" and the "paired list" methods, as these two techniques are termed, do appear to introduce considerably more error into the data set than more straightforward questions. Thus, whereas they might reduce bias in respondents' answers, they also are likely to increase error.

INTERVIEW STRUCTURE

The interview, of course, is only one of a multitude of research techniques available to the social scientist. In the previous section, we detailed some of the types of information that seemed particularly suited to this method. In this section, we discuss the major forms of the research interview. At a general level, the interview approach appears especially suited for research situations in which the existence of basic relationships among social variables is the primary focus: "Is there a relationship between attitudes toward civil authorities and religiosity," or "Is education level related to social class, ethnicity, or attitudes toward the major parties' candidates for the Senate?" In addition, the technique is useful in attempts at hypothesis purification, especially when laboratory reactivity is troublesome.

Now, assume that after extensive consideration of a number of potentially employed alternatives, an investigator has decided to use the interview as his or her principal data-gathering device. Given this decision, what are the available options? The answer to this question depends on the extent of information the researcher possesses about the phenomenon to be studied. If the research problem has been formulated only recently, and no hypotheses have as yet been generated, then the structure of the interview and the form of the questions employed must be adjusted accordingly. However, if on the basis of theory or previous research a definite series of expectations has been developed, then the use of different structures and question forms is indicated. In the pages that follow, we examine some of these alternatives.

The Exploratory Interview

The exploratory interview resembles in general form a participant, nonstructured, free-response observational investigation. In research of this type, neither the questions nor the allowable responses are constrained. There is no "interview roadmap" (structure) to guide the interviewer, whose behavior is dictated by the responses received; he or she is encouraged to follow any leads that appear promising or informative. The number of such leads that ultimately prove productive is usually a function of the technical skill of the interviewer and the extent to which he or she is versed in the theory underlying the issues under study. As such, the less structured the interview, the greater demands on the interviewer's competence and theoretical grounding.

Paradoxically, then, the exploratory interview, while making only minimal demands in terms of data quality, calls for the most highly qualified, technically competent researchers if it is to generate optimally useful data. Costs can be high in exploratory interview settings research. However, these costs are well justified because a failure in the initial hypothesis-clarification phase always adversely affects the remaining research processes, and such failures are difficult to rectify by later adjustments. Without sufficient theoretical and technical competence, the selection of appropriate hypotheses is a matter of luck—thus the necessity for professional personnel in the initial exploratory phase of the investigation.

The Structured-Nonscheduled Interview

Structured-nonscheduled interview techniques are midway between the completely open, nonstructured exploratory approaches and the standardized, structured techniques discussed in the next section. The structured-nonscheduled interview imposes on the researcher the necessity of obtaining certain highly specified types of information (hence the term, *structured*) but does not specify the manner in which the information is to be obtained; that is, no list of prespecified questions (the interview schedule) is employed. The use of this technique is predicated on the assumption either that some form of initial exploratory investigation has been completed or that some theoretical position has allowed a specification of the types of relationships that are likely to exist in the situation under study. The task of the interviewer making use of techniques of this type is well specified. The means to be employed in completing the task are not.

As with exploratory approaches, these techniques are not used to best advantage in testing hypotheses because the stimulus situation varies from respondent to respondent, given the nonscheduled nature of the technique. This interview form, however, often is used in descriptive or classificatory research. In such situations, demographic or other "individual difference" types of variables often are employed as major factors in the classification scheme. Hence, relatively subtle interpersonal distinctions are assessed to provide an indication of the factors that might influence the variables of interest. This interview form requires interviewers of considerable technical competence, because they must be able to channel respondents' thinking along lines of specific theoretical importance, even though there is no schedule of prespecified questions to assist them in this task. The demands for theoretical competence, however, are not as great as in the exploratory interview, because the specific relationships thought to be crucial have been spelled out in advance. Because the interviewer's work consists of investigating prespecified relationships, he or she need not be overly sensitive to responses that occur outside the boundaries established in the initial exploration, which gave rise to the interview in the first place. This "insensitivity" can result in a loss of valuable information because as with all other research techniques, the prespecified focus of the structured-nonscheduled interview results in a constriction of the research field. Although this constriction may result in a loss of information, such techniques provide for a more intensive and focused investigation of the concepts and relationships thought to be most promising.

This is not to suggest that the scope of interviews of this type need be overly restrictive. The monumental research program of Kinsey and his associates (1948) was accomplished primarily through interviews of the structured-nonscheduled variety. This fact provides some insight into the types of situation calling for the use of this interview form. Kinsey understood that questions focused on various sexual practices would affect different respondents in different ways. Thus, the very sequence in which certain topics were introduced was varied accordingly, as these sample instructions indicate:

> For unmarried males, the sequence [should be] nocturnal emissions, masturbation, premarital petting, premarital intercourse with companions, intercourse with prostitutes, animal contacts, and the homosexual. For males who have never gone beyond the tenth grade in school, premarital intercourse can be discussed much earlier in the interview, because it is generally accepted at that social level; but masturbation needs to be approached more carefully if one is to get the truth from that group. (p. 48)

Had Kinsey's interviewers used a prespecified interview schedule, they almost certainly would have alienated a portion of the respondent sample. The use of the structured-nonscheduled interview form is especially appropriate when the sample is diverse, and this diversity can logically be expected to result in different reactions to the questions to be posed. However, if the sample is characterized by a more restricted range of respondent characteristics, or the topics are of such a nature as to affect all respondents in the same way, then the use of this interview form results in unnecessary expense. Technically competent interviewers do not come cheaply. Under relatively restrictive response conditions, the structured-scheduled interview is recommended.

The Structured-Scheduled Interview

As implied earlier, the level of interviewer competence necessary in conducting scheduled research is less than that demanded in the more free-form nonscheduled interview, and this fact is reflected in the cost differences of interviews of this type (Schuman & Kalton, 1985). However, whereas this more constricted interview form places some degree of restriction on allowable interviewer behaviors, it still calls for considerable technical expertise because a poorly trained or unmotivated interviewer can sabotage even the most highly structured research project.

Open and Closed Interview Questions.   Before proceeding with a detailed discussion of this technique, it is important to note a distinction between the types of schedule that can be employed in this form of interview. Differences between schedules are primarily a function of the style of question wording that is used. The more common form employed in scheduled interviews is the *closed* question. Interviews making use of this type of question are analogous to verbal multiple-choice tests. Information is asked of a respondent, who is given a set of allowable answers from which to choose; for example, "Are you a Catholic, Protestant, Jew, or Muslim?" The open form of this question would be, "What is your religion?" Both questions are aimed at the same information, but in the latter case, no constraint is placed on the allowable response, which must be coded by trained judges.

The most obvious administrative difference between these approaches is that the use of open-ended questions places somewhat greater demands on the interviewer, who must transcribe the respondent's replies. At the analysis phase, much greater costs can be incurred, especially on questions allowing for a more wide-ranging series of replies because with this form of question, a system for classifying respondents' answers must be developed before any analysis can proceed (see chap. 13 on the use of content analysis techniques for this purpose). With the closed question form, the classification scheme is provided in advance. This can simplify interviewer's job, in addition to reducing analysis costs. But there is more to it than this.

The seemingly minor administrative differences between open and close-ended questions are associated with major differences in the types of issues that interviews making use of these two question forms typically are designed to address. The structured-scheduled interview making use of close-ended questions allows for the greatest degree of standardization in the respondent–interviewer interaction. As in an experiment, all respondents are provided with a standard set of prespecified, interviewer-produced stimuli (questions), along with a set of allowable answers. Closed schedules are used in situations in which the investigator possesses considerable prior information about the phenomenon of interest. They allow for the most reliable investigation of hypotheses, and it is in this capacity that they are most often employed.

It is important to understand that the required standardization of questions and allowable responses characteristic of the structured-scheduled interview can be accomplished only when the researcher's specification of a participant's potential range of responses is nearly complete. If the researcher unwisely attempts to use closed questions before assuring that the universe of potential responses is adequately defined, the probability is great that much of the obtained data will prove nonusable. Stimuli (interview questions) giving rise to widely different reactions (sometimes called *self-stimulation effects*) can have a very negative impact on the attempt at standardization. If a question elicits an emotional response from 10 percent of the people in a respondent sample, for example, grave problems regarding the comparability of these data with that of the other 90% are indicated (unless, of course, there is some way of differentiating (stratifying) those who respond emotionally from those who do not). The solution to this problem lies in the proper prespecification of questions, responses, and their anticipated effect on respondents. Such prespecification can be assured only after considerable preliminary research.

Self-stimulation effects are not the only problem that a premature use of close-ended questions can produce in the interview. Even more likely are problems brought about by answers that force the interviewer to abandon the preset schedule. To return to our earlier example, suppose that in reply to the question, "Are you Catholic, Protestant, Jew, or Muslim?" our respondent responds "No." At this point, the closed schedule must be abandoned because the obtained response does not fit into the standardized scheme, and there is a good possibility that later questions, contingent on this response, are now palpably inappropriate. Before proceeding in this circumstance, therefore, the interviewer must seek clarification of the respondent's answer. If the respondent meant, "No, I am none of these, I am an atheist," then later questions regarding the intensity of one's religious convictions, attendance at church, synagogue, or mosque, and so on, would be inappropriate. If, however, the respondent's reply on further questioning were found to mean, "No, I am none of these—I am a Buddhist," then many of the questions that follow on the closed schedule probably can be used. The clarification process forced on the interviewer at this juncture, however, destroys the comparability of this interview with that of the others in which the closed format was adequate. As suggested here, the use of a closed interview schedule that does not provide sufficient alternatives with which to encapsulate respondents' possible range of replies can destroy the utility of the obtained data.

To skirt this hazard, and at the same time maintain stimulus comparability among respondents, some researchers recommend the use of an open question format. In this approach, the same questions, scheduled in the same sequence, are asked of all respondents; however, no prespecified list of response alternatives is provided. Techniques of this sort are intermediate to the structured-nonscheduled approaches and the structured-scheduled close-ended methods. Because they approximate the control of the close-ended interview, some have used them in hypothesis-testing research. Given the lack of response restriction inherent in the open-ended question format, and the almost certain noncomparability of responses between respondents (which, in turn, trigger noncomparable interviewer behaviors, self-stimulation effects, etc.), this usage appears ill-advised.[7]

A major potential disadvantage of the closed question interview schedule is that it does not allow the interviewer to respond to any novel information that might be obtained, but that is not a part of the rigidly prescribed schedule. The interviewer must "stick" to the questions as they have been written and cannot react to any new information given by the respondent unless this can be done within the context of the following question or questions. In such circumstances, it is not unusual for the interviewee to assume that the researcher is paying little heed to his or her replies, and under these conditions, maintenance of rapport becomes difficult indeed. Despite these shortcomings, the structured, scheduled, closed-question interview is the interview form that is most likely to be employed in hypothesis testing contexts because of the problems of response- and consequent stimulus-noncomparability inherent in all other types of interview formats. Given the extraordinarily demanding requirements that must be met before the closed question interview can be legitimately employed, it is appropriate to question whether the ideal of a completely comparable interview situation for all respondents can ever be attained in practice. The answer to this query depends principally on the issue or issues on which the interview is focused.

---

[7]Bradburn and Sudman (1979), for example, tape-recorded a number of interviews from a national survey, and found that on the average, one in three questions were read in a way different from that provided in the interview schedule. This lack of standardization of stimuli could make for large variations in respondents' answers.

At first glance it would seem that the degree of controversy of the topic of investigation would play a major role in determining the likelihood that an interview could be employed in hypothesis-testing research. Given the danger of self-stimulation effects, it would seem that the more controversial the issue, the greater the danger involved in the use of the interview as a dependent measure. However, degree of controversy surrounding an issue plays only an indirect role in determining the appropriateness of the structured interview as a means of gathering information. Much more important is the clarity and definitiveness of the potential alternatives provided for response to a given question. If an interview schedule can be constructed in such a way that the list of possible responses that is provided completely specifies the range of possible respondent reactions, then the use of a closed schedule is clearly proper.

These observations reinforce our earlier discussion regarding the effects of an increased focus in research operations. The greater the research constraint (in terms of both researcher and respondent behaviors), the more specific or circumscribed will be the obtained data. Thus, an open-ended schedule might result in considerably more information regarding a respondent's choice of not only a particular response option, but also of the reasons for this choice. If the researcher has correctly decided on a closed format, however, this supplemental information might provide relatively little in the way of new or useful data.

It might at first appear that supplemental information, explaining and qualifying a given response, would never prove superfluous to a researcher who was truly interested in the validity of his or her results, but this observation is not always correct, particularly in situations in which the closed schedule interview is most appropriate. Consider the case of the public opinion pollster hired to determine the chances of a candidate's election to the Presidency of the United States. The desired end product of this research, an accurate assessment of public opinion regarding the available options (i.e., candidates), is clearly specified. The pollster must, even in the most tightly contested race, correctly predict the winner. Given these parameters, the only data of any importance to the successful completion of the research mission are respondents' indication of the candidate they will support with their votes in the general election. Reasons underlying these choices are irrelevant within the boundaries of the research question.

The public opinion poll might be viewed as an atypical example of what is subsumed under the general rubric of "social science research," but it is precisely in settings of this type, or others approximating this degree of constriction of focus (of the research question), that this form of interview is employed most advantageously. This observation might prove discouraging to the researcher hoping to use the interview as a hypothesis-testing tool because issues of social interest often do not offer as limited a choice situation as an election. However, there is some cause for optimism in all of this because techniques enabling a researcher to lend some structure to an ambiguous social situation are available and have been used quite successfully. Most of these techniques involve attempts by the researcher, through the interview schedule, to subdivide a complex choice situation into component parts. Each of these components, in turn, being of a more highly constricted nature than the original, is then investigated through a closed schedule interview. An example clarifies this approach: Suppose that in the early months of an election year, a number of candidates, both Democratic and Republican, announce their intention to run for the Presidency. An interviewer could assess each candidate's chances by presenting their names to a random national sample of 1,000 respondents, who would be asked to name their favorite. Notice that this situation is already more constricted than one in which no alternatives are presented and respondents are free to name anyone.

This approach, however, is quite unlike that of the real election situation, in which one major candidate usually is pitted against only one other. To lend some realism to the survey, therefore, the researcher might ask the respondent to choose the Democrat and the Republican from the list of potential candidates that he or she would most favor, and then to choose between these two. This approach, however, often will result in a pairing of candidates who never survive the nominating conventions. Hence, much information of this type will prove useless from a predictive standpoint. To remedy this problem, a ranking of all candidates might be requested or, better yet, every possible pair of opponents might be presented (see chap. 14), and the respondents asked to indicate their preferences on each pair.

The order in which these options were presented reflects increasing levels of response restriction. Preconditions are imposed, and the respondent is asked to operate within these imposed boundaries. These constraints, in turn, enable the researcher to collect information that is almost certain to prove relevant to the research question.

Examples more complex by far than the one cited here could have been presented, but the process of decomposing complex stimulus situations into more tractable components is comparable across situations. In every instance, an individual is asked to respond within a series of prespecified limits. Conditions concerning the stimulus object are imposed ("Suppose that——were elected, would you ——, ——, etc."), and the respondent is asked to react as if these conditions represented reality. The construction of potential alternatives in such situations is rarely too difficult, but should be undertaken in such a way as to provide for sufficient realism. If the alternatives made available prove unrealistic to the respondent, the interview becomes more an intellectual game than an occasion for the collection of useful information.

QUESTION ADMINISTRATION: CONDUCTING THE INTERVIEW

We described the exploratory interview, the structured-nonscheduled interview, and the structured-scheduled interview as if the operations that characterized these techniques were mutually exclusive. Theoretically, they are. However, in practice, there are elements of all of these research types in almost all interviews. Like most ideals, the descriptions presented earlier are rarely realized, primarily because of the inevitability of uncontrolled, informal behaviors of the interviewer that occur during the administration of the schedule of queries. Previous research (Marquis & Cannell, 1969) employing tape recordings of interviewers' behaviors demonstrated wide variations in the language employed, even when completely structured, close-ended interview schedules were used, and the most experienced interviewers appeared to be the major culprits. A videotaped recording of these same interviews undoubtedly would have revealed even greater variation among interviewers. Changes in seating position and posture, smiles, nods of the head, changes in expression, vocal intonation, and the like would be readily apparent. And although the effects of "paralinguistic" behaviors of this type are not completely understood, it is clear that they could affect the tone and progress of the interview.

The degree of correspondence between the ideal, "pure interview forms" presented earlier and those actually arrived at in practice is a function of a number of variables, and we consider some of the most important of these. However, it should be stressed that the apparent ubiquity of extraneous interviewer behaviors does not necessarily compromise the validity of the interview as a research tool. The so-called extraneous interviewer behaviors that are so apparent in any close inspection of almost any interview at times prove to be necessary adjuncts of this research technique. If an interviewer were not to respond in any way to the behaviors and replies of the respondent, the sensitive person-to-person interaction that plays an important role in any interview might be destroyed, and the quality of the obtained data adversely affected. Researchers employing completely "nondirective" techniques can testify to this fact, for in their attempt to force the interviewee to guide and control the course of the interview, they often succeed only in destroying the rapport that they so diligently courted in the initial phases of the interaction.

Rapport, interviewer-respondent interaction, respondent cooperation—words and phrases of this sort are to be found in almost every interviewing handbook, but as yet, we have presented no indication of the ways and means of generating these conditions. In the section that follows, we intend to remedy this deficiency.

Obtaining Entry

An important task that should precede the administration of the interview concerns the establishment of *entry*, or the gaining of permission to approach an individual or group of individuals for research purposes. Richardson, Dohrenwend, and Klein (1965) distinguished two qualitatively different types of entry situations: those in which a population is insulated from the interviewer by a gatekeeper and those in which the potential respondents are not. It is important to realize that alternate approach strategies should be employed when one encounters one or the other of these circumstances.

Commonly, a *gatekeeper* protects the population of potential respondents. The gatekeeper is an individual who can affect the likelihood of a respondent's cooperating with the interviewer. Attempting to skirt the gatekeeper can be catastrophic and thus should not be considered. Those who doubt this should try to imagine the consequences they would experience if they attempted to interview elementary school children during their afternoon recess or play period without first having secured the gatekeeper's (i.e., the school authority's) permission. It is quite conceivable in this situation that the only information one would gain would be an indication of the speed with which the police in the research locale respond to the call of an agitated educator. Examples of populations secured by a gatekeeper are readily available: elementary and high schools, members of unions, fraternities and sororities, athletic teams, adolescent gangs, rock and roll bands, and so on, are all protected by gatekeepers of one sort or another.

The most obvious and direct strategy in gaining access to a protected group is to approach the person in control and state the aims and methods of the proposed research in a way that is both understandable and nonthreatening. It also is important to provide some rationale as to how participation can benefit the target group. This advice is complicated by the fact that the effective gatekeeper in many settings is not immediately obvious. For this reason, Richardson et al. (1965) suggested that the interviewer not press for an immediate entry decision. If the researcher has misidentified the gatekeeper, but nevertheless convinced this person of the importance of the research, it is possible that this individual might intercede on behalf of the research. Forcing the pseudo-gatekeeper into a premature decision more often than not results in an outright rejection or, in the case in which entry is (apparently) secured, a later reversal by the real gatekeeper. It might appear more difficult to study samples protected by a gatekeeper than to investigate individuals not shielded in this manner. This is not necessarily the case; the approval of the gatekeeper oftentimes helps to legitimize the survey, and encourage the cooperation of the respondents to be sampled. In populations that have no gatekeeper, this potentially facilitative influence is not available.

Two techniques that have been shown to facilitate entry in non-gatekeeper samples are letters of introduction and the "foot-in-the-door" approach. There is some evidence to suggest that a prior letter that alerts the potential respondent that he or she will be contacted later to participate in a research survey helps to increase the rate of participation (Brunner & Carroll, 1969; Cartwright & Tucker, 1969). The foot-in-the-door technique is based on the finding (e.g., Crano & Sivacek, 1982; DeJong, 1979; Freedman & Fraser, 1966) that securing a person's cooperation with a very minor request, and reinforcing this cooperation, facilitates their later cooperation with a more major one. In applying this finding, Groves and Magilavy (1981) asked respondents to participate in a very minimal survey (two questions), and told these people that they might be called later to participate in a larger survey. Those who participated in the minimal survey were significantly more willing to cooperate with the later request than those who did not. Other researchers (e.g., Allen, Schewe, & Wijk, 1980; Hansen & Robinson, 1980; Reingen & Kernan, 1977) have used variations of the foot-in-the-door approach with good success.

Researchers sometimes encounter situations in which even the blessings of the gate-keeper, introductory letters, and the foot-in-the-door technique are not sufficient to secure the cooperation of the entire respondent sample—some people simply will not partici-pate in social research. Respondent self-selection problems of this type are very difficult, because a sufficient number of refusals will negate the assumption of random selection (see chap. 10), and this will seriously limit the generalizability of findings. To see why this is so, consider the following situation. Suppose a researcher wanted to investigate the attitudes of Yale University students toward the New Haven police's Drug Enforcement Squad. In this population, there will be a number of respondents who do not use drugs and who have positive feelings about law enforcement officers; these people will probably cooperate with the interviewer's request. Conversely, there will be a number who do use drugs and who also might be antagonistic to, and suspicious of, the Drug Squad. They might cooperate, or they might fear a police trap and refuse. If the researcher simply disregards these refusals and selects the next person on the list of potential participants (even if the names on the list were drawn randomly), the outcome of the research could be very misleading. The sample of those who actually participate in the research will over-represent the opinions of the negative drug, positive police respondents, and under-represent those of the pro-drug–anti-police respondents. As a result, the findings of such an investigation will prove misleading at best. This suggests that great care be taken not only in the selection of the respondent sample in an interview, but also in assuring that the sample remains intact.

After Entry

Introduction of Purpose. Assuming that the interviewer can at least get a foot in the door, there are a number of introductory procedures that seem to have a positive influence on the likelihood that a person will agree to cooperate. Cannell and Kahn (1968) suggested a series of introductory operations, and their research suggests the wisdom of this approach. They recommend that the interviewer first provide a general description of the research project, then discuss the more specific research objectives, and finally outline the means of attaining these goals. Certainly the language the interviewer uses here will not be technical or scientifically precise, nor is it likely that the initial introduction will be as extensive as that presented when seeking a gatekeeper's approval. Satisfying the respondent's curiosity about the study, and of his or her role in the research process, is both important and necessary if real cooperation is to be secured.

Method of Selection. Having informed the potential respondent of the general nature of the research, some information regarding the manner in which people were selected for study should be provided. If a specific "protected" group is being studied, and the gatekeeper has advanced approval, this fact should be made known. The reasons for selection of the particular group to which the respondent belongs also should be mentioned.

If respondents who are not buffered by a gatekeeper are under study, some information about the sampling procedures employed in their selection should be given. Certainly a treatise on stratified random sampling is not being suggested here, but rather some general information of the chance nature of selection should be mentioned, if such techniques were used. This step is sometimes skipped in the introductory phase of the interview, and this omission is unfortunate because respondents who are unsure about why they were "singled out" for the interview can sometimes prove less than completely candid in their answers.

Agency. Cannell and Kahn's (1968) third step in the introduction process consists of identifying the organization or agency under whose auspices the study is being conducted. This procedure is even more important today than when it was originally suggested. Numerous unethical sales organizations have employed pseudo-interviews to gain access to potential customers, and the public is becoming more and more aware of the fact that persons asking for "a moment of your time to gather information on a very important issue" more often than not are salespersons masquerading as social scientists. This awareness often adversely affects the goodwill of a potential respondent toward legitimate investigators. If satisfactory credentials can be presented, however, this difficulty can be overcome.

Anonymity. Many people who are not trained in the methods of social research assume that all survey responses can be traced directly back to their source; they are unaware that most analyses employ response pooling procedures that aggregate answers over the entire sample (or subsample) to infer general trends. Accordingly, the anonymity of an individual's response should be stressed. It is sometimes profitable in such circumstances to explain the manner in which results will be pooled and analyzed, the large number of projected respondents, and so forth.

A willingness on the part of the potential respondent to submit to the interview might become apparent before Cannell and Kahn's introductory sequence has been completed. The process sketched here paints an unduly pessimistic picture, for individuals often are quite eager to interviewed, and need not be persuaded through a long and intricate introductory process. There are many rewards accruing to the interviewee, including emotional satisfaction at being able to speak out on a matter of personal importance, the pride of being chosen to participate in a scientific investigation, the possibility of affecting public policy, and the opportunity to talk with an attractive interviewer. All of these factors make life much easier for the interviewer. The question then arises, "If I have secured entry by step 2 of the introductory process, should I continue through the entire sequence?" We would answer this question affirmatively because, in addition to securing cooperation, these steps also enhance rapport. Neglecting any of these suggested procedures can compromise the quality of the interaction, and the standardization of the interview across the entire respondent sample.

Interviewer Characteristics: Establishing Rapport

There are many factors other than those mentioned here that can influence the interviewer's chances of obtaining entry and establishing rapport with respondents. Some of these reside in the characteristics of the interviewer. Included among these factors are such things as the interviewer's physical appearance, dress, race, accent, apparent socioeconomic status, ethnic heritage, and the like. Although there is much discussion of this issue, it would seem wise to match, whenever possible, the obvious physical characteristics of the interviewer with those of the expected respondent sample. A complete matching will rarely prove possible, but there are usually some especially salient aspects that should be attended to. One of the most obvious of these is the respective race of the respondent and interviewer. Research suggests the importance of matching the race of the interviewer with that of the respondent (e.g., Hyman, Cobb, Feldman, Hart, & Stember, 1954; Stouffer, Suchman, DeVinney, Star, & Williams, 1949). People seem more reluctant to voice racial dissatisfactions with interviewers of different races. Findings of this type have persisted over the years, especially with racially sensitive issues and appear to hold for black and white respondents alike (Hatchett & Schuman, 1975–1976; Schuman & Hatchett, 1974).

In more long-term interactions, the researcher is well advised to attend closely to a match of other social characteristics that might be important to respondents. Although complete matching is never possible, there usually are some salient features of the respondents' lifestyles that are shared by the interviewer, and which facilitate their interaction. A good example of this form of matching is provided in William Foote Whyte's (1955) investigation of adolescent gang members in "Cornerville." The quality of this research was facilitated greatly by Whyte's extensive knowledge of baseball facts and his bowling skill (!), two interests his respondents shared avidly. Certainly if Whyte had approached his respondents as a Harvard researcher whose interests did not carry him beyond the walls of the sociology library, the classic *Street Corner Society* might never have been written.

In addition to a match on demographic and lifestyle characteristics, there are obviously other personal characteristics of the interviewer that will influence the relationship between interviewer and respondent. These include the interviewer's enthusiasm for the research, his or her level of professionalism, and apparent friendliness and interest in the respondent as a person. Many of these factors cannot be directly controlled, but depend on the availability and selection of experienced and well-trained interview personnel. In the pages that follow, we discuss the more structured aspects of the interview conduct that can be controlled more systematically.

Informal Tactics

Initial Question Sequence. Earlier, we raised the possibility that question order could influence the responses obtained in an interview (see, also, chap. 15). How one answers an early question may have a powerful influence on how later questions are answered. In addition to considerations of this nature, it is important to understand that the early questions in an interview can play a major role in establishing rapport. Accordingly, the least threatening, least demanding, most general, and most easily answered questions should be presented first. (As Kinsey et al., 1948, suggested, this order sometimes will vary as a consequence of respondent characteristics.) Later, once cooperation is assured, and the confidence of the respondent in the integrity of the interviewer is established, more difficult, specific, and sensitive issues may be broached.

Leading Questions. Most of the early manuals on interviewing technique sounded a common injunction against the use of "leading questions." A leading question is one that suggests to the respondent the expected, or preferred, answer (see Table 12.1). A consideration of the effects of experimenter expectancy (chap. 5) would reinforce the apparent wisdom of this warning. Yet, sensible as this advice appears, arguments by

TABLE 12.1
An Example of a Leading-Question Exchange

Speaker	Response
Interviewer	Do you feel you have any biases against people who suffer from mental illness?
Respondent	Of course not.
Interviewer	So you support the half-way house being established in your neighborhood?
Respondent	Are you nuts? I wouldn't risk my children's welfare in that way.
Interviewer	How so?
Respondent	By having a bunch of crazy people running around the neighborhood day and night!

Richardson et al. (1965) suggested that this injunction is in need of some qualification. Richardson suggested that under some, admittedly constrained, research circumstances, the leading question could prove to be a useful and nonbiasing feature of proper interviewer technique. First, we must distinguish between two categories of leading questions, which have been termed *expectations* and *premises*.

A leading question in expectation form is a query whose wording alerts the respondent to the answer that is expected by the interviewer: "You voted for Gore, didn't you?" is an example of such a question form. The premise form of leading question contains within it one or more assumptions that must be accepted if the question is to be answered within the constraints posed: "When did you stop beating your wife?" is a classic leading question of the premise form. It presupposes the premises that (a) at one time, the respondent was or is married; (b) that he did, at least once, beat his wife; and (c) that he has stopped doing so. The general injunction against leading questions of the premise variety has been directed against those queries having premises that were unfounded. But there are times when the premises underlying such questions are well founded, and in these instances, this question form can prove useful. The question presented above, for example, would not appear particularly ill-advised if asked of a respondent with a history of arrests for wife-beating.

It is difficult to phrase questions in a premise-free manner. At the very least, the premise that the respondent shares the same language is a constant aspect of the communication process. Only when the premise is a completely uninformed guess would there appear to be much cause for alarm, not so much because of the potential for biased responses, but rather because it could compromise the interviewer–respondent relationship. Expectations and premises can be combined in the same question, with each varying in degree of strength. However, neither strength nor degree of interrelatedness appears critical when considering the potentially biasing aspects of these question forms. Of central importance is the degree to which the expectation or premise is founded on the interviewer's knowledge of the respondent's likely answer. If an expectation is completely accurate (and very often, accuracy largely can be assumed on the basis of earlier answers obtained in the interview), then there is little danger of bias in making use of it. Queries of this form, based on information generated earlier in the interview, are often used by researchers to reinforce the respondent over the course of the interaction. *Well-informed* expectations and premises indicate that the questioner has been attentive to the responses provided. Thus, contrary to the common assumptions, using *informed* leading questions might paradoxically improve rapport and respondent cooperation.

Although the proper use of the leading question depends on the interviewer's near certain knowledge of the respondent's likely answer, these question forms need not always be used in anticipating the *correct* reply. A tactic used by experienced interviewers that sometimes pays large dividends consists in completely missing the point of the respondent's remarks. This tactic can result in an extensive elaboration of an earlier position, assuming that the interviewer's "misinterpretation" is outrageous enough and that the respondent is motivated to correct it. The danger here is that the misinterpretation is not wrong enough or that the respondent is not sufficiently motivated to correct the errant impression. An apparent complete and total misunderstanding of an individual's opinion, however, often is sufficiently motivating to elicit an elaboration, especially if the issues at hand are of importance to the respondent.

In a slight modification of this approach, Becker (1953) acted the part of a fool in interviewing Chicago school teachers: "I played dumb and pretended not to understand certain relationships and attitudes which were implicit (in the interview)" (p. 31). Using this tactic, Becker "was able to coerce many interviewees into being considerably more frank than they had originally intended" (p. 32) because respondents were forced to elaborate clearly and extensively all of their answers. It should be noted that this tactic was initiated *after* the interviewer had secured respondents' cooperation, and demonstrated his competence—only later in the interview did Becker begin to lose IQ points.

In short, the use of expectations and premises presupposes that rapport has been established, that the interviewer has a very good idea of the respondent's likely response, and that the question be either totally correct or blatantly incorrect. Using partially correct premises or expectations almost always has an adverse effect on the interview. A final observation is also in order here, and has to do with the frequency of use of such question forms: Generally speaking, the effectiveness of any interviewing tactic is inversely related to the frequency of its use within a given interview. To overuse these devices is to demean the intelligence and sophistication of the respondent.

Direction. When reacting to the replies of the respondent, should the interviewer force specific clarifications and amplifications along the lines of research interest, or be completely nondirective, thus enabling the respondent to focus on aspects of the question that are of personal relevance? The question of the degree to which an interviewer should direct the behaviors of a respondent is primarily of relevance when nonscheduled or open-ended question formats are employed, and the answer depends on the projected aims of the research. Suppose, for example, that in response to an inquiry, a respondent were to reply, "Yes, I think property taxes are much too high in this city." A good interviewer might build on this answer in a number of ways. For example, one might direct the respondent's attention to the fact that property taxes support the local schools, and attempt to determine the interviewee's attitudes toward these institutions in light of the expressed opinion regarding taxation. Or, the interviewer might respond simply, "You think taxes are too high," with the expectation that the respondent would be forced to amplify the original statement in response to the interviewer's declaration (note that the inquiry is presented in declarative, rather than interrogative, form).

To a nondirective prod of this type, the interviewee often will amplify and defend the earlier-stated position. Whether, during this process, he or she ever comments on the specific issue of interest to the researcher is an open question. This fact must be considered when gauging the appropriate degree of directiveness to be employed within a given research context. The nondirective approaches appear most useful in exploratory or nonstructured settings, especially if they keep the researcher from imposing his or her own views about what is important in the situation under investigation (because this is what most such research of this form is all about). However, having determined the relevant aspects of the research setting, the issues to be investigated, and so on, the nondirective approaches appear much less appropriate (and certainly less economical). In such situations, more directive approaches should be chosen.

It also is the case that nondirective, typically, open-ended approaches demand much more at the data accumulation and analysis stage. With a completely scripted interview, involving closed (multiple-choice) questions and prespecified question order, the scoring and analysis of the interview data becomes relatively mechanical. However, an interview involving a more fluid, open-ended approach at a minimum requires developing a coding scheme to score the responses that are obtained.

Informal Interviewer Behaviors. As any experienced interviewer will testify, not all respondents are responsive. Merely asking a question is no guarantee that a complete, understandable, and unambiguous response will be obtained. In some cases, the fortunate interviewer is paired with an articulate individual who fulfills the role of the perfect respondent; more often, even with the most cooperative of respondents, some prodding must be used. The informal behaviors an interviewer uses in eliciting an amplification or clarification of an unsatisfactory response, although relatively under-investigated, are of real importance. Moreover, they are a ubiquitous component of all interviews; to deny their existence would be a confession of ignorance of interviewer behavior (see Bradburn & Sudman, 1979; Cannell et al., 1981; Marquis & Cannell, 1969).

One of the most common behaviors (or, in this instance, *non*behaviors) that are employed in attempts to elicit an elaboration of a response is *silence*. It is important to understand that an interview is an interpersonal communication situation, and as such, it is subject to the same informal norms as other communication situations. In most communication settings, the cessation of verbal behavior on the part of one individual is interpreted as a stimulus to the other to begin another verbal exchange. In this way, each communicator's response acts as a stimulus to the other. An interviewer can make use of the reciprocal nature of interpersonal communication in the following manner: If a respondent's answer is not adequate or sufficiently elaborate, the interviewer can fail to respond, that is, fail to re-initiate the conversation. Noting that the answer did not stimulate a response, the interviewee often will elaborate or amplify it. Of course, this tactic can be overused to the discomfort of the respondent (see Chapple, 1953), but it is generally the case that when used sparingly, silence or nonresponse can stimulate interviewees to amplify their answers, with little danger of biasing the obtained data.

A different tactic used by many is makes use of verbal reinforcement. Phrases like "good," "fine," "very interesting," and the like, often are employed to encourage the interviewee to amplify or elaborate a response. By reacting to respondents in this manner, the interviewer demonstrates an obvious interest in their answers, and this can strengthen rapport and assure continued cooperation. Unfortunately, whereas these tactics are unquestionably motivating for respondents, the question of *what* is being motivated in not completely obvious. The "verbal reinforcement" literature in psychology suggests the likelihood that an individual will express a given opinion can be affected by reinforcement. Thus, it is conceivable that an interviewer's reinforcement of a respondent for providing a complete or elaborated answer might be interpreted by the respondent as a reinforcement of the particular *content* of the reply, and this could seriously affect the nature of subsequent answers. More subtle, but equally effective reinforcers are smiles, nods of the head, "uh-huh's," and so on. Actions of this type all serve to encourage the respondent, but again, the biasing effects of such behaviors constitute a real danger.

Recognizing the problems inherent in uncontrolled informal interviewer behaviors (cf. Marquis & Cannell, 1969) caused Cannell and his colleagues (1981) to implement an approach that explicitly provided reinforcement for desirable behaviors. This approach does make for greater control over some informal interviewer tactics, but it appears doubtful that it could possibly control all of them. In addition, it is still likely that in some cases the respondent, who will use the interviewer's actions as a cue to the "appropriate" response, will misinterpret the reinforcement contingency. As such, it is apparent that great care must be exercised in controlling for, or examining the influence of, the informal behaviors emitted by the interviewer over the course of the interaction.

Once the interview data have been collected, what is to be done with them? Although we do not detail here the specific statistical methods to be undertaken in the analysis of such data, the chapter that follows provides an introduction to the general methodological approaches to be used in studying verbal information. As such, it will prove relevant to those making use of the interview, as well as those whose verbal data are obtained by other means (e.g., historic documents, formal and informal communications, rating scales, etc.). Given the historic dependence of most of the social sciences on linguistic data, it should be clear that the chapters that follow should be well learned by anyone wishing to undertake, or interpret, social science research.

SUGGESTED READINGS

Bartholomew, K., Henderson, A. J. Z., & Marcia, J. (2000). Coding semistructured interviews in social psychological research. In H. Reis & C. Judd (Eds.), *Handbook of research methods in social and personality psychology* (pp. 286–312). New York: Cambridge University Press.

Schuman, H., & Kalton, G. (1985). Survey methods. In G. Lindzey & E. Aronson (Eds.), *The handbook of social psychology*, Vol. 2 (3rd ed., pp. 635–698). Reading, MA: Addison-Wesley.

Sudman, S., & Bradburn, N. M. (1982). *Asking questions: A practical guide to questionnaire design*. San Francisco: Jossey-Bass.

13

CONTENT ANALYSIS

The term *content analysis* broadly describes a wide-ranging and diverse domain of techniques designed to describe and explicate a communication or series of communications in a systematic, objective, and quantitative manner. In many ways, the data of most common types of content analyses resemble those obtained in open-ended, exploratory interviews. The exploratory interview imposes no restraints on the questions of the interviewer or the allowable responses of the participant. The researcher has little or no control over the stimuli giving rise to the specific response or the particular form in which the response is framed. Similarly, in most content analyses, the investigator is concerned with a communication that (a) was not elicited by some systematic set of questions chosen by the analyst, (b) probably does not contain all the information he or she would like it to contain, and (c) is almost invariably stated in a manner not easily codified and analyzed. In both research contexts, the interview or content analysis, the investigator must transform these qualitative unstructured messages into useful data for scientific, quantitative analysis.

The research challenge posed by such data is daunting. The dependence of social scientists on the outcome of the communication process as the basic data component of their discipline is readily apparent. Almost every social investigation involves the study of some form of communication. Contrast this with the typical datum of the chemist, physicist, or even physiological psychologist, and the unique dependence of the social scientist on communication and the communication process becomes apparent. Given the role of communication as a major component of social research, it should not prove surprising that many social scientists should specialize in research focused on the communication process per se. Of course, investigation of the total process of communication is quite complicated, calling for, as one classic formula has stated, consideration of "who says what, to whom, how, and with what effect" (Lasswell, Lerner, & Pool, 1952, p. 12). Usually the social researcher focuses on only one or two of the components of this question. The content analyst, although concerned with all of these variables, is particularly interested in the what and the how of the process, that is, with the particular content of a message and the particular manner in which this content is delivered or expressed.

A definition of content analysis that would satisfy all social scientists would be quite difficult to construct, as is evidenced by the following attempts:

"Content analysis is a research technique for the objective, systematic, and quantitative description of the manifest content of communication" (Berelson, 1952, p. 18).

"Content analysis . . . refer[s] to the objective, systematic, and quantitative description of any symbolic behavior" (Cartwright, 1953, p. 424).

"Content analysis, while certainly a method of analysis, is more than that. It is . . . a method of observation. Instead of observing people's behavior directly, or asking them to respond to scales, or interviewing them, the investigator takes the communications that people have produced and asks questions of the communications" (Kerlinger, 1964, p. 544).

"*Content analysis* is a technique used to extract desired information from a body of material (usually verbal) by systematically and objectively identifying specified characteristics of the material" (Smith, 2000, p. 314).

"Content analysis is a research technique for making replicable and valid inferences from data to their context" (Krippendorff, 1980, p . 21).

The diversity of these characterizations suggests that content analysis as a method defies any single simple definition. One important distinction signaled by these definitions should be considered, however. In the first definition, Berelson (1952) limits content analysis to *manifest* content; in the final definition provided, Krippendorff (1980) calls for the analyst to make replicable and valid *inferences* from the data. The dispute about the degree of inference to be engaged in the analysis mirrors the debate evident in discussions of general observational techniques. Some researchers allow no inference in their observations: only observed events (or behaviors) are coded. Others require the observer to make inferences about the motivations or intentions that underlie the observed event. The more inferential approaches are thought to provide a richer, more meaningful picture of the event under study; this richness often is bought at the cost of lowered reliability and validity. This same dispute is evident in the realm of content analysis, where some researchers insist that the technique be applied only to the manifest content of the materials under study, and others allow some degree of inference making, based on the content and the context in which it occurs.

PRELIMINARY CONSIDERATIONS

Before attempting to describe ways in which content analysts have dealt with the scientific study of communication(s), a brief mention of some necessary considerations is in order. Recognizing the similarity between the research operations of the content analyst and those of the social scientist engaging in a more general type of observational investigation will facilitate the transfer of information between the two previous chapters and this one.

General Process Overview

Before embarking on a content analytic investigation, the investigator must first determine whether the technique is compatible with the ultimate goal of the research. Figure 13.1 provides a roadmap of the kinds of decisions that must be made in the process of mounting a content analysis. The first question that should be addressed is whether or not there is a body of text that will provide (or that can generate) the data necessary to answer the research question. This issue is fundamental because a negative response closes consideration of the technique, as it should. However, assume that the question is answered affirmatively.

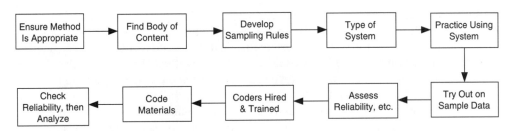

FIG. 13.1. **Steps in the process of developing a content analysis.**

In that case, the researcher must fix rules for gathering evidence and, if necessary, the means by which the information will be sampled. After deciding on the sampling scheme, the next decision concerns the coding system. Should a category or rating system be used? Do either (or both) provide the sensitivity necessary to answer the questions that gave rise to the research project in the first place?

After deciding on the coding system, it is wise to try it out on a sample of data. Usually, the researcher and his or her research team will undertake this *pilot study*. The study is done to answer a simple question: Does the system work? Can it be used reliably, and if so, does it promise to provide useful data? If not, changes need to be made. If so, the analysis is ready to move on the formal research phase. In this step of the process, materials that will serve as the basis of the analysis are gathered, and, perhaps concurrently, coders are trained and provided with materials on which to practice. After reaching acceptable levels of reliability, the critical communications are turned over to the coders. The coding may be done manually or by computer, but even computerized analysis involves considerable human intervention. The data extracted from this process are the raw material for the ultimate summary analysis of the communications, and their subsequent interpretation. The process is complicated, but the rewards can be great if the technique is appropriate for the issue at hand.

Coding Unit

As is true when using any observational method, the content analyst must determine, generally in advance of the analysis, the unit of content that will be employed in the investigation. We qualify this statement somewhat because some analysts allow coding categories and units to emerge empirically during the course of the analysis. This approach is akin to using exploratory approaches in interviewing or general observational methods. We do not believe that the open-ended approach is generally advisable for content analysis. When used in an exploratory fashion, the method can prove costly and cumbersome. Alternate methods are probably more useful in such circumstances.

Once a coding scheme has been decided on, the investigator is faced with a series of decisions, and these decisions parallel those of the general observational methodologist. Consider the questions an observer must answer when attempting to categorize the behaviors of children in a nursery school setting. First, the researcher must decide when or where one unit of behavior ends and another begins. In general observational methodology, time often is employed in the definition of the unit of behavior to be categorized (see chap. 11). In other cases, the attention or focus that a particular child under observation directs toward another object (e.g., a toy, the teacher, another child) defines the unit. When the child's focus shifts from one object to another, a new unit to be categorized is defined. In content analysis, unit issues of a similar type exist, even though we are dealing with text, rather than human actors. Usually, however, a distinction is made between the specific unit to be classified (the *coding unit*) and the context within which its meaning is to be inferred (the *context unit*). Sometimes these units are identical. More often, the unit to be coded is analyzed within a prespecified block of material that constitutes the context unit.

Coding units most commonly employed are the word, the theme or assertion (usually a simple sentence derived from a more complex context), the item (e.g., a news story or editorial) and the character (a specific individual or personality type). From the standpoint of identifiability, the use of the word as the coding unit represents the simplest coding strategy. However, the utility of investigations making use of such units is highly circumscribed. An interesting example of the use of the word as coding unit was provided by Mosteller and Wallace (1964). These investigators used content analytic techniques to determine the authorship of 12 *Federalist Papers* variously attributed either to James Madison or Alexander Hamilton. In a preliminary investigation of Madison's and Hamilton's *known* writings, Mosteller and Wallace identified 265 words that both men used, but with varying frequency. These known frequencies were compared with those of the same words appearing in the disputed papers. By this frequency-of-use comparison, Mosteller and Wallace showed that the data indicated that Hamilton did not author the papers, and, further, that Madison probably did.

Insofar as authorship investigations do not constitute the bulk (or even a sizeable minority) of content analysis research, the more common coding unit is the theme. Berelson (1952) defined the theme as "a simple sentence ... an assertion about a subject matter" (p. 138). Being of greater complexity than a single word, these units often provide more information than can be realized through the use of the word and hence are easier to code; however, they sometimes entail greater research expense in terms of identification, construction, and classification. Consider the problem of the researcher attempting to categorize thematically an editorial writer's attitude toward Bill Clinton's performance as president. The following sentence is encountered: "Clinton demonstrated some remarkably reprehensible character flaws while in the White House; however, his handling of the economy was nothing short of superb, despite a recalcitrant Republican Congress." Can this sentence be judged as an expression of the writer's attitude toward Mr. Clinton? Certainly. Is that attitude favorable or unfavorable? This is a more difficult question to answer. To do so, the researcher's first task is to decompose this sentence into more easily classified assertions or themes. Within this particular sentence, there are three such themes: (a) Clinton had a number of blameworthy flaws; (b) He did a great job with the economy; (c) He did so despite a difficult Republican Congress. Only the first and second of two of these themes reflect the writer's attitude toward Clinton. The first contains an unfavorable evaluation, but the second presents a more positive assessment. The final assertion has nothing to do with the editorialist's attitude toward Clinton (it is concerned with the opposing political party), and hence is discarded from consideration. How one weighs the first two parts of the sentence (and other coded information that is concerned with the former President) will determine the answer to the question of the writer's attitude.

Although this sample sentence was easily broken down into component parts (themes or assertions), not all sentences encountered in a research situation are so amenable to analysis. In the case of more complex stimuli, judges often disagree over the identification of themes, and then about the meaning of themes that are identified. The more complex the stimuli investigated, the more likely it is that such disagreements are encountered. Such disagreements compromise reliability and hence, validity.

If coding problems of this type can be resolved, *thematic analyses*, or those making use of both themes and words as coding units, generally provide more information than analyses based on words alone. A good example of the combination of content units is presented in the work of Stone and Hunt (1963; see also Ogilvie, Stone, & Schneidman, 1966). Stone and Hunt attempted to determine whether they could discriminate between real and simulated suicide notes through content analysis. To study this issue, they collected a group of real suicide notes from court records and asked 15 people who were matched on general demographic characteristics with the victims of these suicides to write simulated suicide notes. Stone and Hunt were able to discriminate between the real and the simulated notes on the basis of three criteria. First, the real notes were more likely to contain references to concrete entities (persons, places, or things); second, real notes were more likely to use the word *love*; finally, fake notes were more likely to elaborate on thought processes or decisions.

Subtracting the first two indices from the third, Stone and Hunt were able to discriminate correctly between real and simulated suicide notes in 13 of 15 instances. To cross-validate their method, they then applied the suicide index to another 18 notes, and correctly identified their authorship (real vs. simulated) in 17 of 18 instances. This "hit ratio" was significantly better than that of independent raters who were not privy to the content coding scheme. The combination of word and theme as coding units in this study enabled a more accurate analysis than that afforded by the use of the more simple (word) unit alone.

Of course, there can be disadvantages involved in the use of more complex coding units. With the word as coding unit, interpretation problems are minimal. Generally, analyses involving simple words as coding units involve an *enumeration* of the occurrence of the word in the document(s) under study. The context in which the word appears is irrelevant to the analysis. These forms of analysis are relatively easy to accomplish today. Most word processors can be used to search and count the occurrence of specific words. However, with more complex coding units, some consideration of the context unit must also be undertaken to allow confident interpretation of the meaning of the coding unit. For example, suppose an investigator were interested in studying a writer's attitudes toward communism, and encountered the following sentence (provided by Danielson, 1963, p. 188): "The communists are taking over the world bit by bit." How is this assertion to be judged? It is impossible to answer this question without some knowledge of the context in which it was embedded. If this quotation had appeared in a speech given by Josef Stalin, it would undoubtedly be seen as a positive reference to communism. If, however, this sentence were part of a keynote address delivered by George Bush to the annual convention of the Daughters of the American Revolution, its implied evaluation of communism would be radically altered. In other words, the context of this assertion would prove extremely important in judging its meaning. The context unit usually is prespecified. It defines "the largest division of context which may be consulted by a coder ... to assign a score to a basic coding unit" (Danielson, 1963, p. 188). The coding and context units employed in an investigation are seldom the same. The context unit, of course, can never be smaller than the coding unit; in the case of highly restricted coding units (e.g., the theme or assertion), context units usually entail more extensive amounts of text.

Limits are placed on the size of the context unit for two purposes. The most important is to insure reliability. If coders were free to peruse as much or as little of the content as they desired in classifying an assertion, differences between coders in amount of context surveyed might cause differences in evaluations. The second reason is economy. Coders are expensive, and some limits must be imposed on the amount of time they are permitted to spend in the classification of a given theme.

Before discussing decisions regarding content sampling, which also are motivated at least partially by economic considerations, two other types of units used in content analysis deserve brief mention. These are units defined by spatial characteristics of the content under consideration (e.g., inches of newspaper column, length of magazine article) or by temporal characteristics of an audio or visual communication (e.g., minutes of time devoted to a topic on a television or radio broadcast). Measures of this type often are used to study the degree of attention devoted in the media to some specific category or categories of information. For example, suppose one wished to investigate the amount of news attention devoted to the President of Mexico, by studying the content of the front pages of a selected sample of North American newspapers. In this case, the front page would constitute the context unit, and the presidential news item the coding unit. In such an investigation, precise measures of amounts of space devoted to a specific category (presidential news) could be obtained. Problems of coder training and category system reliability are usually minimal when using measures of this type. However, the kinds of studies that can be undertaken through the use of spatial and temporal coding units also are limited. Measures of this type tell nothing of the substantive attitudes expressed within the communication under consideration; nor is the quality or veracity of the sampled information noted. Thus, such units are relatively gross measures of communication content.

We might note parenthetically that research by Markham and Stempel (1957) demonstrated that the laborious and time-consuming measurement process required in making use of spatial units is often unnecessary. These investigators found a strong positive relationship between the mere presence of an item (say, a foreign news story) and the number of column inches it occupied. Thus, rather than using space or time units as measures of media attention, a researcher might record the mere presence or absence of a selected content category within a series of predetermined context units. These frequencies often provide the same information as that gained through the use of spatial or temporal units, and can be gathered at significantly less expense.

Sampling

Decisions concerning the way the sample of messages to be analyzed is chosen are closely related to the content analyst's choice of coding and context units. Such sampling usually involves a multistage operation. In the first stage, the particular universe of content and of sources from which all data are to be drawn is identified. Depending on the research problem, the extensiveness of this universe can vary greatly. For example, before one could study the degree of attention that American newspapers focus on the recurrent turmoil in the Middle East, a number of sampling decisions would have to be made. First, the researcher must define the universe of possible sources. Should the sample be drawn from all possible newspapers published in the country? This limits the field somewhat because there are many good papers originating in countries other than the United States Suppose the researcher decides to limit the sample further by studying only U.S. *English-language* daily publications. Should all such newspapers of this type (and there are hundreds that meet these criteria) form the universe? Perhaps, but this would mean that those dailies with circulations of 10,000 or less would be placed on a par with papers whose readership numbers in the hundreds of thousands, even though the influence of the former on mass public opinion is certainly less than that of the large circulation daily. Because the number of papers with huge circulations is not great, a random sample would contain an overrepresentation of the smaller papers—at least in terms of actual readership. To avoid this problem, the researcher can further specify the universe by considering only those papers with circulations greater than 60,000. From this universe, the analyst might then randomly select a specific set of papers as the database.

The sampling process at this point is far from complete because now decisions must be made about the extent of context to be investigated. Surely the researcher does not wish to read the entire edition of each paper in search of Middle East news items. Coding time considerations alone would prohibit such an approach. Suppose that in response to this obvious problem, the investigator chose to sample only front page news. This would not seem to be a particularly bad choice because the major news articles of the day are almost invariably noted on the front pages of most newspapers. However, many newspapers reserve the second page for foreign news; thus, the investigator decides that the first and second pages will be searched for relevant items.

The next question that arises is the particular time period of the sample. Is every possible edition of each sampled paper to be investigated? This will prove difficult because many of the papers constituting the sample will probably have been established many years ago. Suppose, then, that the investigator chooses to sample only those editions published during the years 1996 to 2000 inclusive. Of course, during this time period, the dailies within the sample have each published 1,460 issues [i.e., 4 (years) × 365 (days)]. If the sample is composed of only 50 newspapers, the magnitude of the coding task (i.e., 50 × 1460 × 2, or 146,000 front and second pages to be investigated) becomes enormous. To meet this economically impossible situation, a final sampling strategy might be employed, consisting in sampling days of news copy. Rather than investigating every issue every day, each daily might be sampled every second, third, or fourth day. Or, better yet, within any given 7-day period, one, two, or three issues might be randomly selected from each newspaper. In this way, the coding task is brought into more manageable proportion, and the quality of the obtained data will not be seriously affected.

A schematic representation of the decision points that our hypothetical investigator encountered in generating this sample is presented in Fig. 13.2. This figure illustrates an important distinction between two discrete types of sampling processes, source and content sampling. Decision points 1–4 are concerned primarily with the definition of the source sample from which units of content are to be drawn. Was the paper published in the United States? Was it an English-language paper? Was it a daily? Was its circulation greater than 60,000? All of these questions are concerned with the source of information. From the population fulfilling these requirements, a sample of specific news sources was drawn. The next phase of the research process is concerned with the sampling of content from within this chosen source sample. At this stage, coding and context units are sampled from each source and entered into the content analysis.

This example is presented for illustrative purpose only. The extensiveness of the particular content area from which messages are to be sampled, the coding and context units to be employed, the descriptive or inferential nature of the research all enter into the sampling decision. Not all content analytic studies involve a series of sampling choices as extensive as those outlined here. Consider, for example, the rather limited problem facing the investigator wishing to examine the physical qualities of the heroes of Hemingway's novels. The universe from which the content units are to be drawn, Hemingway's novels, is not extensive. In this instance, *sampling* within this universe would tend to restrict unnecessarily the raw data on which the analysis is to be based. This point deserves consideration. In experimental techniques, we are concerned with the issue of generalizability. Can the results be extended to actors outside the laboratory? In content analysis, we are concerned with a complementary concept, that of *representativeness*. If we severely undersample the content on which our analysis is based, it is likely that our results will not be representative of the more general universe of available content. A balance must be struck between efficiency and representativeness. Too many data result in unnecessary expense; too few and the results do not validly reflect the overall corpus of content.

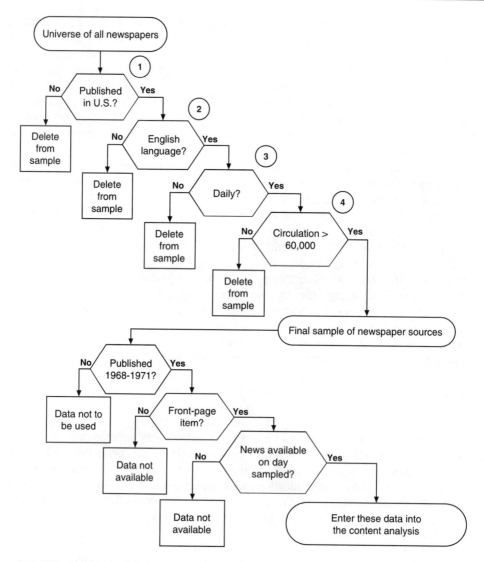

FIG. 13.2. Schematic of decisions made in content sampling from a universe of newspapers.

Many times, an even more restricted selection of text, consisting of a single novel or diary (see Goldman & Crano, 1976; Osgood, 1959; White, 1947) defines the entire universe of sources. In such cases, sampling among sources is both unnecessary and impossible, and only content sampling need be considered. Studies of this type, of course, are almost always purely descriptive. Generalizations based on the analysis of a single message usually are valid only when directed toward that particular message or communication source. To generalize to a universe of communications, one must either analyze that universe, or sample systematically from it and analyze the selected group of chosen messages. The more extensive the universe, the more extensive the sample should be, if the generalization is to be trusted.[1] Thus, it would be foolhardy to attempt to make generalizations regarding

---

[1] In chapter 10, we discussed techniques useful in drawing a survey sample; similar considerations may be applied in the case of content sampling.

all newspapers or all historical novels published over the last 10 years in the United States. Such an ambition would necessitate the use of a nearly unmanageable sample, and would prove to be of limited value even if accomplished, given the diversity and variability of the data that will be included in the sample. This is not to suggest that such a study could not be undertaken. Thanks to the Internet, today's social scientist has available a mass of data amenable for content analysis. Almost all of the world's important (i.e., heavily read) newspapers can be accessed online, and search and abstracting programs can be found with simple on-screen commands. *Lexis-Nexis* is probably the most well-known of the archives. Among other things, it contains a huge database of newspaper reports and a powerful search function. For example, it contains the full text of every *New York Times*, *Washington Post*, and *Christian Science Monitor* article from 1980 onward. The list could be extended almost indefinitely; for example, the *Claremont (CA) Collage* has been abstracted by this service from September, 1998, and the *Columbus Dispatch* from the first day of 1992. *Lexis-Nexis* is available online through many college libraries. Other databases may be found by using common on line search engines. For example, using the keywords "database newspaper" on the Google search engine resulted in 858 entries. Of course, not all of these would be relevant for every specific content analytic research purpose, but it is likely that at least one of them would provide the kind of information sought by the researcher, no matter what the issue. This state of affairs probably will improve over time, with ever-increasing amounts of information available for the analyst. In earlier days, content analytic research was limited by unavailability of data. Now the limits have more to do with the researcher's creativity and motivation.

Category Systems

To achieve scientific respectability, research operations must be systematic. This maxim is true across the methodological spectrum and holds as well in the arena of content analysis. One of the major ways of introducing systematization to this area is through the use of prespecified classification systems in the coding of content. Certainly, intuitive analyses of text are valuable and often quite entertaining. Viewed in this manner, a book review is a content analytic technique, but it is one not usually regarded as having scientific status.

Rather than rely on the intuitive classification of a message or series of messages, therefore, content analysts make use of coding schemes through which relevant dimensions of content are systematically identified and compared in some way. We presented an extensive section dealing with the choice and construction of category systems in connection with observational methods. Those considerations apply as well in the case of content analysis. In observational methodology, the categorization of the action and behaviors of an individual or group occurring within the research situation is of primary interest. In the arena of content analysis, parallel aspects of the content of a communication are of central relevance. Generating a coding system is similar in both cases, but the content coding system is more linguistically oriented because it typically is directed toward the categorization and analysis of a source's verbal or written outputs.

Many different coding systems have been employed by content analysts, studying almost every conceivable aspect of written or spoken messages. One of the major criticisms of this field, in fact, concerns its failure to generate a mutually agreed-on system of coding, through which diverse content can be investigated and compared. It appears that researchers are more intent on individually tailoring a coding scheme to fit their particular research problem than on developing more generally employable techniques. Because the number of systems in the content analysis literature is so extensive, it is likely that an investigator willing to search through the appropriate journals will be able to obtain a "pre-used" coding system suitable for almost any research need. (In two bibiliographic *tours de force*, Holsti (1969, p. 104–116) listed 13 pages of various category systems under the rather modest title of "Categories: Some Examples," and Smith (2000, p. 323), in a table labeled "Some Coding Systems Developed for Social Science Research," cites more than 21 different systems used across 10 major topic areas (e.g., moods and emotions, values, self, life-span development, etc.). The investigator searching for a usable category scheme is urged to consult these valuable sources.

A notable exception to the trend toward the generation of idiosyncratic coding schemes is the approach of computer-oriented investigators whose content analytic systems, although restricted in many ways, are nevertheless becoming attractive to more and more investigators. It seems quite probable at this point that the generalized approaches of this group of scientists will structure this area for some years to come.[2] The basic principles involved in all content analyses, however, do not differ between computer and noncomputer-oriented approaches. To program a computer for content analysis, one must first be able to do the job by hand; that is, to specify in advance the information to be sought, the rules to be applied to code the information and combine data, and so on. The coding rules must be clearly specified in either case. There is no question that the computer is extremely efficient and reliable, but it cannot generate coding rules for the investigator. To be a successful computer-content analyst, one must first become an effective noncomputer-content analyst.

The General Research Paradigm

Before attempting to provide a picture of the scope of this technique and the range of issues to which it has been addressed, a brief mention of the research paradigm usually employed in this area is appropriate. Not surprisingly, the series of operations to be described coincide closely with those discussed in an earlier chapter in conjunction with observational research techniques.

The scientific analysis of message content will usually involve the use of a prespecified coding system. The choice of coding system is best made on the basis of information that is relevant to the data to be categorized. In the case of a content analysis, this means that the researcher, in advance of the choice or construction of a coding scheme, must become thoroughly familiar with the general body of content under consideration. Only then is the investigator in a position to make an informed and reasoned decision regarding the most appropriate classificatory system.

Closely bound to the choice of coding scheme are decisions regarding the appropriate units of analysis, and the particular manner in which these units will be sampled from the larger universe of potential sources. All three decisions must be made in harmony with the others; the goodness of such choices is a function of the extensiveness of the preliminary investigation of message content. As with other techniques, the importance of the preliminary groundwork cannot be overemphasized. Consider for example, our earlier discussion of sampling decisions of newspaper coverage of the Middle East turmoil. If the researcher had decided to limit sampling to front-page news, the strategy could have proved disastrous because many of the newspapers in the sample would have subscribed to the common convention of covering foreign news on page two.

---

[2]An extensive discussion of computer oriented techniques is beyond the scope of this book. The interested reader is directed to the following sources: Barry, 1998; Holsti, 1964; Miles & Huberman, 1994; Seidel, 1991; Stone, 1964, 1968; Stone, Bales, Namenwirth, & Ogilvie, 1962; Stone, Dunphy, Smith, & Ogilvie, 1996.

Prior knowledge of newspaper practices would have prevented such an uninformed choice.

Once coding scheme, units, and sampling rules have been decided upon, and coders trained, the actual content analysis can begin. Coding messages is much like coding observed behaviors, except that the data under investigation are usually in written form.[3] As in all observational research, care must be taken to assure the reliability of the rules (or their application) that are employed to categorize data. Krippendorff (1980) distinguished among three approaches to reliability that have been used in content analysis research. The most simple of these is concerned with stability, that is, the extent to which the *same* coder assigns identical scores to the same content when he or she analyzes it more than once. Failure to obtain adequate test–retest reliability (stability) indicates intra-observer inconsistency; the analyst, that is, did not apply the coding criteria consistently from one session to the other. This could suggest a lack of adequate coder training or a coding system that is so complicated or vague that it is impossible to employ in a consistent fashion. Stability is the minimal form of reliability, and should not be the sole means of demonstrating the reliability of one's content analysis. This is because stability is dependent on the actions of a single coder, who might apply the coding rules consistently, but in an idiosyncratic fashion. Different results might then be obtained if another coder attempted to use the same rules.

A more stringent approach to reliability in content analysis is termed *reproducibility,* which is the extent to which the outcome of a specific coding process "can be recreated under varying circumstances, at different locations, using different coders" (Krippendorff, 1980, p. 131). This approach is most commonly used in establishing the reliability of a coding scheme. Generally, it is termed "intercoder agreement" or "intercoder reliability," because the correspondence between two (or more) coders' estimates of the same content is the measure of this form of reliability. When coding fails to generate reproducible results, the failure can be attributed to intra-observer inconsistencies or interobserver disagreements. Cohen's Kappa is the recommended statistic to assess intercoder reliability. This statistic accounts for chance in assessing the extent of intercoder agreement.[4]

Krippendorff (1980) defined the strictest form of reliability analysis as one that compares the accuracy with which a coding system reproduces, or compares to, some known standard. For example, in Stone and Hunt's (1963) suicide note research presented earlier, the investigators knew which of the notes were real and which were fictitious. To the extent that the coding system accurately reproduced this distinction, it was reliable (or accurate, as this form of reliability is termed). Accuracy can be weakened by intra-observer inconsistencies, inter-observer disagreements, and by the systematic failure of the coding scheme to reflect the standard that is to be used in evaluating the content.[5]

Once the reliability of the coding scheme has been established, the content analysis can proceed in accordance with the particular purposes of the research. If the study is one

---

[3] Some analyses are performed on verbal material, but the audio clips are usually printed before analysis is begun.

[4] We discuss Kappa in detail in chapter 11.

[5] A mirror image of this type of analysis was performed by Hooker (1957), who asked a group of clinicians to content-analyze the projective test reactions of a group of men, some of whom were gay. The issue of the research was to determine if trained analysts could discriminate between homosexual and heterosexual men. At the time, homosexuality was considered a severe form of emotional unbalance. As Hooker expected, the clinicians were unable to distinguish the two groups. Their inability helped change medical opinion; ultimately, homosexuality was no longer considered a psychiatric disorder requiring treatment. We agree with these findings and their policy-related outcome; however, as methodologists, we are obliged to point out the fact that this study made its point by confirming the null hypothesis!

of simple description, the analyst will specify the decision rules employed in assigning a coding unit to a specific category, and present the relative frequencies with which various categories were employed in coding a communication. Sometimes more than one source is analyzed, and the relative frequencies obtained between sources are compared. Shneidman (1963), for example, examined various idiosyncracies in logic that Kennedy and Nixon employed in their first two televised debates. On the basis of his classifications, Shneidman found that Nixon employed the communication strategies of "truthtype confusion," "derogation," and "argumentum ad populism" more often than Kennedy, who instead concentrated on the "irrelevant premise" as his principal idiosyncrasy of reasoning in the debates.

When the aim of the analyst goes beyond that of simple description, the study's potential value is increased, but so is the possibility that faulty generalizations will be produced. Consider, for example, Lowenthal's (1949) analysis of Knut Hamsun's writings. The major themes presented by Hamsun were consistent with the values praised by the Nazis: the importance of race and racial purity, the diminished role of women, and so on. On the basis of this analysis, one could infer that Hamsun was a potential fascist whose true colors were reflected in his written fiction. This inference, in this particular case, would have proved valid, insofar as Hamsun did indeed collaborate with the Nazis during WWII. Many times, however, history is not so cooperative, and drawing inferences from content analytic results is a risky operation.

Inferential content analysis can, of course, be undertaken legitimately, but should be attempted only after some means of testing the validity of such inferences has been determined. Inferential content analyses make many more demands of the researcher than the descriptive variety because they must not only describe content but also provide some statements regarding the motivations of the source responsible for the communication and, finally, present some data bearing on the validity of these propositions. One can, for example, analyze and describe the various propaganda techniques employed by a politician engaged in a close race; whether, on the basis of these findings, the analyst is in a position to comment accurately on the personality structure of this source is an entirely different matter. A good example of this form of analysis is provided by Suedfeld and his colleagues, who, using content analytic techniques informed by strong theory, have produced interesting research assessing the cognitive complexity of statesmen and their resulting decisions (e.g., Suedfeld, Tetlock, & Streufert, 1992).

Attempts by scientists to substantiate the inferences drawn on the basis of content analyses have taken a number of interesting turns. George (1959), for example, was able to check the goodness of the inferences of WWII propaganda analysts through a study of captured Nazi documents. Although this check was made years after the original inferences, it is encouraging to note that the wartime content analysts' records were quite creditable. Because of this need for external verification, the method of content analysis in and of itself is not best suited for testing hypotheses. Many of the arguments presented in opposition to the use of the exploratory interview in hypothesis testing research (see chap. 12) also apply here. Content analysis is, however, a superb technique for the production of hypotheses, which given the nature of their generation, often are supported in later research. The versatility of this method is such that it can be adapted to almost any type of information that can be reduced to textual form (see Viney, 1983).

REPRESENTATIVE EXAMPLES

Having discussed the general features of a content analysis, we can illustrate some of the many forms this technique can assume. Earlier in this chapter, Lasswell et al.'s classic description of the communication process (who says what to whom, how, and with what effect) was cited. Following the lead of Berelson (1954), Holsti (1968, 1969), and a host of others who have surveyed the literature that has made use of this research technique, the remainder of this chapter consists of an investigation of each of the components of this equation as it relates to various forms of content analysis. In this way, some idea of the range of applications of this approach can be imparted within a framework known to be useful to the communications analyst.

Who Said It?

Some of the most interesting studies employing content analysis have focused on the examination of the authorship of various documents. These studies take the form of the classic detective story, and sometimes can prove even more rewarding than the best of the genre. Earlier in this chapter, Mosteller and Wallace's (1964) examination of the probable authorship of 12 disputed *Federalist Papers* was discussed. Yule (1944), in an investigation similar in form, was able to point quite convincingly to the probable author of the classic *The Imitation of Christ*.

Biblical scholars, too, have used content analytic techniques extensively in attempting to settle questions of disputed authorship. While interesting, these studies do not always provide unambiguous results. For example, Morton (1963) identified seven elements of writing style that he felt would clearly distinguish between authors.[6] Using this system, Morton decided that six different authors were responsible for the epistles traditionally ascribed to St. Paul. On the basis of these findings, he challenged the orthodoxy of Christianity either to debunk his results or to revise their traditional views of the early church. The challenge was met by Ellison (1965), who, employing Morton's seven indicators, "discovered" that James Joyce's *Ulysses* was written by five different authors and that none of these individuals could have written *Portrait of the Artist as a Young Man*.

The obvious failure of Morton's coding system, in this particular case, to indicate successfully the single authorship of *Ulysses* and *Portrait of the Artist* placed his contentions regarding the multiple authorship of the Pauline epistles in serious jeopardy. On the basis of these results, we would be forced to conclude that the seven indicators of Morton's analytic system are not sensitive to authorship differences.[7] Validation studies of the type undertaken by Ellison, while sometimes discouraging, are nevertheless valuable because they force the continual revision and improvement of content analytic techniques.

What Was Said?

Problems of validation are not nearly so pressing in studies directed toward answering the question, "What was said?" Investigations of this type typically are descriptive in nature and often attempt to generalize no farther than the messages on which they are based. As Holsti (1969) noted of this type of study, "the content data serve as a direct answer to the research question, rather than as indicators from which characteristics of the sources or audiences are to be inferred" (p. 43). This does not preclude the use of statistical tests to compare differences occurring within and between communications, but hypothesis testing

---

[6]The stylistic indicators employed by Morton were sentence length, frequency of use of the words *and*, *but*, and *in*, frequency of use of definite articles, of all forms of the verb *to be*, and use of the third person pronoun.

[7]As a matter of fact, Ellison analyzed Morton's article and found that by Morton's own criteria, different sections of his report were written by different authors.

research of this type is almost always bounded by the particular messages on which the data are based. The generality of such findings is always in question. The failure to differentiate between the use of statistical tests for content-descriptive, versus inferential, purposes has sometimes resulted in wasted effort in this area.

Probably the bulk of content analytic studies conducted has focused on consideration of the question of "what was said." Because the rate of research of this type has accelerated almost geometrically in recent years, the need for some means of studying the resulting mass is evident. Berelson (1954, pp. 490–495) provided a classificatory system for this purpose, and it is still useful. We employ it, loosely, in an examination of this particular portion of the content analysis literature.

Trends.   One of the most frequent aims of analysts in this research area has been the study of communication trends over time. Has the level of achievement motivation (McClelland, 1961) expressed in the stories included in children's primers changed during the last 50 years? Is the rate of politically inspired movies affected by changing economic conditions? Are the values and goals expressed in the best-selling fiction novels today the same as those of 20 years ago? Questions of this sort are based on the assumption that the mass media act as a barometer, reflecting various aspects of the society they serve. Verification of this assumption is extremely difficult, but the face validity of many of the studies undertaken with this general goal often is quite compelling.

Consider, for example, the research of Yakobson and Lasswell (1949), who studied the content of Russian May Day slogans for the time period 1918–1943. During that period of time, political scientists noted a gradual mellowing of revolutionary zeal on the part of the Soviets. Consistent with this observation, the content analysis of slogans revealed that calls for universal revolutionary activities had steadily diminished, and were replaced with an increased emphasis on nationalistic appeals. A result of this type, while relatively unconvincing when taken alone, proves compelling in conjunction with other, independently arrived at sources of information.

In a nonpolitical vein, Ojemann (1948) analyzed child development articles appearing in *Ladies Home Journal* and *Good Housekeeping* for the years 1904, 1910, and 1940. He found that in the earlier volumes of these magazines, 50% of all communications of this type were attributed to scientific authority, with the remainder based on personal opinion. By 1940 the proportions had dramatically changed, with articles attributed to scientific authority accounting for 98% of all child development messages. It is interesting to note the ease with which a study of this type could be accomplished. The coding system, for example, could be a simple dichotomy: scientific source versus personal opinion. Sampling three years of two different magazines would not seem to demand a great expenditure of coding time. Yet, the results of Ojemann's investigation are quite suggestive of some interesting changes that occurred within this country with respect to attitudes regarding the legitimate sources of advice related to child rearing.

A slightly different variety of trend-relevant content analysis is evident in work by Peterson, Seligman, and Vaillant (1988), who analyzed the optimism expressed by a group of Harvard seniors in a series of open-ended questionnaires. These responses were written in 1946. Thirty-five years later, the researchers analyzed the content of the writing and found a strong relation between pessimism and physical morbidity. Apparently, optimism and pessimism are associated with physical well-being.

Norms.   Research related to the study of trends is evident in the use of content analysis to establish norms. In a representative example of this form of research, Ames and Riggio

(1995) used content analytic techniques to score the responses of a large adolescent sample that had responded to Rotter's incomplete sentences test. The test was scored for evidence of psychological maladjustment and the resulting findings, based on the large sample, used in developing norms.

International Content Differences. One use of content analysis that is both interesting and common is the study of differences in communication content occurring between nations. Similarities or dissimilarities of between-nation content often are thought to reflect important aspects of the countries surveyed. Proving that content differences do, in fact, reflect underlying national differences calls for research operations beyond those of the usual content analytic variety. The descriptive data that studies of this type provide, however, can prove compelling, especially when presented in combination with other, known aspects of the nations under study.

Consider, for example, an investigation undertaken by Lewin (1947), in which he compared the literature of the Hitler Youth with that of the Boy Scouts of America. The major themes of both content samples stressed the value of physical fitness, discipline, and achievement. In the Hitler Youth literature, however, more emphasis was laid on national loyalty and racial pride, whereas the Boy Scout sample stressed generosity and imagination. In conjunction with experiences of WWII, this study provided support for a hypothesis regarding the child training practices that gave rise to the authoritarian Nazi.

Standards. Do news magazines fulfill their objectives of presenting a fair, unbiased discussion of public events? Do they meet the noble standards which the fifth estate has set for themselves? In an examination of the coverage afforded the major candidates in the 1960 presidential nominating conventions by *Time, Newsweek,* and *U.S. News and World Report,* Westley et al. (1963) found, unexpectedly, that the magazines' treatment of the Republican leaders was only very slightly more favorable than that afforded the Democrats. More believable findings were produced when candidates were split along liberal-conservative lines. In this analysis, the favorable news bias of these magazines was clearly directed toward the conservative candidates (Nixon and Johnson) at the expense of the more liberal ones (Rockefeller and Kennedy).

Standards, of course, need not be as nebulous as that of "fair play." Often, specific a priori standards are defined, and communications or sources are compared against this ideal. The Royal Commission on the Press (1949), for example, attempted to study the adequacy of British news coverage through the generation of a priori standards. In the background notes presented before a press conference of the National Coal Board, 33 major facts regarding production, sales, and so on, were presented. The 33 facts represented the standard, and the number of such facts a given newspaper included in the reports and editorials concerning the press conference served as an indicator of the degree to which that paper "measured up." This standard would seem to be realistic if the quality of a newspaper is to a major extent defined by the comprehensiveness of its coverage of major news events. The results of this study of nine newspapers were consistent with professional evaluations, thereby supporting the standard derived by the Royal Commission.

Numerous other approaches have been employed in generating standards. At times, a particularly highly valued source (e.g., the *New York Times* or *Washington Post* among newspapers) is set as a standard, and the degree to which other sources compare to the standard is taken as an indication of their quality on one dimension or another. Sometimes, professional opinion is employed in generating a standard. For example, a group of experts might decide that the ideal TV station would broadcast news shows 20% of the time, public service or educational information 25% of the time, editorial comment 10% of the time, sports 15% of the time, and so forth. Census data, for example, provide a clear picture of the varying proportions of nationality groups within the country. One could use this standard to judge the "reality" of programming in presenting these various groups. If, for example, a particular group represented 11% of the population, it might follow that they should occupy approximately 11% of all broadcast time. If this is not the case, then some form of broadcast bias is taking place, and an interesting study of the nature of this bias immediately suggests itself. Taylor, Lee, and Stern's (1995) analysis of photo ads in a set of selected magazines provides results relevant to this issue. The researchers found that Hispanic models were substantially underrepresented (relative to population figures), and Asian models often were found in stereotypical poses. Research of this type provides an interesting, if indirect, commentary, on the state of race relations in the country, at least as they are reflected by practices of the mass media.

To Whom Was It Said?

It is a frequently observed fact that a presidential hopeful presenting a speech to a meeting of stockholders will stress policies quite different from, and often contrary to, those he or she would discuss in an assembly of labor union members. Given the nature of American politics, this tailoring of messages as a function of the interests and values of the receivers of the communication makes sense. Do the various media likewise tailor their message to the particular population of persons to whom they appeal? Is *Esquire* magazine really directed to the young, hip, liberal, college-educated junior executive? Or is its real appeal to the dirty old man on the park bench? Questions of this sort are generally the focus of investigations of the "To whom?" variety.

Literature that deals with studies of this type is relatively sparse, but what there is of it is intriguing. John Foster Dulles, Secretary of State during the Eisenhower presidential administration was the focus of two such investigations. Both Cohen (1957) and Holsti (1962) found clear evidence that the content of Dulles' communications was guided by a consideration of the audience for whom they were prepared. Similarly, Berkman (1963) found that advertising copy in *Life* and *Ebony* magazines was differentiated in terms of socioeconomic status of product users. Problems of inference can be quite bothersome when dealing with research of this type. Certainly descriptive differences between messages can be discussed. Couple this information with knowledge of the groups typically receiving the messages, and some indication of the source's intent can be obtained, but indications do not constitute acceptable proof. The source, for example, might well have consciously tailored the message to appeal to a specific population of receivers. In this sense, the message might be seen as reflecting the values and attitudes of the target audience. On the other hand, it is just as likely that communications shape, rather than reflect, the views of receivers. This assumes that the media possesses considerable power in molding opinions, an assumption that is not as well supported as might be assumed (e.g., Wartella & Stout, in press). To untangle these two equally likely propositions, researchers would probably have to resort to experimental techniques. It is perhaps for this reason—the inconclusiveness of most obtained results—that analyses focused on the question of "To whom" are relatively underrepresented in the content analysis literature.

How Are the Facts Presented?

Investigations of this question have focused generally on the form or style of the communication. Although the same information might be presented in two communications, one message might prove to be considerably more influential than the other because of the way the facts were presented. Analysis of the way in which messages are structured constitutes the primary goal of investigations of the "How" variety.

Propaganda Analysis.   Propaganda analysts have been particularly active in this area of research. Lasswell (1927), for example, attempting to identify the reasons that underscored the British propagandists' success in WWI and the concomitant German failure, isolated four major goals that both sides attempted to realize. The first consisted of attempts to generate and maintain home front hostility toward the enemy; the second stressed preservation of friendly alliances; the third involved attempts to secure the support of neutral countries; the fourth emphasized the demoralization of enemy soldiers and civilians. Because the propagandistic goals of the British and Germans were essentially the same, to gain an appreciation of the effectiveness of one side over the other, their communications must be analyzed not in terms of *what* was said, but rather in terms of *how* it was said.

One of the major reasons for the British propagandists' success can be traced to the image of a beleaguered England which they attempted to convey. The British pictured themselves as peace-loving islanders, forced to fight so that Western Civilization might be saved from the barbarians. Their goal in the war was "to end all wars," and their methods were strictly humanitarian. German propagandists, conversely, cited the need to extend Germanic *Kultur* as a justification for their war efforts. Humanitarianism was given short shift, and British atrocities were rarely noted. Like their counterparts in the field, the German public relations staff was soundly defeated. It is surprising to note how little they learned in the interval between wars. Their overall performance in WWII was similarly ineffective, although they were successful in generating enthusiasm in Germany for the Nazi cause (e.g., see Riefenstahl's (1935) *Triumph of the Will*) and in portraying the ferocity of their fighting machine, and thereby demoralizing some of their future opponents.

A number of classification systems for the analysis of propaganda have been developed. Lee and Lee (1939) and Lee (1952) described a series of propaganda techniques frequently employed in persuasive appeals. These include, for example, the oversimplification of complex issues, the use of emotional symbols, name-calling, and faulty conclusions from acceptable premises. How the use of these techniques is related to audience response remains unclear, but research on this and similar questions can be facilitated by the use of some standardized coding system.

Stylistic Analysis.   The analysis of propaganda does not exhaust the question of "How?" Considerable research focused on various aspects of literary or linguistic style has been conducted. The diversity of such investigations is noteworthy. Miles (1951), for example, attempted to describe in a quantitative fashion the differing stylistic patterns characteristic of distinct literary periods. Her analyses of poetic writings proved quite successful. Harvey (1953) attempted to discover the major distinguishing characteristics between best selling novels and also-rans. Combining a number of content variables in a prediction equation, Harvey found that he could predict sales with better than 80% accuracy. Not content to confine himself to literary periods or bestsellers, Fries (1940) attempted a structural analysis of the entire English language (as practiced in the United States).

Analyses, of course, need not be confined to languages, novels, items, phrases, or even words. Paisley (1966) studied letter redundancy in translations of Greek communications; this variable was found to distinguish authors.

Horton (1957) completely deserted the arena of literature to concentrate his analysis on the courtship patterns expressed in the popular songs of 1955. He found that the same general progression—from loneliness to fulfillment to loneliness—was expressed in more than 80% of the songs surveyed.

Examples of stylistic analyses could be continued indefinitely, illustrating the point that there are practically no limits on what can be done within the general framework of "How?" In part, this is good, because the scientist is not thereby forced into any overly restrictive series of research activities and topics prescribed by the discipline within which he or she is operating. The diversity of this area, however, reflects a problem as well. The absence of any unifying principle through which the results of various diverse investigations might be integrated may have retarded the development of this research area.

What Effect?

The final general form of content analysis to be considered consists of those investigations focusing on the effects of a communication on its receivers. In other than the most highly restricted situations, potential problems of faulty generalization are acute in such studies. Consider the following example. Immediately following an incendiary speech by a noted radical agitator, the audience riots, burning banks, ROTC buildings, and generally making nuisances of themselves. The riot could conceivably be attributed to (the effects of) the speech, but even in this rather clear-cut instance, the effect of the weather, police actions, unemployment rates, and a host of other possibilities could ultimately prove to have been the major causal culprits. In many content analytic situations, there are no appropriate solutions to such inference problems. Nevertheless, some interesting attempts have been made to link the content of media presentations with specific social effects. For example, sophisticated lagged correlational analyses have been conducted to assess the association between coverage of championship heavyweight boxing matches in the media and increases in homicides in the U.S. population (Phillips, 1983), and Phillips (1982) also presented evidence based on archival records suggesting a link between the occurrence of suicide content in popular television soap operas and the frequency of actual suicides in the population at large (see also Dunand, 1986; Rimé & Leyens, 1988).

Most investigations dealing with the effect of a communication have been undertaken within more constricted boundaries. Studies of the ease with which a communication can be comprehended by a reader (or group of readers) provide a good example of this type of highly restricted research. A number of readability formulas have been devised, and generally consist of considerations of sentence length and vocabulary difficulty (see Dale & Schall, 1948; Flesch, 1943; Gray & Leary, 1935). The usual paradigm of such studies is straightforward. Communications judged by some formula to differ in terms of readability are administered to a group of research participants, whose comprehension is then tested. If comprehension of the message judged more readable is greater than that of the difficult communication, the formula employed in the differentiation of messages is supported.

One of the easiest formulas to apply was devised by Farr, Jenkins, and Patterson (1951). These investigators found the incidence of one syllable words contained in a communication to be a reliable indicator of readability. In addition, they noted that their index, while offering a considerable savings in terms of scoring time, nevertheless correlated positively with scores derived through the use of the popular Flesch (1943) readability formula. Today, readability statistics are commonly available on most commercial word processing programs. Most make use of some variant of the Flesch formula.

All systems of this type, unfortunately, are susceptible to the specialized or idiosyncratic use of language. Gertrude Stein's writing, for example, although characterized by short words and short sentences, is nevertheless quite difficult to comprehend. The contextual qualities of her work, however, would confound almost all standard readability formulas; that is, they would indicate that Stein's writings should be quite readable.

The cloze procedure, a system designed to offset difficulties of this type, was produced by Taylor (1953, 1956). In this system, every fifth, or sixth, or seventh word is deleted from the communication under consideration (see Osgood, 1959, pp. 82–88). The percentage of deleted words that a sample of readers can identify correctly is used in determining the index of readability of the message. In an ingenious and successful study, Taylor (1953) demonstrated the utility of this system under syntactic conditions that had defeated other readability formulas.

Holsti (1969, pp. 90–93) discussed a number of other types of investigation focused on the question of the effects of a communication, but the verification and generalization problems to which most of these are susceptible are nearly insurmountable. For this reason, most studies in this specific area should remain descriptive in nature. This observation could be applied to the great bulk of all content analytic research. Most practitioners of these techniques recognize this, and the quality and utility of their studies clearly reflect this understanding.

As was stated earlier, content analysis is a superb technique for generating and enriching research hypotheses. Using the method to test hypotheses is less common in psychology; it is probably for this reason that content analysis is relatively underrepresented in social psychological research, where theory testing is often valued over hypothesis development. However, there is ample evidence in related disciplines (e.g., communication research and political science) that with appropriate controls and understanding of the boundaries, the technique can be used to test theory. We envision a larger role for this methodology in the future, in all fields of social science research. The ever-increasing availability of data sources, combined with developments in machine-based coding and analysis, bodes well for the field.

SUGGESTED READINGS

Ames, P. C., & Riggio, R. E. (1995). Use of the Rotter Incomplete Sentences Blank with adolescent populations: Implications for determining maladjustment. *Journal of Personality Assessment, 64*, 159–167.

Miles, M. B., & Huberman, A. M. (1994). *Qualitative data analysis: An expanded sourcebook* (2nd Ed.). Thousand Oaks, CA: Sage.

Peterson, C., Seligman, M. E., & Vaillant, G. E. (1988). Pessimistic explanatory style is a risk factor for physical illness: A 35-year longitudinal study. *Journal of Personality and Social Psychology, 55*, 23–27.

14

Scaling Stimuli: Social Psychophysics

Chapters 11, 12, and 13 discussed and examined techniques applicable in general observational research settings. In each of these earlier chapters, constructing, using, and scoring some type of coding scheme or schedule of questions were seen as necessary features of the investigative process if the aim of the observational research was testing, rather than generating, hypotheses. Often, the psychometric quality of the coding systems used in an observational situations is not a major consideration. This lack of attention to the statistical or psychometric properties of the measuring device is attributable to the fact that the coding scheme used by the observational researcher is viewed as a "one-shot" instrument.[1] Most classification systems are constructed to satisfy the needs of a specific investigative setting. Indeed, as we continually suggest throughout this book, observational studies should be designed with the research setting in mind. Thus, considerations of the specific sample of individuals under investigation, their limitations, the physical dimensions of the research context, the behaviors of interest, and so on should all be taken into account in constructing the coding system. This observation suggests that a system suitable for the study of a teenage motorcycle gang in Shaker Heights, Ohio, might not prove useful in studying the adjustment behavior of a group of first-year medical students in Pomona, California.

Tailoring an instrument to the research context (i.e., the respondent sample, the time, or the place in which the research will occur) is characteristic of many of the classification systems employed in social research. However, this degree of instrument tailoring is not typical when investigators attempt to develop scales of high generalizability across time, populations, and contexts. Developing and using scales of high utility, generality, and psychometric quality (i.e., of high reliability and validity) is a common and important feature in the life of the social researcher, and the next two chapters focus on the ways in which such measuring instruments are constructed and interpreted. As we show, some

---

[1]Exceptions to this generalization can be found (e.g., Bales', 1950, classification system, which is still used among researchers investigating small group interaction), but in most instances, the average number of applications of any given coding system appearing in the psychological literature is very close to 1.0.

scales are designed to measure differences among individuals. For example, a scale of anti-Semitism has as its purpose the classification of individuals along a hypothetical continuum: Those at one end of the continuum are defined as the most anti-Semitic and those at the other the least; those scoring in the middle are considered intermediate on their attitudes toward Jewish people. In this form of scaling, all the stimuli used to arrange people on the scale are considered identical, differing only in terms of error. So, on our anti-Semitism scale, we assume that the questions (items) we pose to respondents, which are also used to create our summary measure, all tap the same underlying construct (in this case, anti-Semitic attitudes). Measures of this variety are called *scales of individuals* (or *scales of individual differences*). Individual difference scales are by far the most common form of scale used in contemporary social research. We consider their development and interpretation in chapter 15.

Though far less common, we sometimes are concerned with perceived differences among a set of stimuli, rather than differences among our respondents in their evaluation of these stimuli. Developing scales that tap into perceived differences among stimuli (vs. individuals) is called stimulus scaling. As is shown throughout this chapter, creating stimulus scales calls for an approach and a set of assumptions that are quite different from those used in individual differences scaling. The psychophysicists of 100 years ago attempted to bring the measurement logic of physics into the psychological laboratory, that is, to borrow and apply the methods of measurement used in the physical sciences to the behavioural sciences. They were interested in developing measures of features for which no obvious metric existed (e.g., beauty, taste, etc.), and to do so with high degrees of reliability and validity. A central goal of their efforts was to produce measures that accurately represented the views of the sample on which the measure was based. It is for this reason that Dawes and Smith (1985, p. 515), referred to stimulus scales as "group attitude scales." The real utility of the stimulus scaling approaches is that they allow us to impose a metric on judgments for which no obvious "yardstick" exists. In the physical sciences, this issue usually does not arise. If we wish to know the weight of an object, we can place the thing on a scale; if we wish to know the loudness of a sound, we use a decibel meter. But suppose we want order 10 paintings from most to least beautiful, or to arrange 5 different brands of pizza from most to least delicious. In these instances, no obvious physical yardstick exists. We do not have rulers with which we can unambiguously, and with high consensus, judge beauty or deliciousness. So instead, we apply *psychometric* techniques, which have been under continuous development in psychology since the turn of the 19th century and represent one of the social sciences' major methodological contributions to the study of behavior.

As noted, in stimulus scaling, we are concerned principally with differences between stimuli (or items). As such, variations among stimuli are considered meaningful and important—they are the focus of investigation. However, variations among participants are considered the result of error. This is a very important distinction between stimulus scaling and individual differences scaling, and bears reemphasis. In stimulus scaling, we assume that individual differences in perceptions and evaluations of the stimuli being judged are the result of error. They are not conceptualized as the result of meaningful differences among people. As we show later, the opposite assumption is made in scaling individuals; that is, we assume that there are no differences among the stimuli (i.e., the items) that constitute the measurement instrument. Unless we learn otherwise, all items are assumed to tap the same underlying construct (belief, trait, attitude, etc.). Accordingly, differences that occur between respondents are real and potentially meaningful.

The variations in underlying assumptions between stimulus and individual differences scaling are important. They suggest that the scaling approaches be applied to different problems, which will produce different outcomes and different ways of arranging stimuli and people. Each type of scaling method is valuable in its own right and, as is shown, each satisfies different research needs.

SCALING STIMULI

Although judgments of human respondents are employed in generating scales of stimuli, the focus of stimulus scaling is different from that in which differences among respondents is the central issue of the rating task, and these differences require development of different measurement operations. A typical use of stimulus scaling techniques is found in marketing research, where the researcher is interested in comparative evaluations of different products, brands, or packages. Another use is found in the political arena, where evaluations of competing candidates or social policies might be under scrutiny, or in criminology, where the perceived seriousness of crimes might be at issue.

Typically, in stimulus-scaling investigations, respondents compare one stimulus against all the others, along a specific dimension or quality. These comparisons then are combined across all respondents to form a continuum that represents the aggregate judgment of the entire respondent sample.[2] If certain conditions (discussed farther on) are met, this judgmental continuum provides a precise and accurate summary of respondents' opinions regarding relative differences among the stimulus set. Using this technique, we obtain an ordering of stimuli along the continuum, and, perhaps more importantly, the intervals along the continuum are equal; in other words, the procedure produces scale of interval quality.

In one of the classic stimulus scaling investigations, Louis Thurstone (1927) assessed the beliefs of 266 University of Chicago students regarding the seriousness of a set of 19 different crimes. Among others, the crimes included arson, bootlegging, forgery, homicide, larceny, libel, perjury, rape, and smuggling.[3] Rather than ask the students to rate the seriousness of each crime on 10-point scales, Thurstone paired every crime with each of the others and required his participants to underline the more serious of the two for every comparison. So, on a given judgment, a participant might be asked to judge whether perjury or rape was the more serious crime. On the next judgment, the participant might judge the more serious of libel versus bootlegging. Crano and Cooper (1973) argued that such binary judgments often are more reliable, and less demanding of respondents, than those that require fine-grained ratings or discriminations. It is for this reason, among others, that stimulus-scaling approaches are sometimes preferred to other methods of determining people's beliefs.

Interestingly, Thurstone's results suggested that his sample of university students (in 1927) considered crimes against persons (homicide, rape, kidnapping, assault) as being the most serious, just as students today probably would. Property offenses and victimless crimes (vagrancy, receiving stolen goods, etc.) fell into the less serious segment of the scale. Later replications of this study by Coombs (1967) and Borg (1988) produced results consistent with the early findings, though some the researchers did find some deviations from the original study. For example, in Coombs' (1967) study, 369 University of Michigan students served as participants. They judged rape the most serious offense and homicide

---

[2]This combination of judgments across all respondents requires the assumption, noted earlier, that respondents would all judge the stimuli identically were it not for error. If this assumption were not made, it would not be logical to combine data across all respondents.

[3]Some of the "crimes" Thurstone used in his study (e.g., abortion, adultery) would not be considered illegal today.

TABLE 14.1

Hypothetical Distribution of Scores and Ranks

Participant	Score	Rank
J. Smith	100	1
R. Jones	50	2
D. Williams	49	3
S. Hedrick	48	4
W. Johnson	47	5
J. Davis	2	6
L. Masters	1	7

second most serious, whereas this ordering was reversed in Thurstone's (1927) original study. Coombs' research also disclosed that students of 1967 did not consider bootlegging nearly as serious as Thurstone's participants had, whereas seduction of a minor was considered more serious in the later sample. These variations between studies are probably associated with changing attitudes over time, or with differences in the interpretation of various crime labels, and provide interesting insights into contemporary views of crime.[4]

A central advantage of the stimulus scaling methods described in this chapter is that they produce scales of equal-interval quality. This level of measurement is rarely achieved in most social research, even though the statistics we most commonly use assume it. Typically, our measures are ordinal; that is, the differences they denote between objects (or people) under comparison satisfy the requirement of rank order, but the distance between adjacent ranks are not necessarily equal at all points along the judgment continuum. A brief consideration of the data of Table 14.1 amply demonstrates the difference in understanding that differences between interval and ordinal scales can produce. As shown, our participants appear to vary widely along the continuum we are measuring. However, the ranks do not illustrate the range very well. Smith and Jones are ranked contiguously, even though they are 50 points apart on our measuring instrument. Jones and Williams also are contiguous, but only one point separates them on the instrument. As can be readily seen, the differences in real distance among the respondents are not represented well by the ranking. Higher levels of scale quality provide better representation of the data, a better fit of number to observation (see chap. 1). This is an important advantage of the stimulus scaling methods—if data quality is sufficiently great, they produce scales of equal interval, rather than merely ordinal, quality. The relative neglect of the more psychophysically inspired stimulus scaling methods is a costly lapse.

TECHNIQUES FOR STIMULUS SCALING

The Method of Pair Comparison

Of all the classic psychometric stimulus scaling techniques, two approaches, *pair comparison* and *rank order*, are most common in social research. In the technique known as the method of pair comparison, a group of stimuli of theoretical or practical interest is chosen, and all possible pairs of stimuli are presented to respondents, who are asked to

---

[4]Borg (1988) suggested that participants in Thurstone's (1927) sample might have read "seduction of a minor" as referring to "having sex with a girl under 21," whereas today's students might have read the same item as "molestation of a 3-year-old" (p. 60).

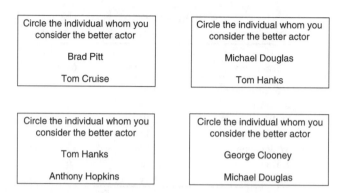

FIG. 14.1.   Examples of stimuli used in the actor-rating pair comparison study.

choose one stimulus over the other with which it is paired on the basis of a quality or dimension defined by the researcher (e.g., beauty, goodness, taste, sex appeal, etc.). This is the method Thurstone (1927) used in his study of the perceived seriousness of crimes. These choices are aggregated over all participants, and if the aggregated judgments can reasonably reproduce the raw data on which they are based, the result provides an accurate and useful summary of the overall opinion of the group.

To lend some degree of concreteness to this discussion, consider the following example. Suppose that we were interested in a group of respondents' attitudes regarding relative differences in acting ability among six popular male actors: Brad Pitt, Tom Cruise, George Clooney, Michael Douglas, Tom Hanks, and Anthony Hopkins.

Notice that we are not concerned that one respondent thinks that Hopkins is a better actor than Clooney, whereas another has the opposite opinion. In stimulus scaling, we are concerned with how the stimuli (our six actors) are arranged along a continuum of acting ability by the total sample. Differences of opinion among the individuals who constitute the sample are not at issue. Indeed, as noted, these differences are considered the result of error.

There is no obvious "acting ability" yardstick that we can use to order these actors, yet the task is far from impossible. Employing the method of pair comparison, we would first assemble every possible pair of actors. In this case, this process would yield 15 nonrepetitive pairs.[5] For example, Pitt would be paired with Cruise, Clooney, Douglas, Hanks, and Hopkins; Cruise with Clooney, Douglas, Hanks, and Hopkins and, as already noted, with Pitt, and so on. Then, each of the pairings would be presented to each respondent, with the instructions to "choose the better actor of each pair." To facilitate this task, and avoid problems that might occur if every participant received the same ordering of pairs, we might place each pair of names on index cards and shuffle the cards before giving them to participants. The index-card stimuli might look like those of Fig. 14.1.

Suppose we administered our set of 15 pair comparison choices to 100 volunteers, 50 men and 50 women. To summarize the obtained data, we could arrange respondents' judgments in a *choice matrix*, as in Table 14.2. In this matrix, the cell entries represent the number of respondents who chose the *column* stimulus over the *row* stimulus. So, in Table 14.2, the data indicate that Clooney was chosen over Cruise by 40 of 100 respondents

---

[5]To calculate the number of pairs that will result from a given number of stimuli, use the following formula: $p = [n\,(n-1)]/2$, where p = number of pairs, and n = the number of stimuli. Thus, in our acting quality study, we would produce $[6 \times 5]/2$ pairs. Thurstone (1927) used 19 different crimes, and thus produced 171 pairs of stimuli.

TABLE 14.2

Example of a Choice (or Similarity) Matrix in a Pair Comparison Study of Acting Ability

Actor	Clooney	Cruise	Douglas	Hanks	Hopkins	Pitt
Clooney	50	60	55	50	70	60
Cruise	40	50	60	70	80	60
Douglas	45	40	50	60	60	45
Hanks	50	30	40	50	60	50
Hopkins	30	20	40	40	50	35
Pitt	40	40	55	50	65	50
Average	42.5	40	50	53.3	63.3	50

Note. The matrix indicates the number of times the column stimulus is chosen over the row stimuli. In this study, $N = 100$ respondents. By convention, a 50% choice proportion is assumed when an object is compared with itself.

(and thus, Cruise was chosen by 60 of 100 participants as a better actor than Clooney). Clooney was chosen by an equal number of respondents when compared with Hanks. The column sum (or mean) gives a reasonable indication of the aggregate group opinion regarding the acting ability of the individuals who constituted the stimulus set. In this instance, the data suggest that the respondents viewed Douglas and Pitt as comparable and superior to Cruise and Clooney; Hopkins and Hanks were judged the best of the lot, with Hopkins a clear favorite of the sample. If this sample were drawn in such a manner as to make it representative of a population (say, of college students, members of the Motion Pictures Academy of Arts and Sciences, citizens of Monaco, etc.), we might generalize these results to the group they represent.

If we wanted to develop a comprehensive index of the respondents' choices that had the property of an *interval scale*, we would transform the choice matrix to a proportion matrix, by dividing each frequency by the total number of respondents. Then, following Guilford (1954, pp. 154–177), we would perform a set of statistical operations on the data to determine if respondents' choices satisfied a set of necessary assumptions. The assumptions are focused on the issue of whether the aggregated (mean) data accurately reproduce the matrix of data from which they were calculated. If they do, the ordering of the stimuli would have equal-interval properties. In other words, the units separating the stimuli would be meaningful (that is, of equal interval). We can infer more from equal-interval data than the mere order of the stimuli (as would be the case if an *ordinal scale* were formed).

One of the central assumptions of the scaling operations employed to transform respondents' preferences into a scale of interval qualities is that the data are *transitive*. Transitivity implies logical consistency in judgment, such that if a respondent feels that Cruise is a better actor than Hopkins, and Hopkins better than Pitt, then he or she should judge Cruise better than Pitt. Such a set of transitive judgments would be expressed as follows:

> If Cruise is better than Hopkins,
> and Hopkins is better than Pitt,
> then Cruise should be judged better than Pitt.

It sometimes happens that a transitive relationship of the type presented here is not obtained (i.e., in this example, Pitt might be judged better than Cruise). Intransitive choices can be generated by a number of factors. For example, the stimuli might be so similar that respondents cannot differentiate them reliably. If a judge were wildly enthusiastic about all the actors, or hated them all more or less equally, he or she would be hard put to differentiate them in a transitive manner. Another possibility is that the scale along which respondents judge the stimuli is multidimensional. In our actor-rating example, it might be that an individual's choice of Cruise over Hopkins was dictated by sex appeal, whereas the choice of Hopkins over Pitt was based on difference in the actors' voice quality; Pitt might be favored over Cruise owing to his appearance in a new movie the respondent enjoyed very much, or by some complex interaction of the voice quality–sex appeal factors (see Tversky, 1969).

A sufficient number of unreliable or intransitive choices will result in a data set that will not satisfy the minimum criteria of scale quality. That is, tests used to determine the reliability of the scale (Mosteller, 1951) will indicate that the data on which the scale is to be based are not sufficiently trustworthy to put any faith in the resulting index. In this situation, the researcher is in a difficult position. It is clear that the scaling process has failed, but it is not completely clear *why* it failed. Some likely avenues to traverse in seeking the source of the problem involve participants' familiarity with the stimulus dimension, the definitional specificity of the choice dimension, the differentiability of the stimuli, and the dimensionality or equivocality of the choice dimension that was required to judge the stimuli.

Participants' familiarity with the stimuli being judged is the easiest issue to assess, but the hardest to offset. It sometimes happens that some fraction of the participant sample is simply unfamiliar with all the stimuli that are to be compared. For example, suppose that some of our participants did not know much about Brad Pitt, and others could not remember what Anthony Hopkins looked like. They could not be expected to compare these actors reliably with others whom they could recall. Comparisons involving these unfamiliar stimulus objects well might prove unreliable, or intransitive, and thus spoil the overall scale.

Sometimes, the choice dimension is not specified clearly, or, if clearly specified, is not one that participants can use consistently. Returning again to our actor example, good acting involves many different qualities. If we are not specific about the particular quality or qualities we wish our judges to use in forming their evaluations, the complexity of the judgment dimension will defeat our attempts at developing a reliable measure.

The issue of specificity is related to the multidimensionality of the choice dimension the participants must use in their judgments. We know that acting can be differentiated along several dimensions. If our judges use one dimension in one comparison and another in a later comparison, there is a good possibility that the judgments will prove intransitive. The shift in dimensions being used from one judgment to another will cause inconsistencies within a judge. If a sufficient number of judgments (or judges) suffer from this problem, the scale will not prove reliable.

The differentiability of the stimuli is not likely to prove a major problem in our actor example, but it can be a major problem in stimulus scale construction. For example, suppose we wanted to order popular brands of beer along a dimension of tastiness. We ask our judges to judge among the following seven beers: Amstel, Beck, Budweiser, Guiness, Heineken, Michelob, and Rolling Rock. Although all of our judges have experienced each brand at one time or another, some of them (not being connoisseurs of the art form) might not be able to distinguish among all, or many, of them. This is not necessarily the result of unfamiliarity. For some, it may be that the difference between the various beers simply are not noteworthy. In this case, the scaling effort will fail. Indeed, it would fail even if the pair comparison study were run as a taste test—that is, if participants were given small glasses of beer to taste and compare, rather than trying to match taste with brand from memory (remember, with 7 stimuli, this would require 21 pair comparisons, or 42 small glasses of beer). If the beers were relatively indistinguishable, or even if two or three of them were, the researcher might find that the resulting choice matrix would not allow for development of a reliable (trustworthy) measurement.

Another problem that can arise when we choose to use a pair comparison approach comes about because of participant fatigue. Recall that $N(N-1)/2$ pairs of choices can be derived from N stimuli. Thus, if our problem involved the judgment of 20 actors' ability, or 20 beers, each respondent would have had to make 190 comparisons. Distortion of results attributable to boredom, fatigue, or, in the case of the beer example, addled judgment, are clearly possible in such situations and would produce a data set that probably would not result in a reliable, equal-interval scale. This problem is difficult to solve. Some researchers scale down the magnitude of the problem by using an incomplete pairing. That is, none of the judges makes the complete set of pair comparisons. Statistical procedures are available to allow this form of pared-down comparative process, but presentation of the complete set of paired stimuli to all judges is preferable. Other researchers divide the task across multiple testing occasions; this tack, too, would lighten participant load, but variations between test days may introduce unacceptable amounts of error into the process. The problem is best solved by using a relatively restricted number of stimuli which, when paired, do not produce an overwhelming demand on participants' stamina.

Lest we paint too gloomy a picture, we should recognize the positive features of the pair comparison approach. Under appropriate circumstances, the method can produce an accurate and concise summary of the judgments of a group even when the dimension along which the judgments are made has no obvious physical metric. The "appropriate circumstances" involve (a) a set of stimuli that are clearly discriminable, (b) with which the respondent sample is familiar, (c) a well-defined and (d) unidimensional choice dimension, and (e) a reasonable number of stimuli, thereby overburdening neither the stamina nor the cognitive capacities of the respondents.

It is important to understand that interval scale results do not allow for *absolute* judgments, or judgments that entail ratios (e.g., this actor [beer] is twice good as the other). Although Anthony Hopkins was rated tops in our hypothetical exercise, for instance, it is possible that in an absolute sense, the majority of respondents consider him a very poor actor. Hopkins falling at the top of the scale does not necessarily imply that the respondents thought him a great, or even a good, actor. Possibly, they simply found him less bad than the others in the comparison group. Only data of *ratio* quality provide a true zero point, which, in the present instance, would allow us to determine whether the aggregate participant sample viewed the top-rated actor as good or bad. If a true zero point had been established (by other scaling methods), we could confidently infer that actors falling above zero had been viewed positively by the respondent sample; those below it were seen as bad actors. In addition, the presence of the true zero would allow us to determine the degree to which one stimulus exceeded another on the dimension used by the judges to differentiate the stimuli.

The Method of Rank Order

The method of rank order is a comparative stimulus scaling technique that enables the researcher to avoid many of the problems inherent in the pair comparison method, while producing results that closely approximate those from the more laborious pair comparison method (Misra & Dutt, 1965). In rank order scaling, respondents order a number of stimuli along a defined choice dimension. To return to our example, we could present our six actors to our participants, and ask them to rank them in order of acting ability, with 1 representing the best, and 6 the worst, actor. From the data obtained in this simple operation, we could construct an equal-interval scale of participants' judgments (see Guilford, 1954, pp. 178–196 for a description of the statistical operations to be used). Notice that this technique avoids two potentially serious problems of the pair comparison approach. First, because all objects of judgment are presented at once, and the respondent ranks all of them in one operation, judgmental intransitivity is physically impossible. If A is ranked over B, and B over C, then A *must* be ranked over C in the rank order approach. In addition, the method of rank order avoids some of the administrative drudgery that can be associated with pair comparisons, especially when large numbers of stimuli are to be compared. Recall that a total of 190 pair comparisons would be generated from a set of 20 stimuli. If the method of rank order were used, the task would be confined to the judgments involved in ordering only those 20. Thus, the technique appears to demand less of the respondents.[6]

Though different on a number of dimensions, the methods of pair comparison and rank order share noteworthy similarities. First, both methods are used to generate *comparative judgments*. Either scaling process, that is, provides information regarding relative differences between stimuli, as judged by the participant sample, and these differences are arranged on a scale of equal intervals, if the data allow for construction of an equal interval scale. As noted, however, neither method provides information regarding the judges' *absolute* appraisal of the rated objects.

Another important similarity between these two stimulus-scaling methods concerns the assumptions regarding differences between participants' ratings. Because responses to stimulus objects are pooled over participants in both methods, differences between participants are ignored. Respondents are viewed as replicates in these methods, and differences between them are attributed to error, or unreliability. In other words, by virtue of the way in which the data are assembled and combined, these approaches assume that all participants would produce the same pattern of choices if their judgments were perfectly reliable. This assumption is necessary to justify the pooling of responses over participants. Fortunately, violations of this assumption can be tested (cf. Guilford, 1954; Torgerson, 1958) and, if the violation is not too extreme, it can be offset.

Multidimensional Scaling Models

The scaling techniques we have discussed to this point are designed to develop unidimensional scales. Indeed, researchers working in this scaling tradition generally strive to achieve unidimensionality in their scales. The reason for this desire is obvious. When judges can slide from one dimension to another when comparing stimuli, the classic psychometric methods fail to produce reliable measures, and this is especially problematic for the method of pair comparison. Some investigators, however, have argued that unidimensional scales do not adequately reflect the complexity we commonly encounter in our everyday lives. Obviously, we can judge actors in terms of "acting ability," especially

---

[6]Nonetheless, some prefer the pair comparison approach in situations involving small numbers of stimuli (say, 10 or fewer). In these situations, participants' responses are thought to be more reliable than in a rank order task because only two objects of judgment are involved in any given pair comparison (cf. Crano & Cooper, 1973). Proponents of the pair comparison method believe that the dimension along which stimuli are to be judged can be held in mind more faithfully when it need be applied in choices involving only two stimuli. In the rank order method, it could be argued that essentially all the stimuli are judged at once.

when that term is strictly defined for us. However, the single dimension that we forced participants to use in our study to judge the goodness or badness of an actor probably grossly oversimplifies the complex judgment scheme that people use in reality. Scott (1968) recognized this fact when he argued that using a single dimension to construe a complex stimulus object (an actor, a beer, etc.) "is patently unrealistic if one takes seriously the widely held psychological principle that any response is multiply determined" (p. 250). Arguments of this nature have proved persuasive to many, and multidimensional scaling approaches have become more widely used in the social sciences. An extended discussion of multidimensional scaling is beyond the scope of this book, and it is fair to say that multidimensional scaling approaches are not nearly as well developed as might be expected. Recall that Scott made his observations nearly 40 years ago. However, some general points, along with the preceding discussion of unidimensional approaches, should prove a useful introduction to these techniques.

Unfolding. Coombs (1964) supplied an appropriate point of transition between unidimensional and multidimensional scaling, and between stimulus and individual difference scaling, with his *unfolding technique*. The problem to which Coombs' approach is addressed is the discovery of the structure or the underlying order among of a set of objects, and the reliable placement of respondents (or stimuli) at some point within this structure in such a way that the ordering of each respondent's pattern of choices can be determined. In this sense, respondents are considered "stimuli" to be ordered along a set of dimension. Coombs' unfolding technique thus bridges the two scaling traditions—stimulus and individual difference scaling—that we consider in this chapter and in chapter 15.

Consider the following example: Sam, Jenny, and Brian are at a point in their college careers when they must choose an academic major. For convenience, we assume that these three students can choose among six different areas, and the rank ordering of their choices is as presented in Table 14.3.

Although their choices obviously are quite distinct, a single preference structure can be constructed that summarizes the inclinations of all three students' toward each of the six possible academic majors, as shown in Fig. 14.2. To determine whether the scale of

TABLE 14.3

Order of Sam's, Jenny's and Brian's Preferences of Academic Majors

Preference	Jenny	Sam	Brian
1	Chemistry	English Lit.	Theatre
2	Physics	Psychology	Psychology
3	Theatre	Art	Chemistry
4	Psychology	Theatre	English Lit.
6	English Lit.	Chemistry	Physics
5	Art	Physics	Art

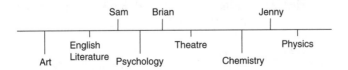

FIG. 14.2. Underlying preference structure for three hypothetical students, with each person's ideal choice noted.

Fig. 14.2 adequately summarizes the choices of our three students, consider the point at which Brian falls on the preference scale. In terms of scale distances, the major closest to Brian is theatre, then psychology, then chemistry, and so on. Thus, Brian's placement on the scale accurately reproduces his preference rankings of Table 14.2. We could create a more graphic illustration of Brian's preferences by "folding" the scale at his ideal point (i.e., the point at which he intersects the scale), hence the term "unfolding technique" to describe Coombs' approach. Using distances from each student's ideal point as indicators of relative preferences, we are able to reconstruct exactly the preference rankings of each of the students, as they were presented in Table 14.3. Inspection of the "ideal points" of Jenny and Sam, and of the distances between their ideal points and the various academic majors, as they are arranged on the scale, will disclose that the scale accurately summarizes their preference patterns as well. As Galanter (1966) observed, "by using this (unfolding) technique, we see . . . that although different people may exhibit different preferences . . . it may very well be the case that the differences in the revealed preferences conceal an underlying consistency in the preference structure" (p. 131).

The utility of the unfolding technique is enhanced if the dimension along which the preference stimuli are ordered is somehow identifiable. In the present example, we could hypothesize that the dimension along which the students arranged their preferences was determined by the degree of mathematical ability required by each of the various academic majors. If we could obtain the school records of our three students and show that Jenny's mathematical aptitude test score exceeded that of Brian's, whose score was greater than Sam's, then our confidence in our description of the critical dimension would be enhanced, as would the utility of the scale.

A good research example of the use of the unfolding technique is provided by Poole (1981), who investigated the ratings that members of the U.S. Senate received from 26 special interest groups, which ranged from Americans for Democratic Action on the left to the National Taxpayers' Union on the right. Poole found that a single dimension, on which Senators were arranged in terms of their liberal or conservative leanings, accounted for nearly 80% of the variance in the special interest groups' ratings. What's more, Senators' votes on a number of crucial issues could be predicted on the basis of their relative standing on the liberal-conservative dimension that Poole derived. And, the accuracy of these predictions surpassed that based on political party affiliation. As Dawes and Smith (1985) observed, "Poole's results are striking. Not only does the unfolding technique yield a single dimension that fits the data well, but in addition, the results are in accord with intuitions about which congressional members are conservative or liberal—and can be used to predict crucial votes" (p. 529).

It is possible that the students' preferences could have been so diverse that a simple one-dimensional preference structure could not have been constructed in such a way that it accurately summarized all choices. For example, suppose that mathematical aptitude and the availability of independent-study courses in each department were the two factors that influenced each student's choices. In this case, the unfolding solution would have required two dimensions, and the students' ideal preference points would be located not on a single scale, but somewhere in the two-dimensional space described by the mathematical aptitude and independent-study availability dimensions.

Multidimensional Scaling Approaches

There are a number of multidimensional scaling (MDS) approaches in addition to Coombs' unfolding model (e.g., see Carroll & Arabie, 1980; Coombs, Dawes, & Tversky, 1970; Guttman, 1968; Kruskal, 1964a, 1964b; Kruskal, Young, & Seery, 1977; Schiffman,

Reynolds, & Young, 1981; Shepard, 1962a, 1962b; Shepard, Romney, & Nerlove, 1971; Torgerson, 1958). Generally, these alternatives rely on judgments of the similarity or dissimilarity among stimuli rather than their preferences to identify the dimensions that respondents use to conceptualize the stimulus class. In an interesting example of the use of multidimensional scaling, Wish, Deutsch, and Biener attempted to determine the dimensions that people employed in judging the similarity among various nations. To accomplish this, Wish et al. drew up a list of 21 nations, and presented all possible pairs of these nations to each of 75 respondents, who were asked to judge their degree of similarity (using a 9-point judgment scale). The degree of similarity between each pair of nations was calculated across respondents, and entered into a similarity matrix, of the type presented in Table 14.2. Multidimensional analysis of these similarity judgments revealed that four dimensions appeared to govern respondents' similarity judgments: the respondents considered the political ideology, the level of economic development, the geography and population, and the culture and race of the paired countries in estimating their degree of similarity or dissimilarity.

Alvaro and Crano (1997) used MDS to estimate the proximity of a set of beliefs held by their participant sample. They presented a set of attitude items, and asked participants to estimate the likelihood that if they changed their attitude about one of the items, they would change their attitude on another. Following is an example of the format they used to investigate perceived similarities and difference among the attitude constructs:

If you changed your mind regarding your position on HOMOSEXUALS IN THE MILITARY, what is the probability that you would also change your position on ABORTION? PROBABILITY = _____ (Note: probabilities may range from 0–100%)

Participants' responses were used to create a matrix of similarities among all of the items. The MDS approach produces a map, or a picture, of the spatial relationships among all the stimuli that are presented. The MDS analysis used by Alvaro and Crano (1997) produced a two-dimensional map of the relationships among the attitude objects which accurately replicated the data from the similarity matrix.[7] To test their theory, Alvaro and Crano were searching for highly proximal attitude objects. So, as expected, the concept of abortion mapped very closely to the concept of contraception. Participants obviously thought that if they were to change their attitude toward abortion, they also would change their attitude toward contraception. The point of the exercise was to find proximal attitude objects that participants did not think were related. These objects, too, were discovered in the MDS, and used in the design of a study that investigated ways in which a persuasive message directed at a specific attitude object affected attitudes on another (see, also, Crano & Chen, 1998). Discovering related attitude objects that participants did not believe to be related could not have been accomplished as efficiently with other techniques. The MDS approach is a highly useful, if underused, method in social research. Although underused, the approach has not been ignored completely.[8] We consider the underuse of stimulus scaling methods in social science a missed opportunity. The techniques are

---

[7]In general, in MDS, if the mapping process is successful, the distances derived from the map will equal those found in the similarity matrix. Increasing the number of dimensions usually results in a better fit of map with matrix, but the trick is to scale the similarity matrix using as few dimensions as possible.

[8]Some of the more intriguing uses of MDS in the social science literature involve studies of the ways in which Alzheimer's patients cluster common objects (e.g., instruments, animals, etc.), as compared with the mappings of elderly non-Alzheimer's patients (Ober & Shenaut, 1999), differences related to variations in music preferences (Tekman, 1998), and factors that affect judgments of emotion in faces (Halberstadt & Niedenthal, 1997).

based on classic psychophysical methods developed over many years, and have proved robust and reliable. They provide relatively fine-grained pictures of beliefs and preferences that exist within a group, and also suggest the degree of unanimity of these beliefs and preferences within the participant sample. Recall that variations among participants are assumed to be a function of error; if sufficient disagreement exists, the scaling procedures will fail; that is, their statistical analysis will suggest that the "summary attitude scale" is not trustworthy. This information may prove useful in itself, but most often the approaches produce trustworthy summary information of high (interval-level) quality. We hope that this brief discussion of some of the more widely known techniques will encourage their use in social research.

SUGGESTED READINGS

Borg, I. (1988). Revisiting Thurstone's and Coombs' scales on the seriousness of crimes. *European Journal of Social Psychology, 18*, 53–61.

Dawes, R. M., & Smith, T. L. (1985). Attitude and opinion measurement. In G. Lindzey & E. Aronson (Eds.), *The handbook of social psychology*, Vol. 2 (2nd ed., pp. 509–566). Reading, MA: Addison-Wesley.

Guilford, J. P. (1954). *Psychometric methods*. New York: McGraw-Hill.

SCALING INDIVIDUALS: QUESTIONNAIRE DESIGN AND RATING SCALE CONSTRUCTION

Studying people's beliefs, attitudes, values, and personalities is a central research preoccupation of the social sciences. This focus on differences among individuals requires that data be organized and conceptualized in a systematic and precise manner, a manner different from that used in stimulus scaling, which we discussed in chapter 14. Whereas we assume in the methods of pair comparison and rank order scaling that all participants would respond identically to the various choice stimuli were it not for random error, the scaling of individual differences requires that we regard variations in responses among participants as meaningful (i.e., as not attributable to error). Conversely, the stimuli used to assess individual differences (typically the questions or "items" in the scale or questionnaire) are assumed to be identical in meaning for all participants, and to be measuring essentially the same idea, knowledge base, or attitude. Differences in participants' responses to these hypothetically "identical" items are the central methodological focus in the scaling of individuals.

QUESTIONNAIRES

Two complementary approaches characterize attempts to establish measures that assess differences among people. For convenience, we will term the slightly less formal measures *questionnaires*, and the more rigorously designed measures *rating scales*. The design tactics used in each help inform the other. Questionnaire and scale construction are integral to many of the data collection methods we discuss throughout this text, so it is important to have a good understanding of their strengths and weaknesses.

In questionnaires, we often do not have the luxury of length. That is, we are unable to use many different items to tap a person's evaluations of a given target such as a person, event, or object. Sometimes, the limitation is imposed because of cost. When conducting a national survey, for example, including even one extra item can be prohibitively expensive, so we must be content with an item or two to assess people's thoughts and feelings on a given topic. In other cases, many different concepts are under scrutiny in the questionnaire, and to use many items to measure evaluations of all of them would create an overly long measuring instrument. Fears of participant fatigue, and the accompanying loss of data quality, motivate fewer items per concept. Of course, some questionnaires are quite lengthy, but here we consider the more typical case. Questionnaires may be administered in the context of an interview study (see chap. 12) or in written form as a self-administered measure. There are no formal rules for questionnaire design, but considerable folk wisdom has grown around their construction, given the intense focus on such measuring instruments over the past 70 years in social science (see Krosnick & Fabrigar, in press). We present some rules of thumb that are commonly adhered to and show that these rules apply, as well, in the development of the more formal rating scales.

Choosing and Wording Questions

The first rule is to ask what you want to know. Whereas indirect methods, which hide the intent of the questioner, sometimes are used (see below), the more direct the question, the more likely is the true meaning of the query to be understood. Questions that are misread or misunderstood cannot possibly provide the sought-for information, and thus should be avoided. A corollary of this rule of thumb is to use short, simple sentences, if possible, when developing questionnaire queries. This rule helps avoid double-barreled questions—compound items that ask more than one question at once. A question such as "Do you think that civil rights activists have gone too far and that the government should crack down on militant organizations in this country" is an example of such a double-barreled question. The problem with such questions, of course, is that it is not easy to know which of the multiple queries contained in the item is the focus of the respondent's answer.

Related to the first rule is its mirror image, namely, do not ask for information that you do not need, simply because others typically do. Often, researchers generate considerable resistance in their respondents by asking for personal information that is irrelevant to their research hypotheses. Asking personal questions—religion, family income, even age—is legitimate if the information will be used in the analysis, and has some relevance to the theory being investigated. However, if the information is simply gathered as a matter of course, or habit, and no plan for its implementation in the analysis exists, then the costs of asking for it should be weighed against its possible relevance in future, secondary, analyses. We recognize the utility of these "added-on" variables in data re-analyses, when questions that were not part of the original study might arise. Being able to use data for proposes other than those for which they were originally gathered is an important advantage to researchers, some of whom might have had nothing to do with the design of the original study. However, we often fail to realize that this value-added feature comes at a cost. Alienating respondents by asking questions they resent, and for which no immediate use is planned, is one such cost.

Using Open-Ended Questions

A distinct advantage of questionnaires, as we are using the term, over scales, is the capacity to use open-ended items. An open-ended item is one that poses a question but does not constrain the answer. The advantage of open-ended questions (e.g., "Who is your favorite mayoral candidate?") over close-ended ones (e.g., "Who is your favorite mayoral candidate, Smith, Jones, or Bradley?") is that the former do not force respondents to choose among a perhaps overly limited set of response options. If the respondent's answer to the questions posed here were "Johnson," the first would capture it, whereas the second would not. Visser, Krosnick, and Lavrakas (2000) argued forcefully that open-ended questions are clearly preferable to closed questions, and in questionnaire construction contexts, we are in general agreement with them.[1] However, whereas open-ended questions may tap respondents' feelings with greater fidelity than close-ended items, their added sensitivity comes with a cost, and that cost involves developing methods of analyzing the free responses that the open items generate. In the mayoral example given, analyzing the content of respondents' open-ended answers would not prove onerous.

Whenever the list of possible answers is relatively constrained, and relatively readily anticipated, coding answers becomes an almost mechanical task. So, for example, if we were to ask, "Whom do you believe is responsible for California's energy problems," the informed respondent would most likely have a rather limited list of possibilities to draw from: the avaricious electric generating companies, bone-headed or unscrupulous politicians, careless consumers, and a few other nefarious eco-villains. However, if the issue is one that admits to a host of possible answers, e.g., "What should the United States do about global warming?" a coding scheme is necessary, and may prove costly. Whether the cost is tolerable depends in part on the researcher's resources, the complexity and importance of the issue under study, and the number of different issues being studied. Obviously, in contexts in which the questionnaire contains a series of different issues, each of which would necessitate construction of a coding scheme, the costs verge on the intolerable. In general, however, "open-ended questions seem to be worth the trouble they take to ask and the complexities in [their] analysis" (Visser et al., p. 238).

Question Ordering

In our discussion of interview methodology (chap.12), we stressed the importance of establishing rapport to help ensure the quality of the interaction, and the truthfulness and completeness of the answers that respondents provide the interviewer. In many questionnaire research contexts, there is little, if any, opportunity to establish rapport. The items are posed by a more or less anonymous questioner, with little attempt at developing any relationship with the research participant, or are presented on a printed page with a brief introduction of purpose. In circumstances like these, question order may become very important. In questionnaire development, the analogue of the rapport-building process requires that the least threatening items be presented first. Only after the respondent has become comfortable with the research, and somewhat committed to it by virtue of answering a number of questions, should more personal or threatening questions be presented. For example, in research on adolescent drug use, it is common that nonthreatening queries be presented before items assessing use of illegal substances are posed. Sometimes the ordering of items can keep a respondent in a study, and this is not a trivial concern.

Another issue related to question order has to do with the possibility that one's earlier answers may affect later ones. For example, suppose we were to ask, "Should freedom of speech be absolutely guaranteed in this country?" Most respondents would answer this question affirmatively. However, the affirmation of this fundamental human right might have ramifications on later answers having to do with the value of freedom—or thought, of expression, and of action. Affirming free speech, that is, probably inclines respondents to a more liberal orientation on later items. However, suppose we were to ask, "Should hate

---

[1]This issue is not relevant in rating scale construction, as the strict formality of scales requires closed questions.

speech be banned?" As before, a reasonable proportion of the respondent sample probably would answer this question affirmatively. In this case, later questions having to do with freedom of expression, thought and action might be colored by this earlier response, but in a way opposite to that exhibited in the first example. The more liberal orientation induced in the first case might be attenuated, and this attenuation would have a discernable effect on later responses.

If the questionnaire items were presented to all respondents in the identical order, this early-item-influence problem could bias the research outcome. To combat this problem, some researchers recommend that questionnaire developers who fear the early-item-influence problem rotate or randomize the order of questionable items (see Tourangeau & Rasinski, 1988).[2] This reordering should not involve the entire questionnaire. The least threatening questions, as noted, always should appear first. However, the order of items that might be mutually reactive should be rotated or randomized within blocks. Thus, if a questionnaire developer anticipates that answers to any of the six items dealing with a particular topic might mutually influence the other answers, the order of the items might be rotated or randomized. Anticipating such interactions among items is not entirely guaranteed, even among researchers intimately acquainted with the content of their items and the likely leanings of their respondents (see Schuman & Presser, 1981).

Drop-Out and the No-Opinion Response Format

Losing respondents is something we want to avoid if at all possible. Whether the respondent loss is attributable to a person's refusal to initiate the questionnaire or to complete it once begun, the loss of respondents represents, at a minimum, a threat to the generalizability of our research results. Persuading potential respondents to take part in our research has been covered elsewhere in this text (e.g., see chap.12). Here we are concerned with respondents who virtually drop out of the research by refusing to answer one or more of the questionnaire's items. Strictly speaking, in these instances, the respondent's entire set of answers should be discarded, and many common statistical routines will, in fact, delete such respondents from the analysis.

One particularly difficult issue that affects the likelihood that a respondent will complete *all* items of a questionnaire is the inclusion or noninclusion of a "no opinion" (or "don't know") option. Some questionnaires allow respondents to indicate that they hold no opinion on an item (or don't know the answer to the question, in a knowledge scale); others allow for a "neutral" response; still others do not provide a "middle of the road" category, forcing respondents to take a stand (albeit, perhaps, a weak stand) on one side or another on the issue. Investigations of the effects of these variations in response format have been conducted for many years (Converse, 1964), and there are good arguments on both sides of the inclusion of the no-response option issue. Respondents generally seem to prefer the no-opinion (or don't know) option (Ehrlich, 1964), and it is our intuition that such attitudes encourage respondents to maintain interest in the questionnaire. Others have suggested that middle of the road responses are inherently ambiguous, reflecting ambivalence, true neutrality, or a reluctance to provide a truthful response (Coombs & Coombs, 1976; Priester, in press; Priester & Petty, 2001). As such, the meaning of the

---

[2]Some researchers even recommend that the order of response options be rotated (e.g., see Krosnick, 1991; Sudman, Bradburn, & Schwarz, 1996). This recommendation is made because of some evidence that suggests that people tend to ascribe more to the initial response options on written questionnaires, and to later options on questionnaires that are read to them by an interviewer (Krosnick & Alwin, 1987; McClendon, 1991).

middle response is difficult to infer. For reasons such as these, some researchers avoid the "don't know" option.

In general, the advantages of allowing a middle option seem to outweigh the negative possibilities. In cases in which a good understanding of participants' feelings about a given issue is particularly critical, it is advisable to provide measures that allow for a clear interpretation of the meaning of such responses, should they occur. Wegener, Downing, Krosnick, and Petty (1995) have suggested a number of different measures that might help us understand the meaning of an apparently neutral response, and we direct the interested reader to this important work.

CONSTRUCTING RATING SCALES

Rating scales are more formalized versions of questionnaires, and are usually designed to measure one specific attitude, value, or personality disposition. Rating scales are the individual difference equivalent of stimulus scales (chap. 14). However, when developing rating scales, a set of central assumptions very different from those of stimulus scales are entertained, and these differences are accompanied by differences in the manner in which data are analyzed. When assessing individual differences on rating (or attitude, or personality) scales, the stimuli are called *items*, and often take the form of a statement the participant is asked to endorse or to reject. Louis Thurstone developed one of the most common forms of such scaling approaches, and although his model has been supplanted by more modern approaches, it forms the basis of many widely used scaling procedures today.

Thurstone's Method of Equal-appearing Intervals

Developing rating scales to measure beliefs, opinions, and attitudes represents a rather recent development in psychology. First attempted by Thurstone (1928, 1931; Thurstone & Chave, 1929), attitude assessment has become one of the social sciences' most important and persistent preoccupations. In the typical Thurstone scale, a respondent is asked to endorse the item or items on the scale with which he or she agrees. Items are designed so that a single item, or a highly restricted range of items, should be endorsed by the respondent, and those that are more extreme and less extreme than the chosen alternative should be rejected. Items of this type have been termed *nonmonotone* (Coombs, 1950) or *noncumulative* (Stouffer, 1950), because it makes little sense to sum a respondent's scores over all of the items of the scale. Agreement with one item, that is, does not imply an increased probability of agreement with any other item on the scale.

In practice, it is very difficult to develop scales of this type. Nunnally (1967) persuasively illustrated this point, by asking, "... how could one find spelling words such that each would be correctly spelled only by persons in a narrow band of the attribute of spelling ability? An item that 'peaked' at the lower end of the scale would be one that is spelled correctly only by rather poor spellers. For an item that peaked in the middle ... very few people with superior ability in spelling would give a correct response" (p. 69). Although the present chapter is not focused on the development of scales of spelling ability, these difficulties are present as well in devising attitude scales based on Thurstone's model. Before discussing the problems involved in Thurstone scales, we consider the means used to develop them. Whereas alternative models of scale construction should be employed in most instances today, understanding Thurstone's approach is important, as it forms the logical basis of many of these more preferred alternatives.

TABLE 15.1

Twelve Items from Thurstone and Chave's (1929) "Attitudes toward the Church" Scale

Item #	Item	Scale Value
1	I think the teaching of the church is altogether too superficial to have much social significance.	8.3
2	I feel the church is petty, always quarrelling over matters that have no interest or significance.	8.6
3	I respect any church-member's beliefs but I think it is all "bunk."	8.8
4	My experience is that the church is hopelessly out of date.	9.1
5	I think the church seeks to impose a lot of worn-out dogmas and medieval superstitions.	9.2
6	I think the church is hundreds of years behind the times and cannot make a dent on modern life.	9.5
7	I think the church is a hindrance to religion for it still depends on magic, superstition, and myth.	9.6
8	The church represents shallowness, hypocrisy, and prejudice.	10.4
9	I regard the church as a static, crystallized institution and as such it is unwholesome and detrimental to society and the individual.	10.5
10	I think the country would be better off if churches were closed and the ministers set to some useful work.	10.5
11	I think the organized church is an enemy of science and truth.	10.7
12	I think the church is a parasite on society.	11.0

The first step in the scale construction process requires the researcher to generate many *potential* items, all of which appear at least initially to relate to the object or attribute of interest. A sufficient number of items to cover the complete range of possible evaluations of the critical object should be assembled. Items should be concise and worded in such a way that their meaning is clear. Double-barrelled items should be avoided, as should items on which either complete acceptance or complete rejection by all the members of the respondent sample can be expected.

In the second phase of the Thurstone scale-construction process, a number of judges are assembled. They independently estimate the degree of favorability or unfavorability that is expressed by each item toward the critical attitude object. A set of items that judges rated in terms of favorability toward a specific attitude object ("The Church") is presented in Table 15.1. This phase of the scale development process is similar to the operations we employ in stimulus scaling, which was discussed in the preceding chapter. Traditionally, an 11-point scale is employed in this process, with the end points of the scale bounded by the phrases "extremely favorable" and "extremely unfavorable." Judges are instructed to disregard their own attitudes in the item-categorization process, and to attempt to ensure that the subjective distances between contiguous points on the 11-point scale are equal.

Once this process is accomplished, the investigator determines the mean favorability rating for each item, and its standard deviation, based on judges' ratings. A large standard deviation is a danger signal, because it suggests that there is considerable disagreement among judges with regard to the favorability of a given item. This result suggests that the meaning of the item probably is ambiguous, and this violates a central assumption, namely that all items are read identically by all respondents. Thus, items exhibiting high standard deviations on the judges' ratings should be discarded.

From the pool of possibilities that remain, a limited number of items (usually 15–25) are chosen to constitute the attitude scale. Items are chosen so that the scale value of the items derived from the judges' ratings cover the entire range of possible opinions toward the attitude object. In addition, items are chosen so that when they are arranged in ascending order with respect to scale values, approximately equal differences are maintained between the means of successive items.[3]

The choice of items completes the final phase of the *scale construction* process. We now move to the *scale utilization* phase. In administering the resulting instrument, the researcher instructs participants to "read all items and choose the two (or three, or four) that best express your feelings on this topic." The average scale value of the items chosen by a respondent is taken as that individual's attitude toward the object or issue under investigation. Instructing respondents to choose two to four items is arbitrary. We suggest, however, that respondents be directed to endorse a limited and specific number of items. Allowing participants to endorse varying numbers of items introduces a degree of variability into the process that most scaling studies might well avoid. A very large number of endorsements should not be requested, because there is a good possibility that this process would force participants to endorse some items that are contrary to their beliefs.

For example, consider the items in Table 15.1, which are drawn from Thurstone and Chave's (1929) *attitude toward the church scale*. These are the 12 statements that express the most unfavorable attitudes on the entire scale. For illustrative purposes, we have presented these items in a manner different from that which a real respondent would experience. First, we have provided the scale values associated with each item. In this instance, higher values represent more negative attitudes. In addition, instead of randomly mixing the items, the usual practice, we have presented them in a systematic order. Now, suppose we asked a respondent to endorse five items. The first four choices are easy for our respondent—they represent her feelings about the church very well. However, the instructions call for five endorsements. Our hypothetical participant might find the slightly more negative statement (Item 8) too extreme, and the slightly less negative statement (Item 3) irrelevant, or too forgiving. By requiring a response to five items, we force the participant to endorse an item (or items) that does not truly express his or her feelings on the critical issue. This, in turn, introduces unnecessary error into the data.

If the scale has been properly constructed, and the respondents are motivated to respond honestly and thoughtfully, it is expected that the items chosen by an individual respondent will be contiguous in terms of mean scale values. If many respondents endorse noncontiguous items, this suggests that the scale is multidimensional, and it should be refined or discarded. Clearly, this noncontinuous item endorsement could occur with the items presented in Table 15.1. Consider item 10, for example. Persons holding extremely negative attitudes toward the institution of the church might not agree with this item because it might suggest to them that the government should impose its sanctions on religion. Although they might not like organized religion, they might feel that freedom of religion is even more important than their dislike of the church. On Item 6, one might agree that the church is indeed hundreds of years behind the times while still acknowledging that it has an enormous, if detrimental, impact on modern life. Items of this sort are not well written because they allow for different interpretations by different people. As such, they should be avoided. As can be seen from Table 15.1, the shorter items appear to avoid the multiple interpretation problem (e.g., see Item 12). It is difficult to misconstrue a simple sentence.

A major common indicator of scale quality—internal consistency (see chap. 3)—is not a meaningful concept in the context of the Thurstone scale construction method, because

---

[3]The equality of intervals separating the scale values of items is an important criterion of Thurstone's technique. If this requirement is met, it suggests that the scale may be treated as being of interval, rather than ordinal, level.

measures of internal consistency make use of participants' responses to all items of a scale. However, test–retest and equivalent forms methods of reliability estimation can and should be undertaken when developing scales of this type. It should be recognized, however, that test–retest reliability is likely to be low in this context, given the method's reliance on a restricted number of item endorsements to represent each individual's attitude. This restriction increases the likelihood that temporal stability will be artificially diminished, because minor changes in scale responses will result in relatively major differences in the mean value of the endorsed items.

In addition to the fact that this scaling model forces the investigator to employ more costly techniques to estimate reliability—and that these are overly susceptible to failure—there are other methodological objections to this approach. For example, whether a judge can be sufficiently objective to disregard important personal feelings in evaluating the favorability of an attitude item is an open question. Hovland and Sherif (1952) found that judges' attitudes toward blacks had a strong influence on the manner in which they viewed the favorability of various items focused on racial prejudice. Items judged as being neutral by racially prejudiced (anti-black) judges were viewed as antagonistic to blacks by blacks and pro-black white judges. On the other hand, Webb (1955) and Upshaw (1965) argued that although the absolute score assigned an item may vary as a function of judges' attitudes, the rank order of the items is maintained (i.e., the *relative* position of items remains unchanged no matter what the judges' attitudes) and thus the utility of Thurstone's stimulus scaling procedure in developing scales of individual differences is maintained. Though this issue is unresolved, there is little disagreement about the fact that the construction of scales through Thurstone scaling techniques is difficult and time-consuming, and, further, that such scales do not take advantages of recent technological developments. For this reason, numerous attempts have been made to improve on and simplify the operations involved in this approach, while at the same time enhancing the quality of the resultant instruments. In the pages that follow, we discuss some of the more popular of the alternative models used in scaling differences among individuals.

Guttman's Scalogram Analysis

One attempt to improve on the Thurstone model was suggested by Louis Guttman (1944, 1947; Guttman & Suchman, 1947). The Guttman scalogram method makes use of the concept of cumulative, or *monotone* items. With items of this type, the more favorable (or extreme) the respondent's attitude, the higher (or more extreme) his or her attitude score. Nunnally's (1967) earlier example of tests of spelling ability here is informative. Presumably, a child who could spell a difficult word would have little trouble with less difficult ones. Similarly, a child who had trouble spelling even easy words would find difficult ones next to impossible to spell correctly. This idea of a cumulative or monotonically increasing level of difficulty (or extremity of belief) lies behind Guttman's approach. The hallmark of the Guttman method is that it presents participants with items of increasing extremity with regard to the issue under investigation. If the scale is of high quality, the individual who endorses an item at a given level of extremity (or favorability) should also respond positively to all less extreme items. Under the most ideal conditions, knowledge of a participant's total score would enable the investigator to reproduce exactly the individual's pattern of responses. Consider the hypothetical scale of Table 15.2.

The items that constitute this scale are arranged in a gradually ascending order with regard to a positive evaluation of (or attitude toward) the socialization of medicine in the United States. If the scale were reliable (or reproducible, to use Guttman's term), we would

TABLE 15.2

Example of Guttman-type Monotone Items

Item #	Item	Yes	No
1	Socialized medicine might in the long run prove to be beneficial to America.		
2	It is probably a good idea that the US begin a program of socialized medicine.		
3	The socialization of medicine is in the best interests of the country.		
4	Socialized medicine would be a very positive move.		
5	Socialized medicine would be the best thing that ever happened to the people of the US.		

expect that a person who endorsed Item 3 would also have endorsed Items 1 and 2. Further, the knowledge that a respondent endorsed two items should enable us to predict with a high degree of certainty that the chosen alternatives were items 1 and 2 (if, that is, the scale were highly reproducible). If an investigator can reconstruct the specific set of alternatives that were chosen by knowing a respondent's total score, the scale is said to possess a high coefficient of reproducibility. To determine the coefficient of reproducibility, the statistical expression of the extent to which participants' patterns of response can be inferred from their total scores, we need know the total number of responses generated by the total sample of respondents, and the number of times that participants' choices fell outside of the predicted pattern of responses. To calculate this statistic, the following formula is used:

Coefficient of Reproducibility $= 1 -$ (Total Errors/Total Responses)

The scale construction procedures employed in the Guttman system are all designed to result in a scale with a high coefficient of reproducibility. It often is assumed that a highly reproducible scale is unidimensional, and thus, must also be internally consistent. Neither the assumption of unidimensionality nor its corollary—the expectation of internal consistency—is necessarily correct. If the probability of endorsement (i.e., the "popularity" of an item) varies greatly from item-to-item within a given scale, it is possible to obtain a very high coefficient of reproducibility with items that have nothing whatever to do with one another.

The difficulty involved in establishing a trustworthy (internal consistency) reliability coefficient for Guttman's scaling approach has resulted in its relative under utilization. Green (1956), Cliff (1977), and Kenny and Rubin (1977) all discussed this issue and proposed alternate (and generally more conservative) methods of assessing the reproducibility of Guttman scales. Although all of these alternatives represent improvements over the standard method, none as yet has gained widespread acceptance. As such, the tendency among many attitude researchers is to avoid Guttman's approach unless it is very clearly suggested by the research operations. One exception to this general observation is found in the social distance measure devised by Bogardus (1959). This is still a popular measure, used to assess the extent of social distance a person would be most comfortable maintaining between himself or herself and a representative member of some identified group (Catholic, Armenian, dockworker, etc.).

In some situations, Guttman's model appears tailor-made for the research issue. For example, in a study of the factors that influence the likelihood that people will act in accordance with their opinions, Sivacek and Crano (1982) asked people (a) if they were willing to sign a petition on behalf of an action that was clearly consistent with an attitude they had expressed, (b) whether they were willing to volunteer to work on behalf of the cause they had espoused, and finally (c) the amount of time they were willing to devote to the cause. These (monotone) behavioral "items" appear to be perfectly suited for Guttman's scaling approach. We reasoned that if a person were willing to volunteer to work on behalf of a given issue, he or she probably would be willing to sign a petition that fostered that position; similarly, if the participant were unwilling even to sign a petition in support of an issue, he or she would probably also be unwilling to work on its behalf. In this instance, the researchers' insights proved correct. The short 3-item Guttman scale had a strong coefficient of reproducibility, and subsidiary data that were gathered over the course of Sivacek and Crano's (1982) research suggested the validity of the items for measuring commitment to the issue under study.

In many circumstances, the Guttman approach either does not lend itself so neatly to the demands of the research or the research does not provide a means of validating the scale, that is, determining whether the items that constitute the scale accurately represent the construct that they are intended to assess. In circumstances such as these, and they are by far more common than those that foster the use of Guttman's scaling model, the scalogram approach probably should be avoided.

Likert's Method of Summated Ratings

The model of scale construction designed by Renesis Likert (1932) represents one of the two most popular approaches for generating reliable scales of individual differences. When compared with the Thurstone method of equal appearing intervals, or Guttman's scalogram approach, Likert's model proves not only more efficient in terms of time and resource expenditure, but also more effective in developing scales of high reliability (in terms of both internal consistency and temporal stability).

In the Likert method, items are presented in a "multiple choice" format. On each item, participants are asked to pick one of (usually) five alternatives that indicate the extent to which they agree with the position espoused in the item. Response options commonly presented are "Strongly Agree," "Agree," "Neutral or Undecided," "Disagree," and "Strongly Disagree."

So, in a scale of attitudes toward the Army, participants might be asked to respond to the statement, "The U.S. Army has been a positive force for peace throughout the world" through the use of these five alternatives. Presumably, a person with a favorable attitude toward the Army would "agree" or "strongly agree" with the statement, whereas an individual with a negative view of the Army would be more likely to endorse the "disagree" or "strongly disagree" options. If we assign values of 1 to 5 to these response options (with higher scores representing more positive attitudes), then a person's overall attitude toward a given issue or entity would be represented by the *sum* of his or her responses over all of the items on the scale.

The item employed here is an example of a *positively worded* statement because agreement indicates a favorable attitude toward the object in question; in this instance, the Army. An unfavorably worded item (or negatively scored) item is one on which strong agreement indicates a strong negative attitude (and in these instances, the scoring procedure is reversed, i.e., "Strongly agree" is scored +1, whereas "Strongly disagree" is given the score of +5). An example of an item that reverses the intent of the previous example might be, "The Army has had a negative effect on world peace."

The summation process used to calculate a total attitude scale score is an implicit recognition of the fact that any single item is at best a fallible indicator of the underlying cognitive construct (i.e., the attitude) it is intended to represent. By combining a participant's responses over a number of such items, however, we are able to minimize the "noise" or error that the imperfections of the items contribute to the overall score (especially if the items have different sources of error, or invalidity), and thereby arrive at a more precise measure of the construct of interest. If we consider each item in a "Likert scale" as an operational definition of the attitude it is intended to tap, then the logic of this scaling approach is consistent with the logic of multiple operationism. We assume that all of the "operations" (i.e., items) will miss the mark to some extent (that is, no single item will perfectly capture the attitude it is intended to represent), but we attempt to design them such that they miss it in different ways; thus, the resulting scale (i.e., the total score across all items) should provide a more sure identification of the construct of interest than any single item. The scale construction process developed by Likert is undertaken with the aim of eliminating to the extent possible the influence of item "irrelevancies," and thereby arriving at the best operationalization (scale) of people's evaluations on any given issue (Crano, 2000).

The initial steps of scale development undertaken in this scaling method resemble those of both Thurstone and Guttman. As in these earlier mentioned approaches, a large number of potential items are collected, and those that are obviously double-barreled, ambiguous, or confusing are either rewritten or discarded. At this point the similarity to earlier methods ends, for rather than searching for items that represent the entire continuum of possible evaluations, the Likert model calls for items that are *moderately* favorable or unfavorable toward the attitude object under study. Because respondents can indicate their *degree* of agreement with each item, generating items of widely varying degrees of favorability is unnecessary. The response format itself provides the indication of extremity. Given the scale construction procedures employed in developing Likert-type scales, the use of extreme items in the initial research phases would be a waste of effort, because the later scaling operations would almost certainly indicate that such items should be discarded.

After creating a number of items that appear to tap the construct of interest, and to tap it unambiguously, the researcher administers the item set to a group of respondents. It is advisable to multiply the number of items by 5 to 10 when estimating the number of respondents necessary for this phase of the scale construction process; thus, the initial assessment process to determine the quality of a set of 20 items would call for the use of approximately 100–200 respondents.

After collecting participants' responses, the items are scored (typically, on a 1–5 basis, as noted earlier), and these scores are summed over each participant, thereby creating a total score for each person. Then, the complete matrix of intercorrelations between all pairs of items, and between each item and the total score, is calculated. Most computer-based routines used to compute correlation matrices also provide sufficient auxiliary information to allow for the calculation of coefficient alpha as an index of internal consistency (see chap. 3; all that is necessary is information regarding the number of items in the scale, and the standard deviations of the individual items and of the total score). However, it is important to realize that whenever a large number of items are used in this initial scale construction phase, the resulting alpha coefficient will almost certainly be large, if the choice of items was at all reasonable.

The investigator's primary research function at this point is to discover the items that form the best scale, retain these, and discard those that fail to discriminate between individuals who have different attitudes (as inferred from their total scores). Coefficient alpha, an estimate of the internal consistency of the entire set of items, is not useful in an item-by-item analysis of this type. Of more practical utility is the investigation of each item's correlation with the total score (see chap. 3). The logic of this approach is straightforward. As noted, the total score is conceptualized as the best single estimate of the attitude under investigation. However, because this score is the outcome of many items, some of which probably are of low quality, the total score is far from a perfect representation of the underlying construct. To improve the precision of the scale, the investigator must discard the least discriminating items. One useful way to do this is to discard those items that do not correlate strongly with the total score. In developing the final scale, the researcher assembles those items having the highest item-total score correlations. Given the dangers of response bias (discussed later in this chapter), it is advisable to use equal numbers of favorably worded and unfavorably worded statements.

After having decided on the best items, and discarded the worst ones, it is necessary to recalculate the item-total correlation of the "reduced set" of attitude statements, because a new total score emerges any time an item is discarded. If the initially strong correlations are maintained, or improved, the investigator then should recalculate coefficient alpha on the reduced set to determine the degree of interrelatedness among items. An alpha coefficient of .75 or higher suggests that the scale is reasonably reliable (i.e., internally consistent). However, because this scale construction process capitalizes on sample-specific variations (i.e., error), some "shrinkage" in the reliability coefficient must be expected when the item set is readministered to another group of participants. The extent of such attenuation is usually not severe unless the new sample is very different from that on which the scale was developed originally.

If coefficient alpha is weak (e.g., if it falls short of an arbitrary value of .70), the internal consistency can be improved by the addition of more items that correlate positively with the original set and, consequently, with the total score. This item-adding process can be continued until the desired level of reliability has been reached. It sometimes happens that an unreasonable number of items prove necessary to satisfy the criterion of internal consistency; in such cases, the investigator almost certainly has developed a multidimensional scale, which taps more than a single attitude or knowledge base. When this occurs, a factor analytic procedure can be employed to illuminate the source of the difficulties, and to help salvage some of the resources that had been expended to that point in the scale-construction process.

Once the items are selected, they are assembled into the new scale. The scale then can be administered to a new set of participants. If the development process described here was followed carefully, and the participants are drawn from the same general population as those on whom the scale was developed, we can be reasonably sure that the internal consistency of the measure will be maintained. The scale is scored as described in the scale development phase: scores are assigned to each of the (typically) five choices (i.e., strongly agree, agree, neutral, disagree, strongly disagree), such that higher item scores all indicate the same valence. Scale reliability is calculated and, if satisfactory, scale sums are calculated for each respondent.

In Likert-type scales, the usual response format uses five response options, which typically range from strongly agree to strongly disagree. However, recent research suggests that seven point scales might provide data of higher reliability and validity, especially if the scale taps both positive and negative evaluations (i.e., if the scale is bipolar). With unipolar scales (i.e., the participant's judgment can range from none to extreme), five point scales are indicated. Unipolar scales might be used to assess respondents' evaluations of the interest value of a TV ad (from none to lots), the importance of an issue, or the degree to which one policy might be preferred over another (see Krosnick & Fabrigar, in press).

Osgood's Semantic Differential Technique

Although Likert's approach is an important technical advance over both the Thurstone and Guttman methods, it nonetheless shares some of the liabilities of these procedures. All

Socialized Medicine

Good :__:__:__:__:__:__:__: Bad

Kind :__:__:__:__:__:__:__: Cruel

Beautiful :__:__:__:__:__:__:__: Ugly

Pleasant :__:__:__:__:__:__:__: Unpleasant

Unfair :__:__:__:__:__:__:__: Fair

Honest :__:__:__:__:__:__:__: Dishonest

Dirty :__:__:__:__:__:__:__: Clean

Valuable :__:__:__:__:__:__:__: Worthless

Negative :__:__:__:__:__:__:__: Positive

Wise :__:__:__:__:__:__:__: Foolish

FIG. 15.1. Example of a series of semantic differential items used to evaluate the concept of socialized medicine.

three scaling models, for example, require relatively major expenditures of time and effort in the scale-construction process. And, although a computer is not absolutely necessary in this process, it certainly is a useful addition. Finally, all three techniques require the development of a new set of items each time participants' attitudes toward a new person or object are to be assessed.

For these reasons, a technique pioneered by Osgood and his colleagues (Osgood, 1962; Osgood, Suci, & Tannenbaum, 1957; Snider & Osgood, 1969) has become popular in contemporary attitude research. The original development of this scaling model was stimulated by Osgood's attempts to determine the subjective meanings people attach to words or concepts. Rather than asking respondents to respond to a variety of statements concerning the concept under study (as in the Likert or Thurstone approaches, for example), Osgood instead presented the concept directly and asked his participants to react to it through the use of a number of 7-point scales bounded by bipolar adjectives, as in the illustration of Fig. 15.1.[4]

Items of this type are called *semantic differential* scales. Osgood's approach required the administration of a large number of such scales to a great many respondents, who were instructed to use the scales in rating a number of diverse concepts (concepts could range from political figures to current events to respondents' evaluations of themselves). All the ratings made on any one scale were then correlated with those made on each of the other scales, and these data were factor analyzed. The results of this type of analysis provided information regarding the extent to which various bipolar scales clustered together, and were independent from other scales. Scales that "load on the same factor" are highly interrelated with one another and relatively weakly related with other scales that do not load on their factor. It is assumed that scales that cluster together are focusing on the same underlying psychological dimension or construct.

A number of studies of this type were conducted (see Osgood & Luria, 1954, 1976; Osgood et al., 1957; Snider & Osgood, 1969) with widely varying concepts being employed and with respondents from 26 different cultures around the world. Over the past decade, more than 500 different studies making use of the semantic differential method, from

---

[4]Bipolar adjectives are logical opposites, or antonyms.

all parts of the globe, have been published. A consistent finding has emerged: Over all of these investigations, the scales that connote an *evaluation* of the object of judgment generally are highly interrelated and, in addition, tend to account for the most "meaning" in respondents' subjective definitions of the object.

Usually, two clusters of scales focused on connotations other than evaluation also have emerged in studies of the semantic differential, the first consisting of scales connoting the *potency* of the object being assessed (e.g., strong/weak), and the second consisting of scales connoting *activity* (e.g., active/passive). The cluster of evaluative scales, however, proves most interesting to attitude researchers, because they assume that a person's evaluation of an object, and his or her attitude toward the object, are synonymous. Given this reasoning, an investigator can operationally define an individual's attitude as the sum of the person's (semantic differential) evaluative scale responses toward the object in question. So, for example, to use semantic differential scales to measure people's attitudes toward socialized medicine, we might employ the evaluative scales presented in Fig. 15.1. The format of this example is typical of studies of this type. A respondent's attitude in this case is defined as the *sum* of his or her scores over all 10 of the semantic differential evaluative scales when rating the concept of socialized medicine.

In this measurement approach, a respondent checks the point on the scale that best indicates his or her degree of positive or negative reaction to the concept in question. In such investigations, it is common that other scales are interspersed among the critical evaluative items. Scales connoting potency (e.g., strong–weak, rugged–delicate, large–small, hard–soft, heavy–light, etc.), and activity (e.g., active–passive, quick–slow, sharp–dull, excitable–calm, hot–cold) often are included. However, in defining respondents' attitudes only the responses on the evaluative items are summated. The summation process is identical to that involved in Likert scaling, and it involves the same assumptions, dangers, and so on. Usually, as illustrated here, 7-point scales are used in semantic differential research, and higher scores are used to connote positive evaluations of the object.

The semantic differential approach offers many practical advantages. Given the nature of the statistical process through which the various factors or "clusters" of items were developed, it is safe to assume that the internal consistency of such a measurement instrument (in which the total score is based on responses to one particular type of scale) will be high. Likewise, investigations of the temporal stability of such instruments have also provided strong support for this measurement approach (e.g., Jenkins, Russel, & Suci, 1957; Osgood et al., 1957; Snider & Osgood, 1969). The generality of the evaluative response as a major component of an individual's subjective reaction toward any object also is extremely advantageous. The semantic differential technique apparently offers the researcher a ready-made attitude scale for assessing the beliefs and attitudes of almost anyone toward almost anything (see Osgood & Luria, 1954, 1976). As such, it offers a tremendous practical advantage over the more classical forms of attitude assessment, all of which demand considerably greater expenditures in terms of instrument development time.

Of course, care and common sense must be exercised when choosing the specific evaluative scales that are to constitute the measurement instrument, because the specific attitude object under investigation could affect the meaning or appropriateness of the scales employed. For example, the bipolar adjectives fair–unfair appear very appropriate if used to determine people's attitudes toward a Justice of the U.S. Supreme Court; these same qualifiers, however, would be less than optimal if the object of judgment were Blue Bell Natural Ice Cream. In circumstances of this type, the use of inappropriate evaluative scales introduces unnecessary error or imprecision. To detect the presence of this problem (because, sometimes, inappropriate scale-concept pairings are difficult to recognize), it is wise to calculate coefficient alpha and item-total correlations on all scales composed of evaluative semantic differential items. A strong coefficient of internal consistency and high item-total correlations suggest that the scales chosen to measure the critical attitude object were appropriate. Of course, the implications derived from this information would suggest only that the particular semantic differential scales that were chosen appear reasonable.

Indirect Approaches

The unidimensional and multidimensional scaling approaches discussed to this point, in the present and the preceding chapters, have involved the *direct* assessment of peoples' attitudes, preferences, judgments, or knowledge. Over the years, a number of techniques focused on the *indirect* assessment of attitudes have been developed. We introduce the concept of indirect attitude measurement in this chapter, and in chapter 16, we consider in detail some approaches designed to measure implicit thoughts and feelings, of which the respondent often is unaware or unwilling to divulge.

In indirect attitude assessment, "the investigator interprets the responses in terms of dimensions and categories different from those held in mind by the respondent while answering" (Kidder & Campbell, 1970, p. 336). Indirect approaches are used to reduce possible distortions that might come about when respondents, attempting to place themselves in a more favorable light, answer questions in a socially desirable, rather than honest, manner. Many researchers feel that they can obtain more accurate evaluations of respondents by having them focus their attention on irrelevant but compelling features of the experimental task. Using misdirection, it is hoped that respondents will lower their defenses, and thus present a more valid picture of their attitudes. Kidder (1969, cited in Kidder & Campbell, 1970, p. 369) has reported data that support this supposition, but some studies (e.g., Malvin & Moskowitz, 1983; Singer, 1978) indicate that self-report responses on sensitive issues, such as drug use, are essentially the same whether respondents are identified by name (and assured confidentiality) or are anonymous.

A variety of indirect techniques have been developed, but it must be said that the success of such attempts sometimes is less than overwhelming (see Dovidio & Fazio, 1992). Consider the following: suppose a researcher were interested in indirectly assessing respondents' attitudes toward labor unions, and decided to employ a sentence completion task for this purpose. In the instructions, the investigator might ask respondents to be "as creative as possible in completing the following sentence stems," among which would be the following:

"The cost of living . . .

"The Teamsters have . . .

"Unions are . . .

Although the participants might focus on creativity in composing their responses, the researcher would actually be interested in the content of their completions. "Filler" items often are included in such tasks to mask even more completely the intent of the study.

In addition to sentence completion tests, Thematic Apperception Tests (TAT) have been employed to assess attitudes indirectly or surreptitiously. In the TAT format, a respondent views a picture for a brief period, and then generates a story concerning the characters in the picture. The content of the respondent's story can be analyzed in light of the specific issues under investigation. The intent of such a measure is far from transparent, and thus, users of the TAT hope that the method will allow them to obtain more honest and unbiased answers from their respondents than if a more direct means of assessment were employed.

Tetlock and Suedfeld (1988; see also Suedfeld, Tetlock, & Streufert, 1992) helped develop a method of coding the integrative complexity (the capacity to integrate many different features of a complex issue to come to a meaningful synthesis) of political leaders, based on the leaders' own public statements. Expanding on a method developed by Schroder and his colleagues (e.g., Gardiner & Schroder, 1972; Schroder, Driver, & Streufert, 1976), this approach codes public pronouncements and attempts to develop insights into the depth and complexity of leaders' understanding of important issues. This approach has yielded interesting insights into the cognitive features of various leaders, typically in stressful circumstances. It obviously is indirect, in that the leaders probably did not assume that Suedfeld and his colleagues were tapping into their cognitive structures as they delivered their policy statements.

It must be acknowledged that these forms of assessment (the sentence completion, the TAT, the coding of cognitive complexity) make considerable demands on the time and technical expertise of the investigator because the responses typically gathered in these methods do not lend themselves to easy scoring. Generally, coders must be taught how to analyze the content of respondents' responses, and this training is labor intensive and time consuming. In addition, it is necessary that some estimates of the reliability of the scoring procedure be developed—these usually involve an assessment of the extent of agreement among coders (see chap.11). If the reliability level is unacceptable, coders must be retrained. Even given these difficulties, however, indirect measures sometimes provide valuable insights into processes that otherwise could not be studied (imagine President Bush allowing an investigator to measure his cognitive complexity). Despite the difficulties, and particularly in settings where unconscious motives might be involved, indirect approaches may be the only reasonable measurement method available. Under such circumstances, the difficulties involved in data acquisition and scoring must be considered part of the cost of admission.

The systematic measurement of people's underlying beliefs, knowledge, attitudes, and values represents a major achievement of social science research. Owing to the courage and imagination of our psychometric forebears, and the technical virtuosity of those that followed, we have developed in the social sciences a set of techniques that allow us to peer into the thought processes of cooperative respondents (and sometimes, noncooperative ones as well; see chap. 16). Scientifically grounded scaling approaches represent one of our field's greatest achievements. Properly applied, well-designed questionnaires and scales allow us some access to the innermost thoughts and evaluations of our respondents, and help us to understand the will of the group under observation. Because of this, questionnaires and attitude scales are powerful tools for applied and basic research. From scientific polling techniques to theory-testing research, behavioral researchers rely heavily on these self-report instruments as a versatile component of our methodological tool chest.

SUGGESTED READINGS

Priester, J. R., & Petty, R. E. (2001). Extending the bases of subjective attitudinal ambivalence: Interpersonal and intrapersonal antecedents of evaluative tension. *Journal of Personality and Social Psychology, 80*, 19–34.

Snider, J. G., & Osgood, C. E. (Eds.). (1969). *Semantic differential technique.* Chicago: Aldine.

Tourangeau, R., & Rasinski, K. A. (1988). Cognitive processes underlying context effects in attitude measurement. *Psychological Bulletin, 103*, 299–314.

16

SOCIAL COGNITION METHODS: MEASURING IMPLICIT THOUGHTS AND FEELINGS

In social research, as in any other field of science, the use of the scientific method requires that assertions be based on observable phenomena (see chap. 1). Inferences about the causes and processes underlying social behavior must first be grounded in observations that can be recorded and replicated. Research that employs the experimental method involves manipulating some aspect of the physical or social environment, and then observing and recording some type of response on the part of participants in the experimental session. In some studies, the observed response is an overt behavior or action of some kind (e.g., stopping to give help, pressing a button to deliver an electric shock to another person, choosing a gift). More often, however, the observed response is a written or oral report from a participant of his or her reactions to the situation, a judgment, or a decision. Similarly, in survey research involving interviews or questionnaires, the observations consist of respondents' self-reports of their behaviors, feelings, or beliefs. Because inner experiences—personal feelings and mental life—are not directly observable, social researchers must often rely on people's introspective reports of their private experience to acquire data that are amenable to recording and quantification.

Previous chapters raised a number of issues and problems that must be considered in evaluating the validity of self-report measures as accurate assessments of respondents' true feelings and beliefs. When respondents are aware that they are participants in a scientific investigation, evaluation apprehension and social desirability concerns may lead them to censure or adjust their responses to meet personal or social standards or expectations (see chap. 6). In many situations, participants may be unwilling to report on their true feelings or reactions, particularly when embarrassing, sensitive, or politically charged issues are at stake.

Even when respondents are willing to provide truthful and candid accounts, they may be *unable* to report accurately on their own inner feelings or mental states. For example, Nisbett and Wilson (1977) argued that individuals do not have conscious access to many of the mental processes that underlie their behaviors or decisions, at least not in a manner that they can verbalize or and articulate.

Given the evidence that respondents are often either unwilling or unable to provide valid reports on certain aspects of their inner experiences or mental processes, exclusive reliance on introspective self-reports as the principal source of information about internal reactions is problematic. Fortunately, over the past few decades, social researchers have developed an armory of new techniques and procedures for tapping the "inner world" of cognitive processes and affective experiences that do not rely on conscious self-report. Because many of these techniques for "getting inside the head" (Taylor & Fiske, 1981) have been adapted from methods developed by cognitive scientists, they are often referred to collectively as *social cognition methodologies*, although some are intended to assess affect, emotions, and motives as well as cognitive processes. The methods described in this chapter cannot fully replace self-report measures as a mainstay of social research, but they can augment more traditional methods by providing different types of information that are not susceptible to the same motivational or capability limitations.

INFORMATION PROCESSING: ATTENTION AND MEMORY

Many of the methods for assessing cognition derive from a general model of information processing that assumes that knowledge about the world and experiences is acquired and remembered through four stages or operations: *attention* (what information is taken in), *encoding* (how that information is understood and interpreted at the time of intake), *storage* (how information is retained in long-term memory), and *retrieval* (what information is accessible in memory). Methodologically, these processes are traced or documented by way of various techniques for assessing selective attention, processing time, and memory.

Measures of Attention

The information processing model assumes that attention is a limited resource that is selectively distributed among myriad visual, auditory, and other sensory stimuli that bombard us at any one point in time. It is further assumed that the particular stimuli that capture and hold a person's attention are those that are most salient or important to the perceiver at the time. Thus, by measuring which inputs a person attends to when multiple alternative stimuli are available, or measuring how long the person attends to some stimuli compared to others, we have an indirect way of assessing what is important, interesting, or salient to that individual.

Visual Attention. The majority of research on attention (and hence, methods for assessing attention) focuses on the processing of visual information—either actual events that are being observed or displays of pictures, words, or other symbols. Measures of visual attention involve tracking direction and duration of eye gaze, that is, when and how long the perceiver's eyes are fixated on a particular object or event in the visual field.[1] Russo and Rosen (1975), for example, assessed visual fixation patterns to analyze consumer choices, using the sequence of eye fixation to trace what aspects of the items were being attended to during the decision process. In another application, McArthur and Ginsberg (1981) used eye tracking to measure selective attention to specific individuals during an impression formation task.

---

[1] In actuality, eye fixations shift three or four times a second within minute distances even while attending to a single object. However, this level of precision is not appropriate for most social research purposes, where more gross assessments of direction of gaze are sufficient.

Precise measurement of eye fixation patterns entails heavy technology and may require that participants hold their heads still in an apparatus so that their eye movements may be tracked and recorded across small distances. Computerized methods for producing visual displays and recording sequential eye movements are routinely used in visual research, but are generally less accessible or useful for social research. For purposes of social information processing, videotaping participants' faces during social interactions or decision making will usually provide sufficient information about location and duration of eye gaze to determine what is being attended to at specific points in time. Olson and Zanna (1979), for example, videotaped participants' eye gaze while they inspected a pair of painting reproductions in a study of selective exposure following decision making. In this case, the measure of interest was how much time participants spent looking at the painting they had chosen while avoiding the unchosen alternative. Eye gaze proved to be a sensitive measure of such selective self-exposure.

Interference as a Measure of Attention.   Another way of assessing how much attention is being paid to a particular stimulus is to determine whether the presence of the stimulus interferes with attending to or processing other information in the environment. The well-known Stroop effect (Stroop, 1935) is an example of an interference-based measure of unintended attention. In this research paradigm, the participant's task is to report the color in which each of a succession of words is written. If the word itself is the name of a color (e.g., the word "red" written in green ink), the semantic meaning of the word interferes with the participant's ability to produce the correct color response. Thus, it takes longer to give the response on trials when an interfering color name has been presented compared with trials in which the word is matched with the ink color or the word is irrelevant to the color naming task. This response interference is an indication that attending to the semantic meaning of the printed word is automatic and cannot be suppressed even when it is not relevant to the task at hand.

The Stroop effect has been adapted as a general measure of automatic attention (see Logan, 1980, and MacLeod, 1991, for reviews). Pratto and John (1991), for example, used the effect to study automatic attention to negative information. Respondents in this experiment were instructed to name the colors in which trait words were written. Some of the words referred to desirable traits (such as "honest") and others referred to undesirable, negative traits (e.g., "sadistic"). Latencies to respond with the correct color name were consistently longer when undesirable words were presented, suggesting that participants had a hard time ignoring social stimuli with strong negative connotations.

Processing Time.   A third method for assessing how important or significant particular information is to the perceiver is to measure the amount of time the individual spends viewing or contemplating the information before making a decision or judgment or moving on to another processing task. Duration of eye gaze is one measure of processing time, but more often this method is used when information is presented sequentially, as, for example, paragraphs displayed successively on a computer screen or successive slides projected on a movie screen. If the participant is given control over the movement from one screen to the next, the amount of time spent viewing a particular item provides a measure of processing time for that information.

As a measure of attention or interest, processing time is somewhat ambiguous because the measure includes time spent encoding or interpreting the stimulus object (the second stage of information processing) as well as simply attending to it. Thus, more complex or ambiguous stimuli may engage longer processing time independent of their interest value. Nonetheless, time spent viewing particular information in a sequence may often provide useful information about what types of information attract the most attention and cognitive effort. For instance, Fiske (1980) found that social stimuli (slides depicting social behaviors) that were rare, extreme, or negative elicited increased processing time. Similarly, Brewer, Dull, and Lui (1981) used looking time to demonstrate that information that is inconsistent with category stereotypes takes longer to process than information that is consistent with stereotypic expectancies.

Measures of Memory

The extent to which individuals can remember information or experiences provides significant clues regarding what information has been encoded and how it is stored in memory. In most social research employing memory as a dependent variable, the memory "test" is introduced unexpectedly, without advance warning, to assess what is encoded and stored spontaneously when perceivers are not deliberately attempting to memorize the information that has been provided. Memory may be assessed in either of two ways: recall or recognition. With recall measures, the participant is asked to report what he or she remembers about information that has been previously presented. This task requires both searching memory for relevant material (retrieval) and assessing whether the retrieved information is correct (i.e., that the person believes it was actually present on the occasion being recalled). Recognition measures, on the other hand, bypass the retrieval stage. The researcher provides items of information and it is the respondent's task to judge whether that information was or was not present at the earlier time.

Recall Measures. The typical paradigm for recall memory experiments involves an initial presentation of stimulus information, which may be anything from a list of words, a series of pictures, a written description or story, or a videotaped event. Usually the participant is given some cover story about why he or she is viewing the information (e.g., evaluating the writing style, forming an impression) that does not involve explicit instructions to remember the material being presented. After the presentation, a specific amount of time is allowed to lapse, and then the participant is asked to report everything they can remember of what was presented earlier.[2] With a *free recall* task, the participant is given no further instructions about what to search for in memory and is free to list anything that he or she thinks is relevant. With *cued recall*, the participant is specifically instructed as to what type of information to remember (e.g., what were the persons in the video wearing, what personality characteristics were listed, what did person X say during the presentation, etc.). In either case, the participant provides a written listing (either specific words or brief summaries) of each thing they can recall from the original presentation.

Memory protocols produced from recall tests can be analyzed in a number of different ways, depending on what the researcher is hoping to learn from the content of the recalled material. The volume or quantity of memory (i.e., the number of different items listed) is sometimes used as a measure of the degree of attention and elaboration the material

---

[2]The time interval between presentation and recall can vary from just a few minutes to a matter of hours or days, depending on whether short-term or long-term memories are being assessed. When the recall measure is taken in the same session within minutes of the original presentation, participants are usually given some unrelated "filler" task to occupy their attention during the interval and prevent active rehearsal of the presented materials. When the recall measure occurs at some later time in a separate session, the researcher has less control over the intervening events and cannot know whether the participant has been thinking about or rehearsing the presentation during the lapsed period of time. However, because participants had not been instructed to remember what they experienced, it is generally assumed that such rehearsal is unlikely.

received when originally presented. A sparse listing of details suggests relatively little active processing of the stimulus materials; greater volume suggests more processing. For this purpose, it does not necessarily matter whether the "recalled" information was actually presented or reflects the perceiver's own internal cognitions generated during the presentation stage (Petty & Cacioppo, 1986). For this reason, the sheer quantity of recall is an imprecise measure of encoding that occurred *during* the original presentation, because we cannot know whether respondents are recording thoughts that they had at the time of the presentation, or thoughts that were generated later, during the recall task itself.

More often researchers are interested in the degree of *accurate* recall represented in the memory protocol, that is, the items listed that match information actually presented at the earlier time. For this purpose, the recall lists must be evaluated and each item scored as correct or incorrect.[3] The final measure may then be the number of items correctly recalled (overall accuracy of recall), or the researcher may be interested in which items were more likely to be accurately recalled (compared to information forgotten or incorrectly recalled). Finally, the researcher may be interested not only in the items correctly recalled, but also in the content of *errors* as represented by the items in the recall list that do not match information actually presented. Such incorrect items are referred to as memory "intrusions" and provide clues as to how the original material was encoded and interpreted before being stored in memory. Unfortunately, intrusion errors in recall protocols provide a very imperfect indicator of encoding processes. First, participants are often very cautious about what items they report on a recall measure (assuming that they are being tested for accuracy) and so do not list items unless they are fairly confident that they actually appeared. As a consequence, the number of intrusions may be very small and unreliable as a measure of cognitive activity. Second, when intrusions do occur, we cannot tell whether they reflect cognitions that were generated at the time of the original presentation or simply bad "guesses" about information that cannot be recalled correctly.[4] For this reason, recognition measures are often more appropriate for the study of memory errors than are recall measures.

A third method of analysis of recall protocols involves paying attention to the *sequencing* of the items recalled, specifically, which items are remembered first or later, and/or which items are recalled together. The former provides information about *accessibility* in memory (i.e., which information is recalled most easily and rapidly and which requires more search time and effort). The latter (measures of *clustering* in recall) provides information about how material has been organized in memory. Clustering measures are most often useful when information has been originally presented in some random or haphazard order but then appears in a different, more systematic order on the recall listings. Clustering measures are indices of the frequency with which items of the same type (or category) appear sequentially in the recall protocol compared to chance.[5] These indices are used to document the kinds of categorizations that perceivers make use of to encode and organize

---

[3]Different standards of accuracy may be applied depending on the type of material being recalled. When very specific items of information have been presented, an exact match may be required for correctness. However, when the information is more complex or ambiguous, items are often evaluated by the "gist" criterion. That is, an item is scored as correct if the coder judges that it captures the general idea of what was presented.

[4]The same problem applies to interpretation of accurate responses because we cannot know whether correct items represent actual memory of the presented materials or simply good "guesses." However, the more detailed and complex the information that has been presented and recalled, the less likely it is that guessing accounts for accuracy.

[5]The two most commonly used clustering measures are the Stimulus Category Repetition index (SCR) developed by Bousfield and Bousfield (1966), and the Adjusted Ratio of Clustering (ARC) measure recommended by Roenker, Thompson, and Brown (1971). See Hamilton et al. (1980) and Ostrom, Pryor, and Simpson (1981) for discussions of the relative merits of each of these indices for social cognition research.

incoming information in memory. For example, Hamilton, Katz, and Leirer (1980) used a measure of clustering in output of recall to show how behavioral information is organized in memory when perceivers are engaged in an impression formation task. In another social information processing study, Pryor and Ostrom (1981) used clustering measures to assess how incoming information about multiple persons in a social situation is processed and organized in memory. They found that when the persons were familiar individuals known to the perceiver, information was encoded and organized by individual person. But when the social stimuli were unfamiliar persons, memory was organized by behavior categories rather than on a person-by-person basis.

Recognition Measures.   As a test of the content of memory, recognition does not require the respondent to retrieve items from the memory store but to identify whether information suggested by the researcher was among the materials presented on a prior occasion. The difference between recall and recognition measures of memory parallels the difference between an essay exam and a multiple-choice exam (Taylor & Fiske, 1981). As with a good multiple-choice exam, the researcher using recognition methods must carefully design and select wrong answers ("foils") that will appear to be correct if the respondent's memory of the earlier material includes cognitions and assumptions that were not actually presented at the time. With recognition measures, the researcher's interest is more often in the types of errors that are made than in the degree of accuracy of memory.

In general, there are two different kinds of recognition tasks. In one paradigm, the respondent's task is to review each item presented by the researcher and indicate whether that item of information was or was not seen before by responding "old" or "new" (or "true," "false"). False recognitions (responding "old" to an item that was not actually present) provide information about how the original materials were encoded and stored along with prior knowledge or inferences that the perceiver brought to bear at the time the information was received and processed. In social psychology, false recognition has been used to study the use of social category stereotypes in forming impressions of individual persons. For example, Cantor and Mischel (1977) demonstrated that participants misremembered trait information that had not actually been presented if it was consistent with the personality type ("introvert" or "extravert") that had been attributed to the person described.

The second type of recognition measure involves assessing memory confusions. In this case, participants are given two or more options and asked to indicate which one corresponds to information presented in the original materials. An interesting application of the recognition confusion method is the who-said-what paradigm originally developed by Taylor, Fiske, Etcoff, and Ruderman (1978). In this paradigm, participants first view an audio-visual presentation of a discussion among a group of six persons. The content of the discussion is presented on audio tape while a picture of the individual group member who is speaking is projected on a screen. Later in the session, the participant is shown an array of photos of the group members and a series of sentences that occurred during the discussion. For each sentence, the participant is to choose which specific group member made that particular statement. What is of interest here is which group members are confused with each other when an incorrect choice is made. In the original experiment using this method, Taylor et al. (1978) varied the composition of the discussion group to determine whether discussants were automatically categorized by sex or race while viewing the presentation. Consistent with the idea of automatic categorization, when the group consisted of three males and three females (or three black and three white males), recognition errors were more likely to involve confusing one male with another male or one female with another female (*intracategory* errors) than attributing a statement made by a female to a male or vice versa (*intercategory* errors). Like clustering measures in recall, recognition confusions are used to assess how persons are classified or categorized in memory, even if they may not be aware of this categorization process.

Both types of recognition task suffer from one major disadvantage as a measure of what has been encoded and stored in memory. Both accurate and false recognition can reflect information that was encoded at the time of presentation, but they can also reflect guessing or inferences made by respondents at the time the memory measure is taken; that is, memory may be constructed (or reconstructed) when the person is tested on what he or she remembers. More sophisticated methods of analyzing recognition and recall errors make use of signal detection models to decompose memory scores and estimate the level of true recognition (Donaldson & Glathe, 1970).

PRIMING: PROCESSING WITHOUT AWARENESS OR INTENT

Even though the memory measures discussed in the preceding section tap unintended memory, in the sense that participants are not aware at the time they receive information that they are going to be asked to remember it later, the memory tests require active, conscious retrieval on the part of participants. As a consequence, these methods can assess only what participants are aware of experiencing and willing to report to the experimenter. Other social cognition methods have been developed that do not require such an active role on the part of respondents, in order to tap cognitive processing and other internal mental states. Specifically, various methods involving *priming* techniques are designed to assess passive cognitive and affective processes that occur without awareness or intent.

Priming refers to the unintended influence that recent or recurrent experiences have on subsequent thoughts, feelings, and behavior (Bargh & Chartrand, 2000). The idea underlying priming effects is that current experiences create a state of mental readiness or preparedness for receiving and interpreting subsequent information. The term priming was first used by Segal and Cofer (1960) to refer to the effect of using a particular concept in one context on the probability that the same concept would be used again in a subsequent, unrelated task. What was particularly interesting about this effect is that exposure to words in the first task influenced word associations in a later task, even though participants were unable to consciously recall those specific words at the completion of the first task (Grand & Segal, 1966). This finding provided initial evidence for a distinction between *implicit* and *explicit* forms of memory (Greenwald & Banaji, 1995; Schacter, 1987). Priming effects reflect implicit memory processes that function independently of what can be consciously retrieved from memory. Because these processes occur automatically and without awareness, the priming effect has come to be utilized in a number of research methods to tap implicit cognition and affect.

Concept Priming

Priming methodology was first introduced to experimental social psychology in a set of studies conducted by Higgins, Rholes, and Jones (1977) that involved priming personality concepts and documenting effects on subsequent impression formation. The experimental procedures used by Higgins et al. (1977) are representative of the basic priming paradigm. In an initial phase of the experiment, participants were given a memorization task that exposed them repeatedly to words related to certain personality traits (i.e., "adventurous" or "independent" or "reckless"). Then, in a second phase, the participants took part in what they believed to be a separate, unrelated experiment during which they were asked to read a story about a person named Donald who was described as engaging in behaviors such as sailing across the ocean alone and preferring to study by himself. The description was intended to be ambiguous in the sense that the specific behaviors could potentially be interpreted in a relatively positive light (e.g., Donald is an independent, adventurous personality) or a relatively negative way (e.g., Donald is reckless and irresponsible). When participants were asked to report their impressions of Donald on a series of personality rating scales, those who had been previously exposed to words related to "adventurous" reported more positive impressions of Donald than did those who had been exposed to words related to "recklessness" in the earlier task. Importantly, this effect was obtained even though participants showed no awareness that there was any connection between the earlier experiment and the impression formation study.

Supraliminal Priming.   The research paradigm used in the Higgins et al. (1977) experiment involved a conscious priming task. During the first phase experiment, participants were aware that they were viewing and processing words, even though they were unaware of the purposes of the word exposure. With such *supraliminal priming*, the participant is fully aware of the priming stimuli but not of the underlying concept that the stimuli are intended to make accessible. Another frequently used supraliminal priming task is the "scrambled sentence task" (e.g., Srull & Wyer, 1979). With this method, participants are told that the study is designed to measure their language ability and their task is to make coherent, grammatical sentences out of each of a string of words (e.g., "him was worried she always," or "knits dependent occasionally he them"). During the course of the scrambled sentence task, the participant is exposed to words (e.g., "dependent," "worried") that are related to the concept that the researcher intends to prime (usually close synonyms). Later, the unintended influence of the activated concept is assessed on a subsequent impression formation or judgment task. Because the nature of the scrambled sentence task disguises the word presentation, participants are almost never aware that the earlier experiment has affected their judgment processes. Thus, supraliminal priming effects demonstrate how biases in person perception and decision making can be introduced without awareness.

Subliminal Priming.   Awareness can be reduced even further by methods that present the priming stimuli in a way that perceivers are not even conscious of seeing them. *Subliminal* exposure is achieved by presenting the prime (usually a word or a picture) very briefly and then immediately masking the stimulus trace by another stimulus (which is supraliminally presented). Subliminal priming was first used in a social cognition experiment by Bargh and Pietromonaco (1982) who used subliminal presentation to replicate the earlier trait concept priming experiments of Higgins et al. (1977) and Srull and Wyer (1979).

The key to subliminal priming is a duration of exposure of the priming stimulus that is too short to be consciously recognized. Usually, the stimulus is projected by a tachistoscope (a device developed by perception researchers to project stimuli at very brief exposures) or on a computer screen, with the participant gazing at a fixation point (e.g., an asterisk) at the center of the screen. The duration of the prime is a matter of milleseconds, although how long the exposure can be and still remain below awareness depends on a number of factors, including where in the visual field the stimulus is projected. With *foveal* processing, the stimulus is presented at the fixation point (within 0–2 degrees of visual angle from the focal point of attention). With *parafoveal* processing, the prime is presented in the periphery or fringe of the visual field, at 3–6 degrees of visual angle from the focal point. Foveal presentation requires extremely short exposure time (on the order of 15 ms) to be subliminal. Because parafoveal presentation is outside of the region of conscious attention, it allows for somewhat longer duration (e.g., 60–120 ms). However, it is somewhat more difficult to implement parafoveal presentation because the researcher has to ensure that the participant's visual focus is on the fixation point at all times.

Regardless of where the priming stimulus is presented, it must be followed immediately by a subsequent presentation (in the same location) of a *masking* stimulus to prevent extended exposure in visual iconic memory.[6] A masking stimulus is a pattern with the same physical features as the prime. So, for example, if the priming stimuli are words, the masking pattern would be a meaningless string of letters ("XQFBZRMQWGBX") that covers the location where the prime was presented.

Because subliminal exposure permits presenting primes without awareness, there is no need to separate the exposure and judgment tasks. Thus, the immediate effects of an activated concept on subsequent judgments or evaluations can be assessed. Subliminal priming has proved to be particularly useful for assessing the biasing effects of social stereotypes when perceivers are not aware that the stereotype has been subconsciously activated. Social category stereotypes have been primed by subliminal presentation of stereotype-related words (e.g., Devine, 1989) or photos of faces of category members (e.g., Bargh, Chen, & Burrows, 1996).

Priming Behaviors and Goals. The influence of primed concepts or social stereotypes extends beyond cognitive processing and judgments. It has been shown that the same priming manipulations (e.g., scrambled sentences, subliminal presentations) can produce behavioral and motivational effects as well as perceptual effects (Bargh & Chartrand, 2000). For example, Bargh et al. (1996) used a scrambled sentence task to activate the concept of rudeness or of politeness. They then waited to see if the participant would interrupt the experimenter (who was engaged in a conversation with a confederate) in order to proceed with the rest of the experiment. Those primed with rudeness-related words were far more likely to interrupt (63%) than those who had been primed with the politeness concept (only 17%). In a second study, it was found that participants who had been primed with words related to the stereotype of the elderly (e.g., "old," "Florida," "wrinkles," "forgetful") were later observed to walk down the hall more slowly than other participants who were primed with unrelated words. The effect was particularly interesting in that participants' behavior was assimilated to an aspect of the elderly stereotype even though the concept of "slowness" itself had not been directly primed.

Assessing Awareness. Whether supraliminal or subliminal priming methods are being used, it is important that the researcher determine that participants were truly unaware of the priming manipulation. Awareness matters because if research participants consciously recognize that there is a relationship between the presentation of the prime and the subsequent judgment task, they are likely to intentionally correct for the potential influences of the prime before making their responses. With supraliminal priming, the issue is whether participants become aware of the researcher's intent to activate certain constructs in the first task that may affect their judgments or behavior in the second task. To avoid awareness, it is important to camouflage the relation between the two parts of the experiment as much as possible, including moving to different rooms, having different experimenters give instructions, and so forth.

Most often, checks for awareness occur during an extensive debriefing session after the experiment is completed, where participants are probed for suspicions or knowledge of the intent of the experiment. This may be accomplished through the use of a *funneled debriefing* (e.g., see Chartrand & Bargh, 1996), a sequence of questions designed to elicit any suspicions or inferences that the participant may have made about the purpose of

---

[6]Unless the visual buffer is erased or overwritten, a visual image remains in short-term memory store even after the stimulus image has been removed from the visual field.

the experiment or the relationship between the priming task and the second experimental task. If a participant reveals any explicit awareness of the priming manipulation during this interview, his or her data may be excluded from the analyses of results of the study.[7]

When subliminal priming techniques are used, possible awareness of the prime presentations can be assessed by somewhat more objective means. The recommended procedure is to tell participants at the end of the experiment that they were exposed subliminally to some stimuli and ask them to try to guess what the content of the presented stimuli was. If they are not able to generate any of the words or images that had been projected, it is safe to assume that they were not consciously aware of the exposure. (However, even one correct guess is sufficient to indicate awareness.) An even more conservative procedure is to give participants a multiple-choice recognition test to see if they can identify the actual primes from among a set of distractor foils. (Because participants may correctly guess some of the correct answers by chance, it is best to compare their performance to that of a control group of respondents who have not actually been exposed to the subliminal stimuli. If the true participants do not guess any more accurately than the controls, it is safe to assume that awareness was not a problem.)

Sequential Priming

Another variation on priming techniques is used to assess automatic associations between mental concepts. The idea behind sequential priming methods is that if one stimulus has become associated with some other concept, feeling, or behavior, then presentation of that stimulus will automatically activate (prime) those associations. In that case, if the prime and the association are presented sequentially, responding to the second (target) stimulus will be facilitated because of the prior preparation produced by the prime.

The basic structure of the sequential priming paradigm is as follows. On each trial, the prime stimulus (a word or a picture) is presented for a short duration (e.g., 150 ms), then erased, and after a brief delay, the target stimulus is presented and the participant makes a judgment about the target by pressing a key to indicate his or her response. The measure of interest is the response latency (speed of reaction time) to make a judgment of the target stimulus. If the target is associated with the prime in memory, then responding to that target should be facilitated when the prime has been presented just before. Thus, if response latencies are shorter when the target is preceded by the prime than when the same target is judged without the presence of the prime, this indicates that the two concepts are automatically associated with each other. Because reaction times are measured in milleseconds, sequential priming requires the use of very precise timing recorders to detect differences in average speed of response.

Although the duration of presentation of the priming stimulus in the sequential priming paradigm is relatively short, it is a supraliminal exposure and hence participants are aware that they are perceiving it. For this reason, the sequential priming method requires some cover story that explains why participants are viewing the primes even though their task is to respond only to the target stimuli. This may be done by telling participants that the study is about people's ability to perform two tasks simultaneously. On each trial, they are being asked to attend to and remember the first stimulus presented while at the same time they are to make a judgment about the second stimulus. In addition, the potential

---

[7]If a significant number of participants (e.g., 5% or more) show such awareness, the whole experiment is cast into doubt, as it then becomes likely that other participants might have had at least some degree of awareness (Bargh & Chartrand, 2000).

effects of awareness are minimized by limiting the time available for making a response. The time between the onset of the prime presentation and the onset of the subsequent target presentation (the *stimulus onset asynchrony*, or SOA) is kept short (usually no more than 300 ms) so that there is no opportunity for conscious processing of the priming stimulus before a judgment about the target is called for. With such brief delays, only automatic (unintended) effects should be able to occur.

Lexical Decision Task.   In one version of the sequential priming technique, the target stimulus is a string of letters and the judgment that the participant is to make is to indicate as quickly as possible whether the string is an actual word or not. If the target is a word, this judgment is made more quickly when it is preceded by presentation of a related word or concept. For instance, when the prime is a category label (e.g., FURNITURE), words representing members of that category (e.g., "chair") are recognized faster than words that do not belong to the category (e.g., "bird"; Neely, 1977). Based on this principle, the lexical decision task can be used to assess automatic activation of stereotypic traits when the prime is a social category label or picture (e.g., Macrae, Bodenhausen, & Milne, 1995).

Automatic Evaluation.   The sequential priming technique was adapted for use in social psychology by Fazio and his colleagues (Fazio, Sanbonmatsu, Powell, & Kardes, 1986) to assess automatic attitudes or evaluative responses to social stimuli. In Fazio's version of the paradigm, the priming stimuli are words or pictures of an attitude object, followed by target words that are evaluative adjectives (e.g., "delightful," "awful"). The respondent's task is to indicate as quickly as possible whether the target word is good or bad (i.e., an evaluative judgment). If the prime automatically elicits an evaluative reaction of some kind, then that evaluative response will carry over to the judgment of the target. If the evaluative meaning of the target matches that of the prime, responding should be facilitated. So, for instance, if the primed stimulus is a concept that the participant has a positive attitude toward (e.g., "party") then it should speed up judgments of positive adjectives (good). Conversely, a positive prime should slow down (inhibit) judgments of a subsequent negative target word (bad). Thus, the pattern of facilitation and inhibition of evaluative judgments provides an indirect (implicit) measure of attitudes toward the prime. If the implicit attitude is positive, presentation of the prime will speed up responding to good adjectives and slow down responding to negative ones. If the attitude is negative, presentation of the prime will speed up subsequent negative judgments and inhibit positive judgments.

Fazio's automatic evaluation paradigm has been used specifically to measure implicit prejudices. For example, Fazio, Jackson, Dunton, and Williams (1995) used photos of White and Black faces as primes in the sequential priming task. Participants were told to attend to and remember the faces for a later recognition test at the same time that they were engaging in the word evaluation task. On some trials, positive or negative adjectives were preceded by presentation of a facial photo of a White person; on other trials the same adjectives were preceded by a photo of a Black person. Implicit prejudice is assessed by comparing (for each participant) the response times on trials with black primes to those obtained on trials with white primes. Automatic negative attitudes toward Blacks are indicated when judgments of negative adjectives are faster following black primes than following white primes while positive judgments are slower. Importantly, individual differences in automatic evaluation were not correlated with explicit self-report measures of racial prejudice. Many participants who scored low on explicit measures of negative attitudes toward Blacks nonetheless revealed negative automatic evaluations of Blacks compared to Whites in the sequential priming task.

Pronunciation Task. An alternative method for assessing implicit evaluation and other automatic associations replaces the judgment reaction time measure with a measure of time taken to pronounce the target word out loud. Again the idea is that if the word has been primed by presentation of a related associate, the time it takes to recognize and speak the word will be shorter than in the absence of a relevant prime. Using the pronunciation task in a sequential priming paradigm, Bargh, Chaikin, Raymond, and Hymes (1996) were able to demonstrate that automatic evaluation effects occur even when the task is not an evaluative one (because pronunciation does not require the respondent to make an explicit good–bad judgment as the Fazio paradigm does). In another interesting application of this method, Bargh, Raymond, Pryor, and Strack (1995) used the pronunciation task in a study of males who were identified as potential sexual harassers. They found that, compared to other participants, harassers showed significant facilitation of pronunciation of sexually related words when they had been primed by a situation of having power. This finding supported the hypothesis that sexual harassment is related to implicit associations between power and sex.

Issues Related to Use of Reaction Time Measures. All of the sequential priming techniques (as well as a number of other social cognition methods) rely on the analysis of reaction times as an indicator of automatic processes. Researchers making use of these methods need to be aware of some methodological issues in using reaction times as a dependent variable. Many factors other than the priming effects of interest can influence response latencies to particular target stimuli, including word length and word frequency. Thus, it is extremely important that these stimulus features be controlled for in making comparisons between priming conditions.

Latency measures also create some problems for data analysis purposes. First, the distribution of response latencies is typically positively skewed (in that very long latencies occur occasionally, but extremely short latencies are impossible). For this reason, various transformations of the reaction time measure (e.g., taking the square root, the natural logarithm, or the reciprocal of the raw latency) may need to be used to normalize the distribution for purposes of analysis. Second, the researcher needs to be concerned about *outliers* in each participant's reaction time data, that is, excessively long latencies that indicate the respondent wasn't paying attention at the time of presentation of the target stimulus, or excessively short reaction times that reflect anticipatory responding before the target was actually processed. Such outliers should be removed from the data set before analyses are conducted. Typically, latencies shorter than 300 ms are trimmed as too fast to represent true responses (Bargh & Chartrand, 2000). But rules for deleting latencies that are too long are more difficult to specify. In general, only very extreme outliers should be trimmed (e.g., times that are more than 3 standard deviations above the respondent's mean reaction time), and care should be taken that deletions are equally distributed across the different priming conditions.

Other Measures of Automaticity

The purpose of sequential priming methods is to assess responses that are elicited spontaneously or automatically, without intent or effort on the part of the respondent. Most automatic responding is presumed to occur early in information processing; given additional time and cognitive effort, some automatic processes may be overridden or corrected by more thoughtful, deliberative cognitive processing. Hence the importance of short SOA in the sequential priming paradigm, since brief times preclude the opportunity for deliberative processing. Alternative methods for assessing automatic responses rely on different strategies for reducing the influence of intentional processing.

Cognitive Busyness. Capacity for conscious processing can be limited by various techniques for creating cognitive overload, either presenting a lot of information very rapidly (e.g., Bargh & Thein, 1985) or occupying cognitive resources with a secondary task (what Gilbert, Pelham, and Krull, 1988, referred to as *cognitive busyness*). A typical cognitive busyness manipulation is to require participants to hold an eight-digit number in memory as they are engaging in a judgment task or while the stimulus information is being presented. Gilbert and Osborne (1989) used this method to test a two-stage model of attribution processes. Some participants were given a number to remember throughout the entire time they were viewing a videotape of a woman engaging in a discussion with a stranger; other participants viewed the same tape without the secondary memory load task. After the video presentation, participants were asked to make attributions about the causes of the actor's behavior. As predicted, those in the cognitive overload condition gave more dispositional attributions than participants in the control condition, who provided more situational explanations for the behavior. These findings were consistent with the theory that dispositional judgments occur automatically and effortlessly, whereas situational attributions require more deliberation and cognitive effort. In later studies, Gilbert and Hixon (1991) used a similar cognitive overload manipulation to assess automatic activation and use of social stereotypes in impression formation.

Checks on the effectiveness of the cognitive load manipulation are important when this method is being used to assess automatic processes. The secondary task should be sufficiently difficult to keep the participant mentally occupied, but it should be one that the participant can perform if trying hard enough. One way to determine whether the overload task has been effective is to test the participant on the secondary memory task at the end of the processing period. If the manipulation was sufficiently demanding, the participant should be able to perform well enough to demonstrate that he or she was actually trying to do the required task, but not perform perfectly, which might indicate that the task was too easy.

Response Interference Methods. Responses that are automatically elicited can be expected to interfere with production of other responses that are incompatible with it. We have already mentioned the use of interference effects in connection with the Stroop color-naming task as a measure of automatic attention allocation. The Stroop effect demonstrates that performance of an intended response can be inhibited when an incompatible response is automatically elicited by the stimulus. Thus, the occurrence of such interference can be interpreted as an indication of automatic processing at work.

Another example of the use of response interference as a measure of automatic processes is the Implicit Association Test (IAT) developed by Greenwald, McGhee, and Schwartz (1998). Like the sequential priming technique, the IAT assesses automatic associations between mental concepts, but it uses a different procedure. In the IAT task, participants are required to make category judgments as quickly as possible about two concepts simultaneously. A stimulus word, name, or picture is presented and the respondent presses a key to indicate whether it is an exemplar of one of two categories (e.g., an African American name or an unpleasant word). In different phases of the experimental task the response keys are switched so that the pairing of categories is reversed. For example, in the first phase, the right-hand key may refer to Black or unpleasant, and the left-hand key to White or pleasant. In the second phase, the pairings are changed so that the right-hand key is Black or pleasant and the left-hand key is White or unpleasant. If the concepts are associated in memory, then trials where the concept pairings are congruent (e.g., Black–unpleasant and White–pleasant) will have shorter reaction times than trials where the pairings are reversed and incongruent. Thus, the difference in speed of responding between congruent and incongruent trials is a measure of degree of implicit association between concepts. The IAT has been widely used in social psychological research to assess implicit prejudice (associations between category names and evaluative words) and stereotype content (associations between category names and specific traits).

SOCIAL PSYCHOPHYSIOLOGY: PHYSICAL TRACES OF AFFECT AND COGNITIVE PROCESSING

The various priming techniques described in the preceding section have the advantage of tapping processes and subtle responses that may not be accessible to conscious awareness. However, they all share the disadvantage that the researcher must be concerned that participants not become aware of the true purpose of the priming manipulation, as awareness can influence the critical responses. Internal physiological responses are less susceptible to alteration by conscious awareness and thus provide the possibility for yet less reactive methods for assessing implicit, unintended responses.

The use of measures of physiological responses has a long history in social research, in attempts to assess internal states such as interpersonal attraction, aversion, specific emotions, or stress. Most of these early investigations relied on single unitary physiological measures such as respiration, pulse rate, finger temperature, and skin conductance (see Blascovich, Mendes, Hunter, Lickel, & Kowai-Bell, 2001; Guglielmi, 1999). Social researchers were relatively unsophisticated about underlying physiological processes and, as a consequence, most of these early attempts did not result in valid or reliable assessments of the psychological states of interest. One major problem is that there is rarely, if ever, a simple one-to-one relationship between a single physiological response and some specific internal psychological state (Blascovich, 2000). The often-used Galvanic skin response (GSR), for instance, provides an indicator of general arousal, which may arise from any number of positive or negative states including stress, excitement, aversion, or sexual desire. Changes in heart rate may signal physical exertion, attention, anticipation, or arousal, with relatively little differentiation when measured in isolation of other physiological responses.

Fortunately, recent advances in theory and methodology now allow for multivariate physiological assessments that are capable of distinguishing different motivational states, positive and negative affect, attention, and active cognitive processing. Because these indicators are potentially relevant to many phenomena of interest to social researchers, such as assessment of prejudice, social emotions, social stress, and interpersonal motives, the availability of sophisticated physiological measures has given rise to a new subfield of *social psychophysiology* (Cacioppo & Petty, 1983) designed to capitalize on these methods for understanding the interrelationships between psychological and physiological states. The downside of this development is that these techniques require expensive equipment, sophisticated programming, and more than superficial training in physiology and neuroscience to make good use of the available methods. Nonetheless, the capability for conducting experiments that include physiological measures is gradually expanding, and social psychophysiological methods are taking their place among the tools for assessing implicit cognition and feelings.

Most physiological measures used in social research involve noninvasive techniques, that is, ways of recording internal physiological responses from the surface of the body.

Usually some form of electrophysiological recording is involved because various physiological events produce detectable electrical signals at the surface level (Blascovich, 2000). Depending on the location and type of recording, electrophysiological measures record signals of neural, cardiovascular, or endocrine system activity occurring in response to current situational inputs. In modern methods, it is the patterns of responses from multiple signals over time that serve as markers of specific psychophysiological states. Some examples of uses of these physiological measures in social research are described in the following sections.

Cardiovascular Indices

Although heartrate alone is an inadequate marker of any specific arousal state, measures of heartrate in combination with other recordings of cardiac and vascular performance can differentiate different states of anticipation or stress (Blascovich & Kelsey, 1990). Tomaka, Blascovich, Kelsey, and Leitten (1993), for example, demonstrated that specific patterns of cardiovascular responses can distinguish between feelings of threat versus challenge as motivational states in anticipation of potentially difficult or stressful situations such as performing difficult arithmetic problems or preparing for a public speech. Threat is marked by responses indicating increased pituitary-adrenocortical activity (PAC), which is associated with negative physiological consequences of stress. A challenge response to the same situation, however, is marked by increased sympathetic-adrenomedullary activity (SAM), which is associated with benign states and improved performance (Dienstbier, 1989).

Tomaka and Blascovich (1994) validated the usefulness of this distinction for assessment of psychosocial processes by demonstrating that individuals with a high belief in a just world (as measured by self-report questionnaire) showed a challenge response to a potentially stressful performance situation and performed better than individuals with low beliefs in a just world, who showed a threat response pattern to the same situation. In another study, Blascovich et al. (2001) found that White participants showed a predominance of threat response in anticipation of engaging in a team task with an African American partner, compared to participants who were anticipating working with a White partner and who showed more challenge response.

Facial Measures of Affective States

One of the difficulties of many physiological indicators of arousal is that these measures do not distinguish between arousal due to positive affect or attraction and negative affect or aversion. Facial expressions, however, do vary in ways that correspond to specific positive or negative social emotions (Ekman, 1993). Ekman and Friesen (1978) developed and validated an elaborate facial action coding system (FACS) to assess various emotional states on the basis of detailed aspects of spontaneous facial expressions. This method of measuring internal states has a number of drawbacks, however. First, training to use the FACS is extensive and requires a considerable investment of time and effort. Second, although facial expressions are usually produced without conscious intention, it is possible to control facial responses if one makes an effort to do so. Thus, facial expression is not always a valid measure of implicit affect.

Facial Electromyograph. Although overt facial expressions are potentially controllable, individuals are not able to control the tiny, visually imperceptible movements of specific facial muscles that occur at the onset of an emotional or affective response to stimulus events. Thus, Cacioppo and his colleagues (e.g., Cacioppo & Petty, 1981; Cacioppo, Petty, Losch, & Kim, 1986) have recommended the use of facial electromyograms (EMG) specific to targeted facial muscles as physiological markers of positive and negative affective states. EMG measures focus in particular on specific muscles of the eyes and mouth associated with corrugator ("frown muscles") and zygomaticus ("smile muscles") activity. Electromyographic recordings obtained from electrodes distributed across areas of the face indicate that corrugator EMG activity increases and zygomaticus activity decreases during negative affect. Conversely, zygomaticus EMG increases and corrugator EMG decreases signal positive affect (Cacioppo et al., 1986). Interestingly, the EMG recordings successfully discriminate between different affective states even when judges observing videotapes of the participants' overt facial expressions are unable to identify whether the affect is positive or negative.

Vanman, Paul, Ito, and Miller (1997) made use of the diagnostic capability of EMG activity to assess implicit attitudes toward members of racial outgroups. In their experiments, White participants were shown slides of Black or White individuals and were asked to imagine themselves in a situation in which they were partnered with that individual in a cooperative task. On overt self-report ratings of the potential partners, respondents tended to show preferential ratings for Black targets. EMG facial measures, however, showed the opposite pattern, with more negativity exhibited toward Black partners.

Startle Eyeblink Reflex. Another minute facial muscle measure that may prove useful to index affective states is electromyograms specific to reflexive eyeblinks (Blascovich, 2000). The startle eyeblink response refers to the reflexive blinks that occur when individuals perceive an unexpected, relatively intense stimulus, such as a loud sound. The startle eyeblink reflex is negatively toned. Hence, Lang and his colleagues (Lang, Bradley, & Cuthbert, 1990, 1992) have reasoned that the eyeblink response should be facilitated or enhanced if the perceiver is currently in a negative affective state and inhibited if the perceiver is experiencing ongoing positive affect. Subsequent research has demonstrated that the strength or intensity of the startle eyeblink reflex as measured by EMG activity is sensitive to affective states as predicted. Thus, the eyeblink reflex may prove useful, as well as other EMG indices, as a measure of covert affect.

EMG techniques require sophisticated equipment and technology to implement and have the added disadvantage that participants must sit still (with electrodes planted on various parts of their faces) and minimize extraneous head movements while responses are being recorded. Thus, the method is hardly unobtrusive and the kinds of stimulus situations in which the technology can be used are limited to relatively passive viewing conditions such as presentations of slides or video displays. Nonetheless, EMG recordings have proved to be valid indicators of implicit affect that individuals may be unaware of or unwilling to express overtly. Thus, EMG measures can be a useful tool for testing theories about activation and influences of nonconscious affect, even if their practical application may be limited.

Measures of Brain Activity

Indicators of cognitive and affective processing are also evident from various noninvasive measures of brain activity, including readings of electrical activity from specific locations on the scalp (EEG) and neuroimaging. Again, these techniques require access to expensive and sophisticated equipment (much of it developed for medical research), but they are finding their way into social research applications.

EEG Studies.   Use of EEG measures in social research include studies of hemispheric asymmetry (differential activation of the right or left hemispheres of the brain under different stimulus conditions or tasks) and computation of the EEG waveform (event-related potential, ERP) that follows presentation of a stimulus event. In either type of measure, the location and timing of differential brain activity is being used to assess emotional responding, categorization, and evaluative reactions (Guglielmi, 1999). For example, Cacioppo and his colleagues (e.g., Cacioppo, Crites, Berntson, & Coles, 1993; Cacioppo, Crites, Gardner, & Berntson, 1994) made use of one component of ERP (the late positive potential, LLP, which occurs approximately 300 ms after onset of a stimulus) to mark implicit positive and negative evaluative reactions. The amplitude of the LLP is larger when a presented stimulus is unexpected or categorically distinct from previously presented stimuli. Thus, to measure whether a stimulus is reacted to negatively, participants are first presented with a series of (known) positive stimuli and then the target stimulus. If LLP amplitude increases significantly in response to the target, it is assumed that a shift to negative evaluation has been registered, even when respondents are unwilling (or unable) to report a negative evaluation overtly.

Neuroimaging.   Advances in brain imaging techniques have seen widespread application in the field of cognitive neuroscience and are gradually finding application in social research as well. Regional cerebral blood flow, as measured by positron emission tomography (PET) has been used to investigate the relationship between regional brain activity and induction of various emotions, but different studies have produced discrepant findings about the regional differentiation of specific emotions (e.g., Lane, Reiman, Ahern, Schwartz, & Davidson, 1997; Robinson, 1995). PET scans have also been used to assess differences in processing of information relevant to the self compared to processing of information about others (Craik et al., 1999). More recently, functional magnetic resonance imaging (fMRI) has been used to track brain activity during various social and nonsocial cognitive tasks. One intriguing finding with potential social implications is fMRI evidence that processing faces of racial outgroup members generates more amygdala activity than processing faces of ingroup members. Further, White individuals whose amygdalas fired up the most also scored higher on two other measures of implicit attitudes toward Blacks (Phelps et al., 2000).

The output of brain imaging studies is subject to a great deal of statistical variation across individuals and across occasions with the same individual. Thus, interpretation of imaging patterns is still in early stages of development. Whether imaging proves to be a reliable and robust technique for assessing social processes remains to be seen.

CONCLUSION

The social cognition methods reviewed in this chapter are intended primarily to assess implicit cognitions and feelings that respondents are unwilling or unable to report on more explicit measures of internal states. Thus, measures of attention, processing time, memory, reaction time, and physiological responses provide a different perspective on mental processes than that provided by traditional self-report methods. When these different types of assessment all converge on the same diagnosis, we have impressive convergent validation of the construct under investigation. But often, as we have seen, the results of implicit and explicit measures of internal states produce discrepant findings. Such differences in outcome raise the issue of which methods assess the "true" attitude, feeling, or cognitive process more accurately.

One possibility is that discrepancies between explicit and implicit measures of attitudes, feelings, and beliefs reflect the fact that respondents are hiding or misrepresenting their true responses on overt self-report measures. In that case, implicit measures provide a more valid assessment of their actual feelings because they are less susceptible to intentional control or deception. And, indeed, it is most often the case that discrepancies between implicit and explicit measures occur with respect to assessments of attitudes or beliefs that are undesirable or politically sensitive, such as racial prejudices, stereotyping, or negative emotional states. Nonetheless, it may be that explicit and implicit responses differ in these cases not because individuals are misrepresenting their conscious beliefs or feelings but because their conscious attitudes are in actuality different from their subconscious responses. Explicit attitudes that derive from controlled cognitive processing may reflect what the individual consciously and intentionally believes and values, even though they may hold residues of more negative affective reactions and beliefs at the level of automatic, unintentional processes. In this case, explicit self-report measures may be more valid than implicit measures, if one presumes that most of social life is carried out under consciously controlled processing conditions.

Most researchers who use implicit measures do not contend that such measures are more valid than traditional self-report measures of respondents' true mental or affective states. Rather, most believe that implicit or automatic responses reflect different underlying processes than responses on explicit measures. In that case, the challenge is to determine what processes and outcomes are related to these implicit measures that are not predicted or accounted for by other methods of assessment. As we have already discussed, automatic processes may be more likely to emerge when individuals are under cognitive overload or responding under extreme time pressure. There is also some evidence that measures of automatic evaluation predict subtle nonverbal behaviors in certain social situations better than do explicit attitude measures. For example, in the study we described previously by Fazio et al. (1995), which used sequential priming to assess automatic racial prejudice, the reaction time measure of automatic evaluation was not correlated with participants' scores on a self-report measure of racial attitudes. However, when participants interacted with a Black confederate of the experimenter after the attitude measurement session, subsequent ratings by the confederate of the participant's friendliness and interest during the interaction proved to be significantly correlated with the individual's evaluative bias in the priming task. Thus, the automatic evaluation measure did seem to successfully predict other subtle, nonverbal (and probably nonconscious) overt behavior. Other studies of the predictive validity of implicit measures such as this are needed to better understand the relationship between implicit cognitive and affective processes and social behavior.

SUGGESTED READINGS

Bargh, J. A., & Chartrand, T. L. (2000). Studying the mind in the middle: A practical guide to priming and automaticity research. In H. Reis & C. Judd (Eds.), *Handbook of research methods in social and personality psychology* (pp. 253–285). New York: Cambridge University Press.

Blascovich, J. (2000). Using physiological indexes of psychological processes in social psychology. In H. Reis & C. Judd (Eds.), *Handbook of research methods in social and personality psychology* (pp. 117–137). New York: Cambridge University Press.

Nisbett, R. E., & Wilson, T. D. (1977). Telling more than we can know: Verbal reports on mental processes. *Psychological Review, 84,* 231–259.

CHAPTER

17

METHODS FOR ASSESSING DYADS AND GROUPS

The preceding chapters on measurement and social cognition dealt with methods for assessing characteristics and behaviors of individual persons. Properties of single persons are known as *monadic* variables. A person's attitude toward abortion, for instance, may be considered monadic because it refers only to the individual's own attitude. In many areas of social science, however, social scientists may be interested in studying persons who are interacting in dyads (pairs) or small groups. In this case, we are not assessing properties of the individuals separately, but rather the nature of their relationship, or the structure or process or outcomes of their interaction. A *dyadic* measurement refers to characteristics of the relationship between two persons; *group* measures refer to characteristics of interacting groups of three or more persons. This chapter considers how to assess variables that are fundamentally dyadic or group level phenomena.

Measures of behaviors or attitudes of interacting persons are a special case because the assessments taken from each of the actors are *interdependent*. Consider the following examples of measures that might result from a study of an interacting dyad:

- How much Tom likes Peter.
- How much Dick smiles when interacting with Paul.
- How intelligent Harry thinks Mary is.

In each of these three interactions, the person who produces the measure (the actor) is an individual person, but the outcome of the measure is influenced not only by the characteristics of the actor but by the particular partner as well. For instance, Tom's liking of Peter is, in part, a consequence of something about Tom, but it is also influenced by what Peter is like and by the nature of the relationship between the two of them. Thus, all three of these cases are examples of dyadic measurements because there are two persons (and their interaction) involved in each.

The terms *partner* and *actor* correspond to stimulus and responder in a dyadic situation. The actor is the responder, and the partner the stimulus. With dyadic data the person can be both stimulus and responder. Although we generally use the terms *actor* and *partner* here, other terms can be used. For instance, Cronbach (1955) used the terms *judge* and *target*, and Swann (1984) used the terms *perceiver* and *target*. In the area of nonverbal communication, the terms *receiver* and *sender* as well as *decoder* and *encoder* correspond to actor and partner. We prefer the terms *actor* and *partner* because they are not specific to any one area of research, as the others appear to be.

One of the things that make dyadic variables different from monadic variables is that they can take the same measurement treating the actor as the partner and the partner as the actor. For some dyadic variables, the distinction between actor and partner is unnecessary. How similar Pat is to Leslie is the same as how similar Leslie is to Pat. It is not necessary to designate Pat or Leslie as the actor. For variables such as the degree to which two persons are similar, the actor–partner distinction is not necessary because for purposes of analysis, the persons are interchangeable. Other examples of dyadic variables for which we do not have to distinguish actor from partner are the physical distance between persons, mutual gaze, and simultaneous speech, as these are all symmetric measures—the same measure serves for both members of the dyad.

Sometimes it is possible to have a dyadic variable, but the resulting data can be considered monadic. This happens when one of the two persons interacting is a confederate or an accomplice of the experimenter. In studies involving confederates, there are usually many actors (participants), but usually only a single partner (the accomplice). When all the actors interact with the same partner, the data from each actor can be considered monadic, particularly if the confederate's behavior has been scripted by the researcher.[1] For example, consider the case in which the researcher measures the degree to which each subject likes the confederate. There is a common partner in this study—the one confederate. This is similar to a study of attitudes, in which there is one persuasive message. Thus, in this study, the measurements of liking can be treated as if they were monadic. This chapter focuses on the study of truly dyadic, not monadic, measures.

DERIVING DYADIC AND GROUP LEVEL MEASURES

Some measures of dyadic or group properties involve direct assessments of the interacting group as a whole. For instance, the level of attraction between two persons may be scored by an observer who watches an interaction between them and then rates that interaction in terms of degree of warmth, engagement, and mutuality expressed by the pair. Similarly, group *cohesion* (the group-level counterpart to interpersonal attraction) can be rated by observers of group process considering the group as a whole. Or the performance of a group on a collective task may be assessed by evaluating the group product, independent of the contributions of individual members.

More often, however, group-level measures are derived from measures taken from the component individuals. Sometimes the aggregate score is the *sum* of the scores of the participating individuals. For instance, attraction between Peter and Tom may be the sum (or the *mean*, which is simply the sum divided by two) of the degree of liking that Peter

---

[1] Interactions that are computer-mediated (e.g., real or simulated "chat rooms") lend themselves to this type of design. The partner in a computerized interaction is often a simulated creation of the experimenter, in which case the interest is in the behavior or responses of the single participant who is reacting to a preprogrammed stimulus person (e.g., Crano & Hannula-Bral, 1994). Sometimes, however, the researcher is studying real online interactions between two or more actual persons (e.g., see McKenna & Bargh, 2000). In this case, the measurements would be dyadic or group-level variables.

expresses for Tom and the liking that Tom expresses for Peter. At the group level, cohesion may be the sum (or mean) of all of the group members' expressed liking for the group as a whole. In other cases, the dyadic measure is based on the *difference* between the ratings or behaviors of the two actors/targets. For instance, dyadic belief similarity is usually measured as the difference between the attitude expressed by person A of the pair and the attitude expressed by person B. The physical distance between two persons is also a dyadic score based on the difference between the physical location of the two participants. At the group level, belief similarity (or rather, degree of dissimilarity) is assessed by some measure of the degree of variance (e.g., standard deviation) of the attitude scores of individual members. Such variance measures often are used as operational definitions of group *consensus*.

Although most dyadic measures are simple additive combinations (sum or difference scores) of the component measures, group measures can sometimes be considerably more complex. For instance, sociometric measures (discussed later in this chapter) are derived from ratings taken from individual group members of each of the other members, but group-level scores are then calculated from complex mathematical formulas.

Whatever the method of combination, dyadic and group-level variables may be derived from measures taken from individuals, but they refer to properties that are meaningful only at the level of the dyad or group. Group size provides a good concrete example of what we mean here. Size is measured by counting individuals who compose the group— each individual contributes to the total measure. However, size as a conceptual variable is something that exists only in the total score, not in the individual bodies that have been counted. Dyadic similarity is another example. Although individual A has an attitude that can be measured monadically, as does individual B, the degree of similarity between those two attitudes is a characteristic of them as a pair. It is not meaningful at the individual level.

Although both direct and derived measures of dyadic and group properties can be found in the social science literature, the challenges of measurement come from assessments of groups that are derived from measures taken from individuals. Thus, the remainder of this section is devoted to discussion of some of these derived measures of dyadic and group-level variables.

Measuring Reciprocity or Mutuality

When working with dyadic measures, a number of issues arise that do not occur when working with monadic measures. When there are scores from both members of the dyad— so that each person serves as both actor and partner—it is possible that the two scores are correlated. The degree to which the two scores are correlated may be a matter of some theoretical importance. Consider some examples:

- In a study of randomly paired couples, Walster, Aronson, Abrahams, and Rottman (1966) were interested in discovering why, after the first date, some couples liked each other and other pairs did not. They were interested, that is, in the degree of *reciprocity* of attraction between the individuals who constituted the dating couples.

- Concerning studies that measure the degree of self-disclosure in two-person relationships, numerous theorists (e.g., Derlega & Berg, 1987; Derlega, Metts, Petronio, & Margulis, 1993; Jourard, 1971; Rubin, 1975; Won-Doornink, 1979) have discussed the conditions in which persons disclose, or resist disclosing, themselves to each other. Of particular interest is whether disclosure from one person stimulates comparable disclosure from the other member of the pair. It is then theoretically useful to measure the degree of reciprocity in self-disclosure.

- Communication scientists have speculated that in communicative social interactions, one person will tend to be dominant and the other submissive. If we take the number of interruptions as a measure of domination, we may want to see if in dyads there is one person who interrupts the other repeatedly while the other is infrequently the interrupter. In this case, the behavior is not reciprocated, but rather compensated, and the predicted correlation between measures is negative rather than positive.

- Social psychologists regularly have people play laboratory games, such as the Prisoner's Dilemma (see chap. 5). Of interest in such settings might be the degree of reciprocity between players. Thus, if one person is generally cooperative, is the other person cooperative too? And, conversely, if one person is competitive, is the other competitive?

- Consider a study that examines pairs of children interacting. One way to index the degree to which two children are engaging in true social interaction is to measure the degree of reciprocity in their behavior. For example, we could measure the number of utterances of both children in the interaction. If the two children are interacting, then there should be some degree of correspondence in their number of utterances. If the young children were only speaking to themselves, the number of utterances of the two would be unrelated.

These illustrations demonstrate that it is essential for many research questions to be studied in such a manner to allow for the investigation of reciprocity. The measure of reciprocity depends on whether the dyad is symmetric or asymmetric. A *symmetric dyad* is one in which persons are indistinguishable from the perspective of the analysis. Examples of symmetric dyads are friends or roommates. In *asymmetric dyads*, the persons are clearly distinguishable by some factor, such as their respective roles or status in the relationship. For instance, married couples are distinguishable by their gender. Other examples of asymmetric dyads are teacher–student, parent–child, and boss–employee.

For asymmetric dyads, the degree of reciprocity can be measured by the ordinary Pearson correlation coefficient. So, for instance, to measure the degree to which members of a couple agree on how satisfied they are with their marriage, one simply correlates the husband's satisfaction with that of the wife's. For symmetric dyads, there is no rule on how to measure the correlation because there is no clear rule for how to call one person's data the X variable and the other's the Y variable. There are two common, yet faulty, solutions to this problem. The first is to find some way of distinguishing the two members of the dyad. For example, if the dyads are siblings, they can be distinguished by the relative age of the members of each dyad. The second way is to distinguish the actor from the partner in some arbitrary fashion. For instance, one uses a coin flip to designate one individual as Person 1 and the other as Person 2. To measure reciprocity correlationally, we treat the score of Person 1 as the X variable and that of Person 2 as the Y variable.

Neither of these two approaches is ideal. The first, which calls for the discovery of a variable by which to distinguish people, is not always feasible because often there may be no reasonable way to distinguish actor from partner. The second approach, making use of an arbitrary (or relatively meaningless) rule to distinguish actor and partner, is also misguided because as is shown, minor variations in who occupies the arbitrarily defined actor or partner role can have an effect on the obtained results. The correct approach makes use of a specialized measure of association called the *intraclass correlation coefficient*. We denote the two scores in the dyad as X and X' and the mean of all scores as M. The

TABLE 17.1

Trust Scores from Eight Pairs of
College Roommates

Pair	Scores	
A	7	10
B	8	8
C	7	7
D	8	7
E	7	8
F	7	8
G	4	6
H	6	6

number of dyads is n. The formula for the intraclass correlation is based on the following two quantities:

$$MS_B = \frac{2\left[\dfrac{\sum(X + X')}{2} - M\right]^2}{n - 1}$$

$$MS_W = \sum(X - X')^2/2n$$

The intraclass correlation is defined as:

$$r = \frac{MS_B - MS_W}{MS_B + MS_W}$$

For dyads, the intraclass correlation, like an ordinary correlation coefficient, varies from -1 to $+1$, with zero indicating no relationship between the variables of interest. The intraclass correlation is the most appropriate measure of reciprocity for symmetric dyads, such as friends and roommates.

Table 17.1 presents scores from eight pairs of college roommates. The scores indicate the extent to which an individual trusts his or her roommate. The intraclass correlation for these pairs of roommates is .43, which indicates that the roommates reciprocated their trust in one another; that is, if one member of a pair had high trust in the other, it is likely that his or her roommate would also indicate relatively high trust. A standard Pearson correlation coefficient on the data of Table 17.1 would reveal a slightly different result ($r = .51$). However, as noted earlier, the Pearson r is susceptible to variations in the placement of the data components; thus, if the scores of Pair A of the table were reversed, the Pearson r would be affected (now, $r = .48$), whereas the intraclass correlation would not. For this reason, the intraclass correlation is clearly preferable in research situations of this type.

Round Robin Designs

One of the problems with measures derived from individual scores is that is it often difficult to distinguish monadic and dyadic components of the derived score. For instance, the total attraction between Tom and Harry (the sum of their ratings of each other) may reveal something about the nature of the relationship between the two of them, something that is unique to them as a specific dyad. However, the total score also reflects something about

Tom and Harry as individuals. Perhaps Tom is the kind of person who expresses liking for everyone he meets. In that case, any dyad with Tom as a member would have a high attraction score, but this may be more a property of Tom than of the relationship with that particular partner. Even a distance score may be determined by the behavior of one component individual and reveal nothing about the dyadic relationship. When there is only one dyad with Tom as a member, it is impossible to tease apart how much the total attraction score is due to Tom alone and how much is a reflection of the dyad.

So far, we have assumed that each person under study is a member of one and only one dyad. In such cases, if there are a total of 16 persons, as there was in the earlier example in Table 17.1, there would be a total of 8 dyads. If the researcher wants to sort out the monadic and dyadic components of relationship measures, it is necessary to employ a more complicated design. The most common design for extending measures of dyadic relationships is a *round robin design*. In a round robin design, all possible pairs of persons in a given set are created. For instance, consider the now classic study of Theodore Newcomb (1961), who studied a group of 17 men living in the same university house. He asked each of these college men to state how much they liked each of the others. With 17 respondents, the total number of dyads that can be formed (to compare the liking of each actor for each potential partner in the group) is $17 \times 16/2$, or 136 dyads.

Round robin designs are employed infrequently in the social sciences, but when they are used, they often occur in significant studies. In research on interpersonal attraction, not only did Newcomb use a round robin design, but in their replication of the Newcomb (1961) study, Curry and Emerson (1970) also used the same method. Round robin designs have also been used to study communication in monkeys (Miller, Caul, & Mirsky, 1967), intertribe relations in East Africa (Brewer & Campbell, 1976), and defense mechanisms in person perception (Campbell, Miller, Lubetsky, & O'Connell, 1964).

There are two major advantages in collecting data using a round robin design. First, many more observations are obtained without increasing the number of participants needed. This gain in the number of comparisons lends added power to the statistical analysis of the data that are collected. Second, with a round robin design one can determine how a person responds generally *to* others, and how that same person is responded to *by* others. It is then possible to describe the score of a given actor with a given partner as being a function of (a) the group that the set of actors is in, (b) how the actor responds in general, (c) how others respond in general to the partner, and (d) how the actor uniquely responds to the particular partner with whom he or she is interacting. Such an analysis of two-person relationships was termed the Social Relations Model by Kenny and LaVoie (1984; see also Kashy & Kenny, 2000).

Table 17.2 presents an illustration of a round robin design. The numbers in the table give the attraction of six persons toward each other. The rows in the table are the actors, and the columns are the partner. So, for instance, the table indicates that John likes Paul (with a score of 12 on the liking scale), whereas Paul's liking for John is only 9. We have left blank the entries in which the same person is both actor and partner to signify that those numbers are not gathered (it is difficult to ask people how much they like themselves!).

By reading down each column of Table 17.2, we can see who is popular overall and who is not. It appears that Bill is the most popular person in the group and Phil the least popular. Reading across rows, we can see who in the group generally likes the others most and who likes the others the least. In this case, it appears that John likes other group members most and that Dave likes them the least. We can view the general tendency to like (or dislike) others as a *response set*, a tendency to respond in a consistent fashion.

TABLE 17.2

Example of Data from a Round Robin Design

	Partner					
Actor	John	Paul	Mike	Bill	Dave	Phil
John	—	12	12	15	15	10
Paul	9	—	4	13	11	4
Mike	14	9	—	15	15	9
Bill	11	8	7	—	9	7
Dave	6	8	7	8	—	4
Phil	12	10	8	15	13	—

With a round robin design, it is possible to obtain a more refined measure of reciprocity than we can get from pair data. Consider what would happen if persons who were popular in the group tended not to like the other persons in the group. If this were true, it would build a negative bias into the reciprocity correlation. For instance, for the data in Table 17.2, the intraclass correlation for the dyads is −.38. Once overall popularity and liking response sets are controlled, however, the correlation becomes .65. Thus, removing the effects of popularity and the liking response set can dramatically influence a correlation. To measure reciprocity in attraction more validly, we need to subtract from each score the extent to which the actor likes the other group members, in general, and the extent to which the partner is liked by the others.[2] The removal of popularity and the response set for liking provides a more valid measure of reciprocity (Kenny & LaVoie, 1982).

Sociometric Analysis

A methodology similar to the round robin design can also be used to measure properties of groups, such as cohesion and communication structure. Earlier, we discussed the measurement of members' attraction toward their group as a whole. In this context, measurement involves rating scales similar to those used to measure other social attitudes. A different approach to the measurement of attraction in group settings was developed in the 1930s by J. L. Moreno (1934), whose methods gradually became known as *sociometry*. Sociometry refers to the assessment of social choices and rejections within a given group, obtained by asking each group member which of the other group members he or she likes or dislikes. Social psychologists fairly commonly ask group members to state who in the group they like, and so they employ what can be called a *sociometric design*. For example, Clore, Bray, Itkin, and Murphy (1978) asked children in a summer camp to identify their best friends. They used these measures to assess the degree to which children chose other children who were members of different ethnic groups.

In a sociometric design, there are two different kinds of choices that can be made. First, the participants can be asked whether they accept other specific group members. Examples of acceptance are choices indicating liking, preferring to work with, preferring to to be on the same team with, and the like. The second type of choice is rejection. Examples of rejection are measures of disliking and preferences of not being associated with the

---

[2]We cannot take a simple average across rows to measure the response or a simple average across columns to measure popularity. More complicated methods are required because people do not interact with themselves (Kenny, Lord, & Garg, 1984; Warner, Kenny, & Stoto, 1979).

TABLE 17.3

Sociomatrix for a Six-Person Group

		Person Being Rated					
		A	*B*	*C*	*D*	*E*	*F*
	A		+	+	0	−	−
	B	+		0	−	0	−
Person Doing	C	0	0		+	−	−
the Rating	D	−	0	+		0	−
	E	−	−	0	0		+
	F	−	−	0	0	+	

Note. + indicates acceptance, − indicates rejection, and 0 represents no choice.

other. The researcher can ask the participant to make acceptances, rejections, or both, but in most studies, only acceptance choices are required.

When gathering sociometric data, the investigator has the option of restricting the number of choices a person can make. For instance, it is common to ask all respondents to choose their three best friends in a group (an "acceptance" choice). Although it seems more natural not to place any restrictions on the number of choices the participant can make, it is advisable to do so. If the number of choices is not set by the researcher, the data will be biased in such a way that the person who makes few choices appears to be more popular, and the person making many choices less popular, than is actually the case. This bias is similar to the response set problem that was discussed earlier in connection with round robin designs.

Participants' choices can be represented in what is called a *sociomatrix*. In a sociomatrix, each individual in the group is represented by a row and a corresponding column with his or her response recorded in the appropriate cell, as in the following example for a group of six, as in Table 17.3. In this matrix, choices are represented by a "+," rejections by a "−," and non-choices by a "0."

A sociomatrix employs a round robin design. All possible pairs of persons are measured. Although the design is round robin, the data are of a different type than those presented earlier in this chapter. The data in a sociomatrix are at the nominal level of measurement, whereas in the earlier example (presented in Table 17.2), they were at the interval level.

There are a number of interesting questions that can be answered by analyzing the data of a sociomatrix (Terry, 2000). One type of question concerns whether the group is in *balance*. According to Heider's (1958) theory, if A likes B, and B likes C, then A also should like C. Measures of the degree of balance in a sociomatrix of N participants are given in Holland and Leinhardt (1978).

From a sociomatrix, it is possible to measure the popularity of individuals within the group. We need simply to count the number of acceptances received by each person, and subtract from this sum the number of rejections, if any. This simple counting strategy is valid when the number of choices is set by the investigator. If respondents are free to choose (accept or reject) any number of others, somewhat more complicated methods must be employed to assess popularity.

We can also determine from a sociomatrix the degree of reciprocity in the group. We begin by counting the number of pairs who reciprocate attraction and divide this quantity by the total number of pairs. The resulting number is the proportion of reciprocated pairs. This quantity should be compared to a baseline proportion of reciprocated pairs that would be expected if respondents' choices were completely random. One useful baseline measure

TABLE 17.4

Liking Choices among Monk Trainees

| | | Monk Trainee Chosen | | | | | | | | | | | | | | | | | |
		A	B	C	D	E	F	G	H	I	J	K	L	M	N	O	P	Q	R
	A		+	+		+													
	B			+		+	+												
	C		+					+	+										
	D		+	+		+													
	E		+	+			+												
	F		+			+						+							
	G		+	+	+														
	H							+		+			+						
Monk	I							+			+				+				
Trainee	J							+	+				+						
Choices	K							+	+		+								
	L							+		+				+					
	M							+		+					+				
	N							+				+	+						
	O		+										+						+
	P															+		+	+
	Q							+									+		+
	R							+									+	+	

Note. A + sign indicates that the individual indicated by the row entry likes the individual indicated by the column entry; a blank indicates no choice.

involves calculating the total number of choices actually made in the group, dividing this number by the total number of choices possible, and squaring the resulting proportion. For example, if there were nine persons in a group, and each made three acceptances, the total number of choices made is 9×3, or 27, and the total number of pairs is 72 (because choices are made by both members of each pairing). The baseline proportion of reciprocal choices thus is $(27/72)^2$, or .141. This baseline proportion would be compared to the actual number of reciprocated choices to determine the extent of reciprocation in the group under study.

From a sociomatrix, we can also detect the presence of *cliques* or subgroupings that exist with a group. Table 17.4 presents an example of a sociomatrix whose data were gathered by Sampson (1969) from monks in a Catholic monastery. Each of the 18 trainee monks was asked to state which 3 other monks they liked the most. The matrix is arranged to show the three clear subgroups that were formed. The subgroups are indicated in the table by boxes. Sampson labeled the first group (Monks A through G) as the "traditionalists," the second group (H through N) as the "Young Turks," and the third group (Monks O through R) as the "outcasts." These subgroupings were determined by a procedure called *block modeling* (White, Boorman, & Breiger, 1976; note that Monk A is an isolate in that no other monks choose him among their most liked, but he is included in the first grouping because all of his choices fall in that traditionalist group).

The sociomatrix can be drawn into a figure to indicate who likes whom, and who does not. Such a drawing is called a *sociogram*. If Person A likes Person B, the two are connected by an arrow going from A to B and vice versa. If rejection measures are made, they too are indicated by directional arrows, but acceptance is indicated by a plus, and rejection by a minus. We have taken the sociomatrix in Table 17.3 and redrawn it as a

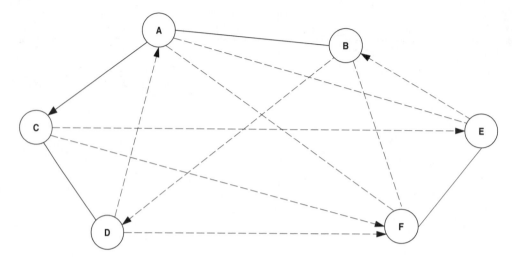

FIG. 17.1. Sociogram of Relations Presented in Table 17.3.

sociogram in Fig. 17.1. Sociograms are more useful than sociomatrices if the number of respondents is less than 10. If we were to draw a sociogram for the monastery study, the resulting diagram would be much too unwieldy to interpret with any degree of confidence.

Social Network Analysis

Sociometric analysis is concerned with the affective ties among members of a social group. Network analysis is a related methodology concerning the communication links or connections among units (individuals or organizations) in a social system. Like sociometry, *social network analysis* utilizes dyadic relations as the basic unit of analysis, with the resulting data organized into matrix representations. However, the two methodologies differ in a number of ways. Whereas sociometry is usually applied to studies of relatively small, bounded groups, social network analysis often involves large social systems where the "actors" may be organizations or political units as well as individuals. The basic measure in a sociometric analysis is the affective relationships among group members, but the basic measure in a network analysis is some index of connectedness, communication, or exchange between component units. The specific kind of linkage being studied depends on the researchers' objectives and interests, but some common measures are exchanges of information or commodities (i.e., trade relations), presence or absence of telecommunication links, shared memberships (e.g., overlapping Boards of Directors), kinship relations, or collaborative efforts (e.g., co-authored publications). Data regarding the existence of linkages may be obtained from self-report questionnaires or interviews with the actors (or organizational representatives) or from archival sources, such as publication citation indices, trade records, or IRS reports.

As with sociometry, the raw data on linkages for a social network analysis are compiled into an $N \times N$ matrix (where N is the number of actors).[3] When the linkage data are symmetrical (e.g., the presence of trade or kin relations), only the $N(N-1)/2$ elements below the diagonal in the matrix are needed for the database, but when measures are

---

[3]When the number of actors in a system is very large (as is often the case), network analyses require access to very large computer facilities.

asymmetrical (e.g., A initiates communication with B, vs. B with A), the full matrix is used. Measures derived from this matrix data can relate to individual units or the system as a whole (Knoke & Kuklinski, 1982; Scott, 1991; Wasserman & Faust, 1994), and statistical techniques often use advances in graph theory and other complex mathematical models. Actor-based measures include number of direct linkages to other units in the system, closeness (ease of interaction with others), and centrality. Other measures describe the nature of the linkages themselves, such as stability, symmetry, or strength. Finally, other analyses focus on characteristics of the network as a whole, such as measures of degree of connectedness (saturation), centralizational, and other structural features. Because of the versatility of this methodology, it is used widely across the social science disciplines interested in the study of social systems as a whole, including sociology, communication science, anthropology, science and technology studies, and organizational science (e.g., see Burt, 1982; Monge, 1987; Rice, 1994; Trotter, 2000).

DESIGNS TO STUDY GROUPS

The study of dyads is an essential feature of almost all social sciences. Also essential is the study of the behavior of the individual members of small groups and the manner in which the total group affects the individual. Studying groups calls for different methodological perspective than that employed when studying individuals within groups.

The Issue of Unit of Analysis in Nested Designs

The major design used by social psychologists to study people in interacting groups is the *hierarchically nested design*. In such a design, each person is a member of one and only one group. Consider a study of jury deliberation. If a researcher seeks to have 10 juries, each with 12 members, he or she would need 120 people for the study. Each person would be a member of one jury. Generally, the scores of two people who are the members of the same group are more similar than the scores of two people who are members of different groups. This similarity of scores happens because of conformity, social norms, modeling, and other social influence that occurs within interacting groups. Even when the members of a group do not interact directly, they may be exposed to common experiences or events that have similar effects on all of them. For instance, children in a single classroom not only interact with each other, they also share a common teacher and a common environmental setting that may influence them all. Because of these shared social factors, the scores of people in the same group are likely to be *nonindependent*; this nonindependence must be considered in the data analysis.

   With data from the hierarchically nested design, one can use either the person, or the group, as the unit of analysis. So for the given jury example, if person is the unit of analysis, correlations and other statistics are computed across 120 persons. When the group is the unit of analysis, the researcher first computes a mean for each group, and these means serve as the data for the computation of various statistics. For the jury example, then, the sample size would be 10 when group is used as the unit of analysis (vs. 120 if person were the unit).

   When scores are independent, then the individual can be used as the unit of analysis. This is desirable because it permits a more powerful statistical analysis of data. Differences, if they do exist, are more likely to be observed if more, rather than fewer, units are employed in the analysis. However, if the scores of person within groups are not independent, then the group, with its lower degrees of freedom (and lower statistical power), is the appropriate unit of analysis. A general approach to the assessment of dependence in dyadic and group data is given by Kenny and Judd (1996; also see Kashy & Kenny, 2000; Sadler & Judd, 2001).

The intraclass correlation (described earlier in this chapter) can be used to estimate the degree of interdependence in data from group members. Because the intraclass correlation is a conservative measure of the degree of nonindependence of group member data, it is recommended that a liberal rule for statistical significance be applied (e.g., alpha = .20; Kashy & Kenny, 2000). If the size of the intraclass correlation falls below this level of significance, it is fairly safe to conduct analyses at the individual unit of analysis without seriously increasing the chances of either Type I or Type II errors. However, if the degree of nonindependence as assessed by the intraclass correlation is significant at alpha <.20, the group is the appropriate unit of analysis to use in statistical tests. (See Kenny & Judd, 1986, for a more extended discussion of the consequences of violating assumptions of independence in the analyses of group data.)

Other Group Designs

Two other designs, although used much less frequently than the hierachically nested design in studying groups, nevertheless deserve mention. They are the *generations design* and the *rotation design*. In the generations design, one begins with a group of a given size—say, three units or actors. One makes the appropriate measurements on Persons A, B, and C. Then Person A is removed from the group and a new person, Person D, is added. After measurements are taken, Person B is removed, and Person E is added. The process of removing a person and adding another is continued, and eventually the group consists of no original members. This laboratory design mimics the life and death replacements of cultures. The design was first used by Jacobs and Campbell (1961) to study the persistence of norms in groups. Jacobs and Campbell inserted a confederate into an original group of five persons, and the confederate influenced the group members to give a certain response. The confederate was then removed, a new (naive) participant took his place, and the behavior of the group was studied. Jacobs and Campbell were able to show that adherence to the norm set by the confederate was still evident many "generations" after the confederate, and all the original group members, had been removed from the group. Although used infrequently, the generations design can be used to answer some questions much more effectively than many of the more popular alternatives.

Another design that can be used in small group research is the rotation design. In the rotation design we begin with a set of, say, nine persons. Then we have each person be in a group with each other person once and only once. With nine persons and a group size of three, each person would be in four different groups. So if we denote the persons as 1 through 9, we would have the following sets of groups as depicted in Table 17.5.

TABLE 17.5

The Rotation Design

		Time			
		I	*II*	*III*	*IV*
	A	1,2,3	1,5,9	1,6,8	1,4,7
Group	B	4,5,6	2,6,7	2,4,9	2,5,8
	C	7,8,9	3,4,8	3,5,7	3,6,9

At each time, three different groups, labeled A, B, and C are formed. No two persons are in the same group more than once. For instance, Person 3 is in a group with Persons 1 and 2 at Time 1, with Persons 4 and 8 at Time 2, with Persons 5 and 7 at Time 3, and with Persons 6 and 9 at Time 4. The person is in a group with each of the eight others once and only once, thus satisfying the requirements of the rotation design.

Barnlund (1962) used a rotation design to study whether the same person emerged as a group leader. He had groups of five people, and each person interacted in six sessions. No two persons were in the same group more than once. At each of the six sessions, the groups worked on a different type of task: artistic, construction, intellectual, co-ordination, literary, and social. Barnlund found that there was a fair amount of stability in leadership. The rotation design, though used infrequently, can be employed to examine the stability of a person's behavior across different groups and situations.

MEASURING GROUP PROCESS AND OUTCOMES

Most of the methods for assessing dyadic and group level variables that we have discussed thus far involve measuring structural features of the social unit, such as similarity, consensus, or communication networks. Many of these measures can be obtained without actually observing the group in interaction, through reports from group members or from archival records. Many of the more interesting and challenging issues in the study of groups arise from attempts to code and quantify the processes of group interaction itself, as well as the group performance, decisions, or products that arise from those processes. The study of group interaction process is a topic of interest within a number of social and behavior science disciplines, including social psychology, communication sciences, administrative sciences, sociology, education, and clinical psychology (McGrath & Altermatt, 2001). As a consequence, the nature of such measures are as varied as the purposes and composition of groups themselves, so a complete cataloging of measures and data collection techniques is beyond the scope of this chapter (for overviews, see Kerr, Aronoff, & Messé, 2000; McGrath, 1984; McGrath & Altermatt, 2001). However, we can provide some discussion of the most common methodological issues and paradigms that arise in these types of studies.

Interaction Processes

Process measures are sometimes derived from retrospective reports and ratings by group members after interaction has taken place. However, most studies of group process involve observation of the actual interactions among group members as they unfold in real time—either through direct observation or by videotaping the group in process and then analyzing the video record. In chapter 11, we talked about the most well-known observational system for classifying and recording interactive behaviors within groups—Bales' (1950, 1970) Interaction Process Analysis (IPA). The IPA and related observation systems (e.g., Borgatta & Crowther, 1965) provide a detailed record of what takes place during group interaction. Using the IPA generates categorical data representing the sequence of occurrence of interactive acts. Various methods of aggregating or summarizing the data from these records can be used to characterize the processes that have taken place in that group. For example, member contributions can be measured by aggregating each member's speaking turns during the group session and computing the proportion of total speaking turns for each.

Data from the IPA also permit quantitative summaries of the content of member contributions. For instance, Slater (1955) used IPA records to identify the roles that evolve among group members as they interact. He distinguished between two important types of functions that could be carried out by different group members: (a) socioemotional functions (behaviors that help to maintain good relationships among group members) and (b) task functions (behaviors that contribute to getting the group's job done). Subsequent research on group effectiveness has used these two variables, as well as other role measures derived from IPA data, to assess how well specific groups are functioning (Forsyth, 1990).

The frequency data generated from interaction process analyses can be analyzed using various statistical techniques for analyzing categorical data, such as chi-square contingency analysis or loglinear and logit models (Argesti, 1996). However, the dynamic nature of group process often involves studying groups over time, which adds to the complexity of data analyses. In analyzing measures taken from the same interacting group at sequential points in time, we must take into account *serial dependence* among behaviors over time. Just as measures taken from members within the same group are nonindependent (i.e., correlated with each other), so, too, each behavior in a group is to some extent dependent on the behavior that occurred just prior to it. Sequential analyses (e.g., Gottman & Roy, 1990) are used to assess the degree of serial dependence in a data set. (See chap. 9 for further discussion of time series analyses.)

Cognitive Processes in Groups

In addition to behavioral acts that can be observed during the course of group interaction, groups also have a cognitive life, that is, the knowledge structures and information processing that are brought to bear to make group interaction and coordination possible. The study of group cognition has generated considerable interest in the social sciences (see Tindale, Meisenhelder, Dykema-Engblade, & Hogg, 2001). For this purpose, novel methodologies have had to be developed to assess such things as how much and what information is shared among group members, how information is distributed, what group members know about each other's knowledge and skills, and what kind of "mental models" group members have about their task and structure.

The distribution of knowledge in a group may be analyzed by coding the contents of each member's knowledge prior to group interaction and assessing the degree of overlap between information held by one member and that of other members of the group (e.g., Kameda, Ohtsubo, & Takezawa, 1997). The degree of overlap prior to interaction can be compared with that obtained after the group interaction. The amount of shared information that members have at the outset of the group process can also be experimentally manipulated, as in the *hidden profile* technique developed by Stasser and Titus (1987). In this paradigm, members of four-person groups are given the task of choosing the best out of three political candidates. Before discussion begins, each of the members is given a set of information (some positive, some negative) about each of the three candidates. Some of the information is given to all four persons (shared knowledge) and some information is given to just one (unshared knowledge). If all of the available information (shared + unshared) is distributed during the group discussion, Candidate A is clearly the best choice. However, no one individual member of the group has enough information to know this at the outset. Thus, the group's decision (to choose Candidate A vs. B or C) will reflect how much the unshared information is brought up and used in the group discussion. Using this paradigm, researchers have found that shared knowledge is more likely to be discussed than is unshared knowledge, and as a result, groups often miss the hidden profile of information and fail to choose the best candidate.

In addition to the knowledge and information that individual group members bring to a task, they also develop *metacognitions* as the group interacts across time (Hinsz, Tindale, & Vollrath, 1997). At the group level, metacognition refers to the knowledge members have about the knowledge and skills that other group members have (sometimes called *transactive memory*; Wegner, 1987) and about their understanding of the group task (sometimes called *shared mental models*; Klimoski & Mohammed, 1994). Tindale et al. (2001) provided a good illustration of group metacognition in their description of sports teams:

> For example, each of the nine members of a baseball team must have an understanding of the rules of the game and the roles for each player . . . for the team to work together. Thus, team players must have a mental model of the task (rules of the game) and the group (the roles of each player) . . . to play effectively. However, this knowledge must be shared among the members in order for it to aid in team effectiveness. Two players who have different models of how to react in a given situation could each behave in ways that would interfere with the other's behavior. (p. 18)

The importance of giving groups opportunity to develop shared mental models and transactive memory was demonstrated experimentally by Moreland, Argote, and Krishnan (1998). They found that when three-person groups were trained together (in a common session, without direct interaction) to perform a radio assembly task, they were subsequently able to perform the same task significantly better than groups who had been trained on the same task individually. Methods such as those used by Moreland and his colleagues are teaching group researchers a great deal about the role of cognition in group process and coordination.

Computer-Mediated Group Interaction

Another innovation in the study of small groups comes from the advent of computer-mediated communication, which provides new ways of recording interactive behaviors and group process, as well as new questions to be addressed by group researchers. Computers can be used as a tool for accomplishing group tasks, as when group members work together at a single computer or work at individual computers with shared access, a process known as *groupwork* (e.g., McGrath & Hollingshead, 1994; Olson, Olson, Storreston, & Carter, 1994). But most often computers are used by groups as a medium of communication among members who are not in face-to-face contact (e.g., Latané & L'Herrou, 1996). Research comparing computer-mediated communication with face-to-face group interaction addresses interesting questions about the role of nonverbal cues in group process and interpersonal coordination, effects of status cues on rates of participation, and amount of information shared among group members (for reviews, see Hollingshead & McGrath, 1995; Kiesler & Sproull, 1992). For example, the importance of paralinguistic and nonverbal communication to transactive memory in dyads was documented in experiments by Hollingshead (1998) in which dating couples worked together on a general knowledge test either through computer-mediated communication or face-to-face. Face-to-face couples performed significantly better than the computer-mediated pairs, apparently because they were able to use nonverbal cues to assess which partner knew the correct answer. Couples who did not know each other prior to the experiment did not show this advantage, suggesting that the effective use of nonverbal information is part of a transactive system that develops over time.

Computer-mediated groups also become more effective over time. In a longitudinal study comparing computer-mediated and face-to-face communication, Hollingshead, McGrath, and O'Connor (1993) examined task performance of work teams in an undergraduate psychology class where the task involved writing a joint paper on course materials. The groups met weekly in 2-hour lab sessions over the course of 13 weeks. Results showed that the computer-mediated groups had poorer task performance than face-to-face groups initially, but after 3 weeks, there were no differences in the quality of papers produced by the two types of teams. Because of the role of learning in all forms of group process, the results of longitudinal studies of groups may show very different results from those obtained in single-shot experiments.

Comparing Groups and Individual Performance

A long-standing issue in the study of groups is that of evaluating the "value-added" by having people work together in groups rather than as lone individuals. Some tasks clearly require the concerted effort of multiple individuals working together because the nature of the task itself is beyond the capabilities of any one person to accomplish (e.g., moving a very large and heavy structure, fighting an invading force, getting to the moon). For many intellectual or physical tasks, however, it is not always clear whether groups of persons working cooperatively together produce more or better products than could be attained by having individuals work separately and then pooling the output of their individual efforts. To address this question, social researchers developed the method of comparing performance (or products) of real, interactive groups, with the products of so-called *nominal groups*. Nominal groups are composed of the same number and types of people as the real groups, but the members work independently rather than in interaction, and the group product is some combination of their individual performances or output.

One interesting example of the evaluation of group performance comes from the study of *brainstorming* groups. Brainstorming was initially developed by an advertising executive (Osborn, 1957) as a method for enhancing the generation of creative ideas through group interaction. The idea of a brainstorming group is that members throw out ideas in a free-wheeling fashion, without evaluation or censure, builiding on ideas as they are generated. Based on the notion that interaction would both stimulate and inspire new ideas and combinations of ideas, Osborn made some very strong assumptions about the importance of group process for creative output. For example, he claimed that "the average person can think up twice as many ideas when working with a group than when working alone" (p. 229).

How has this claim held up to the results of systematic research? Alas for Osborn's credibility, the results of several reviews of studies comparing interacting brainstorm groups with similarly instructed nominal groups consistently show that real groups generally produce fewer and poorer quality ideas than nominal comparison groups (Diehl & Strobe, 1987; Mullen, Johnson, & Salas, 1991). Findings such as these have led group researchers to study the concept of *process loss*, that is, those aspects of group interaction and coordination that inhibit or interfere with group production. For instance, in the case of brainstorming, the fact that group members must take turns talking may block production of ideas, and social psychological processes, such as social comparison and evaluation apprehension, may also be contributing factors to inhibit output (Stroebe & Diehl, 1994). By reducing some of these influences, process gains may override process losses, producing conditions under which real groups outperform the nominal group baseline (e.g., Dennis & Valacich, 1993).

CONCLUSION

The study of persons in dyads and groups allows for the testing of a number of important hypotheses that could not be tested otherwise. Hypotheses concerning reciprocity, interpersonal attraction, and similarity can best be tested with dyadic measures. To accurately understand the processes that are actually operating in the study of groups and dyads, it is necessary to go beyond a naive and intuitive analysis of the data. Often we must take a score obtained from a dyad or group and break it up into component parts to interpret its meaning accurately. Such a partitioning was illustrated in the discussion of the round robin design, the measurement of attraction, and the analysis of scores of interacting groups. We need to divide a score into components to reflect that different processes operate at different levels, and these processes influence the observed score. It might seem that all of the difficulties encountered when dealing with dyadic and group data diminish the charm and interest that these areas might otherwise have had as subjects of research. We prefer to view these complications as interesting challenges which, once confronted and conquered, reveal some fascinating and vital aspects of social life.

SUGGESTED READINGS

Kashy, D. A., & Kenny, D. A. (2000). The analysis of data from dyads and groups. In H. Reis & C. Judd (Eds.), *Handbook of research methods in social and personality psychology* (pp. 451–477). New York: Cambridge University Press.

Kenny, D. A., & La Voie, L. (1984). The social relations model. In L. Berkowitz (Ed.), *Advances in Experimental Social Psychology*, Vol. XVIII. New York: Academic.

McGrath, J. E., & Altermatt, T. W. (2001). Observation and analysis of group interaction over time: Some methodological and strategic choices. In M. Hogg & R. S. Tindale (Eds.), *Blackwell handbook of social psychology: Group processes* (pp. 525–573). Oxford, UK: Blackwell.

PART

IV

CONCLUDING PERSPECTIVES

18

SYNTHESIZING RESEARCH RESULTS: META-ANALYSIS

All sciences progress by the gradual accretion of knowledge. Although surely inspired, Einstein's classic formula relating energy, mass, and velocity was not drawn out of thin air. His was an enormously creative insight based on a synthesis and extension of the available knowledge of the time (Clark, 1971; Kuhn, 1970). Over the years, social scientists have relied on a similar process of intuition and integration of prior findings to develop new insights, which sometimes lead to the accumulation of yet more knowledge. To the extent that the existing literature on a phenomenon is accurate and that we have surveyed it comprehensively and fairly, we can develop an understanding of the structure of interrelationships that underlie it. Current knowledge is the foundation of future discoveries. In the past, this integrative, constructive process was based on a careful reading and interpretation of research results (a *narrative review*, as Johnson and Eagly, 2000, termed it) combined with creative theory-based insights.

This time-honored integrative process has been supplemented in recent years by the development of methods of *quantitative synthesis*, sometimes termed *meta-analysis* (i.e., a summary analysis of cumulated, earlier analyses). These methods allow for the quantitative assessment of factors that affect, or help define, a given phenomenon or construct. The earlier, narrative approach has served us well, but its critics suggest that it is prone to important shortcomings, including (a) narrative analysts' occasional tendency to fail to survey the existing knowledge base completely[1], (b) the lack of clearly stated rules for inclusion or noninclusion of studies in their analyses, and (c) the failure to use a common statistical metric to combine findings across different studies. A competent, systematic meta-analysis is intended to avoid all of these problems and thereby develop a more comprehensive understanding of a construct, or of a relationship between variables. The ultimate goal of such analyses is to construct a secure foundation on which to build a

---

[1] Of course, it is not fair to blame the narrative method for reviewers' failures to perform complete literature searches. However, the tradition of the narrative method does not necessarily call for a complete survey, and the lack of a full survey often produces biased results.

knowledge base. Quantitative assessment techniques require a thorough command of the research literature, good intuition and creativity, and a dogged work ethic; however, they offer a clearer path to understanding the true strength of the variables that affect (or define) a construct than the less formalized narrative approach characteristic of earlier methods of knowledge synthesis.

As a method of combining empirical data, meta-analysis had its beginnings many years ago, but the technique has become more commonly used in the social sciences only over the past 20–30 years (Cooper, 1979; Rosenthal, 1968).[2] Over this short period of time, important and thought provoking syntheses have been produced, and they have helped popularize this general approach (e.g., see Cooper, 1979; Eagly, Ashmore, Makhijani, & Longo, 1991; Eagly, Karau, & Makhijani, 1995; Eagly, Makhijani, & Klonsky, 1992; Sulloway, 1996; Wood, Lundgren, Ouellete, Busceme, & Blackstone, 1994). The shift from narrative to quantitative syntheses was not met with open arms. Many admitted in principle that meta-analysis could be a useful technique if its technical issues could be solved, but even then questioned its necessity. We believe that meta-analysis offers a means of addressing problems that the more traditional narrative analysis cannot. It represents yet another valuable tool for the social scientist, particularly when research on a phenomenon has been multimethodological, a general approach to research that we champion through-out this book. In effect, meta-analysis provides a way of assessing *construct validity* of research findings that involve different methods of design and measurement.

A simple example helps illustrate the role that meta-analysis can play in interpreting findings from different types of research. Suppose a researcher were interested in people's reactions to others on the basis of these others' physical attractiveness. In short, the scientist hypothesizes that people respond more positively to attractive than unattractive people. To test this idea, the researcher shows pictures of target people to a large group of participants who are asked to evaluate each of the targets. The hypothesis is that the good-looking targets will score significantly higher on ratings of pleasant, good, kind, thoughtful, and nice. The ratings on these measures are highly related, so the researcher combines them into an overall "liking" score. Statistical analysis discloses that the physically attractive targets receive scores that are significantly more positive than the unattractive targets (at $p < .05$). The researcher concludes that the results confirm the hypothesis: Attractive targets stimulate significantly more positive evaluations than unattractive targets.

To extend the conceptual and external validity of these results, a second researcher conducts a field experiment in which male and female accomplices are dressed to look either very attractive or very unattractive. They then individually approach strangers in a shopping mall and ask for quarters to make a phone call. The dependent measure is the (positive or negative) response of the participants to the request. Unfortunately, owing to a lack of time, the researcher cannot collect data from many participants. The results of this study suggest that the differences in contributions to attractive and unattractive accomplices are not statistically significant.

What conclusion could a reader draw from these two studies? Is there a relation between physical attractiveness and evaluation, as suggested in the first study, or was the effect an artifactual outcome of the laboratory setting? Or, was the second (null) finding the result of a lack of statistical power to detect a true difference, or a poor conceptualization of evaluation (donating $.25 to a stranger in need of a pay phone)? We find ourselves in a quandary because the conclusions from the two studies are different, at least as we can infer

---

[2]Stigler (1986) found evidence of rudimentary quantitative synthesis in the 1800s; Thorndike (1933) pro-vided a somewhat more contemporary example.

from differences in their respective levels of statistical significance. The problem with this comparative approach is that statistical significance is affected by a host of factors that are not necessarily related to the validity of a research result, such as sample size or the reliability of measures. Probability values are not directly comparable between studies; yet, it is on this basis that we have determined that the results of the two studies are in conflict. To compare the studies properly requires a *common metric* to express the size of the effects obtained in the two investigations. This is the basic insight and contribution of meta-analysis—to convert the results of different studies into a common metric and then combine and compare the results across studies.

STAGES IN THE META-ANALYSIS PROCESS

When two (or more) operationally different but conceptually similar studies produce similar results (or produce results similar in terms of the sizes of their effects), our confidence in both the external and construct validity of our findings is enhanced. However, as our attractiveness example suggests, when results appear to differ among studies, it may be difficult to identify the source(s) of the discrepancy. Differences in outcomes among studies could result from meaningful interactions involving settings, participant populations, or process variables, or from the methodological differences that characterize the discordant studies. With only two studies to compare, it rarely is possible to determine which of the possible reasons for the difference is responsible for the variation in outcome. However, when many studies of the same relationship or phenomenon have been conducted, it is possible to use meta-analytic methods to sort out the sources of variation in results across studies, and thereby develop a more insightful understanding of the phenomenon. The particular outcomes of the various steps in the analysis may vary from analysis to analysis, but the steps to be followed are the same.

Understanding the Literature

The first step, as in any other approach to reviewing research literature, requires that we have a good understanding of the scientific results on the phenomenon chosen for study. Techniques of quantitative synthesis are most effective when they are focused on a relationship between (usually two) variables that can be specified with a high degree of precision. That is, we begin with a specific hypothesis linking an independent variable with a dependent variable, or we specify a relationship between two dependent variables if correlational methodology was the primary method used in past research to investigate the phenomenon. On the basis of theory and prior research, we also may wish to consider the moderating or mediating effects of other variables, but the starting point is always the simple A–B relationship, whether causal or correlational. Returning to our example, we assume that physical attractiveness elicits more positive evaluations; people respond better to beautiful, or handsome, others. This is a simple cause–effect hypothesis relating two variables, and as such is an ideal candidate for meta-analysis. We might want to qualify the hypothesis, for example, by postulating that the relationship is stronger when people of the opposite sex are involved, or that the effect will be stronger when men are the actors and women the attractors (Buss, 1989). Including such moderating variables in the analysis has paid dividends in this research approach when competing theorists have specified factors that impinge on the fundamental relationship under study (see Bond & Titus, 1983; Wood et al., 1994), but the basic necessity for undertaking a meta-analysis is that a relationship between two variables (independent–dependent or dependent–dependent) has been specified.

A second basic requirement is that there be sufficient past research on the relationship of interest. If there are very few studies of the particular relationship to be synthesized, it is not likely that quantitative analysis will produce persuasive results. In general, a meta-analysis requires a relatively large number of studies, with all of them focused on the critical relationship, before its true power as an integrative force can be realized. Thus, the first step in the analysis requires that we have a good grasp of the literature, of what has been done, to have some general idea of the number of studies that have been conducted on the critical relationship we wish to study, along with the potential moderators that may affect the basic relationship. To plunge into the analysis before developing a strong command of the literature is foolhardy. Meta-analysis is labor intensive. To realize halfway through the project that some important variables have been missed, or that the basic relationship under study has not been specified correctly, usually results in an abandoned study and a great loss of time and effort.

Making Choices and Gathering Studies

The importance of specifying the critical relationship clearly becomes apparent in this phase, which entails choosing and accumulating studies to be included in the analysis. To choose studies, the researcher must decide on the criteria to be used to determine the relevance of a particular study. The issue of how broadly or narrowly to define the relationship or construct being investigated affects this choice. Problems may be framed at different levels of specificity or abstractness. A review of the effectiveness of a particular form of one-to-one psychotherapy is relatively narrow, or specific, in comparison to a study of the overall effectiveness of all types psychotherapeutic interventions. A review of the effects of cooperative tasks on Black–White relations is more concrete and focused than a review of the effects of task reward structure on intergroup relations in general.

Choosing studies involves two distinct processes: the first requires a *tentative* specification of inclusion rules, that is, which studies of the critical relationship will be included in the synthesis and which excluded.[3] Studies are included if they meet a specific criterion, or set of criteria. For example, if a meta-analyst wishes to estimate the strength of the *causal* relationship between the chosen independent and dependent variable, then studies that made use of a correlational methodology will not be included in the analysis. Being correlational, they cannot unambiguously support causal interpretations. Alternatively, the researcher may wish to summarize only studies published after a certain date. If there are defensible theoretical reasons for these qualifications, the researcher is fully justified in choice of criteria. A word of caution is in order, however; sometimes, the criterion variable can provide important information. For example, in meta-analysis of studies reporting sex differences in terms of perceived quality of life, Wood, Rhodes and Whelan (1989) found that men reported higher life-quality in studies published after 1978, whereas women reported a better quality of life in studies published before that date. This difference cannot be interpreted causally, of course, because cohort variations are not the result of systematic manipulation. However, Wood et al.'s results provide considerable grist for the speculative mill. If the timing of studies had not been noted and used to differentiate studies, the result could not have emerged.

Published meta-analyses in the social sciences range from those that include as few as 20 or 30 independent studies (e.g., Williams, Haertel, Haertel, & Walberg, 1982) to

---

[3]The specification is tentative because as the analysis progresses, the rules may be changed to better account for the available data.

those containing more than 300 studies (e.g., Rosenthal & Rubin, 1978; Smith & Glass, 1977). In general, the number of studies available for analysis varies as a function of the specificity of the construct being examined. Generally speaking, the more broadly we conceptualize the nature of our construct, the more we will be dealing with conceptual rather than exact replications, and the more we stand to learn about the construct validity of our research operations. It is also the case that more broadly defined constructs are more likely to reveal meaningful differences among studies that are systematically related to effect size, that is, the more likely we are to discover moderators that affect the strength of the critical relationship.

To return to our attractiveness→evaluation example, we might allow only studies that have used attitude scales to define evaluation. More broadly, we might also include studies that involved prosocial actions, donations, eye contact, and so on. In general, more broadly defined variables might be preferred. However, the decision about the allowable breadth of variables must be made in terms of the goals of the study and the number of studies available for analysis. In some cases, a very constricted range of allowable variables will be chosen because this range is specifically relevant to a theoretical controversy. In other circumstances, range will be constricted because there are not enough studies available to support a broader analytic approach. For example, we may study attraction very narrowly, by defining the variable in terms of observable behaviors that must include a relationship of extended duration. Conversely, attraction may be defined by any number of measures, ranging from a simple checkmark on a scale to more extended indications of liking, including relationship duration. More studies will be available with the less constricted definition, but we must be able to satisfy ourselves that the different measures are assessing the same phenomenon, and this requires a reasonable number of studies of all measures, thereby allowing us to compare the results obtained from the different types of measurement approaches. After all, we are interested in the substantive relationship, not measurement variance. If enough studies are not available for comparison among methods, it becomes considerably more difficult to determine whether the studies are focused on the same phenomenon; this is especially problematic if different methods appear to be associated with different outcomes.

A broadly defined construct will require that we break studies down by theoretically relevant *moderator variables*. At a minimum, method of measurement will be one such moderator whose effect must be studied. Therefore, the total number of studies used in the analysis must be large. Each time we break the sample of studies on the basis of a moderator variable, relevant comparisons are based on ever-smaller units. Meta-analysis is not useful for analyzing small sets of studies that differ widely in methods and constructs (Cook & Leviton, 1980). However, if studies are comparable in terms of methods, measures, and participant populations, then relatively few studies may meaningfully be combined to estimate the size of an effect of one variable on another, or the relationship between two variables.

There is some debate about the inclusion or exclusion of studies on the basis of quality. Some suggest that studies that do not meet some common methodological standard (e.g., no control group, no manipulation check information, underpowered, etc.) be excluded (e.g., Greenwald & Russell, 1991; Kraemer, Gardner, Brooks, & Yesavage, 1998). We believe, however, that meta-analysts generally should not exclude studies that meet substantive inclusion criteria, even those that are methodologically suspect. If the study meets the selection rules, it probably is wise not to go over the individual investigations and decide that some are to be excluded from the sample because they do not meet some high standard of methodological requirements. In our view, rather than eliminate studies on the basis of methodological purity, a more promising approach entails rating the methodological rigor of each study and then entering this rating as a potential moderator variable whose effect on the critical relationship may be assessed in the analysis. Such an assessment may show, for example, that only weak studies exhibit the postulated relationship. This result could prove useful and interesting, and would not be available if the weak studies were excluded a priori from the analysis. Conversely, it may be that our "quality of research" indicator is not related to the effect size found in the analysis. In this case, we would have lost statistical power by deleting the studies that did satisfy our methodological inclusion criterion.

After deciding on the inclusion rules, the researcher must gather every possible study that meets the criteria. This process can be accomplished with considerably more ease than it could a few short years ago. Computerized database literature searches in the social sciences are now possible by using sources such as those available in the Social Science Citation Index (Social SciSearch), the Education Resources Information Center (ERIC), Psychological Abstracts, PsycINFO, Sociological Abstracts, and Comprehensive Dissertation Abstracts. These bibliographic sources are available at most university libraries and are online for ease of access. One need only enter the appropriate search terms (usually one or more variants of the critical variables), and the entire literature can be searched. The American Psychological Association's PsycINFO database, for example, contains studies dating back to the 1880s, and the Dissertation Abstracts database extends back to 1861. Of course, social scientists are notorious for coining their own terms, so it is wise to employ search term and criteria broadly, and to exhaustively survey the archives for potentially relevant research. Campbell (1963), for example, listed more than 75 distinct terms used in the literature to refer to the general concept that nonscientists would identify as *attitude* or *opinion*. Thus, if we wished to study the effects of self-interest on resistance to opinion change, it would be dangerous to search only for studies that combine the terms self-interest and opinion. Other names for the opinion construct (*attitude, belief, value, acquired behavioral disposition,* etc.) would also be useful search terms, just as *attitude importance, vested interest, outcome involvement,* and *commitment* might access relevant studies on self-interest. We know the appropriate search terms by being familiar with the research literature and by learning more about the literature as we begin to search it. Meta-analysis is meant to provide an accurate picture of a literature. If the literature search is deficient, that is, if it does not produce the necessary raw materials for study, the analysis will fail. The picture it paints may be pretty, but it will not reflect reality.

A second way of using the automated databases is through a forward search process, by which we specify an important (earlier) study and then find all the subsequent studies that have cited it. By an important study, we mean one that is clearly focused on the construct that is the center of the meta-analysis and that is widely recognized as definitive, or as a classic in the field. Usually, there is relatively good consensus surrounding such studies, and if more than one is available, all should be used. This form of search is possible using Social SciSearch, the automated database of the *Social Sciences Citation Index.*

In addition to the automated databases, it is a good idea use backward search procedures, that is, to search the literature for comprehensive reviews of the particular phenomenon that is the focus of the meta-analysis and to use the references cited in these studies to find additional relevant studies. These studies, in turn, can be used for additional backward literature searches and the process continued until nothing new is found.

Some of the literature sources listed here are important because they include unpublished studies. ERIC, for example, contains a relatively large store of papers presented at major scientific conferences. Often, such papers are not published, and their information would be lost were it not for this archive. Unpublished research is important to include in a meta-analysis because we know that scientific journals are biased toward positive results. Indeed, it is an unusual editor who publishes results that are statistically nonsignificant. A number of comparative reviews demonstrate that published studies tend to show larger effects than unpublished ones. Smith and Glass (1977), for example, examined the standardized effect size obtained in 375 studies of the effectiveness of psychotherapy and found that studies published in books and journals had effect sizes that averaged between .7 and .8, whereas dissertation studies averaged .6 and other unpublished studies only .5. If the goal of the meta-analyst is to describe the universe of studies that deal with a specific relationship or construct, then this positive publication bias could prove misleading. In the worst of all possible worlds, we might be seeing only the 5% of studies that, by chance, have exceeded the $p < .05$ level of statistical significance (Greenwald, 1975).

The existence of inadvertently excluded unpublished studies in an area of research is known as the *file drawer problem* (Bradley & Gupta, 1997; Rosenthal, 1979, 1991), and the extent to which it creates a problem for the outcome of any particular meta-analysis can never be fully known. However, Rosenthal (1979, 1991) suggested a resolution to the problem that allows us to estimate the extent to which it may be an issue. This approach involves calculating the number of studies with null results (i.e., effect size of zero) that has to exist "in the file drawers" before the significance level of the overall effect obtained from the analysis of known studies reaches .05 (i.e., just barely significant). The size of this number helps us evaluate the seriousness of the threat to conclusions drawn from the meta-analysis. If the number of unknown studies that has to exist is very large, then it is not likely that studies in the file drawer will compromise the conclusions we reach on the basis of the available evidence. However, if only a few studies with null results reduce our obtained effects to the edge of statistical nonsignificance, we have to regard the file drawer problem as a potential threat to the validity of our analysis and interpretation.

Calculating and Analyzing Effect Sizes

If we are satisfied that our literature search procedures have succeeded in producing an archive of all (or most) studies relevant to our interests, we are ready to begin the computational phase of the analysis. In this stage, we calculate and analyze the magnitude of the effect size indices that we have drawn from the data. The effect size index is the fundamental, basic unit of all meta-analysis. To synthesize a literature, we need to be able to reduce all results to the same metric. The effect size index represents this metric. Effect size analysis is a simple statistical exercise that often is made difficult by published studies' failure to provide the data needed to calculate effects. As we have noted, the goal of effect size analysis is to develop a statistical indicator of the strength of a given manipulation or treatment on an outcome measure, or the strength of relationship between critical variables in the meta-analysis. To allow direct comparison of the strength of results of different studies requires that the studies each present some form of quantitative analysis of the strength of the critical effect, and that this quantitative analysis is presented in sufficient detail that it can be reduced to a common metric. In practice, this means that before a study can be used in a meta-analysis, it must present results in terms of correlations, means and standard deviations (analysis of variance or t tests), χ^2, or proportions. These values can be transformed so that they indicate the size of a given effect. Once all the results across a set of studies are transformed (into effect sizes) so they are all on the same metric, the transformed value(s) from one study can be compared directly with the transformed values from other studies.[4]

One common effect size index is the correlation coefficient, which sometimes is corrected for skew (e.g., see Hays, 1988), or the standardized mean difference index, which typically is used to transform t and F (analysis of variance) values.[5] These indices represent the strength of a relationship independent of the N on which it is based and, as such, allow comparison among studies that might have used widely varying participant samples. (The details of effect size calculation are beyond the scope of this book. Good sources for this information are Feingold, 1995; Hedges & Friedman, 1993; Hunter & Schmidt, 1990; Johnson & Eagly, 2000.)

Once effect sizes are calculated for all studies, they are aggregated (averaged) in an analysis. Usually, the more reliable results (i.e., those based on larger Ns, and thus, having less error variance) are more heavily weighted in the meta-analysis (Hedges & Olkin, 1985; Hunter & Schmidt, 1990). A confidence interval is computed around the resulting weighted mean, and if the interval does not contain the null value (zero), it is taken to suggest a reliable relationship between the cause and effect variables. If the confidence interval contains the null value, it may be concluded that there is no reliable effect of the cause on the hypothesized effect (or outcome) variable. However, this interpretation should not be made until the homogeneity of the variances of the effect size indices is tested. If there is substantial heterogeneity of effect size variance, then the assumption that the weighted effect size index is an accurate summary of its component parts (the individual effect size estimates from the studies in the analysis) is not supported. In this case, variables that may moderate the relationship between hypothesized cause and effect must be sought.

Coding and Selecting Moderator Variables

Obviously, the effect size indices from one study to another will not be identical. Some random variation among the estimates size is to be expected. However, if there is significant variance among the indices, above and beyond that expected from sampling error, the results cannot be regarded as homogeneous across different studies. Heterogeneity among studies in the size and direction of effect sizes may provide important insights into potential moderators. Of course, potentially relevant *moderator variables* should be selected in advance, on the basis of theory or empirically based hunches, but even post hoc moderators can prove enlightening. Moderators may include methods factors, such as

---

[4]If the necessary information cannot be extracted from published versions of otherwise relevant studies, it sometimes can be obtained from the researcher directly; however, this is not always possible or practical. If many of the relevant studies do not contain adequate statistical information, the analyst may have to resort to simpler quantitative methods, such as combining and comparing p values only (Rosenthal, 1979; Rosenthal & Rubin, 1978, 1982). Such analyses do not provide nearly as much information about the magnitude and variability of effects, but they do utilize more information than the traditional counting methods characteristic of narrative analyses in cumulating results across studies.

[5]The general formula for computation of the standardized mean difference is

$$d = \frac{M1 - M2}{s}$$

where s is some measure of within-group standard deviation. Computation methods differ as to which measure of s is most appropriate to use. Glass (1977; Smith & Glass, 1977) employed the control group standard deviation; others (e.g., Hunter, Schmidt, & Jackson, 1982) recommended the pooled within-group variance. In either case, the statistics r and d are algebraic transforms of each other.

TABLE 18.1

Hypothetical Results of 10 Studies of Message
Source Effects

Study No.	Source Type	Effect Size
1	Expert	.64*
2	Expert	.84*
3	Expert	.40
4	Expert	.16
5	Expert	.64*
6	Attractive	−.04
7	Attractive	−.24
8	Attractive	.20
9	Attractive	.44*
10	Attractive	−.04

*Significant at the $p < .05$ level

whether the study was conducted in a field or lab setting, whether self-report or behavioral measures were used, whether the experimental design involved within- or between-group comparisons, and so forth. Other variables selected for analysis could be theoretically relevant third factors that may interact with the treatment under consideration to determine the effect obtained. Controversies among different theories about the interpretation of an effect, or the conditions under which it will occur, provide good sources for identifying potential moderator effects of interest (see Pillemer & Light, 1980; Wood et al., 1994; for illustrations).

Once one or more potential moderator variables have been selected, each study in the analysis is coded on each of those characteristics (i.e., whether the characteristic is present or absent in the experimental operations or procedures, or the level that was present). The effects of the presence or absence of these moderators are then examined to determine whether it can explain the heterogeneity among the effect sizes of the different studies that constitute the meta-analysis.

The effect of the moderator on the hypothesized cause–effect relationship can be tested in one of two ways. The first method involves dividing the total set of studies into subsets that differ on the characteristic in question, to determine whether the average effect sizes computed within the subsets differ significantly from each other (Rosenthal & Rubin, 1982). To illustrate this approach, consider the hypothetical data in Table 18.1, which represent the hypothetical results of 10 different studies of the effect of the source of a persuasive message on attitude change. In each study, the same message was attributed either to a source that was rated very positively or neutrally by participants.[6] The effect size is the difference in average attitude change obtained under the two source conditions. The researcher is aware that positive source characteristics are effected in different ways in the studies that constitute the analysis. In half the studies, the positive source was someone who was characterized as an *expert* in the field; in the other studies, the positive source characteristic was *attractiveness*; the source was not necessarily an expert, but did possess traits that were highly appealing to the target audience. Both of these variables have been shown in past research to produce greater persuasion (see Brewer & Crano, 1994). Cumulating across all 10 studies, the average weighted effect size is computed as $d = .30$.

---

[6]Of course, different messages were used in the different studies.

TABLE 18.2

Hypothetical Results of 12 Studies of the Effect of
Argument Number of Attitude Change

Study No.	No. Arguments	Effect Size
1	4	−.27
2	4	−.07
3	4	−.22
4	4	−.17
5	3	.37
6	3	−.12
7	3	.42
8	3	.52*
9	2	.47*
10	2	.57*
11	2	.47*
12	2	.17

*Significant at the $p < .05$ level

A confidence interval is drawn around this value, and it is established that the effect is significantly greater than zero ($p < .05$),[7] indicating an overall positive effect for expert or attractive sources. However, an assessment of the variance in effect sizes indicates significant heterogeneity among the effect size indices of the studies, even though the standardized mean difference indices have been corrected for sampling error.

To determine whether this variance is related to the nature of the source manipulation (expertise vs. attractiveness), the researcher separates the studies into those that used expertise-based sources and contrasts the obtained standardized mean difference effect size indices with those that obtained when attractiveness was used. For the expert studies, the average effect size is found to be .54, whereas in the attractiveness studies, the mean effect size is .06. Furthermore, within the two subsets, the variance among effect size estimates reduces to nearly 0 once corrected for the different types of source manipulation. This finding suggests that all of the systematic differences between the two types of studies in their estimates of effect size can be accounted for by the moderator variable of how the positive source was defined or created.

A second method for assessing the contribution of a potential moderator variable to variance in results across studies is to enter the coded variable into a correlation (or multiple regression) analysis with effect size as the dependent measure (Glass, 1978). This method is most appropriate when the variable under consideration is defined quantitatively. For an example of this method, consider again a set of studies on attitude change, this time taking into account differences among the studies in the number of persuasive arguments included in the message attributed to an expert or neutral source, as in Table 18.2. In this analysis, the average effect size of message source is only .15, but as before, there is significant variation in effect sizes from study to study. However, if one correlates the number of arguments used in each study with the size of effect obtained in that study, the correlation is negative and significantly larger than zero (chap. 8 discusses the interpretation of correlations). This suggests that there is an effect of source across studies, but that this effect appears only when the message content is low in number of

---

[7]That is, the confidence interval that encloses the aggregated effect size does not include the null (0) value.

persuasive arguments. When the message has a larger number of arguments, source has little impact on attitude change. Without considering this factor, the results of the overall meta-analysis are misleading.

Interpreting Results

Interpreting the meaning of the effect size indices found in a meta-analysis is, in part, determined by the pattern of results obtained. If the mean effect size over all studies is small and not statistically significant, it is important to determine that the null finding is not a result of a heterogeneous data set, as discussed. If we have some strongly positive and some strongly negative effect size estimates in the analysis, it is important to determine whether a moderator-variable analysis might help differentiate the investigations. Finding potential moderators is usually facilitated by theory; however, if an obvious atheoretical moderator is suggested by the data pattern, it should be used to differentiate the studies and thereby provide a possible new direction for future research. It should be recognized that serendipitous findings of this type are post hoc and should be treated accordingly, in a tentative, hypothesis-generating fashion. They do not unambiguously support causal explanations.

To show why this is so, suppose a researcher were to conduct a meta-analysis on prior research investigating the fundamental attribution error, the tendency of observers to explain others' behavior in terms of personal, rather than situational, factors (Gilbert & Malone, 1995; Ross, 1977). If a competent review of the literature were done, the researcher would find that the effect sizes varied considerably from study to study. Indeed, the variation might be so great that the average effect size was zero. However, being in close touch with the data, the researcher realizes that almost all the positive findings of the bias are found in research conducted in Western cultures (the United States, Europe, Australia), whereas the effect is strongly diminished, and sometimes reversed, in non-Western ones (China, Japan, etc.; see Choi, Nisbett, & Norenzayan, 1999; Fiske, Kitayama, Markus, & Nisbett, 1998). Using culture as a moderator, the analysis would disclose strong results, which help clarify an apparent inconsistency among results in the area. This result should be used as the basis for hypotheses regarding the effects of cultural variations on the attributional bias, but it should not be offered, post hoc, as an explanation of the difference. Interpreting serendipitous findings in a causal fashion is always a mistake, no matter what the methodological source of their discovery (Kerr, 1998).

Some meta-analyses might find a distribution of mean effect size indices that is not notably heterogeneous, but still produces nonsignificant results. The hypothesized effects appear to be too weak to matter. Before jumping to this conclusion, it is important to be sure that the statistical power of the study is sufficient. If too few studies are used, the likelihood of discovering a reliable result is minimized. Effect sizes are often interpreted as small, medium, or large as a function of the amount of variance they explain. Cohen (1988) suggested that aggregated effect sizes that account for approximately 1% of the variance ($r = .10$) be termed *small*; those that explain approximately 9% be termed *medium*, and those accounting for 25% or more be termed *large*. This description is generally understood and provides a convenient shorthand for describing the strength of relationships tapped in the analysis. It also allows calculation of the approximate number of studies that should be used to detect an effect (see Cohen, 1988).

Even apparently small effect sizes discovered in a meta-analysis should not be dismissed lightly. Rosenthal and Rubin (1982) proposed a method of interpreting effect sizes in terms of differences in positive or negative outcomes that are found between the treatment groups that form the basis of the meta-analysis. Using their binomial effect size display (BESD) sometimes provides graphic evidence of the practical importance of treatments that produce only small effect sizes. Suppose, for example, that a researcher is interested in the hypothesis that differences in the membership group of a message source would have an impact on the source's persuasive effectiveness. The researcher gathers studies that investigate source characteristics, and determines each source's group membership: Is the source part of the group being persuaded, or is the source from outside the targeted group? The results suggest that in-group sources are more effective than out-group sources, but the mean effect size is between small and medium by Cohen's definition ($r = .20$). Rather than becoming depressed, the researcher turns to Rosenthal and Rubin's BESD and calculates the difference between persuasive success and failure as a function of the source's group membership. The statistic reveals that the persuasive effect is 20% higher when the source of persuasion is in-group. A marketing executive might find this result to be a very important argument for targeting messages on the basis of source–audience similarity. Even though the effect is not large statistically, in practical terms it is well worth considering.

Narrative vs. Quantitative Syntheses: Some Comparisons

Conclusions drawn from quantitative meta-analytic techniques often can be very different from more traditional, qualitative, narrative reviews of the literature. The latter often are characterized by what has been called the *box-score* or *voting count* method of tabulating results across studies. These methods basically involve counting the number of studies in which statistically significant and statistically nonsignificant result have been obtained. We argue that direct comparison of probability values generally is not a wise course, but the narrative review approach often is completely dependent on such counts. The problem is twofold: (a) Probability values between different studies are not directly comparable, and perhaps more importantly, (b) this approach loses considerable information. It does not readily allow for consideration of the magnitude of effects, nor does it provide information on the direction, or trend, observed in statistically nonsignificant results. Because of these differences in the amounts of information used and obtained, estimates of the overall effects of a treatment obtained in a meta-analysis tend to be less conservative than those based on simple tabulation methods (see Cooper & Rosenthal, 1980).

To illustrate the differences in conclusions that might be drawn from meta-analytic versus narrative review methods, consider again the data in Tables 18.1 and 18.2. In Table 18.1, only 4 of 10 studies reported statistically significant effects, although most of the studies had outcomes in the same, positive direction. In Table 18.2, the tabulation results in an even poorer picture, with only one third of the studies showing a significant effect. In both cases, our traditional narrative analysis would have led us to conclude that source of message had no reliable effect. Conversely, the results of the meta-analyses showed a significant overall effect in the first case, and a qualified effect in the second. The difference in conclusion comes from taking into account the nature of the results from all the studies. In a meta-analysis, even studies with small (and nonsignificant) effect sizes add information about the general direction of effect obtained. This added information is often important in clarifying the relationship between variables. To ignore it, as is done in the box-score approaches, is dangerous and wasteful.

CONCLUSION

It should be obvious that methods of quantitative synthesis have much to offer. They promise to facilitate the growth and development of the social science enterprise and, as such, should become a normal practice in the field. This is not to suggest that these techniques should supplant primary data collection or even narrative reviews. Meta-analysis obviously cannot supplant primary data collection because such data are the fundamental inputs of the meta-analysis. Without primary data, there is nothing to meta-analyze.

Clearly, quantitative syntheses should—and will—play a larger role in the research enterprise in social science. Their advantages are too great to minimize or ignore, despite the enormous efforts that such analyses entail and despite the continuing controversy surrounding the proper statistical derivation and calculation of effect size indices. Even so, these advantages do not take the place of good qualitative reviews of the literature. Narrative reviews still have their place to complement and enrich the interpretation of more quantitative data summaries. The two approaches are best used in combination. Particularly where there are significant variations across studies in effects obtained, a careful examination of substantive and methodological differences among the studies included in the analysis is essential for drawing any meaningful conclusions. Such an examination is part and parcel of both qualitative and quantitative analyses. Bolstering the quantitative precision of the meta-analysis with the creative insights of the narrative analysis affords the best of both possible worlds.

SUGGESTED READINGS

Hunter, J. E., & Schmidt, F. L. (1990). *Methods of meta-analysis: correcting error and bias in research findings*. Newbury Park, CA: Sage.

Johnson, B. T., & Eagly, A. H. (2000). Quantitative synthesis of social psychological research. In H. Reis & C. Judd (Eds.), *Handbook of research methods in social and personality psychology* (pp. 496–528). New York: Cambridge University Press.

Rosenthal, R. (1991). Meta analysis: A review. *Psychosomatic Medicine, 53*, 247–271.

19

SOCIAL RESPONSIBILITY AND ETHICS IN SOCIAL RESEARCH

The social sciences share with all scientific endeavors the need to balance scientific zeal with other values that derive from the social context in which all scientific work takes place. To some extent, the scientific ideal of objectivity inevitably conflicts with humanistic values, and all scientists must at some time come to grips with this conflict. The issue, however, is particularly acute for social scientists because the focus of their research is the behavior of other human beings, and thus not only the goals of research but the very process of data collection is subject to value conflicts. This chapter first considers those ethical issues that are related specifically to research with human respondents and then focuses on the more general issues of concern to all scientists in their choice of research problem and strategy of data reporting.

ETHICS OF RESEARCH DESIGN AND METHODOLOGY

Because the subject matter of the social scientist is human behavior and the processes that mediate that behavior, it is inevitable that scientific interests will conflict at times with values placed on the rights of individuals to privacy and self-determination. The guidelines for behavioral and social research set by the American Psychological Association's Committee on Ethical Standards (1983; 1992) and by the President's Panel on Privacy and Behavioral Research (Surgeon General's directive, 1967) stress the idea of recruiting participants for research on the basis of *informed consent*—that is, that participation be voluntary and with the volunteer's full knowledge of what participation will involve. However, it is recognized that many phenomena could not be researched at all if this ideal were fully met, and that the rights of participants must be weighed against the potential significance of the research problem. Resnick and Schwartz (1973), for example, demonstrated in a verbal conditioning experiment that a complete description of methods and hypotheses eliminated the phenomenon they were attempting to investigate.

In cases where full information cannot be provided, the panel report recommends that "consent be based on trust in the qualified investigator and the integrity of the research institution." Thus, the ethical code does not provide absolute standards that relieve the scientist of important value judgments. Rather, judgments as to the relative importance of research programs and researchers' responsibility for the welfare of their participants are the fundamental bases of research ethics.

Deception in the Laboratory

When research is conducted in the psychological laboratory, there is seldom any question concerning the individual participant's knowledge that he or she is the subject of a scientific investigation. The extent to which participation is fully voluntary is in many cases debatable, given the social and institutional pressures to take part in research that are sometimes involved. But generally, participants in laboratory experiments at least know that they are taking part in a research study. Beyond that, however, the information provided to participants in laboratory investigations is usually minimal, at best, and often intentionally misleading as to the purposes of the research study.

As we emphasized in chapter 5, the methodological strategy of most laboratory research is directed toward motivating the participant to behave spontaneously and unselfconsciously while the researcher maintains careful control over the stimulus conditions to which the participant responds. To this end, the procedures of the research study are often presented and justified in terms of an elaborate "cover story" designed to control the participant's perception of the research setting and influence his or her motivational "set." Thus, the researcher often goes beyond merely withholding information from the participant to deliberate misrepresentation of the details of his or her participation. (The importance of this form of control to the validity of experimental research was discussed in previous chapters of this book.) Yet, such deception is undeniably in violation of values of interpersonal trust and respect.

To what extent this violation is justified by serving scientific goals and the potential advancement of human welfare is a matter of considerable controversy. Some critics argue that no deception is ever justified and that it should not be permitted in the interests of social research (Ortmann & Hertwig, 1997). Most researchers, however, take a more moderated view, recognizing that there is an inevitable trade-off between values of complete honesty and informed consent and the potential value of what can be learned from the research itself. Just as the "white lie" is regarded as acceptable when used in the service of good manners, so a minimal amount of deception may be tolerated in the service of obtaining trustworthy research data. However, there is some debate over whether behavioral scientists have exceeded this acceptable minimum in their research.

For some years the practice of deception in laboratory experiments was accepted with equanimity by most experimenters. However, an article by Herbert Kelman (1967) reflected a growing concern with the widespread, and apparently unquestioned, use of deception in research in social psychology. Kelman's article called into question this practice on both ethical and practical grounds. Ethically, he argued, any deception violated implicit norms of respect in the interpersonal relationship that forms between experimenter and research participant. In addition, the practice might have serious methodological implications as participants become less naive and widespread suspiciousness begins to influence the outcomes of all human psychological research. To offset these problems, Kelman recommended that social psychologists (a) reduce the unnecessary use of deception, (b) explore ways of counteracting or minimizing its negative consequences when deemed necessary, and (c) develop new methods, such as role playing or simulation techniques, which substitute active participation for deception.

Experimentation with these alternative methodologies has been attempted, but the results are mixed, at best (see chap. 5), and it remains ambiguous whether the results of a role-playing simulation can be interpreted in the same way as those obtained under the real experimental conditions. Thus, the general consensus in the research community is that some level of deception is frequently necessary to create realistic conditions for testing research hypotheses, but that such deception needs to be justified by the nature and importance of the research question being studied. As Rosenthal (1994) put it, "The behavioral researcher whose study may have a good chance of reducing violence or racism or sexism, but who refuses to do the study simply because it involves deception, has not solved an ethical problem but only traded one for another" (p. 129).

Deception and Participant Well-being

Apart from the issue of the relationship between experimenter and participant, the ethical acceptability of some deception experiments has been challenged on the grounds that the situations set up by the experimenter sometimes place the research participant in a position of psychological stress or other discomfort. This potentially violates the other major canon of ethical research—to "do no harm" to those who participate. The extent to which such potential distress to participants is tolerable in the name of scientific research is also a matter of debate. As usual, the extremes are fairly well established—no potentially permanent physical or psychological harm to the human participant is ever permissible. However, consensus as to the acceptability of temporary or reversible psychological distress is more difficult to achieve. The Asch (1956) studies, for example, which provided the paradigm for much research on social conformity, clearly placed the naive participant in a position of psychological stress as he weighed the evidence of his own senses against the judgments of presumably sincere fellow students. Most researchers seem to agree that the significance of this line of research and the transitory nature of the psychological discomfort involved justified its undertaking.

The studies of destructive obedience conducted by Milgram (1974), on the other hand, have aroused considerably more variability in reaction. The design of Milgram's research (which has been mentioned in a number of contexts in this volume) involved deceiving participants into believing that they were administering possibly harmful shocks to a fellow participant (actually the researcher's accomplice who was not really receiving any shocks) while being pressured by the experimenter to continue the procedure. In his initial reports of the results of this research, Milgram gave detailed illustrations of evidence of psychological stress on the part of those participants who continued in the experiment. Of one such participant he observed that "within 20 minutes he was reduced to a twitching, stuttering wreck, who was rapidly approaching a point of nervous collapse" (Milgram, 1963, p. 377).

As a consequence of these rather dramatic depictions of participant distress, the publication of Milgram's initial experiments was met with quite a bit of critical reaction (e.g., Baumrind, 1964). Milgram's (1964) response to this criticism emphasized the significance of the research, particularly with regard to the unexpected nature of the results, and the care that had been exercised in the experimental and postexperimental procedures to assure that participants suffered no long-term psychological damage. Milgram also suggested that the vehemence of the critical response to his research may have been largely a function of the nature of his findings. If more participants had behaved in a humane and independent fashion, and refused to administer shocks at high voltage levels, the same research procedures might not have come under such intense critical attack. If so, it would seem that it was not so much the fact of deception that was being criticized, but rather the way participants reacted to the treatment in this particular case. Yet those very reactions— unexpected as they were—are what made the experiments so valuable to social science and our understanding of human nature.

Debriefing: Explaining the Study to Participants at the End

Debate over the ethical acceptability of Milgram's experiments has revealed that whereas social scientists disagree somewhat about the frequency and extent of the use of deception that can be tolerated, few would hold that no research involving deception should ever be done. Where deception is deemed necessary to the exploration of some research problems, attention turns to the best method of counteracting the negative implications of its use. For this purpose, considerable emphasis has been given to the importance of the "debriefing" session, following participation in an experiment, in which the participants are informed of the true nature and purpose of the experimental treatments. Kelman (1967) placed enough value on such debriefing procedures to regard their inclusion in the experimental design as an "inviolate" rule. Milgram's (1964) justification of his research procedures relied heavily on his use of extensive debriefing sessions during which participants were reassured about the nature of their responses and encouraged to express their reactions in what was essentially a psychotherapeutic setting.[1]

When such attention is devoted to the content and handling of debriefing sessions, they may serve not only to "undeceive" the participants (and thereby relieve the researcher's pangs of conscience) but also to enrich the participant's own experience in terms of under-standing or self-awareness. (For a detailed description of the conduct of a debriefing session, see Aronson, Wilson, & Brewer, 1998.) However, we must caution against consider-ing the debriefing session as a panacea for all ethical aches and pains of social research. Some research suggests that when used routinely or handled perfunctorily, debriefing procedures can cause more harm than good (Holmes, 1976a, 1976b; Ross, Lepper, & Hubbard, 1975; Walster, Berscheid, Abrahams, & Aronson, 1967).

Many researchers warn that routine debriefing may produce widespread suspicion and potential dishonesty among populations frequently tapped for participation in psycholog-ical research. Some research has been directed toward this issue, the results of which are interesting, though not entirely consistent. Brock and Becker (1966) exposed participants to one experiment followed by no debriefing, partial debriefing, or complete debriefing, and then tested their responses in a subsequent deception experiment. No differential reactions to the second experiment were obtained except when a strong deception cue was made available through a common element in the two experiments, in which case only the completely debriefed participants reacted with suspicion. On the other hand, Silverman, Shulman, and Wiesenthal (1970) compared students whose first experimental participation had been a deception experiment with others who had participated first in a nondeception memory study. They found significant differences in responses to a second study involving a series of psychological tests. Examination of these differences indicated that the previously deceived participants responded in the direction of more favorable self-presentation than did the nondeceived participants.

---

[1] A follow-up survey of participants in these experiments revealed that 84% expressed positive reactions regarding their participation, whereas only 1.3% had any negative reactions (Milgram, 1964). This finding was supported in a replication by Ring, Wallston, and Corey (1970).

The preceding two studies involved students who had participated in only one experiment prior to testing. Other studies have investigated the effects of multiple participations on attitudes and behavior related to behavioral research. Holmes (1967) found that the more research experience participants had, the more favorable were their attitudes toward psychological experiments, and the more they intended to cooperate in future research. Holmes's study, however, did not take into account the extent to which his participants had experienced deception in the studies in which they had served. A more direct test of the effects of frequent deception was provided by Smith and Richardson (1983), who tested the attitudes of more than 400 research participants who had served in a variety of experiments over the course of an academic quarter. They found that participants who had been in deception experiments evaluated their research experience *more* positively than those who had not been deceived, and that effective debriefing appeared to eliminate the negative feelings of those who felt they had been harmed by deceptive practices. Those who had participated in deception experiments reported that they received better debriefing, enjoyed their experiences more, received greater educational benefits from the research, and were more satisfied with the research program than those who had not been involved in deception experiments.[2] We speculate that some of these variations might be a function of differences between the types of experiments that made use of deception and those that do not. Often, deception-based studies are inherently interesting—they involve complex decision making, arguing against a strong counter-attitudinal communication, making judgments about people and social events, and so on. Those that do not involve deception might require participants to memorize long lists of nonsense syllables, respond as rapidly as possible to randomly presented visual stimuli, deciding which two of three tones are most similar, and so forth. These latter types of studies often are ethically pristine, but they might not be very enjoyable.

With effective debriefing, the negative aspects of the deception studies might be offset, leading to more positive evaluation of the research experience on the part of participants. This requires, however, that the debriefing be conducted in such a way, and with enough thought and effort, that participants leave feeling that they have learned something by the experience and that their time has not been wasted.

Effective debriefing is also important for gaining participants' commitment to the purposes of the research and their agreement not to tell other future participants about the deception. As a result of communication among members of a research participant "pool," the effects of debriefing-generated suspicion may extend beyond those who actually have participated in deception experiments. Weubben (1965) provided some indication of the extent of such inter-subject "contamination" by finding that of 113 participants who had agreed to secrecy following an experimental debriefing session, 72 revealed the nature of the research to other potential participants. Reviews of deception research (Striker, 1967; Striker, Messick, & Jackson, 1967) indicate that there is inadequate assessment of such prior knowledge or suspicion on the part of participants and that the implications of such suspicion for the validity of laboratory experiments are still not well understood. Because of this, badly done debriefings—those that do not succeed in gaining participants' confidence, trust, and cooperation—can potentially harm the scientific enterprise.

Apart from these methodological considerations, debriefing has been criticized because it may not always be effective in relieving the effects of certain kinds of deception manipulations. Walster et al. (1967) reported that for highly concerned participants, even lengthy

---

[2]They also, however, were somewhat more likely than nondeceived subjects to doubt the trustworthiness of psychologists!

debriefings were not successful in removing reactions to false information feedback involving personal adequacy. Ross et al. (1975), too, found that the effects of deception often were exceptionally difficult to offset. Particularly when the nature of the experimental manipulation has involved providing false information of some kind about the participant's personality, competence, or self-esteem, an extensive form of debriefing known as "process debriefing" (Ross et al., 1975) may be required. Such a debriefing procedure includes discussing with participants how the deception may have temporarily influenced their own self-perceptions and the processes by which these effects might occur. Previous research has shown that this type of systematic debriefing is more successful in eliminating any lingering effects of the deception than a standard debriefing in which participants are simply told that the information was untrue but without discussion of process (Ross et al., 1975).

Ethical Issues in Field Research

Although much of the debate about the ethical implications of deception focuses on laboratory experimentation, research conducted outside the laboratory often raises a host of other ethical issues and concerns. In addition to issues related to consent to participate, researchers also must consider issues of privacy and confidentiality when research data are collected in field settings. Because a major advantage of field research, from a scientific standpoint, is the possibility of obtaining samples of behavior under naturally occurring conditions, it frequently is advantageous to conduct such studies under conditions in which the nature of the research is disguised. Thus, the participants may not only be deceived about the purpose of the research, but may even be unaware that they are the subject of research in the first place. The use of "unobtrusive" measures (cf. Webb et al., 1981) highlights this strategy, but even more traditional methods of data collection, such as the interview or questionnaire, are frequently presented in such a way as to disguise their true purpose.

Some scientists regard the practice of concealed observation or response elicitation as acceptable as long as it is limited to essentially "public" behaviors or settings normally open to public observation. Campbell (1969b), for instance, provided a review of settings and behaviors for which disguised research strategies have been employed, including studies ranging from pedestrian violations of traffic signals (Lefkowitz, Blake, & Mouton, 1955), to mailing of "lost letters" (Milgram, 1969), interpersonal interaction in employment offices (Rokeach & Mezei, 1966), arranged encounters between strangers in public streets (Feldman, 1968), fund collection (Bryan & Test, 1967), and door-to-door solicitation (Freedman & Fraser, 1966). All of these involve behaviors that Campbell regards as falling within the "public domain" and thus not requiring permission from participants nor subsequent debriefing. However, there remains the question of subjective definitions of what constitute "public" behaviors, particularly in urban settings where social norms lead to the expectation of anonymity in public places. Some social scientists (e.g., Miller, 1966) regard any form of unaware participation in research as an intolerable invasion of the individual's right to privacy. Even though some settings may readily allow for interpersonal observation, if individuals in these settings do not normally expect to be observed (or, rather, expect *not* to be), the issue of privacy remains. A case in point is provided in the research of Middlemist, Knowles, and Matter (1976), who studied the effects of "spatial invasion" in a men's room by secretly observing participants' behavior at a urinal.

Because by definition field experiments involve some intervention on the part of the researcher in the stimulus conditions to which the unaware participants are exposed, ethical considerations about hidden observation are further complicated by concern over the nature of such manipulations. Examples of experimentation in field settings include systematic variation of the content of applicant briefs sent to prospective employers (Schwartz & Skolnick, 1962), differential behavior on the part of salesmen toward customers (Brock, 1965) or customers toward salesmen (Jung, 1959; Schaps, 1972), varied content of requests for a dime from passing strangers (Latané, 1970), and the apparent condition of the victim of a feigned collapse in a New York subway train (Piliavin et al., 1969). To varying degrees these all fall within a "normal range" of human experience in public places, the only difference being their systematic manipulation by the researcher. Yet, collecting data about individual behavior in these situations clearly violates the spirit of "informed consent," especially when researchers decide it is best not to inform those who have been observed even after the fact.

Privacy on the Internet. The advent of the World Wide Web as a venue for social research creates a new wrinkle in the continuing issue of what constitutes "private" behavior or invasion of privacy. In addition to archival records of communications that are exchanged through various web-based interest groups and bulletin boards, researchers are more and more often becoming involved as "participant observers" in such groups, including introducing experimental manipulations in the form of messages designed to test research hypotheses. Currently, the prevailing philosophy is that Internet messages constitute "public domain" and therefore can be observed and recorded without obtaining consent, although there is an expectation that information about identity of the senders would be protected. However, the use of Internet communications for research purposes is becoming a matter of public debate (e.g., *USAToday*, 2000), and more protections of privacy of such communications may be called for in the future.

Protecting Confidentiality of Data

One justification that researchers use for keeping participants uninformed about their inclusion in a field study (or Web study) is that the data collected from such studies are essentially anonymous, with no possibility of personally identifying the persons associated with the data recorded. Of course, if video or other recording techniques are used that preserve individuating information about the participants, the data are not anonymous and participants should be given the right to consent whether their data will be used. However, when data are recorded without any identifying information of any kind, any invasion of privacy is temporary and confidentiality of the data is insured in the long run.

Even when research is not disguised, avoiding recording of individual identifying information to maintain confidentiality of data is usually a good idea. Assuring participants of the confidentiality of their responses is not simply for their benefit but can also increase the likelihood that they will be open and honest in their responses (Blanck, Bellack, Rosnow, Rotheram-Borus, & Schooler, 1992; Boruch & Cecil, 1979). An experiment conducted by Esposito, Agard, and Rosnow (1984) compared responses on a personality test given by participants who had been assured that their responses would be "strictly confidential" to those given by participants who had not been given such assurances. Those in the confidentiality condition provided data that were less influenced by social desirability biases than those in the control condition. This effect was obtained even though participants recorded their names on the tests that they took.

Protecting confidentiality is relatively easy when no identifying information (e.g., names, social security numbers, etc.) is recorded with the collection of data from individual participants. In many cases, however, participants' names are recorded for various reasons, and under those circumstances protection of confidentiality can present legal or ethical dilemmas for researchers (Blanck et al., 1992). This can occur when the research involves sensitive information (e.g., testing for HIV) or potentially illegal or dangerous behavior (e.g., child abuse) where reporting to partners or authorities may be seen as an ethical or legal responsibility. Research data in situations such as these is subject to subpoena, and researchers have sometimes been put into a painful conflict between their ethical responsibilities to research participants and their legal obligations. For research on some sensitive topics it is possible to obtain a "certificate of confidentiality" from the Public Health Service (cf. Sieber, 1992) that protects participant information from subpoena, but most research involving human participants is not protected in this way.

Databanks and Archival Research. Related to the general issues of invasion of privacy and confidentiality is the debate over creation of various national "databanks" for research purposes. Such databanks would centralized computer storage of data from the Census Bureau, Internal Revenue Service, Social Security Administration, and other federal agencies. Current computer technology and storage capacity have made such linked databases effectively a reality for administrative purposes, so the issue is one of access for researchers.

Longitudinal and correlational research requires that data records be kept by individual respondents, but these techniques do not require that those individuals be personally identifiable. Thus, any systematic controls on access to data designed to protect individual anonymity would not necessarily be inconsistent with research aims. In their review of the potential benefits and risks associated with the creation of a national data center, Sawyer and Schecter (1968) proposed several standards of operation that would provide safeguards for privacy. Among their major suggestions are the following:

- Only objective information be included in data storage.
- Individuals be given the right to review their files for accuracy and to have errors corrected.
- Research analyses be restricted to random samples.
- Files be identified only by code numbers, with access to personal identification strictly restricted.
- Security precautions be instituted for screening data users and access to the types of information provided.

These last two suggestions are related to the fact that some identification of individual files would be required for adding new information to particular files or for producing a file for review at the individual's own request. To assure limited access to the translation between file code numbers and personal identification, some sort of "link" system (involving a mediating step between access to a particular file and association between file number and name), as developed by the American Council on Education (Astin & Boruch, 1970), can be employed. Developing linking systems of this kind can be expensive, but such costs balance the scientific usefulness of large databanks against the risks to individual privacy.

The Regulatory Context of Research Involving Human Participants

Our preceding discussion of ethical dilemmas is intended to convey the idea that there are no simple, absolute rules for deciding whether a particular research practice or method is ethical or not. Rather, considerable judgment is involved in weighing the potential value of the research against potential stress or other costs to research participants. Except for obviously dangerous or damaging actions on the part of the researcher, ethical decision making involves a cost–benefit analysis rather than the promulgation of absolute strictures and rules. Much of the responsibility for making this assessment falls on the individual scientist, but an individual researcher alone is not always the best judge of what is valuable and necessary research and what is potentially harmful to participants. In fact, there is good evidence that biases enter into scientists' assessments of the utility of their own research (Kimmel, 1991). For that reason, the conduct of research that meets reasonable ethical standards and procedures is not just a matter of personal judgment, it is the law.

Almost all social and behavioral research that is supported by federal funds or conducted in educational or research institutions that receive federal funding (of any kind) is subject to federal regulations regarding the conduct of research involving human participants. The primary directive is 45CFR46 in the Code of Federal Regulations, known as the "Common Rule." The code (last revised in 1998) stipulates certain principles for protecting the welfare and dignity of human participants in research and prescribes policies and procedures that are required of institutions in which such research is carried out. As we mentioned in chapter 5 in connection with the initial planning stages of any research study, failure to comply with the procedures dictated by federal regulations can have dire consequences not only for the individual researcher involved but for the whole institution in which he or she works.

Internal Review Boards.   Much of the responsibility for complying with federal regulations is delegated to the institutions (e.g., universities) in which the research is conducted. Every institution in which federally funded research is carried out is required to set up an internal reviewing board (IRB) that evaluates, approves, and monitors all research projects in that institution with respect to ethical requirements and practices. The IRB is appointed by the university administration but with certain requirements for representation by members of the community and legal experts, as well as scientists from departments across the institution. Before any program of research is begun, it is the principal investigator's responsibility to submit a complete description of the proposed research purposes and procedures to the IRB for review. Based on the information provided by the investigator, the members of the IRB evaluate the potential costs and risks to participants in the research as well as the potential benefits of the research if it is conducted as planned. A schematic representation of the IRB review process as it is practiced in most research universities is provided in Fig. 19.1.

If the research described appears to meet ethical standards as set by the IRB committee, approval will be given to the investigator to conduct the research as described. Approvals are extended for a maximum of 12 months; if the research has not been completed within that time, the project must be resubmitted for continuing approval. If the IRB does not feel that the researcher has provided sufficient information to assess the potential risks of conducting the study, or if the proposed procedures do not appear to be fully justified, the proposal will be sent back to the investigator with contingencies or changes that must be made before the research can be approved. In the majority of cases, the review process ultimately results in a project that can be approved for implementation, but on occasion, the IRB can, and will, refuse to allow certain research studies to be done because they are deemed to be unethical or excessively risky.

Although many scientists regard the IRB review process as cumbersome and time consuming, most recognize that it is now a standard part of the design and conduct of research

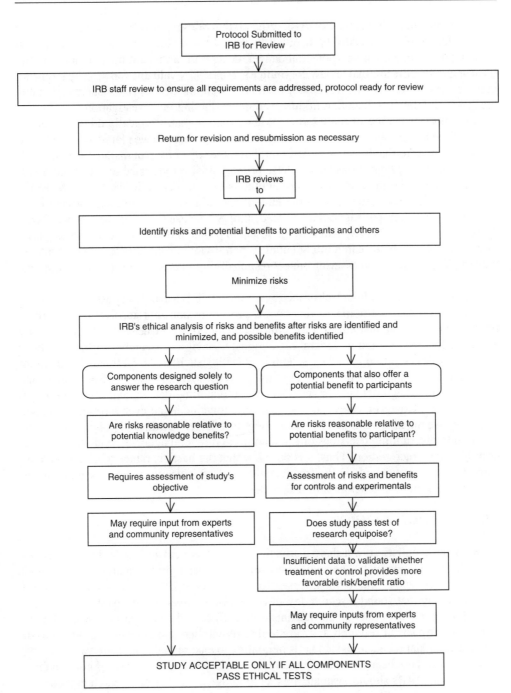

FIG. 19.1. Process of IRB review, including risks and potential benefits (adapted from the National Bioethics Advisory Commission).

involving human participants. Low-risk research that does not involve deception or issues of confidentiality can usually be handled by expedited review. In other circumstances, most notably those involving potential danger, deception, or blatant manipulation of one form or another, the internal review committee serves a very valuable function by requiring the researcher to defend the legitimacy of the research, the necessity for the questionable practices, and the cost–benefit ratio involved in conducting the investigation.

An important feature of the internal review group is that it typically does not consist solely of the researcher's colleagues (many of whom, perhaps, have planned or conducted research similar to that under consideration) but rather of a group of disinterested individuals, scientists and laypersons alike, whose primary goal is the protection of participants' rights. As such, the internal review committee is not "too close to the forest to see the trees." This body can often alert conscientious investigators to a potential problem that neither they nor their colleagues had noticed, simply because they were too involved with the technical and theoretical details of the research problem to notice the threats to participants' rights that the research might entail. When it works well, the IRB review process plays an important role in assuring ethical responsibility in contemporary social research.

Codes of Ethics.   Although clearance by the local IRB is a mandatory aspect of research that involves human participants, this review procedure does not absolve the researcher from any further responsibility for the ethical conduct of his or her research. In addition to the procedures dictated by federal regulations, behavioral researchers also are subject to codes of ethics promulgated by scientific societies such as the National Academy of Sciences (1995) and the American Psychological Association (1992). Such codes and principles provide guidelines for scientists in the planning, design, and execution of research studies. However, rules can always be circumvented, and even a formal code will be ineffective unless sanctioned by social support reflected in editorial policies of professional journals, funding decisions of foundations and federal agencies, and other sources of professional recognition. Thus, it is our view that the best guarantee of continued concern over ethical standards is the frequent airing of ethical issues in a way that ensures exposure to each new generation of researchers.

METHODOLOGY AS ETHICS

Some social scientists draw a sharp distinction between ethical and methodological issues in the design and conduct of behavioral research, but others think that ethics and methodology are inextricably intertwined. Rosenthal and Rosnow (1984), for instance, promote the philosophy that sound research design is an *ethical imperative* as well as a scientific ideal. Taking into account that participants' time, effort, and resources are involved in the conduct of any social research, they argue that researchers are ethically obligated to do only research that meets high standards of quality, to ensure that results are valid and that the research has not been a waste of participants' time. Rosenthal (1994) has gone so far as to suggest that IRBs should evaluate the methodological quality of research proposals as part of the cost–benefit analysis in their decisions about the ethicality of proposed research projects. Critics of this proposal (e.g., Parkinson, 1994; Sears, 1994) argue that ethical concerns and evaluation of the scientific merits of projects should be kept separate because they involve different expertise and different types of standards.

We are sympathetic to the general idea that the participants' investment of time and effort in research studies should be a factor in evaluating the costs of conducting research, and that there is some ethical obligation to be reasonably sure that the research project is worth doing before such costs should be incurred. However, we also agree that IRBs should not be in the business of evaluating the methodological purity of research proposals, beyond some very general evaluations of the justification for the project and the qualifications of the principal investigators. As we hope the previous chapters in this book have conveyed, the criteria for good methodology are neither static nor absolute. Multiple methodological approaches are needed to meet different criteria and purposes of research, and no one study is likely to have high internal validity, construct validity, and external validity at the same time. The value of a particular research project must be evaluated in terms of the contribution it will make to a body of research employing various methods, rather than as an isolated enterprise. One responsibility of the social science methodologist lies in the development of recommendations that contribute to a balanced approach to scientific advance. In one sense, this guideline refers to promoting the use of varied research strategies and methods of assessment, as is advocated throughout this book. In a broader sense, however, this responsibility extends to one of precluding an overly narrow and rigid interpretation of the conduct of science to the exclusion of other forms of inquiry.

A rigorous, cumulative science is inherently conservative, but this does not imply that there is no room in the scientific process for imaginative speculation. Ideally, the methodologist will be skeptical, but not cynical. By this we mean that he or she should be unwilling to accept naively any "scientific" finding without first being satisfied of its methodological rigor. However, the methodologist should not be so cynical that the findings are rejected even in situations where new approaches are being tested. An overly cynical approach can prove even more stultifying to scientific advance than an overly naive one. The productive social scientist is one who can maintain a perspective somewhere between the extremes of sterile cynicism and naive acceptance of intuitively appealing ideas.

Honesty in Reporting Methods and Results

One arena in which ethical principles and scientific ideals converge is the prescription to report results of research and the methods by which they were obtained honestly and completely. Sadly, in all branches of science there are cases in which out-and-out fabrication of findings has been uncovered (Broad & Wade, 1982). Such cases clearly violate both scientific and moral principles. However, there are other areas of reporting where the boundaries between ethical and unethical practice are not so clear-cut. Selective reporting of some results of a study and not others often occurs, and data from some participants are dropped from analyses if they are suspect in some way. Such practices can be justified to reduce unnecessary error in understanding and interpreting results of a scientific study, but these practices can be abused if used to distort the findings in the direction of reporting only what the researcher had hoped to demonstrate. To avoid such abuses, researchers need to use clear criteria for dropping data from their analyses and be scrupulous about reporting how these criteria were applied.

Researchers are expected to be honest about reporting results that do not support their hypotheses as well as results that do support their predictions. In addition, researchers need to be honest about what their predictions were in the first place. Quite often, the results of a research study are somewhat unexpected. This should be valued as part of the research enterprise. If we only got expected results, there would be some question about whether there was any need to undertake the research in the first place! When unexpected findings are obtained, we can usually generate explanations post hoc about why things came out that way. This is a valuable part of the research process: Post hoc explanations become hypotheses for new research. However, it is important to distinguish between interpretations of findings that are made after the fact and predictions that were made before the study began. If post hoc explanations are reported as if they had been predictions, this is a practice that Norbert Kerr labeled "HARKing"—Hypothesizing After the Results are Known (Kerr, 1998). In the long run, this practice could compromise the validity of social research by increasing the prevalence of Type II errors.

ETHICAL ISSUES RELATED TO THE PRODUCTS OF SCIENTIFIC RESEARCH

The development and use of atomic power in the 1940s quite effectively exploded the myth that scientific research is immune from considerations of morality and social values. Since that time, each scientist has had to come to grips with the issues of moral responsibility for the potential uses to which his or her research discoveries may be put. Some resolve this issue by rejecting all responsibility, claiming that scientific knowledge is essentially neutral, potentially serving good or evil depending on decisions outside the scientist's control. Others feel that if scientists are in a reasonable position to foresee the immediate applications of their research efforts, then they must accept responsibility for the consequences of their continuing in that line of research. This issue becomes most acute when the factor of research sponsorship is considered. When a research project is financed wholly or in part by some governmental or private agency, the researcher is usually obligated to report results directly, perhaps exclusively, to that agency. In such cases, the purposes of the sponsoring agency will clearly determine at least the immediate application of information or technical developments derived from that research, and the scientist can hardly deny foreknowledge of such applications, whatever other potential uses the discovery may have. Given the growing costs of research in the physical and social sciences, more and more projects must rely on sources of funding other than those provided by such presumably neutral agencies as universities, and more and more scientists are facing a choice between abandoning a particular line of research or conducting it under the auspices of some non-neutral private agency.

With respect to the long-range goal of social research, that is, understanding human behavior in social settings, every researcher must be aware that as such knowledge accumulates, the potential for using it as a means of gaining control over other people also increases. Thus, the ethical considerations of any researcher in this area must include who will be privy to this knowledge in the long run, and what chances there are for it to come under the exclusive control of one segment of the social system (cf. Kelman, 1968, 1972). Of more immediate concern is the current usage of information collected, or techniques developed, in the course of social research. For example, in research devoted to diagnosing attitudes or personality variations, various "disguised" or "projective" techniques have been developed, which purportedly assess the trait of interest under the guise of measuring something else. What is the responsibility of the designers of these techniques when they are used by corporate personnel officers to weed out unsuspecting employees with potential anti-management values or attitudes? Or, alternatively, what is the responsibility of the researcher whose correlational study of social and attitudinal factors associated with student radicalism is used by university admissions officers to develop screening criteria for rejecting applicants?

The issue of social responsibility is made even more complex when it is realized that the conclusions to be drawn from research results or psychological tests are often grossly misperceived by naive analysts. In the preceding example, for instance, the users of disguised tests or screening criteria might be largely unaware of the high degree of error (i.e., potential misclassification) associated with such selection devices when applied to individuals. Similar issues are raised with respect to research involving results that indicate differences (e.g., in intelligence or personality variables) between different ethnic or racial groups. Because the ethnic variable is inextricably confounded with cultural factors in contemporary Western society, the source of such differences in terms of genetic or cultural factors cannot usually be determined, and most researchers should (and do) report such results in a highly qualified fashion. However, there is no guarantee that other persons might not use the reported results to serve as justification for discriminatory practices based on the premise of innate differences between ethnic or racial groups.

Such potential misrepresentation of ambiguous research results has led some social scientists to suggest that a moratorium be declared on research involving race differences— either that such research not be conducted or that differences, if found, not be reported. Some scientists are horrified at the implication derived from this suggestion that research data should be withheld on the basis of subjective moral judgments of individual researchers, whereas others take the more extreme position that because individual scientists may vary considerably in what they consider morally reprehensible or desirable, some kind of scientific commission should be formed to determine the distribution of research efforts and results.

After reviewing these various policy suggestions, we have come to the position that the moral dilemmas faced by the scientist-researcher cannot be solved by any centralized decision-making body, which may place restrictions on the kind of research that can be undertaken or on the reporting of research outcomes. Rather, we feel that public interests will best be served by programs that actively promote alternative lines of research and competing theoretical (or philosophical) positions. To this end, we offer three suggestions:

- That research programs that currently rely on exclusive sources of support instead be multiply sponsored, or receive support from a combined scientific research fund supported by budget allotments from several different agencies.

- That to the maximum extent possible, all technical reports, research techniques, and research summaries be made available for public distribution.

- That emphasis be given to the social responsibility of individual scientists, or groups of scientists, to educate the public on the nature of their research techniques and results in ways that will enhance understanding of both the conclusions *and* the qualifications and limitations that must be placed on the generalization of those conclusions.

In this view, scientists are encouraged to resist associating with research programs that involved controlled access to scientific data and, similarly, to avoid placing the stamp of scientific respectability on research that is inconclusive, owing to methodological difficulties, or whose limitations are not clearly specified. These suggestions reflect our conviction that open knowledge and education are our best weapons against the misuse of scientific data or instrumentation.

SUGGESTED READINGS

American Psychological Association. (1983). *Ethical principles in the conduct of research with human participants*. Washington, DC: Author.

Kerr, N. L. (1998). HARKing: Hypothesizing after the results are known. *Personality and Social Psychology Review, 2*, 196–217.

Sieber, J. E. (1992). *Planning ethically responsible research*. Newbury Park, CA: Sage.

References

Abelson, R. P. (1968). Simulation of social behavior. In G. Lindzey & E. Aronson (Eds.), *The handbook of social psychology: Vol. 2. Research Methods* (2nd ed., pp. 274–356). Reading, MA: Addison-Wesley.

Abelson, R. P. (1997). On the surprising longevity of flogged horses: Why there is a case for the significance test. *Psychological Science, 8*, 12–15.

Abelson, R. P., & Carroll, J. D. (1965). Computer simulation of individual belief systems. *American Behavioral Scientist, 8*, 24–30.

Abernathy, J. R., Greenberg, B. G., & Horvitz, D. C. (1970). Estimates of induced abortions in urban North Carolina. *Demography, 7*, 19–29.

Adair, J. G., & Epstein, J. (1967, May). *Verbal cues in the mediation of experimenter bias.* Paper presented at the meeting of the Midwestern Psychological Association, Chicago, IL.

Adorno, T. W., Frenkel-Brunswik, E., Levinson, D. J., & Sanford, R. N. (1950). *The authoritarian personality.* New York: Harper.

Agnew, N. M., & Pike, S. W. (1969). *The science game. An introduction to research in the behavioral sciences.* Englewood Cliffs, NJ: Prentice-Hall.

Aiken, L. S., & West, S. G. (1991). *Multiple regression: Testing and interpreting interactions.* Newbury Park, CA: Sage.

Ajzen, I. (1982). On behaving in accordance with one's beliefs. In M. P. Zanna, E. T. Higgins, & C. P. Herman (Eds.), *Consistency in social behavior: The Ontario symposium* (Vol. 2, pp. 3–16). Hillsdale, NJ: Lawrence Erlbaum Associates.

Alfred, R. H. (1976). The Church of Satan. In C. Y. Glock & R. N. Bellah (Eds.), *The new religious consciousness* (pp. 180–202). Berkeley, CA: University of California Press.

Allen, C. T., Schewe, C. D., & Wijk, G. (1980). More on self-perception theory's foot technique in the pre-call/mail survey setting. *Journal of Marketing Research, 17*, 498–502.

Altemeyer, B. (1988). *Enemies of freedom: Understanding right-wing authoritarianism.* San Francisco: Jossey-Bass.

Altemeyer, B. (1996). *The authoritarian specter.* Cambridge, MA: Harvard University Press.

Alvaro, E. M., & Crano, W. D. (1997). Indirect minority influence: Evidence for leniency in source evaluation and counter-argumentation. *Journal of Personality and Social Psychology, 72*, 949–965.

American Psychological Association. (1983). *Ethical principles in the conduct of research with human participants.* Washington, DC: Author.

American Psychological Association. (1985). *Standards for educational and psychological testing.* Washington, DC: Author.

American Psychological Association. (1992). Ethical principles of psychologists and code of conduct. *American Psychologist, 47*, 1597–1611.

Ames, P. C., & Riggio, R. E. (1995). Use of the Rotter Incomplete Sentences Blank with adolescent populations: Implications for determining maladjustment. *Journal of Personality Assessment, 64*, 159–167.

Anderson, C., & Anderson, D. (1984). Ambient temperature and violent crime: Tests of the linear and curvilinear hypotheses. *Journal of Personality and Social Psychology, 46*, 91–97.

Anderson, C., & De Neve, K. M. (1992). Temperature, aggression, and the negative affect escape model. *Psychological Bulletin, 111*, 347–351.

Andrews, F. M., & Withey, S. B. (1976). *Social indicators of well-being.* New York: Plenum.

Argesti, A. (1996). *An introduction to categorical data analysis.* New York: Wiley.

Armstrong, J. S. (1975). Monetary incentives in mail surveys. *Public Opinion Quarterly, 39*, 111–116.

Aronson, E., & Carlsmith, J. M. (1968). Experimentation in social psychology. In G. Lindzey & E. Aronson (Eds.), *The handbook of social psychology: Vol. 2. Research methods* (2nd ed., pp. 1–79). Reading, MA: Addison-Wesley.

Aronson, E., Fried, C., & Stone, J. (1991). Overcoming denial and increasing the intention to use condoms through the induction of hypocrisy. *American Journal of Public Health, 81*, 1636–1638.

Aronson, E., & Mills, J. (1959). The effect of severity of initiation on liking for a group. *Journal of Abnormal and Social Psychology, 59*, 177–181.

Aronson, E., Wilson, T., & Brewer, M. B. (1998). Experimentation in social psychology. In D. Gilbert, S. Fiske, & G. Lindsey (Eds.), *The handbook of social psychology: Vol. 1* (4th ed., pp. 99–142). Boston: McGraw-Hill.

Asch, S. (1946). Forming impressions of personality. *Journal of Abnormal and Social Psychology, 41*, 258–290.

Asch, S. E. (1948). The doctrine of suggestion, prestige, and imitation in social psychology. *Psychological Review, 55*, 250–277.

Asch, S. E. (1951). Effects of group pressure upon the modification and distortion of judgment. In H. Guetzkow (Ed.), *Groups, leadership, and men* (pp. 177–190). Pittsburgh, PA: Carnegie Press.

Asch, S. E. (1956). Studies of independence and conformity: A minority of one against a unanimous majority. *Psychological Monographs, 70*, No. 9 (Whole No. 416).

Aspinwall, L., & Taylor, S. E. (1992). Modeling cognitive adaptation: A longitudinal investigation of the impact of individual differences and coping on college adjustment and performance. *Journal of Personality and Social Psychology, 63*, 989–1003.

Astin, A. W., & Boruch, R. F. (1970). *A "link" system for assuring confidentiality of research data in longitudinal studies.* Washington, DC: American Council on Education Research Reports, 5, No. 3.

Atwood, R. W., & Howell, R. J. (1971). Pupillometric and personality test score differences of female aggressing pedophiliacs and normals. *Psychonomic Science, 22*, 115–116.

Austin, W. G. (1979). Sex differences in bystander intervention in a theft. *Journal of Personality and Social Psychology, 37*, 2110–2120.

Axelrod, R. (1984). *Evolution of cooperation.* New York: Basic Books.

Bakeman, R. (2000). Behavioral observation and coding. In H. Reis & C. Judd (Eds.), *Handbook of research methods in social and personality psychology* (pp. 138–159). New York: Cambridge University Press.

Bakeman, R., & Casey, R. L. (1995). Analyzing family interaction: Taking time into account. *Journal of Family Psychology, 9*, 131–143.

Bakeman, R., & Gottman, J. M. (1997). *Observing interaction: An introduction to sequential analysis* (2nd ed.). New York: Cambridge University Press.

Bales, R. F. (1950). *Interaction process analysis.* Cambridge, MA: Addison-Wesley.

Bales, R. F. (1970). *Personality and interpersonal behavior.* New York: Holt, Rinehart, & Winston.

Bales, R. F., & Cohen, S. P. (1979). *SYMLOG: A system for multiple level observation of groups.* New York: Free Press.

Bales, R. F., & Isenberg, D. J. (1980). *SYMLOG and leadership theory.* Paper presented at the Sixth Biennial Leadership Symposium, Carbondale, IL.

Barclay, A. M., Crano, W. D., Thornton, C., & Werner, A. (1971). *How to do a university.* New York: Wiley.

Bargh, J. A., Chaiken, S., Raymond, P., & Hymes, C. (1996). The automatic evaluation effect: Unconditionally automatic attitude activation with a pronunciation task. *Journal of Experimental Social Psychology, 32*, 185–210.

Bargh, J. A., & Chartrand, T. L. (2000). Studying the mind in the middle: A practical guide to priming and automaticity research. In H. Reis & C. Judd (Eds.), *Handbook of research methods in social and personality psychology* (pp. 253–285). New York: Cambridge University Press.

Bargh, J. A., Chen, M., & Burrows, L. (1996). Automaticity of social behavior: Direct effects of trait construct and stereotype activation on action. *Journal of Personality and Social Psychology, 71*, 230–244.

Bargh, J. A., & Pietromonaco, P. (1982). Automatic information processing and social perception: The influence of trait information presented outside of conscious awareness on impression formation. *Journal of Personality and Social Psychology, 43*, 437–449.

Bargh, J. A., Raymond, P., Pryor, J., & Strack, F. (1995). The attractiveness of the underling: An automatic power-sex association and its consequences for sexual harassment and aggression. *Journal of Personality and Social Psychology, 68*, 768–781.

Bargh, J. A., & Thein, R. D. (1985). Individual construct accessibility, person memory, and the recall-judgment link: The case of information overload. *Journal of Personality and Social Psychology, 49*, 1129–1146.

Barnlaud, D. C. (1962). Consistency of emergent leadership with changing tasks and members. *Speech Monographs, 29*, 45–52.

Baron, R. A., & Bell, P. A. (1975). Aggression and heat: Mediating effects of provocation and exposure to an aggressive model. *Journal of Personality and Social Psychology, 31*, 825–832.

Baron, R. A., & Bell, P. A. (1976). Aggression and heat: The influence of ambient temperature, negative affect, and a cooling drink on physical aggression. *Journal of Personality and Social Psychology, 33*, 245–255.

Baron, R. A., & Lawton, S. F. (1972). Environmental influences on aggression: The facilitation of modeling effects by high ambient temperatures. *Psychonomic Science, 26*, 80–82.

Baron, R. M., & Kenny, D. A. (1986). The moderator-mediator variable distinction in social psychological research: Conceptual, strategic, and statistical considerations. *Journal of Personality and Social Psychology, 51*, 1173–1182.

Barry, C. A. (1998). Choosing qualitative data analysis software: Atlas/ti and Nudist compared. *Sociological Research Online, 3*, http://www.socresonline.org.uk/socresonline/3/3/4.html.

Bartholomew, K., Henderson, A. J. Z., & Marcia, J. (2000). Coding semistructured interviews in social psychological research. In H. Reis & C. Judd (Eds.), *Handbook of research methods in social and personality psychology* (pp. 286–312). New York: Cambridge University Press.

Barton, A. H., & Lazarsfeld, P. H. (1969). Some functions of qualitative analysis in social research. In G. J. McCall & J. L. Simmonds (Eds.), *Issues in participant observation.* Reading, MA: Addison-Wesley.

Baumrind, D. (1964). Some thoughts on ethics of research: After reading Milgram's "Behavioral study of obedience." *American Psychologist, 19*, 421–423.

Becker, H. S. (1953). Field methods and techniques: A note on interviewing tactics. *Human Organization, 12*, 31–32.

Becker, H. S. (1958). Problems of inference and proof in participant observation. *American Sociological Review, 23*, 652–660.

Beecher, H. K. (1966). Pain: One mystery solved. *Science, 151*, 840–841.

Bell, P. A. (1992). In defense of the negative affect escape model of heat and aggression. *Psychological Bulletin, 111*, 342–346.

Bell, P. A., & Baron, R. A. (1990). Affect and aggression. In B. S. Moore & A. M. Isen (Eds.), *Affect and social behavior* (pp. 64–88). Cambridge, England: Cambridge University Press.

Bem, D. J. (1965). An experimental analysis of self-persuasion. *Journal of Experimental Social Psychology, 1*, 199–218.

Bem, D. J. (1967). Self-Perception: An alternative interpretation of cognitive dissonance phenomena. *Psychological Review, 74*, 183–200.

Bentler, P. M. (1995). *EQS structural equations program manual.* Encino, CA: Multivariate Software, Inc.

Berelson, B. (1952). *Content analysis in communication research.* Glencoe, IL: Free Press.

Berelson, B. (1954). Content analysis. In G. Lindzey (Ed.), *Handbook of social psychology.* Reading, MA: Addison-Wesley.

Berk, R. A., Hoffman, D. M., Maki, J. E., Rauma, D., & Wong, H. (1979). Estimation procedures for pooled cross-sectional and time series data. *Evaluation Quarterly, 3*, 385–410.

Berkman, D. (1963). Advertising in Ebony and Life: Negro aspirations vs. reality. *Journalism Quarterly, 40*, 53–64.

Berkowitz, L., & Donnerstein, E. (1982). External validity is more than skin deep: Some answers to criticisms of laboratory experiments. *American Psychologist, 37*, 245–257.

Berry, D. S., & McArthur, L. Z. (1985). Some components and consequences of a babyface. *Journal of Personality and Social Psychology, 48*, 312–323.

Berry, D. S., & McArthur, L. Z. (1986). Perceiving character in faces: The impact of age-related craniofacial changes on social perception. *Psychological Bulletin, 100*, 3–18.

Berry, W. D., & Lewis-Beck, M. S. (1986). *New tools for social scientists: Advances and applications in research methods.* Beverly Hills, CA: Sage.

Bhaskar, R. (1978). On the possibility of social scientific knowledge and the limits of behaviorism. *Journal for the Theory of Social Behavior, 8*, 1–28.

Bhaskar, R. (1982). Emergence, explanation, and emancipation. In P. F. Secord (Ed.), *Explaining social behavior: Consciousness, behavior, and social structure* (pp. 275–310). Beverly Hills, CA: Sage.

Bickman, L., & Rog, D. J. (Eds.). (1998). *Handbook of applied social research methods.* Thousand Oaks, CA: Sage.

Birnbaum, M. H. (2000a). Introduction to psychological experimentation on the internet. In M. H. Birnbaum (Ed.), *Psychological experiments on the internet* (pp. 3–34). San Diego, CA: Academic Press.

Birnbaum, M. H. (Ed.). (2000b). *Psychological experiments on the internet.* San Diego, CA: Academic Press.

Bishop, G. R., Oldendick, R. W., Tuchfarber, A. J., & Bennett, S. E. (1980). Pseudo-opinions on public affairs. *Public Opinion Quarterly, 44,* 198–209.

Bixenstine, V., & Wilson, K. (1963). Effects of level of cooperative choice by the other player on choices in a prisoner's dilemma game. *Journal of Abnormal and Social Psychology, 67,* 139–147.

Blalock, H. M. (1985). *Causal models in panel and experimental designs.* New York: Aldine.

Blanck, P., Bellack, A., Rosnow, R., Rotheram-Borus, M. J., & Schooler, N. (1992). Scientific rewards and conflicts of ethical choices in human subjects research. *American Psychologist, 47,* 959–965.

Blascovich, J. (2000). Using physiological indexes of psychological processes in social psychology. In H. Reis & C. Judd (Eds.), *Handbook of research methods in social and personality psychology* (pp. 117–137). New York: Cambridge University Press.

Blascovich, J., & Kelsey, R. M. (1990). Using cardiovascular and electrodermal measures of arousal in social psychological research. In C Hendrick & M. Clark (Eds.), *Research methods in personality and social psychology. Review of personality and social psychology* (Vol. 11, pp. 45–73). Newbury Park, CA: Sage.

Blascovich, J., Mendes, W., Hunter, S., Lickel, B., & Kowai-Bell, N. (2001). Perceiver threat in social interactions with stigmatized others. *Journal of Personality and Social Psychology, 80,* 253–267.

Block, J. (1965). *The challenge of response sets.* New York: Appleton-Century-Crofts.

Blumberg, H. H. (1994). Group decision making and choice shift. In P. Hare & H. H. Blumberg (Eds.), *Small group research: A handbook* (pp. 195–210). Norwood, NJ: Ablex.

Boekeloo, B. O., Schamus, L. A., Simmens, S. J., & Cheng, T. L. (1998). Ability to measure sensitive adolescent behaviors via telephone. *American Journal of Preventive Medicine, 14,* 209–216.

Bogardus, E. S. (1959). *Social distance.* Yellow Springs, OH: Antiocit Press.

Bogden, R. (1972). *Participant observation in organizational settings.* Syracuse, NY: Syracuse University Press.

Bond, C. F., Jr., & Titus, L. J. (1983). Social facilitation: A meta-analysis of 241 studies. *Psychological Bulletin, 94,* 265–292.

Borg, I. (1988). Revisiting Thurstone's and Coombs' scales on the seriousness of crimes. *European Journal of Social Psychology, 18,* 53–61.

Borgatta, E. F., & Crowther, B. (1965). *A workbook for the study of social interaction processes.* Chicago: Rand-McNally.

Borgida, E., & Nisbett, R. F. (1977). The differential impact of abstract versus concrete information on decisions. *Journal of Applied Social Psychology, 7,* 258–271.

Bornstein, B. H. (1999). The ecological validity of jury simulations: Is the jury still out? *Law and Human Behavior, 23,* 75–91.

Boruch, R. F., & Cecil, J. S. (1979). *Assuring the confidentiality of research data.* Philadelphia: University of Pennsylvania Press.

Boruch, R. F., McSweeney, A. J., & Sonderstrom, E. J. (1978). Randomized field experiments for program planning, development, and evaluation: An illustrative bibliography. *Evaluation Quarterly, 2,* 655–695.

Bourgeault, I. L. (2000). Delivering the "new" Canadian midwifery: The impact on midwifery of integration into the Ontario health care system. *Sociology of Health and Illness, 22,* 172–196.

Bousfield, A. K., & Bousfield, W. A. (1966). Measurement of clustering and sequential constancies in repeated free recall. *Psychological Reports, 19,* 935–942.

Box, G. E. P., & Jenkins, G. M. (1970). *Time series analysis: Forecasting and control.* San Francisco: Holden-Day.

Bradburn, N. M., & Sudman, S. (1979). *Improving interview method and questionnaire design.* San Francisco: Jossey-Bass.

Bradley, M. T., & Gupta, R. D. (1997). Estimating the effect of the file drawer problem in meta-analysis. *Perceptual and Motor Skills, 85,* 719–722.

Brady, J. (1958). Ulcers in "executive monkeys." *Scientific American, 199,* 95–100.

Brechner, K. (1977). An experimental analysis of social traps. *Journal of Experimental Social Psychology, 13,* 552–564.

Brehm, J. W., & Cole, A. H. (1966). Effect of a favor which reduces freedom. *Journal of Personality and Social Psychology, 3,* 420–426.

Brehm, J. W., & Cohen, A. R. (1959). Re-evaluation of choice-alternatives as a function of their number and qualitative similarity. *Journal of Abnormal and Social Psychology, 58,* 373–378.

Brehm, J. W., & Cohen, A. R. (1962). *Explorations in cognitive dissonance.* New York: Wiley.

Brewer, M. B. (1979). In-group bias in the minimal intergroup situation: A cognitive-motivational analysis. *Psychological Bulletin, 86,* 307–324.

Brewer, M. B. (1997). The social psychology of intergroup relations: Can research inform practice? *Journal of Social Issues, 53,* 197–211.

Brewer, M. B. (2000). Research design and issues of validity. In H. Reis & C. Judd (Eds.), *Handbook of research methods in social and personality psychology* (pp. 3–16). New York: Cambridge University Press.

Brewer, M. B., & Campbell, D. T. (1976). *Ethnocentrism and intergroup attitudes: East African evidence.* Beverly Hills, CA: Sage.

Brewer, M. B., Campbell, D. T., & Crano, W. D. (1970). Testing a single-factor model as an alternative to the misuse of partial correlations in hypothesis-testing research. *Sociometry, 33,* 1–11.

Brewer, M. B., & Crano, W. D. (1994). *Social psychology.* Minneapolis/St. Paul: West.

Brewer, M. B., Dull, V., & Lui, L. (1981). Perceptions of the elderly: Stereotypes as prototypes. *Journal of Personality and Social Psychology, 41,* 656–670.

Brewer, M. B., & Miller, N. (1984). Beyond the contact hypothesis: Theoretical perspectives on desegregation. In N. Miller & M. B. Brewer (Eds.), *Groups in contact: The psychology of desegregation* (pp. 281–302). Orlando, FL: Academic Press.

Brickman, P., Folger, R., Goode, E., & Schul, Y. (1981). Micro and macro justice. In M. J. Lerner & S. C. Lerner (Eds.), *The justice motive in social behavior* (pp. 173–204). New York: Plenum.

Broad, W., & Wade, N. (1982). *Betrayers of the truth.* New York: Simon and Schuster.

Brock, T. C. (1965). Communicator-recipient similarity and decision change. *Journal of Personality and Social Psychology, 1,* 650–654.

Brock, T. C., & Becker, L. A. (1966). "Debriefing" and susceptibility to subsequent experimental manipulations. *Journal of Experimental Social Psychology, 2,* 314–323.

Brody, R. A. (1963). Some systematic effects of nuclear weapons technology: A study through simulation of a multi-nuclear future. *Journal of Conflict Resolution, 7,* 663–753.

Brunner, G. A., & Carroll, S. J., Jr. (1969). The effect of prior notification on the refusal rate in fixed address surveys. *Journal of Advertising, 9,* 424–4.

Brunner, J. A., & Brunner, G. A. (1971). Are voluntarily unlisted telephone subscribers really different? *Journal of Marketing Research, 8,* 121–124.

Brunswik, E. (1956). *Perception and the representative design of psychological experiments* (2nd ed.). Berkeley, CA: University of California Press.

Bryan, J. H., & Test, M. A. (1967). Models of helping: naturalistic studies in aiding behavior. *Journal of Personality and Social Psychology, 6,* 400–407.

Buchanan, T. (2000). Potential of the internet for personality research. In M. H. Birnbaum (Ed.), *Psychological experiments on the internet* (pp. 121–140). San Diego, CA: Academic Press.

Burger, G. (1999). The foot-in-the-door compliance procedure: A multiple-process analysis and review. *Personality and Social Psychology Review, 3,* 303–325.

Burgoon, M., Alvaro, E. M., Grandpre, J., & Voloudakis, M. (in press). Revisiting the theory of psychological reactance: Communicating threats to attitudinal freedom. In J. Dillard & M. Pfau (Eds.), *Handbook of persuasion.* Beverly Hills, CA: Sage.

Burt, R. S. (1982). *Toward a structural theory of action: Network models of social structure, perception, and action.* New York: Academic Press.

Buss, D. M. (1989). Sex differences in human mate preferences: Evolutionary hypotheses tested in 37 cultures. *Behavioral and Brain Sciences, 12,* 1–49.

Byrne, D. (1971). *The attraction paradigm.* New York: Academic Press.

Cacioppo, J. T., Crites, S., Berntson, G., & Coles, M. (1993). If attitudes affect how stimuli are processed, should they not affect the event-related brain potential? *Psychological Science, 4,* 108–112.

Cacioppo, J. T., Crites, S., Gardner, W., & Berntson, G. (1994). Bioelectrical echoes from evaluative categorizations: I. A late positive brain potential that varies as a function of trait negativity and extremity. *Journal of Personality and Social Psychology, 67,* 115–125.

Cacioppo, J. T., & Petty, R. E. (1981). Electromyograms as measures of extent and affectivity of information processing. *American Psychology, 36,* 441–456.

Cacioppo, J. T., & Petty, R. E. (Eds.). (1983). *Social psychophysiology: A sourcebook.* New York: Guilford.

Cacioppo, J. T., Petty, R. E., Losch, M, & Kim, H. (1986). Electromyographic activity over facial muscle regions can differentiate the valence and intensity of affective reactions. *Journal of Personality and Social Psychology, 50,* 20–268.

Cain, P. S., & Treiman, D. J. (1981). The dictionary of occupational titles as a source of occupational data. *American Sociological Review, 46,* 253–278.

Caldwell, B. M. (1968). A new "approach" to behavioral ecology. In J. P. Hill (Ed.), *Minnesota symposia on child psychology* (Vol. 2, pp. 74–109). Minneapolis: University of Minnesota Press.

Campbell, D. T. (1963). Social attitudes and other acquired behavioral dispositions. In S. Koch (Ed.), *Psychology: A study of a science: Vol. 6. Investigations of man as socius* (pp. 94–172). New York: McGraw-Hill.

Campbell, D. T. (1969a). Definitional versus multiple operationism. *Et al., 2,* 14–17.

Campbell, D. T. (1969b). Prospective and control. In R. Rosenthal & R. L. Rosnow (Eds.), *Artifact in behavioral research* (pp. 351–382). New York: Academic Press.

Campbell, D. T. (1969c). Reforms as experiments. *American Psychologist, 24,* 409–429.

Campbell, D. T., & Erlebacher, A. (1970). How regression in quasi-experimental evaluation can mistakenly make compensatory education look harmful. In J. Hellmuth (Ed.), *The disadvantaged child: Vol. 3. Compensatory education: A national debate* (pp. 185–225). New York: Brunner-Mazel.

Campbell, D. T., & Fiske, D. W. (1959). Convergent and discriminant validation by the multitrait-multimethod matrix. *Psychological Bulletin, 56*, 81–105.

Campbell, D. T., Miller, N., Lubetsky, J., & O'Connell, E. J. (1964). Varieties of projection in trait attribution. *Psychological Monographs, 78* (entire issue 592).

Campbell, D. T., Siegman, C. R., & Rees, M. B. (1967). Direction of wording effects in the relationships between scales. *Psychological Bulletin, 68*, 293–303.

Campbell, D. T., & Stanley, J. C. (1963). Experimental and quasi-experimental designs for research on teaching. In N. L. Gage (Ed.), *Handbook of research on teaching* (pp. 171–246). Chicago: Rand-McNally. Reprinted as *Experimental and quasi-experimental designs for research*. Chicago: Rand-McNally, 1966.

Campbell, J. P., Daft, R. L., & Hulin, C. L. (1982). *What to study: Generating and developing research questions*. Beverly Hills, CA: Sage.

Cannell, C. F., & Kahn, R. L. (1968). Interviewing. In G. Lindzey & E. Aronson (Eds.), *The handbook of social psychology: Vol. 2. Research methods* (2nd ed., pp. 526–595). Reading, MA: Addison-Wesley.

Cannell, C. F., Miller, P. V., & Oksenberg, L. (1981). Research on interviewing techniques. In S. Leinhardt (Ed.), *Sociological methodology* (pp. 389–437). San Francisco: Jossey-Bass.

Cantor, N., & Mischel, W. (1977). Traits as prototypes: Effects on recognition memory. *Journal of Personality and Social Psychology, 35*, 38–48.

Carlopio, J., Adair, J. G., Lindsay, R. C. L., & Spinner, B. (1983). Avoiding artifact in the search for bias: The importance of assessing subjects' perceptions of the experiment. *Journal of Personality and Social Psychology, 44*, 693–701.

Carlsmith, J. M., & Anderson, C. A. (1979). Ambient temperature and the occurrence of collective violence: A new analysis. *Journal of Personality and Social Psychology, 37*, 337–344.

Carlson, J., Cook, S. W., & Stromberg, E. L. (1936). Sex differences in conversation. *Journal of Applied Psychology, 20*, 727–735.

Carlson, R. (1971). Where is the person in personality research? *Psychological Bulletin, 75*, 203–219.

Carlston, D. E., & Cohen, J. L. (1980). A closer examination of subject roles. *Journal of Personality and Social Psychology, 38*, 857–870.

Carroll, J. B., & Arabie, P. (1980). Multi-dimensional scaling. *Annual Review of Psychology, 31*, 607–649.

Cartwright, A., & Tucker, W. (1969). An experiment with an advance letter on an interview inquiry. *British Journal of Preventive Social Medicine, 23*, 241–243.

Cartwright, D. P. (1953). Analysis of qualitative material. In L. Festinger & D. Katz (Eds.), *Research methods in the behavioral sciences* (pp. 421–470). New York: Holt.

Cattell, R. B. (1972). *Personality and mood by questionnaire*. San Francisco: Jossey-Bass.

Chapin, W. D. (1998). The Balance of Power game. *Simulation and Gaming, 29*, 105–112.

Chapman, L. J., & Campbell, D. T. (1957a). An attempt to predict the performance of three-man teams from attitude measures. *Journal of Social Psychology, 46*, 277–286.

Chapman, L. J., & Campbell, D. T. (1957b). Response set in the F scale. *Journal of Abnormal and Social Psychology, 54*, 129–132.

Chapman, L. J., & Campbell, D. T. (1959a). Absence of acquiescence response set in the Taylor Manifest Anxiety scale. *Journal of Consulting Psychology, 23*, 465–466.

Chapman, L. J., & Campbell, D. T. (1959b). The effect of acquiescence response-set upon relationships among F scale, ethnocentrism, and intelligence. *Sociometry, 22*, 153–161.

Chapple, E. D. (1953). The standard experimental (stress) interview as used in Interaction Chronograph investigations. *Human Organization, 12*, 23–32.

Chartrand, T. L., & Bargh, J. A. (1996). Automatic activation of impression formation and memorization goals: Nonconscious goal priming reproduces effects of explicit task instructions. *Journal of Personality and Social Psychology, 71*, 464–478.

Choi, I., Nisbett, R. E., & Norenzayan, A. (1999). Causal attribution across cultures: Variation and universality. *Psychological Bulletin, 125*, 47–63.

Cialdini, R. B. (1988). *Influence: Science and practice* (2nd Edition). Glenview, IL: Scott, Foresman.

Cialdini, R. B., Borden, R. J., Thorne, A., Walker, M. R., Freeman, S., & Sloan, L. R. (1976). Basking in reflected glory: Three (football) field studies. *Journal of Personality and Social Psychology, 34*, 366–375.

Cicourel, A. V. (1964). *Method and measurement in sociology*. New York: Free Press.

Clark, R. D. (1971). *Einstein: The life and times*. New York: World Publishing.

Cliff, N. (1977). A theory of consistency of ordering generalizable to tailored testing. *Psychometrika, 42*, 375–399.

Clore, G. L., Bray, R. M., Itkin, S. M., & Murphy, P. (1978). Interracial attitudes and behavior at summer camp. *Journal of Personality and Social Psychology, 36*, 107–116.

Cochran, W. G. (1977). *Sampling techniques*. New York: Wiley.

Cohen, B. D. (1957). *The political process and foreign policy: The making of the Japanese peace settlement*. Princeton, NJ: Princeton University Press.

Cohen, J. A. (1960). A coefficient of agreement for nominal scales. *Educational and Psychological Measurement, 20*, 37–46.

Cohen, J. A. (1968). Weighted kappa: Nominal scale agreement with provision for scaled disagreement or partial credit. *Psychological Bulletin, 70*, 213–220.

Cohen, J. A. (1988). *Statistical power analysis for the behavioral sciences* (2nd ed.). Hillsdale, NJ: Lawrence Erlbaum Associates.

Cohen, J. A. (1992). A power primer. *Psychological Bulletin, 112*, 155–159.

Cohen, K. J., Dill, W. R., Kuehn, A. A., & Winters, P. R. (1964). *The Carnegie Tech management game*. Homewood, IL: Irwin.

Coleman, J. S., Campbell, E. Q., Hobson, C. J., McPartland, J., Mood, A. M., Weinfeld, F. D., & York, R. L. (1966). *Equality of educational opportunity*. Washington, DC: Government Printing Office.

Condon, J. W., & Crano, W. D. (1988). Implied evaluation and the relationship between similarity and interpersonal attraction. *Journal of Personality and Social Psychology, 54*, 789–797.

Congressional Information Service. (1990). *American statistical index*. Bethesda, MD: Author.

Converse. P. E. (1964). The nature of belief systems in mass publics. In D. E. Apter (Ed.), *Ideology and discontent* (pp. 168–189). Reading, MA: Addison-Wesley.

Cook T. D., & Campbell, D. T. (1979). *Quasi-experimentation: Design and analysis issues for field settings*. Chicago: Rand-McNally.

Cook, T. D., & Diamond, S. (1972). *An introduction to field experiments*. Unpublished manuscript, Northwestern University, Evanston, IL.

Cook, T. D., & Leviton, L. C. (1980). Reviewing the literature: A comparison of traditional methods with meta-analysis. *Journal of Personality, 48*, 449–472.

Cook, T. D., & Shadish, W. R. (1994). Social experiments: Some developments over the past fifteen years. *Annual Review of Psychology, 45*, 545–580.

Coombs, C. H. (1950). Psychological scaling without a unit of measurement. *Psychological Review, 57*, 145–158.

Coombs, C. H. (1964). *A theory of data*. New York: Wiley.

Coombs, C. H. (1967). Thurstone's measurement of social values revisited forty years later. *Journal of Personality and Social Psychology, 6*, 85–91.

Coombs, C. H., & Coombs, L. C. (1976). "Don't know:" Item ambiguity or response uncertainty? *Public Opinion Quarterly, 40*, 497–514.

Coombs, C. H., Dawes, R. M., & Tversky, A. (1970). *Mathematical psychology.* Englewood Cliffs, NJ: Prentice-Hall.

Cooper, H. M., & Rosenthal, R. (1980). Statistical versus traditional procedures for summarizing research findings. *Psychological Bulletin, 87*, 442–449.

Cooper, S. L. (1964). Random sampling by telephone—An improved method. *Journal of Marketing Research, 1*, 45–48.

Craik, F., Moroz, T., Moscovitch, M., Stuss, D., Winocur, G., Tulving, E., & Kapur, S. (1999). In search of the self: A Positron Emission Tomography study. *Psychological Science, 10*, 26–34.

Crano, W. D. (1981). Triangulation and cross-cultural research. In M. B. Brewer & B. E. Collins (Eds.), *Scientific inquiry and the social sciences: A volume in honor of Donald T. Campbell* (pp. 317–344). San Francisco: Jossey-Bass.

Crano, W. D. (1983). Assumed consensus of attitudes: The effect of vested interest. *Personality and Social Psychology Bulletin, 9*, 597–608.

Crano, W. D. (1997). Vested interest, symbolic politics, and attitude-behavior consistency. *Journal of Personality and Social Psychology, 72*, 485–491.

Crano, W. D. (2000). The multitrait-multimethod matrix as synopsis and recapitulation of Campbell's views on the proper conduct of social inquiry. In L. Bickman (Ed.), *Research design: Donald Campbell's legacy* (chap. 3, pp. 37–61). Beverly Hills, CA: Sage.

Crano, W. D., & Chen, X. (1998). The leniency contract and persistence of majority and minority influence. *Journal of Personality and Social Psychology, 74*, 1437–1450.

Crano, W. D., & Cooper, R. E. (1973). Examination of Newcomb's extension of structural balance theory. *Journal of Personality and Social Psychology, 27*, 344–353.

Crano, W. D., & Crano, S. L. (1984). Interaction of self-concept and state/trait anxiety under different conditions of social comparison pressure. In R. Schwarzer (Ed.), *The self in anxiety, stress, and depression* (pp. 159–169). Amsterdam: Elsevier.

Crano, W. D., & Hannula-Bral, K. A. (1994). Context/categorization model of social influence: Minority and majority influence in the formation of a novel response norm. *Journal of Experimental Social Psychology, 30*, 247–276.

Crano, W. D., & Mendoza, J. L. (1987). Maternal factors that influence children's positive behavior: Demonstration of a structural equation analysis of selected data from the Berkeley Growth Study. *Child Development, 58*, 38–48.

Crano, W. D., & Messé, L. A. (1985). Assessing and redressing comprehension artifacts in social intervention research. *Evaluation Review, 9*, 144–172.

Crano, W. D., & Sivacek, J. M. (1982). Social reinforcement, self-attribution, and the foot-in-the-door phenomenon. *Social Cognition, 1*, 110–125.

Crano, W. D., & Sivacek, J. M. (1984). The influence of incentive-aroused ambivalence on overjustification effects in attitude change. *Journal of Experimental Social Psychology, 20*, 137–158.

Cronbach, L. J. (1951). Coefficient alpha and the internal structure of tests. *Psychometrika, 16*, 297–334.

Cronbach, L. J. (1955). Processes affecting scores on "understanding of others" and "assumed similarity." *Psychological Bulletin, 52*, 177–193.

Cronbach, L. J. (1975). Beyond the two disciplines of scientific psychology. *American Psychologist, 30*, 116–127.

Cronbach, L. J., Gleser, G. C., Nanda, H., & Rajaratnam, N. (1972). *The dependability of behavioral measurements: Theory of generalizability for scores and profiles.* New York: Wiley.

Cronbach, L. J., & Snow, R. (1977). *Aptitude and instructional methods.* New York: Irvington.

Cronkite, R. C. (1980). Social psychological simulations: An alternative to experiments? *Social Psychology Quarterly, 43*, 199–216.

Crutchfield, R. F. (1955). Conformity and character. *American Psychologist, 10*, 191–198.

Curry, T. J., & Emerson, R. M. (1970). Balance theory: A theory of interpersonal attraction? *Sociometry, 33*, 216–238.

Dabbs, J. M., Jr., & Milun, R. (1999). Pupil dilation when viewing strangers: Can testosterone moderate prejudice? *Social Behavior and Personality, 27*, 297–302.

Dale, E., & Schall, J. S. (1948). A formula for predicting readability. *Educational Research Bulletin, 27*, 11–20, 37–54.

Daniel, W. W. (1975). Nonresponse in sociological surveys: A review of some methods for handling the problem. *Sociological Methods and Research, 3*, 291–307.

Danielson, W. A. (1963). Content analysis in communication research. In R. O. Nafziger & D. M. White (Eds.), *Introduction to mass communications research* (pp. 180–206). Baton Rouge, LA: Louisiana State University Press.

Darley, J. M., & Batson, C. D. (1973). "From Jerusalem to Jericho": A study of situational and dispositional variables in helping behavior. *Journal of Personality and Social Psychology, 27*, 100–108.

Darley, J. M., & Latané, B. (1968). Bystander intervention in emergencies: Diffusion of responsibility. *Journal of Personality and Social Psychology, 10*, 202–214.

Davis, R. N. (1999). Web-based administration of a personality questionnaire: Comparison with traditional methods. *Behavior Research Methods, Instruments, and Computers, 31*, 572–577.

Dawes, R. M. (1988). *Rational choice in an uncertain world.* San Diego, CA: Harcourt Brace Jovanovich.

Dawes, R. M., & Smith, T. L. (1985). Attitude and opinion measurement. In G. Lindzey & E. Aronson (Eds.), *The handbook of social psychology*, Vol. 2. (2nd ed., pp. 509–566). Reading, MA: Addison-Wesley.

Dawson, E. J., Crano, W. D., & Burgoon, M. (1996). Refining the meaning and measurement of acculturation: Revisiting a novel methodological approach. *International Journal of Intercultural Relations, 20*, 97–114.

DeJong, W. (1979). An examination of self-perception mediation of the foot-in-the-door effect. *Journal of Personality and Social Psychology, 37*, 2221–2239.

Deluse, S. R. (1999). Mandatory divorce education: A program evaluation using a 'quasi-random' regression discontinuity design. *Dissertation Abstracts International: Section B: Sciences & Engineering, 60*(3-B), 1349.

Dennis, A. R., & Valacich, J. S. (1993). Computer brainstorms: More heads are better than one. *Journal of Applied Psychology, 78*, 531–537.

DePaulo, B. M., Kashy, D. A., Kirkendol, S. E., Wyer, M. M., & Epstein, J. A. (1996). Lying in everyday life. *Journal of Personality and Social Psychology, 70*, 979–995.

Derlega, V. J., & Berg, J. H. (Eds). (1987). *Self-disclosure: Theory, research, and therapy.* New York: Plenum.

Derlega, V. J., Metts, S., Petronio, S., & Margulis, S. T. (1993). *Self-disclosure.* Newbury Park, CA: Sage.

Devine, P. G. (1989). Stereotypes and prejudice: Their automatic and controlled components. *Journal of Personality and Social Psychology, 56*, 680–690.

Diehl, M., & Stroebe, W. (1987). Productivity loss in brainstorming groups: Toward the solution of a riddle. *Journal of Personality and Social Psychology, 53*, 497–509.

Dienstbier, R. A. (1989). Arousal and physiological toughness: Implications for mental and physical health. *Psychological Review, 96*, 84–100.

Dijkstra, W., & van der Zouwen, J. (Eds.). (1982). *Response behavior in the survey-interview.* New York: Academic Press.

Dillard, J. P. (1991). The current status of research on sequential-request compliance techniques. *Personality and Social Psychology Bulletin, 17*, 283–288.

Dillman, D. A. (1972). Increasing mail questionnaire response in large samples of the general public. *Public Opinion Quarterly, 36*, 254–257.

Dillman, D. A. (1978). *Mail and telephone surveys.* New York: Wiley.

Dillman, D. A., Carpenter, E. H., Christenson, J. A., & Brooks, R. M. (1974). Increasing mail questionnaire response: A four state comparison. *American Sociological Review, 39*, 744–756.

Dion, K. K. (1980). Physical attractiveness, sex roles, and heterosexual attraction. In M. Cook (Ed.), *The bases of human sexual attraction* (pp. 3–22). London: Academic Press.

Dion, K. K., Baron, R. S., & Miller, N. (1970). Why do groups make riskier decisions than individuals? In L. Berkowitz (Ed.), *Advances in experimental social psychology* (Vol. 5, pp. 306–378). New York: Academic Press.

Dion, K. K., Berscheid, E., & Walster, E. (1972). What is beautiful is good. *Journal of Personality and Social Psychology, 24*, 285–290.

Dion, K. K., & Dion, K. L. (1995). On the love of beauty and the beauty of love: Two psychologists study attraction. In G. G. Brannigan & M. R. Merrens (Eds.). (1995). *The social psychologists: Research adventures* (pp. 115–127). New York: McGraw-Hill.

Dipboye, R. L., & Flanagan, M. F. (1979). Research settings in industrial and organizational psychology: Are findings in the field more generalizable than in the laboratory? *American Psychologist, 34*, 141–150.

Donaldson, S. I. (in press). High potential mediators of drug abuse prevention program effects. In W. D. Crano & M. Burgoon (Eds.), *Mass media and drug prevention: Classic and contemporary theories and research.* Mahwah, NJ: Lawrence Erlbaum Associates.

Donaldson, W., & Glathe, H. (1970). Signal-detection analysis of recall and recognition memory. *Canadian Journal of Psychology, 24*, 42–56.

Douglas, J. D. (1976). *Investigative social research.* Beverly Hills, CA: Sage.

Dovidio, J. F., & Fazio, R. H. (1992). New technologies for the direct and indirect assessment of attitudes. In J. M. Tanur (Ed.), *Questions about questions: Inquiries into the cognitive bases of surveys* (pp. 204–237). New York: Russell Sage Foundation.

Druckman, D. (1968). Ethnocentrism in the Inter-nation Simulation. *Journal of Conflict Resolution, 12*, 45–68.

Dunand, M. A. (1986). Violence et panique dans le stade football de Bruxelles en 1985: Approache psychosociale des evenements [Violence and panic in the Brussells football stadium in 1985: A psychosocial approach to these remarkable events]. *Cahiers de Psychologie Cognitive, 6*, 235–266.

Duncan, O. D. (1984). Measurement and structure. In C. F. Turner & E. Martin (Eds.), *Surveying subjective phenomena* (Vol. 1, chap. 6). New York: Russell Sage Foundation.

Duval, S., & Wicklund, R. (1973). Effects of objective self-awareness on attribution of causality. *Journal of Experimental Social Psychology, 9*, 17–31.

Duval, S., & Wicklund, R. A. (1972). *A theory of objective self awareness.* New York: Academic Press.

Eagly, A. H., Ashmore, R. D., Makhijani, M. G., & Longo, L. C. (1991). What is beautiful is good, but . . . : A meta-analytic review of research on the physical attractiveness stereotype. *Psychological Bulletin, 110*, 109–128.

Eagly, A. H., & Chaiken, S. (1993). *The psychology of attitudes.* Ft. Worth, TX: Harcourt Brace Jovanovich.

Eagly, A. H., Karau, S., & Makhijani, M. G. (1995). Gender and the effectiveness of leaders: A meta-analysis. *Psychological Bulletin, 117*, 125–145.

Eagly, A. H., Makhijani, M. G., & Klonsky, B. G. (1992). Gender and the evaluation of leaders: A meta-analysis. *Psychological Bulletin, 111*, 3–22.

Eisenberg, N. (1991). Meta-analytic contributions to the literature on prosocial behavior. *Personality and Social Psychology Bulletin, 17*, 273–282.

Ekman, P. (1993). Facial expression of emotion. *American Psychologist, 48*, 384–392.

Ekman, P., & Friesen, W. V. (1978). *Facial action coding system: A technique for the measurement of facial movement.* Palo Alto, CA: Consulting Psychologists Press.

Ellison, J. W. (1965). Computers and the testaments. In *Proceedings: Conference on computers for the humanities* (pp. 64–74). New Haven, CT: Yale University Press.

Esposito, J. L., Agard, E., & Rosnow, R. L. (1984). Can confidentiality of data pay off? *Personality and Individual Differences, 5*, 477–480.

Estes, W. K. (1997). Significance testing in psychological research: Some persisting issues. *Psychological Science, 8*, 18–20.

Fabrigar, L. R., & Krosnick, J. A. (1995). Attitude importance and the false consensus effect. *Personality and Social Psychology Bulletin, 21*, 468–479.

Farr, J. N., Jenkins, J. J., & Patterson, D. G. (1951). Simplification of the Flesch reading ease formula. *Journal of Applied Psychology, 35*, 333–337.

Fazio, R. H., Jackson, J. R. Dunton, B. C., & Williams, C. J. (1995). Variability in automatic activation as an unobtrusive measure of racial attitudes: A bona fide pipeline? *Journal of Personality and Social Psychology, 69*, 1013–1027.

Fazio, R. H., Sanbonmatsu, D. M., Powell, M. C., & Kardes, F. R. (1986). On the automatic activation of attitudes. *Journal of Personality and Social Psychology, 50*, 229–238.

Feingold, A. (1995). The additive effects of differences in central tendency and variability are important in comparisons between groups. *American Psychologist, 50*, 5–13.

Feldman, R. E. (1968). Response to compatriot and foreigner who seek assistance. *Journal of Personality and Social Psychology, 10*, 202–214.

Festinger, L. (1957). *A theory of cognitive dissonance.* Stanford, CA: University of California Press.

Festinger, L., & Carlsmith, J. M. (1959). Cognitive consequences of forced compliance. *Journal of Personality and Social Psychology, 58*, 203–210.

Festinger, L., Riecken, H. W., & Schachter, S. S. (1956). *When prophecy fails.* Minneapolis, MN: University of Minnesota Press.

Fiske, A. P., Kitayama, S., Markus, H. R., & Nisbett, R. E. (1998). The cultural matrix of social psychology. In D. Gilbert, S. Fiske, and G. Lindzey (Eds.), *The handbook of social psychology*: Vol. 2 (4th ed., pp. 915–971). New York: Oxford University Press.

Fiske, D. W., & Campbell, D. T. (1992). Citations do not solve problems. *Psychological Bulletin, 112*, 393–395.

Fiske, S. T. (1980). Attention and weight in person perception: The impact of extreme and negative behavior. *Journal of Personality and Social Psychology, 38*, 889–906.

Fleiss, J. L. (1981). *The design and analysis of clinical experiments.* New York: Wiley.

Flesch, R. (1943). *Marks of readable style.* New York: Teachers College, Columbia University.

Fletcher, J. F. (2000). Two-timing: Politics and response latencies in a bilingual survey. *Political Psychology, 21*, 27–55.

Fode, K. L. (1960). The effect of nonvisual and nonverbal interaction of experimenter bias. Unpublished master's thesis, University of North Dakota.

Fode, K. L. (1965). The effect of experimenters' and subjects' anxiety and social desirability on experimenter outcome-bias. Unpublished doctoral dissertation, University of North Dakota.

Forgas, J. P. (Ed). (2000). *Feeling and thinking: The role of affect in social cognition.* New York: Cambridge University Press.

Forsyth, D. R. (1990). *Group dynamics* (2nd Ed.). Pacific Grove, CA: Brooks/Cole.

Freedman, J. L. (1969). Role playing: Psychology by consensus. *Journal of Personality and Social Psychology, 13*, 107–114.

Freedman, J. L., & Fraser, S. C. (1966). Compliance without pressure: The foot-in-the-door technique. *Journal of Personality and Social Psychology, 4*, 195–202.

Fries, C. (1940). *American English grammar.* New York: Appleton-Century-Crofts.

Galanter, E. (1966). *Textbook of elementary psychology.* San Francisco: Holden-Day.

Galton, F. (1885). Regression towards mediocrity in hereditary stature. *Journal of the Anthropological Institute, 15*, 246–263.

Gamson, W. A. (1969). *SIMSOC, simulated society: Participant's manual with selected readings.* New York: MACM.

Gardiner, G. S., & Schroder, H. M. (1972). Reliability and validity of the Paragraph Completion Test: Theoretical and empirical notes. *Psychological Reports, 31*, 959–962.

Gardner, W. L., Pickett, C. L., & Brewer, M. B. (2000). Social exclusion and selective memory: How the need to belong influences memory for social events. *Personality and Social Psychology Bulletin, 26*, 486–496.

Geller, E. (1955). Systematic observation: A method in child study. *Harvard Educational Review, 25*, 179–195.

George, A. L. (1959). *Propaganda analysis.* Evanston, IL: Row Peterson.

Gerard, H. B., & Mathewson, G. (1966). The effects of severity of initiation on liking for a group: A replication. *Journal of Experimental Social Psychology, 2*, 278–287.

Gerard, H. B., Wilhelmy, R. A., & Conolley, E. S. (1968). Conformity and group size. *Journal of Personality and Social Psychology, 8*, 79–82.

Gergen, K. J. (1973). Social psychology as history. *Journal of Personality and Social Psychology, 26*, 309–320.

Gergen, K. J. (1976). Social psychology, science and history. *Personality and Social Psychology Bulletin, 2*, 373–383.

Gilbert, D. T., & Hixon, J. G. (1991). The trouble of thinking: Activation and application of stereotypic beliefs. *Journal of Personality and Social Psychology, 60*, 509–517.

Gilbert, D. T., & Malone, P. S. (1995). The correspondence bias. *Psychological Bulletin, 117*, 21–38.

Gilbert, D. T., & Osborne, R. E. (1989). Thinking backward: Some curable and incurable consequences of cognitive busyness. *Journal of Personality and Social Psychology, 57*, 940–949.

Gilbert, D. T., Pelham, B. W., & Krull, D. S. (1988). On cognitive busyness: When person perceivers meet persons perceived. *Journal of Personality and Social Psychology, 54*, 733–740.

Glaser, B. G., & Strauss, A. L. (1967). *The discovery of grounded theory: Strategies for qualitative research.* Chicago: Aldine.

Glass, D., & Singer, J. (1972). *Urban stress.* New York: Academic Press.

Glass, G. V. (1978). Integrating findings: The meta-analysis of research. *Review of Research in Education, 5*, 351–379.

Glasser, G. J., & Metzger, G. D. (1972). Random-digit dialing as a method of telephone sampling. *Journal of Marketing Research, 9*, 59–64.

Glasser, G. J., & Metzger, G. D. (1975). National estimates of nonlisted telephone households and their characteristics. *Journal of Marketing Research, 12*, 359–361.

Godow, R. A. (1976). Social psychology as both science and history. *Personality and Social Psychology Bulletin, 2*, 421–427.

Goldman, R. M., & Crano, W. D. (1976). Black Boy and Manchild in the Promised Land: Content analysis in the study of value change over time. *Journal of Black Studies, 7*, 169–180.

Goodstadt, B., & Kipnis, D. (1970). Situational influences on the use of power. *Journal of Applied Psychology, 54*, 201–207.

Goodstadt, M. S., & Gruson, V. (1975). The randomized response technique: A test on drug use. *Journal of the American Statistical Association, 70*, 814–818.

Gottman, J. M., & Roy, A. K. (1990). *Sequential analysis: A guide for behavioral researchers.* New York: Cambridge University Press.

Grand, S., & Segal, S. J. (1966). Recovery in the absence of recall. *Journal of Experimental Psychology, 59*, 138–144.

Gray, W. S., & Leary, B. E. (1935). *What makes a book readable.* Chicago: University of Chicago Press.

Green, B. F., Jr. (1956). A method of scaleogram analysis using summary statistics. *Psychometrika, 21*, 79–88.

Greenfield, T. K., Midanik, L. T., & Rogers, J. D. (2000). Effects of telephone versus face-to-face interview modes on reports of alcohol consumption. *Addiction, 95*, 277–284.

Greenwald, A. G. (1975). Consequences of prejudice against the null hypothesis. *Psychological Bulletin, 82*, 1–20.

Greenwald, A. G. (1976). Transhistorical lawfulness of behavior: A comment on two papers. *Personality and Social Psychology Bulletin, 2*, 391.

Greenwald, A. G., & Banaji, M. R. (1995). Implicit social cognition: Attitudes, self-esteem, and stereotypes. *Psychological Review, 102*, 4–27.

Greenwald, A. G., McGhee, D. E., & Schwartz, J. (1998). Measuring individual differences in implicit cognition: The implicit association test. *Journal of Personality and Social Psychology, 74*, 1464–1480.

Greenwald, S., & Russell, R. I. (1991). Assessing rationales for inclusiveness in meta-analytic samples. *Psychotherapy Research, 1*, 17–24.

Greenwood, J. D. (1983). Role-playing as an experimental strategy in social psychology. *European Journal of Social Psychology, 13*, 235–254.

Groves, R. M., & Kahn, R. L. (1979). *Surveys by telephone.* New York: Academic Press.

Groves, R. M., & Magilavy, L. J. (1981). Increasing response rates to telephone surveys: A door in the face for the foot-in-the-door? *Public Opinion Quarterly, 45*, 346–358.

Guba, E. (1980). *The evaluator as instrument.* Unpublished manuscripts, Indiana University.

Guetzkow, H., Alger, C., Brody, R., Noel, R., & Sidney, R. (1963). *Simulation in international relations: Developments for research and teaching.* Englewood Cliffs, NJ: Prentice-Hall.

Guglielmi, R. S. (1999). Psychophysiological assessment of prejudice: Past research, current status, and future directions. *Personality and Social Psychology Review, 3*, 123–157.

Guilford, J. P. (1954). *Psychometric methods.* New York: McGraw-Hill.

Gulliksen, H. (1950). *Theory of mental tests.* New York: Wiley.

Guttman, L. (1944). A basis for scaling qualitative data. *American Sociological Review, 9*, 139–150.

Guttman, L. (1947). The Cornell technique for scale and intensity analysis. *Educational and Psychological Measurement, 7*, 247–279.

Guttman, L. (1968). A general nonmetric technique for finding the smallest coordinate space for a configuration of points. *Psychometrika, 33*, 469–506.

Guttman, L., & Suchman, E. A. (1947). Intensity and zero point for attitude analysis. *American Sociological Review, 12*, 57–67.

Halberstadt, J. B., & Niedenthal, P. M. (1997). Emotional state and the use of stimulus dimensions in judgment. *Journal of Personality and Social Psychology, 72*, 1017–1033.

Hamilton, D. L., Katz, L. B., & Leirer, V. O. (1980). Organizational processes in impression formation. In R. Hastie, T. Ostrom, E. Ebbesen, R. Wyer, D. Hamilton, & D. Carlston (Eds.), *Person memory: The cognitive basis of social perception* (pp. 121–153). Hillsdale, NJ: Lawrence Erlbaum Associates.

Hansen, R. A., & Robinson, L. M. (1980). Testing the effectiveness of alternative foot-in-the-door manipulations. *Journal of Marketing Research, 17*, 359–364.

Harris, M. J., & Rosenthal, R. (1985). Mediation of interpersonal expectancy effects: 31 meta-analyses. *Psychological Bulletin, 97*, 363–386.

Harris, M. J., & Rosenthal, R. (1986). Four factors in the mediation of teacher expectancy effects. In R. S. Feldman (Ed.), *The social psychology of education: Current research and theory* (pp. 91–114). NY: Cambridge University Press.

Harris, R. J. (1976). Two factors contributing to the perception of the theoretical intractability of social psychology. *Personality and Social Psychology Bulletin, 2*, 411–417.

Harvey, J. (1953). The content characteristics of best-selling novels. *Public Opinion Quarterly, 17*, 91–114.

Hastie, R., & Stasser, G. (2000). Computer simulation methods for social psychology. In H. Reis & C. Judd (Eds.), *Handbook of research methods in social and personality psychology* (pp. 85–114). New York: Cambridge University Press.

Hatchett, S., & Schuman, H. (1975–1976). White respondents and the race-of-interviewer effect. *Public Opinion Quarterly, 39*, 523–528.

Hays, W. L. (1988). *Statistics* (4th Ed.). New York: Holt, Rinehart & Winston.

Heberlein, T. A., & Baumgartner, R. (1978). Factors affecting response rates to mailed questionnaires: A quantitative analysis of the published literature. *American Sociological Review, 43*, 447–462.

Hedges, L. V., & Friedman, L. (1993). Computing gender differences in the tails of distributions: The consequences of differences in tail size, effect size, and variance ratio. *Review of Educational Research, 63*, 110–112.

Hedges, L. V., & Olkin, I. (1985). *Statistical methods for meta-analysis.* Orlando, FL: Academic Press.

Heider, F. (1958). *The psychology of interpersonal relations.* New York: Wiley.

Henle, M, & Hubbell, M. B. (1938). 'Egocentricity' in adult conversation. *Journal of Social Psychology, 9*, 227–234.

Herman, J. B. (1977). Mixed-mode data collection: Telephone and personal interviewing. *Journal of Applied Psychology, 62*, 399–404.

Hess, E. H. (1965). Attitude and pupil size. *Scientific American, 212*, 46–54.

Hess, E. H., Seltzer, A. L., & Shlien, J. M. (1965). Pupil responses of hetero- and homosexual males to pictures of men and women: A pilot study. *Journal of Abnormal Psychology, 70*, 165–168.

Heyns, R. W., & Zander, A. F. (1953). Observation of group behavior. In L. Festinger & D. Katz (Eds.), *Research methods in the behavioral sciences* (pp. 353–385). New York: Holt, Rinehart, & Winston.

Higgins, E. T., Rholes, W. S., & Jones, C. R. (1977). Category accessibility and impression formation. *Journal of Experimental Social Psychology, 13*, 141–154.

Hinsz, V., Tindale, R. S., & Vollrath, D. (1997). The emerging conceptualization of groups as information processes. *Psychological Bulletin, 121*, 43–64.

Hodge, R. W., Siegel, P. M., & Rossi, P. H. (1964). Occupational prestige in the United States. *American Journal of Sociology, 70*, 286–302.

Hofstede, G. J., & Pedersen, P. (1999). Synthetic cultures: Intercultural learning through simulation games. *Simulation and Gaming, 30*, 415–440.

Holland, P. W., & Leinhardt, S. (1978). An omnibus test for social structure using triads. *Sociological Methods and Research, 7*, 227–256.

Hollingshead, A. B. (1998). Retrieval processes in transactive memory systems. *Journal of Personality Social Psychology, 74*, 659–671.

Hollingshead, A. B., & McGrath, J. E. (1995). Computer-assisted groups: A critical review of the empirical research. In R. Guzzo & E. Salas (Eds.), *Team effectiveness and decision making in organizations* (pp. 46–78). San Francisco, CA: Jossey-Bass.

Hollingshead, A. B ., McGrath, J. E., & O'Connor, K. M. (1993). Group task performance and communication technology: A longituinal study of computer-mediated versus face-to-face work groups. *Small Group Research, 24*, 307–333.

Hollingshead, A. de B. (1949). *Elmstown's youth, the impact of social classes on adolescents*. New York: Wiley.

Holmes, D. S. (1967). Amount of experience in experiments as a determinant of performance in later experiments. *Journal of Personality and Social Psychology, 7*, 403–407.

Holmes, D. S. (1976a). Debriefing after psychological experiments: I. Effectiveness of postdeception dehoaxing. *American Psychologist, 31*, 858–867.

Holmes, D. S. (1976b). Debriefing after psychological experiments: II. Effectiveness of postdeception desensitizing. *American Psychologist, 31*, 868–875.

Holsti, O. R. (1962). The belief system and national images: John Foster Dulles and the Soviet Union. Unpublished doctoral dissertation, Stanford University, Palo Alto, CA.

Holsti, O. R. (1964). An adaptation of the 'General Inquirer' for the systematic analysis of political documents. *Behavioral Science, 9*, 382–388.

Holsti, O. R. (1968). Content analysis. In G. Lindzey & E. Aronson (Eds.), *Handbook of social psychology: Vol. 2. Research Methods* (pp. 596–692). Reading, MA: Addison-Wesley.

Holsti, O. R. (1969). *Content analysis for the social sciences and humanities*. Reading, MA: Addison-Wesley.

Hooker, E. (1957). The adjustment of the male overt homosexual. *Journal of Projective Techniques, 21*, 18–31.

Hoppe, M. J., Gillmore, M. R., Valadez, D. L., Civic, D., Hartway, J., & Morrison, D. M. (2000). The relative costs and benefits of telephone interviews versus self-administered diaries for daily data collection. *Evaluation Review, 24*, 102–116.

Horowitz, I. L., & Rothschild, B. H. (1970). Conformity as a function of deception and role playing. *Journal of Personality and Social Psychology, 14*, 224–226.

Horton, D. (1957). The dialogue of courtship in popular songs. *American Journal of Sociology, 62*, 569–578.

Horwich, P. (Ed.). (1993). *World changes: Thomas Kuhn and the nature of science*. Cambridge, MA: MIT Press.

Hovland, C. I., & Sherif, M. (1952). Judgmental phenomena and scales of attitude measurement: Item displacement in Thurstone scales. *Journal of Abnormal and Social Psychology, 42*, 215–239.

Hovland, C. I., Lumsdaine, A. A., & Sheffield, F. D. (1949). *Experiments on mass communication*. Princeton, NJ: Princeton University Press.

Howard, W. D., & Crano, W. D. (1974). Effects of sex, conversation, location, and size of observer group on bystander intervention in a high risk situation. *Sociometry, 66*, 255–261.

Hoyle, R. H. (1995). *Structural equation modeling*. Thousand Oaks, CA: Sage.

Hunter, J. E. (1997). Needed: A ban on the significance test. *Psychological Science, 8*, 3–7.

Hunter, J. E., & Schmidt, F. L. (1990). *Methods of meta-analysis: Correcting error and bias in research findings*. Newbury Park, CA: Sage.

Hunter, J. E., Schmidt, F. L., & Jackson, G. B. (1982). *Meta-analysis: Cumulating research findings across studies*. Beverly Hills, CA: Sage.

Hyman, H. H., Cobb, W. J., Feldman, J. J., Hart, C. W., & Stember, C. H. (1954). *Interviewing in social research*. Chicago: University of Chicago Press.

Insko, C. A., Worchel, S., Songer, E., & Arnold, S. E. (1973). Effort, objective self-awareness, choice, and dissonance. *Journal of Personality and Social Psychology, 28*, 262–269.

Instone, D., Major, B., & Bunker, B. (1983). Gender, self confidence, and social influence strategies: An organizational simulation. *Journal of Personality and Social Psychology, 44*, 322–333.

Internet.com LCC. (1999). One-quarter of US households on line [WWW document]. Available URL: http://www.cyberatlas.com/big_picture/demographics/household.html.

Isen, A. M., & Levin, P. F. (1972). The effect of feeling good on helping: Cookies and kindness. *Journal of Personality and Social Psychology, 21*, 384–388.

Isenberg, D. J. (1986). Group polarization: A critical review and meta-analysis. *Journal of Personality and Social Psychology, 50*, 1141–1151.

Jackson, D. N., & Messick, S. (1962). Response styles on the MMPI: Comparison of clinical and normal samples. *Journal of Abnormal and Social Psychology, 65*, 285–299.

Jacobs, R. C., & Campbell, D. T. (1961). The perpetuation of an arbitrary tradition through several generations of laboratory microculture. *Journal of Abnormal and Social Psychology, 62*, 649–658.

Janis, I. L. (1958). *Psychological stress*. New York: Wiley.

Janisse, M. P. (1973). Pupil size and affect: A critical review of the literature since 1960. *Canadian Psychologist, 14*, 311–329.

Jastro, J. (1900). *Fact and fable in psychology*. Boston: Houghton Mifflin.

Jenkins, J. J., Russel, W. A., & Suci, G. J. (1957). An atlas of semantic profiles for 360 words. In *Studies on the role of language in behavior*. Technical Report No. 15. Minneapolis: University of Minnesota.

John, O. P., Hampson, S. E., & Goldberg, L. R. (1991). The basic level in personality-trait hierarchies: Studies of trait use and accessibility in different contexts. *Journal of Personality and Social Psychology, 60*, 348–361.

Johnson, B. T., & Eagly, A. H. (2000). Quantitative synthesis of social psychological research. In H. Reis & C. Judd (Eds.), *Handbook of research methods in social and personality psychology* (pp. 496–528). New York: Cambridge University Press.

Johnson, J. E., & Leventhal, H. (1974). Effects of accurate expectations and behavioral instructions on reactions during a noxious medical examination. *Journal of Personality and Social Psychology, 29*, 710–718.

Jones, E. E. (1990). *Interpersonal perception*. New York: Freeman.

Jones, S. (Ed.). (1999). *Doing internet research: Critical issues and methods for examining the net*. Thousand Oaks, CA: Sage.

Jöoreskog, K. G., & Sörbom, D. (1993). *LISREL 8: User's reference guide*. Chicago: Scientific Software.

Jöreskog, K. G. (1973). A general model for estimating a linear structural equation system. In A. S. Goldberger & O. D. Duncan (Eds.), *Structural equation models in the social sciences* (pp. 85–112). New York: Seminar Press.

Jourard, S. M. (1971). *Self disclosure*. New York: Wiley.

Jung, A. F. (1959). Price variations among automobile dealers in Chicago, Illinois. *Journal of Business, 32*, 315–326.

Kahneman, D., Slovic, P., & Tversky, A. (1982). *Judgment under uncertainty: Heuristics and biases*, Cambridge, England: Cambridge University Press.

Kalton, G. (1983a). *Compensating for missing survey data*. Ann Arbor, MI: Survey Research Center, University of Michigan.

Kalton, G. (1983b). *Introduction to survey sampling*. Beverly Hills, CA: Sage.

Kalton, G., Collins, M., & Brook, L. (1978). Experiments in wording opinion questions. *Applied Statistics, 27*, 149–161.

Kameda, T., Ohtsubo, Y, & Takezawa, M. (1997). Centrality in sociocognitive network and social influence: An illustration in a group decision-making context. *Journal of Personality and Social Psychology, 73*, 296–309.

Kanuk, L., & Berenson, C. (1975). Mail surveys and response rates: A literature review. *Journal of Marketing Research, 12*, 440–453.

Kashy, D. A., & Kenny, D. A. (2000). The analysis of data from dyads and groups. In H. Reis & C. Judd (Eds.), *Handbook of research methods in social and personality psychology* (pp. 451–477). New York: Cambridge University Press.

Kelman, H. C. (1967). Human use of human subjects: The problem of deception in social psychological experiments. *Psychological Bulletin, 67*, 1–11.

Kelman, H. C. (1968). *A time to speak: On human values and social research*. San Francisco: Jossey-Bass.

Kelman, H. C. (1972). The rights of the subject in social research: An analysis in terms of relative power and legitimacy. *American Psychologist, 27*, 989–1016.

Kennedy, J. L., & Uphoff, H. F. (1939). Experiments on the nature of extrasensory perception: III. The recording error criticism of extrachance scores. *Journal of Parapsychology, 3*, 226–245.

Kenny, D. A. (1979). *Correlation and causality*. New York: Wiley.

Kenny, D. A., & Judd, C. (1986). Consequences of violating the independence assumption in analysis of variance. *Psychological Bulletin, 99*, 422–431.

Kenny, D. A., & Judd, C. (1996). A general procedure for the estimation of interdependence. *Psychological Bulletin, 119*, 138–148.

Kenny, D. A., & La Voie, L. (1982). Reciprocity of attraction: A confirmed hypothesis. *Social Psychology Quarterly, 45*, 54–58.

Kenny, D. A., & La Voie, L. (1984). The social relations model. In L. Berkowitz (Ed.), *Advances in Experimental Social Psychology* (Vol. 18, pp. 141–182). New York: Academic Press.

Kenny, D. A., Lord, R., & Garg, S. (1984). *A social relations model for peer ratings*. Unpublished paper, University of Connecticut.

Kenny, D. A., & Rubin, D. C. (1977). Estimating chance reproducibility in Guttman scaling. *Social Science Research, 6*, 188–196.

Kerlinger, F. N. (1964). *Foundations of behavioral research: Educational and psychological inquiry*. New York: Holt.

Kerr, N. L. (1998). HARKing: Hypothesizing after the results are known. *Personality and Social Psychology Review, 2*, 196–217.

Kerr, N. L., Aronoff, J., & Messé, L. A. (2000). Methods of group research. In H. Reis & C. Judd (Eds.), *Handbook of research methods in social and personality psychology* (pp. 160–189). New York: Cambridge University Press.

Kershaw, D., & Fair, J. (1976). *The New Jersey income-maintenance experiment*. New York: Academic Press.

Kidder, L. H. (1969). *Comparisons of a direct and indirect attitude test: Their relative susceptibility to distortion.* Unpublished master's thesis, Northwestern University, Evanston, IL.

Kidder, L. H. (1981). Qualitative research and quasi-experimental frameworks. In M. B. Brewer & B. E. Collins (Eds.), *Scientific inquiry and the social sciences* (pp. 226–256). San Francisco: Jossey-Bass.

Kidder, L. H., & Campbell, D. T. (1970). The indirect testing of social attitudes. In G. Summers (Ed.), *Attitude measurement* (pp. 333–385). Chicago: Rand-McNally.

Kiesler, S., & Sproull, L. (1992). Group decision making and technology. *Organizational Behavior and Human Decision Processes, 52*, 96–123.

Kiesler, S., & Sproull, L. S. (1986). Response effects in the electronic survey. *Public Opinion Quarterly, 50*, 402–413.

Kimmel, A. J. (1991). Predictable biases in the ethical decision making of American psychologists. *American Psychologist, 46*, 786–788.

Kinsey, A. C., Pomeroy, W. B., & Martin, C. E. (1948). *Sexual behavior in the human male.* Philadelphia: Saunders.

Kish, L. A. (1965). *Survey sampling.* New York: Wiley.

Klein, R. D., & Fleck, R. A. (1990). International business simulation/gaming: An assessment and review. *Simulation and Gaming, 21*, 147–165.

Klimoski, R., & Mohammed, S. (1994). Team mental model: Construct or metaphor? *Journal of Management, 20*, 403–437.

Kluegel, J. R., & Smith, E. R. (1982). Whites' beliefs about blacks' opportunity. *American Sociological Review, 47*, 518–532.

Klumb, P. L., & Baltes, M. M. (1999). Validity of retrospective time-use reports in old age. *Applied Cognitive Psychology, 13*, 527–539.

Knoke, D., & Kuklinski, J. H. (1982). *Network analysis.* Beverly Hills, CA: Sage.

Komorita, S. (1965). Cooperative choice in a prisoner's dilemma game. *Journal of Personality and Social Psychology, 2*, 741–745.

Kraemer, H. C., Gardner, C., Brooks, J. O., III, & Yesavage, J. A. (1998). Advantages of excluding underpowered studies in meta-analysis: Inclusionist versus exclusionist viewpoints. *Psychological Methods, 3*, 23–31.

Kramer, R. M., & Brewer, M. B. (1984). Effects of group identity on resource use in a simulated commons dilemma. *Journal of Personality and Social Psychology, 46*, 1044–1057.

Krantz, J. H., & Dalal, R. (2000). Validity of Web-based psychological research. In M. H. Birnbaum (Ed.), *Psychological experiments on the internet* (pp. 35–60). San Diego, CA: Academic Press.

Krantz, J. H., Ballard, J., & Scher, J. (1997). Comparing the results of laboratory and World-Wide-Web samples on the determinants of female attractiveness. *Behavioral Research Methods, Instruments, and Computers, 29*, 264–269.

Krippendorff, K. (1980). *Content analysis: An introduction to its methodology.* Beverly Hills, CA: Sage.

Krosnick, J. A. (1991). Response strategies for coping with the cognitive demands of attitude measures in surveys. *Applied Cognitive Psychology, 5*, 213–236.

Krosnick, J. A., & Alwin, D. F. (1987). An evaluation of a cognitive theory of response order effects in survey measurement. *Public Opinion Quarterly, 51*, 201–219.

Krosnick, J. A., & Fabrigar, L. R. (in press). *Designing great questionnaires: Insights from psychology.* New York: Oxford University Press.

Kruskall, J. B. (1964a). Multidimensional scaling: A numerical method. *Psychometrika, 29*, 1–27.

Kruskall, J. B. (1964b). Multidimensional scaling by optimizing goodness of fit to a nonmetric hypothesis. *Psychometrika, 29,* 115–129.

Kruskall, J. B., Young, F. W., & Seery, J. B. (1977). *How to use KYST 2: A very flexible program to do multi-dimensional scaling and unfolding.* Murray Hill, NJ: Bell Telephone Labs.

Kubey, R., Larson, R., & Csikszentmihalyi, M. (1996). Experience sampling method applications to communication research questions. *Journal of Communication, 46,* 99–120.

Kuhn, T. S. (1970). *The structure of scientific revolutions* (2nd ed.). Chicago: University of Chicago Press.

Lachenmeyer, C. W. (1970). Experimentation—A misunderstood methodology in psychology and social psychological research. *American Psychologist, 25,* 617–624.

Lana, R. E. (1959). Pretest-treatment interaction effects in attitude studies. *Psycholgical Bulletin, 56,* 293–300.

Lane, R. D., Reiman, E., Ahern, G., Schwartz, G., & Davidson, R. (1997). Neuroanatomical correlates of happiness, sadness, and disgust. *American Journal of Psychiatry, 154,* 926–933.

Lang, P. J., Bradley, M. M., & Cuthbert, B. N. (1990). Emotion, attention, and the startle reflex. *Psychological Review, 97,* 377–395.

Lang, P. J., Bradley, M. M., & Cuthbert, B. N. (1992). A motivational analysis of emotion: Reflex-cortex connections. *Psychological Science, 3,* 44–49.

Langer, E. J. (1975). The illusion of control. *Journal of Personality and Social Psychology, 32,* 311–328.

Langer, E. J. (1997). *The power of mindful learning.* Reading, MA: Addison-Wesley.

Langer, E. J. (2000). Mindful learning. *Current Directions in Psychological Science, 9,* 220–223.

Langer, E. J., & Rodin, J. (1976). The effects of choice and enhanced personal responsibility for the aged: A field experiment in an institutional setting. *Journal of Personality and Social Psychology, 34,* 191–198.

LaPiere, R. T. (1934). Attitudes vs. actions. *Social Forces, 13,* 230–237.

Larson, R., & Csikszentmihalyi, M. (1978). Experiential correlates of solitude in adolescence. *Journal of Personality, 46,* 677–693.

Larson, R., & Csikszentmihalyi, M. (1980). The significance of time alone in adolescent development. *Journal of Current Adolescent Medicine, 2,* 33–40.

Larson, R., & Csikszentmihalyi, M. (1983). The experience sampling method. In H. T. Reis (Ed.), *Naturalistic approaches to studying social interaction* (pp. 42–56). San Francisco: Jossey-Bass.

Larson, R., Csikszentmihalyi, M., & Graef, R. (1980). Mood variability and the psychosocial adjustment of adolescents. *Journal of Youth and Adolescence, 9,* 469–490.

Lasswell, H. D. (1927). *Propaganda technique in the world war.* New York: Knopf.

Lasswell, H. D., Lerner, D., & Pool, I. de S. (1952). *The comparative study of symbols.* Stanford, CA: Stanford University Press.

Laszlo, J. P., & Rosenthal, R. (1967). *Subject dogmatism, experimenter status, and experimenter expectancy effects* (Mimeograph). Cambridge, MA: Harvard University, Department of Social Relations.

Latané, B. (1970). Field studies of altruistic compliance. *Representative Research in Social Psychology, 1,* 49–61.

Latané, B. (1997). Dynamic social impact: The societal consequences of human interaction. In C. McGarty, N. Haslam, & S. Alexander (Eds.), *The message of social psychology: Perspectives on mind in society* (pp. 200–220). Oxford, England: Blackwell.

Latané, B., & Darley, J. M. (1968). Group inhibition of bystander intervention. *Journal of Personality and Social Psychology, 10,* 215–221.

Latané, B., & Darley, J. M. (1970). *The unresponsive bystander: Why doesn't he help?* New York: Appleton-Century-Crofts.

Latané, B., & L'Herrou, T. (1996). Spatial clustering in the conformity game: Dynamic social impact in electronic groups. *Journal of Personality and Social Psychology, 70*, 1218–1230.

Lavrakas, P. J. (1993). Telephone survey methods: Sampling, selection, and supervision. *Applied social research methods series* (2nd ed., Vol. 7). Newbury Park, CA: Sage.

Lavrakas, P. J. (1998). Methods for sampling and interviewing in telephone surveys. In L. Bickman, & D. J. Rog (Eds.), *Handbook of applied social research methods* (pp. 429–472). Thousand Oaks, CA: Sage.

Lee, A. M. (1952). *How to understand propaganda.* New York: Rinehart.

Lee, A. M., & Lee, E. B. (1939). *The fine art of propaganda.* New York: Harcourt Brace.

Lefkowitz, M., Blake, R. R., & Mouton, J. S. (1955). Status factors in pedestrian violation of traffic signals. *Journal of Abnormal and Social Psychology, 51*, 704–706.

Lehman, B. J., & Crano, W. D. (in press). The pervasive effect of vested interest on attitude-criterion consistency in political judgment. *Journal of Experimental Social Psychology.*

Leigh, B. C. (1993). Alcohol consumption and sexual activity as reported with a diary technique. *Journal of Abnormal Psychology, 102*, 490–493.

Leventhal, H., & Sharp, E. (1965). Facial expressions as indicators of distress. In S. Tomkins & C. E. Izard (Eds.), *Affect, cognition, and personality* (pp. 76–82). New York: Springer.

Levin, H. M. (1983). Cost-effectiveness analysis and the communication of evaluation results. In E. Struening & M. B. Brewer (Eds.), *Handbook of evaluation research: University edition* (pp. 345–379). Beverly Hills, CA: Sage.

Levy, L. (1960). Studies in conformity behavior: A methodological note. *Journal of Psychology, 50*, 39–41.

Lewin, H. S. (1947). Hitler youth and the Boy Scouts of America: A comparison of aims. *Human Relations, 1*, 206–227.

Likert, R. (1932). A technique for the measurement of attitudes. *Archives of Psychology*, No. 140.

Linsky, A. S. (1975). Stimulating responses to mailed questionnaires: A review. *Public Opinion Quarterly, 39*, 82–101.

Lofland, J. (1971). *Analyzing social settings: A guide to qualitative observation and analysis.* Belmont, CA: Wadsworth.

Logan, G. D. (1980). Attention and automaticity in Stroop and priming tasks: Theory and data. *Cognitive Psychology, 12*, 523–553.

Lord, C. G., & Saenz, D. S. (1985). Memory deficits and memory surfeits: Differential cognitive consequences of tokenism for tokens and observers. *Journal of Personality and Social Psychology, 49*, 918–926.

Lowenthal, L. (1949). The sociology of literature. In W. Schramm (Ed.), *Communications in modern society* (pp. 100–125). Urbana, IL: University of Illinois Press.

Luce, R. D., & Raiffa, N. (1958). *Games and decisions.* New York: Wiley.

MacLeod, C. (1991). Half a century of research on the Stroop effect: An integrative review. *Psychological Bulletin, 109*, 163–203.

Macrae, C. N., Bodenhausen, G. V., & Milne, A. B. (1995). The dissection of selection in person perception: Inhibitory processes in social stereotyping. *Journal of Personality and Social Psychology, 69*, 397–407.

Mahl, G. F. (1964). Some observations about research on vocal behavior. *Disorders of Communication, 42*, 466–483.

Malvin, J. H., & Moskowitz, J. M. (1983). Anonymous versus identifiable self-reports of adolescent drug attitudes, intentions, and use. *Public Opinion Quarterly, 47*, 557–566.

Manicas, P. T., & Secord, P. F. (1983). Implications for psychology of the new philosophy of science. *American Psychologist, 38*, 399–413.

Manis, M. (1976). Is social psychology really different? *Personality and Social Psychology Bulletin, 2*, 428–437.

Mariampolski, H., & Reichel, P. L. (1978). *New frontiers for the sociological snooper: Problems and prospects for the technology of concealed observation in social research.* Paper presented to the Southern Sociological Society, New Orleans, LA.

Markham, J. W., & Stempel, G. H. (1957). Analysis of techniques in measuring press conference performance. *Journalism Quarterly, 34*, 187–190.

Marks, G., & Miller, N. (1987). Ten years of research on the false-consensus effect: An empirical and theoretical review. *Psychological Bulletin, 102*, 72–90.

Marquis, K. H., & Cannell, C. F. (1969). *A study of interviewer-respondent interaction in the urban employment survey.* Ann Arborr, MI: Survey Research Center, University of Michigan.

Marsh, H. W., & Bailey, M. (1991). Confirmatory factory analyses of multitrait-multimethod data: A comparison of alternative models. *Applied Psychological Measurement, 15*, 47–70.

Marwit, S. J., & Marcia, J. E. (1965). Tester-bias and response to projective instruments. *Journal of Consulting Psychology, 31*, 253–258.

Masling, J. (1965). Differential indoctrination of examiners and Rorschach responses. *Journal of Consulting Psychology, 29*, 198–201.

Masling, J. (1966). Role related behavior of the subject and psychologist and its effects upon psychological data. *Nebraska Symposium on Motivation, 14*, 67–103.

McArthur, L. Z., & Ginsberg, E. (1981). Causal attribution to salient stimuli: An investigation of visual fixation mediators. *Personality and Social Psychology Bulletin, 7*, 547–553.

McAuliffe, W. E., Geller, S., LaBrie, R., Paletz, S., & Fournier, E. (1998). Are telephone surveys suitable for studying substance abuse? Cost, administration, coverage and response rate issues. *Source Journal of Drug Issues, 28*, 455–481.

McCain, L. J., & McCleary, R. (1979). The statistical analysis of the simple interrupted time-series quasi-experiment. In T. D. Cook & D. T. Campbell (Eds.), *Quasi-experimentation: Design and analysis issues for field settings* (pp. 233–294). Chicago: Rand McNally.

McCall, G. J., & Simmons, J. L. (Eds.). (1969). *Issues in participant observation: A text and reader.* Reading, MA: Addison-Wesley.

McClelland, D. C. (1961). *The achieving society.* Princeton, NJ: Princeton University Press.

McClendon, M. J. (1991). Acquiescence and recency response-order effects in interview surveys. *Sociological Methods and Research, 20*, 60–103.

McDonald, D. (1998). The art of negotiating. *Simulation and Gaming, 29*, 475–479.

McDowell, D., McCleary, R., Meidinger, E., & Hay, R. (1980). *Interrupted time-series analysis.* Beverly Hills, CA: Sage.

McGahuey, C. A., Gelenberg, A. J., Laukes, C. A., Moreno, F. A., Delgado, P. L., McKnight, K. M., & Manber, R. (2000). The Arizona sexual experience scale (ASEX): Reliability and validity. *Journal of Sex and Marital Therapy, 26*, 25–40.

McGrath, J. E. (1966). A social psychological approach to the study of negotiation. In R. Bowers (Ed.), *Studies of behavior in organizations: A research symposium* (pp. 101–134). Athens, GA: University of Georgia Press.

McGrath, J. E. (1984). *Groups: Interaction and performance.* Englewood Cliffs, NJ: Prentice-Hall.

McGrath, J. E., & Altermatt, T. W. (2001). Observation and analysis of group interaction over time: Some methodological and strategic choices. In M. Hogg & R. S. Tindale (Eds.), *Blackwell handbook of social psychology: Group processes* (pp. 525–573). Oxford, UK: Blackwell.

McGrath, J. E., & Hollingshead, A. B. (1994). *Groups interacting with technology*. Thousand Oaks, CA: Sage.

McGrath, J. E., & Julian, J. W. (1963). Interaction process and task outcomes in experimentally-created negotiation groups. *Journal of Psychological Studies, 14*, 117–138.

McGraw, K. O., Tew, M. D., & Williams, J. E. (2000). The integrity of web-delivered experiments: Can you trust the data? *Psychological Science, 11*, 502–506.

McGuire, W. J. (1973). The yin and yang of progress in social psychology. *Journal of Personality and Social Psychology, 26*, 446–456.

McGuire, W. J. (1997). Creative hypothesis generating in psychology: Some useful heuristics. *Annual Review of Psychology, 48*, 1–30.

McKenna, K., & Bargh, J. A. (2000). Plan 9 from Cyberspace: The implications of the internet for personality and social psychology. *Personality and Social Psychology Review, 4*, 57–75.

McNemar, Q. (1940). A critical examination of the University of Iowa studies of environmental influences upon the I.Q. *Journal of Psychology Bulletin, 37*, 63–92.

McNemar, Q. (1969). *Psychological statistics* (4th ed.). New York: Wiley.

Mehan, H., & Wood, H. (1975). *The reality of ethnomethodology*. New York: Wiley.

Mehta, R. & Sivadas, E. (1995). Comparing response rates and response content in mail versus electronic mail surveys. *Journal of the Market Research Society, 37*, 429–439.

Mellon, P. M., & Crano, W. D. (1977). An extension and application of the multitrait-multimethod matrix technique. *Journal of Educational Psychology, 69*, 716–723.

Messick, D. M., & Brewer, M. B. (1983). Solving social dilemmas: A review. In L. Wheeler & P. Shaver (Eds.), *Review of Personality and Social Psychology* (Vol. 4, pp. 11–44). Beverly Hills, CA: Sage.

Messick, D. M., Wilke, H., Brewer, M. B., Kramer, R. M., Zemke, P., & Lui, L. (1983). Individual adaptations and structural change as solutions to social dilemmas. *Journal of Personality and Social Psychology, 44*, 294–309.

Messick, S. (1989). Validity. In R. L. Linn (Ed.), *Educational measurement* (3rd ed., pp. 13–103). New York: Macmillan.

Middlemist, R., Knowles, E., & Matter, C. F. (1976). Personal space invasions in the lavatory. *Journal of Personality and Social Psychology, 33*, 541–546.

Miles, J. (1951). *The continuity of English poetic language*. Berkeley: University of California Press.

Miles, M. B., & Huberman, A. M. (1994). *Qualitative data analysis: An expanded sourcebook* (2nd ed.). Thousand Oaks, CA: Sage.

Milgram, S. (1963). Behavioral study of obedience. *Journal of Abnormal and Social Psychology, 67*, 371–378.

Milgram, S. (1964). Issues in the study of obedience: A reply to Baumrind. *American Psychologist, 19*, 848–852.

Milgram, S. (1965). Some conditions of obedience and disobedience to authority. *Human Relations, 18*, 57–75.

Milgram, S. (1969). The lost-letter technique. *Psychology Today, 3*, 30–33, 66–68.

Milgram, S. (1974). *Obedience to authority*. New York: Harper & Row.

Miller, A. G. (1972). Role playing: An alternative to deception? A review of the evidence. *American Psychologist, 27*, 623–636.

Miller, J. D. (1984). *A new survey technique for studying deviant behavior*. Unpublished doctoral dissertation, George Washington University, Washington, DC.

Miller, R. E., Caul, W. F., & Mirsky, I. A. (1967). Communication between feral and socially isolated monkeys. *Journal of Personality and Social Psychology, 3*, 231–239.

Miller, S. E. (1966). Psychology experiments without subjects' consent. *Science, 152*, 15.

Mills, R. T., & Krantz, D. S. (1979). Information, choice, and reactions to stress: A field experiment in a blood bank with laboratory analogue. *Journal of Personality and Social Psychology, 37*, 608–620.

Misra, R. K., & Dutt, P. K. (1965). A comparative study of psychological scaling methods. *Journal of Psychological Research, 9*, 31–34.

Mixon, D. (1972). Instead of deception. *Journal for the Theory of Social Behavior, 2*, 145–177.

Moghaddam, F. M., & Studer, C. (1998). *Illusions of control: Striving for control in our personal and professional lives.* Westport, CT: Praeger.

Moll, A. (1898). *Hypnotism.* (4th ed.). New York: Scribner's.

Monge, P. R. (1987). The network level of analysis. In C. R. Berger & S. H. Chaffee (Eds.), *Handbook of communication science* (pp. 239–270). Newbury Park, CA: Sage.

Mook, D. G. (1983). In defense of external invalidity. *American Psychologist, 38*, 379–387.

Moore, B. S., Underwood, B., & Rosenhahn, D. L. (1973). Affect and altruism. *Developmental Psychology, 8*, 99–104.

Moreland, R. L., Argote, L., & Krishnan, R. (1996). Socially shared cognition at work: Transactive memory and group performance. In J. Nye & A. M. Brower (Eds.), *What's social about social cognition? Research on socially shared cognition in small groups* (pp. 57–84). Thousand Oaks, CA: Sage.

Moreland, R. L., Argote, L., & Krishnan, R. (1998). Training people to work in groups. In R. S. Tindale et al. (Eds.), *Social psychological applications to social issues: Applications of theory and research on groups* (Vol. 4, pp. 37–60). New York: Plenum Press.

Moreno, J. L. (1934). Who shall survive? Washington: *Nervous and Mental Disease Monograph,* No. 58.

Morgan, C. A., III., Grillon, C., Southwick, S. M., Davis, M., & Charney, D. S. (1996). Exaggerated acoustic startle reflex in Gulf War veterans with posttraumatic stress disorder. *American Journal of Psychiatry, 153*, 64–68.

Moriarty, T. (1975). Crime, commitment, and the responsive bystander: Two field experiments. *Journal of Personality and Social Psychology, 31*, 370–376.

Morton, A. Q. (1963). A computer challenges the church. *The Observer*, Nov. 3.

Moser, C. A., & Kalton, G. (1972). *Survey methods in social investigation* (2nd ed.). New York: Basic Books.

Mosteller, F. (1951). Remarks on the method of paired comparisons: III. A test of significance for paired comparisons when equal standard deviations and equal correlations are assumed. *Psychometrika, 16*, 207–218.

Mosteller, F., & Wallace, D. L. (1964). *Inference and disputed authorship: The Federalist.* Reading, MA: Addison-Wesley.

Mullen, B., Johnson, C., & Salas, E. (1991). Productivity loss in brainstorming groups: A meta-analytic integration. *Basic and Applied Social Psychology, 12*, 3–24.

Murdock, G. P. (1967). Ethnographic altas: A summary. *Ethnology, 6*, 109–236.

Murdock, G. P., & White, D. R. (1969). Standard cross-cultural sample. *Ethnology, 8*, 329–69.

Musch, J., & Reips, U. D. (2000). A brief history of web experimenting. In M. H. Birnbaum (Ed.), *Psychological experiments on the internet* (pp. 61–87). San Diego, CA: Academic Press.

Napolitan, D. A., & Goethals, G. R. (1979). The attribution of friendliness. *Journal of Experimental Social Psychology, 15*, 105–113.

Nas, T. F. (1996). *Cost-benefit analysis: theory and application.* Thousand Oaks, CA: Sage.

National Academy of Sciences. (1995). *On being a scientist: Responsible conduct in research.* Washington, DC: National Academy Press.

Neely, J. H. (1977). Semantic priming and retrieval from lexical memory: Roles of inhibition-less spreading activation and limited-capacity attention. *Journal of Experimental Psychology: General, 106*, 226–254.

Newcomb, T. M. (1961). *The acquaintance process.* New York: Holt, Rinehart, & Winston.

Nezlek, J. B., Wheeler, L., & Reis, H. T. (1983). Studies of social participation. In H. T. Reis (Ed.), *Naturalistic approaches to studying social interaction.* San Francisco: Jossey-Bass.

Nisbett, R., & Ross, L. (1980). *Human inference: Strategies and shortcomings of social judgment.* Englewood Cliffs, NJ: Prentice-Hall.

Nisbett, R. E., & Wilson, T. D. (1977). Telling more than we can know: Verbal reports on mental processes. *Psychological Review, 84*, 231–259.

Noble, I., Moon, N., & McVey, D. (1998). 'Bringing it all back home'—Using RDD telephone methods for large-scale social policy and opinion research in the UK. *Journal of the Market Research Society, 40*, 93–120.

Notz, W. W., Staw, B. M., & Cook, T. D. (1971). Attitude toward troop withdrawal from Indochina as a function of draft number: Dissonance or self-interest? *Journal of Personality and Social Psychology, 20*, 118–126.

Nunnally, J. C. (1967). *Psychometric theory.* New York: McGraw-Hill.

Ober, B. A., & Shenaut, G. K. (1999). Well-organized conceptual domains in Alzheimer's disease. *Journal of the International Neuropsychological Society, 5*, 676–684.

Ogilvie, D. M., Stone, P. J., & Schneidman, E. S. (1966). Some characteristics of genuine versus simulated suicide notes. In P. J. Stone, D. C. Dunphy, M. S. Smith, & D. M. Ogilvie, D. M. (Eds.), *The general inquirer: A computer approach to content analysis* (pp. 527–535). Cambridge, MA: MIT Press.

Ojemann, R. H. (1948). A functional analysis of child development material in current newspapers and magazines. *Child Development, 19*, 76–92.

Oldendick, R. W., & Link, M. W. (1994). The answering machine generation: Who are they and what problem do they pose for survey research? *Public Opinion Quarterly, 58*, 264–273.

O'Leary, A., Ambrose, T. K., Raffaelli, M., Maibach, E., Jemmott, L. S., Jemmott, J. B., III, Labouvie, E., & Celentano, D. (1998). Effects of an HIV risk reduction project on sexual risk behavior of low-income STD patients. *AIDS Education and Prevention, 10*, 483–492.

Olson, J., & Zanna, M. (1979). A new look at selective exposure. *Journal of Experimental Social Psychology, 15*, 1–15.

Olson, J. S., Olson, G., Storreston, M., & Carter, M. (1994). Groupwork close up: A comparison of the group design process with and without a simple group editor. *ACM Transactions on Information Systems, 11*, 321–348.

O'Neil, M. J. (1979). Estimating the nonresponse bias due to refusals in telephone surveys. *Public Opinion Quarterly, 43*, 218–232.

Orne, M. (1962). On the social psychology of the psychological experiment. *American Psychologist, 17*, 776–783.

Ortmann, A., & Hertwig, R. (1997). Is deception acceptable? *American Psychologist, 52*, 746–747.

Orwin, R. G. (1997). Twenty-one years old and counting: The interrupted time series comes of age. In E. Chelimsky & W. R. Shadish (Eds.), *Evaluation for the 21st century: A handbook* (pp. 443–465). Thousand Oaks, CA: Sage.

Osborn, A. F. (1957). *Applied imagination.* New York: Scribner's.

Osgood, C. E. (1959). The representational model and relevant research methods. In I. de S. Pool (Ed.), *Trends in content analysis* (pp. 33–88). Urbana, IL: University of Illinois Press.

Osgood, C. E. (1962). Studies on the generality of affective meaning systems. *American Psychologist, 17*, 10–28.

Osgood, C. E., & Luria, Z. (1954). Applied analysis of a case of multiple personality using the semantic differential. *Journal of Abnormal and Social Psychology, 49*, 579–591.

Osgood, C. E., & Luria, Z. (1976). A postscript to "The three faces of Eve." *Journal of Abnormal Psychology, 85*, 276–286.

Osgood, C. E., Suci, D. J., & Tannenbaum, P. H. (1957). *The measurement of meaning.* Urbana, IL: University of Illinois Press.

Ostrom, T. M., Pryor, J. B., & Simpson, D. D. (1981). The organization of social information. In E. T. Higgins, C. P. Herman, & M. Zanna (Eds.), *Social cognition: The Ontario Symposium* (Vol. 1, pp. 3–38). Hillsdale, NJ: Lawrence Erlbaum Associates.

Paisley, W. J. (1966). The effects of authorship, topic, structure, and time of composition on letter redundancy in English texts. *Journal of Verbal Learning and Verbal Behavior, 5*, 28–34.

Parker, S. D., Brewer, M. B., & Spencer, J. R. (1980). Natural disaster, perceived control, and attributions to fate. *Personality and Social Psychology Bulletin, 6*, 454–459.

Parkinson, S. (1994). Scientific or ethical quality? *Psychological Science, 5*, 137–138.

Parry, H. J., & Crossley, H. M. (1950). Validity of responses to survey questions. *Public Opinion Quarterly, 14*, 61–80.

Peters, M. L., Sorbi, J. J., Kruise, D. A., Kerssens, J. J., Verhaak, P. F. M., & Bensing, J. M. (2000). Electronic diary assessment of pain, disability, and psychological adaptation in patients differing in duration of pain. *Pain, 84*, 181–192.

Peterson, C., Seligman, M. E., & Vaillant, G. E. (1988). Pessimistic explanatory style is a risk factor for physical illness: A 35-year longitudinal study. *Journal of Personality and Social Psychology, 55*, 23–27.

Petty, R. E., & Cacioppo, J. T. (1986). *Communication and persuasion: Central and peripheral routes to attitude change.* New York: Springer-Verlag.

Petty, R. E., & Cacioppo, J. T. (1996). Addressing disturbing and disturbed consumer behavior: Is it necessary to change the way we conduct behavioral science? *Journal of Marketing Research, 33*, 1–8.

Pezdek, K., & Banks, W. P. (Eds.). (1996). *The recovered memory/false memory debate.* San Diego, CA: Academic Press.

Phelps, E. A., O'Connor, K. J., Cunningham, W. A., Funayama, E. S., Gatenby, J. C., Gore, J. C., & Banaji, M. R. (2000). Performance on indirect measures of race evaluation predicts amygdala activation. *Journal of Cognitive Neuroscience, 12*, 729–738.

Phillips, D. P. (1982). The impact of fictional television stories on U.S. adult fatalities: New evidence of the effect of the mass media on violence. *American Journal of Sociology, 87*, 1340–59.

Phillips, D. P. (1983). The impact of mass media violence on U.S. homocides. *American Sociological Review, 48*, 560–568.

Pierce, A. H. (1908). The subconscious again. *Journal of Philosophy, Psychology, and Scientific Methods, 5*, 264–271.

Piliavin, I. M., Rodin, J., & Piliavin, J. A. (1969). Good Samaritanism: An underground phenomenon? *Journal of Personality and Social Psychology, 13*, 289–299.

Pillemer, D. B., & Light, R. J. (1980). How to use research evidence from many studies. *Harvard Educational Review, 50*, 176–195.

Polifroni, M. A., von Hippel, W., & Brewer, M. B. (2001). Nazis on the Web: Support for image theory in the internet communications of white supremists. Paper presented at the annual meeting of the Midwestern Psychological Association. Chicago, IL (May).

Politz, A., & Simmons, W. (1949). I. An attempt to get the 'not at homes' into the sample without callbacks. II. Further theoretical considerations regarding the plan for eliminating callbacks. *Journal of the American Statistical Association, 44*, 9–31.

Ponder, E., & Kennedy, W. P. (1927). On the act of blinking. *Quarterly Journal of Experimental Physiology, 18*, 89–110.

Poole, K. T. (1981). Dimensions of interest group evaluation of the U.S. Senate, 1969–1978. *American Journal of Political Science, 25*, 41–54.

Popper, K. R. (1959). *The logic of scientific discovery*. New York: Basic Books.

Popper, K. R. (1963). *Conjectures and refutations: The growth of scientific knowledge*. London: Routledge.

Pratto, F., & John, O. P. (1991). Automatic vigilance: The attention-grabbing power of negative social information. *Journal of Personality and Social Psychology, 61*, 380–391

Priester, J. R. (in press). Sex, drugs, and attitudinal ambivalence: How feelings of evaluative tension influence alcohol use and safe sex behaviors. In W. D. Crano & M. Burgoon (Eds.), *Mass media and drug prevention: Classic and contemporary theories and research*. Mahwah, NJ: Lawrence Erlbaum Associates.

Priester, J. R., & Petty, R. E. (2001). Extending the bases of subjective attitudinal ambivalence: Interpersonal and intrapersonal antecedents of evaluative tension. *Journal of Personality and Social Psychology, 80*, 19–34.

Pryor, J. B., & Ostrom, T. M. (1981). The cognitive organization of social information: A converging-operations approach. *Journal of Personality and Social Psychology, 41*, 628–641.

Quinn, R. P., Gutek, B. A., & Walsh, J. T. (1980). Telephone interviewing: A reappraisal and a field experiment. *Basic and Applied Social Psychology, 1*, 127–153.

Rahn, W. M., Krosnick, J. A., & Breuning, M. (1994). Rationalization and derivation processes in survey studies of political candidate evaluation. *American Journal of Political Science, 38*, 582–600.

Ramirez, J. R., & Crano, W. D. (in press). An interrupted time series analysis of California's three strikes law on instrumental, violent, minor, and drug-related crime: Deterrence and incapacitation. *Journal of Applied Social Psychology*.

Raser, J. R., & Crow, W. J. (1964). *WIN SAFE II: An inter-nation simulation study of deterrence postures embodying capacity to delay response*. La Jolla, CA: Western Behavioral Sciences Institute.

Raser, J. R., & Crow, W. J. (1968). A simulation study of deterrence theories. In L. Kriesberg (Ed.), *Social processes in international relations* (pp. 100–125). New York: Wiley.

Ratliff, E. A. (1999). Women as "sex workers," men as "boyfriends": Shifting identities in Philippine go-go bars and their significance in STD/AIDS control. *Anthropology and Medicine, 6*, 79–101.

Ray, J. J. (1985). Defective validity in the Altemeyer authoritarianism scale. *Journal of Social Psychology, 125*, 271–272.

Ray, M. L., & Webb, E. J. (1966). Speech duration effects in the Kennedy news conferences. *Science, 153*, 899–901.

Reed, C. F., & Witt, P. N. (1965). Factors contributing to unexpected reactions in two human drug-placebo experiments. *Confina Psychiatrica, 8*, 57–68.

Reichardt, C. S., & Mark, M. M. (1998). Quasi-experimentation. In L. Bickman & D. J. Rog (Eds.), *Handbook of applied social research methods* (pp. 193–228). Thousand Oaks, CA: Sage.

Reingen, P. H., & Kernan, J. B. (1977). Compliance with an interview request: A foot-in-the-door, self-perception interpretation. *Journal of Marketing Research, 14*, 365–369.

Reips, U. D. (2000). The web experiment method: Advantages, disadvantages, and solutions. In M. H. Birnbaum (Ed.), *Psychological experiments on the internet* (pp. 89–117). San Diego, CA: Academic Press.

Reis, H. T. (1982). In introduction to the use of structural equations: Prospects and problems. In L. Wheeler (Ed.), *Review of Personality and Social Psychology, 3* (pp. 255–287).

Reis, H. T., & Gable, S. L. (2000). Event-sampling and other methods for studying everyday experience. In H. T. Reis & C. M. Judd (Eds.), *Handbook of research methods in social and personality psychology* (pp. 190–222). New York: Cambridge University Press.

Researchers monitoring Net support groups (2000, September 22). *USA Today.* Available online: http://www.usatoday.com/life/cyber/tech/cti535.htm.

Resnick, J. H., & Schwartz, T. (1973). Ethical standards as an independent variable in psychological research. *American Psychologist, 28,* 134–139.

Rhodes, N., & Wood, W. (1992). Self-esteem and intelligence affect influenceability: The mediating role of message reception. *Psychological Bulletin, 111,* 156–171.

Rice, R. E. (1994). Network analysis and computer-mediated communication systems. In S. Wasserman & J. Galaskiewicz (Eds.), *Advances in social network analysis: Research in the social and behavioral sciences* (pp. 167–203). Thousand Oaks, CA: Sage.

Richardson, S. A., Dohrenwend, B. S., & Klein, D. (1965). *Interviewing: Its forms and functions.* New York: Basic Books.

Riefenstahl, L. (1935). *Triumph of the will (Triumph des Willens).* (Film: B/W, 110 min). Available: http://www.filmsondisc.com/dvdpages/triumph_of_the_will.htm.

Rimé, B., & Leyens, J.-P. (1988). Violence dans les stades: La response des psychologues [Violence in the stands: The response of psychologists]. *La Recherche, 19,* 528–531.

Ring, K., Wallston, K., & Corey, M. (1970). Mode of debriefing as a factor affecting subjective reaction to a Milgram-type obedience experiment: An ethical inquiry. *Representative Research in Social Psychology, 1,* 67–88.

Roberts, R. R., & Renzaglia, G. A. (1965). The influence of tape recording on counseling. *Journal of Consulting Psychology, 12,* 10–16.

Robinson, A., Bradley, R. H., Stanley, T. D. (1990). Opportunity to achieve: Identifying mathematically gifted Black students. *Contemporary Educational Psychology, 15,* 1–12.

Robinson, B. F., & Bakeman, R. (1998). ComKappa: A Windows 95 program for calculating kappa and related statistics. *Behavioral Research Methods, Instruments, and Computers, 30,* 731–732.

Robinson, J. P., & Goodbey, G. (1997). *Time for life: The surprising ways Americans use their time.* University Park, PA: Pennsylvania State University Press.

Robinson, R. G. (1995). Mapping brain activity associated with emotion. *American Journal of Psychiatry, 152,* 327–329.

Roenker, D. L., Thompson, C. P., & Brown, S. C. (1971). Comparison of measures for the estimation of clustering in free recall. *Psychological Bulletin, 76,* 45–48.

Rokeach, M. (1960). *The open and closed mind.* New York: Basic Books.

Rokeach, M., & Mezei, L. (1966). Race and shared belief as factors in social choice. *Science, 151,* 167–172.

Rorer, L. G. (1965). The great response style myth. *Psychological Bulletin, 63,* 129–156.

Rosenberg, M. J., & Abelson, R. P. (1960). An analysis of cognitive balancing. In C. I. Hovland & M. J. Rosenberg (Eds.), *Attitude organization and change: An analysis of consistency among attitude components* (pp. 112–163). New Haven, CT: Yale University Press.

Rosenthal, R. (1966). *Experimenter effects in behavioral research.* New York: Appleton-Century-Crofts.

Rosenthal, R. (1979). The "file drawer problem" and tolerance for null results. *Psychological Bulletin, 86,* 638–641.

Rosenthal, R. (1991). Meta analysis: A review. *Psychosomatic Medicine, 53,* 247–271.

Rosenthal, R. (1994). Science and ethics in conducting, analyzing, and reporting psychological research. *Psychological Science, 5*, 127–133.

Rosenthal, R., & Fode, K. L. (1961). The problem of experimenter outcome-bias. In D. P. Ray (Ed.), *Series research in social psychology*. Symposia studies series, No. 8. Washington, DC: National Institute of Social and Behavioral Science.

Rosenthal, R., & Fode, K. L. (1963). Three experiments in experimenter bias. *Psychological Reports, 12*, 491–511.

Rosenthal, R., & Jacobson, L. (1968). *Pygmalion in the classroom*. New York: Holt, Rinehart & Winston.

Rosenthal, R., & Lawson, R. (1964). A longitudinal study of the effects of experimenter bias on the operant learning of laboratory rats. *Journal of Psychiatric Research, 2*, 61–72.

Rosenthal, R., Persinger, G. W., Vikan-Kline, L., & Fode, K. L. (1963). The effect of early data returns on data subsequently obtained by outcome-biased experimenters. *Sociometry, 26*, 487–498.

Rosenthal, R., & Rosnow, R. L. (1984). Applying Hamlet's question to the ethical conduct of research. *American Psychologist, 39*, 561–563.

Rosenthal, R., & Rosnow, R. L. (1975). *The volunteer subject*. New York: Wiley-Interscience.

Rosenthal, R., & Rubin, D. B. (1978). Comparing significance levels of independent studies. *Psychological Bulletin, 86*, 1165–1168.

Rosenthal, R., & Rubin, D. B. (1982). Comparing effect sizes of independent studies. *Psychological Bulletin, 92*, 500–504.

Rosnow, R. L., & Suls, J. M. (1970). Reactive effects of pretesting in attitude research. *Journal of Personality and Social Psychology, 15*, 338–343.

Ross, L. (1977). The intuitive scientist and his shortcomings. In L. Berkowitz (Ed.), *Advances in experimental social psychology* (Vol. 10, pp. 174–221). New York: Academic Press.

Ross, L., Greene, D., & House, P. (1977). The "false consensus" effect: An egocentric bias in social perception and attribution processes. *Journal of Experimental Social Psychology, 13*, 279–301.

Ross, L., Lepper, M. R., & Hubbard, M. (1975). Perseverance in self-perception and social perception: Biased attributional processes in the debriefing paradigm. *Journal of Personality and Social Psychology, 32*, 880–892.

Rossi, P. H., Wright, J. D., & Anderson, A. B. (Eds.). (1983). *Handbook of survey research*. New York: Academic Press.

Royal Commission on the Press 1947–1949. (1949). Report, Appendix VII. London: His Majesty's Stationery Office.

Rubin, Z. (1975). Disclosing oneself to a stranger: Reciprocity and its limits. *Journal of Experimental Social Psychology, 11*, 233–260.

Rugg, D. (1941). Experiments in wording questions: II. *Public Opinion Quarterly, 5*, 91–92.

Russell, B. (1930). *The conquest of happiness*. New York: Horace Liveright.

Russo, J. E., & Rosen, L. D. (1975). An eye fixation analysis of multialternative choice. *Memory and Cognition, 3*, 267–276.

Sadler, M. S., & Judd, C. M. (2001). Overcoming dependent data: A guide to the analysis of group data. In M. Hogg & R. S. Tindale (Eds.), *Blackwell handbook of social psychology: Group processes* (pp. 497–524). Oxford, UK: Blackwell.

Samph, T. (1969). The role of the observer and his effects on teacher classroom behavior. *Occasional Papers, 2*, Pontiac, MI: Oakland Schools.

Sampson, F. (1969). *Crisis in the cloister*. Unpublished doctoral dissertation, Cornell University, Ithaca, NY.

Sawyer, J., & Schecter, H. (1968). Computers, privacy, and the national data center: The responsibility of social scientists. *American Psychologist, 23*, 810–818.

Schacter, D. L. (1987). Implicit memory: History and current status. *Journal of Experiment Psychology: Learning, Memory, and Cognition, 13*, 501–518.

Schaps, E. (1972). Cost, dependency, and helping. *Journal of Personality and Social Psychology, 21*, 74–78.

Schaps, E., & Sanders, C. (1970). Purposes, patterns, and protection in a campus drug-using community. *Journal of Health and Social Behavior, 11*, 135–145.

Schiffman, S. S., Reynolds, M. L., & Young, F. W. (1981). *Introduction to multidimensional scaling: Theory, methods, and applications*. New York: Academic Press.

Schlenker, B. R. (1974). Social psychology and science. *Journal of Personality and Social Psychology, 29*, 1–15.

Schlenker, B. R. (1976). Social psychology and science: Another look. *Personality and Social Psychology Bulletin, 2*, 384–390.

Schmitt, N., Coyle, B. W., & Saari, B. B. (1977). A review and critique of analyses of multitrait-multimethod matrices. *Multivariate Behavioral Research, 13*, 447–478.

Schmitt, N., & Stults, D. M. (1986). Methodology review: Analysis of multitrait-multimethod matrices. *Applied Psychological Measurement, 10*, 1–22.

Schneider, S. R. (1998–1999). Overcoming barriers to communication between police and socially disadvantaged neighbourhoods: A critical theory of community policing. *Crime, Law, and Social Change, 30*, 347–377.

Schroder, H. M., Driver, M. J., & Streufert, S. S. (1967). *Human information processing*. New York: Holt, Rinehart & Winston.

Schuldt, B., & Totten, J. (1994). Electronic mail vs. mail survey response rates. *Marketing Research, 6*, 36–39.

Schultz, D. (1969). The human subject in psychological research. *Psychological Bulletin, 72*, 214–228.

Schumacker, R. E., & Lomax, R. G. (1996). *A beginner's guide to structural equation modeling*. Hillsdale, NJ: Lawrence Erlbaum Associates.

Schuman, H., & Hatchett, S. (1974). *Black racial attitudes: Trends and complexities*. Ann Arbor, MI: Institute for Social Research, University of Michigan.

Schuman, H., & Kalton, G. (1985). Survey methods. In G. Lindzey & E. Aronson (Eds.) *The handbook of social psychology*, Vol. 2, 3rd ed. (pp. 635–698). Reading, MA: Addison-Wesley.

Schuman, H., & Presser, S. (1981). *Questions and answers in attitude surveys: Experiments on question form, wording, and context*. New York: Academic Press.

Schwartz, H., & Jacobs, J. (1979). *Qualitative sociology: A method to the madness*. New York: Free Press.

Schwartz, M. S., & Schwartz, C. G. (1955). Problems in participant observation. *American Journal of Sociology, 60*, 343–354.

Schwartz, R. D., & Skolnick, J. H. (1962). Two studies of legal stigma. *Social Problems, 10*, 133–142.

Schwarz, N., & Clore, G. L. (1983). Mood, misattribution, and judgments of well-being: Information and directive functions of affective states. *Journal of Personality and Social Psychology, 45*, 513–523.

Schwarz, N., & Strack, F. (1991). Evaluating one's life: A judgment model of subjective well-being. In F. Strack & M. Argyle (Eds.), *Subjective well-being: An interdisciplinary perspective* (pp. 27–47). Oxford, England: Pergamon Press.

Schwarz, N., & Strack, F. (1999). Reports of subjective well-being: Judgmental processes and their methodological implications. In D. Kahneman & E. Diener (Eds.), *Well-being: The foundations of hedonic psychology* (pp. 61–84). New York: Russell Sage Foundation.

Schwarz, N., Strack, F., Kommer, D., & Wagner, D. (1987). Soccer, rooms, and the qualify of your life: Mood effects on judgments of satisfaction with life in general and with specific domains. *European Journal of Social Psychology, 17,* 69–79.

Scodel, A. (1962). Induced collaboration in some non-zero-sum games. *Journal of Conflict Resolution, 6,* 335–340.

Scott, J. (1991). *Social network analysis: A handbook.* London: Sage.

Scott, W. A. (1968). Attitude measurement. In G. Lindzey & E. Aronson (Eds.) *Handbook of social psychology*: *Vol. 2. Research methods* (2nd ed., pp. 204–273). Reading, MA: Addison-Wesley.

Scriven, M. (1967). The methodology of evaluation. In R. Tyler, R. Gagne, & M. Scriven (Eds.), *Perspectives on curriculum evaluation* (pp. 39–83). Chicago: Rand McNally.

Scriven, M. (1993). *Hard-won lessons in program evaluation.* San Francisco: Jossey-Bass.

Scriven, M. (1997). Truth and objectivity in evaluation. In E. Chelimsky & W. R. Shadish (Eds.), *Evaluation for the 21st century: A handbook* (pp. 477–500). Thousand Oaks, CA: Sage.

Sears, D. O. (1986). College sophomores in the laboratory: Influences of a narrow data base on social psychology's view of human nature. *Journal of Personality and Social Psychology, 51,* 515–530.

Sears, D. O. (1994). On separating church and lab. *Psychological Science, 5,* 237–239.

Seaver, W. B., & Quarton, R. J. (1976). Regression discontinuity analysis of dean's list effects. *Journal of Educational Psychology, 68,* 459–465.

Sechrest, L. (1963). Incremental validity: A recommendation. *Educational and Psychological Measurement, 23,* 153–158.

Secord, P. F. (Ed.). (1982). *Explaining social behavior: Consciousness, human action, and social structure.* Beverly Hills: Sage.

Segal, S. J., & Cofer, C. N. (1960). The effect of recency and recall on word association. *American Psychologist, 15,* 451.

Seidel, J. (1991). Method and madness in the application of computer technology to qualitative data analysis. In N. Fielding & R. M. Lee (Eds.), *Using computers in qualitative research* (pp. 107–116). London: Sage.

Shames, M. L., & Adair, J. G. (1967). *Experimenter bias as a function of the type and structure of the task.* Paper presented at the meeting of the Canadian Psychological Association, Ottawa, Ontario.

Shepard, R. N. (1962a). The analysis of proximities: Multidimensional scaling with an unknown distance function. I. *Psychometrika, 27,* 125–140.

Shepard, R. N. (1962b). The analysis of proximities: Multidimensional scaling with an unknown distance function. II. *Psychometrika, 27,* 219–246.

Shepard, R. N., Romney, A. K., & Nerlove, S. (Eds.). (1971). *Multidimensional scaling: Theory and applications in the behavioral sciences.* New York: Academic Press.

Shneidman, E. S. (1963). Plan II. The logic of politics. In L. Arons & M. A. May (Eds.), *Television and human behavior* (pp. 80–99). New York: Appleton-Century-Crofts.

Sieber, J. E. (1992). *Planning ethically responsible research.* Newbury Park, CA: Sage.

Sigelman, L. (1986). Basking in reflected glory revisited: An attempt at replication. *Social Psychology Quarterly, 49,* 90–92.

Silverman, I. (1966). *The effect of experimenter outcome expectancy of latency of word association.* Paper presented at the meeting of the American Psychological Association, New York.

Silverman, I., Shulman, A. D., & Wiesenthal, D. L. (1970). Effects of deceiving and debriefing psychological subjects on performance in later experiments. *Journal of Personality and Social Psychology, 14,* 203–12.

Singer, E. (1978). Informed consent: Consequences for response rate and response quality in social surveys. *American Sociological Review, 43,* 144–162.

Sivacek, J. M., & Crano, W. D. (1982). Vested interest as a moderator of attitude-behavior consistency. *Journal of Personality and Social Psychology, 43*, 210–221.

Slater, P. E. (1955). Role differentiation in small groups. *American Sociological Review, 20*, 300–310.

Smith, E. R. (2000). Research design. In H. Reis & C. Judd (Eds.), *Handbook of research methods in social and personality psychology* (pp. 17–39). New York: Cambridge University Press.

Smith, E. R., & Kluegel, J. R. (1984). Beliefs and attitudes about women's opportunity. *Social Psychology Quarterly, 47*, 81–95.

Smith, M. L., & Glass, G. V. (1977). Meta-analysis of psychotherapy outcome studies. *American Psychologist, 32*, 752–760.

Smith, S. S., & Richardson, D. (1983). Amelioration of deception and harm in psychological research: The important role of debriefing. *Journal of Personality and Social Psychology, 44*, 1075–1082.

Smoker, P. (1968). *International processes simulation: A man-computer model.* Unpublished manuscript, Northwestern University, Evanston, IL.

Snider, J. G., & Osgood, C. E. (Eds.). (1969). *Semantic differential technique.* Chicago: Aldine.

Soskin, W. F., & John, V. P. (1963). The study of spontaneous talk. In R. G. Barker (Ed.), *The stream of behavior* (pp. 228–281). New York: Appleton-Century-Crofts.

Srull, T. K., & Wyer, R. S., Jr. (1979). The role of category accessibility in the interpretation of information about persons: Some determinants and implications. *Journal of Personality and Social Psychology, 37*, 1660–1672.

Stasser, G., & Titus, W. (1987). Pooling of unshared information in group decision making: Biased information sampling during discussion. *Journal of Personality and Social Psychology, 53*, 81–93.

Stigler, S. M. (1986). *History of statistics: The measurement of uncertainty before 1900.* Cambridge, MA: Harvard University Press.

Stone, J., Aronson, E., Crain, A. L., & Winslow, M. P. (1994). Inducing hypocrisy as a means of encouraging young adults to use condoms. *Personality and Social Psychology Bulletin, 20*, 116–128.

Stone, P. J. (1964). *An introduction to the General Inquirer: A computer system for the study of spoken or written material.* Unpublished paper, Harvard University and Simulmatics Corp.

Stone, P. J. (1968). *User's manual for the General Inquirer.* Cambridge, MA: MIT Press.

Stone, P. J. Dunphy, D. C., Smith, M. S., & Ogilvie, D. M. (Eds.). (1966). *The General Inquirer: A computer approach to content analysis.* Cambridge, MA: MIT Press.

Stone, P. J., & Hunt, E. B. (1963). A computer approach to content analysis using the General Inquirer system. In. E. C. Johnson (Ed.), *American Federation of Information Processing Societies, Conference Proceedings* (pp. 241–256). Baltimore, MD:

Stone, P. J., Bales, R. F., Namenwirth, J. Z., & Ogilvie, D. M. (1962). The General Inquirer: A computer system for content analysis and retrieval based on the sentence as a unit of information. *Behavioral Science, 7*, 484–494.

Stoner, J. A. F. (1961). *A comparison of individual and group decisions involving risk.* Unpublished master's thesis, Massachusetts Institute of Technology, Cambridge.

Stouffer, S. A. (1936). Evaluating the effects of inadequately measured variables in partial correlation analysis. *Journal of the American Statistical Association, 31*, 348–360.

Stouffer, S. A. (Ed.). (1950). *Measurement and prediction.* Princeton, NJ: Princeton University Press.

Stouffer, S. A., Suchman, E. A., DeVinney, L. C., Star, S. A., & Williams, R. M., Jr. (Eds.). (1949). *The American soldier: Adjustment during army life.* Princeton, NJ: Princeton University Press.

Strauss, A. (Ed.). (1991). *Creating sociological awareness: Collective images and symbolic representations.* New Brunswick, NJ: Transaction Publishers.

Streufert, S. (1997). Complexity: An integration of theories. *Journal of Applied Social Psychology, 27,* 2068–2095.

Striker, L. J. (1967). The true deceiver. *Psychological Bulletin, 68,* 13–20.

Striker, L. J., Messick, S., & Jackson, D. N. (1967). Suspicion of deception: Implications for conformity research. *Journal of Personality and Social Psychology, 4,* 379–389.

Stroebe, W., & Diehl, M. (1994). Why groups are less effective than their members: On productivity losses in idea-generating groups. In W. Stroebe & M. Hewstone (Eds.) *European Review of Social Psychology* (Vol. 5, pp. 271–303). London: Wiley.

Stroop, J. R. (1935). Studies of interference in serial verbal reactions. *Journal of Experimental Psychology, 18,* 643–662.

Struening, E. L., & Brewer, M. B. (Eds.). (1983). *Handbook of evaluation research*: University edition. Beverly Hills, CA: Sage.

Sudman, S. (1976). *Applied sampling.* New York: Academic Press.

Sudman, S. (1980). Reducing response errors in surveys. *Statistician, 29,* 237–273.

Sudman, S., Bradburn, N. M., & Schwarz, N. (1996). *Thinking about answers: The application of cognitive processes to survey methodology.* San Francisco: Jossey-Bass.

Suedfeld, P., Tetlock, P. E., & Streufert, S. (1992). Conceptual/integrative complexity. In C. P. Smith & J. W. Atkinson (Eds.), *Motivation and personality: Handbook of thematic content analysis* (pp. 393–400). New York: Cambridge University Press.

Sulloway, F. H. (1996). *Born to rebel: Birth order, family dynamics, and creative lives.* New York: Pantheon Books.

Surgeon General's directives on human experimentation. (1967). *American Psychologist, 22,* 350–359.

Swann, W. B. (1984). The quest for accuracy in person perception: A matter of pragmatics. *Psychological Review, 91,* 457–477.

Tajfel, H., Billig, M., Bundy, R., & Flament, C. (1971). Social categorization and intergroup behavior. *European Journal of Social Psychology, 1,* 149–178.

Tanur, J. M. (1983). Methods for large-scale surveys and experiments. In S. Leinhardt (Ed.), *Sociological methodology 1983–84* (chap.1, pp. 1–71). San Francisco: Jossey-Bass.

Taylor, C. R., Lee, J. Y., & Stern, B. B. (1995). Portrayals of African, Hispanic, and Asian Americans in magazine advertising. *American Behavioral Scientist, 38,* 608–621.

Taylor, S. E., & Aspinwall, L. G. (1996). Mediating and moderating processes in psychological stress: Appraisal, coping, resistance, and vulnerability. In H. B. Kaplan (Ed.), *Psychological stress: Perspectives on structure, theory, life-course, and methods* (pp. 71–110). San Diego, CA: Academic Press.

Taylor, S. E., & Fiske, S. T. (1981). Getting inside the head: Methodologies for process analysis in attribution and social cognition. In J. Harvey, W. Ickes, & R. Kidd (Eds.), *New directions in attribution research* (Vol. 3, pp. 459–524). Hillsdale, NJ: Lawrence Erlbaum Associates.

Taylor, S. E., Fiske, S. T., Etcoff, N., & Ruderman, A. (1978). The categorical and contextual bases of person memory and stereotyping. *Journal of Personality and Social Psychology, 36,* 778–793.

Taylor, W. S. (1953). "Cloze Procedure"; A new tool for measuring readability. *Journalism Quarterly, 30,* 415–433.

Taylor, W. S. (1956). Recent developments in the use of 'Cloze Procedure.' *Journalism Quarterly, 33,* 42–48.

Tekman, H. G. (1998). A multidimensional study of music preference judgments for excerpts of music. *Psychological Reports, 82*, 851–860.

Terry, R. (2000). Recent advances in measurement theory and the use of sociometric techniques. In A. H. N. Cillessen, & W. Bukowski (Eds.), *Recent advances in the measurement of acceptance and rejection in the peer system* (pp. 27–53). San Francisco: Jossey-Bass.

Tetlock, P. E., & Suedfeld, P. (1988). Integrative complexity coding of verbal behaviour. In C. Antaki, (Ed.), *Analysing everyday explanation: A casebook of methods* (pp. 43–59). London: Sage.

Thistlethwaite, D. L., & Campbell, D. T. (1960). Regression-discontinuity analysis: An alternative to the ex post facto experiment. *Journal of Educational Psychology, 51*, 309–317.

Thompson, M. S. (1980). *Benefit-cost analysis for program evaluation*. Beverly Hills, CA: Sage.

Thompson, S. C., & Collins, M.A. (1995). Applications of perceived control to cancer: An overview of theory and measurement. *Journal of Psychosocial Oncology, 13*, 11–26.

Thornberry, O. T., Jr., & Massey, J. T. (1988). Trends in United States telephone coverage across time and subgroups. In R. M. Groves, P. P. Biemer, L. E. Lyberg, J. T. Massey, W. L. Nicholls, & J. Waksberg (Eds.), *Telephone survey methodology* (pp. 25–50). New York: Wiley.

Thorndike, R. L. (1933). The effect of the interval between test and retest on the constancy of the IQ. *Journal of Educational Psychology, 25*, 543–549.

Thorndike, R. L. (1942). Regression fallacies in the matched groups experiment. *Psychometrika, 7*, 85–102.

Thorne, B. (1988). Political activist as participant observer: Conflicts of commitment in a study of the draft resistance movement of the 1960s. In P. C. Higgins & J. M. Johnson (Eds.), *Personal sociology* (pp. 133–152). New York: Praeger.

Thurstone, L. L. (1927). Method of paired comparisons for social values. *Journal of Abnormal and Social Psychology, 21*, 384–400.

Thurstone, L. L. (1928). Attitudes can be measured. *American Journal of Sociology, 33*, 529–554.

Thurstone, L. L. (1931). The measurement of attitudes. *Journal of Abnormal and Social Psychology, 26*, 249–269.

Thurstone, L. L., & Chave, E. L. (1929). *The measurement of attitudes*. Chicago: University of Chicago Press.

Tindale, R. S., Meisenhelder, H. M., Dykema-Engblade, A., & Hogg, M. A. (2001). Shared cognition in small groups. In M. Hogg & R. S. Tindale (Eds.), *Blackwell handbook of social psychology: Group processes* (pp. 1–30). Oxford, UK: Blackwell.

Tomaka, J., & Blascovich, J. (1994). Effects of justice beliefs on cognitive appraisal of and subjective, physiological, and behavioral responses to potential stress. *Journal of Personality and Social Psychology, 67*, 732–740.

Tomaka, J., Blascovich, J., Kelsey, R. M., & Leitten, C. L. (1993). Subjective, physiological, and behavioral effects of threat and challenge appraisal. *Journal of Personality and Social Psychology, 65*, 248–260.

Torgerson, W. S. (1958). *Theory and methods of scaling*. New York: Wiley.

Torres, M., & Macedo, J. (2000). Learning sustainable development with a new simulation game. *Simulation and Gaming, 31*, 119–126.

Tourangeau, R., & Rasinski, K. A. (1988). Cognitive processes underlying context effects in attitude measurement. *Psychological Bulletin, 103*, 299–314.

Tracy, P. E., & Fox, J. A. (1981). The validity of randomized response for sensitive measurements. *American Sociological Review, 46*, 187–200.

Trochim, W. (1984). *Research design for program evaluation: The regression-discontinuity approach*. Beverly Hills, CA: Sage.

Troffer, S. A., & Tart, C. T. (1964). Experimenter bias in hypnotist performance. *Science, 145*, 1330–1331.

Troldahl, V. C., & Carter, R. E., Jr. (1964). Random selection of respondents within households in phone surveys. *Journal of Marketing Research, 1*, 71–76.

Trotter, R. T., II. (2000). Ethnography and network analysis: The study of social context in cultures and society. In G. L. Albrecht & R. Fitzpatrick (Eds.), *The handbook of social studies in health and medicine* (pp. 210–229). London: Sage.

Tunnell, G. B. (1977). Three dimensions of naturalness: An expanded definition of field research. *Psychological Bulletin, 84*, 426–437.

Tversky, A. (1969). Intransitivity of preferences. *Psychological Review, 76*, 31–48.

Underwood, B., Berenson, J., Berenson, R., Cheng, K., Wilson, D., Kulik, J., Moore, B., & Wenzel, G. (1977). Attention, negative affect, and altruism: An ecological validation. *Personality and Social Psychology Bulletin, 3*, 54–58.

Upshaw, H. S. (1965). The effects of variable perspectives on judgments of opinion statements for Thurstone scales: Equal appearing intervals. *Journal of Personality and Social Psychology, 2*, 60–69.

Vallacher, R. R. (1978). Objective self awareness and the perception of others. *Personality and Social Psychology Bulletin, 4*, 63–67.

Van Maanen, J. (in press). Notes on the production of ethnographic data in an American police agency. In R. Luckman (Ed.), *Anthropological methods in the study of legal systems*. New York: Academic Press.

Vanman, E. J., Paul, B. Y., Ito, T. A., & Miller, N. (1997). The modern face of prejudice and structural features that moderate the effect of cooperation on affect. *Journal of Personality and Social Psychology, 73*, 941–959.

VanDusen, R. A., & Zill, N. (Eds.). (1975). Basic background items for U.S. household surveys. Washington, DC: Center for Coordination of Research on Social Indicators, Social Science Research Council.

Vidmar, N., & McGrath, J. E. (1967). *Role structure, leadership, and negotiation effectiveness* (Tech Rep. No. 6). Urbana, IL: University of Illinois, Department of Psychology.

Viney, L. L. (1983). The assessment of psychological states through content analysis of verbal communications. *Psychological Bulletin, 94*, 542–563.

Visser, P. S., Krosnick, J. A., & Lavrakas, P. J. (2000). Survey research. In H. Reis & C. M. Judd (Eds.), *Handbook of research methods in social and personality psychology* (pp. 223–252). Cambridge: Cambridge University Press.

Vrij, A., & Winkel, F. W. (1991). Characteristics of the built environment and fear of crime: A research note on interventions in unsafe locations. *Deviant Behavior, 12*, 203–215.

Waksberg, J. (1978). Sampling methods for random digit dialing. *Journal of the American Statistical Association, 73*, 40–46.

Walster, E., Aronson, V., Abrahams, D., & Rottman, L. (1966). Importance of physical attractiveness in dating behavior. *Journal of Personality and Social Psychology, 5*, 508–516.

Walster, E., Berscheid, E., Abrahams, D., & Aronson, E. (1967). Effectiveness of debriefing following deception experiments. *Journal of Personality and Social Psychology, 4*, 371–380.

Walther, J. B. (1993). Impression development in computer-mediated interaction. *Western Journal of Communication, 57*, 381–398.

Ware, M. E., & Johnson, D. E. (Eds.). (2000). *Handbook of demonstrations and activities in the teaching of psychology: Vol. III: Personality, Abnormal, Clinical-Counseling, and Social* (2nd ed.). Mahwah, NJ: Lawrence Erlbaum Associates.

Warner, R. M., Kenny, D., A., & Stoto, M. (1979). A new round robin analysis of variance for social interaction data. *Journal of Personality and Social Psychology, 37*, 1742–1757.

Warner, S. L. (1965). Randomized response: A survey technique for eliminating evasive answer bias. *Journal of the American Statistical Association, 60*, 63–69.

Wartella, E. A., & Stout, P. A. (in press). The evolution of mass media and health persuasion models. In W. D. Crano & M. Burgoon (Eds.), *Mass media and drug prevention: Classic and contemporary theories and research*. Mahwah, NJ: Lawrence Erlbaum Associates.

Wasserman, S., & Faust, K. (1994). *Social network analysis: Methods and applications*. New York: Cambridge University Press.

Weaver, C. N., & Swanson, C. L. (1974). Validity of reported date of birth, salary, and seniority. *Public Opinion Quarterly, 38*, 69–80.

Webb, E. J., Campbell, D. T., Schwartz, R. D., & Sechrest, L. (1966). *Unobtrusive measures: Nonreactive research in the social sciences*. Chicago: Rand McNally.

Webb, E. J., Campbell, D. T., Schwartz, R. D., Sechrest, L., & Grove, J. (1981). *Nonreactive measures in the social sciences*. Boston: Houghton-Mifflin.

Webb, S. C. (1955). Scaling of attitudes by the method of equal-appearing intervals. *Journal of Social Psychology, 42*, 215–239.

Webber, S. J., & Cook, T. D. (1972). Subject effects in laboratory research: An examination of subject roles, demand characteristics, and valid inference. *Psychological Bulletin, 77*, 273–295.

Webster, D. M., & Kruglanski, A. W. (1994). Individual differences in need for cognitive closure. *Journal of Personality and Social Psychology, 67*, 1049–1062.

Wegener, D. T., Downing, J., Krosnick, J. A., & Petty, R. E. (1995). Measures and manipulations of strength-related properties of attitudes: Current practice and future directions. In R. E. Petty & J. A. Krosnick (Eds.), *Attitude strength: Antecedents and consequences* (pp. 455–487). Hillsdale, NJ: Lawrence Erlbaum Associates.

Wegner, D. M. (1987). Transactive memory: A contemporary analysis of the group mind. In B. Mullen & G. Goethals (Eds.), *Theories of group behavior* (pp. 185–208). New York: Springer-Verlag.

Weick, K. E. (1968). Systematic observational methods. In G. Lindzey & E. Aronson (Eds.), *The handbook of social psychology: Vol. 2. Research Methods* (2nd ed., pp. 357–451). Reading, MA: Addison-Wesley.

Weick, K. E. (1985). Systematic observational methods. In G. Lindzey & E. Aronson (Eds.), *The handbook of social psychology* (3rd ed., pp. 567–634). Reading, MA: Addison-Wesley.

Welsh, J. A., & Null, C. H. (1991). The effects of computer-based instruction on college students' comprehension of classic research. *Behavior Research Methods, Instruments, and Computers, 23*, 301–305.

Westley, B. H., Higbie, C. E., Burke, T., Lippert, D. J., Maurer, L., & Stone, V. A. (1963). The news magazines and the 1960 conventions. *Journalism Quarterly, 40*, 525–531.

Weubben, P. L. (1965). Honesty of subjects and birth order. *Journal of Personality and Social Psychology, 5*, 350–352.

Wheeler, L., & Nezlek, J. B. (1977). Sex differences in social participation. *Journal of Personality and Social Psychology, 35*, 742–754.

Wheeler, S. R., & Austin, J. (2000). The loss response list: A tool for measuring adolescent grief responses. *Death Studies, 24*, 21–34.

White, H., Boorman, S., & Breiger, R. (1976). Social structure from multiple networks, I: Blockmodels of roles and positions. *American Journal of Sociology, 81*, 730–779.

White, R. K. (1947). "Black Boy": A value analysis. *Journal of Abnormal and Social Psychology, 42*, 440–461.

Whyte, W. F. (1955). *Street corner society*. Chicago: University of Chicago Press.

Willems, E. P. (1976). Behavioral ecology, health, status, and health care: Applications to the rehabilitation setting. In I. A. Altman & J. F. Wohlwill (Eds.), *Human behavior and environment* (pp. 220–230). New York: Plenum.

Williams, K. D. (1997). Social ostracism. In R. Kowalski (Ed.), *Aversive interpersonal behaviors* (pp. 133–170). New York: Plenum.

Williams, K. D., Cheung, C., & Choi, W. (2000). Cyberostracism: Effects of being ignored over the internet. *Journal of Personality and Social Psychology, 79*, 748–762.

Williams, K. D., & Zadro, L. (in press). Ostracism: On being ignored, excluded, and rejected. In M. Leary (Ed.), *Interpersonal rejection*. New York: Oxford Press.

Williams, P. A., Haertel, E., Haertel, G., & Walberg, H. (1982). The impact of leisure-time television on school learning: A research synthesis. *American Educational Research Journal, 19*, 19–50.

Williamson, J., & Karp, D. (1977). *The research craft: An introduction to social science methods*. Boston: Little-Brown.

Wilson, G. D., & Patterson, J. R. (1968). A new measure of conservatism. *British Journal of Social and Clinical Psychology*, 264–269.

Wilson, J. P., & Petruska, R. (1984). Motivation, model attributes, and prosocial behavior. *Journal of Personality and Social Psychology, 46*, 458–468.

Winer, B. J. (1971). *Statistical principles in experimental design* (2nd ed.). New York: McGraw-Hill.

Wish, M., Deutsch, M., & Biener, L. (1970). Differences in conceptual structures of nations: An exploratory study. *Journal of Personality and Social Psychology, 16*, 361–373.

Won-Doornink, M. J. (1979). On getting to know you: The association between stage of a relationship and reciprocity of self-disclosure. *Journal of Personality and Social Psychology, 15*, 229–241.

Wood, W., Lundgren, S., Ouellette, J. A., Busceme, S., & Blackstone, T. (1994). Minority influence: A meta-analytic review of social influence processes. *Psychological Bulletin, 115*, 323–345.

Wood, W., Rhodes, N., & Whelan, M. (1989). Sex differences in positive well-being: A consideration of emotional style and marital status. *Psychological Bulletin, 106*, 249–264.

Wood, W., & Stagner, B. (1994). Why are some people easier to influence than others? In S. Shavitt & T. Brock (Eds.), *Persuasion: Psychological insights and perspectives* (pp. 149–174). Boston, MA: Allyn & Bacon.

Wortman, C. B., & Rabinowitz, V. C. (1979). Random assignment: The fairest of them all. In L. Sechrest, S. West, M. Phillips, R. Redner, & W. Yeaton (Eds.), *Evaluation Studies Review Annual* (Vol. 4). Beverly Hills, CA: Sage.

Wrightsman, L. S. (1965). Characteristics of positively scored and negatively scored items from attitude scales. *Psychological Reports, 17*, 898.

Yakobson, S., & Lasswell, H. D. (1949). Trend: May Day slogans in Soviet Russia. In H. D. Lasswell, N. Leites, R. Fadner, J. M. Goldsen, A. Gray, I. L. Janis, A. Kaplan, D. Kaplan, A. Mintz, I. de S. Pool, & S. Yakobson (Eds.), *The language of politics: Studies in quantitative semantics* (pp. 100–125). New York: George Stewart.

Yule, G. U. (1944). *The statistical study of literary vocabulary*. London: Cambridge University Press.

Zanna, M. P., & Cooper, J. (1974). Dissonance and the pill. An attribution approach to studying the arousal properties of dissonance. *Journal of Personality and Social Psychology, 29*, 703–709.

Zegiob, L. E., Arnold, S., & Forehand, R. (1975). An examination of observer effects in parent-child interactions. *Child Development, 46*, 509–512.

Zillman, D. (1979). *Hostility and aggression.* Hillsdale, N.J.: Lawrence Erlbaum Associates.

Zillman, D. (1996). Sequential dependencies in emotional experience and behavior. In R. Kavanaugh & B. Zimmerberg, (Eds.), *Emotion: Interdisciplinary perspectives* (pp. 243–272). Mahwah, NJ: Lawrence Erlbaum Associates.

Zimbardo, P. G., Haney, C., Banks, W. C., & Jaffe, D. A. (1973 April 8). Pirandellian prison: The mind is a formidable jailer. *New York Times Magazine*, Section 6, 36, ff.

Zinnes, D. A. (1966). A comparison of hostile state behavior in simulated and historical data. *World Politics, 18*, 474–502.

AUTHOR INDEX

SUBJECT INDEX